THE CHANGING IMAGE OF
BEETHOVEN

Franz Klein, Bust of Beethoven, *c. 1812,*
bronzed plaster, Beethovenhaus, Bonn.

Alessandra Comini

THE CHANGING IMAGE OF
BEETHOVEN

A Study in Mythmaking

First published in the United States of America in 1987 by
Rizzoli International Publications, Inc.
597 Fifth Avenue, New York, NY 10017

Library of Congress Cataloging-in-Publication Data

Comini, Alessandra.
The changing image of Beethoven.

Includes index.
1. Beethoven, Ludwig van, 1770–1827.   I. Title.
ML410.B4C73   1987   780'.92'4   85-42961
ISBN 0-8478-0617-0

55, 522

Jacket illustrations
Beethoven Monument by Max Klinger, 1902
Photographs by Christoph Sandig, Leipzig
Courtesy VEB E.A. Seemann Verlag, Leipzig

Composition by Rainsford Type, Ridgefield, CT
Printed in the United States

For Eleanor Tufts

CONTENTS

PREFACE

This very long book began as a short slide lecture fifteen years ago. The triggering stimulus for both was the fascination I experienced in the photographic presence (I had not yet seen it in marmorian flesh) of a curiously compelling cult statue—Max Klinger's polychromatic image of Beethoven enthroned. First exhibited to wild acclaim by the Vienna Secession at the beginning of this century, Klinger's three-dimensional Beethoven fell out of favor and was neglected as colossal kitsch fifty years later in a post-World-War-II era. But recently, in 1981, it was again sanctioned as edifying public monument by virtue of its theatrical installation in the small foyer of the Neu Gewandhaus in Leipzig.

Although I have since thrice made the physical pilgrimage to Klinger's Leipzig-based Beethoven, my initial encounter with this arresting apotheosis and with the concept of mythmaking was through the lens of Vienna-focused research. As a young instructor and then assistant professor of art history at Columbia University during the 1960s I had recently completed a doctoral dissertation on the Viennese Expressionist artist Egon Schiele. Tracing the sources of Schiele's trenchant style involved me with turn-of-the-century Vienna and I became acquainted with the elegant art and ambitious activities of the Secession, an avant-garde group of artists led by the Art Nouveau master Gustav Klimt. Klimt was a friend of Gustav Mahler and in 1902 the two men participated in the Secession's salute to the Leipzig sculptor Klinger, whose life-size marble effigy of Beethoven, seated on a bronze throne, was the centerpiece in a temple dedicated to Vienna's musical idol. Klinger's riveting yet almost overwhelming image of Beethoven—more Zeus-like than Promethean, more philosopher than musician—struck me as a strange, quixotic deification. In its physical loftiness and earnest symbolism (figures and scenes on the throne) Beethoven the man, and even Beethoven the composer, seemed mysteriously, almost ludicrously remote, muffled in the sensibilities, values, and aesthetics of an age quite removed from his own, yet an age for which he was clearly a special and necessary hero.

In wondering how all this came about, I began to collect and compare earlier images of Beethoven, beginning of course with verbal and visual portraits rendered during his lifetime. It soon became obvious that the mythmaking process had begun while the composer was still alive and that he, by his conduct as well as by his music, had contributed to it. Surprisingly few contemporary descriptions of Beethoven stuck to the physical data; Beethoven's mannerisms, manners, and moods invariably colored the "facts" of his physiognomy. The musical "intentions" of his compositions molded his protean mien, or, conversely, his "character" charged his music. The visual portraits differed drastically from one another. For each contributor to the collective image of Beethoven, a particular concept of Beethoven was also involved. These concepts of Beethoven changed and grew along cultural and psychological lines, and were inherited, embellished, or redefined according to the interests and needs of each articulator.

Gradually, I realized that to trace the changing image of Beethoven in the visual arts—drawings, lithographs, engravings, paintings, and sculptures—was to consider only the effect, not the cause. I would have to explore the *interior* image of Beethoven held by all those who contributed to his mythmaking mystique, especially those composers, performers, artists, writers, and critics who consciously engaged with him as a musical or "moral" force in their own lives. This meant consulting not only Beethoven's contemporaries, but also interrogating those who came after him—plumbing a full century and combing several countries and cultures. A chapter conceived of as "The Musicians' Musician," beginning with Haydn and ending with Brahms, grew to the length of the rest of the book put together. Liszt, Berlioz, and Wagner demanded, and gave, lengthy Beethoven interpretations. Chatty notes (for which I thank my publishers for their spatial tolerance) began to sketch out a second book—curiosities, inconsistencies, and rich cross-references from the realms of primary and secondary sources—as the methodology of art history was harnessed to the disciplines of biography and musicology. Mythmaking lurked everywhere, even in objective data, and my self-imposed task expanded to the inclusion and evaluation of fiction as well as fact, of legend as well as history. The *terminus ad quem* of my study would be the Klinger-Klimt-Mahler climax of 1902, but rapidly taking shape was an appendix (which will have to be a second book) of intriguing, sometimes outrageous Beethoven imagery that extended to the 1980s—much of it supplied to me with gusto by colleagues, friends, and students who had heard of my apparently never-ending study of the changing image of Beethoven.

It is to these colleagues and friends in America, England, and Europe that I should like to express my thanks in general for their positive reception to and encouragement of my project. Some of them know me as an amateur musician who has greedily transcribed Beethoven violin sonatas for flute, more of them know me as an art historian "gone bonkers on Beethoven"; all of them are happily associated in my mind with the rewards of passionate pursuit and well-tempered reflection. In particular, and at the risk of leaving many deserving names out, I should like to mention the following persons to whom, for various Beethovian reasons they will recognize, the final form of this study in mythmaking is indebted: Ingeborg Allihn, Pamela Askew, Egbert Begemann, Jan Beren, Eugene Bonelli, Jean Bony, George Braziller, Ralph Broadwater, Elaine Brody, James Brooks, Mari Coffee, William Dworkin, Viktor Fogarassy, the late Franz Glück, Philip Gossett, David Greene, Robert Gutman, Virginia Hancock, Julius Held, Ingrid Hillebrand, Hans Hillerbrand, William Hipp, William Jordan, Joseph Kerman, Karl Kilinski, Walter Koschatzky, Gordana Lazarevich, Steffen Lieberwirth, Edward Lippman, the late Edward Lowinsky, Otto Luening, Richard Martin, William McClung, Christopher Minnes, Donald Mitchell, Christian Nebehay, Schubert Ogden, Larry Palmer, Pamela Pellar, Robert Rifkind, Michael Rosenthal, the late Walter Rundell, Howard Shanet, Robert Skinner, Maynard Solomon, Claudio Spies, Leonard Stein, Richard Strawn, Alan Tyson, Vladimir Ussachevsky, Erick-Christian Varnhaagen Henriksen, Paul Vellucci, Gregory Warden, William Weaver, Keith Weber, William Wise, Christoph Wolff, Elizabeth Wood, George Zeiss, James Zumberge, and Wieland Zumpe.

In addition, I should like to single out the following: for involving me in Gewandhaus symposia on Brahms and Mahler and hence making it possible for me to study Klinger's Beethoven in situ, Kurt Masur; for allowing me to photograph the Klimt Beethoven frieze in temporary installation during the 1985 Vienna *Traum und Wirklichkeit* exhibition, Robert Waissenberger; for patiently reading and reacting to this book in manuscript form, Raiberto Comini, Isabelle Emerson, Lili Jensen, and Eleanor Tufts; for generous aid in the translation of difficult German passages, Dorothea Carus, Jutta Heinrich Clifford, and Margareta Deschner; and for subtle problem solving and persistent editing of the many parts and revisions of this lengthy book, Brenda Gilchrist.

Finally, I am grateful to several institutions for timely impetus and aid regarding my pursuit of Beethoven. As the 1972–73 Alfred Hodder Fellow at Princeton University I was given a year's freedom from teaching responsibilities and full license to utilize the rich resources there. At my own institution, Southern Methodist University, three summer travel grants and a sabbatical for 1981–82 awarded by the Meadows School of the Arts permitted me to spend the necessary untrammeled periods of time at crucial libraries and archives in New York, London, Bonn, Berlin, Leipzig, and Vienna.

An ultimate spiritual debt is cheerfully acknowledged: the gratifying "obligation," as this book progressed, to listen, time and time again, to Beethoven's music through the ears of other musicians. These articulate transcribers or defiers of the Beethoven mystique provided, each in his or her own way, the phenomenological continuity for the ever-changing image of Beethoven that visits us still today. It is my hope that the reader of this book will enjoy the mythmaking process revealed as much as the author delighted in the tracking of it. We are all beneficiaries of Beethoven's mythopoesis.

Dallas, December 1985

Author's Note

The changing image of Beethoven has extended to practices in the hyphenation of his name. In German, following the sense of the Flemish origin of the name and its probable meaning "beet yard," the first syllable is considered to be "Beet" and hyphenation is accordingly: "Beet-hoven." This division is usually adhered to in British English (see *The New Grove Dictionary of Music and Musicians*), but American English (with Webster as paradigm) hyphenates the name as though its bearer were a member of the *Apis mellifera* family: "Bee-thoven." It is not without a stinging sense of reluctance then, that, in the typesetting of this book, the author has submitted to her publisher's desire to follow Webster's Apian Way.

Chapter One

INTRODUCTION:
MYTHMAKING AS
CULTURAL HISTORY

On a spring day in April 1902, two years after the twentieth century had begun a roll call for which history seemed destined to provide more villains than heroes, the cultural elite of the city of Vienna turned out to honor two adopted idols, one living and in the prime of life, the other dead for seventy-five years. The hallowed objects of this collective pilgrimage were Max Klinger from Leipzig, creator of extraordinary visual icons, and Ludwig van Beethoven from Bonn, composer of nine symphonies, the last of which had fascinated other musicians from Schubert to Schönberg. Critics of the day enthusiastically referred to the life-size statue of Beethoven on special display at the new Secession building as "Klinger's Ninth Symphony" (Figs. 163, 187, 205, 206). And it was exactly that total, united-work-of-art, or *Gesamtkunstwerk*, aspect of Beethoven's Ninth Symphony, with its "inevitable" combination of instrument and voice in the fourth movement, which Klinger strove to approach in his technically extravagant and multicolored marble monument, gleaming with ivory and precious-stone inlay. He provided not only a Zeus-like image of the composer, his features remote and brooding, but also an Olympian environment, with throne, mountain peak, and empyrean eagle.

(Colorplate 10)

All Vienna joined forces to create an appropriate setting for this marmorean Beethoven incarnate. Gustav Klimt, spellbinding exponent of Austrian Art Nouveau, painted a great frieze with allegories referring to Schiller's "Ode to Joy," the poem Beethoven had set to music in his Ninth Symphony. Gustav Mahler reorchestrated the fourth movement of the Ninth for wind and brass instruments only and conducted the Vienna Opera chorus at the exhibition on the opening day. The enthralled public was caught up in the multiple spectacle, which inundated the senses and swayed the emotions through its seductive suggestion of a national "mystique."

This twentieth-century enactment of the title of Wagner's 1840 essay *Pilgrimage to Beethoven*, just a dozen years before the outbreak of World War I, recalls with ironic hindsight Nietzsche's description of the Ninth Symphony: "The Dionysian is approached, as, awestruck, the millions bow down to the dust." Now, more than two hundred years after the composer's birth in 1770, millions of persons around the world not only have surrendered to the sound of Beethoven's music, but have gazed in reverence, or, at the very least, in curiosity, at the image of Beethoven the man. His life span—1770–1827—slightly preceded that full blossoming of the Romantic movement in which, for artist and public alike, large-scale personalities were linked with grandiose work, as in the cases of Berlioz, Liszt, and Wagner. But, as with his contemporaries Napoleon and Byron, the posthumous *interpretation* of Beethoven approached its subject with the full arsenal of nineteenth-century Romanticism at its command. Musical judgments shifted from contemporaneous complaints that Beethoven's compositions, especially the late string quartets and the Ninth Symphony, were inaccessible and incomprehensible to analytical or passional assessments of the music's revelatory dimensions— a process still at work in the 1980s when we find public television presenting an international pilgrimage to Beethoven to the masses through the medium of a white-haired Leonard Bernstein conducting the Vienna Philharmonic.

No less a dramatic change and intensification of meanings is evident in the stream of nineteenth- and early twentieth-century biographies—interpretative studies of Beethoven's personality that saw Beethoven sometimes as temperamental tunesmith, but more often as lonely, self-isolating titan. In the visual arts the metamorphosis began even before the composer's death, and veered from maudlin verisimilitude to obfuscating idealism. It culminated in the great Vienna apotheosis of 1902. The two-hundred-year-long transformation of the image of Beethoven from musician to "tone hero" (Wagner's epithet) invites more than art-historical explanation. Such a radical shift in the representation of Beethoven from recluse to cultural idol mirrors a basic evolution in European intellectual history, the furthest reaches of which, by the turn of the century, had brought the German-speaking world to a peak of cultural efflorescence and to the brink of political crisis. To trace the changes in an apparently simple constant—Beethoven's physical appearance—is to catch sight of some of the fundamental cultural impulses that determined Europe's social destiny. A mythmaking "conspiracy" of the arts and sciences cumulatively combined the musical authority of Liszt, Wagner, and Berlioz—among others—with fertile speculations of phrenology and psychology to produce a remarkable extramusical imago of Beethoven. The imago was not only irresistible, it was true: the triumph of greatness over adversity. By the end of the nineteenth century, this larger-than-life legend of the deaf composer whose music sounded new spheres provided a mythic answer to society's nostalgic yearning for a *cultural* rather than political or military hero—a timely if ineffective spiritual antidote to the materialistic age of Bismarck and Kaiser Wilhelm II. The ecstatic Ode to Beethoven orchestrated by Klinger, Klimt, and Mahler in 1902 Vienna patently summed up the previous century's conviction that "redemption through art" was available to all.

Mythmaking is as old as civilization. The need for myth—that recasting of figures and events into archetypes and epics—has characterized all peoples and societies. As the vehicle through which a collective consciousness signals its cultural identity, the hero often displays unusual powers of self-assertion against gigantic odds, which then, whether frustrated or victorious, are subsumed into universal meaning. Through the alchemy of suffering even the basest metal—the rawest personality—can become gold. Why Beethoven and not Bach, or Mozart, or Wagner, or Brahms became the paradigm of Germanic musical genius for nine-teenth-century Europe has as much to do, and perhaps even more so, with posterity's perception of his life and character as it does with an appreciation of his musical achievements, towering as they were.

Beethoven. We are obliged to stop in front of the name itself even before we start our exploration of the Beethoven mystique. Not because of its origin—Flemish; or its meaning—most probably "beet yard"; but for its sheer sound. For those alert to the aural qualities of words, and for those in pursuit of how, as well as why, myths are made, an immediate observation must be noted. The composer's name was subject to two different pronunciations. As a Rhinelander who spent the first twenty-one years of his life in Bonn, Beethoven pronounced his name with the accent on the first syllable, *Bee*thoven. When he moved to Vienna permanently in 1792, his name, in accordance with the Viennese custom regarding compound words, was pronounced with the accent on the second syllable, Bee-*tho*ven. The acoustical, and possibly the psychological, effect is that of a different persona. This change was accompanied by an orthographic transformation of Beethoven's full name that led to specific consequences: the Rhenish name van Beethoven was pronounced and printed in newspaper reviews in Vienna as "von Beethoven." Hence the humble "van" of Dutch and Flemish origin, meaning no more than "of," became the explicit "von" of German-speaking lands, signifying aristocratic ties. For the next twenty-five years the assumption that Beethoven was of noble birth was widely circulated (even Goethe wrote his name as "von Beethoven"). This was a presumption Beethoven did nothing to correct and in fact depended upon when trying to win sole guardianship of his luckless nephew, Karl, before a court of law. (The ploy backfired when Beethoven could not furnish proof of nobility and his lawsuit was transferred from the Landrecht, the nobles' court, to a civil court for commoners in December 1818.) Thus one of the earliest Beethoven "myths"—that he was of the nobility—was encouraged by Beethoven himself in an attempt to force reality into paralleling what he felt and needed to believe about himself—that he was indeed of a "noble nature."[1]

"Beethoven!" Just the *sound* of his name, unhindered by accent placements, minus a plebeian "van" or aristocratic "von", was enough for Schumann, who revered in both the man and the music something beyond hereditary nobility, something he designated as a "never-ceasing moral force."[2] After attending a performance of the Ninth in 1841 Schumann wrote: "BEETHOVEN—what a word—the deep sound of the mere syllables has the ring of eternity."[3]

"I am Beethoven." The sound of Beethoven's name did not suffice to rescue its unkempt-looking bearer from embarrassment when a far-ranging peregrination took him into a suburb where he was not known and his singular, absentminded demeanor attracted hostile attention. He was mistaken for a beggar and arrested in Wiener Neustadt by the local policeman who, seeing that he had no hat and wore an old coat, flatly informed the protesting stranger that he was a tramp ("Ein Lump sind Sie") and that the famous Beethoven "doesn't look that way" ("So sieht der Beethoven nicht aus").[4] Probably, as far as the intrepid constable was concerned, the "tramp" had not even pronounced the great composer's name correctly!

These two acoustical offerings on the name Beethoven typify the extremes to which the proliferating Beethoven legends would range—from the sublime to the uncouth. There was to be no middle ground for one whom mythopoesis had chosen to embrace.

And yet Beethoven welcomed the mythmaking process, sometimes consciously, sometimes unconsciously. That the impetus for the unresolved oscillations between the anecdotal and the mythic in the Beethoven mystique was provided by Beethoven himself is repeatedly confirmed in the composer's own writings and actions as well as in the reminiscences (already subject, of course, to distortion) of his contemporaries. If Wagner would later call him a "tone hero," Beethoven had already suggested this noble appellation by referring to himself as a "tone poet" ("Tondichter") when discussing his desire to raise music to the level of poetry.

During the course of the nineteenth century two approaches were taken concerning the mundane and mythical faces of the original Beethoven coin: his outer appearance and inner life were made to resemble the gamut of emotions perceived in his music, and his music was interpreted as embodying the passions (and in some cases the defects) of his mercurial personality. This double vision, in which, in the service of myth, the man was matched to his music and vice versa, may have contained contradictions, but it also embraced a larger truth that facts could not pierce. Truth, like time, does not stand still, but is propelled by changing currents of meaning. The power of myth does not depend on correspondence with the facts, but rather upon its capacity to color facts with relevance for later generations. It is the metamorphosis that is the stuff of mythmaking.

Like a greedily feeding shark, the mythmaking process swallows up the flotsam of fantasy along with morsels of reliable data. A robust example of the responsiveness of the Beethoven-as-hero concept to the needs and expectations of successive generations is the lasting popularity of the so-called Incident at Teplitz, furnished by Bettina Brentano von Arnim (1785–1859) some two decades after the event.[5] Since the "incident" reportedly provoked drastically contrasting reactions from two of Germany's greatest geniuses—Beethoven and Goethe—(introduced to each other through the agency of their mutual friend Bettina) every detail of the story was rapaciously consumed and memorized by the German public. The setting was a park in Bohemia's oldest spa, Teplitz, and the date was 1812—one year before Napoleon's enemies would assemble there to sign a coalition treaty against the self-proclaimed emperor who had so disappointed Beethoven and so bedazzled Goethe. A letter[6] allegedly written by Beethoven to Bettina from Teplitz in August of 1812 and published by her in 1839 describes what occurred while he and Goethe were taking a walk together: "On the way home yesterday we met the entire imperial family. From a distance we saw them approaching, and Goethe slipped away from me to stand to one side; say what I would, I could not induce him to advance a step further. I pulled my hat down on my head, buttoned my overcoat, and with folded arms pushed through the thickest part of the crowd. Princes and sycophants drew up in line; Archduke Rudolf took off his hat; the Empress was the first to greet me. Persons of rank know me. To my great amusement, I saw the procession file past Goethe; hat in hand, he stood at the side, bowing deeply."[7]

An amusing nineteenth-century print (Fig. 1) deftly catches the salient points of the drama. The proud figure of Beethoven, his top hat slammed securely on the back of his head and his arms crossed behind him, strides defiantly forward, the sole occupant of the lower half of the picture plane. Engrossed in his own thoughts, he is—apparently—oblivious of the Habsburg promenade through which he has just barged. At the same time, to the upper left, the tall, distin-

1 *Willibrod Josef Mähler*, Portrait of Beethoven with Lyre, *c. 1804,*
oil, Historisches Museum der Stadt Wien, Vienna.

2 *Gustav Leybold,* Beethoven's Study in the Schwarz-spanierhaus *(showing "contemporary" Beethoven bust by Anton Dietrich), 1827, color lithograph, Historisches Museum der Stadt Wien, Vienna.*

3
Ferdinand Schimon,
Portrait of Beethoven
1818–1819, oil,
Beethovenhaus, Bonn.

4
Joseph Karl Stieler,
Portrait of Beethoven,
1819, oil, Collection
Walter Hinrichsen, New York.

Josef Danhauser,
Liszt at the Piano,
1840, oil on wood,
Nationalgalerie,
Berlin, on loan
to the Musical
Instrument Museum,
Berlin.

6   *Ferdinand Georg Waldmüller,*
     Portrait of Beethoven, *1823,*
     oil, formerly possession
     of Breitkopf and Härtel,
     Leipzig (destroyed).

Kaspar Clemens Zumbusch, 7
Beethoven Monument,
*1880, bronze and
granite porphyry,
Beethoven-Platz,
Vienna.*

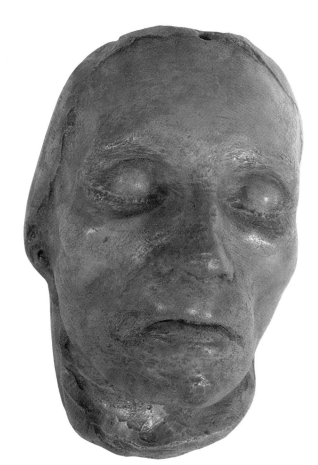

Josef Danhauser, 9
Death Mask of
Beethoven, *1827,
plaster,
Historisches
Museum der Stadt
Wien, Vienna.*

8

Ernst Julius Hähnel,
Beethoven Monument, *1845,
bronze, Münster-Platz, Bonn.*

10   *Max Klinger*, Beethoven Monument, *1902, various colored marbles, ivory,
        precious stones, polished gold, and bronze, Museum der bildenden
        Künste, Leipzig, on loan to the Gewandhaus, Leipzig.*

guished figure of Goethe bows with the greatest ceremony to the royal couple. Goethe's etiquette is servilely correct: his eyes are lowered, he touches his heart with one hand and swings his hat low to the ground with the other. Beethoven looks and acts like a bull by comparison. Emperor Franz I and his wife, Maria Ludovica, acknowledge the grand old man of Weimar with courtly restraint, while to the right of the picture, a highly idealized figure who is supposed to be the young and genial Archduke Rudolf, Beethoven's pupil and loyal patron, turns around with open-mouthed astonishment, his hat suspended in mid-doff, to stare at the composer's rudely turned back.

Certainly, if true, this was indeed an "incident" at Teplitz—one that could not fail to fascinate an age in which, ever since the French Revolution, many Europeans had begun to question the rights and even the very existence of the aristocracy. We may note in passing that, for this vignette—presented to the world in print by Bettina just nine years before the revolutions of 1848—the earlier image of Beethoven's supposed noble birth was not only inappropriate but already discarded. The plain, dark overcoat, which he had buttoned up defiantly, made this unfettered god of music a man of the people—perfect symbol for the battle against tyranny.[8]

But was the Teplitz story true? How much was Wahrheit and how much was Dichtung? Bettina had also described the incident herself in a letter of 1832. Even greater belligerence is ascribed to Beethoven: "While they were walking there came towards them the whole court, the Empress and the dukes; Beethoven said: 'Keep hold of my arm, they must make room for us, not we for them.' Goethe was of a different opinion, and the situation became awkward for him; he let go of Beethoven's arm and took a stand at the side with his hat off, while Beethoven with folded arms walked right through the dukes...on the other side he stopped and waited for Goethe, who had permitted the company to pass by him where he stood with bowed head. 'Well,' he said, 'I've waited for you because I honor and respect you as you deserve, but you did those yonder too much honor.' "[9]

If, as is now generally held, Bettina's two-part presentation of the Teplitz tale (Beethoven's "letter" to her of 1812; her reminiscence letter of 1832) indulges in poetic emphases, the substance of the narrative is corroborated by both Beethoven and Goethe. Concerning Beethoven's bullish behavior, for example, Goethe wrote his close friend the musician Carl Friedrich Zelter a frank but compassionate critique of the man he had just recently met: "I made the acquaintance of Beethoven in Teplitz. His talent amazed me. However, unfortunately, he is an utterly untamed personality, not at all in the wrong, if he finds the world detestable, but he thereby does not make it more enjoyable either for himself or others. He is very much to be excused on the other hand, and very much to be pitied, as his hearing is leaving him, which, perhaps, injures the musical part of his nature less than his social. He, by nature laconic, becomes double so because of this lack."[10]

Beethoven's disdain for what he considered to be Goethe's lackeying to the nobility was real, and his chatty—for him—excursion into this "defect" of the German language's greatest poet somewhat self-consciously adorns an otherwise ordinary business letter to his Leipzig music publishers Breitkopf and Härtel, written a few weeks after the Teplitz encounter: "Goethe delights far too much in the court atmosphere, far more than is becoming to a poet. How can one really say very much about the ridiculous behavior of virtuosi in this respect, when poets, who should be regarded as the leading teachers of the nation, can forget everything else when confronted with that glitter."[11]

Other than the fact that Beethoven was showing off a bit to his publishers about having met Goethe, his tone signals not only disapproval but disappointment that Goethe the man did not live up to the lofty role of Goethe the poet. For years Beethoven had carried his own Goethe "myth" in his heart (as demonstrated by the 1809 and 1810 song settings of Goethe texts and the inspired composition of the *Egmont* music during the same years). In an earlier letter to his Leipzig publishers also written from Teplitz, he had announced almost breathlessly in the midst of technical instructions: "Goethe is here"; and in his next letter to them he positively glowed with pride, reporting: "That Goethe is here I have already told you. I spend some time with him every day."[12] When his idol disappointed him ("köstlich"—"beautiful"—was all Goethe had had to say about Beethoven's playing the piano for him), Beethoven may have decided to lash out at him, even teach him a lesson, in front of the *false* idols of the nobility. Certainly something happened at Teplitz to steer the smoker (Beethoven liked a pipe) and the nonsmoker (Goethe detested tobacco) out of each other's orbits. Bettina von Arnim's Incident at Teplitz may be partly aggrandized, even partly falsified, but it is not fictitious. And to the mythmaking process such distinctions are peripheral. The fact of the story's existence, not the story's facts, is what matters.

Looking again at our nineteenth-century print, let us give Bettina's descriptive talents a final hearing, as we match her eyewitness impression of Beethoven's physical appearance with the image before us: "In person he was small (for all his soul and heart were so big), brown, and full of pockmarks. He is what one terms repulsive, yet has a divine brow, rounded with such noble harmony that one is tempted to look on it as a magnificent work of art."[13]

Posterity, building on the raw materials provided by Beethoven, Goethe, and Bettina von Arnim, did indeed make a "work of art" out of the Teplitz anecdote. Both the *how*—three aspects of the same event—and the *why*—the pre-1848 revolutionary mood of Europe that was disposed to see in Beethoven a fellow fighter against repression—of this particular canto of the Beethoven myth provide us with compelling clues to the cultural history of an entire epoch.

History's Ode to Beethoven has been and will continue to be reorchestrated by each new century. As the stanzas are voiced in many languages, harmony is not always the result. The pinnacle of universality upon which Beethoven's music is so frequently placed has not been impervious to political assault. At first glance it would seem as though no one in the family of nations would disagree with the following internationalist statement made in the early 1940s: "[Beethoven's] nine symphonies represent the highest and noblest type in existence of music that appeals to the mass of the people as well as to fastidious connoisseurs . . . they are popular in the sense that they express the dim emotional longings of a vast mass of people agitated by common griefs, joys, aspirations, and ideals. Here is music of a universal validity—not merely German, not merely religious, but intelligible through its fervor, its eloquence, its force, and its beauty, to all humanity, regardless of the nation, language, or creed."[14]

And yet three decades later, in the 1970s, the party newspaper of the People's Republic of China singled out the music of Beethoven for special condemnation. In an article headlined "Works of Music without Titles Don't Reflect the Class

Spirit," the daily *Jenmin Jih Pao* denounced "numbered works" by the "German capitalist musician Beethoven," and especially what is called Sonata no. 17 (op. 17, Sonata for Piano and Horn in F Major; the fourth movement of which is described by Czerny as "tempestuous"), comparing it with Shakespeare's *The Tempest* as another example of the "filthy nature of the bourgeoisie." The article dismissed the idea that music was a common language transcending national boundaries and reminded its readers that Beethoven composed in an epoch during which "cruel oppression and exploitation of peasants and workers" existed.[15]

Unlike China, Russia was able to read class struggle right into Beethoven's scores: the fourth movement of the Ninth, characterized as the "anthem of human freedom," was performed before the Supreme Soviet with the approval of the purge-prone Stalin, and Lenin freely confessed to Gorky once that he found Beethoven's *Appassionata* Sonata "formidable, super-human music."[16]

Nazi Germany's use and abuse of the Beethoven myth could fill a volume. Hitler's fanatical contempt for his Austrian homeland prompted him to dispute Vienna's historical claim to its famous citizen by churlishly pointing out on the eve of the Anschluss that Beethoven came from the Rhineland.[17] But even the "Germanness" of Beethoven's music could not protect a Jewish performer of it: as early as April 1933 Artur Schnabel was suddenly cut off the air in the middle of broadcasting a cycle of the thirty-two piano sonatas over the Berlin radio.[18] Across the English channel, the ironic weapon of a Beethoven boomerang was nightly hurled at those Germans who listened in secret to British shortwave broadcasts during World War II. A stirring "V for Victory" was signaled before each BBC transmission by playing the opening four notes of the Fifth Symphony, which parallel in their duration the three dots and one dash that stand for the letter *V* in international Morse code.

In another medium and on a different battlefield—that of conjugal maneuvering—Tolstoy had brilliantly used the emotional power of Beethoven's music to undo its listeners as the long-delayed denouement for his 1889 novella *The Kreutzer Sonata*. The jealous husband, Vasa Pozdnischeff, masochistically imagines to himself what is occurring between his wife—"a creature of instinct"—and their bachelor acquaintance, the "well-fed, sleek" moustached Trookhatschevsky, while he is away from Moscow on business in the country. Music—"the most refined lust of the senses"—muses Vasa, had brought them together a week before, and he bitterly recalls the soirée at his home when his wife, at the piano, and his rival, armed with violin, performed the *Kreutzer* Sonata. Vasa speculates on "the terrible effects that music occasionally produces," adding, "In China music is a state concern, and this is as it ought to be." A veritable torrent of music-triggered madness is then unleashed: "Take the 'Kreutzer Sonata,' for example: is it right to play that first *presto* in a drawing-room to ladies in low dresses? to play that *presto*, then to applaud it, and immediately afterward to eat ice creams and discuss the latest scandal?[19] Such pieces as this are only to be executed in rare and solemn circumstances of life. . . . It is meant to be played and then to be followed by the feats for which it nerves you. . . . Upon me, at least, this piece produced a terrible effect; it seemed as if new feelings were revealed to me, new possibilities unfolded to my gaze, of which I had never dreamed before."

Remembrance of the power of Beethoven's music has "ravished" Vasa out of himself, has made possible the awful recognition of his wife's supposed unfaithfulness: "How could I have been foolish enough to leave the city?... Was it not as clear as daylight that everything was consummated between them on that evening?..."

Irrevocably convinced of the truth of his fantasy, Vasa rushes back to Moscow and discovers—just as he had imagined—the couple together in his house. They are at dinner and start to express their surprise. "But neither he nor she finished what they were going to say. The insane frenzy... had again taken possession of me; once more I experienced the same mania for destroying, for using violence, for assuring the triumph of madness; and I yielded myself up to it body and soul."[20] Their protestations of innocence are to no avail. The long-burning fuse of the *Kreutzer* Sonata has ignited Vasa's *voluntary* insanity and he mortally stabs his (evidently guiltless) wife.

Tolstoy's demonic employment of Beethoven—the sound of Beethoven—as the psychological trigger for maniacal action would be repeated in the twentieth century in an even more satanic key by the Anthony Burgess/Stanley Kubrick 1971–72 collaboration of the disturbing, violence-focused movie *A Clockwork Orange*.

The association of Beethoven with violence received its most extreme expression in the self-destructive conduct of the young Jewish author Otto Weininger (1880–1903). In 1903, at the age of twenty-three, he published the sensational best-seller, *Sex and Character*, a malevolent and bizarre tract on women, Jews, and bisexuality. He was not able, however, to resolve the corrosive conflicts within himself that had generated this self-revelatory book. In a pathetic attempt to link himself with genius, he rented a room in the house where Beethoven had breathed his last, wrote two notes announcing his intentions, and on 3 October 1903 shot himself in the heart. The inscription on his grave is a tragic and twisted testimonial to Beethoven: "This stone marks the resting place of a young man whose spirit found no peace in this world. When he had delivered the message of his soul, he could no longer remain among the living. He betook himself to the place of death of one of the greatest of all men, the Schwarzspanierhaus in Vienna, and there destroyed his mortal body."[21]

Identification with Beethoven—a phenomenon not confined to Austria, as we shall see—did have its lighter moments. As a young man, Arnold Schönberg was catapulted into earning his living as a full-time musician by getting himself fired from a low-paying, monotonous bank job when he signed a customer into the account books as "L. van Beethoven."

The conception of Beethoven—the man and his music—prompted antiphonal responses in the arts as well as in real life. Search for the identification of the "Immortal Beloved" alone has animated a genre of literature that runs from the crude to the shrewd, embracing fantasy novellas and psychobiographical detective work.[22] And music "in response" to Beethoven abounds: Meyerbeer composed a choral work after visiting the musician's grave entitled: *Le Voyageur au tombeau de Beethoven* (1845), but less eponymously all of the great symphonists since Beethoven, from Schubert and Schumann to Bruckner, Brahms, Tchaikovsky, Dvořák, and Mahler, have acknowledged and benefited from the liberating example of Beethoven before them, especially the monumental Ninth Symphony.

It is in the visual arts, however, that the image of Beethoven most directly recorded the fluctuating pulse beat of the mythmaking process. Before the mass acoustical access to Beethoven made possible by twentieth-century technology—

radio, records, tapes, cassettes, chips, television—it was the visual Beethoven that enjoyed the widest currency. That historical coinage, minted mostly by nineteenth-century fabricators, still gleams with cultural content. It is the changing image of Beethoven that now invites our closer scrutiny as we reach for a magnifying glass to examine how Beethoven the man became Beethoven the myth.

Chapter Two

BEETHOVEN ALIVE: EYEWITNESS ACCOUNTS AND CONTEMPORARY LIKENESSES

"Yet, why should Beethoven's features look like his scores?" This remark—half admonishing, half astonished—concludes the brief physical description of Beethoven by the Berlin music critic Ludwig Rellstab (1799–1860) in 1825. Rellstab was given to visual analogies: it was his comparison of the first movement of the Piano Sonata op. 27, no. 2 to a moonlit vista of Lake Lucerne that prompted the (unknown to Beethoven) identifying title of *Moonlight* Sonata. By the time the romantically inclined and hero-worshiping young Rellstab met Beethoven in person the composer was internationally acclaimed. Through the recently invented technique of lithography his image had been extensively circulated both on the continent and abroad. Hence Rellstab's surprise, even disappointment, that Beethoven in the flesh evinced "nothing that expressed that brusqueness, that tempestuous, unshackled quality which has been lent his physiognomy in order to bring it into conformity with his works." In fact, up close the myth appeared to be only a man. "His features at first glance seemed lacking in significance: his face was much smaller than I had pictured it in accordance with the likeness which has forcibly constrained it to an appearance of powerful, genial savagery."[1]

Of which likeness was the moonstruck Rellstab thinking? Which image of Beethoven, in circulation prior to Rellstab's visit of 1825, gave the composer a look of "powerful, genial savagery"? Attempts to chart a simple, straight course to the correct answer bring us to the looming tip of the vast iconographical iceberg of Beethoven portraits. Consider the complications involved in tracking this single image with accuracy. First of all, although Rellstab's visit to Beethoven took place in early April 1825—two years before the composer's death at the age of fifty-six—Rellstab, who was twenty-six at the time of his Vienna visit, did not write about this encounter and the impressions it made on him until several decades later. His Beethoven vignette did not appear in print until a year after Rellstab's own death, when it was included in the critic's posthumous memoirs of 1861.[2] Thus, even before we turn down the lights and scrutinize a lineup of portrait suspects, we have to concede that our logical cut-off date of 1825 may actually be misleading. Rellstab's memory of the "powerful, genial savagery" likeness of Beethoven might, by the end of his life, have included one or more of the increasingly demonic-looking images of Beethoven produced after 1825.

Then, too, we must ascertain the medium of the specific likeness referred to by Rellstab: was it a painting in oil, a drawing, an etching, or a lithograph? Knowing in which medium the likeness was executed would be a welcome aid since there is a great deal of data concerning the dates and circumstances of the various oil portraits and sketches from life for which Beethoven sat. The prints also are rather thoroughly documented: both portrait lithographs and portrait engravings were made of the composer during his lifetime. Then, at first only in Vienna, but later elsewhere, there were busts of Beethoven available for public contemplation. But even if Rellstab had conveniently mentioned the medium of the Beethoven "likeness" to which Beethoven-in-person did not, in his opinion, correspond, we would still be dealing with three categories of Beethoven imagery in existence both before and after the 1825 visit. First, there are the likenesses made by artists in front of the model himself—with the knowledge and compliance of the sitter. Second, there are the unauthorized copies of these originals, which, either due to ineptitude or avoidance of legal complications, present altered and sometimes drastic variations on the original theme. Such copies also have a history of switching from medium to medium—an "original" oil painting may be based on a well-known print, or an independent "new" engraving, slightly reduced or enriched in detail, and pulled of course in reverse, may be siphoned from the undiluted oil original. Third, and finally, there are the likenesses comprising caricature and fantasy. It must have been about one of the former that Beethoven exploded in a letter to a friend: "You said something yesterday about that likeness of me. . . . Try to get hold of the thing, if it is at all possible to do so. I assure you that after this experience I will appeal in the Press to all painters not to paint me again without my knowledge. I really did not think that this face of mine would ever cause me embarrassment. . . ."[3]

An embarrassing caricature is probably the one likelihood we can safely exclude in our pursuit of Rellstab's reference. We may also, a shade less safely, temporarily ignore the few oil portraits for which Beethoven sat.

We shall return to the oil portraits, but in the meantime compelling circumstantial evidence invites our speculation that a print was the medium through which Rellstab's acquaintance with Beethoven's likeness was most probably first made. The prevalence and easy availability of etchings and lithographs immediately suggests this theory, and the following witness may be brought in to testify. Proceeding backwards from the 1825 visit, we find an account of 1823 entitled "A Day with Beethoven" written by an English musician with a German surname, Edward Schulz, and published less than four months after the event in a London music magazine. Schulz visited the composer in one of his favorite summer retreats, the picturesque village of Baden outside Vienna, and wrote from strenuous first-hand experience: "Beethoven is a famous pedestrian, and delights in walks of many hours, particularly through wild and romantic scenery."[4] Aside from this set-designer's bonanza for later contributions to the Beethoven-in-nature iconography, another remark by Schulz informs us of Beethoven's visual presence across the channel: "The portrait you see of him in the music shops is not now like him, but may have been so eight or ten years back."[5]

Like Rellstab, Schulz found a contrast between Beethoven in person and the

Beethoven of portraiture. Unlike Rellstab, the Englishman was not glimpsing Beethoven for the first time; he had met him once before, briefly, in 1816. Now he found Beethoven considerably altered and was struck by the thought that the composer looked "very unhappy." By referring to the appropriateness of London music-shop imagery to the Beethoven of "eight or ten years ago," Schulz has helped, possibly, to date the print, of which we are in pursuit. Subtracting eight to ten years from the date 1823 brings us back to the days of the Congress of Vienna, which convened from September 1814 to June 1815. This was the time of Beethoven's greatest public popularity—the handsomely apropos *Wellington's Victory* (op. 91, 1813) was ecstatically received by anti-Napoleonic audiences thronging Vienna for the Congress. Beethoven was presented to the assembled empresses and monarchs by a proud Archduke Rudolf (apparently unmiffed by the Incident at Teplitz). There was a sudden demand for mementos of the composer and the Vienna art-and-music publishing firm Artaria and Co. commissioned an engraved portrait of Beethoven for popular distribution. The French miniature portrait painter and pastel artist Louis Letronne (1790–1842), who was active in Vienna from 1805 to 1817, made a crayon sketch of the composer from life. The Viennese engraver Blasius Höfel (1792–1863) was hired to transfer the drawing to copper plate. The interpretive gap possible twixt one artist's crayon and another's burin is dramatically displayed in the contrast presented by the two images (Figs. 2 and 3).

The French master's rendition is without myth: it is plain, rapidly executed, visual rapportage. It records the Beethoven topography at an even-handed, unemotional level. The forty-three-year-old composer looks surprisingly youthful. His flowing white cravat is most chic. Letronne had shown the surface, but Vienna wanted the psyche. Blasius Höfel complained about the unsatisfactory quality of the drawing and despaired over the preliminary lines on his copper plate. Then he hit on an idea: he would ask the favor of an additional sitting from Beethoven, whom he often saw from a distance at the Artaria firm. His request was granted—a most unusual occurrence—and the young artist was allowed to visit Beethoven in his own quarters for two separate sittings of almost an hour each. During these sessions the composer, after posing obediently for a few minutes, turned to the piano, began to extemporize, and quite forgot the artist's presence, thus providing Höfel with an unparalleled opportunity for close study.[6] The result is a very different Beethoven from that of Letronne's. Mythopoesis has been at work. The line of the brow is now intensified by means of a stipple shadow that connects the eyebrows and suggests a faint frown of concentration. By this one feature alone the bland passivity of the Letronne drawing is converted into keen mental activity in Höfel's engraving. Although the eyes are bright and alert, their meditative aspect is enhanced by the recessed left eye denoting inwardness—a conventional device hinted at by Letronne but firmly emphasized by Höfel. The flat, broad nostrils are slightly more flared in the Höfel version and a pronounced shadow runs the length of the nose, straightening it while lending it greater prominence. The fleshy cheeks and jaws of Letronne's drawing are squared and tightened in the Höfel print. Beethoven's lips are less mobile in the engraving and more tightly set—in keeping with the intensity of expression—and the thick, somewhat protruding lower lip is more harmoniously matched to the thin upper lip. The pronounced rounded chin observed by Letronne is carefully preserved and enhanced in the engraving, where a slight cleft has been added. Beethoven's unruly locks of dark, curly hair have been somewhat thickened without causing them to lose any of their bristling vibrancy and the height of the forehead is carried over into Höfel's image. The composer's collar and cravat have been meticulously copied from the Letronne drawing, as though the engraver were relieved not to have to redo a knot well done. Höfel also added the missing metal button to Beethoven's jacket, a detail not without anecdotal significance, for, when the composer was in one of his convivial, talkative moods, he was reported to have said of himself that he was "all unbuttoned." For this formal portrait, occasioned by his sudden fame during the Congress of Vienna, Beethoven was quite buttoned up as he sat for the foreign artist from France, who scrutinized his facade for posterity. Höfel, ambitious and reverent, and with the benefit of having watched the composer at his music making, attempted to pull forth from his copper plate an impression of the *interior* Beethoven.

But, we must now ask, is Höfel's engraved likeness of Beethoven the one Rellstab remembered as exhibiting powerful, genial savagery? We might stare long and hard at the image and, especially in contrast to the mild mien offered by Letronne, decide yes. Yes, there does seem to be a play between forceful and friendly impulses animating this elemental face. But can we trust our reaction? Have *we* not been brainwashed by two centuries of Beethoven lore? Haven't our eyes been barraged by a hundred different depictions of the "titan" captured in vinyl between the covers of colorful record jackets? Can we be as certain as the policeman who arrested that hatless tramp over a century and a half ago was about how Beethoven really looked? Or did not look?

Regardless of verisimilitude, is it not still possible for the idealized Höfel engraving to be the repository of that powerful, genial savagery noted by Rellstab? Rellstab was already dealing with myth in the face of reality, since, as he pointed out, the Beethoven he saw in 1825 did *not* resemble the Beethoven pictured by the visual arts. The evidence furnished by our English visitor concerning Beethoven's appearance in 1823 and of "eight or ten years" previous, sent us back to the Letronne-Höfel collaboration of 1814. Where do we go from here? We must now determine whether to Beethoven's acquaintances of 1814 the print of 1814 seemed "savage" (already conceptual, mythical) or "accurate" (verisimilitude in accord with perceived reality), or—also possible—*both* (concept affirmed by subjective perception; objective perception colored by preconception based on accrual of behavior impressions).

It is historically convenient that the Höfel portrait of 1814 coincides with Beethoven's making the acquaintance in March of that year with the man who would become his devoted, unpaid secretary and factotum, and first major biographer. This man was Anton Felix Schindler (1795–1864) (Fig. 4), a former law student who had switched to music and made his living as a violinist and orchestra director. With the exception of a rift in 1825, healed the next year after the suicide attempt by Beethoven's nephew, Schindler was—especially from late 1822 onwards—in constant and intimate contact with the composer. Nothing, not even Beethoven's often humiliating treatment of him, deflected the loyalty of this voluntary "slave" to his master. To Schindler's credit, he recognized the genius of Beethoven *during* his lifetime and appreciatively, if sycophantically (and later self-servingly to the point of falsifying documents), garnered every manifestation of Beethoven the mortal and Beethoven the immortal.[7]

Schindler's reaction, therefore, to the 1814 Höfel likeness can be counted upon to be fastidiously critical and possessively protective, reminding us that the wellsprings of fact and fiction can share a common source. Here is Schindler's judgment as, writing in 1860, he ponders the question of Beethoven portraits: "It has often been asked which of the various later portraits is the most faithful representation of the composer. The answer is without a doubt the engraving by Höfel after the drawing by Letronne, made in 1814 and published by Artaria and Co. It shows the master at the peak of his fame . . . with brilliant, sharply observant eyes, full cheeks, a countenance bursting with good health."[8]

This is a thoroughly positive picture of a picture. Höfel's carefully wrought ennoblement as opposed to Letronne's instant journalism is a peccadillo entirely forgiven, in fact, ignored, by the approving and knowledgeable Schindler. Schindler's assertion that Beethoven's countenance was bursting with "good health" is such welcome news that we forget for a moment to wonder what Beethoven's physical condition was actually like in 1814. The many different doctors who attended him in Vienna and the composer himself left ample testimony. In addition to the progressive deterioration of his hearing, Beethoven's general health profile at the age of forty-three is not encouraging. Even before leaving Bonn he had suffered from a "wretched abdomen" and by his thirty-first year he was complaining of "violent diarrhea" and severe digestion problems. The chronic intestinal and stomach troubles that plagued him from then on culminated in the illness that would eventually take his life, cirrhosis of the liver. In addition his ears often hummed and buzzed "day and night."[9] As to the state of his mind and its impact upon his health, ever since the Heiligenstadt Testament of 1802, written when he was in near suicidal despair over his deafness, Beethoven had with tremendous effort been resigning himself ("Resignation, what a wretched resource! Yet it is all that is left to me."[10]) to his physical fate. The profound irony was not lost upon him. A year before writing the Heiligenstadt Testament he had blurted out his awful secret to the physician Franz Gerhard Wegeler: "I must confess that I lead a miserable life. For almost two years I have ceased to attend any social functions, just because I find it impossible to say to people: I am deaf. If I had any other profession I might be able to cope with my infirmity; but in my profession it is a terrible handicap. And if my enemies, of whom I have a fair number, were to hear about it, what would they say?"[11]

Beethoven was only thirty when he wrote these despairing words. By the time of Höfel's portrait, some thirteen years later, his deafness was known to the world. If the image of Beethoven created by Höfel struck Schindler as one surging with good health, the impression is due far more to the composer's great emotional resilience and naturally rugged constitution than to the etcher's solicitous imagination. Schindler stressed Beethoven's ability to overcome depression: " . . . I had always seen the master only momentarily out of sorts or occasionally depressed. Very soon he would regain his composure, carry his head erect, stride ahead with his customary purpose and vigor, once more master in the workshop of his genius as though nothing had happened."[12]

Schindler did not say whether he saw anything of powerful, genial savagery in the Höfel portrait. Beethoven himself was most pleased with the engraving and we know that he presented copies of it to visitors and friends.[13]

What is needed at this juncture in our iconographical pursuit of the rightness or wrongness of Rellstab's characterization of a particular Beethoven likeness— whether or not it is the Höfel print—is a description of what Beethoven actually looked like. After all, Rellstab's complaint was that his host did *not* look like the "forcibly" constraining likeness he had in mind. Now, by all rights, Schindler should be a rich and trustworthy source in this regard. As the person who, during the last few years of the composer's life, saw Beethoven more times a week than anyone else (including the truant nephew, Karl), Schindler's account of the composer's physical appearance is crucial. Here is what the reverent biographer had to say in his section on Beethoven portraits: "Of all the famous musical geniuses, perhaps Beethoven had the head with the most distinctive features, starting with the thick mass of hair and continuing with the forehead, eyes, mouth, and chin in harmonious proportions, in which the only dissonance was the rather broad nose."[14]

Dissonance? We recall that Schindler was a musician. We can expect, perhaps, a sostenuto of details to follow. But instead, Schindler interrupts himself to turn his attention to the following: "It would be difficult to make a bad likeness of such strongly characteristic features, or even to make a caricature of them. Nevertheless, we have both."[15]

He returns to Beethoven now, but it is the picture of good health he most wishes to remember: "Up to his fiftieth year Beethoven's countenance presented a pleasing impression of physical well-being and highest mental capacity. It was Jupiter who sometimes looked out from his face."[16]

We have not gleaned much specific data about Beethoven's looks, but we have certainly gained a touching (and caution-inducing) impression of Schindler's doxology. Schindler may have been Fides to Beethoven's Jupiter, but he was no Zenodorus. *His* Colossus gives us little concrete knowledge of what he himself described as "distinctive." But scattered elsewhere in Schindler's life of Beethoven more exact data is forthcoming. Here is an ensemble: "Beethoven can scarcely have measured more than five feet, four inches, Vienna measure. His body was thickset, with a powerful bone structure and strong muscles; his head was unusually large, overgrown with long, stubby . . . hair, which not infrequently hung neglected about his head and . . . lent him a somewhat unkempt appearance. His forehead was high and broad; his brown eyes which when he laughed were hidden in his head, were small. On the other hand, they would suddenly be projected in unusual size, flashing as they rolled about, the pupils almost always turned upward or, immovable, staring down before them as soon as some idea seized him."[17]

Waxing lustrously on this latter aspect, Schindler contributes an appealing motif for future iconography: "Therewith, however, his whole outward appearance would in the same way suddenly undergo a startling transformation, would assume a visibly inspired and imposing semblance, so that his slight figure, like his soul, would tower before one in gigantic size. These moments of sudden inspiration often would surprise him in the midst of the gayest company or in the street, and usually attracted the liveliest attention of all passersby."[18]

More myth-inspiring information follows, interspersed with physical notations: "What was going on within him was reflected only in his radiant eyes and face, for he never gesticulated, either with his head or with his hands, save when he stood before the orchestra. His mouth was well-shaped and his lips symmetrically proportioned (when younger his lips are said to have projected somewhat) and his nose was broad. His smile lent his whole face a something exceptionally kind and amiable. . . . His laughter on the other hand, often was excessively reverberant and distorted his intellectual and powerfully marked features; then his great head would swell, his face would grow still broader, until the whole effect was that of a grinning mask. It was well that it always lasted but a moment."[19]

The cleft in Beethoven's chin observable in Höfel's engraving is remarked upon in detail by Schindler and confirms the artist's attempt at physiological fidelity: "His chin had an elongated depression in the middle and on either side, which gave it a shell-like conformation and a special peculiarity."[20]

In the changing image of Beethoven, this cleft chin—authenticated by the scribe Schindler himself—would inspire convoluted and dramatic variations.

Reading through Schindler's list of physical traits that frequently coalesce into character traits we discover that we have a psychosomatic image of "powerful, genial savagery." And so we come full circle to Rellstab. But we do not return empty-handed, for the voyage back to the 1814 portrait artifact and forward to the remembered impressions of Rellstab and Schindler written many years after Beethoven's death has given us a panoramic view of the complex components of mythonomy.

Complex and sometimes conflicting are these components. Schindler mentions Beethoven's "brown" eyes. Rellstab discusses Beethoven's "light-gray" eyes. Schindler twice refers to the composer's "broad" nose—the only dissonance, he opines, in Beethoven's features. Rellstab reports that Beethoven's nose was "narrow and sharp."[21] With contemporaries of the great musician providing such differing details, it comes as no surprise that the visual images of Beethoven fashioned during his lifetime could also evince discrepancies.

The virtuoso violinist, who would have preferred to have been remembered as a composer, Louis Spohr (1784–1859) was personally acquainted with Beethoven (whose Ninth Symphony he reluctantly found "monstrous and tasteless") and saw him during the years 1812 to 1816. In 1820, while living in London and giving private lessons, he acquired an eccentric elderly pupil who had such a passion for Beethoven that she played no other music and had her room decorated with all the portraits of the composer she had been able to collect. Spohr reminisced: "As many of these were rather dissimilar, she required me to tell her which was the best resemblance. She had a number of souvenirs of Beethoven. . . . among them a button from his nightgown. . . ."[22] This amusing vignette not only testifies to the wide variety of portrait likenesses of Beethoven in existence while he was still alive but also to the canonization process, complete with sacred relics, that was well under way.

A few more samplings of Beethoven's outer appearance as given by friends and acquaintances would be appropriate in rounding out the Rellstab-Schulz-Schindler accounts. Time and again, personality quirks and qualities strike the writers as apposite to the enumeration of physical traits. Spohr's description is a laconic example: "He was a bit rough, not to say uncouth, but an honest eye peered out from beneath bushy brows."[23] Carl Maria von Weber used just two words to sum up the conduct and the appearance of the famous man who congratulated him on Der Freischütz: "rough" and "repellent."[24]

One reporter thought to comment on Beethoven's teeth, and he was a musician, not a dentist. This was the long-lived and winsome Darmstadt composer Louis Schlösser (1800–1886) who, after an interval of sixty-three years, published his recollections of first spying upon and then getting to meet Beethoven in 1822. Time had not dimmed the vivid impression of his youth. He caught sight of Beethoven for the first time at a performance of Fidelio: "I saw, familiar to me from engravings and paintings, the features of the creator of the opera I had just heard, Beethoven himself. . . . I followed the Desired One and his companions (Schindler and Breuning, as I later discovered) like a shadow through crooked alleys and past high, gable-roofed houses, followed him until the darkness hid him from sight."[25]

The very next day Schlösser had the wonderful luck to introduce himself to the composer under the best possible circumstances as the bearer of a letter of financial good tidings from his countryman the grand duke of Hessen. Beethoven's reception was cordial and Schlösser, at last in the presence of the "Desired One," was sensitive to both the exalted and the mundane aspects of what his joyful eyes beheld: "Standing so near this artist, crowned with glory, I could realize the impression which his distinguished personality, his characteristic head, with its surrounding mane of heavy hair and the furrowed brow of a thinker, could not help but make on every one. I could look into those profoundly serious eyes, note the amiably smiling expression of his mouth when he spoke. . . . My visit probably occurred shortly after he had eaten breakfast, for he repeatedly passed the napkin lying beside him across his snow-white teeth, a habit, incidentally, in which I noticed he often indulged."[26]

Beethoven beckoned the young man to speak into his ear trumpet and what next transpired shows that the composer was only too aware of the legends circulating about him: "Though Beethoven was so impervious to flattery of any kind, my words which came stammering from the depths of my soul, nevertheless seemed to touch him, and this induced me to tell about my nocturnal pursuit of him after the performance of *Fidelio*. 'But what prevented you from coming to see me in person?' he asked. 'I am sure you have been told any amount of contradictory nonsense; that I have been described as being an uncomfortable, capricious and arrogant person, whose music one might indeed enjoy, but who was personally to be avoided.'"[27]

Indeed Schlösser had been told, ever since his arrival in Vienna some months before, that a stranger's chances of meeting the great recluse were doomed to failure. But Beethoven in the flesh showed the greatest sociability, causing Schlösser to ask himself afterward: "Was this actually the incomparable tonal hero, accorded the most devoted reverence by all classes, whose genius, by striking the shackles from the infinity of the psychic, had called into being a new era of culture . . . ?"[28]

Schlösser remembered and wrote down what he asked himself in such high-flung language in the 1880s, not in the 1820s, and it should therefore not amaze us to find his language studded with favorite catch phrases and key words from the legacy of Romanticism—"striking the shackles," "infinity," and "psychic."

In addition to its general interest this literary portrait of Beethoven demonstrates how every nuance of his behavior as well as every detail of his appearance were absorbed into the mythic memory, whether recounted by eyewitnesses for history with love or with rancor. In publishing his reminiscences the eighty-five-year-old Schlösser was not unaware that his positive account of the composer's conduct would stand alongside colorful evidence to the contrary. He made a plea for equal time: "For all that a more rigorous examination can not free Beethoven from the reproach of momentary loss of temper and disregard for the forms of good society, these lesser shadows, in view of the very limited intercourse with the outside world entailed by his deafness and his ever-increasing absorption in the inner world of his own thoughts, after all, establish a just claim to consideration where he is concerned. . . . I consider quite as open to question the credibility of a number of anecdotes current about him in Vienna regarding his eccentricities and extravagances. . . ."[29]

And so, at the end of his long life, we have one of the myth-reporters reproaching the mythmaking process with a shake of his Romantic walking stick.

It is difficult, as we have seen, to keep our exploratory voyage confined to the narrow course of Beethoven's outer appearance, which, at every bend, is fed into by so many anecdotal streams. Is there not one contemporary observer of Beethoven who kept an unswerving line of pure physical description? The answer is, largely, no: not of any sustained length. The recollections given by those who knew Beethoven in his extreme youth touch on his physique but feature his precocious behavior, musical or otherwise. Quite self-conscious of the fact that he was now describing a famous man, the master baker Gottfried Fischer (1780–1864), son of the couple who owned the house in the Rheingasse where Beethoven grew up in Bonn, took care to label his narrative "Former physique of Herr Ludwig van Beethoven." He continued: "Short and thick-set, broad across the shoulders, short neck, large head, rounded nose, dark-brown complexion; always leaned forward a little in walking. When still a boy they used to call him 'der Spagnol' (the Spaniard) in our house."[30]

This report, attesting and emphasizing Beethoven's unusually dark "foreign" complexion even as a boy, would have unforeseen consequences in America during the 1970s when, as an offshoot of the Civil Rights movement and growing black pride, a popular slogan was formulated: "Beethoven was black." This particular myth was given a curious boost in currency by the fact that the earliest known image of Beethoven is a silhouette cut out in black paper by the otherwise unknown artist Joseph Neesen (Fig. 8). It shows Beethoven at about the age of sixteen, with typical eighteenth-century pigtail and jabot. His "rounded nose" contrasts with his full, slightly receding forehead and his lips are pushed forward by teeth that protrude a bit. His chin is powerful and his neck is short—all physical characteristics of the mature Beethoven.

One of the first people to commit Beethoven's features to memory after his reputation began to grow in Vienna was a gifted teenage pianist identified as Fraülein von Kissow. Around 1796, barely fourteen years old, she greatly impressed the composer by her excellent playing of his recent sonatas. She had ample opportunity to observe him and her frank description did not repress the disfiguring smallpox scars she had noticed: "He was short and insignificant, with an ugly red face full of pockmarks. His hair was very dark and hung fairly tousled about his face."[31]

The facial scars noted by this female reporter and, we may remember, by Bettina Brentano von Arnim, were artfully concealed by the painter Christian Horneman (1765–1844) in the portrait miniature he painted of a very comely[32] Beethoven in 1803 (Fig. 6). The dark "tousled" hair is abundantly in evidence as is a quite pronounced cleft chin. The eyelids are thin and recede somewhat under the prominent brows—a feature consistently repeated with amazingly little variation in the later portraits from life—but the long nose is unreconcilable with the verbal descriptions we have gathered. Patching up after a quarrel, Beethoven made a gift of this appealing, if misleading, portrait to his friend Stephan von Breuning (1774–1827) (spotted by the young Schlösser when he followed Beethoven and Schindler home from the fateful *Fidelio* performance). Like Beethoven, von Breuning had recently moved from Bonn to Vienna where he would pursue a successful career in law, becoming a Hofrat in 1818. The intimate gift that passed between these two lifelong friends had no impact on contemporary Beethoven imagery since it was never reproduced as a print (and is certainly not a candidate for Rellstab's "savagery" likeness), but the idealized image foreshadows later Romantic attempts at nasal enhancements and complexion cures.

Some of the most unembellished and direct information about Beethoven's physical appearance comes from people who were children when they met the composer. Carl Czerny (1791–1857), of later pedagogical fame, was taken to meet his future piano teacher when he was about ten years old. The sight of Beethoven at once reminded him of "the picture in Campe's *Robinson Crusoe*. . . . His coal-black hair, cut *à la Titus*, bristled shaggily about his head. His beard—he had not been shaved for several days—made the lower part of his already brown face still darker."[33] Told to play something, Czerny began to play a Mozart piano concerto. Beethoven became interested, sat down beside him, and filled in the orchestral melody over Czerny's accompanying passages, giving the boy a chance to observe that "his hands were overgrown with hair and his fingers, especially at the ends, were very broad."[34]

Another child, the droll young son of Stephan von Breuning, was an almost daily visitor to the composer during the last year of his life. Gerhard von Breuning (1813–1892) was impressed by Beethoven's "dazzlingly white and unbroken rows of teeth" (not that common a sight in nineteenth-century Europe) and had many things to say about his friend's outward appearance as it was affected by "that indifference to dress peculiar to him"—a subject to which we shall return for the origin of some of the most cherished Beethoven legends.[35]

We have now assembled enough written data on Beethoven's physical appearance to produce a reasonably reliable ensemble for use as a matrix in judging the portraits. Putting aside the visual images we have examined so far, let us recapitulate the physical impression of Beethoven yielded up by eyewitness accounts. Beethoven was stocky and on the short side, with powerful shoulders. His complexion was brownish, and later a sickly yellow. He was hirsute and the hair on his head grew in thick black, and later gray, tufts of somewhat bristly texture. He had broad hands with short, spatulate fingers. His square face was topped by a rounded and high forehead. His jawbone was muscular and his chin quite prominent, with a pronounced cleft. He had bushy eyebrows, narrow eyelids, and small, piercing brown eyes that either rotated agitatedly upward or glazed into thoughtful stasis. His nose was flat and his mouth strong, with a slightly protruding lower lip. Usually his lips were set tightly closed, but when he laughed, perfect white teeth were revealed. The expression of his countenance could radiate, in rapid and unpredictable sequence, geniality, melancholy, or total oblivion of his surroundings.

Could such an external semblance be the shell for "powerful, genial savagery"? Rellstab had said that Beethoven in the flesh displayed "nothing which expressed that brusqueness, that tempestuous, unshackled quality which has [in portraiture] been lent his physiognomy in order to bring it into conformity with his works."

The modern reader, whether or not discovering such qualities in Beethoven's music, cannot fail to recognize the litany of traits just recited. They are part of the Beethoven mystique—a mystique solidifying while the composer was still alive. They are not myth but fact, and spring from the character of the man himself. Too much testimony and too many tales concerning the abrupt, stormy, unfettered nature of Beethoven exist to be ignored. If Beethoven was indeed the first composer consistently to voice extramusical ideas in his music, he was expressing (as Van Gogh would do later in paint) himself. It was the dualism of tenderness and turbulence, a spirit assailed yet assailing, which Beethoven's personality bridged and displayed—in his demeanor as well as in his music. He *did*—frequently—look like, that is, *act* like, *feel* like, his scores. This was what Höfel and not Letronne had seen. Beethoven *was* a genius; his character partook of this special gift and in part shaped it, but only in his music, his best music, did he transcend human frailty. A unison of his personality with his work was what hero worshipers (and later biographers) expected, needed to find and so frequently did not. Friends and strangers alike experienced the Beethoven of distrustful, tyrannical, rebellious, melancholy moods. His nephew, Karl, was driven to attempt suicide as an escape from the uncle who insisted on being his father. And yet this same man could infuse his music with lofty purpose. His noble motives could become moral motifs and are experienced as such by countless performers and listeners. His philosophy of resignation, reverence for nature, capacity for passionate feeling, emotional resilience, acceptance of struggle, and stubborn hope for humanity all resonate in his music. Not always, of course. Just as with his letters, he could also write funny, irreverent, witty, and even raucous music. His oeuvre has been seen and can be seen as a continuous personal confession: a great humanist's dialogue with life. "Ich schreibe Noten aus Nöten" ("I write notes from need"), Beethoven used to say, succumbing to his universal love of puns (so natural for this man of sharpened aural awareness) and acknowledging quite simply the elemental force that drove him to "speak" in music, just as, finally, he compelled music and voices to speak in the Ninth.

The mythicization of Beethoven, both contemporary and posthumous, was facilitated partly because, more than with most artists, much of the style was the man. How to convey that much of this man was also very like his style became the self-appointed task of a volunteer army of eyewitnesses, painters, sculptors, and biographers.

We recall that our eyewitness Rellstab had expected to see, and then reprimanded himself for the thought, a Beethoven who looked like his scores. But the Beethoven he saw in April 1825 was a seriously sick man. His painful intestinal troubles had briefly incapacitated him, and he had been warned by physicians that he was in danger of an inflammation of the bowels. "I am not quite well, I have been ill," Beethoven told Rellstab in the first moment of their meeting.[36] As Rellstab sat beside the "sick, melancholy sufferer," he read "sadness, suffering and kindness in his face; yet I repeat not a trace of harshness, not a trace of the tremendous boldness which characterizes the impetus of his genius was even evanescently noticeable."[37] But we have a probable and very practical explanation of why Beethoven did not now resemble his earlier portrait likenesses. Edward Schulz had already commented on the "considerable alteration" in Beethoven's appearance by 1823, and now even Schindler removed his rose-colored glasses: "The illness of 1825 dimmed the fire in [Beethoven's] eyes so that, like so much of his internal and external being which at that time had begun to undergo a metamorphosis, the strange look in his eyes was no longer to be seen."[38]

Slowly, then, the fires that sustained the "powerful, genial savagery" of Beethoven's life and likeness were burning down. This sharp decline in health is certainly one reason why, to the young, idolizing Rellstab, Beethoven did not look like his scores.[39]

The iconographic quest for the "complete" Beethoven—that matching of the outer with the inner man—got an extremely helpful boost in 1812 because of an ambitious project conceived by Beethoven's good friend, piano maker Johann Andreas Streicher (1761–1833). As decoration for his private concert hall on the Ungargasse, Streicher wished to have the busts of famous musicians placed on wall brackets around the room. The Viennese anatomical sculptor Franz Klein (1779–after 1836), whose procedure of taking life masks from his sitters before modeling their busts had earned him the nickname "Professor Head Lopper," was engaged for the task of adding the forty-one-year-old Beethoven to Streicher's hall of celebrities. Klein encountered some resistance from his famous subject, who was sure the wet gypsum with which his whole face had been plastered would suffocate him. The first attempt ended in failure, but the result of the second attempt is a priceless legacy. Physical comparison with the verbal portraits of Beethoven is, thanks to this uncannily accurate artifact, made possible. The squarish head is not really unusually large (as remembered by Schindler and the Bonn baker, for example); the vertical stretch from chin to hairline measures just short of eight inches (19.75 centimeters). But the forehead *is* large: pronounced, powerful, wide, rounded, and prominent without being really high. In profile view it bulges slightly forward above the furrowed brow. The nose is indeed flat and broadens out over the lower cartilage. A marked vertical groove—the philtrum—runs from under the nose to just above the middle of the upper lip. Seen level at full face the nostril wings flare ever so slightly, inspiring the "lion-muzzle" analogy of certain descriptions. If the life mask is picked up and observed from below, the orifices of the nostrils are seen to be of uneven circumference, with the left much smaller and a bit higher than the right. The contracted brow and drooping set of the firmly clamped lips are partially due to the uncomfortable procedure of plaster casting, but do agree with contemporary descriptions of Beethoven's facial expression when not animated. Most striking are the scar on the right side of the nose, the deep scar on the right side of the chin, and the pronounced cleft. When one actually touches the mask this cleft can be felt to throw up a mound of flesh on either side—the "shell-like conformation" mentioned by Schindler. This strange configuration at the tip of the chin is not the result of a bony chin but of an overdeveloped mentalis muscle that raises the chin and pushes up the lower lip.

The fidelity of Klein's life mask extends even to the reproduction of Beethoven's skin pores and facial scars. While contemporary accounts uniformly referred to the many blemishes as smallpox scars, there are some lumpy areas around the chin and mouth, on the cheeks, and especially above the nose between the eyebrows not explained by smallpox. Here is a modern (1970) medical description and analysis of the physical evidence fixed in plaster:

> The excellent life-mask of 1812 . . . shows marked lumpiness and induration of the skin at the root of the nose, on the cheeks and around the mouth and chin. In the middle of the forehead at the root of the nose, in a large area measuring 5 cm. from side to side and 2 cm. vertically and extending for a further 2 cm. down the nose, there are eight deep punched-out scars. Five of these are circular and from 0.75 to 0.5 cm. in diameter; three are elongated and measure 2 cm. by 0.4 cm., and the rest are of varying shapes and smaller size. The thickened skin of the cheeks is similarly, though not so deeply, scarred and there is

33

much similar disfigurement about the mouth and chin. The right side of the nose shows an elongated (1.5 by 0.5 cm.) atrophic scar particularly suggestive of lypus. . . . there is no record of [Beethoven's] having had smallpox; and although some of the scars, both discrete and confluent, could be due to smallpox, the larger lesions and indurations are not anything like it.[40]

Whatever the medical cause of Beethoven's pustular facial eruptions—and a secure diagnosis is admittedly difficult—the formidable impression conveyed by Klein's austere life mask of seriousness and intense concentration (again, due partly to the plastering discomfort) would be seized upon by all later image makers as appropriate to the Beethoven aura.[41] But the pockmarks—hardly conducive to hero worship—would be left behind.

If we imagine this white face crowned by a full surround of unruly, "bristly" hair, the sense of an imposing, even massive head is projected, and this is exactly what is conveyed in the plaster-of-Paris bust painted to look like bronze Klein produced. Had Rellstab visited Streicher's piano salon and seen this likeness of Beethoven on display, his indelible impression of powerful, genial savagery could only have been strengthened. Circling this life-size bust to obtain the informative profile view, we do indeed feel closer to the "complete" Beethoven, at least his outer shell. The extraordinary variety of foster homes and the metamorphic vicissitudes through which copies of Beethoven's life mask passed are subjects to which we shall return. Suffice it to say here that the Beethovenhaus in Bonn has for many years quenched the thirst of icon-hunting pilgrims with smoothly poured new drafts of gypsum in the likeness of Beethoven!

With the literary and life-mask portraits firmly ensconced in our visual memory, let us now evaluate the major effigies for which Beethoven sat during his lifetime. What will prevail? Realism? Idealism? Caricature? Or fantasy? The one factor in common is that they are all different. Even during his lifetime the visual Beethoven was a theme with intriguing and independent variations.

"A bullet,"[42] was the reaction of the first major artist to portray Beethoven, Willibrord Joseph Mähler (1778–1860), as he studied the musician's aggressively bulging forehead. The twenty-six-year-old fellow Rhinelander, newly arrived in Vienna, was promptly taken round to meet the composer in the late summer of 1804 by their mutual friend Stephan von Breuning. They found Beethoven in the midst of completing the Third Symphony. In fact, the *Eroica* was so much on the composer's mind that when Mähler begged him to perform something, he complied with the first movement of the new symphony and, without a break, extemporized upon it for a full two hours. This munificent encore gave Mähler plenty of time to observe Beethoven's broad hands and muscular fingers and to notice that he played almost without moving his hands, "the fingers alone doing the work."[43] A cordial friendship developed between the two men based on mutual admiration. Beethoven kept the three-quarter-length oil portrait Mähler soon painted of him (1804–5;) with him for the rest of his life—no mean feat, since during the thirty-five years he lived in Vienna he changed residences over forty times.

Beethoven lost most of his furniture and some of his books and personal possessions during these frequent, often precipitous moves, but one of the few things he did not lose (and which was commented upon as late as 1822 by Schlösser as the only ornament he could see in Beethoven's large but bare apartment) was what might be considered the inspiration for Mähler's picture, an oil portrait by Leopold Radoux (flourished 1754–1781) of the beloved grandfather whose

(Colorplate 1)

34

name he bore, Ludwig van Beethoven (1712–1773), former Kapellmeister at the electoral court in Bonn (Fig. 5). Radoux's picture shows a large, elegantly dressed man with fur-trimmed jacket, velvet robe, and octagonal hat, seated in an interior before an open musical score to which he directs attention by pointing at it with his right hand. His face is long with a high forehead and cleft chin. It was this serious-looking, successful musical ancestor whom Beethoven venerated (in contrast to his inept, alcoholic father) and whose image he craved to have with him at all times. In the same letter of 29 June 1801 to Franz Wegeler in which he had revealed the secret of his deafness to his far-off friend in Bonn, Beethoven had urgently requested that his grandfather's portrait be sent to him by mail coach as soon as possible. Now, four years later, the grandson's own portrait in oil must have seemed to Beethoven a fitting companion piece for the worthy Ludwig van Beethoven, the elder. Both paintings survived the composer's peregrinations and were inherited by his nephew, Karl. Here is Mähler's own description of his portrait of the Bonn Kapellmeister's famous grandson: "Beethoven is represented, at nearly full length, sitting; the left hand rests upon a lyre, the right is extended, as if, in a moment of musical enthusiasm, he was beating time; in the background is a temple of Apollo."[44]

Where Radoux had been literal, Mähler was allegorical: *his* Beethoven does not hold actual music but the age-old symbol of music and attribute of Apollo, the lyre. Ludwig van Beethoven, the younger, does not, in bourgeois fashion, point to music already set down; instead his hand rises, palm outward, in response to music heard and to be written down for the future. The inspired composer's red-lined coat has fallen from his shoulders and twines around his lower torso like a classical garment, as with a contrapposto twist his figure looms large against the backdrop of nature. The Mähler portrait is a charming if awkward balance—with its attributes of temple, lyre, outdoor setting, and dramatic blasted tree motif—of conventional "old-fashioned" neoclassicism and the new Romanticism. Mähler had studied three years in Dresden with Germany's most famous portrait painter, Anton Graff (1736–1813), but the idea of placing the creator of the *Eroica* in the world of nature with the hint that he not only communed with but commanded the elements was his own. In deference to the divine spark he wished to suggest, Mähler, like Christian Horneman before him (Fig. 6), overlooked the scarred surface of Beethoven's face and concentrated instead on the ruddy complexion, piercing eyes, and tousled hair. Also similar to the Horneman miniature of the year before, Beethoven's naturally squarish face had been somewhat elongated by emphasis on the sideburns and by depicting the nose as thinner and longer than it really was. We hear no complaint about this deviation from reality from Beethoven, who was in fact so tickled with this Apollonian reflection of himself that he wrote Mähler, who had borrowed the picture temporarily, the following urgent request: "Dear Mähler! I most earnestly request you to return my portrait to me as soon as you have made full use of it—Should you still require it for any purpose, please make haste at any rate—I have promised it to a stranger, a lady who saw the portrait at my place, so that she may have it in her room during her stay of a few weeks in Vienna—and who can resist such *charming advances*? It is clearly understood, of course, that if all kinds of *favors are going to be bestowed* on me for this, *your share* will not be forgotten—Wholly your, Bthvn"[45]

This candid letter from the thirty-three-year-old Don Juan to his worthy Leporello reveals a robust Beethoven at that randy level which was to give his two major nineteenth-century biographers—Schindler and Thayer—so many problems later on.[46] The musician has collaborated with the artist in this felicitous pictorial presentation and the mythmaking process has been given a nudge by the hero himself.

In reading Beethoven's letter to Mähler another aspect of the visual Beethoven comes to light, which, considering the insight it gives to the interior Beethoven, is worth comment. This is the "self-portrait" presented by Beethoven's letter style (so frequently *calamo currente*, as Emily Anderson, translator of the letters into English, summed it up[47]), his unregulated orthography, and his largely illegible handwriting. Beethoven's use of poignant "thought" dashes—there are four of them in the letter to Mähler quoted above—as a punctuation preferable to periods (a duty often assigned by him to commas) and his enthusiastic underlinings—twice in the Mähler letter—attest the celerity of thought that so frequently sped ahead of his pen and his passion for affirmation through attention-holding emphases. In spite of his deafness, his inconsistent orthography—especially with proper names—reflects an aural rather than a visual memory, and his native Rhenish dialect persists alongside Viennese colloquialisms. Graphologists have had a field day with Beethoven's handwriting (Fig. 7), matching its chronologically progressive (1812–19) illegibility and later (after 1819) extremely large size with periods of creative infertility, anxiety over his nephew, and onset of total deafness. If many of Beethoven's melodies emphasize the first beat, the pen pressure he exerted during the writing of a word was on the downstroke of individual letters. These downstrokes moved into agitated side-strokes as his deafness progressed. His innate rebellion against convention surfaces in the calligraphic solution he devised for avoiding the angular German script by writing in a curved manner that encompasses all directions.[48] It was the aggregate of these characteristics—presented for public memorization in the large number of facsimiles accompanying books and articles on Beethoven—that helped to flesh out the effigy of the composer being constructed by his admirers.

Returning to the Mähler portrait we might ask what the faithful amanuensis Schindler thought of it. It was, after all, an image cherished by Beethoven and one that greeted Schindler silently but emphatically every time he entered the composer's lodgings. We might imagine that it would be the object of Schindler's careful attention since, as he (mistakenly) wrote: "there are only three oil portraits of Beethoven for which he posed." Here is what he leaves history concerning the Mähler likeness: "The first [oil portrait] is a three-quarter-length portrait showing the master, about thirty years of age, seated. It is in the possession of his family and has not been copied because of its mediocrity."[49]

Mediocrity? Mähler's portrait may show a prettified Beethoven, but it certainly is not a mediocre work of art. One explanation for Schindler's contemptuous dismissal of the portrait could be the fact that the Beethoven *he* came into almost daily contact with, especially after 1819, was a man some fifteen years older than the permanent souvenir of youth staring out so challengingly at the beholder. But, as we shall presently see, there was another, all too human reason for Schindler's reluctance to admit the Mähler portrait into the Beethoven iconography. In the meantime the impression we are receiving of Schindler himself seems to suggest that just as he would not allow any detraction from Beethoven by others, neither would he permit any flattery of the master. Beethoven was *his* to idealize, no one else's.[50]

A nonheroic likeness—almost like a candid shot in its offhand, unposed manner—is the profile sketch of Beethoven (Fig. 9) done some four or five years after the Mähler oil. The drawing was probably done by Ludwig Ferdinand Schnorr von Carolsfeld (1789–1853) (uncle of Wagner's favorite Tristan, Ludwig Schnorr von Carolsfeld), who had settled in Vienna in 1804 and studied portraiture at the Academy. He may have had the chance to sketch Beethoven at the house of the Malfatti family, in whose possession the sketch remained for many years.[51] The fact that Beethoven looks so at ease in this drawing, indeed almost smiling, may reflect the contentment he felt at being included in such a warm and cultured family circle. So at home did he begin to feel with the Malfattis, in fact, that he allowed himself to fall in love with the eighteen-year-old daughter, Therese, a talented pianist whose cordial receptivity and reverence for the composer twice her age encouraged him to make a formal proposal of marriage—a proposal that was tactfully but firmly rebuffed by Therese and her parents sometime in the summer of 1810.[52] Schnorr von Carolsfeld's portrait sketch shows important agreement with the Klein life mask, with the protruding, rounded forehead and flat nose broadening at the tip all attentively reproduced. Beethoven's carefully groomed sideburns and dapper appearance in this drawing reflect the sudden attention he was lavishing on his person and dress at this "courtship" time. Under the Malfatti spell he dispatched two urgent letters to a cellist friend asking him to lend him, not his cello, but his looking glass until he could buy one like it, as his was broken.[53] The tables have been turned on mythmaking for once: it is Beethoven who has consciously and carefully provided the Schein; the artist has merely responded to it, not embellished it. The Sein of the man—equated with his music once again—is interestingly summed up by Wilhelm Karl Rust (1787–1855), a young musician from Dessau who reported back home in a letter of July 1808 on the Beethoven of this period: "He is as original and singular as a man as are his compositions; usually serious, at times merry but always satirical and bitter. On the other hand he is also very childlike and certainly very sincere. He is a great lover of truth and in this goes too far very often; for he never flatters and therefore makes enemies."[54]

No wonder the Malfatti family was kindly but cautious about the genius in its midst.

In August 1815 Beethoven obligingly sat again for his friend Mähler, who, in the wake of Congress of Vienna fever, wished to make a portrait for himself—since Beethoven had kept the first one—to add to what had become known as his "gallery of musicians." Only a year had passed since the youthful Letronne-Höfel likeness had been published, but the Beethoven of Mähler's new oil portrait looks distinctly aged (Fig. 10).[55] This portrait (of which he made at least two known copies[56]) has eschewed the stilted posturing and symbolic attributes of the earlier conception and presents a more straightforward and "interior" image. The results are eminently successful through understatement. Concentrating exclusively on Beethoven's head and upper torso, and with no gestures or setting to distract attention, Mähler has created a highly convincing counterpart in color to Klein's white life mask. The portrait agrees with the mask in all essential points and picks up on aspects only hinted at in the plaster, such as the tendency of Beethoven's eyebrows to thin into two separate grooves as they grow outwards and the undulating hairline of the forehead, which was beginning to recede at the sides, leaving a tuft of vigorously upward growing hair at the center, as supplied by Klein for his plaster bust. In the oil portrait Beethoven's hair is shown as still blackish brown (he was forty-four now), but the sufferings caused by deafness are now stamped clearly upon his face, and the expression of his small brown eyes, while alert and sparkling, denotes a certain withdrawal into a tremendously absorbing and demanding inner life. Mähler's bust portrait of Beethoven was displayed along with his portraits of other famous local musicians, and an admiring reviewer reported that he did not know which to admire more: the "perfect similitude" or the "truthful soul painting."[57] Five other contemporary musicians painted by Mähler for his portrait gallery would later have the unhappy honor of serving as pallbearers at Beethoven's funeral.[58]

Standing forgotten in some attic may be the large canvas that is a documented, but missing, link in the chain of oil portraits for which Beethoven sat. The painting was large because it was a life-size rendition, and an ambitious one at that, for, according to a lengthy contemporary description of it published in 1818,[59] it was a double portrait: an outdoor scene set in the Mödling countryside outside Vienna showing Beethoven with his then twelve-year-old nephew, Karl. The boy was pictured dozing under a tree while his famous uncle was caught in an attitude of harkening to an inner voice, his eyes inspired and rolling far to one side, while his stubby hands clutched a half-rolled sheet of music paper and thick carpenter's pencil. Beethoven's pose can be reconstructed in two preparatory drawings that have survived, one of his face (Fig. 11) and the other a study of the position of his hands across his chest (Fig. 13). The creator of these two sketches was the twenty-five-year-old artist August Carl Friedrich von Klöber (1793–1864), newly arrived in Vienna from having fought against Napoleon's armies in Germany and France. Before taking up the call to arms he had studied painting at the Berlin Academy and now the lure of Correggio and Rubens had brought him to the great collection of those masters in Vienna. But he was yanked from contemplation of past art by the request of his brother-in-law, the baron von Skrbenski—inspired perhaps by the example of Mähler's Tonkünstler-Galerie—to paint him a row of portraits of famous Viennese personalities, including the poets Karoline Pichler and Franz Grillparzer, and Beethoven. The former soldier Klöber has left a vivid account of his campaign and conquest of Beethoven: "Making Beethoven's acquaintance was a difficult task, and it was still more difficult to get him to sit for me . . . a friend of Beethoven's, the cellist Dont, . . . advised me to wait until the summer, since Beethoven usually spent the summer at Mödling and was then at his most easy-going and accessible. In a letter, our mutual friend told Beethoven that I would be arriving in Mödling, and also that I wished to draw him. Beethoven agreed, on condition that he would not have to sit for too long a time. Early in the morning I went to call on him . . . [he] came in and said, 'You want to paint me, but I am very impatient.' . . . Beethoven then sat down, and the boy [Karl] had to begin practicing the piano . . . Beethoven, despite his deafness, corrected every mistake the boy made. . . ."[60]

Karl's music lesson gave the painter time to sketch and study Beethoven's face: "Beethoven always looked very serious, his extremely lively eyes usually wandered, looking upwards somewhat darkly and low-spiritedly, which I have attempted to capture in the portrait. His lips were shut, but the expression about the mouth was not unfriendly. . . . In friendly conversation . . . he took on a genial and mild expression. . . . Every mood of his spirit was immediately and violently expressed in his countenance."[61] Then what Beethoven had warned him of concerning his impatience happened: "After roughly three quarters of an hour he became restless; remembering Dont's advice, I now knew it was time to stop, and asked him only if I could come again the next day, since I was staying in Mödling. Beethoven was quite agreeable and said, 'Then we can meet more often for I can not sit still too long at one time; you must also have a good look at Mödling, for it is quite lovely here, and as an artist you must certainly be a nature lover.' "[62]

During the days that followed, Klöber ran into Beethoven several times on his walks in the woods around Mödling, but, remembering Dont's advice not to greet him under these cirumstances, he pressed on, pretending not to notice him. Actually he noticed as much as he could about the composer's intense communion with nature: "Once . . . I saw him climbing up the hill opposite from the defile which separated us, his broad-brimmed gray felt hat pressed under his arm; once at the top, he lay down full length under a pine tree and looked at the sky for a long while."[63]

From watching the composer on his walks Klöber got the idea for how he might picture his subject in the painting: " . . . it was most interesting to see him, a sheet of music paper and a stump of a pencil in his hand, stop often as though listening, look up and down and then write a few notes on the paper."[64]

The two portrait studies capture the impressions described by Klöber in his verbal portrait of the composer, and we may presume that the final oil was faithful to the preparatory drawings. We have the model's reaction, as reported by the artist: "When Beethoven saw my portrait, he mentioned that he liked the way the hair was done; other painters have always done it too elegantly dressed, as though he were appearing before a court official, and he was not like that at all."[65]

What was this approved-of hair like in the final oil? A hint of the wildly flowing luxury of locks is rapidly indicated in Klöber's pencil study of the face (a drawing the artist kept all his life), and a second study by Klöber of Beethoven's head, fleshed out with chalk over charcoal (Fig. 12), gives a full accounting of what had pleased Beethoven. A lithographic copy of this charcoal study was made in 1841[66] and its distribution helped to spread the wild-haired image of the composer so acceptable to Beethoven and his mythographers alike.

If Klöber's pictorial legacy had not inspired the increasingly leonine mane and blazing eyes rampant in later Beethoven imagery, his verbal portrait would have. Consider the impact of this concluding statement of Klöber's (who, writing over forty years later, wrongly remembers the color of Beethoven's eyes) on succeeding heroizing generations: " . . . his hair was the color of blued steel, having begun to change from black to grey. His eyes were blue-gray [brown] and quite lively. When his hair was tossed about by the wind, he had something absolutely Ossian-like and demoniacal about him."[67]

By alluding to one of the period's most admired literary "finds"—Macpherson's *Ossian* (even Goethe was taken in by this great literary hoax)—our objective recorder of physical data, Herr August von Klöber, has suddenly gone over to the subjective camp. He has also intoned one of the key words of the second half of the nineteenth century—"demoniac"—soon to be recruited into the service of the "dionysian," through which there could then be "redemption." Schopenhauer, Wagner, and Nietzsche were just waiting in the wings.

Undeniably, Klöber's Beethoven evinces that "powerful, genial savagery" of which our friend Rellstab spoke, and it is possible that, with the addition of this "Ossian-like" image to the century's visual repertoire, another of the obviously aggregate sources from which Rellstab retained that memory of Beethoven's pictorial likeness he had found so different from his hero in the flesh has been pinpointed and identified. For we must remember that more than three decades of additional and posthumously issued Beethoven imagery had intervened between the time the Berlin critic had met Beethoven and the time he wrote about that meeting. Not even one who had experienced Beethoven the man could be free from the cluster of mythic images that accrued to his figure with the passing of time.

It is good to know that Beethoven liked the Klöber portrait, hair and all. Dare we ask what the self-appointed protector of Beethoven lore and likeness—Schindler—thought of it? Since the original double-portrait oil had already entered the collection of Klöber's celebrity-collecting brother-in-law, the baron von Skrbenski, at his estate in far-off Silesia by the time Schindler entered the scene, the feckless biographer could only know it through the lithographic print, executed, as we have noted, after Beethoven's death. We have so far consulted Schindler's aesthetic judgment in connection with the Letronne-Höfel print, which he praised, and the first Mähler oil of Beethoven—a likeness he had disdained to discuss because of its "mediocrity." We now continue with Schindler's account of the portraits made of Beethoven during his lifetime: "In time the Höfel engraving was followed by a lithograph [1841] by Klöber of Berlin. On the sheet in written, 'Drawn from nature in Mödling. . . .' The contrast between this life-size head and the 1814 engraving is so great that one who knows no better would be thrown into much confusion, for the two are as opposite as the poles. In the Klöber drawing, even the contours of the face are wrong, and the uncouth features show no trace of intelligence. It is the countenance of a worthy brewer, not that of an artist, and it certainly is not Beethoven. Of all the poor likenesses of our master, this one must be considered the most plebeian."[68]

Schindler pulls no punches. And, writing in 1860, he has—slyly—one more thing to say about this plebeian image, the author of which was still alive and famous as a history painter in Berlin: "In both northern and western Germany it is the one most generally known. . . . Truly, Berlin has not been fortunate in the matter of Beethoven portraits. If only the publishers felt any sense of devotion to accuracy concerning historical persons, even in respect to their portraits . . . the one by Klöber would be removed immediately from circulation out of respect for our master."[69]

The unhappy Schindler has learned the hard lesson that one can (in his view) transcribe myth but one can not harness it. Perhaps this was why he—proud biographer of Beethoven who, according to Heinrich Heine, had his visiting card inscribed "L'ami de Beethoven"—had his own likeness photographed (see Fig. 4). Charity forbids comment on this pristine and pious document of Schindler's self-mythology. But why, we find ourselves asking, did Schindler display so much hostility (or pretended ignorance) toward so many of the pictures of Beethoven, pictures with which the composer had declared himself pleased? For the most part these images were as idealized as was Schindler's purifying biographical portrait. The answer comes with our examination of the next oil portrait in the Beethoven chronology. It was painted by Ferdinand Schimon (1797–1852) and a copy of it was owned, till the day of his death, by Schindler.

(Colorplate 3)

At first glance the portrait looks almost ludicrous: the eyes roll wildly in their sockets and invisible wind blasts at the snaking locks of flying hair. When we learn that the creator of this picture was only twenty-one or twenty-two (references to him in Beethoven's conversation books allow us to date the portrait 1818 or 1819) and that he was also a singer and an actor, we might well wonder— on the basis of this crude drama on canvas—whether the young man's career potential lay in one of the other arts. In fact Schimon was such a fine dramatic tenor that his friend Franz Schubert did succeed in persuading him to give up painting, and in 1821 Schimon received an appointment with the Royal Theater of Munich, where he spent the rest of his life. Let us turn to Schindler's reaction to this work of Schimon's youth: would he be put off by the amateur artistic quality? "Schimon's portrait is not a significant work of art, yet it is faithful to Beethoven's character. No other likeness succeeded so well in portraying the characteristic expression of the eyes, the majestic brow, that domicile of so many powerful and lofty ideas, his coloring, the firmly closed mouth and the muscular chin."[70]

At least, Schindler was never lukewarm, either in condemnation or in praise. And again we notice the tendency, not unique to Schindler, to equate Schein with Sein; Beethoven's appearance with his character—leading naturally to an analogy with the music—"powerful and lofty ideas." The biographer informs us of the provenance of the work: "The original, which unfortunately has darkened greatly [a further sign of Schimon's amateur procedure], was at first in my possession. It is now in the Royal Library in Berlin, and I have a considerably improved copy by Professor Schmid of Aachen."[71]

Schindler does have interesting things to say about the conditions under which young Schimon's portrait came into being, addressing in particular the problem of depicting the eyes:

> At my request the painter, who was still very young, was granted permission to set up his easel next to the master's study and to work there as he wished. Beethoven categorically refused a sitting, for he was then hard at work on the *Missa Solemnis* and protested that he could not spare a single hour's time. But Schimon had already followed him on his walks in the country; he had already made quite a collection of sketches, and was entirely satisfied to be allowed to paint as the master worked. When the portrait was finished but for the most important feature, the expression of the eyes, it seemed advisable to do this most difficult task perfectly, for in Beethoven's face the eyes were remarkable, registering a whole gamut of emotions, from wild and defiant to tender and loving, just like the whole gamut of his states of mind.[72]

A testimonial from a very different source begs intrusion here because of its close corroboration of the above. Almost four decades after having met Beethoven in the flesh (1822), Rossini reminisced to Wagner in Paris in 1860 about Beethoven's appearance: "The portraits of Beethoven that we know, reproduce fairly well his physiognomy. But what no etcher's needle could express was the indefinable sadness spread over his features—while from under heavy eyebrows his eyes shone as from out of caverns and, though small, seemed to pierce one."[73]

Schindler's insistence on the importance of capturing the characteristic expression of Beethoven's eyes is not to be belittled. When we compare the torpid quality of Klein's life mask (protective shields had been placed over the closed eyes and these protrusions were what the plaster recorded) with the sparkling sense of inner life conveyed by the Mähler, Klöber, and Schimon portrayals, we realize that—as often with a still photograph today—the expression of the eyes is the crucial and deciding factor between a successful and an unsuccessful likeness. The anxious biographer was simply pleading for the animation that memory, capable of being serial in its cumulative and simultaneous recollections, lent to the remembered Beethoven of his mind's eye and life experience.

Just how Schimon was able to determine what aspect to give his subject's eyes was explained by Schindler: "It was the master himself who came to his aid. The hardy, unaffected nature of the young academician, his forthright bearing as if he were in his own studio, his coming without saying 'Good day' and his departure with no 'Adieu' made more of an impression on Beethoven than what was on the easel. In short, the young man began to interest him, and he invited him to coffee. Sitting thus opposite the composer at the coffee-table, Schimon was able to do the eyes. A second invitation to take a cup of coffee 'with sixty beans' was sufficient for the painter to complete his work, with which Beethoven was well pleased."[74]

We may well imagine how gratified Schindler was when he became the owner of a portrait for which he had persuaded his revered master to sit and of which, it seems, he had heard hearty approval from Beethoven himself. For the jealously possessive Schindler, all other portraits of the tone hero must measure up to his Schimon portrait, which, once we understand the "rightness" of the roving eyes, no longer seems so alien to Beethoven iconography. Schindler magnanimously shared Schimon's image with the world at large (incidentally authenticating his closeness to the Schimon-Beethoven encounter) when he commissioned an engraved reproduction of it as frontispiece for the first edition of his Beethoven biography. Thus yet another image of powerful, genial savagery entered the mainstream of mythography.

Beethoven voiced his view of the ordeals of portraiture in a letter written to Zmeskal, the friend from whom during the ill-fated Therese Malfatti courtship he had begged the loan of a mirror. The letter is undated but was probably written in 1818 or 1819. It is not possible to determine whether Beethoven was referring to August von Klöber or Ferdinand Schimon, but the sentiments expressed show us a poignant reason—not at all concerned with loss of composing time—why Beethoven so disliked playing the role of painter's model: "I can not [be responsible] either for the good fortune (if the *painter* considers it so) to have drawn me, or for the misfortune to have *made a bad drawing* of me—But as he attaches so much importance to *my face*, which is really not so very significant, then in *God's name* I will sit for him, although I regard sitting as a kind of penance—Well, so be it—But why you should attach so much importance to my doing this, I can hardly understand and, what is more, refuse to understand. . . . Good God! How pestered one is when one has such a wretched ["fatales"] face as I have."[75]

The composer had not forgotten about his pockmarks, even if most artists were blind to them. Perhaps this is why he liked those portraits, like the Klöber and the Schimon, in which attention was drawn away from his face and to his full head of hair. His conscious endorsement of these two "demoniac" portrayals gave impetus to the proliferation of increasingly frenzied images of later and posthumous vintage. (A look at the iconography engendered by Europe's greatest showman of the nineteenth century—Paganini, fervent admirer of Beethoven—reveals sophisticated complicity with and manipulation of the century's obsession with artistic "possession" by demoniac forces.)

Unlike Rellstab, some visitors to Beethoven during the final years of his life saw in him a living confirmation of his famous portrait likenesses. There exists for example the discussion of Beethoven by a certain Sir John Russell who published a journal of his travels on the continent in 1824. His account of how the composer looked in 1821 not only perpetuates but quite colorfully contributes to the myth-making process:

> Though not an old man, he is lost to society in consequence of his extreme deafness, which has rendered him almost unsocial. The neglect of his person which he exhibits gives him a somewhat wild appearance. His features are strong and prominent; his eye is full of rude energy; his hair, which neither comb nor scissors seem to have visited for years, overshadows his broad brow in a quantity and confusion to which only the snakes round a Gorgon's head offer a parallel. . . .
>
> I have heard him play; but to bring him so far required some management, so great is his horror of being anything like exhibited. . . . The amateurs were enraptured; to the uninitiated it was more interesting to observe how the music of the man's soul passed over his countenance. . . . The muscles of the face swell, and its veins start out; the wild eye rolls doubly wild, the mouth quivers, and Beethoven looks like a wizard overpowered by the demons whom he himself has called up.[76]

Just on the borderline between caricature and portraiture are two drawings of Beethoven done either at the end of 1819 or early in 1820 by the young engraver Josef Daniel Böhm (1794–1865) (Figs. 14 and 15). It would seem as though Beethoven could never turn down a young artist, and although we do not know what the answer was, an entry in one of the conversation books for 1820 phrased in characteristic Viennese modalities makes the following request: "Böhm wishes that you might like to give him another sitting."[77] "Sitting" is not quite the right word for what Böhm came up with, since both of his "portraits" show the composer standing, striding in fact. Beethoven's low top hat is planted firmly on the back of his head, as in the Incident at Teplitz days, and he clutches the ubiquitous, mandatory notebook behind his back as, almost in cinema sequence, we see the great man hurry past us, absorbed in his thoughts, first in profile view (Böhm has accentuated the flat nose and protruding lips with almost Neanderthal result) and then, in the second view, with the retreating figure seen from the back. Similar to depictions of other famous personalities whose formidable appearance in public discourages greetings or acknowledgment, Böhm's hurried sketches emit a surreptitious aura.[78] The sight of Arthur Schopenhauer and his poodle on their daily walk in Frankfurt was to inspire a similar discreet (or frantic?) portrait from the back (Fig. 16). In the twentieth century Arnold Schönberg would pay jocose homage to Beethoven in his little *Self-Portrait Walking, Seen from the Back* (Fig. 17).

Böhm may only have had access to the Beethoven in motion, but another aspiring young artist, Anton Dietrich (1796/7–1872), not only had admittance to a stationary Beethoven, but also the benefit of Klein's life mask from which to work. This time it was a sculptor to whom Beethoven could not say no. There is even an apologetic letter from the composer written in early 1820 begging Dietrich not to be annoyed that he must put off their visit until the following morning.[79] Young Dietrich made a small model of Beethoven's head and then modeled some six copies of it, some with life-size proportions. The replicas—all plaster casts—were of two varieties. One, with longish hair billowing over the ears and unabbreviated, blocked-in torso, was meant to suggest the contemporary Beethoven (Fig. 18); the other, with shorter hair revealing the ears and the back of the undraped torso left hollow, was intended to present a more timeless, "classical" Beethoven, *à l'an-*

tique (Fig. 19).[80] Neither version is anchored to the relentless realism of the Klein life mask (although the cleft and scar on Beethoven's chin were retained) and the idealization seems to have pleased both the artist and his model. Here is Dietrich's side of the conversation that ensued when he enthusiastically reported to Beethoven in one of the conversation books about having shown the original head at a recent exhibition of the Academy of Fine Arts, a show which featured "Busts of Great Composers": "—Your head looks particularly good from the front, and it was so appropriate, because on one side there was Haydn and on the other side Mozart. —Before the next art exhibition I am going to make your portrait again, but completely life-size. —I saw the majordomo and he is so stingy that he only wanted to give 10 or 12 florins [$50–$60] for your bust, and that is impossible since I still have a week's work to do on it. If the countess were well she would undoubtedly have the bust made up in marble."[81]

Apparently no marble copy of Dietrich's bust was ever realized, but if we look at a wash drawing of 1827 made by Johann Nepomuk Hoechle (1790–1835) (Fig. 20) showing Beethoven's study[82] in the Schwarzspanierhaus—his final residence—we can certainly see where at least one of the life-size plaster replicas Dietrich spoke of making went. It ended up in Beethoven's own collection, providing a three-dimensional companion for the treasured Mähler portrait of 1804–5. In the drawing we see the bust placed precariously on the right window ledge, quite visible behind the drawn but transparent curtain. That this effigy is the Dietrich portrait bust seems to have been overlooked in the Beethoven literature, but the visual evidence is overwhelming. With quick strokes Hoechle has caught the sculptor's summary of Beethoven's characteristic profile—receding but upward curling thick hair; prominent, bulgy forehead; flat, almost "pug" nose; protruding lips; and rounded, muscular chin. The scroll-like hollow torso and short hair revealing the ear confirm that this is one of Dietrich's classicizing busts. Schindler never mentions Dietrich or his sculptural efforts by name, but he did make the following sweeping pronouncement: "Nor do most of the sculptured busts of Beethoven bear close examination. Most of them are coarse masses."[83]

Hoechle's "portrait" of the room was made three days after the composer's death. The idea was to preserve, in visual form at least, the way Beethoven's last dwelling place had looked. The next step was to convert the wash drawing into a medium that could be widely reproduced, and for that purpose the artist Gustav Leybold (1794–after 1842) was commissioned by the Viennese publisher Trentsenky to work up a lithograph based on the Hoechle *delineavit ad Natura* original. Leybold obliged with at least two separate but generally very similar black-and-white lithographs and one striking color lithograph. With the debut of this second image (Figs. 21, 22, 23) onto the stage of Beethovenian iconography we have a unique opportunity to watch a mythmaker in action. Or is this a mythoclast? The classical Beethoven bust of the wash drawing is gone. In its place is an aquiline-nosed individual with high but regular brow and long, slicked-down hair. This new head is supported by an extended and solid torso. What is this? A figment of the artist's imagination or a very knowledgeable if somewhat inaccurate reference to the Beethoven of Dietrich's other, more contemporary conception? But the aquiline nose is out of place in either replica. How far can we trust the lithographer's fidelity? In other parts of the picture we see that he has given and he has taken away. A brilliant moon now shines in through the window on the left, throwing the silhouette of Saint Stephen's Cathedral into dramatic relief, and two enticing stacks of neatly piled music (highly uncharacteristic of Beethoven

alive from all accounts) now stand on the floor by the renowned Broadwood mahogany piano (which is rendered in extremely faithful detail). The door on the
left now has a handle and overhead panel, and gold-tipped curtain rods have
been provided, with the curtains rehung a touch more elegantly. On the piano
the plain brass candlestick to the left has been replaced by an ornamental one
with a winged figure sitting at its base. On the minus side the rococo stucco design in the ceiling is gone, one of the burned-down candles is missing, and, most
peculiar of all, the classical statuette (a replica of the Apollo Belvedere) on the top
shelf of the bookcase has disappeared. In its stead is a large bird with outspread
wings whose gaze is fixed upon the bust in the window.

We might think these changes part and parcel of poetic license, but the appearance of the cupid-adorned candlestick where it was not in evidence before
argues strongly for the fact that our lithographer artist was specifically acquainted
with at least one object in Beethoven's estate. In Schindler's listing of those
personal effects of the composer that "passed" into his collection the following
item is noted: "a brass candlestick with shade—it shows a cupid sitting in a
boat, supporting the shade with both hands."[84] This "Amor" candle holder,
without the "sail" shade but with its supporting mast silhouetted against the
open window, is what we are looking at in the color lithograph. With such
access to Beethoven's objects on the part of the artist, we might even theorize
that *both* versions of Dietrich's plaster busts were in Beethoven's apartment (even
though they were not mentioned in the official estate list, but then neither is
Beethoven's portrait of grandfather Ludwig or the Mähler portrait of 1804–5,
both of which went immediately into nephew Karl's possession). Perhaps the
artist himself decided to substitute the less classical, more "romantic" effigy in
this second drawing of the room. And perhaps what we read as an aquiline
nose is just a slip of the hand (in Leybold's black-and-white lithographic copies
—Fig. 22— the nose has in fact been altered to look less prominent), for certainly
the other details—blocked in torso and long hair—agree with Dietrich's other
version.

Beethoven's estate was not auctioned off until eight months after his death,
and his lodgings were actually left relatively unguarded, allowing Schindler
secretly to amass quite a trove of important documents and memorabilia. Hence
it seems possible that both Hoechle and Leybold, the exact dates of whose
lithographs are unknown, had entry to Beethoven's apartment before Schindler's
surreptitious pilfering had made serious headway. In fact if the color lithograph
attesting to the absence of the Apollo figure is based on what the artist saw in
the actual room, rather than on what he was copying from the wash drawing,
then the print serves as a sort of criminologist's document of the progress of
Schindler's thievery, for we know that he gathered up a number of Beethoven's
statuettes of male figures. This excursion into the pictorial metamorphosis of
the Dietrich Beethoven bust, already rendered in two variations by the sculptor
himself, is but one turn in the labyrinthine windings our tracing of the mythmaking process can elect to follow. Another turning would lead us to the transformation effected when a Viennese portrait lithographer by the name of Josef
Kriehuber (1800–1876), who in his lifetime tossed off more than seven thousand
portraits, "copied" Dietrich's Beethoven bust (Fig. 24), making him look like
Goethe, with the lengthened nose. Yet another unexpected bend awaits us when
we view the drawing that Dietrich himself made of Beethoven in 1826, based
upon his busts and the Klein life mask, and reproduced through the taming

intervention of yet another hand, the lithographer Faust Herr (active in Vienna 1834–1849) (Fig. 25).

Let us return, possibly with relief, to the relatively straightforward circumstances and fascinating result of Beethoven's next encounter with an artist determined to secure his likeness for posterity. The artist was Joseph Karl Stieler (1781–1858), whose name history would link not with Vienna but with Munich, where, at the behest of King Ludwig I, he created over a period of twenty-seven years the famous Schönheitsgalerie of thirty-six beautiful women who had caught the monarch's appreciative and wandering eye. (The entire Gallery of Beauties is still in place in the Nymphenburg Palace, and, among other femmes fatales, Lola Montez continues to dazzle the modern-day visitor.) Stieler was also a painter of famous men and by the end of his life he could boast of having portrayed Goethe, Tieck, Humboldt, and Schelling. In the fall of 1819 he presented himself to Beethoven. Schindler gives an approving account of the painter's winning ways: "He was highly recommended and was already an artist of repute. His personality and appearance added to his popularity. He had the knack of making the temperamental master conform to his wishes. Sitting after sitting was granted [three sessions in all], without a single complaint about loss of time."[85]

Schindler then describes the portrait, commenting on the almost overnight aging of the now gray-haired Beethoven: "It shows Beethoven dressed in his grey indoor coat standing in a grape-arbor; in his left hand is a sheet of paper with the words 'Missa Solemnis,' and his right hand holds a pencil. The startling difference between the Schimon portrait and that by Stieler is explained by the long illness that had intervened."[86]

Entries in the composer's conversation book for 1–14 April 1820 continue the narrative: "[Stieler]: In what key is your Mass? I just want to write on the page Mass in . . . [Beethoven]: D Missa Solemnis in D."[87]

Some modern viewers who read the inscription placed by Stieler on the manuscript Beethoven holds in his painting may wonder whether a mistake has been made by the artist since the designation clearly reads "Missa Solemnis in D#." This apparent inconsistency is explained by the fact that in nineteenth-century Germany sharps were frequently used to signify major keys (Beethoven himself inscribed the *Leonore* Overture no. 1 in C Major as "Ouvertura in C#"). Hence the key of D Major was often referred to as D sharp—as we see it printed in Stieler's picture.

The conversation-book evidence does not record what passed in Stieler's mind when he saw Beethoven's treasured portrait of Ludwig van Beethoven, senior, on the wall. But Stieler's identical rectangular format and complementary pose—the grandson is shown in equal torso length and also directs attention with his right hand to the music he holds—are mute witnesses to the painter's resourceful and inventive approach. Was the Munich-based painter also in silent competition with the Mähler "allegorical" portrayal of Beethoven done fifteen years before? This new image of Beethoven certainly displays a determined effort to trace an anatomy of melancholy—genius incarnate—close to and still of this world, yet removed from the commonplace by transfiguring inspiration.

Schindler was impressed with Stieler's professionalism—the artist had quite confidently determined the ultimate pose and basic colors of the painting, down to the red cravat, in a quickly rendered oil sketch[88]—but he had a nagging reservation about the final portrait, so very different from his own Schimon depiction: "The whole painting seems to be executed in a style of simplicity. As for the natural, characteristic expression, the moment was well captured and the reaction has been favorable. On the other hand, the attitude the painter so loves to depict in men of genius, with the head inclined, is contradictory to Beethoven's character, for the master in his middle years was never known to bear himself otherwise than with his head proudly erect, even in moments of physical suffering. A painter personally acquainted with Beethoven would not have painted him in this attitude."[89]

We can check for ourselves this observation of Schindler's about the Munich painter's predilection for showing men of genius with their heads inclined by looking at Stieler's portrait of Goethe (Fig. 26) done some eight years later. The illustrious author is shown seated at a table, holding a piece of paper with the concluding lines of a poem by Ludwig I (the king had commissioned Stieler to do Goethe's portrait for him). Goethe's head is anything but inclined, rather its attitude is one of cocked attentiveness, with eyes rolling far to the right, as if responding to something beyond the picture plane—Stieler's flattering way of suggesting the great sitter's mental occupation with the amateur literary effort before him. One thing the two portraits have in common, aside from the painter's device of intimating deep thought by showing the eyes in upward or sideward orbit, is the awkwardness of the arms and hands. Only one hand is shown in the Goethe painting, while the unfolded sheet of paper conveniently blocks the view of most of the arm. The other arm, cut off above the hand, hangs woodenly to the side. Stieler had well over a month in Weimar to work on Goethe's portrait, but in his three sittings with Beethoven there was only time to concentrate on the composer's face. Stieler had to complete the background and body away from his model, with the result that Beethoven's arms are not convincingly attached to his shoulders. Later variations of Stieler's arresting portrait would solve that problem by simply doing away with the arms altogether (Fig. 27), focusing attention on an increasingly idealized face with the cicatrized chin miraculously healed and the bushy eyebrows handsomely arched and under control. Josef Kriehuber, whose "copy" of Dietrich's bust we have just looked at, made his own copy of the Stieler painting (Fig. 28), thereby provoking Schindler's indignant characterization of him as "that master of convention and flattery."[90] Looking at the Kriehuber image we can not help but agree with Schindler: the artist simply could not resist lengthening Beethoven's nose while narrowing the face and heightening the forehead.[91]

Stieler's Beethoven portrait was exhibited in the same exhibition of 1820 as Dietrich's head of the composer, and it excited much favorable comment according to Beethoven in the conversation books for that spring.[92] Certainly all the elements dear to future mythmakers are present in Stieler's heroizing conception: genius inspired by inner voices in the presence of nature, with leonine hair writhing wildly in symbolic parallel to the seething turbulence of creativity. Even Schindler had written, reprovingly, that "to present the master with short hair is like painting a lion with its mane cut off."[93] It would be Stieler's romantic image of Beethoven that, through extensive lithographic reproduction,[94] would exert the greatest influence on Beethoven iconography. And there is no doubt that Beethoven was pleased with the painter's lionization; when his publisher Artaria issued prints of the portrait he ordered copies to distribute as gifts to his friends.[95]

A description cited by Schindler to demonstrate the closeness of his own preferred Schimon portrait to the Beethoven of reality can be applied by the modern reader to the Stieler depiction with interesting findings. This description was written by the person Beethoven purportedly designated on his death bed to be his official biographer, Friedrich Johann Rochlitz (1769–1842), leading music critic and first editor of the Leipzig *Allgemeine musikalische Zeitung*. The two men had finally met in person in the summer of 1822 and Rochlitz, although declining the task of writing the composer's biography, did publish, just a year after Beethoven's death, the letter in which he had reported on the momentous meeting: "If I had not been prepared for it, the sight of him would have disturbed me, as it has so many others. It was not the distracted, almost savage exterior, not the thick black hair that hung shaggily around his face [had Stieler's portrait of two years earlier exaggerated Beethoven's graying hair?], nor any other single feature, but the whole impression of his presence. Picture to yourself a man of about fifty years [the composer was almost fifty-two], somewhat shorter than the average yet of powerful, stocky build. His bone structure is compact and very strong, something like Fichte's but heavier, especially in the full face."[96]

Rochlitz's allusion to the German philosopher Johann Gottlieb Fichte in regard to Beethoven is of special interest, not because of the aptness of any physiognomic parallels—they were both short with piercing eyes—but because of the insistence with which their names would be associated by mythographers with German patriotism. The recently deceased (1814) Fichte had actively linked himself with the German cause by his, still famous, fiery *Addresses to the German Nation* urging resistance against Napoleon. In his writings he sounded very much like the "unbuttoned" conversationalist, letter writer, and composer of *Fidelio*. The philosopher declared, for example: "The system of freedom satisfies my heart; the opposite system destroys and annihilates it. To stand cold and unmoved, amid the current of events . . . this existence is impossible for me. I scorn and detest it. I will love; I will lose myself in sympathy; I will know the joy and grief of life."[97]

For Rochlitz, Fichte's eyes, bulging somewhat in his head (Fig. 32), must have been a commanding feature of the physical makeup that led him to make a comparison with Beethoven. Rochlitz was particularly impressed by Beethoven's smaller but compelling eyes: "His eyes are restless, glowing, and, when his gaze is fixed, almost piercing; if they move at all, the movement is darting, abrupt. The expression of his countenance, especially of his eyes, so full of intelligence and life, is a mixture or a vacillation, sometimes in a flash, between shyness and the most sincere kindness. His whole bearing bespeaks that tension, that restless, careful listening of the deaf, that is so deeply touching . . . this is the man who has given happiness to millions—pure, spiritual happiness."[98]

The cost of creating that music which, in Rochlitz's admiring opinion, was to give so much happiness, and the strange circumstances under which the deaf composer was wont to work when seized by inspiration, were described by Schindler in regard to the *Missa Solemnis*:

It was four o'clock in the afternoon. . . . In the living room, behind a locked door, we heard the master singing parts of the fugue in the *Credo*—singing, howling, stamping. After we had been listening a long time to this almost awful scene, and were about to go away, the door opened and Beethoven stood before us with distorted features, calculated to excite fear. He looked as if he had been in mortal combat with the whole host of contrapuntists, his everlasting enemies. His first utterances were confused, as if he had been disagreeably surprised at our having overheard him. Then he reached the day's happenings and with obvious restraint he remarked: "Pretty doings, those! Everybody [his frequently disappearing servants] has run away and I haven't had anything to

Fig. 1 Carl Röhling, The Incident at Teplitz, *c. 1887, lithograph.*

Fig. 2 Louis Letronne,
Beethoven, *1814,*
pencil drawing,
private collection, Paris.

Fig. 3 Blasius Höfel,
Beethoven, *1814,*
engraving after
a pencil drawing
by Louis Letronne.

Fig. 4 Anton Felix Schindler, photograph of 1862.
Beethoven's amanuensis and one of his first mythmakers.

Fig. 5
(opposite, above)
Leopold Radoux, Ludwig van Beethoven *c. 1750, oil on*
canvas, private collection, Vienna. This portrait of Beethoven's
grandfather was one of the composer's most prized possessions.

Fig. 7
(opposite, below)
Beethoven's handwriting, from a letter of 1820, private
collection, Vienna.

50

*Fig. 6 Christian Horneman,
Beethoven, 1803,
miniature on ivory,
Collection Dr. H. C. Bodmer,
Beethovenhaus, Bonn.*

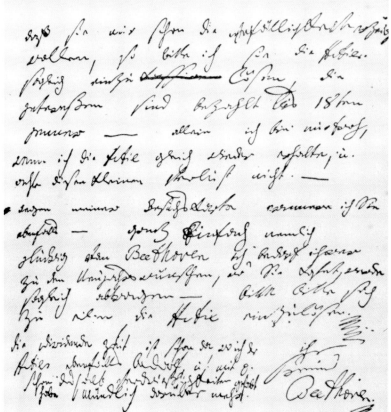

*Fig. 8 Joseph Neesen (attributed),
Silhouette of Beethoven,
c. 1786, Beethovenhaus, Bonn.*

51

*Fig. 9 Ludwig Ferdinand
Schnorr von Carolsfeld*,
Beethoven, *pencil drawing,
c. 1808 or 1809,
original now lost.*

Fig. 10 Willibrord Joseph Mähler,
Beethoven, *1815,
oil on canvas,
Gesellschaft der
Musikfreunde, Vienna.*

Fig. 11 *August von Klöber*, Study of Beethoven's Face, *1818, pencil drawing, Collection Dr. H. C. Bodmer, Beethovenhaus, Bonn.*

Fig. 12
August von Klöber,
Study of Beethoven's
Face, *1818, charcoal*
with chalk, formerly
Collection C. F. Peters,
Leipzig, disappeared 1945.

Fig. 13 *August von Klöber*, Study of Beethoven's Hands, *1818, pencil drawing, Collection Dr. H. C. Bodmer, Beethovenhaus, Bonn.*

Fig. 14
Josef Daniel Böhm,
Beethoven Walking,
late 1819 or early 1820,
drawing, Beethovenhaus,
Bonn.

Fig. 15
Josef Daniel Böhm,
Beethoven Walking,
Seen from the Back,
late 1819 or early 1820,
drawing, Beethovenhaus,
Bonn.

Fig. 16 Wilhelm Busch, Caricature of
Schopenhauer and His Poodle, Seen
from the Back, *c. 1860, drawing for*
Fliegenden Blätter.

Fig. 17 Arnold Schönberg, Self-Portrait Walking,
Seen from the Back, *1911, oil on cardboard,*
Arnold Schoenberg Institute, University of
Southern California, Los Angeles.

Fig. 18 (right) *Anton Dietrich,* Beethoven
("Contemporary"), *1821, plaster bust, Historisches*
Museum der Stadt Wien, Vienna.

Fig. 19 (far right) *Anton Dietrich,* Beethoven
("Classical"), *1822, plaster bust,*
formerly Collection Henrietta Dux, Vienna,
photograph of 1908.

Fig. 20 Johann Nepomuk Hoechle,
Beethoven's Study in the
Schwarzspanierhaus *(detail
showing "classical"
Beethoven bust by Anton
Dietrich), 29 March 1827,
wash drawing, Historisches
Museum der Stadt Wien,
Vienna.*

Fig. 21 Gustav Leybold,
Beethoven's Study in
the Schwarzspanierhaus
*(detail showing "contemporary"
Beethoven bust by Anton
Dietrich), 1827, color
lithograph, Historisches
Museum der Stadt Wien,
Vienna.*

Fig. 22 Gustav Leybold,
Beethoven's Study in the
Schwarzspanierhaus
*(detail showing variation on the
"contemporary" Beethoven bust
by Anton Dietrich), c. 1827,
black-and-white lithograph,
Historisches Museum der
Stadt Wien, Vienna.*

Fig. 23 Gustav Leybold, Beethoven's Study in the Schwarzspanierhaus, *c. 1827, black-and-white lithograph, Historisches Museum der stadt Wien, Vienna.*

Fig. 25 Faust Herr, Beethoven, *c. 1840, lithograph after a pencil drawing by Anton Dietrich.*

Fig. 24 Josef Kriehuber,
Anton Dietrich's Bust of Beethoven,
c. 1822–27, lithograph.

Fig. 26 Joseph Karl Stieler, Johann Wolfgang
von Goethe, *1828, oil on canvas,*
Neue Pinakothek, Munich.

58

Fig. 27 Anonymous artist, Beethoven, after 1820, oil, copy after the oil portrait of Beethoven by Joseph Karl Stieler of 1819–20, private collection, Turin.

Fig. 28 Josef Kriehuber, Beethoven, after 1819, lithograph after the oil portrait of Beethoven by Joseph Karl Stieler of 1819–20.

Fig. 29 Johann Josef Neidl,
Beethoven, c. 1801, engraving after
a drawing by Gandolph Ernst
Stainhauser von Treuberg of 1800,
published by Cappi.

Fig. 30 Ferdinand Georg Waldmüller, Portrait of the
Engraver François Haury, 1834, oil on wood, Galerie des
Neunzehnten Jahrhunderts im Oberen Belvedere,
Österreischische Galerie, Vienna.

Fig. 31 Johann Heinrich Ramberg,
Beethoven, 1820,
oil on copper, Collection Jo Beth
Apperson Milton, Smyrna, Georgia.

Fig. 32 Friedrich Burg, Johann Gottlieb Fichte,
c. 1810, lithograph.

Fig. 33 Johann Stefan Decker, Beethoven, May 1824, chalk drawing with white heightenings, Historisches Museum der Stadt Wien, Vienna.

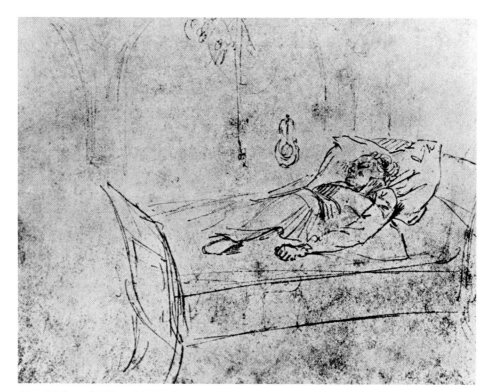

Fig. 34 Joseph Eduard Teltscher, Beethoven in a Coma, *26 March 1827, pencil drawing, formerly Collection Stefan Zweig.*

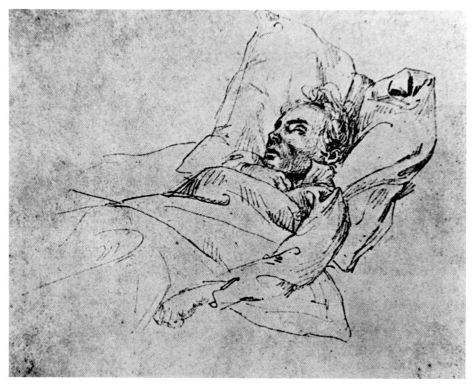

Fig. 35 Joseph Eduard Teltscher, Beethoven on His Deathbed, *26 March 1827, pencil drawing, formerly Collection Stefan Zweig.*

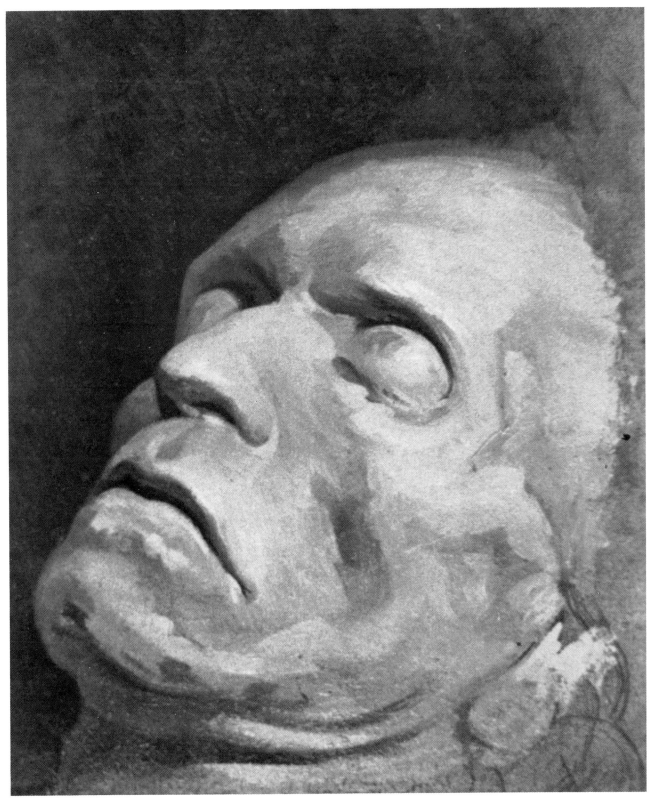

Fig. 36 Josef Danhauser, Beethoven on His Deathbed, *28 March 1827, oil sketch, Beethovenhaus, Bonn.*

Fig. 37 Josef Danhauser, Beethoven on His Deathbed, *1827, lithograph.*

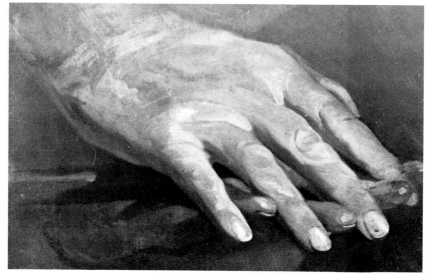

Fig. 38 Josef Danhauser, Beethoven's Hands, *28 March 1827, oil sketch, Beethovenhaus, Bonn.*

eat since yesternoon!" I tried to calm him and helped him to make his toilet. . . . Never, it may be said, did so great an art work as is the *Missa Solemnis* see its creation under more adverse circumstances.[99]

A—probably apocryphal, but worthy of examination at this point—portrait of Beethoven looking exactly like Schindler's description, with "distorted features, calculated to excite fear," recently surfaced in an American private collection.[100] It is a small oil done on copper by the prolific Hanover portrait painter, book illustrator, caricaturist, and engraver Johann Heinrich Ramberg (1763–1840), monogrammed and dated 1820. The image is one of a scowling Beethoven, of rugged complexion with fixed and level gaze, standing before a table upon which are music and note papers. He faces and stares at the beholder and in a feat of apparent double-jointedness holds a quill pen in his right hand that is bent parallel to the table-top plane. A dressing gown or coat is thrown over his jacket and gold vest and, unique in Beethoven iconography, he wears a cloth cap (six night caps were listed in the inventory of the composer's household effects after his death). Neither Schindler nor Thayer report the creation of this formidable image. Is it a fantasy of post-Beethoven-making, a pictorial response to earlier images of the composer, a memory based on a personal encounter (oil on copper calls for painstakingly slow execution), or a portrait for which Beethoven—in all his *terribilità* (Fig. 31)—actually posed? Can we trust the date—1820—placed in the upper left-hand corner, suggesting that the music at hand is possibly the *Missa Solemnis*? Was Ramberg in Vienna in 1820? (He is documented only as having passed through in the early 1790s on his way to Rome.) Did he perhaps create this scowling summary of Vienna's most famous living composer for his close friend Baron von Greiffenegg, who during the years 1816 to 1823 was the Austrian chargé d'affaires to the Hanover court? Is the painting just a concoction based on myth? Might Ramberg's great nephew—a Viennese born too late to have been more than a child when Beethoven died—Arthur Georg Freiherr von Ramberg (1819–1875), a history and genre painter whose monogram is confusingly like that of his Hanover relative, have composed the image much later in the century? Such are the problems that plague the authenticity of undocumented Beethoven portraiture. For our vigil in keeping watch over the processes of mythmaking, it is not necessary to establish the answers to these very legitimate questions, desirable as it is to know for sure, since it is the sheer physical existence of such an image that concerns us. Nevertheless, it is important to speculate upon whether this particular icon—genuine or fanciful—had any impact of its own upon the snowballing mythicization of Beethoven. Since the portrait was not reproduced in the print medium and seems to have remained in private hands until the twentieth century, the answer to this question at least is, with certainty, no.[101]

And yet how similar in spirit is Ramberg's sullen Beethoven to the next and final documented oil portrait for which Beethoven sat. This glowering image is posterity's least favorite likeness; it is the least copied, least reproduced contemporary portrait of Beethoven. It is not the picture of a hero. But it is certainly a picture of Beethoven. It is the nonheroizing work of a fanatical pursuer of reality, Ferdinand Georg Waldmüller (1793–1865), a superb genre and landscape painter who excelled in portraiture as well. Known as the Austrian Ingres, he combined photographic verisimilitude with rhythmical harmonies of precise form and subdued color chords. The plenitude of the detailed observations of his sitters was usually posited against a neutral but richly mottled background, as with his pic-

(Colorplate 6)

ture of Beethoven. Comparison of this Beethoven portrait of 1823 with one done by Waldmüller eleven years later of the engraver François Haury (Fig. 30)[102] verifies the stark eschewal of Romanticism Waldmüller's motto "back to nature" implied. Here, under the cool scrutiny of Biedermeier realism,[103] is one instance in which we may surely suppose we are gazing at a reliable mirroring of physiological fact. And yet, according to Schindler, Waldmüller's way was strewn with Beethovenian thorns: the composer experienced a sudden dislike for the courteous thirty-year-old academician and refused to let him return for a second sitting. Here is Schindler's detailed account of the abortive meeting between Vienna's greatest honorary citizen and Vienna's greatest portrait painter:

> At the beginning of 1823 the publishing firm of Breitkopf and Härtel wanted to own a portrait of our master, and chose Waldmüller, professor at the Academy[104], to paint it. But there were obstacles; Beethoven felt the pressure of work, his eyes were giving him constant trouble, and he was almost always in a bad temper. After much wrangling, an appointment was made for the first sitting. Waldmüller's behavior on this occasion was reverential and far too self-effacing, a bearing that Beethoven generally found most irritating. We have just seen how both previous painters [Schimon and Stieler] had succeeded in their work by taking the opposite approach. No matter how much Waldmüller hurried with sketching the head and roughing out the portrait, the preoccupied master was impatient to get back to his work, and would repeatedly stand up, pace the floor irritably, and go to his writing-table in the next room.
>
> The under layer of paint had not yet been completed when Beethoven made it clear that he could tolerate the procedure no longer. When the painter had left, the master gave vent to his spleen and called Waldmüller the worst artist in the world because he had made him sit with his face toward the window. He obstinately refused to hear any arguments in the man's defence. No further sittings took place and the artist completed the portrait from memory. . . .[105]

What important information is betrayed by Schindler's repetition of Beethoven's naïve assertion that Waldmüller was the world's worst painter because he made him sit facing a natural light source! If anything, this confirms the impression given by the Mähler, Schimon, and Stieler portraits of interesting, but second-rate talents at work. Now at last Beethoven sat vis-à-vis an artist of superior gifts, and that artist's utterly professional approach was found wanting—by a Beethoven who professed to detest flattery but was (unconsciously?) used to it in portraiture. Who else but the truth-seeker Waldmüller, who did not hesitate to record the wart on the upper lip of one of his female sitters, had the gall to ask his pockmarked model to sit facing a window? Schindler speaks of Waldmüller's application of an under layer of paint and of the roughing out of the portrait on the spot. How skilled the painter was at quickly grasping the minutiae of human gestalt is exemplified in his observation of the disparate nostril openings so clearly indicated in the portrait. Back in his studio, working from memory, as Schindler said, the painter did not indulge in answering rudeness with documentation of Beethoven's facial scars. One of the things that seared Waldmüller's memory, however, was the disgruntled aura radiated by the composer, for the portrait fairly bristles with Beethoven's discontent. The incipient frown captured in Klein's life mask is now pervasive and seemingly habitual; the restless rolling of the eyes noted by Schimon and Stieler is accurately recalled by Waldmüller, as are the narrow eyelids. This is the first and only painted image of Beethoven in which the flat nose of the composer has not been subtly recast. The large, slightly sagging jowls, previously so firm and muscular, are also rendered with unideal-ized fidelity. Waldmüller's keen eye had noted the receding hairline of his sitter and the silver-streaked strands of long hair contrast jarringly with the still-dark eyebrows and red-flushed cheeks.

Was this the way the fifty-two-year-old composer really looked? What would Schindler's verdict be—he who according to his own testimony had tried to give arguments in Waldmüller's defense? Here is the verdict: "In a word, the Wald-müller portrait is, if possible, further from the truth than any other. It is the like-ness of a venerable pastor whose thoughts are occupied with elaborating a hom-ily for the edification of his congregation."[106]

But if Schindler saw a parson in Waldmüller's austere portrait of Beethoven, others spied something far less tame in the real-life Beethoven of this period—the period during which the composer's mind was on the Ninth Symphony. The mu-sician Julius Benedict (1804–1885), still in his teens, was taken along by his mentor Weber to meet Beethoven a few months after the Waldmüller picture had been completed. Years later he recalled his vivid impressions of Beethoven for Weber's son, and the description sounds familiar: "King Lear or the Ossianic bards must have resembled him in appearance. His hair was thick, grey, and bristly, here and there altogether white; his forehead and skull had an exceptionally broad curve and were high, like a temple; his nose was four-square, like that of a lion, the mouth nobly shaped and soft, the chin broad, with those wonderful shell-formed grooves in all his portraits, and formed by two jaw-bones which seemed meant to crack the hardest nuts. A dark red overspread his broad, pockmarked face; be-neath the bushy, gloomily contracted eyebrows, small radiant eyes beamed mildly upon those entering; his cyclopean, four-cornered figure, which towered but slightly above that of Weber, was covered by a shabby house-robe, with torn sleeves."[107] Julius Benedict certainly had a wonderful memory, but the suspicion that it had been substantially aided by Schindler's biography in its third, 1860 edi-tion will have to remain in the offing.

Another teenage witness to this late period, the singer Wilhelmine Schröder-Devrient (1804–1860), whose Leonore gave *Fidelio* its first lasting success, left a different sort of word portrait of the hopelessly deaf composer, who, with strange gestures and weird sounds, attempted (against the better judgment of his friends) to conduct a rehearsal of his opera in November 1822: "I felt as though I were gazing at one of Hoffmann's fantastic figures which had popped up before me."[108]

This familiar reference to E.T.A. Hoffmann, one of the most influential expo-nents of German Romanticism, and, in his music criticism, one of the very first to appreciate Beethoven's music, is an important link in the process of how Bee-thoven the man became, even in his lifetime, through his actions and appear-ance, Beethoven the myth. We shall soon take up the implications for mython-omy of the Kreisler ("mad" musician of E.T.A. Hoffmann's publications) image as associated in the public mind with Beethoven.

Waldmüller's glum portrait of the preoccupied, prematurely aged composer re-ceived distribution in the form of an engraving circulated by Breitkopf and Här-tel, struck a few decades after Beethoven's death. The imprint made by this mel-ancholy mien on future Beethoven iconography—which on the whole rejected the aged aspect of the composer—was only slightly ameliorated by the last pic-ture for which the composer knowingly posed—a chalk drawing by the Paris-trained Johann Stefan Decker (1784–1844) in May 1824 (Fig. 33). A happy event occasioned this brooding final portrait. It was the "Grand Musical Concert by Herr L. v. Beethoven," which took place on 7 May 1824 and included the first performance of "A Grand Symphony with Solo and Chorus Voices entering in the finale on Schiller's Ode to Joy." The concert, with Beethoven himself conducting and aided by Michael Umlauf (whom the orchestra and singers had secretly been instructed to follow), was wildly and enthusiastically received and a second performance was given on 23 May. Decker's portrait drawing was made a few days after either the first or the second concert and a lithographic reproduction was printed as a supplement to the *Wiener Allgemeine Musikalische Zeitung* on 5 June 1824 along with a laudatory review of the new music. Decker's sympathetic and elegant portrait confirms many of the observations made by the uncompromising realist Waldmüller but presents them in more palatable (to the public and to Beethoven) form. The contraction of the brows, tight-set drooping lips, jowls beginning to sag, and dramatic contrast of black eyebrows with white, receding hairline are all there. Yet through the simple device of turning Beethoven's head a fraction to one side, Decker has deftly avoided the inescapable reality presented by a frontal view of Beethoven's broad nose, and has in fact strengthened it with a corrective shadow while permitting a *di sotto in su* view to exhibit a flattering, slight flare of the nostrils. (How easily Waldmüller, had he *wished* to do so, could have done the same thing, but he was out to record unmanipulated truth.) The stiff collar and still-fashionable white cravat are in perfect order, and a barber's scissors and comb seem to have visited Beethoven's hair. (Sir John Russell would have been astonished.) It was this last, short-haired aspect of the portrait drawing that caused Schindler to sneer that depicting the composer with short hair was like painting a lion without its mane. When, after Beethoven's death in March 1827, an engraving of the Decker likeness was made by Joseph Steinmüller (1795–1841) for circulation by Artaria in the fall of that same year, Schindler's wrath knew no bounds: "The blatant contrast between this bit of fantasy and the lithograph made from Stieler's portrait [about which Schindler had been only mildly enthusiastic previously] . . . is sufficient to condemn it. . . . Moreover, this likeness shows Beethoven as much too old, while the expression of his character has nothing in common with the creator of great works of art."[109]

Schindler can certainly not be faulted for avoiding skirmishes. But in contrast to Schindler's disapproving opinion of the Decker-Steinmüller print (and it is touching to see how, at the end of his own life, writing in 1860, he refused to accept imagery that made his hero look old), we have a second opinion by one of Beethoven's contemporaries that is very positive. Czerny, who, we remember, as a boy had sat close enough to the composer to memorize his hairy hands and broad fingers, declared that the Decker-Steinmüller portrait was "the only correct likeness that has been published" of Beethoven.[110]

For a final time we can seek to inquire what Beethoven himself thought of his latest portrait. He was apparently pleased about having been the object of yet another artist's attentions, for when sending a copy of the Stieler picture to his Bonn friend Franz Wegeler, he boasted in a letter of 7 December 1826, that "the portrait I am sending with this letter is certainly an artistic masterpiece, but it is not the latest one which has been done of me."[111] And he approved of the Decker likeness enough to dedicate a copy of it to his Paris publisher.[112] Other copies were also no doubt distributed by the composer as gifts to his friends at home and abroad. Perhaps, in spite of the premature aging Decker's likeness faithfully recorded, Beethoven had been able to accept the truism he had marked in his much-thumbed copy of Homer's *Odyssey*: "For quickly doth misfortune make men old."[113] This was the last image of himself over which Beethoven might ever exercise control. Henceforth—although his earthly sojourn would be recorded on two more occasions—the inexorable forces of mythmaking would fashion a larger-than-life-size likeness of the man who, while still alive, had become a legend.

There is no doubt that Beethoven was proud of the fact that since his twenty-ninth year painters and sculptors had asked to portray him and that publishing houses had issued lithographic and engraved copies of his likeness. His years in Vienna commenced and ended with the firm Artaria's commissioning artists to sketch the composer's portrait for reproduction and commercial distribution. Beethoven delighted in being able to send back to Bonn the first such efforts (Fig. 29), dating from the year 1800. He sent it to Franz Wegeler, and his accompanying letter of 29 June 1801 happily bragged that "this portrait is being published here by Artaria who like many other art dealers in foreign countries too has often asked me for one."[114] A quarter of a century later Beethoven was still posting images of himself back to Wegeler, as we have seen. Since the recipient was in both cases the same faithful friend of his youth—the person to whom Beethoven had once confessed the horrible secret of his deafness—it might be well to read how, only three months before his death, Beethoven summed up his life for the ever-caring Wegeler. Our mind's eye can wander, as Wegeler's must have done, through a Beethoven portrait gallery of twenty-five years of imagery, ranging from the hopeful, if unprepossessing-looking, black-haired youth of the Artaria-initiated awkward conception of 1800 (Fig. 29) to the resigned gray-haired titan of Decker's reverent rendition of 1824:

My beloved old friend!

. . . Each of us had to pursue the purpose for which he was intended and endeavor to attain it. Yet the eternally unshakeable and firm foundations of good principles continued to bind us strongly together. Unfortunately I can not write to you today as much as I should like to, for I have to stay in bed. So I shall confine myself to answering a few points in your letter. You say that I have been mentioned somewhere as being the natural son of the late King of Prussia. Well, the same thing was said to me a long time ago. But I have adopted the principle of neither writing anything about myself nor replying to anything that has been written about me. Hence I gladly leave it to you to make known to the world the integrity of my parents, and especially of my mother. . . .

As for my diploma I merely mention that I am an Honorary Member of the Royal Scientific Society of Sweden and likewise of Amsterdam, and also an Honorary Citizen of Vienna. A short time ago a certain Dr. Spiker took with him to Berlin my latest grand symphony with choruses; it is dedicated to the King, and I had to write the dedication with my own hand. . . . On that occasion something was said to me about the Order of the Red Eagle, Second Class. Whether anything will come of this, I don't know, for I have never striven after honors of that kind. Yet at the present time for many other reasons such an award would be rather welcome.—In any case my motto is always: Nulla dies sine linea; and if I let my Muse go to sleep, it is only that she may be all the more active when she awakes. I still hope to create a few great works and then like an old child to finish my earthly course somewhere among kind people. . . .[115]

Fifteen weeks later, with plans for a Tenth Symphony sounding in his head, Beethoven did finish his earthly course. The people around him were, for the most part, kind. The items they found in the secret drawer of an old cabinet—among them the letter to the "Immortal Beloved"—would forever fan the flames of curiosity and mythmaking. Two pathetically intimate, and ultimate, portraits of the living—or rather not quite dead—Beethoven (Figs. 34 and 35) leave no doubt as to the physical suffering endured by the composer during the four months of his mortal illness. The poignant drawings, hastily sketched in pencil, show Beethoven in the coma from which he was not to regain consciousness. The eyes are already permanently shut, the fists tightly clenched, and the mouth gapes open, obdurately gasping for breath. The arms and shoulders are emaciated. Underneath the sheets the once powerful frame is horribly swollen with the dropsy for which the abdomen had four times been tapped. Edema, hemorrhages, and jaundice accompanied the final stages of his cirrhosis of the liver. The physician in attendance, Dr. Andreas Ignaz Wawruch, reported that his patient knew the end had come: "Beethoven in gloomy hours of presentiment, foretold his approaching dissolution after his fourth tapping, nor was he mistaken. No consolation was able longer to revive him; and when I promised him that with the approaching spring weather his suffering would decrease, he answered with a smile: 'My day is done; if a physician still can be of use in my case (and then he lapsed into English) his name shall be called wonderful.' This saddening reference to Handel's *Messiah* so profoundly moved me that in my inmost soul and with the deepest emotion I was obliged to confirm the truth of what he said."[116]

Towards evening on 24 March 1827, after swallowing a few spoonfuls of twenty-year-old Rhine wine sent to him at his urgent request from Mainz, Beethoven, mercifully, lost consciousness. Gerhard von Breuning describes the death struggle: "During the next day and the day following the strong man lay completely unconscious, in the process of dissolution, breathing so stertorously that the rattle could be heard at a distance. His powerful frame, his unweakened lungs, fought like giants with approaching death. The spectacle was a fearful one."[117]

It was this fearful spectacle that the young painter Joseph Eduard Teltscher (1801–1837), a close friend of Schubert and destined to die a tragic death by drowning a decade later, courageously attempted to record for history. He may have been called to the scene for this purpose by Beethoven's composer colleague from Graz, Anselm Hüttenbrenner (1794–1868), who, through the timing of fate, would be the person supporting Beethoven's head at the moment of death. Hüttenbrenner's report, written to Thayer thirty-three years after the event, explains why the artist's drawings remained unfinished: "When I entered Beethoven's room on March 26, 1827 at about three o'clock in the afternoon, I found there Court Councillor [Stephan von] Breuning, his son [Gerhard] . . . and my friend Joseph Teltscher, portrait painter. I think that Prof. Schindler was also present."[118]

Hüttenbrenner told Thayer that Teltscher then began to draw Beethoven's face, and this so upset Breuning that he protested, causing the painter to retire in embarrassment. Depressed and restless from their long bedside vigil, Breuning and Schindler left the Schwarzspanierhaus a short time later themselves and went out to the Währing Cemetery for the sad purpose of picking a grave site. They were delayed in returning to take up the death watch by snow and a sudden, severe thunderstorm. Thus it was that a mere acquaintance and not an intimate of Beethoven's was at his side when death came. Hüttenbrenner's effusive account of the final moments has done far more than Teltscher's private portraits of moribund resistance to contribute to the legend of Beethoven as titan and defier of the gods.[119] Here, first, are the facts as educed from Hüttenbrenner's report: "After Beethoven had lain unconscious, the death-rattle in his throat from three o'clock in the afternoon till after five, there came a flash of lightning accompanied by a violent clap of thunder, which garishly illuminated the death-chamber. (Snow lay before Beethoven's dwelling.) After this unexpected phenomenon of nature... Beethoven opened his eyes, lifted his right hand and looked up for several seconds with his fist clenched and a very serious, threatening expression. . . . When he let the raised hand sink to the bed, his eyes closed half-way. . . . Not another breath, not a heartbeat more!"[120]

And here is Hüttenbrenner's report again, this time unabridged and with his own running commentary:

> After Beethoven had lain unconscious, the death-rattle in his throat from three o'clock in the afternoon till after five, there came a flash of lightning accompanied by a violent clap of thunder, which garishly illuminated the death-chamber. (Snow lay before Beethoven's dwelling.) After this unexpected phenomenon of nature, which startled me greatly, Beethoven opened his eyes, lifted his right hand and looked up for several seconds with his fist clenched and a very serious, threatening expression as if he wanted to say: "Inimical powers, I defy you! Away with you! God is with me!" It also seemed as if, like a brave commander, he wished to call out to his wavering troops: "Courage, soldiers! Forward! Trust in me! Victory is assured!" When he let the raised hand sink to the bed, his eyes closed half-way. My right hand was under his head, my left rested on his breast. Not another breath, not a heartbeat more! The genius of the great master of tones fled from this world of delusion into the realm of truth!—I pressed down the half-open eyelids of the dead man, kissed them, then his forehead, mouth and hands. At my request Frau van Beethoven [the woman present was probably not one of Beethoven's sisters-in-law but his maid Sali who had been in faithful attendance during the last months] cut a lock of hair from his head and handed it to me as a sacred souvenir of Beethoven's last hour.[121]

Thus our well-intentioned, if imaginative, reporter also becomes, by his own admission, the first to collect a lock of Beethoven's hair as a relic. There would be others.

About the unexpected phenomenon of nature, the sudden thunderstorm that lent its own drama to the timing of Beethoven's death, there is agreement in all accounts—in fact it is corroborated by records at the Vienna weather bureau for that day—but again it is instructive to see how each witness provides his own coloration of the fact. Not even Dr. Wawruch was free from subjective speculation concerning the storm, which he sets a little later in the day: "The twenty-sixth of March was stormy, and clouded. Toward six in the afternoon came a flurry of snow, with thunder and lightning—Beethoven died. Would not a Roman augur, in view of the accidental commotion of the elements, have taken this apotheosis for granted?"[122]

It would certainly be remiss not to inquire how Schindler portrayed his revered master's death. He did not, he could not, claim to have been present. His account is straightforward and specifies Beethoven's exact age—an important detail since so many future biographers, neglecting to note that the composer was born in

December (he was baptized on the seventeenth; there is still uncertainty as to what day in December he was born), would blithely subtract the birth year 1770 from the death year 1827 and come up with the pronouncement that Beethoven died at the age of fifty-seven. Here is Schindler's terse account of the final hours:

> On the morning of twenty-four March the master asked for the last sacrament which he took in a spirit of true devotion. At about one o'clock in the afternoon he showed the first signs of his approaching death. A frightful struggle between death and life began, probably as a result of his extraordinary strong nervous system, and continued without respite until a quarter to six on the evening of twenty-six March, when during a heavy hailstorm the great composer gave up his spirit. He was fifty-six years, three months, and nine days old.
>
> The fortunate one who was able to close our friend's eyes in the hour of death was the esteemed composer and music-lover Anselm Hüttenbrenner, who had hurried to Vienna from Graz so that he might see Beethoven again. Breuning and this author had gone that afternoon to the village graveyard at Währing to seek out a suitable last resting place. The storm prevented our quick return. When we entered the sick room someone called out to us, "It is finished."[123]

(Colorplate 9)

But the portraiture of Beethoven was not quite finished. Before his body was lowered into the ground on March 29, three more eyewitness likenesses were made of his physical remains: oil sketches were made of his face (Fig. 36) and his hands (Fig. 38), and his death mask was taken. The artist to whom these eschatological images were vouchsafed was a twenty-one-year-old Viennese—the youngest artist ever to approach the mortal Beethoven. Josef Danhauser (1805–1845) had studied violin extensively as a boy and his veneration for Beethoven sprang from a genuine appreciation of the composer's music. He was the son of the great furniture owner whose wares played a role in creating the Viennese Biedermeier (Louis Letronne had worked for the Danhauser firm as a drawer of furniture designs) and had been sent to the Vienna Academy to study art. A statement by his brother Carl, written sixty-four years after the event in 1891, was recently discovered and explains what happened after Stephan von Breuning consulted by letter with Schindler on the day after Beethoven's death concerning the following quandary he found himself facing: "Tomorrow morning a certain Danhauser wishes to take a plaster cast of the body [sic]. He says it will take five minutes, or at the most eight. Write and tell me whether I should agree. Such casts are often permitted in the case of famous men, and not to permit it might later be regarded as an insult to the public. Vienna, 27 March. Breuning."[124]

Schindler obviously gave his benediction and, ever the conscientious historian when it served *his* image of Beethoven, reported: "This plaster cast (taken by Danhauser, who later became renowned as a sculptor) still exists. The facsimile of this letter from Breuning [about Danhauser's request] is given at the end of this volume. It proves the authenticity of the death mask, and is an example of the handwriting of the friend who for so many years remained true and constant to the great composer."[125]

Why, we may wonder, should Schindler wish to confirm the death mask's authenticity? One plausible reason is that he probably owned a copy of it and was providing a pedigree, but another reason is aesthetic: the mask, with its hollow, sunken cheeks and sagging features, simply does not—at first glance—look like Beethoven; at least not the Beethoven of Klein's life mask. But this pathetic, emaciated face is not the Beethoven of life. It is the ineffable palimpsest of wasting disease and many years of emotional and extreme physical pain. Furthermore it is not a complete effigy, for the plaster gruesomely records the disfiguration of Beethoven's head and temples caused by the autopsy of March 27 when the temporal bones were sawed out and removed along with parts of the ears for the purpose of determining the reason for Beethoven's deafness.[126] Carl Danhauser's memoir takes up what occurred next and how he and his brother got involved in taking Beethoven's death mask. A fellow Academy art student, Johann Mathias Ranftl (1805–1854), woke the two brothers early in the morning[127] with the momentous news then spreading through Vienna that Beethoven had died.

CHAPTER TWO
BEETHOVEN
ALIVE:
EYEWITNESS
ACCOUNTS

> Since we had plaster casting in our firm, my brother Josef, who had been motivated to try that kind of work in his study of heads, immediately got the idea of taking a mask of the great departed one. We dressed quickly, ordered the carriage to be got ready, and since in the meantime Hofmann, the plasterer employed by our factory, had arrived we took him with us in the carriage.
>
> It was still very early in the day when we arrived at the house of the departed and we couldn't find anyone who might give us information. Finally a woman let us go up the stairs and above we found an open foyer with the door leading to the adjoining room ajar. We clutched at the latch and went inside. Against the main wall of this room stood a bed and in this bed lay Beethoven's corpse. Since the dead man's beard had grown quite thick during his sickness we sent the plasterer to get a barber who shaved away the beard.[128]

While the two boys were waiting for the barber to come Josef made two drawings which he then worked up into oil sketches (Figs. 36 and 38), one of the dead man's face and the other of his hands, catching in swift, impressionistic strokes the well-known stubby fingers, which in death were stiffly folded together. Before the barber's arrival the Danhausers also discreetly acquired their own Beethoven relics: "Meanwhile we had cut off two locks of hair from where they lay profusely over each other at the temples as a souvenir of the illustrious head and then set to work. My brother, who understood less about this sort of thing than the experienced plasterer, was very happy to have his help and so soon a good cast was taken which we, preserving it securely, carefully took home, for my brother had gotten the idea that as a painter he might try his hand at modeling and at making a bust of Beethoven. He went to work immediately and succeeded actually in creating a bust of the master which astonished everyone and prompted admiration for the young artist. Several casts were made."[129]

Where the original death mask and Danhauser's modeled bust of Beethoven later went we shall discover shortly. What was immediately made available to the sensation-loving public was the lithograph—with all locks of hair restored—that the enterprising young artist produced of Beethoven on his deathbed (Fig. 37). This wrenching, great-browed, hollow-cheeked image of suffering left behind was the last "portrait" for which the mortal Beethoven ever posed. Henceforth, it would be the immortal Beethoven whom posterity would pursue as its model.

Chapter Three

BEETHOVEN DEAD: SHAPING THE POSTHUMOUS PORTRAIT

"When I heard of Beethoven's death it seemed to me as if a god had departed, and I shed bitter tears."[1] This devastated reaction was that of a seven-year-old boy in Hagen—Charles Hallé (1819–1895), the Westphalian musician whose later brilliant career as a conductor took him to England where he founded the still-famous Hallé Orchestra at Manchester. His adoration of Beethoven was life-long. At the age of seven he was already playing the piano part of the *Archduke* Trio; as an adult he was the first pianist to play all the Beethoven sonatas in both Paris and London, and he regularly played the entire cycle of sonatas until the last year of his life. On the evening of his death he was rehearsing Beethoven's Piano Concerto no. 3.

Those who actually had the chance to witness Beethoven's funeral on the afternoon of 29 March 1827 were no less overwhelmed by the loss, especially since the procession (Fig. 39) was one of the most impressive of its kind ever seen in Vienna. Beethoven, who in life had contributed his share toward establishing his status as a genius, was accorded a burial by his adopted city that far exceeded his social rank, a burial that paid homage to his artistic citizenship in world creativity. Schools were closed for the event, and, as Schindler proudly reported, nearly twenty thousand persons followed the procession from the Schwarzspanierhaus to the parish church in the Alserstrasse, a distance of little more than one long city block that, because of the huge crowd, took more than an hour and a half to cover. The composer's brother Johann—whose name Beethoven had gone out of his way to avoid uttering or writing—Stephan and Gerhard von Breuning, and Schindler were the chief mourners following the ornately decorated bier; Hummel and seven other Kapellmeisters[2] were the pallbearers, and among the torch-bearers were Czerny and Schubert, with bouquets of lilies pinned to their shoulders. After the blessing of the body, two hundred coaches, including several imperial ones, joined in the cortege that accompanied the hearse, drawn by four horses, out to the Währing Cemetery.

At the gates of the cemetery an event took place that gave immediate impetus to the mythicization of Beethoven. This was the recitation of a moving funeral oration written by no less a poet than Franz Grillparzer (1791–1872) (Fig. 40), Austria's foremost dramatist and long a personal friend of the composer's. Schindler had come to him a few days before with the news that Beethoven was dying and a request that he compose the funeral oration. Grillparzer had set to work on the speech when "Schindler came again and told me that Beethoven had just died. Then something snapped inside me; the tears rushed from my eyes, and I could not finish the speech as elegantly as I had begun. . . . I had really loved Beethoven."[3]

Grillparzer's oration was delivered in ringing, emotional tones by a well-known actor from the Burgtheater, Heinrich Anschütz (1785–1865), another personal friend of the composer. The speech not only expressed the acute sense of historical loss felt by the city, but also provided a whole program for the interpretation of Beethoven as unifying cultural concept. Here are the essential parts:

CHAPTER THREE
BEETHOVEN
DEAD: SHAPING
THE
POSTHUMOUS
PORTRAIT

Standing by the grave of him who has passed away we are in a manner the representatives of an entire nation, of the whole German people. . . . The heir and amplifier of Handel's and Bach's, of Haydn's and Mozart's immortal fame is now no more, and we stand weeping over the riven strings of the harp that is hushed.

The harp that is hushed! Let me call him so! For he was an artist, and all that was his, was his through art alone. The thorns of life had wounded him deeply, and as the castaway clings to the shore, so did he seek refuge in thine arms, O thou glorious sister and peer of the Good and the True, thou balm of wounded hearts, heaven-born Art! To thee he clung fast, and even when the portal was closed wherethrough thou hadst entered in and spoken to him, when his deaf ear had blinded his vision for thy features, still did he ever carry thine image within his heart, and when he died it still reposed on his breast.

He was an artist—and who shall arise to stand beside him? As the rushing behemoth spurns the waves, so did he rove to the uttermost bounds of his art. From the cooing of doves to the rolling of thunder, from the craftiest interweaving of well-weighed expedients of art up to that awful pitch where planful design disappears in the lawless whirl of contending natural forces, he had traversed and grasped it all. . . . Ye children of the voices divided thrice and four times! heaven-soaring harmony: "Freude, schöner Götterfunken," thou swan song! Muse of song and the seven-stringed lyre! Approach his grave and bestrew it with laurel!

He was an artist, but a man as well. A man in every sense—in the highest. Because he withdrew from the world, they called him a man-hater, and because he held himself aloof from sentimentality, unfeeling. . . . An excess of sensitiveness avoids a show of feeling! He fled the world because, in the whole range of his loving nature, he found no weapon to oppose it. He withdrew from mankind after he had given them his all and received nothing in return. He dwelt alone, because he found no second Self. But to the end his heart beat warm for all men, in fatherly affection for his kindred, for the world his all and his heart's blood.

Thus he was, thus he died, thus he will live to the end of time.

You, however, who have followed after us hitherward, let not your hearts be troubled! You have not lost him, you have won him. No living man enters the halls of the immortals. Not until the body has perished, do their portals unclose. He whom you mourn stands from now onward among the great of all ages, inviolate forever. Return homeward therefore, in sorrow, yet resigned!

And should you ever in times to come feel the overpowering might of his creations, like an onrushing storm, when your mounting ecstasy overflows in the midst of a generation yet unborn, then remember this hour, and think, We were there, when they buried him, and when he died, we wept.[4]

Grillparzer's impassioned oration opened the floodgates of several kinds of consciousness: a national awareness of the artist as a man alienated from and made to suffer by an uncomprehending society; and, finally, a historical consciousness of the man, the moment, and its meaning—a legacy to the future. The oration also contained, in its characterization of Beethoven's music, the germ of what would become a certain kind of response: the tendency to see his music as something encompassing extremes and spiraling upwards from reasoned stratagems to elemental lawlessness—celestial and chthonic all in one.

Of the many eulogies, reminiscences, and documents that soon began to appear in print after Beethoven's death, none was to contribute more poignantly to history's romanticized image of the deaf composer than a letter written by Beethoven himself—the Heiligenstadt Testament of 6 and 10 October 1802. It was discovered by Schindler in a pile of the composer's private papers and although it was quickly bought at auction by Artaria, Schindler had already made copies of it and mailed them to Moscheles in London and to Rochlitz—the man who would turn down the task of writing Beethoven's biography—in Leipzig. Rochlitz may not have felt up to writing a full-scale life of the composer but he recognized gripping copy when he saw it, and this, Beethoven's agonized confessional of self-justification, certainly was. Ostensibly addressed to his two brothers, Carl and Johann (a space eloquently "identifies" the younger brother whose name Beethoven could not bring himself to write down) (Fig. 41), the document alternates between appeals to "fellowmen" and "mankind" in general, speaks of having overcome the temptation to do away with himself, and cites the likelihood of ultimate deafness as the reason for the author's self-isolation and despair. The document is also written—unusual for Beethoven—in a careful and legible hand. It is a fair copy, written with an audience in mind. By publishing it in the 17 October 1827 issue of the *Allgemeine musikalische Zeitung*—fewer than seven months after Beethoven's death—Rochlitz was fulfilling the wish expressed in the Heiligenstadt Testament that as soon as he was dead Beethoven's deafness be revealed to the world so that it might be "reconciled" to him. But that death did not come for another twenty-four and a half years, and just as the young Goethe had let a fictional Werther carry out the suicidal urges engendered by the failure of a real-life love affair, so Beethoven's sheer act of writing the Heiligenstadt Testament, with its references to suicide contemplated and overcome, seems to have granted its author the will to go on with life, turning even the defeat of deafness into a victory of will. Here are the crucial passages from Beethoven's outpouring of 1802 that dictated posterity's obsession with the Beethovenian topoi of suffering and triumph:

For my brothers Karl and   Beethoven

Oh you men who think or say that I am malevolent, stubborn or misanthropic, how greatly do you wrong me. You do not know the secret cause which makes me seem that way to you. From childhood on my heart and soul have been full of the tender feeling of goodwill, and I was ever inclined to accomplish great things. But, think that for 6 years now I have been hopelessly afflicted, made worse by senseless physicians, from year to year deceived with hopes of improvement, finally compelled to face the prospect of a *lasting malady*

CHAPTER THREE
BEETHOVEN
DEAD: SHAPING
THE
POSTHUMOUS
PORTRAIT

(whose cure will take years, or, perhaps, be impossible). Though born with a fiery, active temperament, even susceptible to the diversions of society, I was soon compelled to withdraw myself, to live life alone. If at times I tried to forget all this, oh how harshly was I flung back to the doubly sad experience of my bad hearing. Yet it was impossible fo me to say to people, "Speak louder, shout, for I am deaf." . . . Oh I cannot do it, therefore fogive me when you see me draw back when I would have gladly mingled with you. My misfortune is doubly painful to me because I am bound to be misunderstood; for me there can be no relaxation with my fellow-men, no refined conversations, no mutual exchange of ideas. I must live almost alone like one who has been banished, I can mix with society only as much as true necessity demands. If I approach near to people a hot terror seizes upon me and I fear being exposed to the danger that my condition might be noticed. . . . But what a humiliation for me when someone standing next to me heard a flute in the distance and *I heard nothing*, or someone heard a *shepherd singing* and again I heard nothing. Such incidents drove me almost to despair, a little more of that and I would have ended my life—it was only *my art* that held me back. . . . Oh fellow-men, when at some point you read this, consider that you have done me an injustice. . . . You my brothers Carl and
     as soon as I am dead if Dr. Schmid[t] is still alive ask him in my name to describe my malady, and attach this written document to his account of my illness so that so far as it is possible at least the world may become reconciled to me after my death. . . .[5]

Beethoven wrote this moving document when he was thirty-one; he thought enough of it to take it with him through many changes of residence and summer sojourns in different lodgings. When he died, at the age of fifty-six, the world already knew of his deafness. But his request that his malady be described and revealed to the world, once published and circulated through Rochlitz's Leipzig journal, was to add fuel to the fire of morbid inquisitiveness that accompanied the new interest in phrenology, and Beethoven's remains would be twice exhumed and examined—in 1863 and again in 1888.[6]

A less morbid but far more incendiary component in the mythmaking process was the literary contribution by E.T.A. Hoffmann (1776–1822) (Fig. 42) that led to a spontaneous combustion of Beethoven's image into the full-flamed Romantic conception of Beethoven as a mad genius. We have already seen how, even during the composer's lifetime, his sometimes inexplicable antics and "Ossian"-like looks had inspired some eyewitnesses to think in terms of demoniac possession, and that the impressionable young singer Wilhelmine Schröder-Devrient felt as though she were gazing at one of "Hoffmann's fantastic figures." There are several levels at which the names of Beethoven and Ernst Theodor Amadeus (originally Wilhelm; Amadeus was the name he gave himself in honor of Mozart) Hoffmann connect.

The first is in real life. Although his profession was law, the multitalented Hoffmann had managed to pursue his real loves—music, literature, and painting—with tremendous intensity and some success. His productivity was extraordinary. As a composer he wrote ten operas, including *Undine* (forerunner to Weber's *Der Freischutz* in its mingling of the supernatural with the natural), two masses, several cantatas, two symphonies, incidental music to over a dozen plays, motets, and a great deal of chamber and piano music. As a writer of fiction he invoked music whenever possible in his fantastic stories, and sometimes illustrated their themes himself in a wiry lined, energetic style that bristles with nervous energy. The happy combination of musical and literary gifts served him admirably

as a music critic and he contributed some one hundred reviews of great originality and perception to the *Allgemeine musikalische Zeitung* through the titillating medium of essays written by the fictitious violinist and Kapellmeister Johannes
Kreisler. These ''Kreisler papers''—Kreisleriana—which contained appreciative
analyses of Beethoven's music, were issued as part of Hoffmann's first book, *Fan-
tasiestücke in Callots Manier*, published in four volumes between 1814 and 1815, and
it was in this form that the peripatetic music critic and his work were brought to
Beethoven's attention. In the conversation book for March 1820 a visitor wrote:
''In the Phantasie-Stücke by Hoffmann, you are often spoken of. Hoffmann was
musical director in Bamberg; he is now Government Councillor.—Operas of his
composition are performed in Berlin.''[7]

Beethoven, studying the new entry in his conversation book, reacted first to
the pun inherent in the critic's name and wrote down the following response:
''Hofmann [*sic*] du bist kein *Hof-Mann* [Hofmann you are no courtier].''[8]

He also must have read what the author had to say about his music for on the
twenty-third day of the same month, March, he spontaneously wrote Hoffmann—now in Berlin—the following cordial letter: ''I am seizing the opportunity
through Herr Neberich [a local wine merchant] to approach a man so full of life
and wit as you are—Also you have written about my humble self. Also our *weak
Herr Starke* [Beethoven is trying to be witty for Hoffmann as he now modifies Herr
'Strong' with the antonym 'weak'] showed me some lines of yours about me in
his album. Thus I am given to believe that you take some interest in me. Allow
me to say that this from a man with such distinguished gifts as yourself pleases
me very much. I wish you everything that is beautiful and good and remain with
high esteem yours faithfully Beethoven.''[9]

Hoffmann's response, if any, has not been preserved, but we can certainly find
out what it was that he had written concerning Beethoven's music that so pleased
the composer. The writer whose fantastic stories would provide musical inspiration for Adam (*La Poupée de Nuremberg*), Offenbach (*Le Roi Carotte, Les contes d'Hoffmann*), Delibes (*Coppélia ou La fille aux yeux d'email*), Tchaikovsky (*Nutcracker*), Busoni (*Die Brautwahl*), and Hindemith (*Cardillac*), among others, would, in his
musical analysis of Beethoven, set the style for a new genre of music criticism,
one which would be emulated by such composer-critics as Weber, Schumann,
Berlioz, and even Wagner. After a century of dry, rationalistic criticism, Hoffmann's poetic volleys, subjective rains of emotion, sultry enthusiasms, and almost plastic perception of spiritual values in music presented a strange, new hothouse environment for the swiftly growing romantic reverence for music. And it
is at this second level that Hoffmann's name is irrevocably linked with Beethoven's, for Hoffmann's Beethoven was the Beethoven of romanticism. Henceforth
an entire century would view the composer through Hoffmann's tinted glasses.
Let us look at what he published in 1814 on instrumental music and Beethoven's
unique contribution to it. He begins: ''When we speak of music as an independent art, should we not always restrict our meaning to instrumental music,
which, scorning every aid, every admixture of another art (the art of poetry),
gives pure expression to music's specific nature, recognizable in this form
alone?''[10]

So far this might sound like an argument (anticipating Eduard Hanslick) for
absolute music. Beethoven had not yet ''admixed'' the art of poetry to induce
a grand symphony to ''speak,'' so Hoffmann—destined to die two years before
the Ninth Symphony's first performance—never had the occasion for a possible

CHAPTER THREE
BEETHOVEN
DEAD: SHAPING
THE
POSTHUMOUS
PORTRAIT

conversion. But two words used by Hoffmann in his very next sentence direct us to the subjective arena in which he sees the victory of instrumental music take place: "It is the most romantic of all the arts—one might almost say, the only genuinely romantic one—for its sole subject is the infinite."[11] With these words our bewitching representative of German Romanticism unhesitatingly applies the term "romantic" in its adjectival capacity to lead music and his readers to that goal of Romanticism, union with the "infinite." Now he explains how invocation of the infinite conjures up not sunrises and tempests but mysterious yearnings and fathomless feeling:

> The lyre of Orpheus opened the portals of Orcus—music discloses to man an unknown realm, a world that has nothing in common with the external sensual world that surrounds him, a world in which he leaves behind him all definite feelings to surrender himself to an inexpressible longing.
>
> Have you even so much as suspected this specific nature, you miserable composers of instrumental music, you who have laboriously strained yourselves to represent definite emotions, even definite events? . . . Your sunrises, your tempests . . . and the rest. . . .
>
> Mozart and Haydn, the creators of our present instrumental music, were the first to show us the art in its full glory; the man who then looked on it with all his love and penetrated its innermost being is—Beethoven! . . . Beethoven's instrumental music opens up to us also the realm of the monstrous and the immeasurable. Burning flashes of light shoot through the deep night of this realm, and we become aware of giant shadows that surge back and forth, driving us into narrower and narrower confines until they destroy *us*—but not the pain of that endless longing in which each joy that has climbed aloft in jubilant song sinks back and is swallowed up, and it is only in this pain, which consumes love, hope, and happiness but does not destroy them, which seeks to burst our breasts with a many-voiced consonance of all the passions, that we live on, enchanted beholders of the supernatural! . . . Beethoven's music sets in motion the lever of fear, of awe, of horror, of suffering, and wakens just that infinite longing which is the essence of romanticism. He is accordingly a completely romantic composer. . . .[12]

Certainly no critic in the Age of Enlightenment had ever written about music in this way. In fact no one had ever written about music like this! Whether or not Beethoven accepted Hoffmann's generous label as a completely Romantic composer is unconfirmed, but Hoffmann would have been enchanted by the laconic description of his tone realm written by Beethoven, in the same year as Hoffmann's review, to his close friend Count Franz Brunsvik: "As regards me, great heavens! my dominion is in the air; the tones whirl like the wind, and often there is a like whirl in my soul."[13]

Hoffmann's encomium goes on bravely to confront and quash current Beethoven criticism: "The musical rabble is oppressed by Beethoven's powerful genius; it seeks in vain to oppose it. But knowing critics, looking about them with a superior air, assure us that we may take their word for it as men of great intellect and deep insight that, while the excellent Beethoven can scarcely be denied a very fertile and lively imagination, he does not know how to bridle it! Thus, they say, he no longer bothers at all to select or to shape his ideas, but, following the so-called daemonic method, he dashes everything off exactly as his ardently active imagination dictates it to him."[14]

Such a characterization of anti-Beethoven criticism was not—in contrast to Hoffmann's story style—based on fantasy. As early as 1806 the mighty symphonic overture to *Fidelio* had provoked the following hostile (anonymous) report: "All impartial experts and music lovers have unanimously been of the opinion that never has such incoherent, shrill, confused, ear-shocking music been written. The most cutting dissonances follow each other in really horrible harmony."[15]

That Beethoven's "horrible" harmonies were not dashed off in the first flashes of demonic inspiration is substantiated by the hundreds of drafts, workings-out of passages in hardly altered form, revisions, and experimental notations in Beethoven's compositional sketchbooks.[16] And Beethoven himself had given a description of how he worked to Louis Schlösser, the young musician visitor from Darmstadt who, we have seen, retained such a vivid memory of Beethoven's "snow-white teeth." When Schlösser timidly asked how he attained his musical goals Beethoven answered unaffectedly:

> I carry my thoughts about with me for a long time, sometimes a very long time, before I set them down. At the same time my memory is so faithful to me that I am sure not to forget a theme which I have once conceived, even after five years have passed. I make many changes, reject and reattempt until I am satisfied. Then the working-out in breadth, length, height and depth begins in my head, and since I am conscious of what I want, the basic idea never leaves me. It rises, grows upward, and I hear and see the picture as a whole take shape and stand forth before me as though cast in a single piece, so that all that is left is the work of writing it down. . . . You will ask me whence I take my ideas? That I cannot say with any degree of certainty; they come to me uninvited, directly, or indirectly. I could almost grasp them in my hands, out in Nature's open, in the woods, during my promenades, in the silence of the night, at earliest dawn. They are roused by moods which in the poet's case are transmuted into words, and in mine into tones, that sound, roar and storm until at last they take shape for me as notes.[17]

This is an important rebuttal of the "musical rabble's" critique of how Beethoven composed, but in the interests of the chronological unfolding of a Beethoven mythology, we must remember that Schlösser's valuable account was not published and hence not available to the collective—and corrective—consciousness until 1885. In the meantime those apologists seeking the elusive method in Beethoven's "madness" had to make do with Schindler's description of the composer's work habits, a description that would itself inspire the most maudlin motifs, to say nothing of horrible harmonies, in the visual arts: "Beethoven's Daily Routine: Beethoven rose every morning the year round at dawn and went directly to his desk. There he would work until two or three o'clock, his habitual dinner hour. In the course of the morning he would usually go out of doors once or twice, but would continue to work as he walked. These walks would seldom last more than an hour, and may be compared to a bee's excursions to gather honey."[18]

It is not surprising that even after the Schindler and Schlösser accounts were in print, popularizers and spreaders of the posthumous portrait still preferred to emphasize the demoniac aspect of the "possessed" composer, which Beethoven's self-admitted inspiration in the presence of nature suggested so seductively.

Returning to Hoffmann's 1814 defense of Beethoven's music we can not help but admire his instinctive comprehension of the interior Beethoven. He challenges and instructs the musical rabble:

> Yet how does the matter stand if it is *your* feeble observation alone that the deep inner continuity of Beethoven's every composition eludes? If it is *your* fault alone that you do not understand the master's language as the initiated under-

CHAPTER THREE
BEETHOVEN
DEAD: SHAPING
THE
POSTHUMOUS
PORTRAIT

stand it, that the portals of the innermost sanctuary remain closed to you? The truth is that, as regards self-possession, Beethoven stands on a par with Haydn and Mozart and that, separating his ego from the inner realm of harmony, he rules over it as an absolute monarch. In Shakespeare, our knights of the aesthetic measuring-rod have often bewailed the utter lack of inner unity and inner continuity, although for those who look more deeply there springs forth, issuing from a single bud, a beautiful tree . . . thus, with Beethoven, it is only after a searching investigation of his instrumental music that the high self-possession inseparable from true genius and nourished by the study of the art stands revealed.[19]

In coupling the composer's name with that of Shakespeare's, our rhapsodic defender of the ''deep inner continuity of Beethoven's every composition'' has revealed his early Romantic pedigree and strengthened with the most up-to-date arguments his plea for our understanding of Beethoven's instrumental music, which, because of the very fact that it opened up ''also the realm of the monstrous,'' was *not* beautiful—that is *not* classical, eighteenth-century, and subject to the rules of reason; but, rather, *sublime*—that is nonclassical, nineteenth- century, rich with variety and irregularity, and free from constraint. All of these arguments had been used by the earlier Romantics in their enthusiastic revaluation of Shakespeare, who had previously been seen by French classicists as having broken all the rules and therefore unworthy. Herder's essay (1773) ranking the English playwright above Corneille, Racine, and Voltaire and the superb translations into German of Shakespeare undertaken jointly by Ludwig and Dorothea Tieck and August and Caroline Schlegel (from 1797 on) were of monumental importance for one of nineteenth-century Germany's great gifts to human thought: the idea of *aesthetic relativism*.[20]

German appreciation of Shakespeare's ''sublime'' nonconformity and inner coherence had an exciting parallel in the new reverence for Gothic (''German'') architecture and Strassburg Cathedral in particular, as eulogized by the youthful Goethe of *Sturm* and *Drang* in his essay ''Of German Architecture'' (''Von Deutscher Baukunst,'' 1772). In one inspired blow Goethe had refuted neoclassical animadversion towards Gothic ''confusion.'' He explained the seeming capriciousness of the cathedral's decorative surfaces as ''like the trees of God,'' hence sheathing an organic unity in which all the thousands of details had a hidden interaction that harmonized with the whole. For the early German Romantics Shakespeare and Strassburg had revealed the sublimity of the nonbeautiful; for a late German Romantic like Hoffmann, Beethoven's music—saturated with sensory expectancy—afforded a bittersweet and enthralling glimpse of infinite longing.

Almost as though he were consciously imitating Goethe's glowing account of Strassburg Minster, Hoffmann now turns his pyrotechnical prose to the task of igniting admiration for a monument by Beethoven—the Fifth Symphony: ''Can there be any work of Beethoven's that confirms all this to a higher degree than his indescribably profound, magnificent symphony in C minor? How this wonderful composition, in a climax that climbs on and on, leads the listener imperiously forward into the spirit world of the infinite! . . . No doubt the whole rushes like an ingenious rhapsody past many a man, but the soul of each thoughtful listener is assuredly stirred, deeply and intimately, by a feeling that is none other than that unutterable portentous longing, and until the final chord—indeed even in the moments that follow it—he will be powerless to step out of that wondrous spirit realm where grief and joy embrace him in the form of sound."[21]

Hoffmann's vaulted language, his transports of contradictory feeling are literary echoes of the passions unleashed in Beethoven's music; the "unutterable longing" was the common emotional property of both men's epoch—an epoch steeped in the concept of struggle. This struggle was perceived not only in the personal sense of Goethe's dictum "Streben, immer streben" ("Strive, always strive") but—ever since the revelations of the French Revolution—in the social sense as well. The "liberal" longings and utterances of both Beethoven and Hoffmann were based upon this broadened prospect of life on a continent that had seen political upheaval effected by the power of one individual, Napoleon. The much-desired Romantic unity sought for the fragmented self that had been buffeted about by social turbulence was sighted by Hoffmann in Beethoven's Fifth: "The internal structure of the movements, their execution, their instrumentation, the way in which they follow one another—everything contributes to a single end; above all, it is the intimate interrelationship among the themes that engenders that unity which alone has the power to hold the listener when he overhears it in the connecting of two movements or discovers it in the fundamental bass they have in common; a deeper relationship which does not reveal itself in this way speaks at other times only from mind to mind, and it is precisely this relationship that prevails between sections of the two Allegros and the Minuet and which imperiously proclaims the self-possession of the master's genius."[22]

The insistence, repeated here, on Beethoven's "self-possession" is a necessary counter to the external threat of hostile criticism from the musical rabble, and to the internal phenomenon of musical *raptus* (Beethoven's own word for the grip that suddenly and without warning transported him from the world of every day to the orbit of creativity). Self-possession also denotes and fends off possession by someone or something else—a factor affecting the tightrope between sanity and madness upon which Hoffmann, in his alter ego Johannes Kreisler, and Beethoven, in the estimation of some contemporaries, precariously walked. (Even Goethe, for example, thought most of Hoffmann's writing was "sick," and there was much in Beethoven's music that, as we shall see, had he allowed himself to be open to, would have upset the hard-won serenity of his old age.) Hoffmann's analysis of the Fifth Symphony has not come to an end, but now suddenly we hear from the fictitional Kreisler who, with the eerie ease of a true Hoffmannesque doppelgänger, tangentially substitutes his voice and a very different tone into the review we have been reading of Beethoven's instrumental music. With only a paragraph indentation to signal any break of continuity, Hoffmann's (schizoid) text abruptly addresses Beethoven personally and in the "Du" form reserved for intimates or gods:

How deeply thy magnificent compositions for piano have impressed themselves upon my soul, thou sublime master; how shallow and insignificant now all seems to me that is not thine, or by the gifted Mozart or that mighty genius, Sebastian Bach! With what joy I received thy seventieth work, the two glorious trios [for Piano, Violin, and Cello in D Major—the *Ghost*—and E-flat Major], for I knew full well that after a little practice I should soon hear them in truly splendid style. And in truth, this evening things went so well with me that even now, like a man who wanders in the mazes of a fantastic park, woven about with all manner of exotic trees and plants and marvelous flowers, and who is drawn farther and farther in, I am powerless to find my way out of the marvel-

CHAPTER THREE
BEETHOVEN
DEAD: SHAPING
THE
POSTHUMOUS
PORTRAIT

ous turns and windings of thy trios. The lovely siren voices of those movements of thine, resplendent in their many-hued variety, lure me on and on. The gifted lady who indeed honored me, Kapellmeister Kreisler, by playing today the first trio in such splendid style, the gifted lady before whose piano I still sit and write, has made me realize quite clearly that only what the mind produces calls for respect and that all else is out of place.[23]

In this impassioned, almost raving hymn to Beethoven (with its evocation, then passing up, of the sensual—"the gifted lady"—for the spiritual) we touch upon the third level at which the names Beethoven and Hoffmann were joined, this time by posterity's fascination with the concept of "mad" genius. In his Kreisler fragments Hoffmann had created a tortured musician estranged from the world and feverishly worshiping "only what the mind produces"—his art. Kapellmeister Kreisler was frequently at the brink of being possessed by Satan or other dark forces. What was eventually to befall this pursuer of a higher vision, for whom earthly harmony and domestic happiness were impossibilities, is shown to us graphically by Hoffmann in a drawing made during the last year of his life and titled *Kreisler im Wahnsinn* (*Kreisler in Delirium*) (Fig. 43). We see the gaunt, unkempt figure of the musician, his wild hair on end, holding his long-stemmed pipe aloft as he dances a bizarre jig. Hoffmann had already given his readers the clue to Kreisler's emotional instability in a description of the unhinging process that took place when the musician played a fortissimo C Major chord on the piano. At the sound of the chord a frenzy overtook him: "In mad joy let us dance over the open graves. Let us shout for joy—they don't hear it down there. Hurrah—Hurrah—dance and jubilation, the devil enters with drums and trumpets!"[24] Then, at the sound of the C Minor chord played also fortissimo: "Don't you know him? Don't you know him? See—with glowing claws he grabs for my heart! He disguises himself in all sorts of mad masks, a huntsman, a concertmaster, or a quack doctor. . . . Kreisler, Kreisler, pull yourself together. Do you see it, lying in wait, the pale specter with the red sparkling eyes—stretching toward you its bony, clawlike fists out of the torn cloak, shaking its crown of straw on its smooth, bald skull! It is madness!"[25]

Insanity—the specter that haunted the fictional Kapellmeister Kreisler, author of such rapturous appreciations of Beethoven—was easily ascribed in the public mind by extension to Kreisler's creator, Hoffmann, who in his habitual late-night sipping of flaming punch seemed to court derangement, and to Beethoven, whose substantial enjoyment of alcohol had quickly been promoted by amateur pathologists into the cause of his liver ailment. A sublime madman was to the Romantic century's taste, and Hoffmann's archetypal mad musician provided an enduring mold into which Beethoven's eccentricities, both biographical and musical, were inextricably blended.[26]

Negligible in size and artistic quality, but fascinatingly significant as a document visually linking Beethoven and Hoffmann, is a pen and ink drawing made six years after Beethoven's death (Fig. 44), in 1833. The sketch was made not in Vienna but in Hamburg, and by a thirty-year-old amateur artist whose odd life and gifts were a combination of the two deceased heroes he had resuscitated on paper. The artist's name was Johann Peter Lyser (1803-1870) and the drawing, as an inscription on the upper right hand corner tells us, "was sketched by Herr Lyser with a pen in 5 minutes on the 26th of June 1833 at K.'s with a pen, and in fact standing up." Two other personages grace the page: Paganini, tall and thin—placed between Beethoven and Hoffmann—and, to the far right in a bust profile,

Lyser himself. All four figures—two living, two dead—are identified in the artist's handwriting. The figure of Beethoven to the far left, standing in a characteristic pose with arms behind his back and low top hat pulled securely down on his head, confronts the other three figures who face him in descending heights. First is Paganini, the tallest, with hands in his pockets, then Hoffmann, holding a walking stick and doffing his top hat in homage, his wild hair on end, and finally a reverent Lyser who views the parade of extraordinary personalities he has created with approbation.

How is this drawing to be explained? It is not necromancy, for Paganini was still alive; in fact we know that the "demon" violinist had been in Hamburg since the eleventh of June of that year and that he is supposed to have drunk punch at the Alster pavillion with Heine and Lyser.[27] We know further that Paganini sat for a profile sketch by Lyser that was considered so good Heine praised the artist as the only man who "has succeeded in putting his true physiognomy on paper."[28] The answer to the puzzle of the peculiar assemblage in the drawing before us lies in the personality of Lyser himself. The son of an actor, he was born in Flensburg (at that time a Danish possession) and very early showed remarkable linguistic, artistic, literary, and musical talent. He learned to speak French, Italian, and English fluently, taught himself to paint in oils, and played the piano, violin, and flute. The further development of his musical talents was dealt a tragic blow when at the age of sixteen he lost his hearing after a severe case of grippe. His increasingly restless nature led him to sea for a brief period, then to various employments as actor, scene-painter, art teacher, and free-lance writer, until he settled permanently in Hamburg in 1827 where he served as whimsical music critic—in spite of his deafness!—for several local periodicals and made regular serious contributions to major German music reviews including the *Neue Zeitschrift für Musik*. He wrote dozens of short stories, fairy tales, novels, and romances in the style of Hoffmann, including a work called *From the Sketchbook of a Deaf Painter*. He consciously emulated Hoffmann, but he also identified to an extraordinary (Hoffmannesque) extent with Beethoven, whose affliction of deafness he shared.

The Beethoven-Hoffmann ensemble is not the only Lyser sketch of the deaf composer. He was responsible for one of the most popular and frequently reproduced images of Beethoven—a drawing published in 1833 in the music periodical issued by B. Schott and Sons in Mainz, *Cäcilia* (Fig. 45), and briefly edited by Lyser. Lyser, who had never set eyes on Beethoven (he is not documented as ever having been in Vienna prior to 1845), accompanied his little fantasy sketch with a brief printed explanation in which he wrote that the picture of Beethoven was "drawn truthfully after nature, as, in the last years of his life he leaped and ran rather than walked through the streets of Vienna."[29] The drawing is awkward and poorly proportioned but eloquently captures the contemporary impression (as remembered by Gerhard von Breuning[30]) of the preoccupied composer, oblivious to his surroundings. Whether it is based on the Böhm profile drawing of 1819–20 (see Fig. 14) or on an intermediary work now lost is difficult to conjecture, but Beethoven's features have been made to appear less Neanderthal than in the Böhm prototype. Just how far Lyser could stray from the reality of Beethoven's facial silhouette is evidenced in a tentative and sketchy drawing (Fig. 46) in which the composer is shown striding with his left foot forward. This sketch was obviously a tryout for the drawing with right foot in the lead that Lyser elected to publish in *Cäcilia*, where he filled in a "Viennese" setting and presented as a foil

CHAPTER THREE
BEETHOVEN
DEAD: SHAPING
THE
POSTHUMOUS
PORTRAIT

two "elegant" pedestrians in the background, so we may see for ourselves the full measure of Beethoven's long, unstylish coat length.[31] The Böhm original also shows Beethoven leading with his right foot, and there exists another right-foot-forward drawing made during his lifetime or immediately after his death by our depicter of Beethoven's Schwarzspanierhaus study (see Fig. 20), Johann Nepomuk Hoechle. Hoechle's amusing picture (Fig. 48) shows Beethoven walking in the rain, huddled inside his great overcoat and staring determinedly ahead from beneath his bedraggled top hat. It was upon drawings similar to the Böhm and Hoechle examples (Böhm had transferred his drawing to silver plate for reproduction) that Lyser based his idolizing imagery.

The left-foot-forward attempt was given another and far more successful[32] try by the artist on a sheet of paper (Fig. 47) that bears a second Beethoven "portrait"—a profile bust facing left with the mandatory unruly hair, frowning brow (the sloping forehead is completely wrong), tight-set, drooping lips, and dark beard stubble. Just beneath this bust portrait Lyser has lovingly embellished an imitation of Beethoven's distinctive signature—"L v Beethoven"—and directly under this floreate forgery he has "confessed" the all-absorbing identification with his deaf hero in a double signature that reads "Lyser Beethoven." The final flourish of this tandem signature whips gracefully and commodiously back in a double loop to underline, unite, and embrace both names. What psychologist could ask for more in this touching and unself-conscious metamorphosis of L(udwig) Beethoven into Lyser Beethoven?[33] Heine had comprehended the intensity of this one-sided relationship, and he left a description of his friend of Hamburg days that, in its satanic and synaesthetic Hoffmannesque suggestions, would certainly have delighted the artist:

> The deaf painter, Lyser . . . with inspired frenzy caught Paganini's head in a few pencil strokes so successfully that one is amused and terrified at the likeness. "The devil guided my hand," the deaf painter said to me, chuckling mysteriously and nodding his head with good-natured irony, as he was in the habit of doing when playing his Till Eulenspiegel pranks. This painter was an odd fellow. In spite of his deafness, he loved music passionately, and he was supposedly able, if near enough to the orchestra, to read the music from the faces of the musicians and to judge from their finger movements whether the execution was successful. Indeed he also wrote critiques of the opera in an estimable Hamburg journal. Is there anything strange in this? In the visible signature of the performance the deaf painter could see the sounds. There are men to whom the sounds themselves are only invisible symbols in which they hear colors and forms.[34]

A literal and aesthetically pedestrian rehash of the Böhm-Hoechle-Lyser "Walking Beethoven" motif was added to the posthumous portrait by the Prague artist Martin Tejček (dates unknown), who published his lithograph of Beethoven on promenade in 1841 (Fig. 49). This arrested-motion image is arresting only in that its owl-faced protagonist in faultlessly foppish attire is so diametrically opposed to the shabby, unheeding genius of the preceding imagery. Tejček, about whom almost nothing is known, is supposed to have observed Beethoven on his daily walk during a sojourn in Vienna in the 1820s,[35] but his fashion-plate study did little to satisfy the Romantic century's appetite for the "real" Beethoven.

This hunger was satisfied, temporarily, by another Lyser visual feast, this time incorporating not only the man but his music and his muse—Nature (Fig. 50)—an absolutely irresistible combination. The title of this graphic concoction is *Bee-*

thoven Composing the "Pastoral" by a Brook. Lyser published the drawing in his 1833 issue of the Taschenbuch für Freunde der Tonkunst, *Cäcilia.* This time Beethoven reclines on a grassy bank against a convenient back-supporting boulder, his walking coat unbuttoned and his top hat (shrunk to medium height again) off but at the ready on a nearby tree stump. Beethoven lounges comfortably with his legs crossed, but his figure is alert and he does not relax completely, for his muse—the babbling brook falling in empathic stepwise fashion parallel to his body—is speaking. The composer hearkens attentively, his facial expression is absorbed and thoughtful, and in his hands he holds staved music paper and a long narrow pen (Lyser apparently did not know about Beethoven's preference for short carpenter's pencils). *This* is the Beethoven portrait craved by posterity. Had not Beethoven himself written concerning the "program" of his *Pastoral* (in an effort actually intended to downplay too literal an interpretation): "Recollection of country life—more expression of feeling than painting,"[36] and had he not designated the second movement specifically as "Murmeln der Bäche" ("Murmuring of the Brooks")?[37] From the sublimity of nature's inspiration we pass to what Schindler would no doubt have branded as a travesty: Lyser has shown his beloved Beethoven wearing a black cravat!

Anachronistic faux pas aside, Lyser's unabashedly Romantic portrait of 1833 (no less romantic than Schindler's own description of Beethoven's revisiting the site of the *Pastoral* Symphony's inspiration[38]) stimulated a whole new genre of Beethoven-by-the-Brook imagery, an imagery that would delight generations of myth-gazers. Just how quickly Lyser's appealing iconographic ensemble was picked up and disseminated is revealed by the fact that his concept of Beethoven reclining and composing by a brook was already appropriated the following year when the *Almanac* of the Zürich Musikgesellschaft for 1834 published a colored lithograph (Fig. 51) by an anonymous artist who improved upon Beethoven's pose and supplied youthful good looks, and added a whole fantasy panorama of the Heiligenstadt-Nussdorf valley. The top hat seems to have floated downstream and out of sight in the process.

A postscript on Lyser's end seems fitting. Unlike his hero, his death passed unnoticed: no crowds or imperial carriages accompanied the body of Johann Peter Lyser to his last resting place, the expenses for which had to be assumed by one of Hamburg's municipal almshouses. This strange minor character on the stage of history ended his life in Hoffmannesque poverty and neglect, wielding his pen only as a forgotten, ill-paid public amanuensis.

The Beethoven of the *Pastoral,* the musician who found his muse in the pantheon of nature, was accessible to all. Once the critical catcalls concerning some of the birdcalls (which Beethoven had allegedly pointed out to Schindler) abated, the Sixth Symphony became the common and easily comprehended property of its age. In the same way that the music professed to represent, at times even to reproduce, a "recollection of country life," Lyser's engaging image of Beethoven-by-the-Brook, and later Schindler's winsome word painting likening Beethoven's forays into nature to a bee's excursions to gather honey, gave welcome substance to that salient theme of Romantic contemplation: the relation of the individual to *nature.* When the individual was of mythic proportions, and when elemental nature was plumbed to reveal its primal conflicts, a "sublime" status inspiring awe resulted. This was the level to which, during a century of biographical exploration and musical analysis, the Sixth Symphony was raised. Written by a cultural idol, this music about humankind's most mutual experience uplifted even the rankest philistine.

With equal lustrousness there blazed in the musical firmament along with the *Pastoral* Beethoven's Third Symphony, the *Eroica*, addressed to that polestar of Romantic meditation: the hero concept. We are not concerned here with Beethoven's ambivalent feelings towards Napoleon, which caused him still to consider titling his grand symphony "Bonaparte" even *after* the famous tearing up of the title page incident in front of his startled friend—Ferdinand Ries (1784–1838)—who had brought him the news of Napoleon's self-proclamation as emperor. The motivations for Beethoven's reluctance to cancel the dedication and title have been amply covered in other studies.[39] The grist for our mythopoetical mill is of a different texture and twofold: posterity's addiction for retelling the story of the destruction of the title page by Beethoven (which actually did take place), and the conflicting and sometimes crackpot interpretations afforded the "heroism" expressed by the mighty music. Lying at the base of both phenomena was the specter—for the German lands—of an unwelcome hero, Napoleon. Twice, in 1805 and 1809, Napoleon had marched across Germany to make a triumphal entry into Vienna. Such military humiliation rankled and would not be avenged in the collective consciousness until Wagner replaced history with myth and routed the memory of the dark Corsican with the blinding light of a blond Siegfried. Until this Lethean deliverance there was the legacy and the reality of a German giant, Beethoven—the man and his music. The man had acted thusly in the face of Napoleonic megalomania according to the account of eyewitness Ries:

> In this symphony [the *Eroica*] Beethoven had Buonaparte in his mind, but as he was when he was First Consul. Beethoven esteemed him greatly at the time [1804] and likened him to the greatest Roman consuls. I as well as several of his more intimate friends saw a copy of the score lying upon his table with the word "Buonaparte" at the extreme top of the title page and at the extreme bottom "Luigi van Beethoven," but not another word. Whether, and with what the space between was to be filled out, I do not know. I was the first to bring him the intelligence that Buonaparte had proclaimed himself emperor, whereupon he flew into a rage and cried out: "Is he then, too, nothing more than an ordinary human being? Now he, too, will trample on all the rights of men and indulge only his ambition. He will exalt himself above all others, become a tyrant!" Beethoven went to the table, took hold of the title page by the top, tore it in two and threw it on the floor.[40]

Schindler, who had not yet entered Beethoven's life at this point, repeated the story as he got it from Count Moritz Lichnowsky, who was by chance with Beethoven when Ries arrived with the shocking news: "The fair copy of the score, with the dedication to the First Consul of the French Republic inscribed simply 'Napoleon Bonaparte' [this already conflicts with Ries's account] on the title page, was ready [to be sent to Paris] . . . when the news reached Vienna that Napoleon had allowed himself to be proclaimed Emperor of the French. It was Count Lichnowsky and Ferdinand Ries [Lichnowsky was already with the composer when Ries arrived] who brought the news to Beethoven. No sooner had the composer heard it than he seized the score, tore out [up!] the title page and, cursing the 'new tyrant,' flung it on the floor."[41] So far there are only minor variations in Schindler's version of the title-page destruction incident. But the gra-

CHAPTER THREE
BEETHOVEN
DEAD: SHAPING
THE
POSTHUMOUS
PORTRAIT

tuitous report that followed concerning Napoleonic exchanges that supposedly took place between Schindler and Beethoven provided a cornucopia for later interpretations of the *Eroica* as musical politics:

> It was a long time before the friends of the democracy-loving composer were able to calm his righteous anger, but finally his passions gave way to quieter reflections on what had occurred. In the end he consented to the publication of the work under the title *Sinfonia Eroica* with the sub-title "Per festeggiare il sovvenire d'un grand Uomo." . . .
>
> The admiration that Beethoven had felt for Napoleon was, however, no more; it had changed into hatred, and not until the emperor met his tragic end on Saint Helena was the composer able to forgive him. Can we not recognize in Beethoven's obstinacy a trait inherited from his Dutch ancestors? But he was able to joke sarcastically about this earth-shaking event and his change of heart. He pointed out, for example, that he had already composed the music appropriate to such a catastrophe, namely the Funeral March in the *Eroica*. He went even further in describing the symbolism of this movement, for the theme of the middle section in C major was supposed to represent a new star of hope in Napoleon's reversed fortunes (his return to the political stage in 1815), and finally the great hero's powerful decision to withstand fate until, at the moment of surrender, he sinks to the ground and allows himself to be buried like any other mortal.[42]

It is tempting to reword the old question and ask: with Schindler as Beethoven's friendly interpreter, who needs analytical enemies? We shall see later how the admiring Berlioz stretched his imagination to the outer limits to explain the "play of funereal kind" in the third movement scherzo that follows the Funeral March of the second movement. To do Schindler justice, however, we must note that his very next remarks on the *Eroica* advised posterity to practice caution: "When I quote his symbolic explanations, however, I do not wish to imply any literal interpretation such as that of the modern Beethoven interpreters. In fact, the master always decried with great energy all such treatment of his, or any, music. . . . We must realize his political temperament at the time when he pretended to find in his Funeral March a specific association with the passing of a greatly admired person. Witty, trenchant minds like our composer's may often let fall a remark that aptly characterizes its object. Yet such a remark taken out of context and broadly published can be very misleading. . . ."[43] Mary Shelley's *Frankenstein* had been published in 1818; perhaps the Schindler of 1860, revising his biography of Beethoven for a third edition some thirty-three years after the composer's death, had witnessed sufficient aberration of his own comments on Beethoven applied out of context that he now knew, with Victor Frankenstein, what small control a creator can exercise over a creation once it assumes a life of its own, whether monster or myth. Here is just one of the grotesque literary interpretations of Beethoven's *Eroica* that had come into being before Schindler's warning was issued. It was printed in the program notes for an 1843 performance of the Third Symphony by the newly formed Philharmonic Society in New York:

> This great work was commenced when Napoleon was First Consul, and was intended to portray the workings of that extraordinary man's mind. In the first movement, the simple subject, keeping its uninterrupted way through harmonies that at times seem in almost chaotic confusion, is a grand idea of Napoleon's determination of character. The second movement is descriptive of the funeral honors paid to one of his favorite generals, and is entitled "Funeral

March on the Death of a Hero." The winding up of this movement represents the faltering steps of the last gazers into the grave, and the listener hears the tears fall on the coffin [the tympani rolls?] ere the funeral volley is fired [louder tympani rolls?], and repeated faintly by an echo. The third movement (Minuet and Trio) describes the homeward march of the soldiery, and the Finale is a combination of French Revolutionary airs put together in a manner that no one save a Beethoven could have imagined.[44]

CHAPTER THREE
BEETHOVEN
DEAD: SHAPING
THE
POSTHUMOUS
PORTRAIT

We run the risk here of rechanneling our interests in midstream from a study of the changing images of Beethoven to a chronicling of the mutations of Beethovenian musical interpretation—but these are mutations that after all played a formative role in what artists would choose to emphasize in their visual presentations, as we have seen in Lyser's Beethoven-by-the-Brook imagery, with its response to the nature source and setting associated with the *Pastoral*. A general awareness of the modulations through which Beethoven's musical works have been taken by interpretative and, more recently, psychological explication is crucial to our recognition of the social inflections animating the posthumous portrait of Beethoven. Without such documentation it would be immensely more difficult to grasp the phenomenon of contradictory appraisals of the "real" Beethoven for what it is: a mapping of the changing topography of human thought. Only when viewed through the telescope of time does later twentieth-century resistance to the nineteenth-century heroic imperative make sense. Two world wars taught thinkers to be wary of Thomas Carlyle's Great Men and of the political consequences of hero-worship, which had begun with Napoleon and ended with Hitler.[45] It is only from this perspective that we can appreciate the diverging analyses of the heroic in Beethoven's *Eroica* represented in the following opinions voiced by two musicologists separated by three-quarters of a century. Writing in 1896 the Englishman George Grove took up where the New York Philharmonic program notes had left off and glossed a memorable passage in the Funeral March with this anglophilic augmentation: "In this noble and expressive passage of fugal music we might be assisting at the actual funeral of the hero, with all that is good and great in the nation looking on as he was lowered into his tomb; and the motto might well be Tennyson's words on Wellington—'In the vast cathedral leave him,/ God accept him, Christ receive him.' "[46]

Seventy-five years later, in 1971, Philip G. Downs, commenting on the simultaneous musical and extramusical arguments in the *Eroica*, theorized: "The music has to be more than music—it has to be a means to a way of life, and the dramatic purpose of the *Eroica* Symphony is to provide a lesson on the conquering of self. It is fruitless to talk about the hero of the symphony being Napoleon or General Abercrombie or even Beethoven himself. . . . The music presents the listener with a musical entity which is anything but heroic, since it lacks the strength to escape from the tonic."[47]

This (temporary) denial of the heroic is an unexpected if authentic yield of technical analysis, but the critic has a motivation for this surprise attack that is more flippant than serious; he is, after a brief flirtation with psychoanalysis, preparing us for a new twentieth-century hero—Reason (surprisingly like the eighteenth-century one): "A destructive force which threatens the existence of the first musical entity is found to be identical with it, but, as it were, out of phase with it. What a musical allegory of those forces which psychological jargon labels as *ego* and *id*! . . . The heroism involved in the first movement is that which, when threatened to the point of extinction, rejects the solution which requires total suppression of the individuality (compromise solution) and rejects that which requires the uncontrolled expansion of self (the turbulent passage which rejects the compromise and is in turn rejected by it). The heroism lies in the rational adjustment of that which is out of phase, and the result is security."[48]

Having allowed heroism, defined on his own terms, reentry into the *Eroica* sphere, this security-seeking twentieth-century critic permits himself a conclusion that outstrips Romantic critiques for magniloquent wish projection: "Many commentators have speculated as to who the hero of the symphony may be, for heroism there certainly is. But it is not the heroism of the military hero, for the man who has the strength to overcome himself is the rarest kind of hero. Beethoven's wish to benefit humanity is realized. The new way which was revealed was one in which Beethoven was able for perhaps the only time in music, to show the listener an analogue of his own potentiality for perfection. *A higher revelation than all wisdom and philosophy.*"[49]

In this twentieth-century example of simultaneous rejection and aggrandizement of the heroic we have, in a sense, taken one step forward and two steps backward, resuscitating favorite aspects of the Enlightenment—humanity's ability to help itself through reason and strength of will—*and* of Romanticism—the triumph of feeling expressed in lofty personal aims. (We have no progress in recognition of the phenomenon that some Beethoven listeners are not male.) Perhaps Carlyle was right. Each epoch craves, even it if does not create, heroes. Demystification of Beethoven leads to greater beatification. The arduous and ardent pursuit of unattainable perfection that propelled the composer from masterpiece to masterpiece, the musical tensions of barriers maintained then surrendered then reasserted, the passionate rebellion erupting alongside feats of willpower, the unremitting exposure of pathos and ecstasy, and above all the coercive feelings of Beethoven himself—all these seem to defy temporal dissection. Just as fragments of a mirror can only reflect a partial picture, so each age's looking glass remakes Beethoven into its own image, hinting at but never fully encompassing the summation of emotional absolutes his music clothes in sound. The inwardness of Beethoven's music, turned inside out, becomes the outwardness of his mythology—the timeless hero who does not go away.

Music critics, whether friendly or hostile, have not been able to step from out of the shadow of Beethoven; even their total disapproval only confirms his lasting prestige. What about musicians? How did Beethoven's successors affect his posthumous portrait? We shall examine Beethoven as musicians' musician in the next chapter, but we might at this point consider the comments and judgments of some of Beethoven's fellow composers to see what their image of their great contemporary was like.

It is tempting to turn to Rossini first of all, since, as we have seen, his description of how Beethoven looked in the year 1822 was not only authoritative—based on personal observation—but even (anticipating art historians?) took into consideration a comparison of the model with his portraits. We recall what he told Wagner about the small, piercing eyes that seemed to shine "as from out of caverns."[50] Rossini said a great deal more to Wagner about his impression of Beethoven, deploring the great composer's ramshackle living quarters, his seeming financial destitution, and the strange indifference to his condition universally expressed by the aristocracy of Vienna when he indignantly raised the question of Beethoven's neglect with them.

All of these colorful elements would surely have been appropriated with cor-

CHAPTER THREE
BEETHOVEN
DEAD: SHAPING
THE
POSTHUMOUS
PORTRAIT

diality into the communal posthumous portrait of Beethoven being assembled by biographers and artists, but there are several circumstances that intervened before Rossini's personal testimony was admitted before the public bar. What is usually the stuff of footnotes must surface occasionally in a cumulative study such as ours, in the shape of chronological mileposts at which the distance still to be traveled from fact to fable can be measured. Our data-collecting journey is actually an uphill one, analogous to the ascent of a reversed pyramid, since each decade following Beethoven's death has deposited information, some of it fact, some of it fiction, but all of it about Beethoven and therefore to be taken into account.

Thus, in the case of Rossini's potential impact on the burgeoning image of Beethoven, the following sequence must be kept pegged to the mythometer's bulletin board:

(1) Sometime during his four-month stay in Vienna (April–July 1822) to supervise the production of his new opera *Zelmira*, the thirty-year-old Rossini, inspired by a performance of the *Eroica*, made vain attempts to meet the composer through Artaria and Salieri and finally managed to visit Beethoven in the company of their mutual friend the Italian poet Giuseppi Carpani.[51]

(2) An entry in Beethoven's conversation book for August 1826 asks: "It is true, isn't it, that Rossini wanted to visit you and you refused to see him?"[52] (Beethoven's answer was not written down, but he must have been irritated that such a rumor was already rampant in a Vienna that loved to pit Italian against German music.[53]

(3) Thirty years later, in 1856, Rossini declared to a visitor that he had met Beethoven.[54]

(4) Schindler erroneously reported in 1860 that Beethoven had not allowed Rossini to call upon him.[55]

(5) Rossini's "Beethoven Conversation" with Wagner took place in March 1860.[56]

(6) Rossini, told in 1867 by three Austrian visitors (including Hanslick) that Schindler "and other biographers" denied that Beethoven had ever received him, confirmed for a second time that he had indeed met and visited with Beethoven.[57]

(7) Wagner made no reference to what was said about Beethoven in his brief account of the Paris visit with Rossini when he published an obituary on Rossini in 1868[58] or in his massive autobiography *Mein Leben* (published posthumously, 1911).

(8) The 1860 Rossini-Wagner "Beethoven Conversation"—immediately jotted down in scrupulous detail afterwards by a third party, the Belgian amateur musician Edmond Michotte (1830–1914), was not published until 1906,[59] almost half a century after Rossini's decanted reminiscence, which was already of a thirty-eight-year-old vintage.

With this complicated chronology behind us and the reminder that we are pursuing Rossini's contribution to the Beethoven legend, and not vice versa, logic dictates that we defer full citation of the "Beethoven Conversation" until the posthumous portrait of Beethoven—passing through the reverent hands of other musicians—is placed upon the easel of one of the most protean of all embellishers of the Beethoven myth, Wagner.

However one link in the unfolding chain of Beethoven commentators that connects the Rossini of the 1820s with the Beethoven of the 1820s can here be taken into consideration. The link is of French forging and appears in the form of

Stendhal's enthusiastic *Vie de Rossini*, published in 1824, when Rossini was only thirty-two, with forty-four years to live. Stendhal's adoration of all things Italian and his obsession with what he called southern "energy" had found its outlet in a manuscript on the history of Italian music from 1800 to 1823 which, at the last minute, he reworked to intertwine leafily with an account of the blossoming career of Rossini, creating an inchoate chimera of anecdotes, chronological tables, libretto extracts, autobiographical footnotes, and categorical analyses of music based on presumed *a priori* national traits. Rossini, being Italian, gets most of the kudos, but Beethoven the German comes in for his share of contagious characterization. Stendhal's concept of Beethoven is one of unbridled Germanic passion. Not to deny the possibility of this to the Italian race, however he does provide an Italian connection: the "wild impulsiveness in the manner of Michelangelo" is "a feature of the music of Beethoven."[60] Then, concerning Beethoven's place in the temple of German music, a non-French, non-Italian quality is allowed full reign: "If the 'uncouth' had been forbidden by law, how could Beethoven, with his wild impetuosity and his outlandish music, have been there to catch up the torch as it fell from the hands of the measured and noble Haydn?"[61]

Wild impetuosity and impulsiveness—two of the proverbial aspects to be ascribed by both German and French Romanticism to Beethovenian "essence"—are codified here as implacable features that, in his pursuit of Rossini, Stendhal almost inadvertently imprinted upon the century's mirror image of Beethoven—an image already dilating to reflect the passions and the prejudices of those who gazed upon it.

A contemporary musician whose critical view of Beethoven was anything but inadvertent was Carl Maria von Weber (1786–1826), who shared with Beethoven the fact of having had his portrait painted by Ferdinand Schimon (Fig. 52). Weber's laconic description of the physical Beethoven has already been noted. The world would not have access to all the details of Weber's 1823 visit to Beethoven until the biography brought out by his son in 1864,[62] but regular readers of the music reviews published in German-language periodicals learned as early as 1809 what the young Weber of twenty-three, already the composer of two symphonies, thought of Beethoven's *Eroica* and his orchestral style in general. A whimsical scene in which the instruments of the orchestra are arguing among themselves about their musical supremacy was fantasized by Weber for his reading audience. Suddenly they are interrupted by the property man responsible for packing them into their cases. He silences their squabbling with an effective threat:

> "Wait!" he shouted, "Are you rebelling again? Just wait! Pretty soon they are going to set out the *Eroica* symphony by Beethoven, and after that I'd like to see which one of you can move a limb or a key!"
> "Oh, no! Not that!" begged all the instruments.
> "Give us an Italian opera; then at least one can get twenty winks from time to time," said the viola.
> "Fiddlesticks!" retorted the property man. "You'll soon learn. In these enlightened times when all traditions are flung aside, do you think that a composer is going to deny his divine, his herculean inspiration just to please the likes of you? God forbid! It is no longer a question of clarity, preciseness, restraint, and emotion, as in the old days of artists like Gluck, Handel, and Mozart. No; listen to the recipe from the newest symphony that I have just received from Vienna, and then tell me what you think. First there is a slow

section, full of short, disjointed ideas, none of which has anything to do with any other. Every quarter of an hour we hear three or four notes. It's exciting! Then there is a muffled roll of drums and a mysterious viola phrase, all adorned with the right number of rests and empty measures. Finally, after the audience has given up all hope of ever surviving the tension and arriving at the Allegro, everything bursts forth in a break-neck tempo, but care is taken that no principal theme emerges, and it is up to the listener to try and make one out. Modulations from one key to another abound, but they need not give you any trouble. Just remember Paer in *Fidelio*: all you have to do is make a chromatic run and stop on any note you like, and there is your modulation. Above all, every rule must be disregarded, for rules only fetter genius."[63]

CHAPTER THREE
BEETHOVEN
DEAD: SHAPING
THE
POSTHUMOUS
PORTRAIT

The next year, in answer to a well-meant comparison by his publisher of his work with that of Beethoven's, Weber, whose direction as founder of German Romantic opera, was leading him along a path very different from that of Beethoven's, wrote a wrathful objection: "You seem to see me . . . as an imitator of Beethoven, and flattered as many might be by this, I don't find it in the least pleasant . . . my views differ too much from Beethoven's for me to feel I could ever agree with him. The passionate, almost incredible inventive powers inspiring him are accompanied by such a chaotic arrangement of his ideas that only his earlier compositions appeal to me; the later ones seem to me hopeless chaos, an incomparable struggle for novelty, out of which break a few heavenly flashes of genius proving how great he would be if he would tame his rich fantasy."[64]

Weber sounds very much like the conservative older critics of Beethoven here, but by 1814 his musical judgment had mellowed, his own compositions were being well received, and, with less to fear from the titan in Vienna, he experienced a real change of heart. The response to his new perception of Beethoven was generous and practical: he began to play and conduct Beethoven's music regularly. With a three-year contract as director of the Prague opera in his pocket, he presented—after an unheard-of fourteen rehearsals—*Fidelio* to the city on 27 November 1814 and was enraged when the Prague audience failed to understand the "truly great things in the music."[65] Nine years later, at the beginning of 1823, with the enormously popular *Der Freischutz* behind him (fifty performances in Berlin in fewer than two years), Weber rehearsed the Dresden opera company for a production of *Fidelio*, debuting in the title role young Wilhelmine Schröder-Devrient (of the Hoffmann analogy concerning Beethoven, when she repeated her role in Vienna a year later). The Dresden production sparked an exchange of four letters from Weber and three from Beethoven and after news of the successful opera production (29 April) reached Beethoven, he referred to Weber as "my dear friend *Maria Weber*."[66] The correspondence between Weber and Beethoven has been lost but we have a draft of Weber's first letter, showing that he had indeed been greatly affected by the experience of his own personal changing image of Beethoven: "Each representation will be a festival to me, giving me the opportunity of offering to your noble spirit a homage springing from my inmost heart, which is filled with mingled admiration and affection for you."[67]

Because of some later Schindler mischief making concerning Weber's relation to Beethoven, it is important to state that it was Beethoven himself who, learning that Weber was in Vienna supervising the premiere of his new opera *Euryanthe*, and making the acquaintance of Weber's young pupil Benedict (from whom we have already heard concerning Beethoven's "Ossianic" appearance) in a music store, issued a pressing invitation that they call on him at Baden, where he was spending the early fall. Even though this meant rising at six A.M. and driving twenty miles, Weber jumped at the chance to meet Beethoven in the flesh and the visit took place on 5 October 1823. A letter to his wife described the encounter in glowing terms: "... the excursion to Baden had been agreed upon for seven-thirty ... unfortunately, however, it rained vilely. The main thing was to see Beethoven. The latter received me with the most touching affection; he embraced me at least six or seven times in the heartiest fashion and finally, full of enthusiasm, cried: 'Yes, you are a devil of a fellow, a fine fellow!' We spent the noon-hour together, very merrily and happily. This rough, repellent man actually paid court to me, served me at the table as carefully as though I were his lady, etc. In short, this day always will remain a most remarkable one for me, as for all who shared it."[68]

Unfortunately Weber, already mortally ill with tuberculosis, would not have long to cherish this memory. Fewer than three years after Beethoven's huge fist had enclosed his thin hand in a warm Auf Wiedersehen, Weber would be dead at the age of thirty-nine. Comparison of the two composers' portraits by their mutual portraitist, Schimon (Fig. 52), shows how the aura of general emaciation brought on by Weber's consuming disease was reflected on his mild countenance. His devoted pupil Julius Benedict—also present at the Beethoven interview—has left one of the best testimonials about the genuine and positive aspect of Weber's final image of Beethoven. When Benedict first approached Weber for lessons, the composer played him some passages from his own works and then proceeded to give a "rendering of Beethoven's sonatas, with a fire and precision and a thorough entering into the spirit of the composer which would have given the mighty Ludwig the best proof of Weber's reverence and admiration for his genius."[69]

(Colorplate 3)

The adamancy of these remarks concerning both the Beethoven and the Weber mystiques was perhaps inspired by the tempest in a teacup brewed by Beethoven's draconian defender Schindler. In his 1840 biography of Beethoven, Schindler had found it fitting to repeat a remark ascribed to Weber that, in regard to the Seventh Symphony, "the extravagances of this genius have now reached the *non plus ultra*, and Beethoven must be quite ripe for the madhouse."[70] Reviews of his book quickly challenged the "madhouse" remark and took Schindler to task for his anti-Weber attitude. In a reply of 31 December 1840 Schindler waffled a bit, saying he was only the reporter of the remark and admitted that "perhaps Weber was not the author of those bitter criticisms of Beethoven's works."[71] But by the time of his revised edition of Beethoven's life twenty years later, Schindler was just too fond of the justifiable indignation that welled in his breast every time he thought of the madhouse allusion to abandon it for lack of mere proof. He had after all found a printed proof of anti-Beethoven sentiments in Weber's instruments-of-the-orchestra parody of 1809 and the letter to Weber's publisher strenuously objecting to the comparison of himself with Beethoven (made public in 1853[72]). Thus in a special appendix to his 1860 edition of the Beethoven biography entitled "Carl Maria von Weber as a Critic of Beethoven," Schindler had his cake and ate it too. He began by practicing tremendous objectivity by benignly characterizing Weber's youthful criticisms as having been written by an "apprentice artist," and magnanimously extending Weber the composer his due by inviting us to compare "his great operas with the statements he had made some ten years earlier," smugly concluding that "there emerges from such a comparison the moral that young musicians should avoid publishing their opinions of works they do not understand."[73] Having demonstrated his scholarly remove from the field

CHAPTER THREE
BEETHOVEN
DEAD: SHAPING
THE
POSTHUMOUS
PORTRAIT

of battle Schindler then serves himself another slice of Torte: he reprints both of the apprentice artist's critiques of Beethoven in their entirety, and then heaps on the final Schlag by reintroducing the spurious Seventh Symphony madhouse quip: "The reader, having read the above specimen of conceit and malice, will not be surprised to hear of a second, far worse pronouncement in which Weber, after hearing our master's A major symphony, declared its composer ready for the madhouse."[74]

Thus with heavy-handed dexterity, the sixty-five-year-old paladin passed the madhouse remark on into legend, and unwittingly bequeathed the very thing he had wished to deny to the Beethoven mythmakers of future generations. Readers remembered only that Schindler had mentioned (not denied) madness in connection with Beethoven, and the blending in the public perception of Hoffmann's fantasy Kreisler with the real-life figure of Beethoven as epitome of genius bordering on insanity continued to take place. Equally counterproductive were Schindler's repetitions of accusations concerning Beethoven's supposed addiction to drink in order to refute them;[75] the communal myth preferred the charge to the acquittal.

One of the bitterest disappointments of Schindler's life must have been the fact that, before his own biography of Beethoven first saw the light of day in 1840, a fellow musician claiming to be an intimate friend of Beethoven brought out a publication on the composer which, in an appendix, presented a self-aggrandizing personal reminiscence of Beethoven's life and character that not only influenced the posthumous perception of Beethoven, but also gave a cue to interpretations "apprentice artists" would make of him. This pretender-to-the-Beethoven throne (who when "exposed" by Schindler dismissed him as "Beethoven's valet") was Ignaz Ritter von Seyfried (1776–1841), and his book was a falsified (as proven in Schindler's day[76]) "edition" of what purported to be a textbook compiled from handwritten notes by Beethoven himself on the essentials of thoroughbass, counterpoint, and composition: *L. van Beethovens Studien im Generalbasse, Contrapuncte und in der Compositionslehre*. Seyfried's book was published by Tobias Haslinger (1787–1842) in Vienna in 1832 and, as Schindler says, it "sold like hotcakes."[77] To make matters worse, as far as Schindler was concerned, Seyfried's hoax was accompanied by another travesty, a fantasy bust portrait of Beethoven produced by the Viennese lithographer who had already incurred Schindlerian wrath, Josef Kriehuber.[78] By the 1850s Seyfried's book had been translated into French, Italian, and English editions, and a Hamburg publisher brought out a second German edition in 1851.

We shall return to what is of mythmaking value in Seyfried's *Anhang*, but now that we have been temporarily derailed from tracking the observations of coeval musicians concerning Beethoven, it might be well to consider the chronology of reminiscences, reviews, memoirs, and reports that, due to their *appearance in print*, had entered the communal well from which heady bucketfuls of Beethoven lore could be drawn. By the time Schindler was ready to publish his first edition of the *Biographie* in 1840 there was already in existence a colorful "group" portrait of his hero. Some of the widely scattered pieces of this fretsaw image were known to him, others were not. For critical reaction to Beethoven's work—and hence by extrapolation his personality—the following important periodicals devoted to music (in addition to the many local and foreign daily newspapers) were rich reservoirs.

GERMAN LANGUAGE:

Vienna: *Wiener allgemeine musikalische Zeitung* (1817–24): contained portraits of celebrated musicians, including Beethoven; edited (1819–20) by Schindler's nemesis Seyfried, but briefly under the editorship of Friedrich August Kanne (1778–1833), an "unequaled eccentric" (Schindler's words), talented poet, and composer much admired by Beethoven. Kanne returned the compliment by demonstrating an unusual (for the time) appreciation for Beethoven's late works. He was a torch bearer at Beethoven's funeral.
Allgemeiner musikalischer Anzeiger (1829–40): edited by Ignaz Franz Castelli (1781–1862), who despite his Italian surname had a critical eye for Italian opera production. A personal friend of Beethoven, who enjoyed his merry pranks, he recorded a number of Beethoven anecdotes in his memoirs (*Memorien meines Lebens*, Vienna, 1861–62).

Leipzig: *Allgemeine musikalische Zeitung* (1798–1848): put out by Beethoven's publishers Breitkopf and Härtel, founded and first edited until 1818 by the man whom Beethoven supposedly designated on his deathbed his biographer, Rochlitz. The foremost German-language musical periodical of its time.
Neue Zeitschrift für Musik (1834–1974; 1975–78 as *Melos/Neue Zeitschrift für Musik*; from 1979 *Neue Zeitschrift für Musik*): founded by the then twenty-three-year-old Schumann as a spirited answer to the "honey-daubing," old-world platitudes into which the earlier Leipzig music periodical had fallen.

Mainz: *Cäcilia* (1824–48, with distribution in Hamburg, Berlin, and elsewhere): issued by the well-known firm of music publishers B. Schott and Sons (the first to use lithography for the printing of music editions, which included Beethoven's last quartets, the *Missa Solemnis*, and the Ninth Symphony) and edited in the 1830s briefly by the deaf Lyser of Beethoven visual imagery fixation. In 1824 *Cäcilia* had written Beethoven directly to find them a Viennese correspondent, and in 1825, due to what even a non-Freudian might now call a Freudian slip on Beethoven's part, *Cäcilia* published a "romantic biography" written by Beethoven joshing his publisher Tobias Haslinger and causing Beethoven a not-too-painful discomfort at what was "only a joke."[79]

Berlin: *Berliner allgemeine musikalische Zeitung* (1824–30): founded by another Beethoven fan, the prolific writer Adolf Bernhard Marx (1795–1866). Marx's perceptive reviews of Beethoven's music in the pages of his influential periodical did much to spread the composer's fame throughout North Germany during his lifetime.

ENGLISH LANGUAGE:[80]

London: *The Quarterly Musical Magazine and Review* (1818–1828): edited by Richard Mackenzie Bacon (1776–1844) of Norwich, this ambitious musical emporium, the initiator of musical journalism in England, contained important references (not always flattering) to the London Philharmonic Society's performances of Beethoven's music.
Harmonicon (1823–33): contained engraved portraits, lives, and memoirs of prominent musicians, reports of foreign musical news (including the vignette already cited by Edward Schulz, "A Day with

CHAPTER THREE
BEETHOVEN
DEAD: SHAPING
THE
POSTHUMOUS
PORTRAIT

Beethoven," in which the author remarked that the portraits of Beethoven in the music shops no longer resembled the aged composer), and concert reviews (puzzled reactions to Beethoven's Seventh, Eighth, and Ninth symphonies).

The Musical World (1836–91): dedicated cosmically to embracing almost anything directly or indirectly related to the world of music (before 1840, mystified critiques of Beethoven; after 1840, quite rich in analyses of Beethoven and hence of keen interest to Schindler for his 1860 revision of the *Biographie*).

FRENCH LANGUAGE:

Paris: *Les Tablettes de Polymnie* (1810–11): edited by the French-Italian team of Alexis de Garaudé (1779–1852), a politically astute court singer, and Giovanni Giuseppi Cambini (1746–c. 1825), an extraordinary fertile composer of 60 symphonies and 114 quartets who had been captured by pirates in his youth and in his more settled years became Boccherini's favorite viola player. This short-lived magazine was responsible for the famous quip that Beethoven's music harbored together "doves and crocodiles" (March 1811).

La Revue musicale; after 1835, *Revue et gazette musicale* (1827–80): published by Beethoven's friend Maurice (Moritz) Adolf Schlesinger (1798–1871), son of the Berlin-based book and music publisher Adolf Martin Schlesinger (1769–1838). Both father and son published music by Beethoven, but as a young man (1819) Schlesinger, Jr., endeared himself to Beethoven by sending a meal of roast veal out to him by carriage in Baden after a visit to the composer who told him a tale of woe about the local tavern's lack of veal that day. Schlesinger's name appears frequently in the conversation books. The periodical attracted some notable pro-Beethoven commentators including Schumann, Berlioz, Liszt, and Wagner.

Le Ménestrel (1833/4–1940): devoted to the music scene around the world.

La France musicale (1837/8–70): included musical biographies and essays.

Schindler, in reviewing this vastly differing journalistic depository, may have felt that he too was encountering doves together with crocodiles. Apart from the culling of Beethoven's musical and—as we have seen, by implication—character representations from these sources, Schindler also had to cope with the small but disparate body of literary portraits and pseudobiographies that had appeared in print prior to 1840. To reenact Schindler's pioneering trek through these murky swamps and flowering pastures is subject matter for another, yet to be written, book, but we can and should take notice at least of the sequence and occasional substance of this often familiar but indistinctly mapped terrain, since close knowledge of it enables us to assign some of the Beethoven myths their date and place of birth. Here then is a chronological but by no means exhaustive ensemble of the far-flung fragments that would go into the shaping of the posthumous portrait of Beethoven.

The first one, we know, was actually read by Beethoven himself, and was printed in the year 1809. This was an account given by the North German composer and indefatigable musical journalist Johann Friedrich Reichardt (1753–1814) in a travelogue written in the form of "confidential letters" and, scattering confidentiality to the winds, published under the alluring title *Vertraute Briefe*.[81] Here are some mythmaking excerpts: "At last I succeeded in finding and visiting the good Beethoven. People here care so little about him that no one could tell me where he lived and it cost me a great deal of effort to discover his address. At last I found him in his large, disorderly, lonely lodgings. He looked at first as gloomy as his apartment, but soon cheered up . . . expressed himself on a number of topics . . . in an honest and charming way. He is of a powerful temperament, his appearance practically Cyclopean, but really quite sincere, cordial, and good."[82]

If people were unable to give Reichardt Beethoven's address it was not necessarily because they were indifferent to the great composer living in their midst but very possibly because they were ignorant of what the latest abode of the precipitately peripatetic composer might be. The evocation of a physical giant through Cyclopean appearance is a germinal stage of the titanism soon to be assigned to Beethoven's music and personality. Our North German celebrity-hunter continues: "Beethoven . . . has the unhappy, hypochondriac, melancholy notion in his head and heart that everyone here persecutes and despises him. His visibly stubborn nature may well frighten away many of the good-natured, gay Viennese. Many among those who do recognize his great talent and merit do not employ enough humanity and delicacy to bring about the means [financial support] for an enjoyment of life which the sensitive, inflammable, and mistrustful artist might gladly receive . . . . It often grieves me very deeply when I see this basically good, excellent man gloomy and suffering, although on the other hand I am convinced that his best, most original works can only be brought forth when he is in such headstrong, deeply sullen [mismütigen] moods."[83]

Here then is the inventory of Beethoven's traits and circumstances that was to be snatched up so enthusiastically by purveyors of the Beethoven myth. Even at this early date (the Beethoven of this account was not yet thirty-eight) the litany included physical disorder, indifference or miscomprehension by society, and a dual personality (anticipating by seventy-seven years Dr. Jekyll and Mr. Hyde) of sincere goodness rent by gloomy mistrust and hair-trigger readiness to take offense.

What did Beethoven think of this thumbnail character sketch? We do not need to speculate: he referred to the just-published *Vertraute Briefe* in a letter to his Leipzig publishers: "What do you say to that silly scrawl of Reichardt's letters? But I must admit that so far I have seen only a few fragments."[84]

The great grumbler seems to protest with purrs of pleasure and even to look forward to more from the pen of Reichardt.

We do not know whether Beethoven was aware of the two separate accounts published in English about him during the year 1824. The earlier reminiscence was by our English friend with the German surname, Edward Schulz, and appeared in the January issue of *Harmonicon*. It described a fortunate day for the visitor, and in many ways it was a fortunate one for Beethoven also, for Schulz, in the company of Haslinger (the same Haslinger of Beethoven's "joking" romantic biography), visited the composer in Baden on one of the rare days he did not need his ear trumpet to hear:

The 28th of September, 1823, will be ever recollected by me as a *dies faustus* . . . Being with Mr. H., I had not to encounter any difficulty in being admitted into his presence. He looked very sternly at me first, but immediately after shook me heartily by the hand. . . . Nothing can possibly be more lively, more animated and—to use an epithet that so well characterizes his own symphonies—more energetic than his conversation, when you have once succeeded in getting him into good humor; but one unlucky question, one ill-judged piece of advice—for instance, concerning the cure of his deafness—is quite sufficient to estrange him from you forever. . . . He introduced his nephew to me, a fine young man of about eighteen, who is the only relation with whom he lives on

CHAPTER THREE
BEETHOVEN
DEAD: SHAPING
THE
POSTHUMOUS
PORTRAIT

terms of friendship. . . . The history of this relative reflects the highest credit on Beethoven's goodness of heart; a most affectionate father could not have made greater sacrifices on his behalf, than he has made.[85]

So far, aside from the inevitable parallel between Beethoven the man and Beethoven's music, this account has touched upon two notable aspects that would hold fascination for future generations: Beethoven's deafness and Beethoven's relation (euphemistically sketched here) with his nephew. Schulz next provided a stage cue that would help inspire the Lyser genre of Beethoven-in-nature visual response and encourage the many stories of Beethoven's absentmindedness: "B[eethoven] is a famous pedestrian, and delights in walks of many hours, particularly through wild and romantic scenery. Nay, I was told that he sometimes passes whole nights on such excursions, and is frequently missed at home for several days."[86]

Next comes another equation of character and creation along with—in Austria's age of police agents and censorship—an important political comment for later readers determined to see the liberal Beethoven as revolutionary: "He is a great enemy to all *gêne* [meant here as constraint], and I believe that there is not another individual in Vienna who speaks with so little restraint on all kinds of subjects, even political ones, as Beethoven. He hears badly, but he speaks remarkably well, and his observations are as characteristic and as original as his compositions."[87]

The other published English account of 1824 is Sir John Russell's travel book, from which we have already quoted the description of Beethoven's hair as unvisited by comb or scissors and the account of Beethoven at the piano with wildly rolling eye, overpowered by the demons he had summoned. We now look at another passage from the journal that happily passes on an anecdote concerning Beethoven's undisciplined, irritable conduct in public, and incidentally mentions an activity that would be picked up the very next year by a London critic and indignantly brought to bear on Beethoven's Ninth Symphony:

> The total loss of hearing has deprived him of all the pleasure which society can give, and perhaps soured his temper. He used to frequent a particular cellar, where he spent the evening in a corner, beyond the reach of all the chattering and disputation of a public room, drinking wine and beer, eating cheese and red herrings, and studying the newspapers. One evening a person took a seat near him whose countenance did not please him. He looked hard at the stranger, and spat on the floor as if he had seen a toad; then glanced at the newspaper, then again at the intruder, and spat again, his hair bristling gradually into more shaggy ferocity, till he closed the alternation of spitting and staring, by fairly exclaiming "What a scoundrelly phiz!" and rushing out of the room.[88]

It was not the self-induced temper tantrum or even the unholy mixing of beer and wine that attracted the attention of the London critic, but the newspapers: "I must ever consider this new symphony as the least excellent of any Beethoven has produced, as an unequal work, abounding more in noise, eccentricity, and confusion of design. . . . Beethoven, we are told, reads of the world, although he sees and hears but little of it, . . . he finds from all the public accounts, that noisy extravagance of execution and outrageous clamour in musical performances, more frequently ensures applause than chastened elegance or refined judgement—the inference therefore that we may fairly make is, that he writes accordingly. He writes to suit the present mania. . . ."[89]

This use—or abuse, rather—of the smallest sliver of Beethoven evidence as slim scaffolding for a fantasy edifice of recrimination, carried on while Beethoven was still alive, demonstrates the facile alacrity with which different constructors of the Beethoven monument were assembling their tangible building blocks.

Yet a third[90] English visitor to Beethoven left a myth-confirming account of the composer during his lifetime, and while it is doubtful that Beethoven read it, we know that he was very happy to receive this particular foreign visitor, for she was the talented daughter of the famous musicologist Sir Charles Burney (1726–1814), whose four-volume history of music was a treasured item in his small personal library.[91] At the conclusion of the visit Beethoven wrote out thirteen measures of a piece for piano and, after carefully ascertaining the correct spelling of her name, dedicated the autograph, taking as few chances with the English language as possible: "Comme un souvenir à Sarah Burney Payne par Louis van Beethoven le 27 Septembre, 1825."[92] Sarah Harriet Burney Payne for her part published a sympathetic account of the outing to Baden to visit "the giant of living composers" in the December 1825 issue of *Harmonicon* (published anonymously), reporting to her London readers: "The people seemed surprised at our taking so much trouble; for, unaccountable as it may seem to those who have any knowledge of or taste for music, his reign in Vienna is over, except in the hearts of a chosen few . . . and I was even taught to expect a rough, unceremonious reception. . . . he addressed us in so gentle, so courteous, so sweet a manner, and with such a truth in his sweetness. . . . He is very short, extremely thin, and sufficiently attentive to personal appearance."[93]

Before leaving the company of the deaf composer she placed the manuscript page of the music he had just written out for her on the Broadwood piano invitingly. Although Beethoven obligingly played it through, prefacing it by three or four chords ("such handfuls of notes"), it was only too apparent that the composer derived no pleasure from doing so, whereupon the visitor delicately took her leave of him—but not before Beethoven spontaneously promised to visit her if he came to England (an unfulfilled dream always dear to his heart).

There is no doubt that the English public avidly read this latest report on Beethoven for it was in England that the composer's music—thanks to the dedicated efforts of Sir George Smart,[94] Charles Neate, Ferdinand Ries, and Ignaz Moscheles—was enjoying its first and greatest foreign success. Twenty-three months after Beethoven's death a critic for *Harmonicon* fairly purred with national pride: "The French seem just to have discovered the merits of Beethoven's symphony in C minor [Fifth Symphony]. At the first performance for the present season of the *Sociéte des Concerts*, on the 21st of December, this stupendous composition was performed, and received with *transports of admiration, almost amounting to frenzy*. It met with nearly as warm a reception at the Philharmonic Concerts, no less than sixteen years ago. . . ."[95]

French honor would be redeemed in the next decade by the heroic efforts of Berlioz and other crusaders of French Romanticism to explain the grandeurs of Beethoven to their fellow citizens. As Beethoven's reputation was tossed back and forth on the waves of internationalism, the emerging imagery would reveal not so much the historical Beethoven of Franz I's Vienna as it would each nation's particular psychic requisites for hero worship.

Returning to the chronology of published reminiscences available to Schindler and the public before 1840, we come to the first posthumous one that, unlike the career-encapsulating obituaries, concentrates on the demeanor and look of the composer. This was the account published by the royal librarian from Berlin mentioned in that final letter of Beethoven's to Wegeler in which he had summed up his life's accomplishments and referred to "a certain Dr. Spiker" who had received from him in person an inscribed copy of his Ninth Symphony for delivery to the king of Prussia. Samuel Heinrich Spiker (1786–1858) published a description of his September 1826 visit to Beethoven in the *Berlinische Nachrichten* on 25 April 1827, within a month of the composer's death. Much of the already legendary portrait outlines are retraced, but the author's eagerness to offset any hardening of the undeniably harsher aspects of his subject is noticeable. In other words Dr. Spiker behaves just like a good mythmaker, even though his intention is to combat myth:

> But very little hope of seeing him had been held out to the writer of these lines himself, who most ardently wished to make Beethoven's personal acquaintance. A certain circumstance, however, facilitated a meeting. . . . Beethoven lived in the suburb on the *glacis* . . . in cheerful, sunny rooms. Owing to his weak state of health, he made frequent use of baths in his last years, and hence we [Spiker was with the unflappable Tobias Haslinger] . . . saw his bathing apparatus in the anteroom. Opening on it was Beethoven's living room, in which, in rather genial disorder, scores, books, etc., were piled helter-skelter, and in the middle of which stood a grand fortepiano made by the admirable artist Konrad Graf [the Broadwood that usually stood end to end with the Graf had been sent out for repairs in May]. The furniture was plain and the whole appearance of the room was probably like that of many another person who pays more attention to inward than to outward order. Beethoven received us very amicably. He was dressed in a plain gray morning suit which went very well with his cheerful, jovial face and his artlessly ordered hair.[96]

This is certainly the first time we have heard of Beethoven's lodgings as "cheerful" and "sunny"! Not to beg the question of weather, which could certainly have played a role, we pass on in silent wonderment to the "genial disorder" of the room and the "artlessly ordered" hair. Such tolerance is new to the Beethoven iconography and is an excellent indication of how quickly the outrage over Beethoven's tempestuous conduct and disheveled appearance abated when he himself was no longer present to shock the sensibilities of the formality-loving Viennese. Spiker's indulgent description, encompassing pleasing morning coat, artlessly ordered hair, grand piano, and genial disorder could almost have dictated the program of a pen-and-ink silhouette produced later in the century by an unknown artist showing Beethoven standing at the piano, sheets of music paper in his right hand, on the floor, and on the piano top, and tentatively sounding a chord with his left hand (Fig. 53).

Spiker the Prussian is circumspect but also a little sly concerning Beethoven's well-documented habit of reacting to strangers and friends alike about his mistreatment from the Viennese and we are treated to a literary vignette of those sketchbooks that had so intrigued Klöber and Stieler as properties to be included in their final portraits of the composer (see Fig. 12): "His own circumstances in Vienna, Beethoven only touched upon fleetingly, and seemed to take pains to avoid recalling them. In general, however, he was exceptionally merry and laughed at every jest with the good-humored readiness of a man without guile who believed in all, something not to have been expected in view of the generally current rumor that Beethoven was very gloomy and shy. It was very interesting to see his musical sketchbook which, as he told us, he always carried with him on

CHAPTER THREE
BEETHOVEN
DEAD: SHAPING
THE
POSTHUMOUS
PORTRAIT

(Colorplate 4)

his walks in order to jot down with his lead pencil any musical ideas which might occur to him. It was full of individual measures of music, suggested figures, etc."[97]

Finally a specific reference by Spiker to a famous earlier portrait of Beethoven suggests an on-the-spot rejection of the sickly individual before him and a myopic nostalgia for the robust image of a Beethoven past: "Among the many pictures of Beethoven extant I consider the one drawn of him in his younger days by Louis Letronne [see Fig. 2] and Riedl's engraving [Riedl was the publisher who released the Letronne-Höfel image] those which most resemble him. There was something unusually alive and radiant in his eyes, and the mobility of his whole being undoubtedly prevented anyone from regarding his death in the near future as probable."[98]

The gleam Spiker saw in the grievously ailing Beethoven's eyes may, speaking from a practical viewpoint, have been temporarily ignited by the composer's cherished hope of real financial, if not titular, reward from King Friedrich Wilhelm III. (We recall the wistful reference in his letter to Wegeler to the possibility mentioned on the occasion of Spiker's visit of his being awarded the Order of the Red Eagle.) The disappointment Beethoven experienced was made doubly acute when the Prussian king sent back in payment to his Bonn-born "subject" (as Beethoven called himself in a transparently obsequious cover letter to the king) neither a decoration nor a money order but a "diamond" ring with a reddish glow, which the Vienna court jeweler appraised as worth only three hundred florins in paper money. Beethoven promptly and contemptuously sold it to the jeweler despite the protestations of his young friend Karl Holz (1798–1858; Schindler's hated rival and replacement during the two-year break in his relationship with Beethoven). Holz had exclaimed, "Master, keep the ring, it is from a king," prompting Beethoven to call out "with indescribable dignity and self-consciousness, 'I too am a King'!"[99]

Spiker's romanticizing ability to read radiance in Beethoven's eyes restores the fire Schindler assures us had been dimmed by the illness of 1825 and passes the aspect of a blazing, Schimon-type portrait of Beethoven through the lines of *Wahrheit* and safely into the camp of *Dichtung*.

While Schindler, by his own not necessarily trustworthy account, was vainly entreating Rochlitz of Leipzig to take on the task of writing Beethoven's biography (letters passed between them in September and October 1827[100]), an opportunist who had scarcely known Beethoven jumped into the breach. His name was Johann Aloys Schlosser and within a few months after the composer's death he rushed into print with a ninety-three-page book entitled *Ludwig van Beethoven: Eine Biographie*. Although the book was published in 1827, a respectful and scholarly interval was suggested by the imprint: Prague, 1828. The frontispiece (Fig. 54), crudely conceived and executed, incised a motif into the Beethoven iconography that would be handsomely appropriated by Klinger at the end of the century as effective pendant to his Beethoven monument: an eagle of awesome proportions and commanding appearance. The illustration to Schlosser's book is humble in size only. Its message is vaulting: to either side of a large lyre standing abandoned in a primordial ravine, scantily clad mortals fall back in wonderment at the specter of a great, majestic eagle—the spirit of Beethoven—aggressively ascending through storm clouds and thunder bolts to the heavens with confident flaps of its outspread wings. Little doubt is left—visually—that the king of musicians is about to reach his rightful celestial perch. Schlosser corroborates this in an unambiguous preamble: "For a long time Germany and all Europe have not been so deeply and painfully moved by a death as that of Beethoven's. He climbed to a level of Art that no one else can come to and which he leaves behind to no one."[101]

The text of the book itself added little information to what was generally known about Beethoven at that time. The author in fact augmented his slim narrative with a collection of opinions concerning Beethoven's music ("Urtheile über Beethoven's Werke") that took up the last seventeen pages of his book. The idea of equating the caliber of Beethoven's music with the quality of his personality was unself-consciously voiced by Schlosser in his preface along with the—to him—altruistic hope that proceeds from this Beethoven biography might aid in erecting a monument to Beethoven's "teacher," Haydn!

This "insult" alone may be why Schindler did not deign even to mention Schlosser's book. But Thayer did, characterizing it as a "wretched little 'biography'" and inviting readers to make their own conclusions concerning the book written by "a man who hastily threw a few pages together soon after the death of the composer, and who begins by adopting the old error of 1772 as the date of his birth, and naming his father 'Anton.'"[102]

The "wretched" Schlosser biography may have been full of errors but at least it conscientiously debunked one myth about Beethoven's childhood: a story (which Schindler also labeled as a "pretty little fable") about a spider that "whenever little Ludwig was playing his violin in his room, descended from the ceiling to sit on the instrument. When his mother discovered her son's companion, she killed it, whereupon the boy smashed his violin to bits."[103] Mythmaking was thus deprived of spinning further arachnoid webs in this one respect.

The next major memoir of Beethoven to include material that would help shape his posthumous portrait was furnished by the very man who had rejected Schindler's petition to write the biography of Beethoven. We have already read Rochlitz's account in the previous chapter of Beethoven's physique— which the North German critic found similar to that of Fichte's—and we also observed that it was Rochlitz who realized what a fine *self*-portrait Beethoven's Heiligenstadt Testament would be in the pages of his *Allgemeine musikalische Zeitung*. In 1828 in the form of letters recording his visit to Vienna and printed as the foreword to his periodical, Rochlitz set forth the impressions gathered in three separate meetings with the composer during 1822. Aside from confirming the phenomenon of Beethoven's "piercing" eyes, Rochlitz's remarks addressed two major areas of interest to future mythographers—the "political" Beethoven and the "bearish" Beethoven. Concerning the first dimension: "He philosophized, or one might even say politicized, after his own fashion. He spoke of England and the English, and of how both were associated in his thoughts with a splendor incomparable. . . . His remarks all were made with the greatest unconcern and without the least reserve. . . . 'Well, it happens that I am unbuttoned today,' he said and the remark was decidedly in order [artists would take this remark quite literally, see Fig. 53]. His talk and his actions all formed a chain of eccentricities, in part most peculiar. Yet they all radiated a truly childlike amiability, carelessness, and confidence in everyone who approached him. Even his barking tirades—like that against his Viennese contemporaries . . . are only explosions of his fanciful imagination and his momentary excitement."[104]

Further embroidery of the generous bolt of "political" cloth contained in the above would be drawn from English and French commentators, but embellish-

CHAPTER THREE
BEETHOVEN
DEAD: SHAPING
THE
POSTHUMOUS
PORTRAIT

ment would also occur in a restless Germany edging toward the revolutions of 1848 and represented by no less an alarmist trumpeter than Richard Wagner. We should be quite correct to imagine that Fidus Schindler would be the first watch-dog to protest this sort of published account of Beethoven as a somewhat naïve and noisy partisan—the sort of account that, as he put it, started "from the premise that he was one of the many so-called harmless tavern politicians, whose ire could be aroused by a single catchword."[105] Citing the same Rochlitz passage we have just read, Schindler, unable to contain his emotion, declared: "What a complete misunderstanding of the character and the person is here! And Rochlitz was to have been Beethoven's biographer?!"[106] Beethoven's mighty protector has succumbed to double punctuation marks here; all that is lacking is Beethoven's own emphatic underlining. In light of the deliberate misinterpretations and license characterizing later mythmakers' analyses of the "political" Beethoven, Schindler's vigilant wariness proves justified.[107]

Rochlitz's second contribution to the mythmaking process was to endow Beethoven's brusque mannerisms with a bruin simile destined forever to fix in the public mind an image of Beethoven as lovable, almost pattable, bear: " . . . once he is in the vein, rough, striking witticisms, droll conceits, surprising and exciting paradoxes suggest themselves to him in a continuous flow. Hence in all seriousness I claim that he even appears to be amiable. Or if you shrink from this word, I might say that the dark, unlicked bear seems so ingenuous and confiding, growls and shakes his shaggy pelt so harmlessly and grotesquely, that it is a pleasure, and one has to be kind to him, even though he were nothing but a bear in fact and had done no more than a bear's best."[108]

We might now feel inclined to add our voices in ursicidal unanimity to Schindler's outburst: "And Rochlitz was to have been Beethoven's biographer?!"

One other item passed by Rochlitz into the Beethoven repertoire is of interest to us in adding a further insight into the Incident at Teplitz story, so dear to the hearts of future mythographers: " 'But,' said he [Beethoven], 'you really live in Weimar, do you not?' He probably thought so because of my address. I shook my head. 'Then it is not likely that you know the great Goethe?' I nodded my head vigorously. 'I know him too,' said Beethoven, throwing out his chest, while an expression of the most radiant pleasure overspread his face. 'It was in Karlsbad [Teplitz] that I made his acquaintance—God only knows how long ago! At that time I was not yet altogether deaf, as I now am, though I heard with great difficulty. And what patience the great man had with me.' "[109]

If we believe Rochlitz's verbatim powers then Beethoven's stressing of Goethe's patience with him may signal the fact that Beethoven had at least some action requiring forbearance on his mind in regard to his conduct with Goethe of ten years before. The Teplitz story does seem to have sprung from some exchange—however minor in origin—that occurred between the two extraordinary men. Our chronology will return us to such speculation shortly, but the march of time has now brought us to Schindler's bête noire, the "apocryphal work on Beethoven," to use his epithet, produced by his rival Ignaz von Seyfried.

Seyfried was no mean musician, either as composer or conductor, and it was in the latter capacity at Schikaneder's Theater-an-der-Wien that he had his closest contact with Beethoven—during the 1805 production and premiere of *Fidelio*. In the biographical supplement to his *Beethoven-Studien* of 1832, Seyfried claimed to have had a thirty-year acquaintance with Beethoven during which their "friendly relationship" was "never weakened, never disturbed by even the smallest quar-rel."[110] Beethoven's friend and yet never a quarrel? This unique assertion, even without the imprecations of Schindler, should make us suspicious. It is cold fact that there was not a single male friend of Beethoven's who did not at least once, and frequently more than once, find himself denounced by the mercurial com-poser; not even his lifelong friends from Bonn days—Franz Wegeler and Stephan von Breuning (to whom he gave the Horneman miniature portrait of himself as a gesture of reconciliation)—had escaped this uniform fate. And even the faithful Schindler had temporarily slipped from Beethoven's favor (to be replaced by the more genial, less obsequious Karl Holz). Thus forewarned, let us allow Seyfried to proceed: "When he composed *Fidelio* [1805] . . . we were living in the same house and (since we were each carrying on a bachelor's apartment) we dined at the same restaurant and chatted away many an unforgettable hour in the confi-dential intimacy of colleagues. . . . No physical ill had then afflicted him [the Heiligenstadt Testament of 1802, which Seyfried also published, contradicts this statement]; no loss of the sense which is peculiarly indispensable to the musician had darkened his life; only weak eyes had remained with him as the results of the smallpox with which he had been afflicted in his childhood, and these compelled him even in his early youth to resort to concave, very strong (highly magnifying) spectacles."[111]

Seyfried has touched here upon an iconographical detail mythographers chose largely to ignore—Beethoven's glasses. Two pairs of his myopic lenses [112] passed into Schindler's "safekeeping" and are now preserved at the Beethovenhaus in Bonn. The fact that up to his thirty-fifth year Beethoven used a lorgnette for dis-tance is confirmed by several accounts, notably by Grillparzer[113] and by Ferdi-nand Ries who, with a touch of humor, reported that as late as 1805 Beethoven, when passing a pretty girl or woman on the street, would turn around and "gaze keenly at her through his glasses."[114] One contemporary artist, whose two oil portraits of the composer (not reproduced in this present book[115]) are so far re-moved from reality—and even from myth—that they seem to be images of an-other person, did indicate a gold chain hanging from the composer's neck—the chain to which presumably a lorgnette, tucked out of sight, was attached. By the 1820s Beethoven was again using his glasses in public: Schindler mentions that in February 1823 the composer employed his "black-ribboned lorgnette to examine attractive window displays,"[116] and Gerhard von Breuning's childhood memory of Beethoven striding through the streets on his daily constitutional during the years 1824 and 1825 includes seeing "the double lorgnette which he wore because of his nearsightedness"[117] hanging down loosely from his neck. Mythmaking and corrective lenses do not necessarily mutually exclude each other—Schubert, mas-ter of more "intimate" music, could be depicted with them, for instance (see Fig. 59), though not always, and Weber, whose thick, round spectacles were abso-lutely indispensable, was even shown wearing them while conducting;[118] but the timeless quality increasingly associated with Beethoven-the-Titan forbade such specificity of flawed mortality.[119] Considering that Beethoven himself gave up wearing the lenses in public for a time, perhaps he shared this perception of ge-nius; his own was already hampered enough by the encumbrance of the ear trumpets forced upon him by deafness. Certainly we have seen that, as his unen-cumbered eyes focused fuzzily on such would-be portrayers as Mähler, Stieler, and Waldmüller, he was solemnly aware of his own image.

CHAPTER THREE
BEETHOVEN
DEAD: SHAPING
THE
POSTHUMOUS
PORTRAIT

But Seyfried's published account of Beethoven the man contained features other than spectacles to offer the Beethoven myth. He was a zestful writer, and several of the personality traits and circumstances upon which he touched, while already familiar, received picturesque confirmation:

> The more his hearing failed, and those intestinal troubles which in the last years of his life also afflicted him gained the upper hand, the more rapidly there also developed the ominous symptoms of a torturing hypochondria. He commenced to complain about a world which was all evil, intent only on delusion and deceit; about malice, betrayal and treachery. . . .
>
> Beethoven never was seen in the street without a little notebook in which he jotted down his ideas of the moment . . . a truly admirable confusion ruled in his household. Books and music were strewn about in every corner; here the fragments of a cold snack, there bottles, still sealed or half-emptied; on his standing desk was the hurried sketch of a new quartet; elsewhere were the débris of his breakfast; here on the piano, in the shape of scribbled-over pages, lay the material for a magnificent symphony, still slumbering as an embryo; there drooped a corrected proof waiting for release. The floor was covered with business and personal letters.[120]

Later artists, especially sculptors commissioned to invent public memorials to Beethoven, found inspiration in Seyfried's description of a Beethoven undeterred by the elements: "No sooner had Beethoven swallowed his last mouthful than . . . he would set forth on his customary promenade, that is to say, he would twice make the circuit of the city in double-quick step, as though something had stung him. Did it rain, snow or hail, did the thermometer stand at sixteen degrees below zero, did Boreas blow with icy breath from puffed cheeks from across the Bohemian border, did thunders roar, lightnings zigzag through the air, winds howl or Phoebus' torrid rays fall vertically on his head as in Lybia's seas of sand? How could any of these things trouble this man filled with a sacred fire. . . ."[121] Moving from a discussion of the composer's daily routine to his character, Seyfried delivered a pro-German pronouncement that would serve manipulators of the myth from Wagner to Hitler: "Beethoven, in the truest sense of the word, was a real German, body and soul. Entirely at home in the Latin, French and Italian languages, he used by preference and whenever possible his native tongue. Had he been able to have his own way in the matter, all his works would have appeared in print with German title pages. He even tried to delete the exotic word 'pianoforte,' and chose in its stead the expressive term *Hammerklavier* ('hammerpiano') as a suitable and appropriate substitute."[122]

Finally, Seyfried's chromatic narration of how Beethoven played the piano set forth a kaleidoscopic paradigm from which later interpreters of the piano sonatas and concertos, from Liszt to Clara Schumann, would select their own favorite views:

> In his improvisations even then [1799] Beethoven did not deny his tendency toward the mysterious and gloomy. When once he began to revel in the infinite world of tones, he was transported also above all earthly things. . . . Now his playing tore along like a wildly foaming cataract, and the conjurer constrained his instrument to an utterance so forceful that the stoutest structure was scarcely able to withstand it; and anon he sank down, exhausted, exhaling gentle plaints, dissolving in melancholy. Again the spirit would soar aloft, triumphing over transitory terrestrial sufferings, turn its glance upward in rev-

erent sounds and find rest and comfort on the innocent bosom of holy nature. But who shall sound the depths of the sea? It was the mystical Sanskrit language whose hieroglyphs can be read only by the initiated.[123]

CHAPTER THREE
BEETHOVEN
DEAD: SHAPING
THE
POSTHUMOUS
PORTRAIT

Seyfried's *Beethoven-Studien* reached the hands of many readers, especially young musicians, who, as a Schindler ally in exposing the deception mused, "went hungry in order to save the money to buy a true relic of Beethoven."[124] Nevertheless, whether Schindler liked it or not, Seyfried's reminiscences, attached to the end of the supposed Beethoven music textbook, did have an impact on posterity's conception of Beethoven. What must Schindler have thought when he learned that upon his rival biographer's death in 1841, his body was placed in the Währinger Cemetery near the grave of Beethoven?

From across the channel an English voice was raised in 1835 to proclaim Beethoven as a worthy successor to the Germanic triad of Handel, Haydn, and Mozart. "He alone is to be compared to them in the magnitude of his works, and their influence on the state of the art," wrote George Hogarth (1783–1870), father-in-law of Charles Dickens, in his book *Musical History, Biography and Criticism.* Enough of Beethoven's personal eccentricities were known to Hogarth to inspire him to "analyse" the composer's work in the following manner: "The music of Beethoven is stamped with the peculiarities of the man. When slow and tranquil in its movement . . . it is grave, and full of deep and melancholy thoughts. When rapid, it is not brisk or lively, but agitated and changeful—full of 'sweet and bitter fancies'—of storm and sunshine—of bursts of passion sinking into the subdued accents of grief, or relieved by transient gleams of hope and joy. . . . The rapid *scherzos* . . . are wild, impetuous, and fantastic; they have often the air of that violent and fitful vivacity to which gloomy natures are liable. . . . and are strikingly illustrative of the character of his mind."[125] Whether eyewitness or distant critic, these early writers on Beethoven evinced the approach we have already seen to be endemic to the Beethoven myth—equation of the man with his music.

Cipriani Potter (1792–1871), an English musician who had visited Beethoven a few times in 1818 and who introduced the composer's Third and Fourth piano concertos to the English public in 1824 and 1825, published his "Recollections of Beethoven" in *The Musical World* of 29 April 1836. He was particularly eager to elucidate the character of his deaf friend (who wrote his name "Botter"):[126]

> Many persons have imbibed the notion that Beethoven was by nature a morose and ill-tempered man. This opinion is entirely erroneous. He *was* irritable, passionate, and of a melancholy turn of mind—all of which affections arose from the deafness which, in his latter days, increased to an alarming extent. Opposed to these peculiarities in his temperament, he possessed a kind heart, and most acute feelings. . . . Another cause for mistaking Beethoven's disposition, arose from the circumstances of foreigners visiting Vienna, who were ambitious of contemplating the greatest genius in that capital, and of hearing him perform. But when, from their unmusical questions and heterodox remarks, he discovered that a mere traveling curiosity, and not musical feeling, had attracted them, he . . . feeling highly offended, was not scrupulous in exhibiting his displeasure in the most pointed and abrupt manner: a reception which . . . did not also fail in prompting them to represent his deportment unfavorably to the world.[127]

Here at last is a mythoclast at work, solicitously attempting to correct the distorted view already held of Beethoven. How Schindler and Thayer, whose biographies repeatedly attempted to rectify mistaken notions, must have approved of Cipriani Potter's (futile) attempt to correct the image of a perpetually glowering genius.

Schindler *did* approve of one of the two authors of the first major source book on Beethoven to appear in print: the 163-page *Biographische Notizen über Ludwig van Beethoven*, published by Bädecker at Coblenz in 1838 by two of the composer's friends from Bonn, Franz Gerhard Wegeler and Ferdinand Ries. The contributor of whom Schindler approved was the physician Wegeler (who had much information on Beethoven's youth to provide), but for his fellow musician Ries, who at the age of seventeen in 1801 had actually received piano lessons from Beethoven, Schindler harbored only jealousy and foreboding since, as he said, Ries believed that "concerning great men everything may be said, for it does not injure them."[128] The fact that Schindler destroyed over half of the four hundred Beethoven conversation books in his possession because of passages he judged harmful or unbecoming to his hero shows he was of an obstinately opposite opinion, the consequence of which was an irredeemable loss to history. Wegeler and Ries wrote their accounts separately, and after Ries's death, which occurred in the same year the book was brought out, Moscheles included parts of it as an appendix to the English version (1841) of Schindler's Beethoven biography. In 1845, on the occasion of the unveiling of a Beethoven monument in Bonn (a literally Victorian event to which we shall return), Wegeler published an appendix to the book and by 1862 the Wegeler-Ries volume had been translated into French.

From the beginning the Wegeler-Ries book was a valuable and reliable (Schindler's misgivings to the contrary) resource for Beethoven scholars, as well as for mythologists, and the book appeared at a good time, only eleven years after Beethoven's death. Thirty-five letters from Beethoven to the authors were also included. Wegeler's part of the book (the first section) relates some of his younger friend's early defiant actions towards his aristocratic patrons and then bravely takes up one of the questions on everybody's mind—Beethoven the bachelor's relationship to women. In doing so Wegeler attempted to slay a dragon of Seyfriedian conjuring: "Among the biographical notices with which Ignaz, Ritter von Seyfield, has provided his study of Beethoven, we find the following sentence, on p. 13: 'Beethoven never married nor, strange to say, did he ever have a love affair.' The truth of the matter, as my brother-in-law, Stephan von Breuning, Ferdinand Ries, Bernhard Romberg [a Bonn cellist and old friend of Beethoven's] and I myself came to know it, is that Beethoven never was out of love, and usually was much affected by the love he was in at the time.... In Vienna Beethoven, at least so long as I was living there, always had some love affair in hand, and on occasion he made conquests which many an Adonis would have found it difficult, if not impossible, to encompass."[129]

We witness here the initial push to a pendulum that has not yet lost its momentum, swinging from puritanical continence (punctured by occasional "genital"—Beethoven's word—relief at brothels) to Don Juanian social conquests and at least one (Immortal Beloved), unfulfilled through self-renunciation, deep love for a member of the opposite sex. The speculation concerning this aspect of the posthumous portrait of Beethoven had already attracted Wegeler's attention in 1838; by the time Schindler published his revised life of Beethoven in 1860 rumor and curiosity had mounted to such an extent that he felt himself compelled to deliver the following revealing invective against mythmakers in general:

We come now to a chapter of Beethoven's life that must be treated with discretion: the matter of his various love affairs. Who would have guessed twenty years ago that one day the world would find this aspect of the composer's life fully as engrossing as his musical works? [Schindler was spared Hollywood at least[130]] . . . in the previous editions of this book . . . I confined myself to a brief, well-documented account, for with the exception of one affair which deeply affected Beethoven's life and work, I felt that the composer's love life was worthy of no greater emphasis than other equally interesting chapters of his life. The literary world disagreed. What I had written was too short and too prosaic for them, and so they distorted the facts, turning the sober musician into a romantic hero crazed with love. For to them any composer whose work is often so wildly passionate—it is on Beethoven's music that these writers based their findings—must be himself a prodigious and passionate lover, certainly no ordinary man with normal emotions! . . . They depict his personal idiosyncrasies as signs of madness, arising from unnatural excesses; they clothe him with totally false attributes. . . . His passions and affairs have been elaborated upon and shamelessly exploited by both French and German writers.[131]

CHAPTER THREE
BEETHOVEN
DEAD: SHAPING
THE
POSTHUMOUS
PORTRAIT

Once again we have, as succinctly charged by Schindler, evidence of Beethoven's musical "proof" being used as testimony for the "facts" of his personal life. The mythmaking process we are pursuing was already well known to Schindler.

Let us now turn to Ries's part of the Beethoven Notizien. We have already heard his voice briefly in regard to the tearing up of the "Napoleon" dedication page incident and also concerning Beethoven vis-à-vis women—that he liked to peer after pretty passersby through his lorgnette.[132] But Ries, who felt that no revelation could dethrone a genius, had much, much more to say about Beethoven. What he did *not* say about the composer is a credit to his character, for the young and then penniless Ries (who had lost an eye from smallpox as a boy) was the butt of many of Beethoven's sullen recriminations and accusations of treachery. This is how he transposed that aspect of his relationship with the composer:

> Beethoven was extremely good-natured, but just as easily inclined to anger or suspicion, motivated by his deafness, but even more by the conduct of his brothers [both Karl (1774–1815) and Johann (1776–1848) had followed Beethoven from Bonn to Vienna, where all three died]. Any unknown could easily defame his most proven friends; for he was all too quick and unquestioning in crediting their lies.[133] He would then neither reproach the person suspected nor yet ask him for an explanation, but his manner toward him would immediately show the greatest haughtiness and the most supreme contempt. Since he was extraordinarily violent in all he did, he would also try to find his supposed enemy's most vulnerable spot, in order to indulge his rage. Hence it often was impossible to tell how one stood with him until the matter was cleared up, in most cases by the merest chance. Then, however, he would try to atone for the wrong he had done as quickly and effectually as possible.[134]

Very suggestive details for the posthumous portrait were provided by Ries concerning Beethoven's physical dexterity: "In his manner Beethoven was very awkward and helpless; and his clumsy movements lacked all grace. He seldom picked up anything with his hand without dropping or breaking it. Thus, on several occasions, he upset his ink-well on the piano which stood beside his writing-desk. No furniture was safe from him; least of all a valuable piece; all was overturned, dirtied and destroyed. How he ever managed to shave himself is hard to understand, even making all allowance for all the many cuts on his cheeks."[135]

Ries, like Wegeler, had tales to tell of Beethoven's proud demeanor in the presence of aristocracy, and one incident gives us some insight into Archduke Rudolf—one of the supposed dramatis personae of the Incident at Teplitz:

> Etiquette and all that etiquette implies was something Beethoven never knew and never wanted to know. As a result, his behavior when he first [c. 1804] began to frequent the palace of the Archduke Rudolf often caused the greatest embarrassment to the latter's entourage. . . . One day, finally, when he was again, as he termed it, being "sermonized on court manners," he very angrily pushed his way up to the Archduke, and said quite frankly that though he had the greatest possible reverence for his person, a strict observance of all the regulations to which his attention was called every day was beyond him. The Archduke laughed good-humoredly over the occurrence, and commanded that in the future Beethoven be allowed to go his way unhindered; he must be taken as he was.[136]

This anecdote is important for the use made of it by later elaborators of the "natural" independence of genius (something in which Beethoven sincerely believed), but it also illustrates how little the role of musician versus royal patron had changed in Beethoven's day from the servile status of eighteenth-century court musicians. Consider the following report given so proudly by Beethoven's contemporary Spohr on the success of his tenacity when invited to play for royalty during his 1819–20 sojourn in London, where the custom of looking upon artists as mere entertainers was even more entrenched than on the continent:

> As we arrived at the ducal palace and a servant showed us to a room where the other artists were waiting, I simply had Johanning hand him my violin case, continuing up the steps, my wife on my arm, before the servant had time to recover from his astonishment. At the entrance to the salon where the invited company was assembled, I gave my name to the servant posted there. When he hesitated to open the door, I made a gesture as if to open it myself. At this the servant opened the door and announced us. The Duchess, mindful of German custom, arose from her seat, approached my wife, and led her to the circle of ladies. The Duke, too, welcomed me cordially and introduced me to the gentlemen. I reckoned that I had brought it all off successfully, but soon noticed that the servants continued to regard me as an intruder, refusing to serve me tea or any of the other refreshments. . . . When time came for the concert to begin the majordomo had the artists summoned one after the other, according to their places on the program. They appeared, notes or instrument in hand, greeted the company with a deep obeisance—acknowledged by no one, as far as I could see, except the Duchess—and played or sang whatever it was that they were supposed to sing or play. It was the elite of the most distinguished artists and virtuosos of London, and their performances were almost all very beautiful. They seemed lost upon the illustrious audience, for conversation continued without a moment's interruption. . . . I had a great desire not to play, and, when my turn came, delayed so long that the Duke himself . . . entreated me to do so. Not until then did I summon a servant to bring up my violin case. Instrument in hand, I began to play, dispensing with the preliminary obeisance. The foregoing must have attracted the attention of the company, for there was complete silence in the room while I played.[137]

Spohr's charming stratagem would not have been necessary a few decades deeper into the century that made a cult of genius. Beethoven, conscious of the possession of genius, sincerely believed this gave him the right to exist outside social convention—as did Mozart to a lesser extent. Beethoven simultaneously desired the acknowledgment of kings and thrived, or rather triumphed, without it. There was a sixteenth-century precedent for this sort of transcending individualism, Michelangelo—a name already linked by Stendhal with that of Beethoven—but even Michelangelo could not ignore the whims of a pope. Beethoven accomplished through oblivious introrseness his independence of the Austrian court. What his nineteenth-century successors would enjoy was the elevated status accorded artists as a result of a society newly in awe of the phenomenon of genius beholden to no one and to no thing except its own genius.

Before we take leave of the Wegeler-Ries account of Beethoven, which we see did not conceal but rather featured the composer's imperious ways, it is only fair to cite a final passage in which Ries—who later worked so loyally on Beethoven's behalf in London—tried to reconcile for himself and for posterity the two conflicting images he had come to know so well: "All in all, he was a dear, good fellow; only his variable humor and his violence where others were concerned, often did him disservice. And no matter what insult or injustice had been done him by any one, Beethoven would have forgiven him on the spot, had he met him when crushed by misfortune."[138]

The next revolution of our chronological carousel takes us forward to January 1839 and back to the Teplitz Incident, with which we began our observation of mythmaking. On this date Bettina Brentano von Arnim (Fig. 55) presented to the world transcriptions of "three" letters written to her when she was in her mid-twenties by Beethoven.[139] One of the side effects of Frau von Arnim's literary fantasias (we recall that only the "middle" letter dated Vienna 10 February 1811 is authenticated by the existence of an autograph) was the entry of her candidacy in the speculations of later researchers for serious nomination as the "Immortal Beloved." Here are some of the lines penned by the forty-year-old Beethoven in the genuine letter of 1811 sent to Bettina in Berlin:

> Dear, dear Bettine! [sic]
> I have already had two letters from you; and I see . . . that you still remember me and, what is more, far too favorably—I carried your first letter about with me during the whole summer; and indeed it often made me feel supremely happy. Even though I do not write to you very often and although you see nothing of me, yet in thought I write a thousand letters to you a thousand times.—You are getting married, dear Bettine, or perhaps you are already married [Bettina married the poet Achim von Arnim on 11 March 1811]; and I have not even been able to see you again before the event. Well, may all the happiness and blessings which marriage bestows upon a wedded couple be yours and your husband's in full measure. . . . If you write Goethe about me, choose all the words which will tell him of my warmest regard and admiration. . . . Now all good wishes, dear, dear B[ettine]. I kiss you sorrowfully on your forehead and thus imprint on it as with a seal all my thoughts for you—Write soon, soon, and very often to your friend   Beethoven[140]

When we read this letter in translation in a language like modern English, which no longer makes any distinction between the formal and intimate forms of address, our first question in pondering the relationship between writer and recipient is to ask what form of address was used in the original German. *Sie* or *Du*? That would tell us something. We have the answer and it is consistent with the multiple image of Beethoven mirrored by myth but so frequently reflected by the figure before that mirror himself. Beethoven, in the original German, displays both forms of address, employing the formal for the opening and the close, and

CHAPTER THREE
BEETHOVEN
DEAD: SHAPING
THE
POSTHUMOUS
PORTRAIT

dartingly changing key just before the finale. Here is the passage that elicited this shift to the tonic of intimacy, followed by an immediate and ''safe'' return to the dominant: "Nun lebe wohl, liebe, liebe Freundin, ich küsse Dich so mit Schmerzen auf Deine Stirne und drücke damit wie mit einem Siegel alle meine Gedanken für Dich auf.—Schreiben Sie bald, bald, oft Ihrem Freund   Beethoven"[141]

If we had the original sheet of paper upon which this letter was written before us, we would notice another feature—one as telling of Beethoven's key-changing liberties as are his shifting forms of address. The words immediately after the phrase "I kiss you" are heavily and thickly scratched out.[142] For once we, if not the mythmakers, can observe an instance of Beethoven's harnessing a first impulse.

But now let us turn to an impulse Frau von Arnim did not restrain with the passage of time—the temptation to represent a more intense relationship than the infatuation that briefly took place between Beethoven and herself. This was accomplished by sandwiching the genuine Beethoven letter of 1811 in between the two slices of spurious missives ''dating'' from the years 1810 and 1812. There is no doubt that some of the sentiments Bettina has Beethoven express ring true and are derived from her vivid recollection of their conversations. But the language in which the thoughts are couched simply does not match the style encountered in any dozen of the more than two thousand Beethoven autographs in existence.

We shall return to the style in a moment, but in the interests of mythmaking milestones let us first briefly examine the escalation of Beethoven's (posthumous) ardor toward his new friend:

From the (unauthenticated) letter of ''11 August 1810'' (written entirely in the formal form of address):
Dearest Bettina,

There has never been a more beautiful spring than this year's, that I do declare, and I feel it too, just because I have made your acquaintance. . . . Alas, unfortunately my ears are a partition through which it is not easy for me to have any friendly communications with human beings. . . . As it was, I could only understand the wide, intelligent look of your eyes, which has made such a strong impression on me that I shall never, never forget it—Dear Bettine, dearest girl! . . . How precious to me are those few days when we two were chattering, or, rather, corresponding. I have kept all the little scraps of paper with your witty, dear, and charming answers. . . . Since you left I have had melancholy hours, dark hours when I could do nothing. . . . But no doubt I shall have a letter from you?—This hope sustains me. . . . Yes, dearest Bettine, do reply to this letter. Let me know what is about to happen to me since my heart has become such a rebel. Write to your most faithful friend   Beethoven[143]

From the (unauthenticated) letter of ''Teplitz, August 1812'' (employing both formal and intimate forms of address):
. . . we [Goethe and Beethoven] had just been talking about you. Dear God! Had I been able to spend as much time with you as that man did, believe me, I should have produced far, far more works, and really great works. . . . the most beautiful themes . . . found their way from your eyes into my heart, themes which will enchant the world some day when Beethoven will no longer be there to conduct. . . . Spirits too can love one another and I shall always pay court to yours. Your praise is more precious to me than that of the whole world. . . . Ah, dearest child, for how long a time now have we been of the same opinion about everything!!! . . . Adieu, Adieu, most charming girl, your last letter

lay on my heart for a whole night and refreshed me there. Musicians can take *every liberty*. Dear God, how I love you!

Your most faithful friend and deaf brother   Beethoven[144]

CHAPTER THREE
BEETHOVEN
DEAD: SHAPING
THE
POSTHUMOUS
PORTRAIT

Even taking into account the high-flung effusions common to early nineteenth-century letter exchanges between friends, this flare-up of intensity smacks of anachronistic fueling. The flames are fed by nostalgia for what a transitory flirtation might have become. An accumulated acquaintance with the facts of Beethoven's life has also telescoped circumstances out of sequence. In the "first" letter of 1810 for instance, Beethoven's reference to keeping "all the little scraps of paper" upon which Bettina had supposedly written her part of the conversation is a discordant detail since the famous conversation books were not necessary until after 1817, when Beethoven's hearing had thoroughly deteriorated. (The earliest known conversation book dates from February and March 1818.) And the "third" letter, allegedly written from Teplitz in "August" of 1812, introduces a month into the Incident at Teplitz story when neither Beethoven nor the Habsburgs were there (Archduke Rudolf is not documented as visiting Teplitz at all in the year 1812). Still, Beethoven often did not date his letters. But the mere fact that the date is given and is wrong by a whole month suggests that Frau von Arnim—transcribing events that had taken place over a quarter of a century before—was helping history out and filling in with generous details when needed, as she had done in her first publication immortalizing a monument, the 1835 *Goethes Briefwechsel mit einem Kinde*. With the publication of her two sets of "letters" from two German geniuses, the newly widowed (1831) author launched not only a literary career[145] but also a flotilla of myth-laden vessels that would help supply the Romantic century's posthumous images of its culture heroes.

Bettina Brentano von Arnim's contribution to the Beethoven myth introduced two bits of Beethoveniana to the world: the composer's supposed infatuation with her (he was, in fact, on the rebound from rejection of his marriage proposal to Therese Malfatti)—taken seriously only by those determined to discover the identity of the "Immortal Beloved"—and the Incident at Teplitz—perhaps one of the most immortally beloved anecdotes ever recounted about Beethoven. Earlier we read the substance of that account; here—in the interest of style—is "Beethoven's" fulminating preface as published by Bettina: "Kings and princes are able, no doubt, to appoint professors, create Privy Councillors, award titles and affix order ribbons. But they cannot create great men or minds which rise above the rabble of this world; that they certainly need not try to do; and therefore great men of that type should be respected—When two such people as Goethe and I meet, the great lords should discover what is really great in men of our type."[146]

Again, some of the sentiments are genuinely Beethovenian—he who, when his brother Johann signed a letter "Land Owner," signed his, "Brain Owner."[147] But the style is not. Let us allow secretary Schindler to comment on what he finds at fault with Beethoven's language as transcribed by Bettina von Arnim:

Beethoven's manner of expressing himself, both in speech and in writing, was always of the utmost simplicity, brevity, and conciseness, as the many letters we have in his hand show. He disliked hearing affected speech or reading an affected style of writing, for in everything he demanded natural straightforwardness without a trace of ostentation. Beethoven did indeed frequently speak and think of his genius as Bettina says, recognizing in it a higher revelation and placing it above any philosophy, yet he always minimized his own worthiness. Beethoven never exhibited the least sign of conceit such as

113

abounds in Bettina's quotations. . . . It is the third letter, dated "Teplitz, August 1812" that I particularly suspect and shall continue to suspect until the whole letter is produced, at least in facsimile. My suspicion is aroused because of what Beethoven writes there about his behavior towards the Emperor's family when he was with Goethe.[148]

Anecdotal allure, not authenticity, is what attracts the mythmaking process however and the Teplitz Incident would continue to be cherished by readers of Bettina's Beethoven. We can treat ourselves to a parting glance at the Schindler–von Arnim controversy in a vignette sketched by Schindler himself. We must imagine the two mythographers, now aged forty-eight and fifty-eight respectively, facing each other across a dark sitting room in Berlin: "During my fairly long stay in Berlin in 1843, I had the honor of making the acquaintance of Frau von Arnim. She told me many interesting things about her literary efforts, about what she had achieved and what she had failed to achieve. About her relationship with Beethoven, however, I could not induce her to say a single word, though she knew of my book about him and knew that she was personally mentioned in the book. Without asking directly if I might examine the famous letters, I hinted that it was extremely important for me to see the originals. The esteemed lady would at such times wrap herself in a deep cloak of silence, pretending to hear nothing I had said."[149]

We can't help but wonder what sort of cloak Schindler-the-Truth-Seeker might have found for himself, had Frau von Arnim asked to see the four hundred Beethoven conversation books in his possession!

The linking of Bettina's name with that of Beethoven's brought about by her 1839 publication of "three" Beethoven letters was not limited to the European confines of a German-reading public. The New World had already trembled at the impact of Beethoven—the man and the myth—as revealed by the music, and no less a person than social critic Margaret Fuller (1810–1850), editor of the transcendentalist journal *The Dial*, published articles on Beethoven from 1840 to 1842. She also translated part of Bettina von Arnim's correspondence and in her memoirs of about 1842 commented: "Bettine [taking Beethoven's spelling of the name] lives and follows out every freakish fancy, till the enchanting child degenerates into an eccentric and undignified old woman."[150] Her severe critique of Bettina however had no power to dam the torrent of emotions she poured into her private journal after hearing a concert of Beethoven's music. Like a latter-day Saint Theresa of Avila, Margaret Fuller the New Englander experienced the ecstasy of mystical-sensual union with her beloved:

To Beethoven, November 25, 1843
   My only friend,
   How shall I thank thee for again tonight breaking the chains of my sorrowful slumber. I did not expect it. For months now I have been in a low state of existence. . . . Thou didst say thou hadst no friend but thy art. But that one is enough. I have no art, in which to vent the swell of a soul as deep as thine, Beethoven, and of a kindred frame. Thou will not think me presumptuous in this saying as another might. I have always known that thou wouldst welcome, wouldst know me, as no other who ever lived upon the earth since its first creation would. Thou wouldst forgive me, Master, that I have not been true to my eventual destiny, and therefore have suffered on every side "the pangs of despised" love. Thou didst the same . . . but thou didst borrow from those errors the inspiration of thy genius. . . .

CHAPTER THREE
BEETHOVEN
DEAD: SHAPING
THE
POSTHUMOUS
PORTRAIT

But thou, oh blessed master! dost answer all my questions, and make it my privilege to be. Like a humble wife to the sage or poet, it is my triumph that I can understand, can receive thee wholly, like a mistress I arm thee for the fight, like a young daughter, I tenderly bind thy wounds. Thou art to me beyond compare, for thou art all I want. No heavenly sweetness of Jesus, no many-leaved Raphael, no golden Plato, is anything to me, compared with thee.... Beethoven, my heart beats. I live again, for I feel that I am worthy audience for thee.... Tonight I had no wish for thee: it was long since we had met. I did not expect to feel again.... Thy touch made me again all human. O save and give me to myself and thee.[151]

This extraordinary outpouring from a Beethoven worshiper halfway across the world as early as the year 1843 brings home a point likely to be obscured in our iconographical quest: that the *power* of Beethoven—that which *made* him so mythic—was his *music*. No other composer's music had meant so much to so many people. No other musician had had the power to affect, to inspire, to terrify, to fascinate, to frustrate, to move so many listeners. The changing image of Beethoven across two hundred years is merely the barometer from which readings of the elemental force of his music can be taken. The critical reception of Beethoven's music in different countries and within individual hearts fashions the materials and the frame for history's portrait of the man.

Our chronology of history's access to the public Beethoven via periodicals and publications has at last taken us to Schindler's own first portrait of the composer, unveiled in 1840 and available in English through the ("interfering," Schindler would say) medium of Moscheles by the following year.[152] From Moscheles's reminiscences[153] of Beethoven, which he added to his edition of the Schindler biography, another one of those contradictory scraps of pithy information emerged that cast a new light upon the man who had adamantly refused Haydn's request to designate himself as "Pupil of Haydn"[154]: "Yet what was my surprise when, one day, in the house of Court-conductor Salieri, who was not at home, I saw a card lying on the table, on which might be read, in his laconic style: 'Pupil Beethoven called!' "[155]

Such a revelation did not, incidentally, poison Moscheles's own attitude towards Salieri. His narrative continues charmingly: "This set me thinking. A Beethoven still could learn something from a Salieri? Then with how much more reason could I."[156] Two contrarily cut pieces of the same portrait puzzle, such as this Haydn versus Salieri "pupil" attitude of Beethoven's, demonstrate how it was possible, even reasonable, for later biographers wishing to cut a broader swath through the field of facts to claim in a single sentence that Beethoven was both haughty and humble. There is no fictionalization here, only generalization. This is what Schindler had already tried to fix for posterity. The fluctuating needs and interests of mythmaking however would often focus on just one of these poles, bending it to the service of fable and distorting it beyond fact. If a proud Beethoven was needed for an increasingly antimonarchist France, then a Beethoven who scorned the rings of kings could be found; conversely, if a simple, unassuming man of the people was required for brotherhood-loving twentieth-century internationalist writers like Romain Rolland and Emil Ludwig, then the following—equally authentic—Beethoven could be broadcast in many languages:

One day [fall 1826] Johann [Beethoven's "Land-Owner" brother] went to Langenfeld and Beethoven ... went with him. The purpose was to visit a surgeon named Karrer, a friend of the brother. The surgeon was absent on a sick-call, but his wife, flattered by a visit from the landowner, entertained him lavishly. Noticing a man who held himself aloof from the company, sitting silently on the bench behind the stove, and taking him for one of her guest's servants, she filled a little jug with native wine and handed it to him with the remark: "He shall also have a drink." When the surgeon returned home late at night and heard an account of the incident he exclaimed: "My dear wife, what have you done? The greatest composer of the century was in our house today and you treated him with such disrespect!"[157]

It was just this sort of reverse Supper-at-Emmaus genre of story that so swelled biographers' literary coffers with Beethoven gems. As with his music, so with his life it was possible to discover a man for all seasons.

A minor event of history may well be the advent of a Schindler for all seasons. Unable to be the first in print on his beloved Beethoven, he seems to have become possessed by a compulsion to produce the *most* in print on Beethoven. His two visits to Paris during the winter and spring 1841 as the newly published Beethoven authority (this must be the period in his life when he handed out his *"ami de Beethoven"* visiting cards, if we can believe a smirking Heine) gave him plenty to write about, and his account of the growing acceptance of Beethoven's music in the French capital was published as an appendix entitled "Beethoven in Paris" in the second (1845) edition of his life of Beethoven. Hence, in a sense, he becomes the first writer consciously to take a sounding of the composer's reputation and, in this case, changing image. The sounding was chauvinistic. With almost childish pleasure Schindler describes how the musicians of the Paris Conservatoire fell to their knees before his portrait of the master. (Of this, more later.) About the music itself Schindler reports that in 1815 the *Eroica* was hesitantly given a first reading under François-Antoine Habeneck but that "at the end of the first movement everyone burst out laughing"; the same fate awaited the other movements, and so it was not until 1820 that, trying a different symphony, the Fifth, an appreciation began to dawn on the instrumentalists and their conductor. Proudly Schindler reports that the musicians he met in 1841 who happened to have taken part in this momentous discovery still remembered it with "noble pride." Apparently in one voice they then confessed to Beethoven's earthly nuncio: "His compositions awakened in us the first consciousness of the dignity and significance of our profession, and when we had gained some understanding of him, we recognized our obligation to make his music heard and known."[158]

This mass Gallic conversion, as witnessed by our German apostle, may strain credulity, but it does bring attention to an important phenomenon concerning the improving social status of music and musicians compared to the situation in the 1820s, which we recently saw through Spohr's eyes. The fact was that in Germany—as opposed to Italy and France—seriousness and a sense of moral purpose seemed inherent in music, especially as defined by philosophers, and these sensed qualities functioned simultaneously with the sheer emotional force of Beethoven's major creations in their effect upon performers and listeners. The exportation of such a highly charged product, if connected with the proper outlet—dedicated conductor, well-rehearsed orchestra—could indeed, in a city accustomed to the "beautiful" rather than the new "sublime,"[159] have convinced its imbibers of the dignified and significant aspects of music making. The respect Beethoven's music demanded for itself accrued to the orchestra performing it and the day of the truly grand, perfection-seeking symphony orchestra was at hand.

It would be the medium through which a new philosopher, Beethoven, could offer his salve to a suffering humanity.

Back in Germany, Schindler's ally in the elevation of Beethoven to the role of spiritual leader was the very "lady of letters" whose transcriptions of Beethoven conversations into letters he had so deplored. There was no doubt however as to the date or the contents of a letter Bettina Brentano had written from Vienna on 28 May 1810 ecstatically reporting her meeting and conversations with Beethoven to Goethe. After Goethe's death in 1832, Bettina won the right to have her letters to him returned and it was this letter exchange of Goethe's "with a child" which she published in her famous *Goethes Briefwechsel mit einem Kinde*. This is an appropriate place to go back and read for ourselves what had once been written for the great Goethe's eyes only, but which since 1835 had sparkled in the firmament spanning the public domain, communicating the fervor of its blazing light to an enthralled readership. Here is the High Priestess presenting a new god to an old god: "When I saw him of whom I shall now speak to you, I forgot the whole world—as the world still vanishes when memory recalls the scene.... It is Beethoven of whom I now wish to tell you, and who made me forget the world and you; I am still not of age, it is true, but I am not mistaken when I say—what no one, perhaps, now understands and believes—he stalks far ahead of the culture of mankind. Shall we ever overtake him?—I doubt it, but grant that he may live until the mighty and exalted enigma lying in his soul is fully developed, may reach its loftiest goal, then surely he will place the key to his heavenly knowledge in our hands so that we may be advanced another step towards true happiness.[160]

Here the stage is already set for Beethoven-as-Revealer—the composer who is ahead of his times and whose compositions when comprehended will give true joy. When Bettina says she is still not of age (in the legal sense; she was a twenty-five-year-old, very literate "child" at the time) and then stresses her precocious comprehension of Beethoven—about whose Ninth Symphony the converted Weber still had secret reservations to the end of his life—we are forced to admire the certitude of her belief in Beethoven's achievements. Even if she embellished this vaulting credo for the 1835 publication of the then twenty-five-year-old letter, with an additional knowledge of Beethoven's late works possibly fortifying her judgment of his genius, Bettina's unstinting and remarkable recognition is still decades ahead of much nineteenth-century music criticism. She next tries to convey the spirit of Beethoven's musical philosophy to Goethe in what (Schindler would and did maintain) were *her* rather than Beethoven's own words: "He himself said: 'When I open my eyes, I must sigh, for what I see is contrary to my religion, and I must despise the world which does not know that music is a higher revelation than all wisdom and philosophy, the wine which inspires one to a new generative process, and I am the Bacchus who presses out this glorious wine for mankind and makes them spiritually drunken.'"[161]

This mixed metaphysical metaphor—crossing spirituality with sensuality—would have tremendous consequence for that supreme musical alchemizer, Wagner. Already, in the same letter, Bettina had presented Beethoven as a divine magician whose "every posture is the organization of a higher existence, and therefore Beethoven feels himself to be the founder of a new sensuous basis in the intellectual life...."[162]

It seems that Beethoven said much more to Bettina on this topic. She hastily wrote it down for Goethe:

CHAPTER THREE
BEETHOVEN
DEAD: SHAPING
THE
POSTHUMOUS
PORTRAIT

"Music, verily, is the mediator between the life of the mind and the senses. . . . The mind wants to expand into the limitless and universal where everything flows into a stream of feelings which spring from simple musical thoughts. . . . There indeed [in Beethoven's symphonies] one feels that something eternal, infinite, something never wholly comprehensible is in all that is of the mind, and although in my works I always feel that I have succeeded, yet at the last kettledrum with which I have driven home to my audience my pleasure, my musical conviction, like a child I feel starting over again in me an eternal hunger that but a moment before seemed to have been assuaged. Speak to Goethe about me," he said; "tell him to hear my symphonies and he will say that I am right in saying that music is the one incorporeal entrance into the higher world of knowledge which comprehends mankind but which mankind cannot comprehend. . . . Write to Goethe if you understand what I have said. . . ." I promised to write you everything to the best of my understanding. . . . Last night I wrote down all that he had said; this morning I read it over to him. He remarked: *Did I say that? Well, then I had a raptus!*"[163]

Indignant howlings from the ghost of Schindler interrupt our contemplation of this fascinating image of Beethoven trying to edit his eloquence. Bettina's *Goethes Briefwechsel mit einem Kinde* publication had not escaped Schindler's eagle eye and in the 1840 biography he attacked the Beethoven portion with unctuous sarcasm: "Anyone reading in Goethe's *Briefwechsel* . . . what in her letter of 28 May 1810 the apparently over-excited Bettina reports Beethoven to have said, will be unable to refrain from thinking what a wit, what a monstrous swaggerer he must have been. The impression will be entirely false. . . . How amazed Beethoven would be to read the words put into his mouth by the prattling Bettina! . . . He would no doubt have exclaimed, 'My dear chatterbox of a Bettina! It was you who must have had a *raptus* when you wrote such things to Goethe!' "[164]

Fairness now demands that we consult the reaction of the third party involved in this portrait of Beethoven—the recipient of Bettina's letter, Goethe. His answer of 6 June 1810 is replete with the caution denied barnstorming youth: "Your letter, heartily beloved child, reached me at a happy time. You have been at great pains to picture for me a great and beautiful nature in its achievements and its strivings, its needs and the superabundance of its gifts. It has given me great pleasure to accept this picture of a truly great spirit. Without desiring at all to classify it, it yet requires a psychological feat to extract the sum of agreement; but I feel no desire to contradict what I can grasp of your hurried explosion, I should prefer for the present to admit an agreement between my nature and that which is recognizable in those manifold utterances."[165]

Even without Schindler's bangings on the alarm gong, the tintinnabulation of Goethe's peal of reason should serve to warn truth seekers not to accept Bettina's Beethoven verbatim. But, tempting as it is to enter and take sides in the arena of authenticity, this is not the goal of the itinerary we have set for ourselves in this book. We are pursuing facts, yes, but facts as transmuted by their individual reporters into fable. *Mundus vult decipi.* The mythmaking process, like the world, *wants* to be deceived—or at the very least enchanted. And this the "child" High Priestess Bettina accomplished when she delivered to the Apollo of Weimar the gist of her encounter with the Dionysus of Vienna. Her message was strikingly similar to E.T.A. Hoffmann's: Beethoven was the first musician to feel an "eternal hunger"; Beethoven's music was the first to express "something eternally infinite." In other words, Beethoven was the first Romantic composer.

The ennoblement of their profession felt by the Paris Conservatoire orchestra and expressed to Schindler in 1841 was but one of the fruits of the rich harvest that Beethoven and Beethoven mythographers had—together—sown. Many of these fruits were collected and displayed in Schindler's revised and final edition of his Beethoven *Biographie* in 1860,[166] only to be fumigated, rinsed, and redisplayed in Thayer's biographical installments of the 1860s and 1870s. But in the meantime other seeds for that harvest had been planted by the musical interpreters of Beethoven, and it is to these musicians we now turn for the Romantic century's evolution of the Beethoven myth.

CHAPTER THREE
BEETHOVEN
DEAD: SHAPING
THE
POSTHUMOUS
PORTRAIT

Chapter Four

BEETHOVEN INTERPRETED: THE MUSICIAN'S MUSICIAN

Part 1: *Haydn to Chopin*

An oft-repeated and reasonably reliable account has it that if Papa Haydn had had his way with history, Beethoven would have designated his indebtedness in his early compositions—at least in the first two trios of opus 1—to Haydn. Ferdinand Ries is the source for this bit of believable lore: "It was Haydn's wish that Beethoven place on his earlier works: 'Pupil of Haydn.' This Beethoven refused to do because, as he said, though he had taken a few lessons from Haydn, he never had learned anything from him."[1] The iconography of mythmaking certainly does not portray Beethoven as a Haydn pupil. A contemporary picture shows the two musicians together, but well over two hundred other people are also in the crowded scene painted by the miniaturist Balthasar Wigand (1770–1846) on a box cover to commemorate Salieri's special concert of 27 March 1808 featuring *The Creation*, and honoring the elderly Haydn on his impending seventy-sixth birthday. Salieri conducted and the younger musicians of Vienna, including Beethoven and Hummel, lined up to pay tribute to the frail septuagenarian who had been carried into the Old University hall in a special armchair.[2] Close scrutiny of the antlike procession of well-wishers converging upon the seated Haydn does not reveal to perfect satisfaction which of the figures might be the definitive Beethoven. It is rather the defiant Beethoven—vis-à-vis Haydn—that tradition has endorsed, if not illustrated, in visual form.

Quite different is the case for pictorial couplings of Beethoven and Mozart—the other great Austrian composer with whom Beethoven is supposed to have had a few lessons. Several anonymous nineteenth-century illustrators responded to the same legendary event: the moment when young Beethoven extemporized on a theme for an approving and astonished Mozart in the presence of Viennese society (Fig. 56):

Beethoven, who as a youth of great promise came to Vienna in the spring of 1787 . . . was taken to Mozart and at that musician's request played something for him which he, taking it for granted that it was a show-piece prepared for the occasion, praised in a rather cool manner. Beethoven, observing this, begged Mozart to give him a theme for improvisation. He always played admirably when excited and now he was inspired, too, by the presence of the master whom he reverenced greatly; he played in such a style that Mozart, whose attention and interest grew more and more, finally went silently to some friends who were sitting in an adjoining room, and said, vivaciously, "Keep your eyes on him; some day he will give the world something to talk about."[3]

Another anonymous illustration of the improvisation event[4] shows an oblivious Beethoven playing a small pipe organ to the left while, from the right, a conspiratorial Mozart—his finger to his lips—tiptoes silently into the room, beckoning and encouraging several listeners to come closer. Both depictions have in common the pronounced contrast between an elegant, bewigged, worldly Mozart and a disheveled, totally engrossed young Beethoven. Both also present visual confirmation of the invisible boundary lines being drawn up by opposing Mozart and Beethoven camps of the "involuntary" versus the "willed" genius—a concept that fascinated scores of nineteenth-century thinkers and stimulated the German philosopher Wilhelm Dilthey's (1833–1911) formulation (1898)[5] of three essential types discernible in the history of thought. Encompassing philosophical and psychological world attitudes, these types of thought could be reduced, according to Dilthey, to (1) positivism (realism), with the intellect in ascendancy (Hobbes and Stendhal fit into this category, for example); (2) objective idealism, with feeling in dominance (Spinoza and Goethe); and (3) dualistic idealism, with the will predominant (Fichte and Schiller). Dilthey's types—drawn from philosophy and literature—were superimposed upon the arenas of music and art by Herman Nohl (1908)[6] with the following interesting if somewhat pat results: Berlioz and Velazquez fit into type one, Schubert and Rembrandt into type two, and Beethoven and Michelangelo (already mentioned in tandem by Stendhal, it will be recalled) into type three—that genus in which neither intellect nor feeling but will reigns supreme, and the spirit functions independently of nature. How handsomely these two great solitaries— Beethoven with his deafness and pock marks, Michelangelo with his broken nose and poor health—locked into this scheme in which a mother lode of genius, imbedded deep within the self, was mined through tremendous mental effort and sheer force of will. And how different, or so it seemed to the German schematizers of human genius, these "willed" qualities of Beethoven and Michelangelo appeared alongside the perpetual cascades of Mozart's uninhibited, natural gifts.

Turning from the iconography of Beethoven rejecting or astounding his two great predecessors, Haydn and Mozart, to examples of his own impact upon other musicians brings us to the portals of a realm where solid fact intertwines with fantasy and fiction. The dimensions of this kingdom in which the musicians' musician—Beethoven—was venerated and interpreted stretched across nineteenth-century Europe. Temporally its inhabitants included those coevals who actually had contact with Beethoven in life, like Rossini and Spohr, and extended to those who came after but addressed themselves to "possessing" Beethoven for their age, like Berlioz and Wagner.

The multiple and changing image of Beethoven nourished in this rarified terrain of fellow musicians centered, understandably, upon the interpretation and meaning of Beethoven's work. Four eminent pianists—Czerny, Hummel, Ries, and Moscheles—who could all claim authentic and close acquaintance with Beethoven's keyboard style, carried four separate gospels to the faithful on how Beethoven should be played. Carl Czerny (Fig. 57), for example, produced a thesis "on the correct performance of all Beethoven's works for piano solo" (*Klavier-schule*), which the ever vigilant Schindler gleefully glossed with deft jabs of his editorial bistoury. Rather eloquently, he considered what was good about Czerny and what, he argued very persuasively, was severely misleading about Czerny "the virtuoso-pedagogue" and his consequent attempts to "virtuositize" Beethoven's compositions.[7] The faithful amanuensis lamented what he called the "influence on Beethoven's music" of both Czerny and Ries since "each of them wished to shine as a composer in his right" and each was of the opinion that Beethoven's "music could be improved by changing it."[8] Sweeping the predatory specters of Czerny and Ries into the same net, Schindler staunchly continued: "It is no small matter when two talented, important pianists, both of whom lived in more or less direct contact with the composer, conceive themselves as correctors of his eternal monuments rather than conforming with the most conscientious exactitude to what he had written and, like faithful apostles, witnessing to the world in a practical way what he had taught them."[9]

We are treated to a dizzying double dose of Schindler's own conservatism in relation to Romanticism and also to the rococo as he calls upon the state of affairs in the visual arts to help clarify the error into which Czerny and Ries had fallen by departing from the classical models in order to adhere to the new piano style: "Both followed much the same course as the plastic arts in France from the time of Louis XIV until the middle of the eighteenth century: the further they got away from the study of antiquity and the more they strove merely for external effect, the more deeply they denigrated into cheap affectations and theatrical excesses, until Jacques-Louis David finally led them back to antiquity."[10]

Schindler published this extraordinary summary of French painting in *1860*! Of the two greatest exponents of French Romanticism, Géricault had been dead for thirty-six years and Delacroix had only three more to live. That Watteau's tenderness, Boucher's naughty eroticism, and Fragonard's light-hearted sentimentality might not have appealed to the somber German visitor to a Paris of the 1840s is understandable, but that David represented the correct quiddity, the ne plus ultra of French art, means that Schindler's thick neoclassical sun shades had done a remarkably thorough job of keeping out the pervasive ultraviolet rays of Romanticism.

Schindler's argument with the incipiently Romantic or "modern trend in piano performance" was, he said, that of Beethoven's as well: the new manner abandoned the sustained style, encouraged bravura passages, trills, octave doublings, an indiscriminate use of the pedal, and—worst of all— distracting physical dramatics on the part of the performer. When we recall the description of Beethoven's almost motionless demeanor at the keyboard while extemporizing upon his *Eroica* for two hours for the painter Mähler, and when we read Schindler's repeated assertions that Beethoven's hands and the upper portion of his body were held quiet while he played, we can understand the genuineness of Schindler's distress over the false image of the composer being projected throughout Europe and abroad. In his agitated if exaggerated words: "Yet, irony of fate! the creator of so many noble works in all the musical media, with his vigorous opposition to all bodily motion at the piano, had to be content to see a herald of this ['modern'] style take an interest in his piano music and hold off for a few years its total disappearance from the concert repertoire. It was Carl Czerny whose contribution must be proclaimed aloud, even for the very piano style that the great master deplored."[11]

Always the master of the backhanded compliment, Schindler appropriately saved his greatest indignation at the distortion of Beethoven's pianistic image for the Romantic century's greatest piano virtuoso: "Anyone who has seen Herr Franz Liszt play the piano has an accurate picture of the mannerisms he learned from his teacher Czerny: hands always in the air, sometimes even flung above the head, the keys struck from a height of two feet above the keyboard, and so forth."[12]

We shall return to Liszt's gymnastic framing of his pyrotechnical presentation of Beethoven, but chronology beckons us back to the images of Beethoven emblazoned on the memories of the two fellow musicians who visited him on his deathbed and who participated in his funeral as pallbearer and torchbearer respectively, Hummel and Schubert.

The Hungarian composer and pianist Johann Nepomuk Hummel (1778–1837) (Fig. 58) was only eight years younger than Beethoven and like him a pupil of Mozart, Haydn, Johann Georg Albrechtsberger (1736–1809), and Salieri. He was considered Beethoven's rival in extemporizing and in fact a certain coolness had developed between them since their first meeting when Hummel was nine and Beethoven seventeen. But when news of Beethoven's mortal illness reached Hummel in Weimar, where he held a court post and was friendly with Goethe, any feelings of enmity were banished and early in March 1827 Hummel rushed back to Vienna to see the dying man. He brought with him his wife, Elizabeth, whom Beethoven had known as a young girl, and a talented fifteen-year-old pupil, Ferdinand Hiller. Hiller's published reminiscences of the four visits made to Beethoven's deathbed with Hummel[13] provided the touching portrait of a reconciliation between Beethoven and his old friend[14] and recorded a thought-provoking outburst from the dying man that later biographers would weave into their Beethoven imagery: the composer's expression of remorse at never having married. Here are the pertinent lines from Hiller's sympathetic account of the four visits to the progressively deteriorating invalid:

First Visit (8 March). "Emaciated by long and severe illness he seemed to me, when he arose, of tall stature; he was unshaven, his thick, half-gray hair fell in disorder over his temples. The expression of his features heightened when he caught sight of Hummel, and he seemed to be extraordinarily glad to meet him. The two men embraced each other most cordially. . . . Beethoven asked about Goethe's health with extraordinary solicitude and we were able to make the best of reports. . . . Concerning his own state, poor Beethoven complained much. 'Here I have been lying for four months,' he cried out, 'one must at last lose patience!'"

Second Visit (13 March). "We found his condition to be materially worse. He lay in bed, seemed to suffer great pains, and at intervals groaned deeply despite the fact that he spoke much and animatedly. Now he seemed to take it much to heart that he had not married. Already at our first visit he had joked about it with Hummel, whose wife he had known as a young and beautiful maiden. 'You are a lucky man,' he said to him now smilingly, 'you have a wife who takes care of you, who is in love with you—but poor me!' and he sighed heavily. He also begged Hummel to bring his wife to see him. . . . "

Third Visit (20 March). "When we stood again at his bedside . . . he was very weak and spoke only in faint and disconnected phrases. 'I shall, no doubt, soon be going above,' he whispered after our first greeting. Similar remarks recurred frequently. In the intervals, however, he spoke of projects and hopes which were destined not to be realized. . . . he would visit Madame Hummel (she had come along with her husband) and go to I do not know how many places. . . . His eyes, which were still lively when we saw him last, dropped and closed to-day and it was difficult from time to time for him to raise himself."

Fourth Visit (23 March). "Hopeless was the picture presented by the extraordinary man when we sought him again on March 23rd. It was to be the last time. He lay, weak and miserable, sighing deeply at intervals. Not a word fell from his lips; sweat stood upon his forehead. His handkerchief not being conveniently at hand, Hummel's wife took her fine cambric handkerchief and dried his face several times. Never shall I forget the grateful glance with which his broken eye looked upon her."[15]

Hummel's visits to his moribund friend were paralleled by another service that contributed enormously to the musical public's knowledge of Beethoven's work. For many decades, long before his instrumental music became the common fare of symphony orchestras, Beethoven's symphonies were made widely available and known through Hummel's arrangements for piano duets. The image of the symphonic Beethoven was kept alive by a former "rival" whose own image was destined to fade from public memory.

FRANZ SCHUBERT

The "indefatigable song composer" (as the Leipzig *Allgemeine musikalische Zeitung* called him in 1827) Franz Schubert's (1797–1828) tremendous admiration for Beethoven and his own untimely death at the age of thirty-one, just twenty months after that of his idol's, whetted public interest in any and all aspects of what might be called Schubert's Beethoven.[16] The musical impact of Beethoven upon the mature Schubert may be perceived in the symphonies and string quartets; but that Schubert's appreciation for Beethoven's innovations needed time to develop is amusingly evident from a passionate diary entry of 16 June 1816, written when the nineteen-year-old Franz was still very much within the pale of his teacher Salieri:

Herr Salieri celebrated his jubilee yesterday, having been fifty years in Vienna and nearly as long in the imperial service; he was awarded a gold medal by His Majesty and invited many of his pupils, male and female. . . . It must be beautiful and refreshing for an artist to see all his pupils, gathered around him, each one striving to give of his best for his jubilee, and to hear in all these compositions the expression of pure nature, free from all the eccentricity that is common among most composers nowadays, and is due almost wholly to one of our greatest German artists; that eccentricity which joins and confuses the tragic and the comic, the agreeable with the repulsive, heroism with howlings and the holiest with harlequinades, without distinction, so as to goad people to madness instead of dissolving them in love, to incite them to laughter instead of lifting them up to God.[17]

This fascinating, opinionated portrait by young Schubert of a Beethoven bent on bizarre effects smacks of the same sort of youthful conservatism we have observed in another "apprentice artist"—Weber. And, as with Weber, Schubert's image of Beethoven changed very much for the better with time. By April 1822 in fact Schubert made his newfound admiration public by dedicating his opus 10— the Variations in E Minor for Piano Duet—to Beethoven. The title page features the name Ludwig van Beethoven in large print, surrounded by a decorative garland below which are the words: "dedicated by his Worshipper and Admirer Franz Schubert."[18]

Did Beethoven know of this dedication? Schindler tells us he did, and even though the veracity of his account has been questioned, it is worth reading because it furnished the mythmaking process with an enthralling subject to ponder: the image of two disparate musicians face to face:

> It went badly with Franz Schubert when in 1822 he brought to the master the variations for four hands that he had dedicated to him. The shy young artist, lost for words, found himself in a very uncomfortable situation, despite Diabelli's bringing him, introducing him, and expressing for him his sentiments for the master. The courage that had stayed with him right to the master's house abandoned him at the sight of the monarch of the arts. And when Beethoven expressed his wish that Schubert himself write down the answers to his questions, Schubert's hand was paralysed as if held in a vice. Beethoven went through the manuscript that had been brought to him and came upon an error in harmony. He pointed it out to the young man in a kindly manner, adding that it was no deadly sin. But Schubert, perhaps as a consequence of this encouraging remark, lost his composure entirely. Once out in the street again, he was able to pull himself together and scolded himself roundly. But he never regained the courage to present himself to the master again.[19]

Schindler's story, as usual, puts his master in favorable lighting, bathing him this time in the golden glow of benign harmony instructor. Schubert's version of the event, as told to his good friend Josef Hüttenbrenner (Anselm's younger brother), was laconically different: he did take the four-hand variations to Beethoven's house, Beethoven was out, so he left them with a servant. Only later Schubert heard, with great happiness, that Beethoven not only had liked the variations but had been playing them through "frequently and gladly" with his nephew, Karl.[20]

To mythmaking's pressing questions—*did* Beethoven and Schubert ever meet? *did* they converse?—a mythmaking answer was thoughtfully provided (fabricated, some think[21]) by that reluctant decliner of a Beethoven biography, Rochlitz. In his letter to Härtel of 9 July 1822 describing how he at last had met Beethoven in the flesh, Rochlitz wrote: "Some two weeks later [after his first, somewhat disappointing encounter with Beethoven] I was about to go to dinner when I met the young composer Franz Schubert, an enthusiastic admirer of Beethoven. The latter had spoken to Schubert concerning me. 'If you wish to see him in a more natural and jovial mood,' said Schubert, 'then go and eat your dinner this very minute at the inn where he has just gone for the same purpose.' He took me with him."[22]

The continuation of Rochlitz's narrative makes no further reference to Schubert and the implication is that Rochlitz entered the inn alone, where he was able to observe Beethoven in a lively "monologue" with those about him and later, at Beethoven's invitation, to converse privately with him in a little side room. Schubert's knowledge of Beethoven, then, included a familiarity with his daily routine but, consonant with his extreme modesty, not the temerity to insinuate himself into it. There is some proof that Beethoven was kept aware of Schubert's activities. Karl reported to his uncle in the conversation book for August 1823 as follows: "They greatly praise Schubert, but it is said that he hides himself."[23]

Neither composer was able to hide himself from a certain persistent portrayer of images whom we have already met, the Prague-born Joseph Teltscher. A year before his grim task of sketching Beethoven on his deathbed (Figs. 34 and 35),

Teltscher, one of the inner circle of "Schubertians," completed a realistic lithographic portrait of his friend Schubert—stocky, plain, and complete with glasses, just as the world knew him (Fig. 59).[24] Small wonder that this young man of unprepossessing appearance and painfully shy disposition did not take advantage of mutual friends to press himself into the presence of the deaf tone master. Better to watch the aging "titan" from afar, on his daily walks or when he took his meals at public inns like the one to which he had conducted Rochlitz. But Schubert never missed a performance of Beethoven's music; he was avid, even fanatical, about hearing the older composer's works. In his early youth, when still seeking his musical metier, Schubert is supposed to have said: "I believe that something could become of me, but who can do anything after Beethoven?"[25] How similar to the lamentations voiced by those later sixteenth-century artists born in the shadow of Michelangelo, and yet mannerism was born. Beethoven had certainly not neglected the art of song writing, but with Schubert the German Lied—or more properly the Art Song—came into its own. Songs poured forth from Schubert's bottomless reservoir of musical inspiration; in a career less than half as long as Beethoven's, Schubert set over six hundred texts to music, an extraordinary oeuvre count for any composer. Two favorite authors whom he set to music— Schiller and Shakespeare—were compared by Schubert to the two musical gods he worshiped: Schiller to Mozart, Shakespeare to Beethoven. Again we have the "polarities" so appealing to the nineteenth-century Romantic mind: the rule perfecters and the rule breakers. A remark characterizing Schubert's own genre of genius was picked up by later writers on music and used to explain and differentiate the two kinds of genius represented, supposedly, by Mozart and Schubert on the one hand, and Beethoven on the other. The remark was purportedly made by the Pizarro of the 1814 revival of *Fidelio*, Johann Michael Vogl (1768–1840), distinguished erstwhile member of the Vienna Hoftheater who tirelessly sang so many of his young friend's songs to Viennese audiences at private and public performances. "Schubert was in a somnambulistic state whenever he wrote music. This explains how, in this visionary condition, the scarcely educated boy could see into the secrets of life, have the emotions, the knowledge."[26] Vogl contrasted Schubert's "truly divine inspirations" and "utterances of a musical clairvoyance"[27] with the laborious method of those who compose "through willpower, effort, reflection, knowledge,"[28] churning up the image of Beethoven as Schubert's opposite—suffering and sweating as he slowly hammered out resistant musical form on the anvil of will.

If we choose to believe Schindler—and most mythologizers chose to—Beethoven was introduced to Schubert's Lieder on his deathbed. Schindler stars as the thoughtful intermediary in an account written by none other than himself:

> As the illness to which Beethoven finally succumbed after four months of suffering from the beginning made his ordinary mental activity impossible, a diversion had to be thought of which would fit his mind and inclinations. And so it came about that I placed before him a collection of Schubert's songs, about sixty in number, among them many which were then still in manuscript. . . . The great master, who before then had not known five songs of Schubert's, was amazed at their number and refused to believe that up to that time (February, 1827) he had already composed over 500 of them. But if he was astonished at the number he was filled with the highest admiration as soon as he discovered their contents. . . . With joyous enthusiasm he cried out repeatedly: "Truly a divine spark dwells in Schubert."[29]

That this—Beethoven's image of Schubert—was known to Schubert appears to have been the case. Not only would Schindler have been pleased to convey the compliment to Schubert, to whom, after Beethoven's death, he passed on several Rellstab poems that had been in Beethoven's possession, but a separate report of Beethoven's "divine spark" praise was given by Anselm Hüttenbrenner[30]—Schubert's intimate friend and the man present by chance, we recall, at Beethoven's death. Indeed it was Hüttenbrenner who seems to have been responsible for adding a new, poignantly mortal dimension to Schubert's idolizing image of Beethoven: "About eight days before Beethoven's death Prof. Schindler, Schubert and I visited the sick man. Schindler announced us two and asked Beethoven whom he would see first. He said: 'Let Schubert come first!' "[31] And, according to legend, a second visit by the grieving Schubert was made to Beethoven's bedside in the company of Josef Hüttenbrenner and Joseph Teltscher, but by this time the dying man could only fix his eyes on them, making gestures none could interpret.[32]

It is fact that Schubert was one of the thirty-eight torchbearers at Beethoven's funeral on 29 March 1827; but what happened immediately afterwards comes to us in two conflicting versions. The diary entry for that date of one of Schubert's drinking companions who had also attended the burial ceremony at the Währinger Cemetery reads: "I went to the 'Castle of Eisenstadt' where I remained with Schober, Schubert and Schwind until almost 1 a.m. Needless to say, we talked of nothing but Beethoven, his works and the well-merited honours paid to his memory today."[33] But "tradition"—that invigorating ally of the mythmaking process—has it that Schubert went to a different inn, the Mehlgrube, with his two fellow composer friends Franz Lachner (1803–1890) and Benedikt Randhartinger (1802–1893), who had also been torchbearers at Beethoven's funeral. At the Mehlgrube Schubert is supposed to have proposed two toasts, the first to Beethoven's memory, and the second to whomever of the trio fate would decree next to follow Beethoven into the grave.[34] Mythopoesis chose the second version. Franz Schubert died on 19 November 1828 from an advanced case of syphilis (legend called it abdominal typhus).

His deathbed delirium, during which he spoke Beethoven's name, was interpreted by his brother in a touching letter to their father to mean that he wished to be buried in the same cemetery as Beethoven:

Most cherished Father,
    Very many are expressing the wish that the body of our good Franz should be buried in the Währing churchyard. Among those many am I too, believing myself to be induced thereto by Franz himself. For on the evening before his death, though only half conscious, he still said to me: "I implore you to transfer me to my room, not to leave me here, in this corner under the earth; do I then deserve no place above the earth?" I answered him: "Dear Franz, rest assured, believe your brother Ferdinand . . . you are in the room in which you have always been so far, and lie in your bed!"—And Franz said: "No, it is not true: Beethoven does not lie here."—Could this be anything but an indication of his inmost wish to repose by the side of Beethoven, whom he so greatly revered?!
    Your afflicted son   Ferdinand.[35]

No one doubted this deathbed "wish"—a consoling one for the survivors—and arrangements were immediately made to bury Schubert in the new Währinger Cemetery; it was even possible to place him just "three graves distant from Beethoven's."[36] Henceforth, for pilgrims to Vienna the physical image of Beethoven's burial place would be associated with that of Schubert's as well, and the link was strengthened in later years when, in 1888, the remains of both Beethoven and Schubert were transferred to graves of honor in the Pantheon of Musicians at Vienna's great Central Cemetery, where they were buried side by side.

An ingenuous visual pairing of the two composers' effigies, united in death by the proximity of their graves (Fig. 60), was contributed to the iconography of mythmaking by a close friend of Schubert, the Vienna-born artist Moritz von Schwind (1804–1871)—one of the drinking companions referred to in the first of the two accounts concerning Schubert's actions right after Beethoven's funeral. The prolific Schwind, whose career after 1827 took him to Munich, released his German Romantic love of mythology, opera, and fairy tales from an apparently inexhaustible cornucopia of richly imagined vignettes drawn with a graphic fluidity that parallels the lyricism of Schubert's musical line. He was a good friend of Grillparzer's as well and his lively cycle of drawings illustrating Mozart's *The Marriage of Figaro* had been brought to Beethoven on his deathbed as a welcome distraction.[37] A music worshiper all his life, Schwind paid homage to the two bygone musical giants of his Vienna days when, in 1862, he created the *Lachner Roll*—a humorous series of forty watercolors narrating high and low points in the life of his friend Franz Lachner (Schubert's drinking companion and fellow composer in the second version of post-Beethoven funeral events). Like Schwind, Lachner had had to leave Vienna in order to further his career. Our illustration (Fig. 60)—episode twenty-three from the *Lachner Roll*—shows a sad moment in Lachner's life: his formal farewell to Vienna, made in the Währinger Cemetery before the graves of Beethoven and Schubert. In a mixture of fact and fantasy, Schwind shows the two grave monuments set, as they were in actuality, against the containing eastern wall; the shapes of the two monuments however (pyramidal "obelisk" for Beethoven, rectangular "temple" for Schubert) have been drastically redesigned into matching slabs, rounded at the top, and punctured with niches for housing life-size portrait busts. The right-hand marker has the letters F. SCHUBERT carved under a friendly looking bust (Schwind's swift approximation of the bronze bust of Schubert by Josef Alois Dialer, placed in the niche between two columns in 1829), but Lachner stands with his hat doffed and his left leg tenderly planted on the adjacent grave—Beethoven's—at the head of which a stern, square-featured countenance surrounded by billowing locks of hair looks down steadfastly upon the meditating pilgrim. This bust was carved out of Schwind's generous imagination. Beethoven's actual monument had no effigy of the composer affixed to it, only a symbolic medallion above a lyre.

Beethoven appears three more times in the *Lachner Roll*: in the very first episode as the tempestuous-looking composer of the *Eroica* in the year of Lachner's birth (a good omen for Lachner); in episode four as an approving spirit supervising Lachner's musical education along with the ghosts of Haydn and Mozart; and in episode fifteen—still broad-nosed and wild-haired—as a performer playing four-handed piano with Lachner. Schubert also appears three more times: serenading by night with Vogl and Schwind (episode seventeen), drinking new wine at Grinzing with Lachner (episode twenty-one), and applauding in the audience at Lachner's Vienna farewell concert (episode twenty-two). This fleeting double quartet of appearances in the *Lachner Roll* almost suggests that Schwind, in his later years, was trying to compensate for not ever having formally portrayed either of his famous contemporaries when they were alive.[38]

Schwind's lionizing depiction of Beethoven in the *Lachner Roll* reached only a very small and intimate circle, but ten years earlier, in 1852, the artist had proclaimed his allegiance to the hallowed Beethoven Way (both he and Lachner were bitterly to oppose Wagner and the "music of the future" all their lives) by painting an almost six-foot-high (5' 10" × 3' 4") four-part "altarpiece" titled simply *The Symphony* and illustrating "loosely" Beethoven's 1808 Fantasia for piano, chorus, and orchestra, op. 80. The painted ensemble, comprising "carved" borders, trompe-l'oeil "statues" (Saint Cecilia and Venus), grisaille bas-relief, medallions, framed and open scenes spread across four registers (the four times of day), is truly a fantasia of Schwind's own making and has more to do with the unfolding love story sparked by the sound of Beethoven than with Beethoven's music. The scenes of encounter, courtship, and wedding trip float above in predictable sonata form, but our thematic attention is attracted by the many-figured predella scene below (Fig. 61) in which Beethoven's music is being performed by real-life musicians under the benign marmorean gaze of Beethoven himself. The laurel-wreathed and garlanded Beethoven bust is set high on a pedestal inside a little four-columned temple. Directly below it stands the director of the orchestra, Franz Lachner. The solo pianist ties us closer to Beethoven for she is Maximiliane Brentano (1802–1861), daughter of Antonia (the "Immortal Beloved"?) Brentano and recipient of Beethoven's dedication of his Piano Sonata in E Major, op. 109. Sitting at her side is her attentive page-turner, Schwind himself. To the far left of the mixed chorus, towards which the diagonal line of the flute directs our attention, a trio of well-known figures from Vienna's past can be identified: standing in profile and towering over the others is the singer Michael Vogl; next to him is Schubert, who concentrates on the music through his spectacles; and next to Schubert, his head supported on the palm of his left hand, is Grillparzer, lost in a reverie. A compositional ritornello directs our view back to the love theme as, following the direction of the gaze of the tall young man standing near the piano to the right, we discover the object of his riveted attention—the graceful singer who rises to perform her solo on the left (and the object of Schwind's own wistful affection, Caroline Hetzenecker, principal singer at the Munich Opera). This is Schubert's and Schwind's Beethoven, then, incarnate in the power of music to stir the emotions and to inspire love.

LOUIS SPOHR

One of the important transmitters of the musical image of Beethoven through performances of his works was a violin virtuoso and conductor who introduced the six string quartets of op. 18 at Berlin and Leipzig as early as 1805. We have met Louis Spohr before—in his double-stopped description of Beethoven as "a bit rough, not to say uncouth" and as he intrepidly crossed social barriers with his wife in London. He was an accomplished amateur painter (Fig. 62)[39] as well as the author of a manual on the art of violin playing (*Violin School*, 1831) still in use today. But it was not until the appearance of his *Autobiography*, published posthumously in 1860 and translated into English five years later, that Spohr's secret image of Beethoven emerged—that same Beethoven whose *Missa Solemnis* and Ninth Symphony he had conducted faultlessly (according to Schindler[40]) at the Bonn Beethoven Festival of 1845. The great violinist's memoirs revealed far more, ultimately, about Spohr than about Beethoven:

> No diminution of Beethoven's creative powers was as yet noticeable. But from that time onward [after 1813], as his increasing deafness made it impossible for him to hear any music at all, it was inevitable that this should adversely affect

his fantasy. His constant striving to be original and to break new paths was no longer subject to aural control. Is it any wonder that his works became steadily less coherent and less intelligible? There are those, to be sure, who flatter themselves that they understand these late works, and in their enthusiasm, go so far as to label them masterpieces. I am not among them, and confess freely that I have never been able to develop a taste for the later Beethoven. I include among these even the much admired Ninth Symphony, whose first three movements, despite flashes of genius, strike me as inferior to any of the movements of the preceding eight symphonies [Spohr also composed nine symphonies], and whose fourth movement I consider so monstrous and tasteless and, in its representation of Schiller's Ode, so trivial that I cannot imagine its having been written by a man of Beethoven's genius.[41]

Such pronounced and passionately expressed musical conservatism from the mouth of a highly respected interpreter of Beethoven comes as a shock. (Schindler, who was still alive when the memoir was published, must have issued primal screams if he read it.) Spohr might have been surprised to learn that Beethoven, on his side, considered the violinist's music "too rich in dissonances."[42] The difficulty of adjusting to Beethoven's Ninth, even for the well-disposed listener, and yet recognition of the ineluctable force of its composer—this paradox, which was obviously Spohr's situation, was summed up succinctly by Grillparzer in four jovial lines of 1843:

Whether I like it or no,	Ob's mir gefällt, ob nicht gefällt,
His fame remains whole and well,	Sein Ruhm bleibt ganz und heil,
For every *Faust*, as we know,	Denn jeder Faust, es weiss die Welt,
Has its Part Two to tell.	Hat seinen zweiten Teil.[43]

Nevertheless, given Spohr's reactionary attitude towards Beethoven's later music, it is all the more astonishing to observe him devoting herculean energy to bringing out the early operas of Schwind's and Lachner's bugaboo, Wagner (*The Flying Dutchman*, Kassel, 1842, and *Tannhäuser*, Kassel, 1853). This he did in spite of finding in Wagner's new music "some things which are ugly and excruciating to the ear."[44]

In the strange tolerance of this conservative of conservatives who was willing to conduct a "choral" symphony he found incomprehensible and to introduce an opera that contained passages of "frightful" music, there lies an important, unspoken premise. Both Beethoven and Wagner were German. Spohr, in his autobiography, is quintessentially chauvinist, solemnly conscious on his concert tours to Russia, England, France, and Italy that he was bringing the message of German musical excellence to the indigenous audiences of lesser climes. And Spohr, for all his patronizing prejudices, was correct: musically, the first half of the nineteenth century was to bear the impress of a Germanic stamp. Romanticism, in music, belonged to Germany. The tradition, craft, and dynamism of Haydn, Mozart, and Beethoven were reverently carried aloft as banners by Spohr. In a century when virtuosos rather than composers dominated the musical scene, Louis Spohr's public performances of Beethoven—whatever his private reservations—drew puissant attention to the image of Beethoven as titan of the age. In his championing of German music Spohr did effectively fulfill the modest entreaty penned to him by Beethoven in his autograph album: "Dear Spohr, wherever you go, and wherever you encounter true art and true artists, please remember me, your friend, Ludwig van Beethoven."[45]

For much of his life Spohr had the distinction, or mortification, of being called Germany's greatest violinist and a virtuoso second in the world only to Paganini. This undisputed, Genoa-born king of the instrument with uniquely Italian flamboyance publicly declared his worship for the musicians' musician in every major city of Europe. Niccolò Paganini's (1782–1840) homage often took the concrete and shrewd form of interspersing Beethoven overtures or movements from the Beethoven symphonies with his own music in his successful, ambitious concert programs in Europe and England. The idea of a trip to the home of his musical idol had long been on Paganini's mind. Prince Metternich, whose violin Paganini had played in Rome in 1819, had urged him to come to Vienna and the invitation had not been forgotten. For many years Paganini had also flirted with asking the composer of the *Pastoral* Symphony to write a special "tempesta" for him, upon which he would play a series of variations. But death had cheated him of the chance to petition Beethoven (who would surely have declined such a project): the Italian musician arrived in Vienna on 16 March 1828, one year too late. The remembrance of this missed opportunity may have partly caused the unchecked tears to flow down Paganini's cheeks as he sat, rigid and immobile, through an outdoor performance of Beethoven's Seventh Symphony at Vienna's Augarten. "È morto," was the only explanation he offered to his surprised companion. Such emotional display was "surely one of the highest and most sincerely felt signs of homage the memory of Beethoven ever received," triumphantly concluded the press account of this little scene.[46]

Paganini's flair for self-dramatization received curious and important impetus during his Vienna sojourn (March–August) when he learned that, like him, his idol had had a harsh father whose vaulting ambition for the musical talents of his son had cast a tyrannical shadow over his childhood. Previous to being in possession of such heartrending and myth-inspiring information Paganini had been extremely reticent about his own youth. In an autobiographical sketch written on 28 February 1828 at the request of a friend just before leaving Milan for Austria, Paganini made only the briefest of references to his father, commenting that he was a commercial broker who taught him mandolin playing and the rudiments of the violin and whose "ear was bad though he was passionately fond of music."[47] But immediately after his Vienna sojourn (Schlosser's life of Beethoven had been out for almost a year), while concertizing for impatient audiences in Prague who had had to wait for the maestro to convalesce from dental surgery and who, in their predilection for snubbing whatever Vienna applauded, were proving unreceptive, Paganini fathered a second autobiographical sketch. The new account was no longer limited to the G-string. Paganini's idea was to sway public opinion in his favor and to put an end to the harmful rumors bordering on slander that were being gleefully reported by the Prague press. The expanded vita was left with his good friend and host the writer Julius Schottky, who affixed it as one piece of a "mosaic" (his word) portrait of Paganini, which he published in 1830. This time, Beethovenian harmonics were clearly audible in Paganini's amplified new rendition of the strains of his early years—a childhood remarkably like (Paganini's image of) Beethoven's childhood:

> My father was a not very well-to-do tradesman and was by no means without musical talent which, however, was in no way comparable to his love of music. He soon recognized my natural talent and I have him to thank for teaching me

the rudiments of the art. His principal passion kept him at home a great deal, trying by certain calculations and combinations to figure out lottery numbers from which he hoped to reap considerable gain [contemporary readers would recall that the reputed principal passion of Beethoven's father—alcohol—frequently kept him at home also]. He therefore pondered over the matter a great deal and would not let me leave him, so that I had the violin in my hand from morn till night. It would be hard to conceive of a stricter father. If he didn't think I was industrious enough, he compelled me to redouble my efforts by making me go without food so that I had to endure a great deal physically and my health began to give way.[48]

When the weird real-life counterpart to E.T.A. Hoffmann's demonic violinist appeared in Beethoven's Vienna at his first concert (29 March 1828), a critic for the *Wiener Theaterzeitung* watching him play made the proper association: "His expression seemed to mirror an inner conflict; the most unspeakable pain, the most ardent longing, the cruelest jest, even the most cutting scorn became discernible, all inevitably reminiscent of Hoffmann's Kreisler."[49] Conflict, pain, longing, jest, scorn—all these labels were used at various earlier times to describe the gamut of Beethoven's musical conduct at the piano, words now used to designate the oscillating moods conjured up by this new musical apparition, this "infernal-divine fiddler,"[50] whose homage to Beethoven was incorporated into the very program, the opening number of which had been the overture to *Fidelio*. Just as Lyser was to unite in his fantasy sketch the figures of Beethoven, Paganini, and Hoffmann, gazed at by his own self-portrait (see Fig. 44), so the *Theaterzeitung* critic of this premier appearance of Paganini in Vienna (a concert attended incidentally by Schubert) seemed to invoke this "Ghost Trio" of Romanticism to share the stage in phantasmagorical juxtaposition.

FELIX MENDELSSOHN

Ten years later in a very different tonal context—Paris—Paganini would link his name with that of Beethoven to spell out a new and astonishing chord, a triad in which the major third would be the thirty-five-year-old Berlioz. But before we peruse French translators of Beethoven let us return to our survey of German interpreters. The familiar figure of a reluctant, wary Goethe enters the scene once again from the wings of historical fact for some much-needed exposure to the true greatness of Beethoven, and this time he shares the stage with a child prodigy out of whose mouth would come the jewels of enlightenment. The person who succeeded where others had failed was Felix Mendelssohn (1809–1847). The date was early November 1821 and the scene Goethe's formidable music room in Weimar (Fig. 63). The twelve-year-old Felix had been brought to the grand old lion (now seventy-two) of Weimar by his teacher, Carl Friedrich Zelter (1758–1832)— that rough-hewn pillar of musical conservatism who, to the dismay of many, wielded enormous influence over Goethe's musical tastes, shielding him successfully from such representatives of modern music as Beethoven and Schubert. With characteristic bluntness—one of the things that endeared him to Goethe— Zelter had by letter prepared Goethe for the precocious phenomenon he wished to present. Felix was his "best pupil," he declared, "a good and pretty boy, vivacious and obedient." Then he added: "Admittedly he is the son of a Jew, though not one himself."[51] Zelter's gratuitous information concerning his pupil's racial heritage (Felix was in fact a grandson of the renowned Jewish philosopher Moses Mendelssohn) was not the only "warning" he wished to impress upon the Weimar reception committee. Before Felix was allowed to join the three string players who had been assembled to play through the Quartets for piano, violin, viola, and cello with their young composer, Zelter had addressed them conspiratorially, solemnly urging them not to show too much amazement at the boy's gifts since up to now he had been able to preserve him "from vanity and overestimation of himself, those damnable enemies of all artistic progress."[52] The musicians and even Goethe himself honored Zelter's request, although as soon as the vivacious boy with dancing black curls that cascaded down the back of his neck had acquitted himself at the piano and been sent to the garden to "cool off," excitement over this "second Mozart" could no longer be suppressed. With Zelter's encouragement Goethe put the young prodigy to the test during a second session at which he performed alone at the piano—first improvising brilliantly on a theme provided by his teacher, then playing from faultless memory a Bach fugue, the minuet from Mozart's *Don Giovanni*, and the overture to *Figaro*. Such apparently effortless mastery of Mozart inspired Goethe to place before the young pianist a neatly written manuscript from his own collection—a Mozart adagio, which Felix sight-read with perfect assurance as though he had known the piece for years. The poet could not have been more intrigued and now he pulled the ace from his deck of musical cards, laying yet another manuscript from his own collection before the excited boy. Half-jestingly and half-seriously Goethe admonished him to take care, for this music would truly gauge his powers. One of the witnesses was Ludwig Rellstab—familiar to us by virtue of his remark pondering whether Beethoven's features should resemble his scores. The Berlin critic described the messy piece of paper Goethe had propped up on the piano: "You could scarcely tell whether they were notes, or whether it was a page lined and spattered with ink in countless places."[53] With growing astonishment Rellstab watched what then occurred:

> Felix burst into a laugh of wonder. "Is that writing? Is a man able to read that?" he called out. Then suddenly he grew earnest, while Goethe uttered the question, "Now guess, if you can, who wrote it?" and Zelter, advancing to the instrument and looking over the shoulders of the lad, said: "That is Beethoven's, one could see that a mile away. He always writes as if he had used a broomstick for a pen, and then brushed down the fresh notes with his sleeve." At the name of Beethoven, Felix became visibly earnest, yes, more than earnest; a holy awe was disclosed in his features. He looked upon the manuscript without turning away his eyes, and then a visible gleam of surprise spread over his features. This all lasted only a few seconds, however, for Goethe allowed no time for preparation, he would have his proof sharply tested: "Did not I say to you," he cried, "that this would catch you? Now try and show what you can do." On this, Felix began to play. It was a simple song, but the notes had been so rubbed out and scratched out that it required a wonderful skill to read them at a glance. On the first playing, Felix often had to correct himself, laughingly striking a false note, and then instantly correcting himself with a "not so." Afterwards, he cried: "Now I will play it to you as it should be," and the second time he did not fail in a note. "That is Beethoven," he cried, " . . . that is Beethoven alone; I should have known it."[54]

Goethe needed no more tests; from that moment he shared Zelter's pride in a Felix for whom even the nadir of incomprehensibility—Beethoven—presented no hurdle. Felix was presented to the Weimar court and daily summoned to play for Goethe who managed to prolong the visit into a stay of sixteen days. Perhaps it was Rellstab's enthusiastic reporting of these events abroad that was responsible for the entry in one of Beethoven's conversation books: "Mendelsohn [*sic*] 12 years old promises much."[55]

If Beethoven had thus at least heard of the boy wonder, Mendelssohn for his part had devoured all there was to know of Beethoven and his music. He dreamed of being allowed humbly to present himself to the world's greatest living composer, but his father had different ideas as to who this composer might be, and so it was to Luigi Cherubini in Paris, rather than Ludwig Beethoven in Vienna, that Abraham Mendelssohn took his gifted son four years later, with the bold request to pass judgment on Felix's talents—a judgment which, though favorable, was regarded by Felix as coming from a "burnt-out volcano."[56] The titan who still hurled mighty bolts of creativity across the Danube riveted young Mendelssohn's attention. While still in his teens he used his phenomenal powers of memorization to acquire, note for note, everything by Beethoven available in print or manuscript copy. Since his wealthy banker father subscribed as a matter of course to all publications of new works by serious composers as they were released by the great music publishing firms of Germany, Austria, and France, Beethoven's music was available to him and Felix eagerly learned the sonatas, piano concertos, and piano reductions of the symphonies by heart. Mendelssohn senior, although willing to condone his son's choice of music as a profession, once the coveted Cherubini approbation had been procured, was never pleased with his son's choice of Beethoven—especially the late, "nonclassical" Beethoven—as musical paradigm. The divergent views of father and son on the Promethean merits of Beethoven erupted into heated arguments and Felix was once ordered to leave the dinner table because of his obstinate praise of Beethoven—an event recalled by the composer in a letter to his sisters several years later.[57] The situation was only aggravated for the older Mendelssohn when he observed that of all the gifted people who were regular visitors to the palatial family home in Berlin, Felix formed the closest relationship with the musicologist and Beethoven champion Adolf Bernhard Marx. For the untroubled, sheltered sixteen-year-old composer of the ethereal Octet for strings (op. 20) the contrast presented by Beethoven's personal tribulations and troubled, strife-filled music must have been irresistible. How romantic to experience what Beethoven had experienced, to suffer as Beethoven had suffered, in fact to *be* Beethoven. And indeed Mendelssohn did once play at being Beethoven. The evidence of this innocent charade has fortunately been preserved. It was precipitated by the twentieth birthday of Felix's favorite sister, Fanny—whose extraordinary musical talent would have to remain, as their father firmly wrote her, "decoration."[58] One day in November a letter appeared at Leipzigerstrasse No. 3 addressed to Fanny Mendelssohn. Written in a distinctive but almost illegible scrawl, it was dated "Vienna, 8 November 1825" and signed "Beethoven." The writer expressed his pleasure at the report brought to him by "some friends" that the dear Fräulein had "succeeded in making a well-educated audience listen to my Concertos in E flat and G" and announced graciously: "I am sending you my Sonata in B-flat (Opus 106) as a present on your birthday, with my heartiest congratulations. I did not write the sonata out of thin air. Play it only if you have ample time. . . . Where your friendship alone cannot attain full understanding, do not hesitate to ask Marx, the great authority on my music [*mein Kenner Marx*]. He will explain everything to you; especially the slow Adagio movement affords him plenty of time to do so. . . . I am enclosing a poor likeness of mine as a present for you. After all, I am a potentate just as good as any other, who gives away his portrait."[59] There were clues in this "letter from Vienna" that pointed to a Berlin origin: the mischievous dig at Marx's expertise and the implied use of one of Abraham Mendelssohn's derogatory labels—"potentate"—for Beethoven. The identity of the gleeful forger must have been easily flushed out to the amusement of all, perhaps even Papa Mendelssohn himself.

If the deaf artist Lyser had identified with Beethoven in a double signature that united his name with his idol's, here was an even bolder blending of psyches. And a revelatory one. For the sixteen-year-old Felix was speaking on his own behalf as well as Beethoven's when he suggested that music as monumental as the Piano Sonata in B-flat did not come "out of thin air." Even the most effortless-appearing inspiration could conceal, as did his own soaring Octet, a secret scaffolding of polyphony. What portrait likeness, we may wonder, did "Beethoven" include in his letter as a present for Fanny? Considering Felix's substantial talent for landscape drawing, an activity in which he found soothing release all his life, it is fairly safe to speculate, and certainly within the bounds of rougish Mendelssohnian family humor, that the cheerful counterfeiter also produced his own "poor" image of Beethoven—perhaps an outrageously exaggerated "etching" with ink still fresh from the press. We do know that Felix owned and treasured a real portrait reproduction of Beethoven. In a charming letter describing the contents of his room, newly arranged after returning to Berlin from a sojourn in London, he commented: "My room is in order, the pictures are hung, Sebastian Bach over the piano, . . . and Rebecca's [his younger sister] portrait side by side with Beethoven and a couple of Raphaels—so the walls are rather a medley."[60]

It was a more serious and also an authentic image of Beethoven that Mendelssohn resolved to hold up to the gaze of his revered but obstinately shortsighted friend Goethe when next they met. Goethe had followed the meteoric career of Zelter's protégé with possessive pleasure. Now, in May 1830, on his way from Berlin to Italy, this surrogate grandson visited Weimar again, no longer a "precious boy" of twelve but an aristocratic young gentleman and master musician of twenty-one. The Jewish dimension of Zelter's introductory description had in the meanwhile taken a curious turn: when Felix's parents paid a courtesy visit to the Weimar bard, Goethe made the eloquent statement to Frau Mendelssohn about her son: "He is my David—and I am Saul."[61] Mendelssohn's visit to the poet was, like his first, an extended one. He stayed fourteen days, due to Goethe's insistence that Felix be sketched by a local artist for his portrait gallery of notable visitors to Weimar. Since "the drowsy old lion" of Weimar usually asked his guests to leave rather than stay, Mendelssohn was honored to oblige, and the great old man was soon addressing him in the "Du" form again. In a letter to his family Mendelssohn reported a most unusual music appreciation class, conducted by him every morning at Goethe's request for an attentive student body of one:

He likes to hear the works of all the different great piano composers in chronological order and have me tell how they have progressed. All this time he sits in a dark corner and his old eyes flash. He wanted to have nothing to do with Beethoven, but I told him I could not let him escape, and played the first part of the symphony in C minor [the Fifth Symphony]. It had a singular effect on him; at first he said, "This arouses no emotion; nothing but astonishment; it is grandiose." He continued grumbling in this way, and after a long pause he began again, "It is very great; quite wild; it makes one fear that the house might fall down; what must it be like when all those men play together!" During dinner, in the midst of another subject, he alluded to it again.[62]

What the gentle but irresistible young Mendelssohn had initiated and was privileged to observe was the reluctant, poignantly touching admission of the emotional force of Beethoven by an iron-willed old man who at the end of his controlled life of the intellect could not afford to be overwhelmed by a power from without. The Romantic Walpurgis Night of *Faust*, Part 1, had long had a rival and a replacement in Goethe's thoughts, for he was involved with the classical Walpurgis Night of *Faust*, Part 2. For Goethe to acknowledge the passions unleashed by Beethoven so late in his own ordered life would be to reopen the flood gates of the emotionalism of his youth, releasing once again those *Leiden* of the young Werther successfully dammed up for so long.

Mendelssohn was not the first Romantic to invade the Weimar citadel and spiritually jar Goethe. Nineteen years earlier, during the height of what might be called Goethe's period of neoclassical retrenchment, the young Sulpiz Boisserée, that charming champion of Romantic medievalism in general and enthusiastic agitator for the completion of Cologne Cathedral in particular, dared to bring his "retrograde" message and drawings of what the Gothic torso would look like if finished to the supreme commander of the enemy camp. The twenty-eight-year-old Boisserée's diary and letters home are a heartwarming record of the capitulation of a man who had chalked up a forty-year record of hostility towards the Romantic cause. For the *Sturm und Drang* Goethe of long ago, whose awestruck essay of 1772 on Strassburg Cathedral—*Von Deutscher Baukunst*—kindled the Gothic Revival in Europe, had since been impatiently disowned by Goethe, the Apostle of Classicism. Here are the highlights of Pilgrim Boisserée's progress during 3 and 8 May 1811 as he attempted to rekindle his sixty-two-year-old adversary's interest in the Romance of German Gothic:

First meeting: "I have just come from Goethe, who received me very coldly and stiffly.... His manner of addressing me could not have been more stiffly distant.... Then we came to the drawings ... 'Yes, yes, quite so, hem, hem.' We proceeded to the work itself, to the fate of medieval architecture and its history ... to all of which he listened as if he'd like to eat me alive.... On departure he gave me either one or two fingers, I am not sure which, but I think we will soon achieve the whole hand."

Second meeting: "I am getting on splendidly with the old gentleman; the first day I only got one finger, the second I already had his whole arm."

Third meeting: "When I was alone with him on Tuesday and showed him the drawings he sometimes positively growled at me like a wounded bear; you saw how he battled with himself and blamed himself for ever having failed to recognize such greatness."

Fourth meeting:"After lunch we sat alone; he praised my work with all possible warmth and emphasis. I had the elevating sense of the victory of a great and noble cause over the prejudices of one of the most intelligent of men ... I experienced the noble joy, which is so seldom vouchsafed to us in life, of seeing one of the greatest of men recant an error, through which he had been untrue to himself."[63]

Mendelssohn's well-tempered image of Beethoven on the piano did not spur Goethe to recant anew, but it did penetrate and penetrate deeply a fissure in the fragile fortress of Goethe's peace of mind. The meeting with Beethoven in Bohemia long before had struck a discordant note, but not in the scale orchestrated by Bettina. From all evidence[64] the Incident at Teplitz briefly exposed the Apollonian Goethe to chaos. Chaos as incarnated by the persona of Beethoven and the chthonian realm of his music. He who had spent a lifetime laboriously constructing a self-contained empire in which feelings were recycled into intellectual material, and outside stimuli carefully sifted and stored, could not risk the Dionysian attraction of Beethoven's abyss. Flight, not fight, was Goethe's reaction to any ungovernable element that threatened his hard-won serenity. And so Goethe had taken secret flight from Beethoven. His silence on Beethoven the man— whose humble letter of 8 February 1823 begging him to persuade the Grand Duke of Weimar to subscribe to the publication of his *Missa Solemnis* received no answer— extended to Beethoven the composer. Not that there was a dearth of performances of Beethoven's music in Weimar; on the contrary, Goethe attended the playing of a good number of the composer's works.[65] But he said nothing. He listened, and, out of an instinct for self-preservation, he took care not to *hear*. We may glean an idea of Goethe's conscious defensiveness from the frank explanation he gave his philologist friend Wilhelm von Humboldt as to why he avoided exploring Indian philosophy: "I have nothing whatever against Indian thought, but I am afraid of it. It would involve my imagination in the pursuit of the formless and the misshapen; I must guard myself more earnestly than ever against this."[66] What Goethe would purposefully stand aloof from in order to preserve his Olympian tranquillity, an entire age would also reject, as the tempest of Romanticism abated between 1815 and 1848 before the windless calm of studied Biedermeier placidity. A whole half-century would pass before an author could describe the unnerving implications of surrendering to the sounds coming up from the Beethovenian abyss. And indeed the aging Tolstoy did not write *The Kreutzer Sonata* until 1889.

The fact that Mendelssohn had made an earnest attempt to transmit his image of Beethoven to Goethe was recounted to old Zelter back at Berlin in two versions, one expansively "Romantic," the other "neoclassic" and cautious. The report penned by Mendelssohn was sent from Munich a few weeks after he had made his sad (and final) farewell to the poet: "I have often played to Goethe in the morning hours. He wanted to get an idea of how music has developed and wished to hear the music of different composers in chronological order. He seemed rather wary of Beethoven; but I could not spare him this acquaintance because he had to hear 'where sounds had turned to,' and so I played for him the first movement of the C minor symphony which he liked very much."[67] Goethe's note to Mendelssohn's former teacher was written at "half-past nine on a morning of beautiful and clearest sky," the moment after Mendelssohn's departure: "His presence was especially beneficent to me. My relationship to music is still the same: I listen to it with pleasure, with participation and with thoughtfulness [but] chiefly I am fond of the historical viewpoint. For how can we understand any apparition unless we can observe it on its journey toward us? Felix too understands this desire to walk step by step; fortunately his excellent memory allows him to draw forth examples at will. Beginning with Bach and his epoch, he brought me living accounts of Haydn, Mozart, and Gluck. He gave me a sufficient idea [*hinreichende Begriffe*] of the modern technicians and finally he made me feel and think about his own creations."[68] Circumvention through silence was Goethe's solution to the Beethoven problem. The greatest of the "modern technicians" ("*grossen neuen Technikern*") was not even mentioned by name![69]

But Mendelssohn himself went out of his way to hear the name of Beethoven pronounced, especially by those fortunate enough to have known him. In a letter written to Fanny from Milan in 1831 he exulted over the chance circumstances that had led him to call upon Beethoven's former piano student, Dorothea Graumann von Ertmann (1781–1849). The baroness, to whom Beethoven had dedicated his Piano Sonata in A major, op. 110, obligingly played for the young Mendelssohn what "not a person in Milan" cared to hear—piano music by Beethoven. Of the personal anecdotes she had to tell her eager listener concerning Beethoven, the following one, noted down by Felix for his sister, has entered the Beethoven legend: "She told me that when she lost her last child, Beethoven at first shrank from coming to her house; but at length he invited her to visit him, and when she arrived, she found him seated at the piano, and simply saying, 'Let us speak to each other by music,' he played on for more than an hour, and, as she expressed it, 'he said much to me, and at last gave me consolation.'"[70]

The picture of Beethoven "speaking" through his piano inspired maudlin visual responses over the decades (Fig. 64), but Mendelssohn's own reaction was of emulation: sixteen years later, for the dangerously ill son of his friend the Leipzig singer Livia Frege, he consoled mother and child by visiting and playing for three hours on the piano—a wordless concert that began with Beethoven's *Moonlight Sonata*.[71]

Characteristically in accord with his active veneration for past geniuses of music, Mendelssohn was not content with presenting Beethoven only in the context of a salon or sick-room situation. His prodigious years as director of the Gewandhaus Orchestra in Leipzig from 1837 until his death in 1847 tipped the scales in favor of "historical" concerts and the instrumental music of Beethoven was played with a regularity second only to the performances of Mozart's work. Mendelssohn's own compositions rank only tenth for frequency of presentation, lagging behind Haydn, Cherubini, Bach, Handel, and Weber. His all-Beethoven concert of 11 February 1841 was enthusiastically described by Schumann as "one of the richest evenings of music, such as we may, perhaps, hear but seldom in this world."[72] For another program Mendelssohn conducted a fascinating lineup: all three *Leonore* overtures plus the *Fidelio* Overture. This novel chance for comparison was discussed with approval by Schumann in his Florestan voice, and by the visiting English music critic Henry Fothergill Chorley (1808–1872) who, commenting on the entire Leipzig season under Mendelssohn's dynamic direction, could not resist the Romantic tradition of linking Beethoven with one of his own countrymen of genius: "Never, indeed, did I hear the Symphonies of Beethoven so intensely enjoyed as at Leipzig and never so admirably performed. As regarded those works of the Shakespeare of music, I felt, for the first time in my life, in 1839, richly and thoroughly satisfied beyond reserve or question."[73]

The common link of Beethoven worship prompted an unusual proposal from Paganini, who was present in London at the premiere of Mendelssohn's *Italian Symphony* on 13 May 1833. On the same program Mendelssohn appeared as soloist in Mozart's Piano Concerto no. 20 in D Minor and Paganini, enchanted by Mendelssohn the pianist, rushed up to him after the concert with the suggestion that they play Beethoven violin sonatas together. Mendelssohn was more than willing,[74] but Paganini's recurring dental disasters chose this time to yank him away from chamber music and so the curious collaboration never took place.

Belief in Beethoven notwithstanding, there was one work by the departed genius that did not fit comfortably even into Mendelssohn's litany, no matter how often or how credulously he evoked it. This was the same magnum opus that had constituted such a stumbling block for Spohr—the Ninth Symphony. Concerning his conducting it at the Lower Rhenish Musical Festival of 1836 in Düsseldorf, Mendelssohn confided to an old family friend from Berlin days: "It is hard to speak about this music at all . . . the instrumental moments belong to the greatest things that I know in art; from the moment where the voices enter, even I do not understand it, i.e., I find only individual details perfect, and when that is the case with such a master, the fault probably lies with us. Or with the execution. . . . In the vocal movement, however, the writing for voices is such that I know of no place where it could go well, and perhaps that is the reason for the incomprehensibility up till now."[75]

Incomprehensibility! This was the word used by the enemies of Beethoven's music, not by believers in Beethoven. And what grim presence was on hand at the Düsseldorf festival, what ubiquitous high priest of Beethoven criticism, ever watchful for signs of failure to render properly the musical intentions of his master? Why Anton Felix Schindler, of course. If Felix expressed private reservations concerning his comprehension of the Ninth, Anton Felix did not hesitate to go public about what he (correctly) perceived to be a doubting Thomas. Here is Schindler, the not-so-secret anti-Semite, berating the grandson of Moses Mendelssohn for his profanation of Germany's national treasure and recalling his own valiant attempts to head him off at the impasse: "When in 1836 this writer had occasion to oppose in the *Kölnische Zeitung* Mendelssohn's treatment of the ninth symphony at the Düsseldorf Music Festival his voice was a solitary one, and was heard with nothing but scorn and derision. At that time it might not have been too late to join forces to erect a dam against the gathering flood or, at least, to make one of the largest streams harmless. But where were they who could dauntlessly have withstood with their better knowledge the musician who had been declared infallible by all the dilettantes and music-lovers of the province?"[76] So much for Westphalia and the Lower Rhineland. But Schindler needed to alert all Germany to the Danger that was not just a provincial menace. As usual he avoided ambiguity:

> In regard to Beethoven's music, it was largely Mendelssohn who set the standard: this was a great misfortune for the music. No music will ever recover from the wounds inflicted upon it by this artist, highly esteemed both as a pianist and as a conductor. [And as a composer? Does Schindler expect us to believe that the premiere of Mendelssohn's oratorio *Saint Paul* at the same Düsseldorf Festival simply escaped his notice?] For the bad seeds he has planted north and south, east and west throughout the musical state have already borne fruit that can never be rooted out, despite the efforts that certain art journals may bend in that direction, for the effects have already poisoned the flesh and blood of a whole generation.[77]

Just what was it about Mendelssohn's noxious Ninth interpretation that so contaminated the musical soil of Germany? After all it was a work that the "pianist" and "conductor" had studied and pondered for years: when it was only two years old and he only seventeen, he had already attempted to reveal its mysteries at the piano keyboard to a group of enthusiasts. And a year later he had been present in Stettin at the first performance in Northern Europe of Beethoven's Ninth Symphony, when the local Musikdirector Carl Loewe had "balanced" the program with the world premiere of two of Mendelssohn's own works.[78] Furthermore, since the age of fifteen, Mendelssohn had also had the benefit of actual instruction by and, later, a lifetime of cordial advice from an authentic Beethoven "Kenner" who became one of Mendelssohn's most intimate and cherished friends—Ignaz Moscheles. Ah! Here was the detested fly in Schindler's ointment again. Moscheles—member of a musical species regarded with suspicion by Schindler: the "piano virtuoso." Moscheles—member of the Hebraic race that so repelled Schindler. Moscheles—editor of the English translation of *his* Beethoven biography, that publication which had inexplicably left *his*, Schindler's, name off the title page. And, worst of all, Moscheles—the talented musician who had known Beethoven and enjoyed his trust and respect during the years *before* (1810– 14) Schindler's appropriation of the master and his official history. In such a manner must the secret, subterranean thoughts of Schindler have flowed as he listened to Moscheles's "product" set the tempi of the Ninth at that famous Düsseldorf performance—tempi discussed with Moscheles and so different from his own. All this found sublimation in Schindler's describing Mendelssohn and other conductors who were also "virtuoso pianists" as chasing "whole orchestras in double-quick step."[79]

Ten years later the *"ami de Beethoven"* was still self-employed as spy for the German nation-at-large when he caught Mendelssohn engaging in another act of musical treason. (One wonders whether Mendelssohn fantasized about barring Schindler from attending his concerts.) This time the victim was Papa Haydn, but the crime was the same—tempo sabotage: "In Haydn's chorus, 'The Heavens are telling the Glory of God,' to interpret the *alla breve* as the norm produces *a presto*. Mendelssohn understood it this way at the 1846 Lower Rhine Music Festival in Aachen, and drove the 500-voice chorus in double-quick march to do it. . . . "[80]

If Schindler's hounding of Mendelssohn was never to abate, neither was Mendelssohn's great reverence for Beethoven. By serendipity and determined pursuit, Mendelssohn had collected and fashioned a compelling image of the dead composer that would move and inspire him to the end of his days. This image had been enhanced by contact with people who had known Beethoven. As early as 1825, when Abraham Mendelssohn had taken the family to Paris to obtain the Cherubini judgment on his son, Felix and Fanny had been allowed to take a few piano lessons from Beethoven's good friend the pianist Marie Bigot, whose memories of the great man were eagerly absorbed by the brother and sister. And in Berlin, although Felix found the intellectual posturing of Bettina von Arnim distasteful, he had listened attentively to this living link's reminiscences of Beethoven. During his musical career he met and interrogated other acquaintances of Beethoven—persons whom we too have met in our mythmaking inquiry: Julius Benedict, Goethe, Ferdinand Hiller, Hummel, Moscheles, Rellstab, Ferdinand Ries, and Rossini. Now, in the last year of his life, Mendelssohn's interior image of Beethoven was so potent, so familiar, that it was second nature to him to quote his dead colleague as an inspiration during difficult times. Attempting, for example, to console a friend on the death of his mother, he wrote: "'Crush evil and keep your head high,' Beethoven closed a letter in 1809 or '10; should one not repeat this today, and be able to write it at the end of every letter?"[81]

Certainly, whether "classical Romanticist" or "Romantic-minded classicist" (as music history was alternately to dub him), Mendelssohn was aware that he was an independent successor of the composer he so venerated, "If I don't die young," he often said, wryly commenting on the prospect of projects at hand. But Mendelssohn did die young, at the age of thirty-eight, on 4 November 1847, of an aneurysm in the brain. Keeping the deathwatch in the bedroom where Mendelssohn lay, partly paralyzed and almost unconscious from the last of several increasingly severe strokes suffered during the week, was the friend of his youth,

Ignaz Moscheles. It was a heartrending scene the older man never forgot. Writing of it years later, Moscheles recalled the great nexus that seemed to him to have had special relevance at the moment of Mendelssohn's passing: "As his breathing gradually became slower and slower, my mind involuntarily recurred to Beethoven's Funeral March, 'Sulla Morte d'un' Eroe,' to that passage where he seems to depict the hero as he lies breathing his last, the sands of life gradually running out. The suppressed sobs of the bystanders, and my own hot tears, recalled me to the dread reality. At twenty-four minutes past nine he expired with a deep sigh."[82]

IGNAZ MOSCHELES

Among the things Ignaz Moscheles (1794–1870) (Fig. 65) surely had told his pupil Mendelssohn about Beethoven were the reminiscences he had attached, as editor, to the 1841 English translation of Schindler's biography, including that winning vignette of Moscheles's decision to study with Salieri after discovering in Salieri's house a calling card pithily inscribed "Pupil Beethoven called." More Beethoveniana was forthcoming from Moscheles's pen, however, for he had kept a diary since his twentieth year, and at the end of his long life these conscientious and sometimes chatty personal journals encompassed a period of almost sixty years. This engaging record of the world of music was lovingly edited and published by Moscheles's wife, Charlotte, two years after his death, and by 1874 translations were available in both Britain and America for English-language devotees of the international music scene.[83] Because they cover a lifetime, Moscheles's comments on Beethoven are of particular interest for the mythmaking mill, not only for their anecdotal content but for their proof of the unswerving primacy of Beethoven in Moscheles's temple of musical giants. Neither the conversion of a Weber nor the secret reservation of a Spohr is the stuff of Moscheles's Beethoven. "We musicians, whatever we may be, are mere satellites of the great Beethoven, the dazzling luminary"[84] he wrote at twenty-two. At seventy-two his judgment was the same. Like Charles Hallé, Moscheles attempted to play the luminary's music at the tender age of seven. His memoirs record the fluctuating temperatures of his first attack of the Beethoven virus and its subsequent "cure":

> Although but seven years old, I actually ventured upon Beethoven's Sonate Pathétique. Imagine if you can how I played it; imagine also the Beethoven fever, to which I fell a victim in those days—a fever which goaded me on to mangle the other great works of the immortal author. My father put a check to this mischief by taking me one day to Dionys Weber [director of the Prague Conservatory of Music]. . . . My mother having decked me out in my Sunday best, I played my best piece, Beethoven's Sonate Pathétique. But what was my astonishment . . . when Dionys Weber finally delivered himself thus: "Candidly speaking, the boy is on the wrong road, for he makes a hash of great works. . . . The first year he must play nothing but Mozart, the second Clementi, and the third Bach; but only that—not a note as yet of Beethoven. . . ."[85]

When, seven years later, Moscheles's recently widowed mother reluctantly allowed him to pursue his musical studies in Vienna, his thoughts flew ahead of him: "Above all, I longed to see and become acquainted with *that man* who had exercised so powerful an influence over my whole being; whom, though I scarcely understood, I blindly worshiped."[86] Over the next few years the budding concert pianist and composer dogged all performances of Beethoven's music (exercising his critical faculties only regarding Beethoven the pianist). He met Beethoven at lunch in 1810, and by 1814 he was able to announce the stunning news to his diary: "The proposal is made to me to arrange the great masterpiece *Fidelio* for the piano. What can be more delightful?"[87] From this collaboration—a project initiated by Artaria and to which Beethoven agreed with the proviso that he might supervise the work as it progressed—much anecdotal grist for the mythmaking mill was yielded up by young Moscheles. The most important was the following: "Under the last number I had written 'Fine mit Gottes Hülfe' (the end with the help of God). He was not at home when I brought it to him; and on returning my manuscript, the words were added, 'O, Mensch, hilf dir selber' (Oh, man, help thyself)."[88] Was Beethoven teasing the dedicated twenty-year-old, or was he in deadly earnest? Such speculation became so widespread that Moscheles, who lived to see his own anecdote annexed into the corpus of Beethoven knowledge, felt compelled at the age of sixty-seven to tell what he could about this dimension of his hero: "In answer to a question about Beethoven's sentiments on the subject of religion, I am under the impression that he was a Catholic, but a free-thinker at the same time. Of his piety I have no doubt, for his music speaks to the hearts of all nations, just as the sacred works of a Bach, a Mozart, or Mendelssohn do."[89] While the designation "freethinker" would help ignite the literary fires of those determined to claim Beethoven for extramusical, radical causes, the grand sweep of effectiveness ascribed by Moscheles to *all* of Beethoven's music (a potency associated by him only with the *sacred* music of the other composers) anticipates the later nineteenth-century insistence on the universal meaning of Beethoven.[90]

If Mendelssohn had once played at being Beethoven by writing a letter in "his" hand, Moscheles occasionally used his familiarity with Beethoven's physical mannerisms to "convey" to the musicians of an orchestra the composer's musical message by indulging in a reverent but nonetheless amusing imitation of Beethoven as conductor—stooping down almost out of sight for the piano passages, standing on tiptoe and leaping upwards at a fortissimo. This innocent, well-intentioned mime of something he had seen many times was a real-life stimulant for the Hoffmann-derived tradition of the stereotypical "mad" conductor. Witnesses tended to remember the telling charade, not Moscheles's disclaimer: "Inasmuch, however, as I cannot emulate the great man in his works, I abstain from copying him in his attitudes; with him it was all originality, with me it would be caricature."[91] But caricature can, in Joseph Conrad's words, put the face of a joke upon the body of truth, and such visible manifestations of Beethoven, even if ersatz, were welcomed, emulated, and passed into the Beethoven lore.[92] What Moscheles attempted to enact for the edification of orchestra players about to sound the musical mysteries of his hero for the first time was what Beethoven as conductor had himself attempted to convey—a *Seelekarikature* in which physical exaggerations urged forth spiritual qualities.

Moscheles, like Mendelssohn, was repeatedly in demand and successful as a conductor in London, and, again like Mendelssohn, he took advantage of the English public's receptivity to things German by scheduling the music of Beethoven. The earnest *Seelekarikature* with which he provided the players of the London Philharmonic when he rehearsed the Ninth in the spring of 1837 was to prove signally effective. Critical reaction to the first London performance of the Ninth, conducted by Sir George Smart on 21 March 1825, had not, as we have seen, been good—the music was characterized as having no intelligible design and Beethoven was accused of writing to suit the "present mania" for noisy extravagance. Moscheles rehearsed the instrumentalists and singers individually so that each "had some knowledge of the colossal work before the time of the first orchestral rehearsal," while the second full rehearsal was used "for the acquirement of light, shade, and expression."[93] After the concert an elated Moscheles reported: "All the newspapers are fairly in raptures with this colossal music, and unanimously insist on its remaining as a fixture in the 'Repertoire,' and being performed, on a grander scale, either in Exeter Hall or at the Birmingham Festival. Suffice it to say that wealthy England has enriched herself by one additional treasure, and how I rejoiced that I have been permitted to disinter it!"[94]

The next year, 1838, Moscheles conducted not one but three performances of the Ninth with the London Philharmonic. So successfully did Beethoven's music become a "fixture" in the English repertoire that Moscheles permitted himself the pedagogical luxury of staging "historical concerts," the better to frame the accomplishments of his empyreal sovereign of music: "I have burrowed again and again into the ash-covered treasures of the musical Pompeii, and brought many grand things to light. Beethoven is great—whom should I call greater?—but as the public is forever listening to his music, alternating with modern pieces written mostly for display, I intend to introduce, first of all, those composers who gave the impetus to Beethoven's eagle flight."[95]

This prototype of the modern orchestral program proved extremely popular and after the second concert Moscheles rewarded his audience with Beethoven's Variations on a Theme by Handel as "dessert." The main course would continue to be Beethoven however and in 1841 Moscheles, who had not that year been reelected as one of the directors of the Philharmonic, was prevailed upon to conduct the Ninth again. Critics no longer complained about the symphony's excesses or incomprehensibility; familiarity with the work was now nudging the pendulum in the opposite direction. The London *Times* summed it up: "Artists and amateurs now are glad to own that Beethoven's Ninth Symphony is as much remarkable for majesty and grandeur as for simplicity."[96]

Certainly Beethoven had not been accused of (or complimented upon) *simplicity* concerning the Ninth before, and the appearance of the two most famous catchwords of neoclassicism—grandeur and simplicity— gives us pause. For in the midst of the gale storms of Romanticism that were blowing through England with as much elemental force as on the continent, the German archaeologist Johann Joachim Winckelmann's (1717–1768) seductive concepts of "noble simplicity" and "serene grandeur"—originally applied in 1755 to Greek sculpture—now seemed, to one critic, at least, applicable to Beethoven's grandest symphony. This differs from the dichotomy of the beautiful (classical) versus the sublime (Romantic) that we came upon regarding the new nineteenth-century grouping of Shakespeare, Strassburg Cathedral, and Beethoven as examples of the sublime. Why, in an England of 1841, would a society primed for the far-flung, labyrinthial intensification of feelings by Romantic writers such as Burns, Blake, Scott, Coleridge, Wordsworth, Keats, Byron, and the Shelleys now require simplicity? Was the Romantic Age dying just as the Romantic Beethoven was being discovered?

Yes and no. The Romanticism unleashed by the implications of the French Revolution and the saga of Napoleon's rise and fall was on the rebound and in its new life it assumed different characteristics. In a humiliated Germany recovering from the bloody Napoleonic invasions we can speak of a Biedermeier Backlash; in an England whose upper middle class was not enfranchised until 1832 we might call the ensuing period a Victorian Visor. Both epochs were prepared to substitute sentiment for passion, to impose routine over disorder, and to laud the intimacy of family life as bulwark against revolution. Symptomatic of this new domesticized Romanticism is Mendelssohn's reaction when, asked by the musical and approving Queen Victoria what she might do for him, he asked to see the Royal Nursery. Expressed musically, the shift in Romanticism towards intimacy was nowhere more clearly manifested than in the rise of salon music. Quieter accents were sought in both music and life; the roar of revolution, politics, and passion subsided. Instead of long, drawn-out Pathétiques and Appassionatas, momentary inspirations and dreamy diary pieces predominated. Moscheles's own successful piano Etudes took on the nature of "characteristic pieces," and the salon genre encompassed Schubert's Impromptus, John Field's Nocturnes, Mendelssohn's forty-eight Songs Without Words, Schumann's Papillons and Fantasies, and Chopin's Preludes. No wonder "simplicity" was looked for in Beethoven's mighty Ninth. The new scrutiny of Beethoven terrain was not completely in vain, for the same composer who grappled with the blows of destiny in his symphonies had corralled lesser motivic pulsations into a collection of twenty-four Bagatelles, the playing of which he left to others, especially his many women admirers. More tranquil rhythms were ushered into the salons after the 1820s, and thus it was that "the other," "simple" Beethoven was discovered floating in the bulrushes by the daughters of Romanticism.

Let us return to Moscheles's own image of Beethoven—certainly one of titanic proportions and not at all subject to the condensed representation favored by the Biedermeier or Victorian drawing room. Quite literally Moscheles could not tolerate a curtailed Beethoven: he took Hummel to task upon noticing ten- and twenty-two-bar cuts in his arrangement of Beethoven's Seventh Symphony, commenting indignantly in his diary: "Hummel, who takes every possible liberty, wishes to improve upon Beethoven's directions to the band, as well as the notes themselves."[97]

A Beethoven portrayal of which Moscheles heartily approved comes to light in a letter written by him in the early fall of 1838, shortly after the coronation of Queen Victoria (an event Moscheles got to witness in person, thanks to his friend Sir George Smart's inspiration to equip him with a surplice and position him as a surplus bass with the choir inside Westminster Abbey), to his wife. Moscheles wrote with some urgency: "I recommend you a small pamphlet by Ries and Wegeler upon Beethoven, it has just been published at Coblenz by Bädeker; and gives one an insight into the wonderful life and works of Beethoven. I consider every part of it authentic."[98]

We might reread this last sentence through Schindler's ashen-tinted spectacles if we wish to measure the full venom of those verbal darts Schindler would soon be unleashing at his rival biographers of Beethoven. Those indiscrete revelations by Ries about the temperamental Beethoven that Schindler had tried with no success to block? Yes. Ries's Beethoven sounded very familiar to Moscheles, and Schindler would never live down his secret resentment that both Ries and Moscheles had known a Beethoven he had not— the younger man of before 1814. But the bomb (Moscheles's English edition of Schindler's biography) had not yet fallen. So far there was no bad blood between Schindler and Moscheles. Schindler had in fact kept Moscheles, far away in London, scrupulously informed by letter of Beethoven's last illness; he had even sent him a lock of hair from the dying man's head.[99] It was Moscheles, after all, who had been responsible for the generous action taken by Sir George Smart and the London Philharmonic, who, when informed of Beethoven's grave illness and financial worries, immediately collected and sent him an "advance" of one thousand florins—a gift that arrived in time to ease the composer's final week of life. After Beethoven's death Schindler continued to communicate with Moscheles in London concerning the legal problems involved in reclaiming the gift of money for the Philharmonic. These lengthy letters of 4 and 11 April and a final one of 14 September are given in full in Moscheles's memoirs and there is no hint of any undercurrent of hostility; in fact we find Schindler sharing this disturbing news with Moscheles: "At Prague, Herr Schlosser has published a most wretched biography of Beethoven."[100] As late as October 1840 Moscheles still seemed to be very much in the good graces of the amanuensis-turned-author, for in a letter to his wife describing a brief stay in Aix-la-Chapelle with Mendelssohn he sketches the following amusing vignette: "The journey was a satisfactory one, and here we have no end of friendly meetings . . . : afterwards in came a long gaunt figure of the Don Quixote kind, and embraced me—it was Schindler. He greeted Mendelssohn, who returned the salutation, although, as I saw, with some mental reserve. . . . Schindler emphatically annihilated music and musicians of the present day."[101]

This thumbnail sketch of the man whose portrait of Beethoven was to become the official account for several decades is fascinating indeed: through Moscheles's twinkling eyes we glimpse a lanky German Don Quixote whose self-imposed mission was to attack with the lance of his critical tongue the hideous windmills of modern music. When Moscheles himself was transformed into one of these offensive targets, Don Anton did not hesitate to charge. Before we examine the attack, the devious tactics of which were to cast a false light upon the image of Beethoven, let us confirm that a search of Moscheles's diary and letters for the period surrounding the fateful year of 1841 reveals no hint of willful wrongdoing regarding giving full credit to Schindler's authorship of the Beethoven biography. Although he discusses his musical publications, Moscheles makes no mention of the 1841 English translation of Schindler's work published in two volumes by the London firm of Henry Colburn or of his part in "editing" it. This omission suggests that Moscheles did not consider his last minute involvement with the publication in any way crucial. He had just been appointed pianist to Prince Albert (1840) and from the publisher's point of view this honorary title, plus the fact of Moscheles's personal acquaintance with the subject of the biography, must have appeared as highly desirable features to incorporate in the packaging of the Schindler book for an English public. Moscheles was not responsible for the title page in which his name and appointment to Prince Albert are mentioned and Schindler as author is not. This was the publisher's doing. In his editor's preface Moscheles does indeed refer to Schindler while at the same time making the character of his "editorial" collaboration quite clear. He writes of "acceding to Mr. Colburn's request that I would add to the English translation of Schindler's Biography of Beethoven which he was about to publish, such explanatory notes, characteristics, and letters as might tend more fully to illustrate and complete the whole," and states emphatically that "the Notes bearing my signature, then, are all that belong to me in these volumes. The Appendix is, however, of my collection."[102]

Thus forewarned, let us now gird our loins for the inevitable Schindlerian attack under the banner of Beethoven. It was unleashed in 1860—nineteen years after the English title-page incident—in the third and last edition of his Beethoven biography. Schindler's opening maneuver was to circle up within striking dis-

tance of his intended victim by relating one of Moscheles's own cheerful anecdotes about the composer and then gratuitously suggesting to the reader an unflattering level of interpretation: "Once Moscheles had to make an arrangement
of a number from [*Fidelio*]. . . . Hummel had already arranged the piece for Artaria, but Beethoven had torn up the manuscript without knowing who had done
the poor work. At the end of his version Moscheles wrote, perhaps fearing that
his work would suffer the same fate: '*Finis*, with God's help.' Beethoven wrote
underneath: 'Man, help yourself.'"[103]

We note the glancing blow delivered to virtuoso pianist Hummel in passing as
we gear up for Schindler's frontal attack. With crocodile tears aflow, the stalwart
biographer reluctantly leaps into the fray: "What the author must now relate as a
parenthetical adjunct to the above is one of the most unpleasant tasks he has ever
had to assume."[104] Somehow courage comes and Schindler's parenthesis continues for three pages. We learn that in a foreword to an edition of Beethoven sonatas, Moscheles wrote that during the years from 1808 to 1820 he had enjoyed
the personal acquaintance of Beethoven. This (basically truthful) assertion released the arrow of Schindler's mighty crossbow of righteous indignation:

> For Moscheles to say while I am still alive that he enjoyed Beethoven's acquaint-
> ance is the most unheard-of audacity that has ever been uttered. In the inter-
> ests of Beethoven's music, I am forced to say frankly that apart from the in-
> stance described above ["Man, help yourself"], Moscheles was in Beethoven's
> company only once. In November 1823, during a short visit that he made to
> Vienna, I took him to see the master and we three dined together. The reason
> for this meeting was that Moscheles wanted to ask Beethoven in person if he
> might use his English grand piano for a public concert that was to take place at
> the Kärntnerthor Theater. . . . Strangely enough, the master's reply was that he
> suspected Moscheles of some kind of financial speculation, since the piano had
> too short a keyboard to be of use to him. Nevertheless he lent him the piano.[105]

We are not allowed breathing space to interrupt or question Schindler as to what
authority fixes the number of encounters between Beethoven and Moscheles at
only two during fifteen years of opportunities, for the very next arrow this relentless wager of verbal warfare lets fly at Moscheles is tipped with poison, and
we can only cringe in discomfort: "But we must mention in this connection another more important obstacle to any familiarity between Moscheles and Beethoven. This was Beethoven's hatred for the children of Israel in the arts, for he
saw how they all turned toward the newest innovations, making profit from the
most lucrative trends."[106] Schindler's Beethoven had, by 1860, absorbed all of the
former secretary's sub-rosa prejudices, and this legend-locked vein of anti-Semitism was not missed or neglected by later miners of the Beethoven myth, including Wagner and Hitler. Schindler's irresponsible misrepresentation of the image
of Beethoven for the sanctimonious, deluded aim of destroying the composer's
"enemies" fulfills the prescient words that Beethoven himself once wrote to him:
"Moreover I have on the whole a certain fear of you, a fear lest some day through
your action a great misfortune may befall me."[107]

If Moscheles discovered himself belittled and even expelled from Schindler's
Beethoven, he was recompensed by continuing to find greatness in Beethoven's
Beethoven—the music. During the politically troubled year of 1848, when peti-
tions, barricades, and riots were springing up across Germany as the Biedermeier
generation was awakened from its slumber by the strident call for civil liberties,
Moscheles found serenity and inspiration in the Ninth Symphony: "This work

revealed new beauties to me . . . [it] stands relatively to other Symphonies like the Cathedral of Cologne to other churches."[108]

How revelatory of the times is Moscheles's choice of cathedrals to compare with the titan of symphonies: it is not Strassburg but Cologne. This nomination is a faithful reflection of the change in focus of the Gothic Revival movement in Germany after young Sulpiz Boisserée's "conversion" of Goethe to the cause. Once the sage of Weimar had swung his weight to the project—he even allowed *Von Deutscher Baukunst* to be reissued in 1823—the drive to finish that most "German" of German cathedrals, Cologne, became a national passion. By 1850 enough work had been done on closing up the nave that it was possible to use the cathedral as the site for the elaborate ceremony installing Archbishop von Geissel as a cardinal. One of the witnesses of this impressive event was Robert Schumann, who, at the end of the same year attempted to convey the Gothic grandeur of the "solemn ceremony" in the fourth, "Cathedral," movement of his Symphony no. 3 in E-flat Major. No wonder that the image of mighty Cologne Cathedral, with its vast proportions and bold harmony of detail, sprang to Moscheles's mind as an appropriate analogy to Beethoven's Ninth.

Something on the magnitude of the Ninth was surely needed to take Moscheles's thoughts off the woes afflicting his homeland. He had come "home" at what soon proved to be a bad time. It had been his devotion to Mendelssohn and the lure of participating in the active musical life of Leipzig that had induced Moscheles in 1846 to say farewell to his loving London public of twenty-five years and take up the post of piano professor at his friend's newly founded Conservatory of Music at Leipzig. Now, two years later, Mendelssohn was dead and Germany alive with revolutionary agitation. Love for Beethoven's music did indeed literally help Moscheles through those troubled times. "Whenever I play, I forget everything. . . . How beautiful the world is, after all; this misery will pass, and liberty will dawn upon us!"[109]

Moscheles also found some satisfaction in conducting *German* musicians in the playing of Beethoven's music, particularly the Ninth Symphony, since he was able to achieve "certain effects and 'nuances' which with all my hearty exertions I could not succeed in bringing out with a London orchestra."[110] Observing the strugglings of promising young German composers with a kindly eye, Moscheles again reached for the model of Beethoven. He appraised Brahms accordingly:

Brahm's [*sic*] compositions are of a really elevated character, and Schumann, whom he has chosen as his model, recommends him as the "Messiah of Music." I find him, like Schumann, often piquant, but occasionally too labored. Even Beethoven's music was objected to, people say, when it first appeared, as being too farfetched, and difficult to understand. True it is, that Beethoven's genius lured him away to paths never trodden before, which are not accessible to everyone, and yet since that time it has been proved, that he not only sought but found what he wished to express in music. Let us hope that this also may be the lot of the younger composer.[111]

Another promising young pianist-composer crossed Moscheles's path at this time (1854–55). He was a young Russian whose exotic, elemental appearance suggested a cherished countenance from the past: "Rubinstein's features and short irrepressible hair remind me of Beethoven." When we compare the unruly-haired Beethoven of August von Klöber's portrait drawing (Fig. 11) with the Anton Rubinstein (1829–94) of photographs (Fig. 66) the Beethoven of Moscheles's recollection appears before us with uncanny immediacy. This is indeed a "Tartar" version of Beethoven, with remarkably similar, squarish features—high forehead, muscular chin, pronounced philtrum, and short, broad nose. This rough-hewn physical resemblance to Beethoven—noted by other comtemporaries as well—did not displease Rubinstein, who venerated him above all other musicians, and who would later surprise and electrify audiences in New York and Saint Petersburg by presenting all-Beethoven piano recitals.[112]

The receptivity of Moscheles's visual memory and the increasing pleasure he took in recalling the past ("Every performance of Beethoven's overture in C, op. 115, is especially interesting to me, for it reminds me of the old Vienna days, when Beethoven lent it me [*sic*] in manuscript for one of my concerts."[113]) conspired in a curious and wonderful way for the seventy-five-year-old Moscheles one night in December of 1869. The image of his long-departed friend Beethoven appeared to him in a dream. So vivid was the impression, so strange the dream-assembled circumstances, that Moscheles carefully wrote a detailed account in his diary:

> Towards morning, after a restless, almost sleepless night, I had the following highly exciting dream. I chanced to hear (I wonder where?) that, since the day of Beethoven's death in Vienna, a couple of old servants were in charge of the room in which he died, and declared that, on each anniversary of Beethoven's birthday, he could be conjured up to appear in bodily form, but only to those with whom he had been personally acquainted in his lifetime. . . . I must go there (I said to myself,) and told Charlotte what I proposed doing. She eagerly caught at the idea, and begged and prayed I would take her with me. I was much embarrassed, and explained to her that such a thing was impossible, as she had not known Beethoven personally. She would not be put off, and begged hard I would allow her at least to see the manes of the great departed; surely I could make him understand that *my* wife ought to be pardoned this act of indiscretion. After much hesitation I consented! On the appointed day we came to Vienna, and demanded admission to the room. We sat upon the bed in which Beethoven had pronounced his last words, "Plaudite, amici, comædia finita est." The servants made some mysterious movements with their hands, and soon afterwards Beethoven, in bodily form, arose slowly like a statue of white marble, the body draped in classical Grecian folds. The apparition came near, and stretched out its cold hands towards me; I clasped them immediately and kissed them. Beethoven turned his head towards me in a kindly way, as if he wanted to ask me questions; I intimated to him by signs that he could not hear my answers. He shook his head sorrowfully, withdrew his hands from mine, and vanished into the upper air—then I awoke.[114]

Three months after recording this poignant dream, old Moscheles, surrounded by his wife Charlotte and their children, quietly expired. He had been allowed to see forty-three more years into the future than had Beethoven, but at the end of his life the impress of that musical genius whom he had known half a century earlier revealed itself as still puissantly distinct. Such was Moscheles's Beethoven then—an image composed in equal measures of authenticity, comprehension, and veneration.

Among his discerning pronouncements on younger German composers, Moscheles had, in 1849, linked the names of Beethoven and Schumann in an interesting comparison: "On a second hearing of Schumann's Symphony in C, I feel more and more that he follows boldly in Beethoven's footsteps, reminding me of him in daring, but scarcely in tenderness."[115]

ROBERT SCHUMANN

In his own estimation Robert Schumann (1810–1856) (Fig. 67) asked only that his name be placed "somewhere near" Beethoven's.[116] Those qualities that characterize much of Schumann's music—dreamy meditation and sanguine ebullience—inform with a sunny warmth the words that streamed so gracefully from Schumann's pen as editor for nine and a half years of the *Neue Zeitschrift für Musik*. One of the century's most articulate and cultured composers, along with Liszt and Berlioz, he created a new "poetic criticism" of music inspired by the literary models of E.T.A. Hoffmann and Jean Paul Richter (1763–1825), but trading the mist-shrouded extremes and extravagances of early Romanticism for lucidity and enthusiasm. The cordiality, integrity, and imagination with which Schumann expressed himself on musical subjects were paradigms of constructive criticism. His belief that a critic's review should attempt to convey the impression created in the original music, bearing the reader aloft from the deserts of dry analysis, introduced and legitimized an empathic alternative to the technical music criticism of the day. He called all manner of poetic devices to his aid in his efforts to reconvey the musical work of art. To give utterance to his words Schumann assembled a partly imaginary league of "Davidites"(the *Davidsbündler*)—art lovers whose passionate disagreements and discussions of music were printed like fragments from a continuous novel in the playful pages of Schumann's *Neue Zeitschrift*. The Davidites' enthusiastic comments were very different from the staid conservatism and ossified platitudes of Leipzig's other musical journal, Rochlitz's august *Allgemeine musiklische Zeitung*. The affection and prominence that Schumann, like his esteemed friend Mendelssohn, gave to great composers of the past not only disseminated music history but *made* music history by amplifying the myth of Beethoven for the nineteenth century.

Schumann's instinctive reverence for two musical geniuses—Beethoven and Schubert—had begun in Saxony, where he was born, and by the time a trip to Austria (1838) was decided upon—as part of his strategy to wrest his beloved Clara Wieck from her father's tenacious grasp—Schumann had assumed the worshipful attitude of a true pilgrim. The pilgrimage route led to Beethoven's grave, and the twenty-eight-year-old Schumann spoke for his generation when he described his romantic odyssey:

> The musician who visits Vienna for the first time delights awhile in the festive life of the streets, and often stands admiringly before the door of Saint Stephen's Cathedral; but he soon remembers how near to the city lies a cemetery containing something worthier of regard to his mind than all the city boasts— the spot where two of the glorious heroes of his art rest, only a few steps apart. No doubt, then, many a young musician, after the first few days of excitement in Vienna, has like me wandered to the Währinger Cemetery to place flowers on those graves, were it but a wild rosebush, such as I found planted on Beethoven's. Franz Schubert's resting place was unadorned. One fervent desire of my life was fulfilled; I gazed long on the two sacred graves, almost envying the person buried between them. . . . [117]

These reverent words had been written for an article to be published in the *Neue Zeitschrift*, the musical review Schumann had cofounded in Leipzig four years earlier and which, with high hopes, he now sought permission from the local authorities to publish in Vienna. For this was the other part of his and Clara's plan— to distance themselves from the treacherous father who played psychological havoc with their plans to marry and to win financial independence through Robert's musical journalism and Clara's piano concerts. During the first few weeks in Vienna Schumann's optimism was strong and in a letter to his brothers back in Saxony he reported a cheering incident that augured success: "Yesterday I went to the cemetery where Beethoven and Schubert are buried. Just fancy what I found on Beethoven's grave—*a pen*, and a steel one [*eine Stahlfeder*] to boot. That seemed to me a good omen, and I shall preserve it as something quite sacred."[118]

Heartened by this symbolic find at the site of Beethoven's mortal remains, Schumann, in a Jean Paul type of reverie, empathically scanned Vienna's horizon: "Often when gazing on the city from the heights above I have thought how frequently Beethoven's eyes may have glanced restlessly toward the distant silhouette of the Alps."[119] But as Schumann's gaze fixed on the details of Vienna life, with its superficiality, frivolous musical tastes, gossip, warring cliques, and ubiquitous officialdom that promised nothing but endless delays and complications for *Neue Zeitschrift* publishing prospects, the idealist quickly became an indignant realist: "Vienna is the city where Beethoven lived; and there is perhaps no place in the world where Beethoven is so little played and mentioned as Vienna."[120]

Did Schumann realize that he was echoing Beethoven's own bitter thoughts, as expressed so frequently in the last years to his foreign visitors? One of those visitors was Schumann's own reluctant future father-in-law, Friedrich Wieck (1785–1873). For two years Robert had lived in the Wieck household as an earnest student of Friedrich Wieck's punctilious piano pedagogy—the same tutelage that had produced the pianistic masterpiece of Wieck's career, Clara. Surely at some time before his heart hardened against the improvident, impetuous lover who threatened the carefully plotted destiny of his own child prodigy, the egotistical Wieck must have related to Schumann the story of the most memorable event of his life—his visit to Beethoven.

Since Schumann's literary image of Beethoven would be disjunctively reflected by the manifestations of the dual self he projected in print so successfully—Florestan and Eusebius—it is interesting that the picture Friedrich Wieck left of the living Beethoven was similarly breathless and multifaceted:

> Under the ruddy grapes the conversation turned on musical conditions in Leipzig . . . the Gewandhaus—his own housekeeper,—his many lodgings, none of which really suited him—his promenades—Hietzing—Schönbrunn—his brother—various silly asses in Vienna—aristocracy—democracy—revolution—Napoleon . . . the perfected Italian opera . . . the archduke Rudolf—Fuchs, then a famous musical personage in Vienna. . . . all was done with a certain heartfelt sincerity, even in his utterances of despair, and with a deep inward rolling of his eyes and clutchings at his head and hair. All was rough, at times, perhaps, a little rude, yet noble, elegiac, soulful, well principled, enthusiastic, anticipatory of political mishap. And then? Then he improvised for me during an hour, after he had mounted his ear trumpet. . . . weaving in the clearest and most charming melodies, which seemed to stream to him unsought, most of the time keeping his eyes turned upward, and with close-gathered fingers. . . . After a hearty farewell . . . I crept away . . . quite exhausted and dissolved in the strangest sensations. . . . [121]

This is the only time Wieck ever came close to sounding like Jean Paul—Schumann's hero—and we half expect to hear the elderly pedagogue exclaim in unison with Eusebius: "BEETHOVEN!"

Whatever the ultimate strength of this percolating portrait of Beethoven as filtered down from Wieck to Schumann, a tremendous reinforcement was absorbed by the composer during his six-month sojourn in Vienna. He became convinced that a new epoch of German music was developing from the doubly fertilized soil of "Beethoven-Schubert Romanticism." But, although Schumann literally made some important Schubert manuscript finds in Vienna, his discovery of Beethoven had begun long before he ever set eyes on the Danube. With the total enthusiasm of youth, the twenty-year-old Schumann had made this notation in 1830: "Beethoven's B-flat quartet, op. 130, heard for the first time. Ultimate goal!"[122] Another of the young composer's ultimate goals was to contribute to the erection of a Beethoven monument in Bonn. (A project dear to the heart of Liszt and one that would be realized, as we shall learn in the next chapter.) With the aid of his Davidsbündler friends—three of them imaginary—he published a discussion of four voices on the subject in the pages of the *Neue Zeitschrift*. First to speak was the irrepressible musical zealot Florestan, who was only too eager to heap scorn upon the pedestrian idea of a physical monument to be financed by penny subscriptions:

> The future monument stands vividly before me already; a moderately high pedestal, a lyre upon it with the dates of birth and death, heaven above, and a few trees about it. . . . Fortunate, Napoleon Buonaparte, that thou art sleeping soundly amid the water, and that we Germans cannot persecute thee with monuments. . . . But as for thee, Beethoven, neither thy D-minor symphony, nor all thy lofty songs of grief and joy are great enough for us to spare thee the honor of a monument; thou shalt not escape our recognition! I see well enough, Eusebius, that I make thee angry, and that out of mere goodness of heart thou wouldst allow thyself to be petrified into a statue for a Carlsbad fountain, were the committee once determined on it. Yet do not I also regret that I never saw Beethoven, that my burning forehead was never pressed by his hand,—and I would gladly give a considerable part of my life to be able to say to the contrary![123]

This is Schumann himself talking, and from the heart: he was sixteen when Beethoven died and the missed possibility of meeting the master face to face, as Wieck had done, haunted him. That he did the next best thing— visited Beethoven's last lodgings—is obvious from what Florestan says next:

> I walk slowly toward No. 200 Schwarzspanierhaus (the house in which Beethoven died), and mount the steps; all is hushed around me; I enter his room; he rises like a crowned lion, yet with a splinter in his paw. He speaks of his griefs. In the same moment, a thousand enraptured listeners roam beneath the pillared temple of his C-minor symphony. But the walls may fall together; he hastens out; he complains that he is left alone, that people care little about him. Then the basses rest on that deepest tone in the scherzo of the symphony; not a breath is heard; silently a thousand hearts are suspended over that fathomless deep; but now the glory of the highest created thing seems to dawn; rainbow on rainbow rises above that splendor.—And still he roams through the streets; no one knows him, no one greets him.—The last chords of the symphony resound; the public rubs its hands, enthusiastic philistines exclaim, "Ha, that is true music."—And thus you treated him during his life; none cared to offer him true companionship; full of grief he died, and, like Napoleon, without a child beside him; alone in the solitude of a city. Erect a monument to him now; perhaps he deserved it; but do not forget to engrave Goethe's verses on the pedestal—

"So long as a great person lives and acts,
   People would gladly stone him.
   But once he's dead and gone,
   They immediately go about collecting huge donations
   To insure that a Monument
   Will honor his life's misery.
   But they should weigh their gain;
   It would be much smarter
   To forget the good man altogether."[124]

Florestan-Schumann has not only linked the epoch's three mightiest figures—Napoleon, Beethoven, and Goethe—he has also used Goethe's sarcastic sermonette to reinforce his own fierce opinion that no amount of posthumous public acknowledgment can sufficiently honor the departed creator who gave but did not receive. He chastizes those Viennese philistines who, surviving Beethoven, boast of the spiritual nourishment they receive from the composer whom, in life, they neglected. Florestan clearly prefers the "abandoned" Beethoven of recently minted myth to the truculent, suspicious, reclusive Beethoven of actuality. The leonine image of physical portraits is revived by Florestan, crowned, and given appropriate pathos by the image of "a splinter in his paw." This allows the ultra-sensitive Romantic to revel in the allegorical wounds of his hero.

The monument-to-Beethoven discussion takes a sardonic turn with the next voice to be heard. Begging to be excused from giving an opinion, Jonathan (the Davidsbündler nickname for Schumann's real-life friend and fellow composer Ludwig Schunke[125]) delivers a jab at the rival cities now claiming Beethoven as their own: "We understand that the Viennese feel jealous of the people of Bonn, and determine to have a monument also: what a farce when people shall ask which of them is the real and correct thing? Both cities hold ownership in Beethoven; he figured in the church registers of both places; the Rhine calls itself his cradle, the Danube (mournful celebrity), his bier. . . . Finally, (Leipzig) will step in as a sort of central ground for German cultivation, with this especial claim to regard, that it was the first city to interest itself in Beethoven's compositions. . . ."[126]

Irony leaves off when Leipzig is mentioned, however, for Schumann and his circle were ready and pleased to acknowledge that old Rochlitz, in spite of his (to them) conservative shortcomings, had done more than any other music critic to promote appreciation of Beethoven in North Germany and especially in Leipzig, home of the *Allgemeine musikalische Zeitung.* And Schumann's present-day idol Mendelssohn had since taken up the Beethoven banner in his capacity as conductor of the Leipzig Gewandhaus concerts. The Davidites could indeed be proud of their own city's (dubbed "Firlenz" in the pages of the *Neue Zeitschrift*) contributions to the cause of Beethoven.

It was the other side of Schumann's musical self—Eusebius—that recoiled at Florestan's nihilistic attitude concerning a monument to Beethoven. Inspired by an image of Beethoven as *German* (a concept that would later enrich the coffers of Nazi ideology), Eusebius began passionately:

One should walk on tiptoe in church,—but your sudden entrance offends me, Florestan. At the present moment, we give our attention to many hundreds of men; the question is German; Germany's noblest artist, the first representative of the German mind, not even excepting Jean Paul, is to be honored: he belongs to *our* art; they have been labouring at the Schiller monument for many years;

that to Gutenberg is yet at the commencement. If you let the affair drop, or even set about it indifferently, you will deserve all the kicks of insolent Byronian poetry. . . . And shall not a whole nation, taught patriotism and greatness of heart by the creations of Beethoven, make public evidence of gratitude . . . ?[127]

Warming to his topic, the creative Eusebius fantasized a spectrum of colorful memorial possibilities:

Were I a prince, I would build a temple in the style of Palladio, to his memory; ten statues should stand within it, and if Thorvaldsen and Dannecker would not execute them all, they should at least see that all were executed under their superintendence; nine they should be, these statues, like the number of the muses, and of his symphonies,—Clio the Eroica, Thalia the Fourth, Euterpe the Pastoral, and so on,—himself the divine Apollo. There the German people should assemble from time to time, to celebrate festivals, and there his own works should be performed in the highest stage of perfection. Or else: take a hundred century-old oak trees, and write his name with them, in giant letters, on a plain. Or carve his likeness in colossal proportions, like Saint Borromeo on Lake Maggiore, that he may gaze above the mountains, as he did when living; and when Rhine ships pass, and foreigners ask the name of that giant form, every child may answer—It is Beethoven. Or would you dedicate to him a living monument, build in his name an academy for German music, where *music, his* word, may be taught, not as a trade that any mechanic may choose, but a school of poets, a school of music in the Grecian sense, to be opened by the hands of a pure priesthood to the chosen ones only. Rise, throw off your indifference, and remember that his monument will also commemorate yourselves![128]

A not-so-invisible Italian itinerary pulsates behind Eusebius's references to Palladian temples and the giant statue of Saint Carlo Borromeo: the seven- week trip through North Italy that Schumann made during the summer of 1829 while still a student at Heidelberg. With his own eyes the nineteen-year-old reluctant student of law admired the somber seventeenth-century bronze effigy of the Milanese saint rising 113 feet above Arona; and, traveling eastward towards Venice by way of Vicenza, Schumann had seen and would always remember the elegant edifices of Palladio. Turning from Renaissance and Baroque prototypes for a monument to Beethoven to contemporary artists, Eusebius-Schumann singles out two of the period's most renowned sculptors, the Dane Bertel Thorvaldsen (1770–1844) and the Swabian Johann Heinrich von Dannecker (1758–1841). Schumann was obviously aware of these artists' portrayals of German heroes—the Schiller and Gutenberg monuments to which Eusebius refers were both projects Thorvaldsen had been commissioned to design: the Schiller monument for Stuttgart (completed 1835) and the Gutenberg monument for the city of Mainz (1833–34; executed by Herman Vilhelm Bissen). Schumann may also have been thinking of Dannecker's colossal marble bust of Schiller, finished in 1810 and destined for the temple of German heroes then abuilding outside Regensburg—Walhalla (completed 1842)—pet project of King Ludwig I. The Bavarian art-loving king had also ordered the busts of Haydn and Gluck (ready since 1825) to be included among his selection of 118 immortals. Surely the differing reactions of Florestan and Eusebius concerning the erection of a Beethoven monument were in part inspired by the epidemic of sculptural memorials then sweeping Schumann's Germany.

The last to sound his opinion on a Beethoven monument in Schumann's quartet of voices is the mediator between Florestan and Eusebius, the wise and older Master Raro (Schumann's ideal, integrated, and whole self, and symbol of the union between himself and Clara—ClaRARObert). Immediately Raro councils a middle road:

> Your ideas need a handle; Florestan is a destroyer, Eusebius allows things to fall of themselves. It is certain that when we act in the manner preferred by the beloved dead, we give the highest proof of reverence and gratitude; but Florestan must acknowledge that any kind of reverence requires an outward manifestation, and that so long as the commencement is delayed, one generation will blame another for procrastination. Under the brave mantle which Florestan throws over the affair, avarice and low motives may here and there take refuge, as well as fear that people may be taken at their word when they incautiously praise monuments in honor of great men. Unite your views![129]

Raro-Schumann not only dispenses wisdom, he suggests a practical plan, citing the names of Beethoven adherents who are already at work:

> Collections should be made throughout Germany; concerts, operatic representations, performances in churches should take place, nor would it be unsuitable to solicit gifts from great singing or music festivals. Ries in Frankfurt, Chélard in Augsburg, L. Schuberth in Königsberg have lately commenced the work, Spontini in Berlin, Spohr in Kassel, Hummel in Weimar, Mendelssohn in Leipzig . . . see! how many honorable artist names I lay before you, and yet what forces, means, and cities remain. May a lofty obelisk or pyramid apprise posterity that the contemporaries of a great man, though they esteemed his intellectual creations as his noblest monument, yet spared no pains to evince their admiration by an extraordinary outward manifestation![130]

The presence of this fanciful four-part choral with varying texts for a monument to Beethoven in the pages of the newborn *Neue Zeitschrift für Musik* is delightful testimonial to Schumann's interest in the project. In the summer of 1836 Schumann channeled his support of a Beethoven monument for the city of Bonn into a different medium—music. He composed the Phantasie in C Major, op. 17, and announced it to Breitkopf and Härtel, the Leipzig publishers whom he had in common with Beethoven, as a Grand Sonata for piano "of which copies will be sold in aid of the monument."[131] Its three movements were to be titled, he suggested, "Ruins," "Triumphal Arch," and "Wreath of Stars," and the dedication would be to Franz Liszt. The work was not published until 1839, however, and then without the "Beethoven" references Schumann had requested—designations considered too fanciful by the publisher.

How to aid the Bonn Beethoven project was still on Schumann's mind as he prepared to leave Leipzig for the ill-fated Vienna foray: writing one of his *Neue Zeitschrift* contributors, he suggested some provocative topics for forthcoming issues of the magazine: "What are your ideas about musical festivals, prize competitions, Beethoven monument?"[132]

Although Schumann claimed that he only used "the letters of the alphabet under compulsion" and preferred "writing symphonies and sonatas directly,"[133] his alphabetic altruism produced a new kind of Beethoven criticism which, because of its messianic fervor, itself became a part of the Beethoven mystique. Paralleling the disparate yet engaged personalities of Florestan and Eusebius, Schumann oscillates between bluster and circumspection, rapture and historicism, slyly delivering analytical observations in the guise of innocent remarks by technically minded "Beethovians" (philistine music lovers or connoisseurs who are the butt of both Florestan's and Eusebius's wit), and overtly fleshing out the conception of Beethoven as Romanticist by applying his credo that musical criticism at its highest "leaves behind it an impression resembling that awakened by its subject."[134] It was with this heady justification that Schumann called upon literature as effective aid to her sister art: "In this sense, Jean Paul, by means of a poetic companion picture, may contribute more to the understanding of a Beethoven symphony or fantasia (even without mentioning either symphony or fantasia) than a dozen so-called art critics, who place their ladders against the Colossus, and measure him carefully by the yard."[135]

In a single stunning sentence Schumann could allegorize, demystify, then re-poeticize the practical tools of his critic's trade: "As a pedagogue, I must search for these objects—roots, flower, and fruit, or for the mechanical, harmonic, melodic, and poetical contents, or for the gain offered to heart, ear, and hand."[136]

Schumann's multiple approach to critical morphosis is nowhere so in evidence as in his attempt to recreate the impression awakened by hearing Mendelssohn conduct consecutive performances of all four overtures to *Fidelio* in one evening. Like the overtures, Schumann's essays on them took four different forms. The earliest (1840) allowed Schumann's three alter egos to express themselves entirely in character:

Eusebius: When it was played for the first time in Vienna and almost wholly failed, it is said that Beethoven wept; in the same situation Rossini would have laughed. Beethoven was induced to write the new one in E Major, which might have been written by some other composer.—Thou didst err; yet thy tears were noble.

Raro: The first conception is always the most natural and the best. The understanding may err, but never the feeling.

Florestan: Ye peddlers in art, do ye not sink into the earth when ye are reminded of the words uttered by Beethoven on his deathbed: "I believe I am as yet but at the beginning"; or Jean Paul: "It seems to me that I have written nothing as yet?"[137]

In Schumann's second attempt, Florestan gets to chastise the Viennese all by himself before leading his readers backstage into the imagined workings of Beethoven's mind:

It should be written in golden letters that last Thursday the Leipzig Orchestra performed—the four overtures to *Fidelio, one after another.*

Thanks to you, Viennese of 1805, that the first did not please you and that Beethoven in divine rage therefore poured forth the three others. If he ever appeared powerful to me, he did so on that evening, when, better than ever, we were able to listen to him, forming, rejecting, altering in his own workshop, and glowing with inspiration. He was most gigantic in his second start. The first overture was not effective; stop! thought he, the second shall rob you of all thought—and so he set himself to work anew and allowed the thrilling drama to pass before him, again singing the joys and sorrows of his heroine. This second overture is demonic in its boldness—even bolder, in certain details, than the third, the well-known great one in C Major. But it did not satisfy him; he laid this one aside also, merely retaining certain passages from which, already more certain and conscious, he formed the third. Afterwards there followed the lighter and more popular one in E Major, which is generally heard in the theater as the prelude. Such is the great four-overture work. Formed after the manner of Nature, we first find in it the roots from which, in the second, the giant trunk arises, stretching its arms right and left, and finally completed by its leafy crown.[138]

We note the words and phrases used by the stormy Florestan to characterize his hero's persona and music interchangeably: "powerful" and "demonic"; "boldness" and "divine rage." The readers are taken to the forge of creativity; it is a Vulcan who hammers and lines up his musical thunderbolts. And the soothing concluding analogy of the tree of nature reminds us that Goethe's simile of Strassburg Cathedral as a tree of God still casts its spell on the generation of 1810.

Schumann appears with his own editorial voice in the third essay on the *Leonore* overtures, pleading for the publication of the scores of all four overtures (the manuscript to the second one in C major was still lying fallow at Breitkopf and Härtel) in one volume. He argues that such a collective edition would not only be a memorable demonstration of conscientiousness, but also an insight into the "more secret workshop of a master," in particular providing an example of "the almost playful creative and inventive power of this Beethoven in whom Nature simultaneously combined the gifts for which she usually requires a thousand vessels."[139]

The linking of Beethoven's gifts with "Nature" thus continues and the concept of Beethoven as titanic receptacle for an overabundance of talent is effectively advanced in this otherwise sober call for publishing completeness. And it is the editor in Schumann who speaks out in the fourth essay (written two years later, in 1842), prompted by the publication of the parts, if not yet the score, to the second *Leonore* overture. How Schindler must have rejoiced to have found himself and his new book cited as ultimate authority for the sequence in which the four overtures were written! This would not prevent the self-appointed Metronome of Beethoven tempi from pillorying Clara Schumann's playing of Beethoven, however, as we shall see. Schumann may have felt respect for some of Schindler's more knowledgeable assertions concerning Beethoven's music, but his kudos concerning an account of Beethoven's life went to Schindler's immediate predecessors in the field, Wegeler and Ries. In a letter to his close friend, the pianist Henriette Voigt, Schumann announced happily: "You will find something interesting to read on your return. Some biographical notices of Beethoven have just come out by Ferdinand Ries and Dr. Wegeler (the latter a faithful schoolfriend of Beethoven's). I will lend you the book—one cannot tear one's self away from it."[140] Nevertheless Schumann may have been the first to have seen the need for an account of the *interior* Beethoven, for he continues: "It is reserved to some future Jean Paul to write Beethoven's history, from within and without—a glorious work, worthy of a second master."[141]

The genial enthusiasm and often pure delight that set Schumann's brand of music reviewing so apart from the unctuous or carping approach of his somber contemporaries is best encountered in connection with Beethoven in an essay responding to a rondo-capriccio manuscript from among Beethoven's posthumous works bearing the "title" "Rage over the Lost Penny, Released in a Capriccio" (op. 129). Schumann uses this endearing "evidence" of Beethoven's membership in the human race to poke fun at certain idolaters: "It is the most amiable, harmless anger, similar to that felt when one cannot pull a shoe off the foot and perspires and stamps while the shoe very phlegmatically looks up at its owner. Now I have you, Beethovenians! I could be angry with you in quite another way when you gush with enthusiasm and cast your eyes to heaven and rave about Beethoven's freedom from earthliness, his transcendental flight from star to star."[142]

In responding to the "content" of this piano piece Schumann could not have known that the title had actually been supplied by the man whose life of Beethoven he respected—Schindler. The helpful inscription, "Rage over the Lost Penny, Released in a Capriccio," had probably been added by the overwrought scribe prior to the auctioning off of Beethoven's effects, for the purchasers, Diabelli and Company, published the piece in 1828 with a title page bearing the motto that caught Schumann's bemused attention: "Die Wuth über den verloren Groschen, ausgetobt in einer *Caprice*."[143] Schumann did not use this particular piece as springboard for an exegesis on program music (as he would Beethoven's Sixth Symphony), possibly because, as he candidly admitted, he had sensed not rage but mirth in the music before noticing the title page inscription: "It would be difficult to find anything merrier than this whim."[144] Instead he developed his cherished counter-theme to Beethoven as titan; that humanizing one of Beethoven as ordinary mortal springing from nature and subject to base humors:

> "Today I feel altogether unbuttoned," was his favorite expression when he was inwardly merry. [Schumann had obviously been reading Rochlitz's reminiscences.] And then he laughed like a lion and beat about him, for he was always untamable! "But with this capriccio I'll get you!" You will think it common, unworthy of a Beethoven, like the melody to *Freude, schöner Götterfunken* in the D Minor Symphony; you will hide it far, far beneath the *Erioca*! And should we have a new renaissance of art—the genius of truth holding the balance with this comic capriccio on one side and ten of the newest pathetic overtures on the other—the overtures would rise as high as heaven. Young and old composers, there is one thing you may learn from it of which, above all things, it is necessary to remind you—Nature, Nature, Nature![145]

How this all too human aspect of converting domestic frustration into musical material must have appealed to Schumann's understanding and experience of the autobiographical dimensions in some of his own compositional inspiration. This *affective* viewpoint was cogently expressed by Schumann to a fellow composer once while attempting to summarize his musical methodology: "I began to compose at once, and even in my early years the simple lyrical style was not enough for me. So I soon got to Beethoven, soon to Bach. Literature, surroundings, mental and physical experience, also influenced me, and now I sometimes ask myself where it will all end."[146] And in a letter to Clara two years before their marriage Robert wrote with even greater specificity of this important ingredient in his Romantic makeup: "Anything that happens in the world affects me; politics, for example, literature, people; and I reflect about all those things in my own way—and these reflections then seek to find an outlet in music."[147]

Predisposed then to comprehend musical form as transformed inner experience, Schumann as critic was nevertheless wary of literal or realistic interpretations. Beethoven's Sixth Symphony was a case in point: "In composing his *Pastoral* Symphony Beethoven well understood the dangers he incurred. His explanatory remark, 'Rather expressive of the feeling than tone painting,' contains an entire aesthetic system for composers. And it is absurd for painters to portray him sitting beside a brook, his head in his hands, listening to the bubbling water!"[148]

This explicit disapproval of Beethoven-by-the Brook imagery, with its conjuring up of Lyser's 1833 portrait in particular (see Fig. 50), shows us a different side of the *Neue Zeitschrift* editor. He did not hesitate to risk offending a fellow contributor, in this case the real-life Davidite "Vater Doles," alias "Fritz Friedrich," otherwise identified by Schumann as "the deaf painter Lyser, a friend of mine."[149] Schumann's reluctance to accept a literal image—either in a portrait of Beethoven or in a passage by Beethoven—is consonant with Romantic ambivalence, which placed more stock in the power to suggest and evoke than in the ability to define. Such titillating vagueness did not however prevent the musicologist in Schumann from speaking out on "certain probably corrupted passages" in Beethoven scores. One sudden, quixotic rest in the first violins in the first movement of the Sixth Symphony, for example, is singled out for correction by Schumann with convincing technical arguments (accepted by later musicologists). In the same breath Schumann the Beethoven worshiper also reasons how it was possible that the musical world had listened to the same passage year after year without violently complaining. The reason "can only be explained by the magic influence of Beethoven's music which moves us so deeply that, while immersed in it, we almost forget to think and hear."[150]

It was partly to distance himself from the magic circle of music, so that he *could* think, *could* hear, that Schumann faceted himself into the several personalities who speak with such different tongues in the pages of his magazine. ("Florestan and Eusebius represent my dual nature, which like Raro, I should like to melt down into a man,"[151] he said accurately of his divided personality and tendency to overstrung emotions, long before the inception of those alternating manic and depressive attacks that announced his mental deterioration.)

Schumann's imaginary trio of Florestan, Eusebius, and Raro scored a fourth and real voice into the animated discussion that followed a performance of Beethoven's Ninth Symphony. The voice was that of the wealthy Leipzig patron of the arts Karl Voigt, husband of Henriette Voigt. He had proven himself worthy of membership in the Davidsbündler by a remark that endeared him forever to Schumann: after hearing a rehearsal of the Ninth, Voigt burst out, enthralled, that he wished to leave part of his fortune to the "divine" work. Evoking and echoing Goethe's discovery of the gothic, Voigt exclaims before the monumental edifice of Beethoven's last symphony: "I am the blind man who is standing before the Strassburg Cathedral, who hears its bells but cannot see the entrance. Leave me in peace, young men; I no longer understand mankind."[152] Eusebius approves of Voigt's groping outburst: "Who blames the blind man if he stands before the cathedral and has nothing to say? Let him only remove his hat reverently while the bells ring above."[153] Florestan leaps in with several, important to the myth-making process, injunctions: "Yes, love him, love him well, but never forget that he reached poetic freedom only through long years of study; and reverence his never-ceasing moral force. Do not search for the abnormal in him, return to the source of his creations; do not illustrate his genius with the Ninth Symphony alone, no matter how great its audacity and scope, never uttered in any tongue."[154] At last Master Raro enters the dialogue, his customary calm giving way to emotion: "No more words on the subject! Let us forever love that lofty spirit who looks down with benignity on that life which gave him so little. . . . Young men, you have a long and difficult road before you. A wonderful glow fills the sky—whether of morning or evening, I do not know."[155] But in fact Raro-Schumann did know: Beethoven's creations had brought music to a new dawning—the new Romantic School. And Beethoven's last symphony was, for

Schumann and his Davidites, "the turning point from the classical to the Romantic period."[156]

Schumann's Beethoven critiques often turned against their articulator in sly Jean Paulian fashion. Concerning the Seventh Symphony, *Neue Zeitschrift* readers were entertained with another droll attack on the excesses of programmatic exposition to which Beethoven was subjected. In a heated discussion of the symphony, the Davidites ridiculed both the deification and the demystification of the composer's music. Eusebius reports a "lecture" given by Florestan as he used Master Raro's piano to punctuate his observations. Playing the opening chords of the symphony, Florestan claims to laugh at those "who eternally preach about the innocence and absolute beauty of music as such," saying that his fingertips itch when he hears "some people say that Beethoven, while writing his symphonies, gave himself up to exalted sentiments—lofty thoughts of God, immortality, and the course of the stars."[157] Almost hidden in Florestan's outcry is this extraordinarily modern-sounding finding: "in some arias of Marschner's *Hans Heiling*, for example, I find beauty without truth, and in Beethoven, on rare occasions, truth without beauty."[158] Not until early twentieth-century Expressionists like Kirchner and Kokoschka attempted to penetrate the facade of forms would truth "without" beauty become a legitimate and major aim of art. Shifting his attention to those who found Beethoven's A Major Symphony not lofty but only literal, Florestan laughs again, this time at a description he had read in the rival journal *Cäcilia*: "it is the merriest wedding; the bride, a heavenly maid with one rose, only one, in her hair. . . . the guests arrive, greeting each other with servile bows; and the airy flutes remind us that in the village, gay with maypoles, gawdy with ribbons, everyone rejoices for and with the bride Rosa."[159]

The spritsail of Schumann's skifflike humor is fully extended before the majestic presence of the Ninth Symphony as, awed by his delight in the music and delighted by his awe, Florestan takes refuge in a parody of those musical pedants who believe that description equals explanation: "When the first chord of the finale burst out, I said to a trembling man next to me: 'What else is this chord, dear cantor, but a common chord with an anticipatory dominant note in a somewhat complicated distribution (because one is uncertain whether to take the A of the timpani or the F of the bassoon for a bass)?' "[160] In his quandary as to how, really, to write about the Ninth without being presumptuous, Schumann again turns to the solution of a divided self—the faceted critic who articulates every possible viewpoint of the professional philistine:

> And I looked at these Beethovenians, as they stood there with their eyes popping out, and said: "That was written by our Beethoven, it is a German work—the finale contains a double fugue—he was blamed for not introducing such forms—but how he did it—yes, this is *our* Beethoven." Another chorus joined in: "The work seems to contain the different genres of poetry, the first movement being epic, the second, comedy, the third, lyric, the fourth (combining all), the dramatic." Still another bluntly began to praise the work as being gigantic, colossal, comparable to the Egyptian pyramids. And others painted word pictures: the symphony expresses the story of mankind—first the chaos—then the call of God "There shall be light"—then the sunrise over the first human being, ravished by such splendor—in one word, the whole first chapter of the Pentateuch in this symphony.
>
> I became angrier and quieter. . . . I grasped Eusebius's arm and went down the stairs with him, surrounded by smiling faces. Below, in the dark of the street lamps, Eusebius said as if to himself: "BEETHOVEN—what a word—the

deep sound of the mere syllables has the ring of eternity. As if no better symbol were possible for this name!" "Eusebius," said I very calmly, "Do you, too, dare to praise Beethoven? Like a lion he would have reared himself before all of you and asked: 'Who are you that you dare be so presumptuous?' I do not mean you, Eusebius, you are a good soul, but does a great man *have* to have thousands of dwarfs in his train?"[161]

Not to praise Beethoven, then, is the only course to take when confronted by the great Inexpressible, Schumann seems to be saying. To experience Beethoven, to feel Beethoven, to *live* Beethoven, this is the only way. In a quieter and completely serious vein, Schumann writes of the Leipzig musical season for 1841: "Finally the Ninth. At last one begins to realize that here a great man has created his greatest work. I do not recall that ever before has it been received so enthusiastically. Saying this we do not mean to praise the work—which is beyond praise—but the audience. . . . "[162]

Publicly counseling silent worship, Schumann now takes his place as the priest of Romanticism's cult of Beethoven. The route to Beethoven—and to oneself—lay through the experiencing of his music: "I am now *living* through some of Beethoven's quartets in the truest sense, and feel even the love and hate in them," Schumann wrote in his own voice to a fellow composer.[163]

In his younger years it had been Schumann's cherished intention to write the lives of both Beethoven and Bach, with a critique of all their works. As he turned from a literary to a musical career however this project was abandoned. But not the outward signs of his veneration. A description of Schumann's bachelor apartment, written just a month before his marriage to Clara, gives us a rare glimpse of the composer in his setting. We are told of Schumann's writing table upon which was displayed a collection of bizarre caricatures of the most famous contemporary musicians—Liszt with four hands, Paganini with rolled-up sleeves contemplating the one unbroken string on his violin—and we hear about a more serious portrait gallery gracing the wall above the grand piano. Next to a haunting deathbed portrait of Ludwig Schunke, the prematurely deceased Davidite whose essay on a Beethoven monument had been signed Jonathan, hung the images of Beethoven and Bach; below them was a "sparkling likeness" of Clara.[164]

CLARA WIECK SCHUMANN

Now that we are to within a month of the long-awaited marriage between Robert Schumann and Clara Wieck (1819–1896) (as father Wieck's last-ditch efforts to prove Schumann a drunkard failed), it would be remiss not to inquire, as Robert had certainly done, into Clara's image of Beethoven (Fig. 68). Whatever Friedrich Wieck's true intentions may have been when he made his pilgrimage to see and talk with Beethoven, the effects of that visit left a pronounced mark upon the piano pedagogy and repertoire the father would impose upon his prize pupil. Rejecting what he considered the mincing technical elegance of the Czerny school, Wieck strove to inculcate Clara's small fingers with a full-bodied, singing touch and her mind with a divinatory sensibility capable of comprehending the fervid pianistic vision of Beethoven—a vision, Wieck said, upon which most of the musical world had turned its back. (Clementi and John Field were exceptions.) In one of the earliest of forty diaries Clara kept through her long life she noted down the high point of attending her first Gewandhaus concert. "I heard a grand symphony by Beethoven," the six-year-old diarist wrote, "which excited

Fig. 39 Franz Stöber, Beethoven's Funeral, *1827, watercolor, Beethovenhaus, Bonn.*

Fig. 40 Moritz Michael Daffinger,
Franz Grillparzer, *1827, watercolor,*
Historisches Museum der
Stadt Wien, Vienna.

161

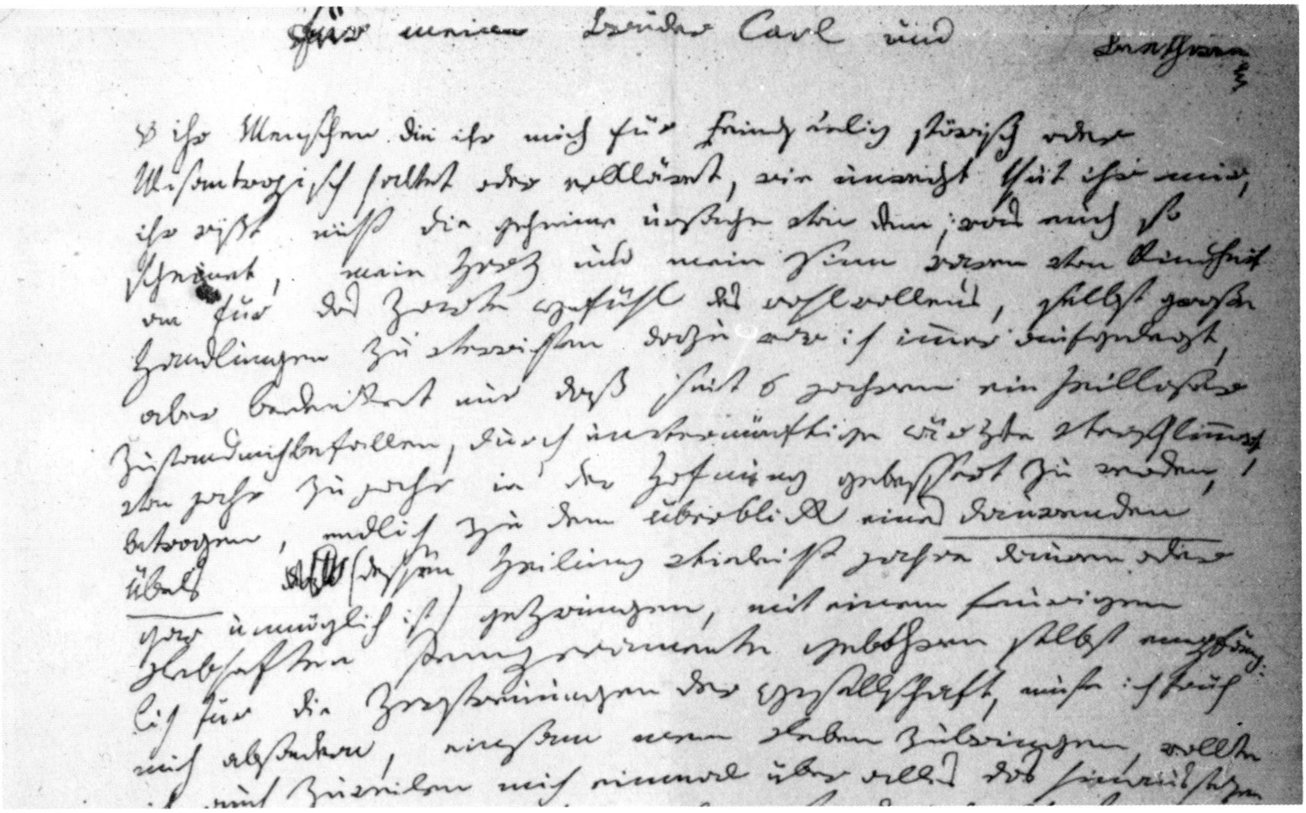

Für meine Brüder Carl und Beethowen

O ihr Menschen die ihr mich für Feindseelig störisch oder
Misantropisch haltet oder erkläret, wie unrecht thut ihr mir,
ihr wißt nicht die geheime ursache von dem, was euch so
scheinet, mein Herz und mein Sinn waren von Kindheit
an für das zarte gefühl des Wohlwollens, selbst große
Handlungen zu verrichten dazu war ich immer aufgelegt,
aber bedenket nur daß seit 6 jahren ein heilloser
Zustand mich befallen, durch unvernünftige Ärzte verschlimmert,
von jahr zu jahr in der Hofnung gebessert zu werden,
betrogen, endlich zu dem überblick eines daurenden
übels (dessen Heilung vieleicht jahre dauren oder
gar unmöglich ist) gezwungen, mit einem feurigen
Lebhaften Temperamente gebohren selbst empfäng-
lich für die Zerstreuungen der Gesellschaft, muste ich früh
mich absondern, einsam mein Leben zubringen, wollte
ich auch zuweilen mich einmal über alles das

Fig. 41 Ludwig van Beethoven, Heiligenstadt Testament, *6–10 October 1802, Stadtbibliotek, Hamburg.*

Fig. 42 Ernst Theodor Amadeus Hoffmann, Self-Portrait, *c. 1800, drawing, Nationalgalerie, Berlin.*

Fig. 43 Ernst Theodor Amadeus Hoffmann, Kreisler in Delerium, *1822, pencil drawing, present whereabouts unknown.*

Fig. 44 Johann Peter Lyser,
Self-Portrait with
Beethoven,
Paganini and
E.T.A. Hoffmann,
26 June 1833,
pen-and-ink
drawing, private
collection, Paris.

Fig. 46 Johann Peter
Lyser, Beethoven Taking
a Walk, *c. 1833, pencil*
drawing, Gesellschaft
der Musikfreunde,
Vienna.

Fig. 45 Johann Peter Lyser, Beethoven Taking
a Walk, *1833, drawing for* Cäcilia, *Beethovenhaus,*
Bonn.

Fig. 48 Johann Nepomuk Hoechle, Beethoven in the Rain, *c. 1827, pen, ink, and watercolor, present whereabouts unknown.*

Fig. 47 Johann Peter Lyser, Sheet of Beethoven Sketches, *c. 1833, lithograph after the original drawing.*

Fig. 49 Martin Tejček, Beethoven Dressed for a Walk, *1841, lithograph.*

Fig. 50 Johann Peter Lyser,
Beethoven
Composing the *Pastoral*
by a Brook, *1833,*
drawing for Cäcilia.

Fig. 51 *Anonymous artist,*
Beethoven Composing
the *Pastoral* by a Brook,
1834, color lithograph for
the Zürich Musikgesellschaft
Almanac *of 1834.*

Fig. 52 *Ferdinand Schimon,*
Carl Maria von Weber, *1825,*
oil, present whereabouts unknown.

Fig. 53 *Anonymous artist,*
Beethoven at the Piano,
c. 1880, lithograph.

Fig. 55 Elizabeth (Bettina) Brentano
von Arnim, *lithograph by
Landshut from the year 1809.*

Fig. 54 *Johann Aloys Schlosser, frontispiece to* Ludwig
van Beethoven: Eine Biographie *(Prague, 1828).*

Fig. 56 Anonymous artist,
Beethoven Playing for Mozart
before Viennese Society,
detail, c. 1850, wood engraving.

Fig. 57 Blasius Höfel,
Carl Czerny, c. 1820,
engraving after a drawing
by Joseph Lanzedelly.

Fig. 58 Catharina Escherich,
Johann Nepomuk Hummel,
c. 1800, oil, present
whereabouts unknown.

Fig. 59 Joseph Teltscher, Franz Schubert, *1826, lithograph.*

Fig. 60 Moritz von Schwind, episode 23 from the Lachner Roll: *''Lachner's Farewell to Vienna and to the Graves of Beethoven and Schubert,'' 1862, pencil and watercolor, formerly private collection, Munich.*

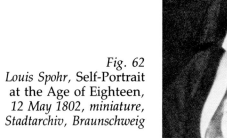

Fig. 61 Moritz von Schwind,
The Symphony, *predella detail,*
1852, oil on canvas,
Neue Pinakothek, Munich.

Fig. 62
Louis Spohr, Self-Portrait
at the Age of Eighteen,
12 May 1802, miniature,
Stadtarchiv, Braunschweig

Fig. 63 Anonymous artist,
The Twelve-Year-Old
Felix Mendelssohn
Playing for the
Seventy-Two-
Year-Old Goethe
(November 1821),
c. 1847, engraving.

Fig. 64 Albert Graefle,
Beethoven Playing
for His Friends,
c. 1877, lithograph.

Fig. 65 Henri François Brandt,
Ignaz Moscheles, *c. 1830, lithograph.*

Fig. 66 Anton Rubinstein,
photograph of c. 1870.

Fig. 67 Robert Schumann,
photograph of 1850.

Fig. 68 Anonymous artist, Clara Wieck-Schumann,
1850, engraving after a photograph of 1850.

Fig. 69 István Halász, At Liszt's First Concert in Vienna,
Beethoven Embraces Him (The Consecration Kiss), *1873, lithograph.*

Fig. 70 Jean Auguste Dominique Ingres, Franz Liszt, *1839, Rome, pencil drawing, formerly in possession of the Wagner family, Bayreuth.*

Fig. 71 Josef Danhauser, Liszt at the Piano, *1840, oil on wood, Nationalgalerie, Berlin, on loan to the Musical Instrument Museum, Berlin.*

Fig. 72
Josef Danhauser,
Beethoven, 1827,
plaster bust (life
size), Beethovenhaus,
Bonn.

Fig. 73 Photograph of
Peter Ilyich Tchaikovsky's
work room at Klin,
c. 1855–57. A lithograph
of August von Klöber's
Study of Beethoven's
Face (Fig. 12)
is on the wall.

Fig. 74 Photograph of Franz Liszt in his study at the Hofgärtnerei house in Weimar, c. 1880. Beethoven's death mask
and a lithograph of August von Klöber's Study of Beethoven's Face (Fig. 12) are on the wall behind him.

Fig. 75 Josef Kreihuber, Niccolò Paganini,
1828, lithograph.

Fig. 76 Henri Grevedon, Gioacchino Rossini,
1828, lithograph.

Fig. 77 Achille Devéria, Victor Hugo,
1829, lithograph.

Fig. 78 Achille Devéria, Alexandre Dumas père,
1829, lithograph.

Fig. 79 Eugène Delacroix,
George Sand, 1834,
oil on canvas,
private collection, France.

Fig. 80 Josef Kriehuber, Matinée at Liszt's, 1846, drawing,
Historical Gallery of the Hungarian National Museum, Budapest.

Fig. 81 Jean Auguste Dominique Ingres,
Portrait of Luigi Cherubini and the
Muse of Lyric Poetry, *1842, oil on
canvas, Louvre, Paris.*

*Fig. 82 Frédéric Chopin,
photograph of 1849.*

Fig. 83 Jean Auguste Dominique Ingres (attributed), Hector Berlioz,
c. 1832, drawing, present whereabouts unknown.

Fig. 84 Léopold Massard, François-Antoine Habeneck, *c. 1840, engraving.*

Fig. 85 Eugène Louis Lami,
Upon Hearing a Beethoven Symphony,
1840, watercolor, present whereabouts unknown.

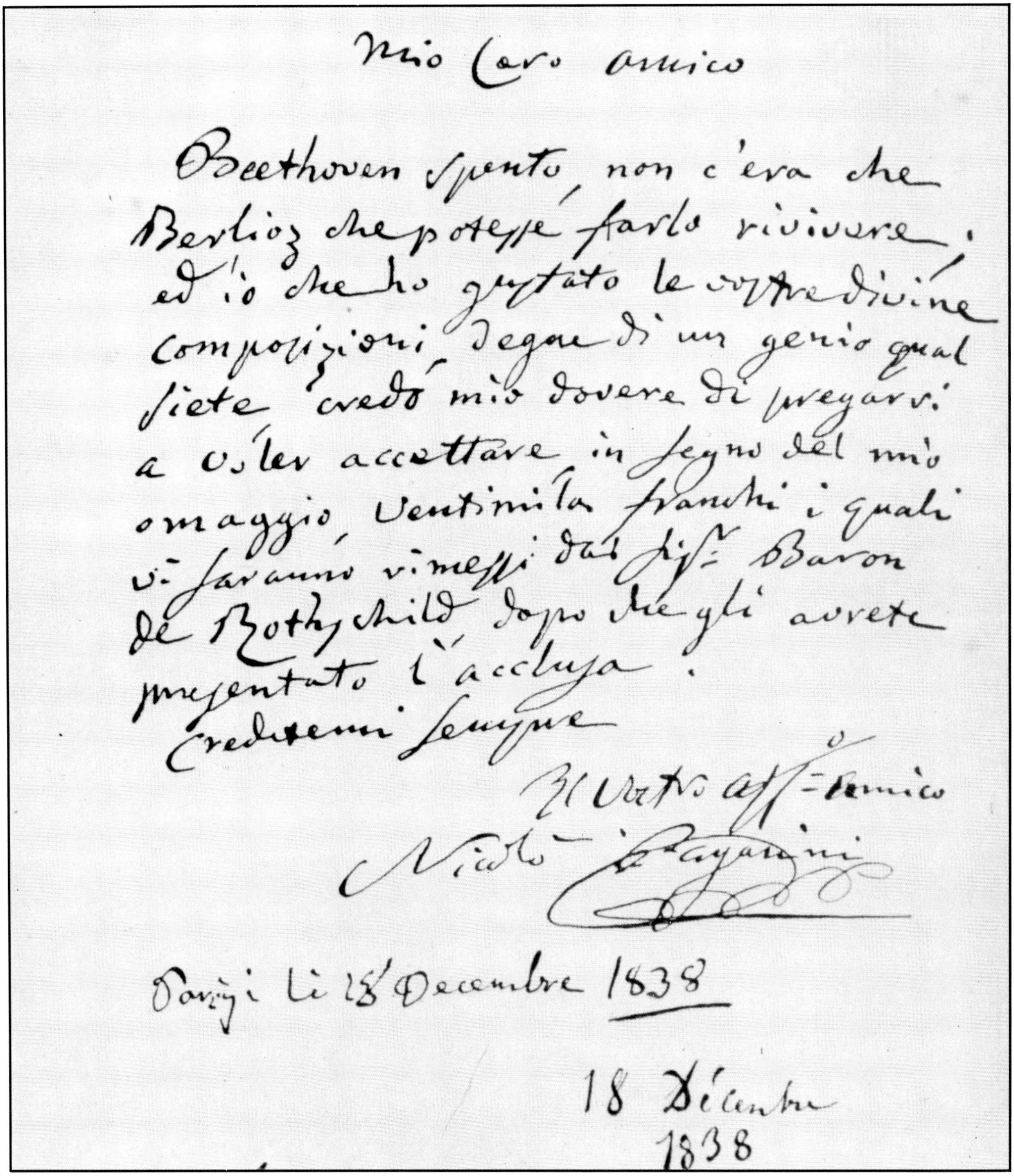

Mio Caro Amico

Beethoven spento, non c'era che Berlioz che potesse farlo rivivere; ed io che ho gustato le vostre divine composizioni, degne di un genio qual siete, credo mio dovere di pregarvi a voler accettare, in segno del mio omaggio, ventimila franchi i quali vi saranno rimessi dal Sigr. Baron de Rothschild dopo che gli avrete presentato l'acclusa.

Credetemi sempre

Il Vostro aff.mo amico

Nicolò Paganini

Parigi li 18 Decembre 1838

18 Décembre 1838

Fig. 86 *Niccolò Paganini's letter to Hector Berlioz of 18 December 1838 giving him, as Beethoven's successor, twenty thousand francs.*

Fig. 87 Georges Bizet, photograph of 1875.

Fig. 88 Romain Rolland, photograph of c. 1927.

182   *Fig. 89 Richard Wagner, calling-card photograph by P. Petit, Paris, March 1860.*

Fig. 90 Richard Wagner, first page of his copy, done in 1830 at the age of seventeen, of the orchestra score to Beethoven's Ninth Symphony. Nationalarchiv der Richard Wagner-Stiftung, Bayreuth.

Fig. 91 Gioacchino Rossini, calling-card photograph by Numa Blanc, c. 1860.

Fig. 92 Franz von Lenbach,
Arthur Schopenhauer, 1868,
oil, formerly in the possession
of the Wagner family,
Bayreuth.

Fig. 93 Cosima (née Liszt) Wagner, photograph of c. 1870.

Fig. 94 Friedrich
Nietzsche,
photograph
of 1867.

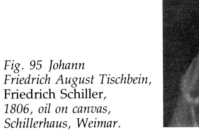

Fig. 95 Johann
Friedrich August Tischbein,
Friedrich Schiller,
1806, oil on canvas,
Schillerhaus, Weimar.

Fig. 96 Photograph of the salon at Richard Wagner's Villa Wahnfried in Bayreuth, after 1880. Robert Krauße's copy of the Portrait of Beethoven by Ferdinand Georg Waldmüller hangs in the center of the back wall.

Fig. 97 Robert Krauße, Copy of Ferdinand Georg Waldmüller's 1823
Portrait of Beethoven, *1869, oil on canvas, formerly Villa Wahnfried, Bayreuth.*

Fig. 98 *Anonymous artist,* Copy after Ferdinand Georg Waldmüller's 1823 Portrait of Beethoven, *1823, engraving, distributed by Breitkopf and Härtel, Leipzig.*

Fig. 99 *George Papperitz,* Richard Wagner in the Circle of His Friends at Villa Wahnfried, *c. 1875, lithograph after the original oil painting. Cosima Wagner is at the left with Siegfried; next to Wagner in front of the window are the Russian painter Paul Zhukovski and the conductor Hermann Levi. Franz Liszt holds forth at the piano and the tenor Albert Niemann stands to the right. Blessing the ensemble is the portrait of King Ludwig II on the wall behind Liszt.*

Fig. 100 *Wilhelm Beckmann,* Life at Wahnfried, *1880, oil, Richard Wagner Museum, Triebschen. Franz von Lenbach's* Portrait of Arthur Schopenhauer *hangs in a place of honor above Wagner's head, while outdoors the bronze bust of King Ludwig II keeps watch.*

Fig. 101 *Hans von Bülow, photograph of c. 1870.*

Fig. 102 Johannes Brahms, photomontage of c. 1898–1908 showing the composer in the music room of his apartment at Karlsgasse No. 4 in Vienna. Brahms's treasured bust of Beethoven is on the wall behind him.

Fig. 103 F. Wichgraf, Sketch of Johannes Brahms, May 1879, pencil drawing. Wickgraf's sketch shows a beardless Brahms standing in the music room of his apartment at Karlsgasse No. 4 in Vienna. The Beethoven bust is already in place on the wall behind him.

Fig. 105 Carl Johann Arnold, Musical Evening in the Home of Bettina Brentano von Arnim, *1854–56, watercolor, present whereabouts unknown.*

Fig. 104 Johannes Brahms and
Joseph Joachim, photograph of 1867.

Fig. 106 Johann Strauss, Jr., and Johannes Brahms
at Bad Ischl, photograph of 1894.

Fig. 107 Eduard Hanslick, photograph of c. 1890.

Fig. 108 Detail of the ceiling decoration (1895) of the Zürich Tonhalle with the images of Johannes Brahms, Ludwig van Beethoven, and Richard Wagner.

me greatly [*was mich heftig aufregte*]."[165] Did the plight of the deaf composer also speak to this small child whose own first years had been overshadowed by the threat of deafness? By the time she was ten it was Paganini who, uncommonly amiable to her in private, thrilled her with his public rendition of the rondo *scherzoso* from the *Kreutzer* Sonata—that and the cantabile of his double stops surpassed "all description,"[166] Clara told her diary. At home it was not only Clara but also "Herr Schumann"—a fellow pupil—who benefited from Wieck's insistence that the works of Beethoven be meticulously explored and memorized. Recognizing Schumann's rare talents as a composer, if not as a pianist, Wieck began to call his musical lodger the "German Chopin" or, even more flattering, a "second Beethoven."

The exaltation of Beethoven in the musical routine of the Wieck household served father and daughter well when it was decided that Clara, like young Felix Mendelssohn before her, should be taken to Weimar and "shown" to Goethe. Calculatingly alert to the formidable publicity that approbation from the great Goethe could provide his protégée, Friedrich, in late September of 1831, packed up Clara—just turned twelve—with their music for an onslaught of Paris by way of Weimar. The fact that he had no introduction to Germany's most besieged celebrity did not discourage Wieck, the insistent entrepreneur. Discovering that a local dignitary was a Beethoven enthusiast, Wieck treated him to a double dose of Clara's execution and his elocution with the result that word spread quickly through Weimar and an invitation from Goethe for the first of October promptly materialized. Wieck was perceptive enough to sense that Beethoven should not be on the agenda for the neoclassical music room overlooking the Frauenplan, and yet it was not the classical masters of the past that he served up. He wanted to stun Goethe, to take him by storm with something new yet not mystifying. And so Clara played the latest music from France, composed by the young virtuoso, Viennese-turned-Parisian Heinrich (Henri) Herz (1806–1888). (The "heartless" pianistic pretensions of Herz would attract punning ridicule from Schumann's *Neue Zeitschrift*.) Goethe was enchanted. The Wiecks were invited back for more vigorous music-making, exciting their eighty-two-year old hoary host to exclaim to Clara that she had "more strength than six boys put together."[167] On the strength of this, and with written endorsements from Goethe, the Wiecks left Weimar in triumph, and Beethoven was restored to Clara's repertoire.

In Paris the Wiecks were astonished to find that Beethoven had preceded them. "The French at present affect to love Beethoven above all else," Wieck cautiously reported.[168] But it was true. As Schindler would happily recount in his "Beethoven-in-Paris" appendix for the second (1845) edition of his *Biographie*, the Conservatoire concerts—under the enlightened and dedicated leadership of Habeneck—had been educating the French public to the wonders of Beethoven. The Wiecks attended four Habeneck concerts during their two-month sojourn in Paris and each program contained Beethoven compositions, including several of the string quartets, played by the combined string sections. They heard the Third, Fifth, Sixth, and Eighth symphonies, and Mendelssohn was the guest soloist in the Piano Concerto no. 4. "Everyone here lives for and demands nothing but Beethoven," concluded Wieck, still not completely credulous—after all, could the superficial French, with their wretched "tough-bones" pianos, their adoration of Herz and Meyerbeer, and their lack of any serious interest in his own Wunderkind, really comprehend a Beethoven? The French foray proved unsuccessful for Friedrich Wieck, and by May father and daughter were back in Leipzig, where

Robert viewed the suddenly more mature Clara with new eyes. "Leonore," he called her, in honor of her plucky qualities. More and more the bond of Beethoven would link these two musicians.

Although Wieck had encouraged his daughter to master the sonatas of Beethoven, along with the fugues of Bach, he had wisely calculated that, until Clara was firmly established as a premiere pianist, her public programs should be showcases for more familiar music rather than precocious attempts to inform and shape musical taste. It is difficult to realize today—with so much of Beethoven's music solidly anchored in concert repertoires ranging from piano to full orchestra—that in the first two decades following the composer's death, most of Beethoven's piano and chamber music was not just neglected, it was virtually unknown. And the solo piano "recital," as opposed to concerts in which the pianist appeared in alternating sequences of solo and ensemble music, sometimes sharing the bill with distinguished vocal soloists, was only on the threshold of development.[169] But as critics began to praise Clara Wieck's musicality as well as virtuoso technique the young pianist's public programs not only depended less and less on the usual orchestral intervals, but also became more daring in their selections. The "safe," crowd-pleasing pieces of Hummel and Herz gave way to new works by Chopin, Liszt, and Mendelssohn. The great keyboard composers of the past were also included and by 1836 Schumann was able to give his favorite pianist and his favorite composers equal space in the Neue Zeitschrift. Of the seventeen-year-old's talent he wrote, not without prejudice and yet not without truth: "To appreciate her resource one must be aware that she stands as a virtuoso at the summit of her time, whence nothing is hidden from her. She has penetrated the depths in which Sebastian Bach has entrenched himself and the heights whence Beethoven stretches his giant fist; is acquainted with the modern musical endeavor that would bridge the space between these depths and heights, and imparts her wisdom to us with girlish charm."[170]

In February 1837 the two Wiecks from Leipzig launched an ambitious campaign of eight public performances on the musical citadel of Berlin. The Prussian capital was the home of Ludwig Rellstab, whose visit to Beethoven a dozen years earlier has prompted the conundrum he posed to himself: "Yet why should Beethoven's features look like his scores?" Another resonating link in the Beethoven chain also resided in Berlin—Bettina Brentano von Arnim. Now in her fifties, but still basking in the limelight of her much-published associations with Goethe and Beethoven, she observed the appearance of a new "Kind" on the cultural block with a wary eye. She was delightful to the young pianist in person but after Clara's first concert, which included, besides Bach, Mendelssohn, and Chopin, the slow movement and finale of Beethoven's Appassionata Sonata—all played by memory—she was not so delightful in her critique of Clara to others. Responding, as did many Berliners, to the "monotony" of a program unrelieved by full orchestral participation and to the innovation, still unknown in Germany, which Clara had picked up in Paris of playing from memory, Bettina pronounced her "one of the most intolerable artists I have ever seen."[171] Clara's feat of memory struck Bettina only as ostentation and lack of respect. "How pretentiously she seats herself at the piano, and without notes, too!"[172] grumbled the erstwhile provider of literary notes Beethoven may never have written, self-righteously. But Clara's concerts were successful in spite of their challenge to custom and her performances warmly reviewed by most of the press. (Rellstab was a holdout.) The Berlin repertoire was expanded to include the Kreutzer Sonata and when the

Appassionata was again performed the program announced without pusillanimity: "the whole work by desire."[173]

Clara Wieck had brought Beethoven's piano music to Berlin and had triumphed for them both; by the end of the year she was ready to be his propagandist in a city notorious for the neglect of its own composers, Vienna. In several private soirées given before her first public concert, set for 14 December 1837, Clara presented the E-flat Trio of Schubert and introduced the music of a composer whose name was known in Vienna only as the editor of the *Neue Zeitschrift*. The success of these private musicales was repeated and grew with each public concert, and when it was announced that Clara Wieck would play the *Appassionata* Sonata—previously heard only in the privacy of the homes of Beethoven amateurs—for her third public appearance on the concert stage, the performance was immediately sold out. On 7 January 1838 Clara Wieck brought Beethoven "home," not presumptuously, not accusingly, but legitimately, through sheer musical weight. The city, awakened to the cultural logic of her choice and reminded of its rightful heritage, was electrified. A writer who had never forgotten Beethoven, Grillparzer, expressed the delight of all by publishing a poem in the *Wiener Zeitschrift für Kunst, Literatur* two days after the concert entitled, pithily, "Clara Wieck und Beethoven." Although hardly on the lofty level of Beethoven's funeral oration, Grillparzer's verses pay charming homage to the performer-interpreter who had achieved the long-overdue introduction of Beethoven's piano music to the public. By crediting Clara with recovering the key to Beethoven, he extends to her the key to the city her "white fingers" had conquered:

> A wondrous man, tired of life and the world,
> Angrily locked up the magic of his soul
> In a diamond-hard and well-kept shrine
> And tossed the key into the sea and died.
> Poor small souls exhaust themselves in the striving—
> In vain! No tool can pry open the obstinate lock
> And so the magic sleeps on as does its master.
> A shepherd's daughter while playing on the beach
> Watches the hasty and senseless search.
> Daydreaming in young girl fashion,
> She sinks her white fingers into the water.
> They seize and lift and hold tight. It is the key!
> Up she jumps, up, with her heart beating faster,
> The shrine looks at her as though it had eyes.
> The key fits. The lid flies open. The spirits
> Ascend, then drop and bow
> To the lovely, innocent mistress
> Whose white fingers lightly guide them as she plays.[174]

In her delighted thank-you letter to Grillparzer for this tribute Clara Wieck responded in the way most congenial to her nature and her heart—by inviting the poet to attend a private performance she was about to give of a "beautiful living picture in tones,"[175] the piano composition *Carneval* by Robert Schumann. Grillparzer did indeed come, as Clara proudly reported to her Robert in a letter written out of range of Friedrich Wieck's ever-watchful surveillance.[176]

On April 11, nine days before the Wiecks' departure from Vienna, the twenty-six-year-old Franz Liszt arrived at their door, engagingly courteous and flatteringly eager to meet the pianist who had just played to such critical acclaim the showpieces by himself and his rival Thalberg on the same concert program. (More of Papa Wieck's crafty campaign strategy.) The Wiecks and Liszt played for and with each other and were mutually dazzled. On successive visits Clara introduced Franz to Schumann's *Carneval* and was gratified by his enthusiastic response. Liszt was to become a staunch supporter of both Robert's music and Clara's playing. They also exchanged musical opinions and one of the measurable effects on Liszt was that he immediately included two Beethoven sonatas in a series of daytime recitals he gave while in Vienna. Thus the sober-minded Saxon Wieck's concept of Beethoven and his piano sonatas as not only suitable but germane to the concert pianist's repertoire was quickly picked up and adopted by the flamboyant virtuoso from Hungary.

The image of Beethoven, as contained in the great *Hammerklavier* Sonata, was Robert's proposal to Clara as part of the very private program he suggested they play for one another in March 1840. This "bride and bridegroom" reunion concert, as Schumann hopefully and defiantly called it, took place a few weeks after Wieck had discharged one of the last poison arrows in his quiver of rage at the couple's marriage plans—an "anonymous" letter vilifying Robert and sent to Clara on the eve of a gala concert she was to give in Berlin. (Somehow Clara managed to perform that night.) "All through," had been Robert's specific injunction concerning their mastery of the arduous Sonata in B-flat,[177] and the consoling safe conduct to a world of unassailable values that Beethoven's piano music represented for both Schumanns was confirmed after their marriage, which took place despite all Wieck's machinations on 12 September 1840, one day before the bride's twenty-first birthday. Less than a year later, despite the time devoted to the joys of unopposed marital and domestic communion, Robert reported contentedly in their mutual marriage diary, with some untranslatable punning: "Clara is studying with real devotion many Beethovenian (as well as Schu-and-husbandian) things [*auch Schu-und-Ehemännisches*]."[178] And again: "Clara has been industriously studying some of Beethoven's sonatas and in her own way [*ganz eigentümlich gefasst*] has assimilated them without at all injuring the original conception. It is a great treat for me."[179] Indeed for both Schumanns it was more than a treat. For the composer Robert, this investigation of Beethoven would reap much inspirational fruit (as with the earlier joint exploration of Bach's fugues); for the concert-artist Clara, the deepening perceptions obtained would enrich her powers of interpretation and enhance the authority with which she played and presented her image of Beethoven to the musical public.

One member of the concert-going public there was, however, who would never, never concede "Frau Schumann" the authenticity which her performances, especially of the Piano Concertos nos. 4 and 5, suggested. We need not linger in guessing at the identity of this bellicose critic. It was Schindler. Constitutionally unable to see what the Romantics saw in Beethoven—Romanticism—Schindler's condemnation sprang from his conservative and intrinsic need to "defend" the classical music of the past against modern times and caprice. His (sometimes justified) contempt for what he called virtuoso-specialists as interpreters of other composers' works only exacerbated the critical frame of mind in which he listened to pianists such as Thalberg, Liszt, Chopin, and Clara Schumann. His severest comments were reserved for the latter, who had the misfortune to cross his path in 1854, and their acidity suggests that the woman-shy bachelor in Schindler was uncorking the vial of stinging reproaches which the musical pedant poured into print:

> In November 1854 Frau Schumann gave two evening recitals in Frankfurt, at which she played the following works: Beethoven's concerto in E flat major [no. 5] and his C major sonata opus 53, the Rondo from Carl Maria von Weber's sonata in C major, the Variations Sérieuses by Mendelssohn. . . . The impression made by these works, especially the Beethoven and the Weber, upon those who truly understood this music, was most painful, and no one could bring himself to say a word of praise at such inartistic treatment of classical music, save the newspapers, which overflowed with dutiful admiration.[180]

Astonishing as it may be to find Schindler lumping Weber, the object of his previous scorn, with Beethoven and classical music, the waxing belligerence of Schindler's attack should come as no surprise:

> Frau Schumann's extraordinary reputation had led us to expect that she understood the art, almost completely lost nowadays, of playing classical music in the classical style, by grasping its very fundamentals and presenting the whole in their light. But we were all wrong; we had to admit reluctantly that she was in this respect just another virtuoso, capable of literally wearing out classical music, but not of truly presenting it. . . . as far as irresponsible treatment of all good music and lack of understanding of all character were concerned, Frau Schumann was no better than the general public, but in respect to her feeling for the psyche of tone and her innocence of the most rudimentary knowledge of musical rhetoric, she has no equal.[181]

What would that other great Beethoven admirer, Friedrich Wieck, have thought of this last comment, so crudely impugning the musical education of his most distinguished pupil? And did Schindler have any basis for his resounding censure other than his own preening self-image as oracle of the old order? Although by training a violinist, Schindler, according to conversation-book notations extending through the years 1820–23, had with some struggle learned all of Beethoven's piano sonatas by heart, playing them for the composer on the piano and benefiting from Beethoven's on-the-spot corrections and explanatory remarks. Not surprisingly, Schindler—although no performing pianist—considered himself an indisputable authority on the orthodoxy of Beethoven piano performance. We recall that Robert Schumann had written in the joint journal of their marriage that Clara had been assimilating the Beethoven sonatas in her own way without in the least encroaching upon the original. Who was right? The *Neue Zeitschrift* critic turned enamored husband, or the peripatetic protector of Beethovenian purity? Perhaps a disinterested, third party's voice is needed. Here is that of a well-trained pianist who became Europe's first fully professional music critic, Eduard Hanslick (1825–1904) (Fig. 107), whose searching reviews of the concert scene appeared in the Viennese press for fifty-three years:

> The artistic subordination of her own personality to the intentions of the composer is, with her, a principle. And she is, indeed, rarely qualified to grasp and to identify herself with those lofty intentions. Brought up on Bach and Beethoven, she has become so much at home in the thoughts of august composers that she finds profound beauties where others only find riddles. . . . As unusual as is the inclusion of Beethoven's Sonata in A Minor, op. 101, in a modern recital, Clara Schumann's programme was just as exceptional in its unblemished purity as a whole.[182]

Well! There is no hint here of the travesties of classical masters Schindler found so distressing. Hanslick had been writing in *Die Presse* about the second of five scheduled concerts given by Clara Schumann in Vienna during January and February of 1856. Schindler was not present but he obviously collected press clippings about this concert series zealously and for a purpose. He found what he was looking for and prefaced the dissenting review with a malicious morality lesson of his own composing and published the ensemble in the 1860 edition of his Beethoven biography. Here is Schindler at his most splenetic:

> Next to Liszt, the most ardently admired star in the constellation of the virtuosi is Clara Schumann. For many years this musician has been acclaimed by all German critics as the greatest model of Beethoven performance. This unbounded enthusiasm shows the extent of the confusion that reigns at present in the ranks of these critics. . . . But every vice eventually comes to judgment, and this case is no exception. It was [the *Monatschrift für Theater und Kunst*] that shattered the general prepossession in favor of Frau Schumann and avenged the Vienna composer whom for more than twenty years she had sorely maltreated. . . . The celebrated, infinitely overrated artist revisited the imperial capital in 1856 after seventeen or eighteen years, perhaps in hopes of finding another Grillparzer who would sing the praises of her and her playing as he had done on the occasion of her first visit. Instead, she was confronted with this journal of reawakened, independent criticism that had nothing in common with popular opinion and declined to lift its songs to her in pure sonnets.[183]

Poor Grillparzer; little could he have known that twenty-two years hence his little "Clara Wieck und Beethoven" poem would meet with such a nasty nemesis. But Schindler's elephantine memory never forgot. Nor did the charging mastodon of music spare the journal he had just praised by overlooking its past sins: "It is one of the long list of misfortunes that befell Beethoven's piano music, starting in the 1820s and culminating with Frau Schumann, that even this periodical gave recognition to the current Viennese opinion."[184] And how had the *Monatschrift* now redeemed itself in Schindler's unblinking eyes? By a disapproving description of Clara Schumann's execution of Beethoven's Sonata in D Minor, op. 31, performed at her first concert. According to the reviewer the first movement "lacked any significance whatsoever," the tempo and tone of the adagio left an impression of "icy frigidity," and "as for the finale, it is not a question here of personal dissatisfaction but of the outrageous conduct of an irresponsible artist. Frau Schumann altered the prescribed Allegretto into a Prestissimo that even her amazingly agile fingers were unable to execute. . . . "[185]

Here we have the crux of the matter so far as Schindler, Keeper of All Beethoven Tempi, was concerned. He agreed heart and soul with the *Monatschrift*'s complaint that Clara Schumann's rushing of runs was the deplorable result of a large phenomenon—"the irresistible desire on the part of today's whole musical world, to take every tempo faster than the composer and the simplest laws of nature, art, and reason would have them."[186]

The history of changing tastes in tempi can be a cultural as well as a musical index to an epoch. Schindler and the *Monatschrift* reviewer found Clara Schumann's Beethoven tempi too brisk in 1856 (Hanslick, writing of the same concert series, indeed praised the "dazzling facility" with which she played fast movements[187]), but Friedrich and Clara Wieck had found the *vormärzliche* tempi of Beethoven's Seventh Symphony, as performed in Vienna's Redoutensaal dur-

ing their 1837–38 sojourn, intolerably and shockingly sluggish.[188] If Clara Schumann's Beethoven tempi were indeed accelerated beyond the norm set for Schindler by Beethoven himself, this is interestingly consonant with the increased
pulse rate of the Mendelssohn-Schumann brand of Romanticism.[189]

What outraged or, more accurately perhaps, really frightened Schindler about
Clara Schumann's image of Beethoven was its *contemporaneity*—due in part to
new piano actions developed since Beethoven's day and to the radical change in
pedal techniques that took place after 1830, endowing the piano with the color of
tone intuited by Beethoven himself. At any rate, after publishing the results of a
"never-before-disclosed" poll in which he had asked two "veteran" critics (read
"conservative" critics) whether, in their opinion, Frau Schumann's Beethoven
was "kept within bounds" or was "almost recognizable . . . because of the tempi
she chose,"[190] Schindler concluded his Clara Condemnations with this novel and
revealing call to arms:

> The state has the authority to call to account and punish any violation of law
> and order in the interests of the whole political structure. But who has the au-
> thority to call to account the artistic violations of an artist . . . ? The *Monatschrift*'s
> attack on Frau Schumann, with its reference to the "outrageous conduct of an
> irresponsible artist," should have come many years sooner, for long before this
> attack competent musicians had recognized from her performances that both
> her training and her limited sensitivity made her playing suitable only for mod-
> ern music. But Frau Schumann has allowed herself to be misled into taking on
> all the classical composers *in order to modernize*—that is, to abuse—all of them.[191]

For the supremely important innovation of introducing Beethoven piano sonatas—especially the late ones—into the public concert repertoire, Frau Schumann
got not the slightest nod of acknowledgment from Herr Schindler.

Did this intractable zealot who labored so unceasingly to undermine the repu-
tations and credibility of other purveyors of the Beethoven image, and who had
himself *destroyed* so much of that part of the composer's self-portrait as mirrored
in the conversation books, did this man ever have bad dreams? Fanatics cannot
afford consciences, but wasn't Schindler ever haunted by a nightmare? The answer is, surprisingly, yes—sort of. And the account was supplied by Schindler
himself. While allowing our narrative and Clara Schumann a moment to recover
from the attacks just cited, we might pause to examine the manifestation of a subterranean Schindlerian anxiety. In the midst of his multiple negotiations during
the early 1840s to sell his deviously assembled collection of Beethoven memorabilia, Schindler was visited by what he called a remarkable dream. So "merkwür-
dig" and real was this dream that he noted down all the details in a diary entry
dated 21 October 1843:

> During the night a dream came to me that I was with Beethoven in the
> Schwarzspanierhaus in Vienna, conversing with him and apprising him of the
> unpleasant experiences that I have gone through here concerning his spiritual
> legacy. He listened to all this in silence, then after some reflection, during
> which he let his head hang down in that singular manner of his, he said: "Don't
> upset yourself over this. Instead, write to the mayor of Bonn and have him wall
> up everything inside the base of the statue that is being erected there—that's
> where it would be stored in the safest way." These words were spoken so
> loudly that they woke me up. Quickly I looked around the room to see whether
> Beethoven was actually there.[192]

This is certainly a significant dream: the defanging resources of Schindler's subconscious mind might have impressed even a Sigmund Freud.

Liszt was in Vienna during Clara Schumann's 1856 concert season and observed at first hand the austere authority with which she compelled the musical public to listen attentively to Beethoven's late and at that time still rarified, unfamiliar works. He marveled at the respect accorded both the "gentle, suffering priestess,"[193] as he called her, and her serious, exacting offering: the Piano Sonata in A Major, op. 101, and the *Hammerklavier* Sonata, op. 106. At her first concert she was called back to the stage fifteen times by a public intrigued, possibly, as much by the personal sorrow which now sanctioned Clara Schumann's revelation of the "tragic" Beethoven, as by her masterly command of the music. For this was no longer the talented young girl who had first enthralled Vienna, but a mature, proven artist and mother of seven children who, as everyone knew, had been left virtually fatherless by a cruel blow of fate. For Robert Schumann, hopelessly insane, was now in an asylum and his thirty-six-year-old wife, forced to become the breadwinner of the family, almost a widow. For the sensation-loving press this was a heady combination and perhaps Schindler was correct in sensing bathos where there should have been pathos.[194]

Shortly before Schumann's frenzied attempt to end his sufferings by drowning himself in the Rhine, on that fateful day of 26 February 1854, there had been several alarming bouts with the imagined sounds that so persistently closed in upon his auditory sensibilities. His abnormal excitability and proneness to respond to the slightest of stimuli are foreshadowed in the apparently harmless obsession with spiritism he had suddenly demonstrated the year before. An earlier favorite preoccupation—Beethoven—occurred to him as the obvious subject with which to test the powers of the magnetic medium before him. Schumann enthusiastically described the results of his experiment with table-turning: "Yesterday for the first time we tipped tables. A wonderful force! Just think, I asked it how the rhythm of the first two measures of the C Minor Symphony [Beethoven's Symphony no. 5] went. It hesitated longer than usual before answering—at last it began—but at first rather slow. When I told it: 'But, dear table, the tempo is faster,' it hastened to rap in the right tempo. . . . We were all beside ourselves with astonishment, as if surrounded by wonders."[195]

The image of Beethoven was again emphatically on Schumann's mind during one of the few lucid intervals he enjoyed just before his final collapse and removal to the asylum at Endenich, near Bonn. Trying to explain the chaos of alternatingly heavenly and demonic tones assailing him, he described his condition as a state in which there was "no outstanding harmony, a good deal like the first chord in the finale of the Ninth Symphony."[196] When we think of the rupturing force of this mighty chord, with its "horrible clamor" (George Grove) fortified by drums and searing spectrum of wind instruments, including even a contra bassoon, we not only gain painful insight into Schumann's sufferings, but are forced to respect the acuity of his self-knowledge. That this particular Beethoven chord could serve as frame of reference by which the abnormal might be conveyed to the normal attests Schumann's musical intelligence as it strove to comprehend its own derangement. (Conversely, one almost wonders at Beethoven's own ability to withstand the jolt administered in this single giant chord.)

For the next two years and five months Clara Schumann was not allowed to see her husband. The doctors held out not even the filaments of false hopes to her.

Others did manage to visit the now usually placid patient, among them—amazingly—the meddlesome Bettina Brentano von Arnim, who greatly upset Clara by writing that Robert was in the hands of an inept physician who was himself a hypochondriac. More soothing reports were sent back by the two young musicians who had entered and gladdened the final months of the Schumanns' last year together—Joseph Joachim and Johannes Brahms. During the first year of his confinement, before his physical condition deteriorated, Schumann was allowed to take daily walks and the goal of these excursions—since Endenich was on the outskirts of Bonn—was the recently erected Beethoven monument in the Münsterplatz, opposite the city's five-towered late Romanesque cathedral. Elated at having encouraging news to convey after spending an entire afternoon with Schumann on 23 February 1855, Brahms wrote his revered Frau Clara a letter, whose solicitous tact was far riper than his twenty-one years: "My most beloved Friend! I feel that I have so many beautiful things to tell you this evening that I really don't know where to begin. From two o'clock til six I was with your beloved husband. . . . When I wished him good-bye he insisted on accompanying me to the station. . . . I never once looked at my watch and in reply to his questions always said that there was no hurry. So we went to the cathedral, and to the Beethoven Monument, after which I brought him back to . . . the Endenich Road."[197]

(Colorplate 8)

Brahms knew how much this walk to salute the effigy of Beethoven meant to Schumann, for in one of the few letters the invalid had written him since his arrival at Endenich he had made specific reference to it: "I always enjoy looking at Beethoven's statue and the magnificent view towards the Siebengebirge."[198] It had been a steel pen fround on Beethoven's grave in Vienna that had inspired the *Neue Zeitschrift* editor; now a bronze monument in Bonn brought solace to the man inscrutable destiny had prematurely propelled across the Rubicon of his life's own musical work. And Brahms grasped out for Beethoven in his attempt to explain to Joachim the ineffable happiness that receipt of a letter written by an apparently rational Robert had brought to Clara: "She could not read it for some time, and then what unspeakable joy; I can only think of the finale in *Fidelio* in F Major, I can describe it in no other way. It is beyond tears—it fills one with a deep and joyful awe."[199]

But the happy reunion of wife and husband in Beethoven's opera was not to take place for the Schumanns in real life. On 23 July 1856 a telegram arrived for Clara from the very doctor who had forbidden her to "excite" Robert by her presence, urging her to come quickly if she wished to see her husband alive once more. Clara arrived at Endenich with Brahms. Her diary preserves the final scene: "I saw him, it was in the evening between six and seven. He smiled at me and with great difficulty, for he could no longer control his limbs, put his arm around me. Never will I forget it. I would not trade this embrace for all the treasures in the world."[200] Schumann died peacefully in his sleep at four o'clock in the afternoon two days later. The Beethoven chain that had banded Clara and Robert together twenty years earlier was graced by a final living link to Beethoven and the Schumanns: Grillparzer. He who had delivered the funeral orations for both Beethoven and Schubert now traveled up to Bonn from Vienna and spoke at the open grave of Schumann. The composer whose radiant image of Beethoven had spread the gospel of Romanticism was gone, but henceforth his music and his musical criticisms would leave their own imprint on humanity's perception of the undying continuum of musical genius. And in the forty long years left to her,

Clara Schumann would, through her exquisite piano playing, focus the attention of the world on a triad sacred to her and to her century—Beethoven, Schumann, and Brahms.

FRANZ LISZT

An ardent Beethoven advocate *not* in Clara Schumann's perfect chord but a prominent contemporary who would nevertheless resoundingly augment the implications of a Romantic Beethoven was Franz Liszt (1811–1886). Liszt's admiration for Beethoven was not only lifelong, it was undeflected by the respect he felt in later years for his son-in-law Wagner's music (one of several reasons that prevented Clara Schumann from wholly approving of Liszt). The image of Beethoven held aloft through Europe by the Hungarian-born virtuoso pianist and composer was a mighty one—it promised deliverance: "For us musicians, Beethoven's work is like the pillar of cloud and fire which guided the Israelites through the desert—a pillar of cloud to guide us by day, a pillar of fire to guide us by night, 'so that we may progress both day and night.' His obscurity and his light trace for us equally the path we have to follow; they are each of them a perpetual commandment, an infallible revelation."[201]

The Old Testament ring of Liszt's stirring words has a New Testament apposition in Liszt's life, for he was able to claim the distinct privilege (denied both Schumanns) of having witnessed the Revelation in person. As a boy of eleven he had been taken to Beethoven's house and introduced to Vienna's living legend. If Mendelssohn and Clara Wieck could claim the personal benediction of Goethe, Liszt could, and did, claim the actual blessing of Beethoven. In fact, regardless of or perhaps just because of the circumstances, which Liszt reported as having taken place in private, mythopoethis had, by 1873, transformed the encounter into a public event, recorded that year in a whimsical Hungarian print (Fig. 69) depicting (as the accompanying title proclaims) Beethoven embracing the boy Liszt at his first concert in Vienna (*The Consecration Kiss* or *Weihekuss*). Because Liszt's credibility had waned in proportion to his waxing as a histrionic virtuoso during the years 1839–47, the Kiss-of-Beethoven story was received with suspicion by detractors everywhere except in Hungary. Intriguing references to the child-prodigy Liszt written by Schindler and a formally worded salutation to the deaf composer on behalf of Liszt are there for our perusal in Beethoven's conversation book for April of 1823, and Schindler's account of *his* role in introducing Liszt awaits us, but first let us read Liszt's own compelling recollection of the event which, looking back upon his life at the age of sixty-four, he called the palladium of his career:

> I was about eleven years of age when my venerated teacher Czerny took me to Beethoven. He had told the latter about me a long time before, and had begged him to listen to me play sometime. Yet Beethoven had such a repugnance to infant prodigies that he always had violently objected to receiving me. Finally, however, he allowed himself to be persuaded by the indefatigable Czerny, and in the end cried impatiently: "In God's name, then, bring me the young Turk!" It was ten o'clock in the morning when we entered the two small rooms in Schwarzspanierhaus which Beethoven occupied; I somewhat shyly, Czerny amiably encouraging me. Beethoven was working at a long, narrow table by the window. He looked gloomily at us for a time, said a few brief words to Czerny and remained silent when my kind teacher beckoned me to the piano.

I first played a short piece by Ries. When I had finished Beethoven asked me whether I could play a Bach fugue. I chose the C-minor Fugue from the Well-Tempered Clavichord. "And could you also transpose the Fugue at once into another key?" Beethoven asked me. Fortunately I was able to do so. After my closing chord I glanced up. The great Master's darkly glowing gaze lay piercingly upon me. Yet suddenly a gentle smile passed over his gloomy features, and Beethoven came quite close to me, stooped down, put his hand on my head, and stroked my hair several times. "A devil of a fellow," he whispered, "a regular young Turk!" Suddenly I felt quite brave. "May I play something of yours now?" I boldly asked. Beethoven smiled and nodded. I played the first movement of the C-major Concerto. When I had concluded Beethoven caught hold of me with both hands, kissed me on the forehead and said gently: "Go! You are one of the fortunate ones! For you will give joy and happiness to many other people! There is nothing better or finer!"[202]

There is also nothing in this version of Liszt's reminiscence that parallels the very public and crowded setting given the encounter in our Hungarian commemorative print of 1873, which illustrates a moment, supposedly at Liszt's musical debut in Vienna, when Beethoven, looking quite slim and agile, bends forward to give the fair-haired lad a spontaneous hug. The bestowal of this reward—far more precious than the ribboned wreath lying conspicuously neglected on the floor—is gazed at with universal approval by the assembled audience of music lovers, all of whom seem to rank fairly highly on the social scale.

How did the Incident of the Kiss-Embrace get transferred from Beethoven's private lodgings to Vienna's elegant Redoutensaal, where the boy Liszt had indeed given a public performance (though not his first) on 13 April 1823? Entries in Beethoven's conversation book covering the month of April are of great interest in this regard. A few days and a few pages before the date of the concert this flowery "introduction," probably written by Liszt's father, Adam, for his son, appears: "I have often expressed the wish to Herr von Schindler to make your high acquaintance and am rejoiced to be able now to do so. As I shall give a concert on Sunday the 13th I most humbly beg you to give me your high presence."[203]

Herr *von* Schindler! No wonder Schindler allowed this entry to reach posterity, although of course it was the practice then in Vienna, even more than now, to allow all possibly important strangers the benefit of high status in address. Did Beethoven attend this Sunday concert? On Saturday "von" Schindler's handwriting conveys a message that shows the invitation must have been repeated along with a bait calculated to capture the great composer's personal interest (the former land-steward Adam Liszt was rapidly learning his new role as impressario for the talented offspring he had brought from the Esterházy estate at Raiding to Vienna): "Little Liszt has urgently requested me humbly to beg you for a theme on which he wishes to improvise at his concert tomorrow. [Some words crossed out] humilime dominationem Vestram, si placeat scribere unum Thema—."[204] Naturally Beethoven's spoken response (also in the Latin both men so enjoyed flexing?) does not appear and can only be surmised, but the existence of some interest in the boy is felt as Schindler's cajoling side of the conversation continues:

He will not break the seal till the time comes. . . .

The little fellow's free improvisations cannot yet, strictly speaking, be interpreted as such. The lad is a true pianist; but as far as *improvisation* is concerned, the day is still far off when one can say that he improvises. . . .

Czerny Carl is his teacher. Just eleven years. . . .

Do come, it will certainly amuse Karl to hear how the little fellow plays. . . .

It is unfortunate that the lad is in Czerny's hands—[205]

Here in this last entry is disheartening proof that Schindler never missed a chance to denigrate a rival, not even when Beethoven was alive. (There is also the strong possibility that many of Schindler's comments were *added* by him to the conversation books *after* Beethoven's death.) And by holding out the lure of nephew Karl's certain company at such an event, Schindler also demonstrates his own expertise at stringing out bait. But now, after a short conversational excursion into another topic, comes an entry that in retrospect has proved puzzling: "Won't you make up for the rather unfriendly reception of the other day by coming tomorrow to little Liszt's concert?"[206]

What "unfriendly reception" is this? The initial gloomy mood in which, according to Liszt's narrative, he and his teacher Czerny found the composer? Or is a chapter missing from the Kiss-of-Beethoven story as remembered by Liszt? Schindler would have us think so, at least in the final edition of his Beethoven biography. He does not deny that Liszt met Beethoven, and the setting is the same as in Liszt's version—Beethoven's apartment—but observe what has been added and what has been subtracted in Schindler's flashback of 1860, when the conversation book with his anti-Czerny remark was already the property of the Royal Library in Berlin and no longer available for his consultation (or further tampering):

> The author knows of only one occasion on which Beethoven's reception of a young artist could not be called friendly. The incident has to do with Franz Liszt whom, in the company of his father, I introduced to the master. Beethoven's lack of cordiality sprang in part from the exaggerated idolatry accorded the lad, whose talent was indeed remarkable; but mainly from the request addressed to the master for a theme on which the twelve-year-old boy might base a free improvisation at his forthcoming farewell concert. It was a request as thoughtless as it was unreasonable. In any case, the excessive enthusiasm for this boy exceeded the bounds of all reason. It was so extreme that, after Beethoven had refused the request with obvious impatience, Emperor Franz, or at least Archduke Rudolf, was approached for a theme upon which the little virtuoso might improvise.[207]

Aside from the fact that righteous indignation has been interjected and Czerny's tutorial presence withdrawn, Schindler's account of 1860, when read in tandem with his own conversation book entries of 1823, is an excellent substantiation of how, over time, memory (and not just Schindler's) tends to compress sequential events into a single occurrence. The presentation of Liszt and his father merges with remarks written several days later and not in their presence by Schindler to Beethoven concerning the request for an improvisation theme and offering a judgment that the boy Liszt could not yet be considered an improviser. What has soured Schindler's memory? We need not thrash about searching for an elusive answer. In the intervening three decades the "true-pianist" child prodigy (whose exact age Schindler misremembers) had become what Beethoven's Defender most abhorred—a keyboard virtuoso. Here is Schindler's stinging denouncement of 1860, by which time there had been plenty of opportunity to observe the envied Czerny's end product: "Anyone who has seen Herr Franz Liszt play the piano has an accurate picture of the mannerisms he learned from his teacher Czerny: hands always in the air, sometimes even flung above the head, the keys struck from a height of two feet above the keyboard, and so forth."[208]

But there was more to deplore about the mature Liszt, and Schindler did not shrink from the summoning trumpet blast of duty:

> Liszt emerged from Czerny's instruction an accomplished pianist, if one can say that at the age of twelve anyone's training is complete. . . . For the two years that Czerny taught the boy he did nothing but train him in the bravura style.[209] It dominated everything that the pupil was ever to practice or to produce in public. . . . But when, in the vicissitudes of Paris salon life, the teacher's influence began to wane, the discipline became more free to develop his own artistic individuality. Yet this individuality, even in the boy, had taken the form of eccentricity, which became apparent in his so-called free fantasies on given themes. . . . We have since learned, however, to what extremes the great virtuoso went in carrying out this improvisation that was so close in spirit to his own inclinations. Could such an artist be a reliable model of classical music, by whatever name it be called, when his performing style was based on no fundamental system but depended largely on state of mind and mood, or on the desire for applause?[210]

Had Schindler been pro rather than contra the new Romanticism in music, what a fine apologist he could have been, for he surely had his fingers on the pulse beat of the movement. A style that "depended largely on state of mind and mood" precisely sums up the nervous sensibility upon which so much of Romanticism, especially that of Schubert, Schumann, and Liszt, draws. And if Schindler saw Liszt as cultivating eccentricity, Liszt himself perceived Beethoven as the Great Eccentric, remarking that "Beethoven was quite right to assert *his* right to allow that which was forbidden,"[211] and praising Beethoven as "the glorious, holy, crazy one."[212]

Schindler had more to say about Liszt as a performer, indeed as a performer of Beethoven, but let us return to that question haunting the Kiss-of-Beethoven story—where did it take place? *Did* Beethoven attend the concert at which legend (if not Liszt) has it the event took place? Schindler had something to say about this, too, but it depends upon which edition of his Beethoven biography we consult. First let us take into account the closing line of Schindler's wheedling conversation with Beethoven on the day before the young Liszt's concert of 13 April 1823: "It will encourage the boy. Will you promise me to come?"[213] And now the chronology of a change of heart: in the second edition of Schindler's book, published when Liszt was thirty-four, mention *is* made of Beethoven's having attended the Wunderkind's concert;[214] in the revised edition of fifteen years later the following universal disclaimer is fired off and in predictable buckshot spray: "Biographical sketches of Liszt have claimed that Beethoven was present at the farewell concert in 1823. Schilling's *Encyclopedia* even adds that Beethoven took the hand of little Liszt after the concert and pronounced him worthy of the name 'artist.' Beethoven did not attend this concert or any other private concert after the year 1816."[215]

Schindler's adamant revisionism had little effect on the Liszt-Beethoven legend. To this day biographers have had to grapple with the image—true or not—of Beethoven's osculatory consecration, the *Weihekuss*, of the lad Liszt.[216]

Before he turned twenty, Liszt had already placed the effigy of a second god in his pantheon. This was a living musician, one who shared his cult for Beethoven and whose monumental technique was matched only by the *terribilità* of his

Mephistophelean showmanship—Paganini. As a nineteen-year-old enthusiast, Liszt was in faithful attendance during the dazzling series of concerts the diabolic virtuoso gave in Paris, beginning on 9 March 1831, and his rapt reaction—including exact notations of some of Paganini's violinistic effects—was sent to a friend in Geneva in a letter that fairly teems with stimuli guaranteed to produce the kind of quivering Romantic jellyfish that Schindler so loved to spear:

> Here is a whole fortnight that my mind and fingers have been working like two lost spirits—Homer, the Bible, Plato, Locke, Byron, Hugo, Lamartine, Chateaubriand, Beethoven, Bach, Hummel, Mozart, Weber, are all around me. I study them, meditate on them, devour them with fury; besides this I practice four to five hours of exercises (3rds, 6ths, 8ths, tremolos, repetition of notes, cadences, etc., etc.). Ah! provided I don't go mad, you will find an artist in me! Yes, an artist . . . such as is required nowadays! "And I too am a painter!" cried Michelangelo the first time he beheld a *chef d'oeuvre*. . . . Though insignificant and poor, your friend cannot leave off repeating those words of the great man ever since Paganini's last performance. . . . what a man, what a violin, what an artist! Heavens! what sufferings, what misery, what tortures in those four strings! . . . As to his expression, his manner of phrasing, his very soul in fact![217]

The stagecraft savoir faire Liszt picked up from Paganini was repaid a hundred-fold by the arduous task the pianist set himself of transcribing some of the twenty-four Capricci (Schumann and Brahms also paid pianistic homage to Paganini[218]).

The reference to Michelangelo in Liszt's epistolary outburst on Paganini reminds us of his direct contact with the masterpieces of that artist when he arrived for the first time in Rome early in 1839. A living painter, known almost as much for his love of music as for his adoration of Italian Renaissance masters, became Liszt's personal guide to the city's art treasures—Jean-Auguste-Dominique Ingres (1780–1867), at that time head of the French Academy in Rome. Ingres was a proficient amateur violinist and *his* homage to Paganini had taken place twenty years earlier (1819) when he produced the pristine thin-line portrait drawing of the violinist with his violin tucked under his arm that, with its sharp focus on undistorted verisimilitude, presents such a cool neoclassical contrast to the dramatic ensemble of shimmering dark and light patches with which in 1832 Delacroix—also an amateur violinist—equated the Romantic phantom of Paganini in concert. "Raphael and Michelangelo make me understand Mozart and Beethoven better,"[219] Liszt wrote his friend Berlioz, attempting to convey the impact of his Italian experience. Ingres favored his new young musician friend with an elegant portrait drawing (Fig. 70) that subtly characterizes the twenty-eight-year-old virtuoso's languid yet defiant self-sufficiency. The drawing is dedicated, in Ingres's hand, to "Madame d'Agoult," the countess who had left her husband and two children in Paris to elope with Liszt in 1835 and who, at the time of their acquaintance with Ingres, was about to give birth to the last of three children she and Liszt would have together.[220] One of these children, Cosima, would later emulate her mother's rejection of husband for musician-lover, although, unlike her mother, she ended by marrying the second man in her life—Richard Wagner.

During the five months Liszt and Marie d'Agoult stayed in Rome their friendship with Ingres refined to the point that the painter played through some of the Beethoven sonatas for violin and piano with Liszt, who was able sincerely to praise Ingres's interpretation of their common hero. In turn Ingres may well have shown Liszt the treasured trio of musical holographs he had acquired from an elderly pensioner of the French Academy—framed fragments of themes by Haydn, Mozart, and Beethoven (preserved today in the Ingres Museum at Montauban). It is tempting to speculate further: Liszt may have told Ingres about the occasion of his boyhood presentation to Beethoven, and Ingres very probably demonstrated his membership in the Beethoven cult by delivering himself of interdisciplinary sentiments similar to those he once expressed to a German artist who had asked him how one could best learn to paint a landscape: "Study Phidias, Raphael, and Beethoven, and you will be the best landscape painter in the world."[211]

It was certainly Ingres who recommended an architect to the Countess d'Agoult when, early in 1840 at Liszt's urgings, she set up the lavish apartment in Paris on the Right Bank at 10 rue Neuve des Mathurins that would become the setting for her own literary aspirations and collecting of luminaries, and the home *away* from which Liszt could continuously be as he concertized across Europe for nine months of the year. The precarious balance of their cooling relationship lasted only another four years, but it was during this period and supposedly against the backdrop of Marie d'Agoult's distinguished Paris salon that one of the most fascinating images of Beethovenian Romanticism—à la Liszt—was created. The image was actually a fantasy potpourri. Originally entitled "Liszt's Moment of Consecration" ("*Eine Weihemoment Liszts*"[222]), it was inspired by a commission from Beethoven's piano-maker friend Conrad Graf (1782–1851), in response to a stunning series of six matinee concerts given by Liszt in Vienna between 18 November and 4 December 1839, and executed by the same artist who, as a young man of twenty-one, had had the temerity to take Beethoven's death mask. The painter was Josef Danhauser and the painting's theme *Liszt at the Piano* (Fig. 71). Liszt was literally "consecrating" his moments at the piano, for all the proceeds from the six gala concerts were to be donated to the realization of the Beethoven Monument in Bonn. And the piano for this high purpose was of course a Graf piano. It is one of ponderous proportions with a casing of decoratively burled, highly polished mahogany.[223] Although the setting of this *Weihemoment* purports to be Parisian, replete with several recognizable French and international personalities—to whom we shall return—the view out the large window that, along with the Graf piano below, dominates the right hand portion of the picture is not of the narrow, winding streets in the Faubourg Saint-Honoré, which we might correctly expect of a pre-Haussman Paris. Instead the (romantically) clouded sky opens to reveal a vast expanse of gently sloping land with a distant forest far beyond. This is a well-known Viennese panorama—the vista over the *glacis* to the Wiener Wald as seen from the city's southern Wieden suburb (the present-day Fourth District). A whole series of Vienna-related harmonics rises from the implications of this patent topographical motif: not only was Wieden on the *glacis* one of Beethoven's favorite walking areas, but the famous "Moonshine House" (auf der Wieden No. 102) of jolly Schubert-Schwind days had become, since 1827, Conrad Graf's piano workshop and showroom. Situated close to Fischer von Erlach's great Baroque church, the Karlskirche, the "imperial and royal fortepiano maker to the Vienna court" proudly displayed this distinctive and historical address on his pianos: "*nächst der Carls Kirche im Mondschein No. 102.*" (The dark label over the keyboard in Danhauser's painting reads simply but clearly "*Conrad Graf—Wien.*") A further local link to this particularized setting emerges: Graf's Mondschein quarters were right next door to the house in which the painter of this hybrid Liszt-Beethoven ensemble had his studio!

(Colorplate 5)

The Austrian artist's own personal connection with the composer whose music Liszt reverently intones is stated in no uncertain terms, for it is Danhauser's life-size plaster bust of Beethoven that crowns the Graf piano and looks benevolently across at the assembled group of communicants. We recall that Danhauser, in his brother's words, after obtaining a good cast of Beethoven's countenance and conveying it safely home, set to work immediately to model a bust of the dead composer whose features were still so vividly impressed upon his mind. The result "astonished everyone" and "several casts were made." Picking up Carl Danhauser's narrative again, we learn of a mishap: "A first, very successful copy, which was sent to Moscheles in London, and in the success of which we placed great expectations—we hoped that it would be executed in marble there—arrived in fragments."[224] At least two more copies of this imposing bust do survive, however, one in the Historisches Museum der Stadt Wien in Vienna and the other in the Beethovenhaus at Bonn (Fig. 72). The frontal view of the head in our illustration of the Bonn copy reveals something difficult to discern in the three-quarter presentation given the bust by Danhauser in his painting: the pupils of the eyes have been drilled (unlike the Klein bronzed plaster casts made from the life mask, and unlike either the "contemporary" or "classical" plaster busts by Anton Dietrich, See Figs. 18 and 19). The specific drilling of the pupils and their high placement within the eye sockets create an effect similar to that produced in the Schimon and Stieler oil portraits: the eyes seem to rove upward, in true Beethovenian fashion. The pronounced cleft chin and animated helmet of hair suggest that Danhauser was familiar with both the Klein and Dietrich busts, while the intimation of heroic nudity and the youthful appearance of Danhauser's Beethoven effigy—in both its plaster and painted versions—effectively blot out any associations with the emaciated death mask from which Danhauser had worked.[225] It was obviously the living, vigorous Beethoven Danhauser wished to commemorate and which, in the painting, despite its chalky pallor, vibrates with an answering resonance to the notes sounded by the real-life disciple and master interpreter, Liszt. The thumb of his right hand seems to be depressing F (F-flat?) above middle C, while the middle finger touches B-flat and the ring finger depresses D-flat; however the accuracy of Danhauser's grouping of the black keys into sequences of twos and threes leaves something to be desired.[226]

(Colorplates 3 and 4)

In spite of the ambiguous placement of Liszt's elegantly drooping right hand, we may surmise with reasonable certainty just what music is sounding from the worthy instrument he has chosen to play, for not only is the Conrad Graf plaque inescapably discernible above Liszt's fingers, but so also, plainly readable, are two unopened (Liszt naturally knew them by heart) compositions propped up on the music rack. The folded sheet in front is titled: "Marcia funebre sulla morte d'un Eroe per L. v. Beethoven." This refers to the slow movement of Beethoven's Piano Sonata in A-flat Major, op. 26 (1802)—one of Liszt's specialties. The cover of the upright sheet of music behind reads simply: "Phantasie von F. Liszt"—denoting another of Liszt's pianistic specialties. The great keyboard artist's own earlier Viennese ties are symbolized by the motivic introduction of an open music book lying on the floor in front of the piano leg. The inscription on the left hand page is conspicuous: "dedié à son Élève Liszt par C. Czerny." (Liszt had recently returned the compliment by dedicating an 1839 publication of piano studies [op. 137] to his former teacher, and in 1852 his *Transcendental Etudes* [op. 139] were published with a dedication to Czerny.) If this is not enough, the Vienna connection is sealed and announced to the world by the wording on the extreme lower left of the painting, written in a handsome script: *"Im Auftrage Conr. Graf's zur Erin-nerung an Liszt gemalt v. Danhauser 1840"* ("Commissioned by Conr. Graf in re-membrance of Liszt painted by Danhauser 1840"). There is one final link in this charmingly chauvinist chain, one which can not be perceived by looking at the picture but only by touching it. It is not canvas but wood. The very surface on which this painting was executed is a Conrad Graf art product, for the enthusias-tic piano maker presented Danhauser with a four-foot by five-foot four-inch panel of his very best and hardest sounding-board wood on which to capture Liszt at the piano.[227]

There is no doubt that, just as Danhauser's depiction of Beethoven's facial fea-tures was based on a first-hand knowledge of his subject, so also was his rendi-tion of the "Dantesque" profile (as it was often called) of Liszt. Danhauser, the former violin student who as a boy had venerated Beethoven, was now, as a pro-fessor of painting at the Vienna Academy, no less a lover of music and had will-ingly fallen under the spell of Liszt's musicianship—an experience he was to re-peat when the virtuoso returned to Vienna for two weeks in February of 1840 for a second concert appearance. The two men had already met and the friendship forged was sufficient to inspire a unique gesture of homage on Danhauser's part: he presented the deeply moved Liszt with a very fine copy of the death mask he had taken of their mutual hero.[228] Liszt kept the precious relic always and it was installed in a place of honor in both of the Weimar houses where he spent so large a part of his later life, first at the spacious Altenburg villa, from 1848–61, with the enduring liaison of his middle and older age, the Princess Carolyne Sayn-Witt-genstein, and then, alone for three months (April, May, June) of every year from 1869 on, in the little four-room Hofgärtnerei house. It is in this latter cozy resi-dence—formerly the house of a gardener, and overlooking the ducal park—that a photograph taken of the aged Liszt seated at his writing table (Fig. 74) reveals to us the exact placement of two hallowed Beethoven images. The Danhauser death mask, crowned with a wreath of some sort to diminish the austere impact of the sunken cheeks and missing cranium, hangs on the wall at the far left, next to the striped Algerian window curtain.[229] Across from it to the right, partially obscured by a light-seeking potted plant but still instantly recognizable, is a framed repro-duction of August von Klöber's Ossian-like image of the Beethoven with tousled hair that had so pleased the original sitter. A lithograph of Klöber's compelling chalk and charcoal portrait study (see Fig. 12) had been made by the artist's stu-dent Theodor Neu in 1841 for mass production and, to jump ahead for a moment to the country Liszt would visit three times in the 1840s, the enduring popularity of Klöber's dramatized Beethoven image is attested by the fact that a copy of the print formed the focal point in Tchaikovsky's musicians' hall of fame as arranged on the wall of his music room at Klin in the mid-1880s (Fig. 73). (Liszt and Tchai kovsky met just once—at the first Bayreuth Festival in 1876.)

Throughout the long life in which Liszt's veneration for Beethoven was con-sistently proven by actions as well as words (our next chapter on the Three-Dimensional Beethoven deals more fully with his fund-raising efforts on behalf of several Beethoven memorials), two more Beethoven relics came Liszt's way. And they were important relics because, unlike the once-removed Danhauser death mask copy or the lithographic reproduction of Klöber's portrait, these pre-cious items had felt the impress of the master at first hand. They were the Heilig-enstadt Testament and the Broadwood piano. Before returning to ponder the dis-tinguished identities of the six characters in search of Beethoven assembled so titillatingly in Danhauser's *Liszt at the Piano,* let us note how two such major Bee-thoven items came to be connected with Liszt—one fleetingly, the other permanently.

It will be remembered that the tragic aspect of the composite Beethoven-as-Romantic image—the private despair in 1802 over his progressive deafness—had been revealed to the world when Rochlitz published the text of the Heiligenstadt Testament in 1827 in his Leipzig *Allegemeine musikalische Zeitung.* The holograph itself passed into the hands of Beethoven's "landowner" brother Johann and next surfaced in London in 1840, when Liszt, apparently as agent for a complicated family cause involving the wives of both Beethoven brothers, [230] offered it for sale for fifty guineas. In 1843 the document was acquired by Liszt's friend and fellow Paganini-admirer, the virtuoso violinist Heinrich Wilhelm Ernst (1814–1865; see Fig. 80)—whose possession of it Schindler actually approved[231]—and in 1855 Ernst gave the autograph to Jenny Lind, thus initiating a musical chairs progression that kept the hallowed holograph within the inner circle of Beethoven lovers for some fifty years.[232]

Concerning the second and larger relic: when Beethoven's estate was put up for sale the Vienna music publisher Carl Anton Spina bought for 180 florins the six octave, mahogany-cased grand piano that Thomas Broadwood had shipped to Beethoven from London via Trieste in early 1818 and which instantly became one of the composer's most cherished possessions. Fellow musicians who had been allowed to play on it by Beethoven had scratched (!) their names into the wood to the right of the keyboard (these included Ferdinand Ries) and it was this magnificent instrument—witness to the birth of Beethoven's last three sonatas for piano, opp. 109, 110, and 111—that Liszt received as a gift in Vienna in 1846 as homage from the virtuoso-struck Spina. Its presence at Weimar was noted with awe by George Eliot when she visited the Altenburg ménage at Weimar in September of 1854,[233] and, unlike the Heiligenstadt Testament, which Liszt had in his hands only briefly, the Broadwood piano remained in Liszt's possession to the end of his days.[234]

Now that the Beethoven-Liszt-Vienna connections in Danhauser's icon of group Romanticism have been explored in their several complexities, let us address the international aspects of the reverent listeners featured so palpably on the left, or "Parisian," side of *Liszt at the Piano.* Reading from left to right across the elegantly appointed music room of 1840 (Danhauser's years of designing furniture for his father's firm served him well in furnishing the Faubourg apartment he visited only in imagination), we encounter Alexandre Dumas *père* (1802–1870), Victor Hugo (1802–1885), George Sand (1803–1876), and, standing in a a brotherly clutch, the musical twosome of Paginini and Rossini. Completing the lineup of living Romantics present at this *Weihemoment* are the "Florentine" profiled Liszt and a floor-ensconced, flaxen-haired Marie d'Agoult seen from the back (thus relieving the conscientious portraitist from having to invent a visage for the only member of the famous ensemble whose physical appearance was unknown to him). Due homage is also paid to the prematurely departed but ever-present prototype of Romanticism Lord Byron (1788–1824), whose gilt-framed profile, hovering adroitly above that of Liszt's, gazes away from the bust of the German hero on the piano and towards the statuette of a Gallic heroine on the far left—Joan of Arc (about whom d'Agoult would later write a play and Liszt two songs). Danhauser has pulled all the stops. And quite appropriately. We can not help but admire his only slightly outdated knowledge of the shifting membership of the

Liszt-d'Agoult circle. (Liszt and the countess would themselves be separating permanently in April of 1844.) By featuring the literary trio of Dumas, Hugo, and Sand in the company of their hostess Marie d'Agoult, our Austrian artist was reassembling a famous cast of characters from earlier and happier days (by 1840 George Sand was not on speaking terms with Marie d'Agoult): the fall of 1836 when, installing themselves in the stylish Hôtel de France at 23 rue Lafitte, d'Agoult and Liszt set up a mutual sitting-room with Sand (who took rooms a floor below). Here the animated gatherings that attracted the capital's cultural elite took place. The discussions of the so-called Humanitarians ranged from theater to left-wing liberal politics to music to Saint-Simonism, and among the opinionated and articulate guests were Hugo, Dumas, and Rossini. That Danhauser coupled the exquisitely urbane Rossini, whose rapier wit had made him one of the untamed social lions of Paris, with the spectral Paganini, whose deteriorating tubercular larynx made it impossible for him to speak above a murmur in society, is not so much the historical acknowledgment of a friendship as it is symbolic affirmation of mutual membership in the clique of Beethoven Venerators. So important to Danhauser was this (authentic) common bond linking three prominent contemporary musicians to the great music master of the past, that unity of time, place, and action fell by the wayside—a necessary sacrifice to the ideal omnium-gatherum of this Paris-Vienna Simultaneous Salon of 1840. (Chronological accuracy for the year 1840 would have placed the desperately ill Paganini in Nice, where he died on 27 May, and Rossini in Bologna, where for several years he had been involved in a zealous administrative attempt to reform that thankless city's Liceo Musicale.)

In 1840 Paganini would have been fifty-seven, Rossini, forty-six. They appear much younger, though by no means idealized, in Danhauser's depiction. When we seek to find pictorial sources for the artist's astonishingly correct portrait verisimilitude we understand why. The well-defined visages of both Paganini and Rossini can be traced back to two widely circulated portrait lithographs produced a dozen years earlier, one immediately upon Paganini's March 1828 arrival in Vienna, the other during Rossini's reign as director of the Théâtre Italien in Paris. Line for line, the gaunt features of Paganini were meticulously taken from a print executed in 1828 (Fig. 75) by an artist who drew the violinist from life and whom we have met before—"that master of convention and flattery," as Schindler kindly called him—Josef Kriehuber (see Figs. 24 and 28). Danhauser's fidelity to the waxen, narrow-faced image in the original[235] even carries over Kriehuber's distinctive device of showing a high white collar framing Paganini's face with one flap standing stiffly up and the other bent under the chin. For his portrayal of Rossini, it would seem that Danhauser turned for help to an 1828 lithograph by the Paris-born artist Henri Grevedon (1776–1860) (Fig. 76).[236] Grevedon, much admired for his large-format portrait lithographs of famous actresses and dancers, had drawn the thirty-six-year-old composer (who in 1828 was considerably less stout than destiny and a gourmet's appetite would leave him) in a pose that faced to the left. Here Danhauser took the liberty of reversing the direction so that Rossini might gaze in tandem with Paganini at the Liszt evocation of Beethoven taking place at the piano. Otherwise, the hairline, arching brows, slightly bulging eyes, circles under the eyes, long nose and ear, pursed lips, and pronounced chin are identical; only the white collar tips above the black cravat have been omitted.

It is quite understandable that Danhauser would have turned to artists who had actually sketched their models in the flesh[237] for his rendition of Paganini and

Rossini, and it is possible to confirm that he followed this procedure in regard to the three French protagonists presented *en face* in the left-hand side of *Liszt at the Piano*. (Danhauser's striking likeness of Byron is recognizable as being derived from the popular 1818 engraving after a profile drawing by George Henry Harlow, and his problem-solving rear view of Marie d'Agoult *is*, incidentally, correct in rendering her as a large, statuesque woman with blonde hair.) The sources for Dumas, Hugo, and Sand are there for the looking, and the most helpful French connection would appear to be Achille Devéria (1810–1857), a history painter who made himself known by a prolific series of lithograph portraits of actors, singers, and authors. His sympathetic rendition of the twenty-seven-year-old Victor Hugo (Fig. 77), with high brow, receding but abundant and silky growth of hair, fine eyebrows, deep-set eyes, pointed nose, narrow chin, and collar-concealing neckcloth, is the obvious source for Danhauser's equally genial treatment of eleven years later. The appositeness of including Hugo as one of the select audience listening to a private rendition of the slow movement of Beethoven's Piano Sonata in A-flat Major may have been explained to Danhauser by Liszt himself, who, during the cholera epidemic in Paris during the spring of 1832, would sometimes sit down at the piano in Hugo's house and vent his anguish at the sight of corpses being collected in the street below by playing the *marcia funebre*.[238] While it might not have been so difficult to acquire the likeness of the author of *Hernani* even in far off Vienna, it is a testament to the box-office fame of playwright Alexandre Dumas, who in 1840 had not yet embarked on his even more successful career as a novelist, that Danhauser was able to come by his portrait likeness as well, possibly but not necessarily Devéria's fetching lithograph of 1829 (Fig. 78). In the case of Dumas, son of a mulatto and hence endowed with a head of wiry black hair, portrait authenticity was of more than usual interest, and although Danhauser did not convey his great physical size (he was over six feet tall), he did convincingly relay not only Dumas's crinkly hair but also his carefully cultivated wisps of moustache and goatee.[239]

Almost as rapt as the floor-riveted Marie d'Agoult in Danhauser's entranced ensemble is the trousered George Sand, who lolls back in her high leather chair and firmly reaches over to quiet the ebullient talker Dumas (who has not lost his place in the book he seems just to have closed, possibly at Sand's imperious cue). Sand, who had eavesdropped with fascination for three months during the summer of 1837 at her Nohant chateau as her houseguest Liszt worked out his piano transcriptions of Beethoven's Fifth and Sixth symphonies, does not lose her grip on the slim, smoldering cigar in her left hand. She has tossed her top hat (and gloves) to the floor behind Liszt's back, where (as with its real-life owner) it competes in its sophisticated, silken black sheen with the multilayered pale pink bonnet of Marie d'Agoult that appears almost to sidle up to the pianist on the piano bench. (D'Agoult's matching gloves are possessively splayed out over the music volumes threatening to slip off the top of the piano to the right.) Because of her chin-length Joan of Arc haircut (of which the eponymous statuette subtly reminds us), pale face, loose white neckpiece, and black velvet jacket, Sand looks like a female Liszt, and we watch as—unknowingly—these twin comprehenders of Beethoven incline their heads towards one another.

Where did Danhauser find the prototype for the supine sursum corda expressed by Sand? This time the painter prince of French Romanticism, Delacroix himself, supplied the image (Fig.79)—a portrait of the young author in men's clothing commissioned by her editor François Buloz for the *Revue des Deux Mondes* from whence it was transmitted to the waiting worlds of letters and scandal. Danhauser has deftly transcribed the large, upward-gazing eyes and three-quarter view of the head with its somewhat unpronounced chin, and given his voracious Vienna viewers (who were shocked by the partially revealed pant's leg) an authentic portrait of Paris's most active femme fatale. Thanks to her platonic (in spite of everything) friendship with Liszt, Lélia-Sand is admitted into the Beethoven temple where all passions become purified, passing through a divine filter in somewhat the same way that these sensation-seeking Romantics drew their smoke through narghiles like the Turkish water pipe Danhauser has gone to such pains to include at the extreme lower left of his music-room drama.

Let us ourselves imbibe for a moment the rarified atmosphere that the "Protector of Beethoven," as one Viennese newspaper had hailed Liszt,[240] was conjuring at the piano. What sort of playing might we expect? Unpredictable, is the safest answer, if we remember Schindler's apt description of Liszt's performance style (and Romanticism in general) as depending largely on state of mind and mood. Let us follow two accounts of how Liszt played the adagio of Beethoven's *Moonlight* Sonata on two different occasions. The narrator in both instances, although not comfortable in the Hôtel-de-France group, is a Romantic par excellence, and one whose own gargantuan image of Beethoven we shall examine later—Hector Berlioz. Here is the first account:

> One day Liszt was playing the adagio of Beethoven's Sonata in C-sharp minor before a little circle of friends, of which I formed part, and followed the manner he had then adopted to gain the applause of the fashionable world. Instead of those long sustained notes, and instead of strict uniformity of rhythm, he overlaid it with trills and the tremolo. I suffered cruelly, I must confess—more than I have ever suffered in hearing our wretched cantatrices embroider the grand air in the "Freischutz"; for to this torture was added my distress at seeing an artist of his stamp falling into the snare which, as a rule, only besets mediocrities. But what was to be done? Liszt was then like a child, who when he stumbles, likes to have no notice taken, but picks himself up without a word and cries if anybody holds him out a hand.[241]

A few years later, at another small party of friends, Berlioz was again present when Liszt held forth at the piano, this time playing Weber at first:

> As he was about to finish, the lamp which lighted the apartment appeared very soon to go out; one of us was going to relight it: "Leave it alone," I said to him; "if he will play the adagio of Beethoven's sonata in C-sharp minor this twilight will not spoil it." "Willingly," said Liszt; "but put the lights out altogether; cover the fire that the obscurity may be more complete." Then, in the midst of darkness, after a moment's pause, rose in its sublime simplicity the noble elegy he had once so strangely disfigured; not a note, not an accent was added to the notes and the accents of the author. It was the shade of Beethoven, conjured up by the virtuoso to whose voice we were listening. We all trembled in silence, and when the last chord had sounded no one spoke—we were in tears.[242]

The occurrence of such apparently schizoid delivery of one and the same Beethoven composition was not confined to a single listener's experience. On 9 June 1840 the *Musical World* reported a London performance of the *Kreutzer* Sonata by Liszt with the Norwegian violinist Ole Bull (1810–1880) during which so many liberties were taken that the "disapprobation of the audience" was called forth.[243] And yet less than a month later, on 2 July, the *Times* reviewed another performance of the *Kreutzer* Sonata by the same pair with total approval, implying that even Schindler "who condemns with inflexible severity all erroneous and imperfect interpretations of the great master's ideas"[244] would have agreed about Liszt that: "There was not a note to which he did not give meaning, and passages which in the hands of other performers would have fallen, as it were, dead on the ear, were prominently brought out . . . and the hearers felt their connection with, and importance to, the beautiful whole."[245]

Not to leave the poles of Liszt's mercurial execution of the *Moonlight* Sonata in perpetual opposition, let us adjoin a third and final account of a performance dating from the 1880s. Liszt's Russian student Alexander Siloti (1863–1919) indiscreetly reported hearing a "marvelous" rendition of the *Moonlight* in Leipzig by his countryman Anton Rubinstein (whom Liszt had nicknamed "Van II" in recognition of his remarkable resemblance to Beethoven). Although this "specialty" of Liszt's youth was never heard at Weimar, Siloti's unreserved assessment of Rubinstein's Beethoven triggered something deep inside his elderly teacher. Suddenly he rose and went to the piano. Siloti reminisced: "Rubinstein had played on a beautiful Bechstein in a hall with very good acoustics. Liszt was playing in a little carpeted room, in which small space thirty-five or forty people were sitting, and the piano was worn out, unequal, and discordant. He had only played the opening triplets however when I felt as if the room no longer held me and when, after the first four bars, the G-sharp came in the right hand, I was completely carried away. Not that he accented this G-sharp; it was simply that he gave it an entirely new sound. . . ."[246]

Here we have perhaps the state of mind and mood of the Beethoven listener assuming as strong a role as that of the Beethoven performer, but Siloti's account (written twenty-seven years later) does channel attention to a distinct phenomenon—Liszt as inspired *interpreter:* one who regarded himself as musical "helmsman," not "oarsman."[247] The piano was an extension of himself and he shared with Beethoven the urge to play old works in new ways—a compulsion that earned them both the label "unpredictable." This designation, at first synonymous with "spontaneous," "possessed" and "heaven-storming" in the vocabulary of early Romanticism, began to lose its luster as the century ripened and fidelity to the letter was seen increasingly as gateway to the spirit of music past. It has been remarked that "classical" playing was a creation of the second half of the nineteenth century, fostered through the controlled re-creations of the textural intentions of earlier composers by performers such as Clara Schumann.[248]

To conclude our inhaling of the atmosphere surrounding Liszt's keyboard launching of his Beethoven montgolfier, let us allow the inflamed words of Liszt's first biographer, Joseph d'Ortigue (1802–1866), to sum up the feelings of the assembled Romantics in Danhauser's international icon *Liszt at the Piano*: "Beethoven is for Liszt a god, before whom he bows his head. He considered him as a deliverer whose arrival in the musical realm has been illustrated through the liberty of poetical thought, and through the abolishing of old dominating habits. Oh, one must be present when he begins with one of those melodies, one of those posies which have long been called symphonies. One must see his eyes when he opens them as if receiving an inspiration from above. . . . One must see him, hear him, and be silent."[249]

Although by 1840 Byronsim was beginning to pale, the pairing of the silhouettes of the English poet with the Hungarian pianist in Danhauser's pictorial social register of Romanticism is exceedingly, indeed presciently, apropos. That Beethoven's own interest had been directed to Byron's writing[250] could hardly have been known by the painter, but presumably Liszt could have told Danhauser while posing for him details not only about Marie d'Agoult's coloring but about the visit he had recently made on his way to Vienna via Venice (October 1839) to see Byron's house and the remarkable coincidence of having hired the same gondolier who had once, for five days fifteen years earlier, ferried the English lord about the city's canals.[251] Perhaps Liszt even discussed which of Byron's works he would most like to put into musical form. The list would have included *Mazeppa* (earliest of several war-horse piano settings, 1839–40; a later orchestrated version with Victor Hugo's poem prefixed to the score, 1851) and, envisioned as operas but never completed, *Sardanapalus* (*Sardanapale*, Italian-style opera in three acts with 111 pages of sketches, 1846–1851) and *Manfred* (scenes for chorus, 1862). What is prophetic about Danhauser's pairing is that Liszt would in a sense share Byron's fate in history. Their adventuresome, Don Juanian lives have been studied more extensively than their work. Both are looked upon as personifications of Romanticism rather than voices of Romanticism. The collective nineteenth-century concept of Beethoven, on the other hand, as symbolized by his prominence in Danhauser's doxology, would honor him not only as the incarnation but the instrument of Romantic aspirations.

After sitting for Danhauser in the Austro-Hungarian capital, Liszt paid a triumphal call on his native village, to which he had not been since his father had taken him away at the age of ten to study with Czerny in Vienna. When he entered the cottage where he had been born, he approached Adam Liszt's ancient piano with delight and commented that the pictures of Haydn and Beethoven with which he had grown up were still in their places on the wall. As a boy, whenever he was asked what he wanted to to be when he grew up, so the tradition to which he was now actively contributing has it, Liszt's response was always the same: ''Like that one,'' pointing to the Beethoven portrait.[252] How intriguing for our examination of Liszt's interior image of Beethoven to know that from his earliest days a physical likeness of his ''god'' looked down upon him in the obscure Hungarian hamlet of Raiding. *Which* Beethoven portrait reproduction might it have been? Liszt left Raiding in the early spring of 1822, making the terminus ante quem for the Beethoven print (and we may presume it was a print) 1821 at the latest. The two tenable candidates then are either the Neidl engraving of about 1800, distributed by Artaria in Vienna showing the youthful Beethoven (see Fig. 29), or, far more likely, that brooding portrait circulated during Beethoven's Congress-of-Vienna days of popularity engraved by Höfel in 1814 (see Fig. 3).

If indeed it was Höfel's melancholy ''Byronic'' image of Beethoven under the eyes of which Liszt thrived as a child, it was a very familiar visage whose ''darkly glowing gaze'' Liszt encountered in person nine years later, thanks to the ''indefatigable'' efforts of his teacher. Local Viennese mythography would not forget this or Liszt's other debts to Czerny. It is responsible for an amusing (and instructive) ''replay'' of Danhauser's Liszt-Beethoven *Weihemoment* in which chauvinism joins hands with an unblushing plagiarism (Fig. 80). Drawn in 1846, the encore is entitled *Matinée at Liszt's*. The creator of this all-too-familiar—despite its reversal—composition includes a pensive self-portrait in striped trousers on the left. It is our acquaintance of several previous iconic occasions, Josef Kriehuber. Since it was this Viennese artist who made the engraved portrait of Paganini (Fig. 75) upon which Danhauser had relied so literally for *his* painting, perhaps Kriehuber's pictorial borrowing is only fair play. At any rate, Kriehuber's contemplative attitude, with one hand supporting the head, would set a norm for future depic-

tions of the proper pose in which to listen to Beethoven. And it is certainly Beethoven whom Liszt is playing (once again by heart) on the Graf piano. The clearly
printed inscription on the taller sheet of music in the center of the music rack
reads: "Sonata AS♭ DUR Beethoven 26ten Werk." But where is Beethoven? The
bust is gone. Implicit perhaps, since this is obviously a moment of pan-Beetho-
venism. Artistic pride also suggests that paraphrasing Danhauser's figural grouping was one thing, but sequestering his singular plaster cast quite another. But
although the king is missing from his round table, his knights are not. There are
Beethoven champions all about. Liszt, the Protector, is there, and so, too, standing in the place of Rossini in the original omnium gatherum, is Beethoven's great
pupil and trainer of future pianists in the Beethoven tradition, Carl Czerny. Liszt's
high opinion of Czerny's Beethoven is worth quoting: "In the twenties, when a
great portion of Beethoven's creations was a kind of Sphinx, Czerny was playing
Beethoven *exclusively*, with an understanding as excellent as his *technique* was ef-
ficient and effective."[253] In this connection we might resuscitate one of Czerny's
own observations on Beethoven's playing, since later pianists' attempts to simu-
late it had an impact on the purist approach of "restrained" Romantics like Clara
Schumann: "[Beethoven] called my attention to the *legato*, which he himself controlled to such an incomparable degree, and which at that time [1800] all other
pianists regarded as impossible of execution on the fortepiano. . . . "[254] The "unrestrained" Romanticism represented by Liszt in his early years may have been
abetted by a second Czerny description of Beethoven's playing as "notable for its
tremendous power, character, unheard-of bravura and facility."[255]

Like a three-dimensional chess game, the invisible presence of a third Beethoven champion is signaled by the staggered placement of two clue pieces. On
the piano music brace to the left is a folded-over sheet of paper (another faithful
iconographical quotation from the Danhauser painting[256]), but although the inscription designates "F. Liszt" as composer, the subject of the "Fantasia" is now
specifically identified. A single word precedes its genre designation, and that
word is "Paganini."[257] Paganini—Liszt's other god and his predecessor as concertizing Beethoven Promoter across Europe. Realization of this implied presence
helps us appreciate the reason for and identity of the bearded violinist seated in
the capacious (and Lélialess) leather armchair on the right. We have met this earnest young virtuoso and proud owner of the Heiligenstadt Testament. It is Heinrich Wilhelm Ernst, who after studying violin at the Vienna Conservatory modeled his performance technique on Paganini by dogging his idol from town to
town. Liszt described him as having a "noble, sweet, and delicate nature."[258] The
Moravian-born Ernst's inclusion in this adumbrated but still decipherable Homage to Beethoven completes the local "Vienna" environment surrounding Liszt.
There is however one person whose identity has not yet been discussed. Presenting as commanding a countenance as that of Liszt, whom he faces, this tall,
thin figure stands in the spot occupied by Paganini in Danhauser's picture, and
yet he is certainly not Paganini. Who is this usurper (whom Czerny, unlike his
demonstrative Rossini counterpart in the Danhauser version, quite clearly does
not embrace)? Here Kriehuber hails a famous foreign Defender of Beethoven—
Berlioz. The cross-connections on a non-Beethovenian scale between Kriehuber's
visible and imputed dramatis personae are legion: Berlioz made the fateful introduction of Liszt to Marie d'Agoult in 1833; Paganini commissioned the viola concerto which ended up in 1834 as *Harold in Italy* (Berlioz's "symphony with viola");
Liszt transcribed it for piano in 1836, and Ernst performed the viola solo under

Berlioz's baton in Russia in 1847. While all this is beyond the scope of our pursuit of Beethovenian mythmaking, it is invigorating to consider that the inviting by-ways which must be passed by here seem so often to converge upon or radiate from the centrum that is Beethoven. And presently we may legitimately take up Berlioz and the ultra-Romantic image of Beethoven that in his role of passionate and astute music critic he was to fashion for himself and the French public.

We can not leave Liszt just yet however. His labors on behalf of Beethoven extended across the entire span of his long and extremely active life and were by no means confined merely to the spectacular period of his career as traveling virtuoso. Indeed he may have identified with Beethoven more deeply than any of his contemporaries (or even modern-day critics) suspected, for his talents and ambitions paralleled those of Beethoven in two ways: he too could play the pianoforte with that "tremendous power, character, unheard-of bravura and facility" ascribed by Czerny to Beethoven, and he also was a composer ("I too am an artist!"). But there the analogy ended, according to much of the outside world. His own music (over seven hundred original works) was on the whole not taken seriously, resented in fact. Chopin reputedly once sneered that his colleague's compositions would be "buried in souvenir albums, together with volumes of German poetry."[259] Was Liszt a prisoner of his own legend? The "transcendental" performer, the ingenious and tireless transcriber, the generous arranger, and devoted editor of other composers' works was simply not highly regarded as a composer by most of his own peers, including—notably—Berlioz and Wagner, whose careers he so substantially forwarded in his role as music director at Weimar (1848–59). We might wonder whether Liszt—at least the young Liszt—remembering the *Weihekuss,* ever dared to dream that history could designate him as a worthy successor to Beethoven. The Heidelberg musicologist Ludwig Nohl (1831–1885), author of a pioneering three-volume biography of Beethoven (1864–77), did in fact assert in 1874 that Liszt was continuing the tradition of great innovation established by Beethoven in a study linking Beethoven, Liszt, and Wagner. But we have the old man Liszt's own reaction to the pairing of his name with Beethoven's. Six years before his death, writing from Italy, he penned the following modest and colorful disclaimer to a Weimer author who was planning to do just that: "I frankly confess that the title of the pamphlet, 'Beethoven and Liszt,' at first frightened me. It called to my mind a reminiscence of my childhood. Nearly fifty years ago, at the Jardin des Plantes in Paris, I used often to notice a harmless poodle keeping company in the same cage with a majestic lion, who seemed to be kindly disposed towards the little chamberlain. I have exactly the same feeling towards Beethoven as the poodle toward that forest king."[260] Liszt a poodle, Beethoven a lion? The leonine image had long since taken root in the mythopoesis of Beethoven, as we know, but not even Liszt's detractors during the *Glanz-Periode* of white gloves and colorful waistcoats had ever barked out such a sobriquet. Liszt's modesty, fashioned from the corroding experience of a half-century of disappointments as a composer, may be considered fundamentally genuine.

Even if in his mature years Liszt no longer entertained the prospect of composing music that ranked on the same level as Beethoven's, he was certainly still capable of being thrilled by parallels between their lives. He took nostalgic pleasure for example in enunciating the following connections in a letter to the brother of his intimate friend Prince Lichnowsky, who had fallen a victim to mob violence in the revolutions of 1848 some twenty-eight years earlier, and whose estates in

Silesia he had visited: "The most grateful recollections ever bind me to the House of Lichnowsky. Your highly endowed father and your admirable brother Feliz showed not less kindness to me, than Prince Carl Lichnowsky showed before that to the young Beethoven, who dedicated his Opus I. (3 Trios) to the Prince Lichnowsky, and felt himself quite at home in the so-called Krzizanowitz 'Palace,' and in the Castle of Grätz."[261]

Liszt's friendly relationship with Beethoven scholars is another example of the proprietary tie felt by the Defender all his life. Nohl was only the last of several Beethoven authorities with whom Liszt had a sympathetic correspondence. When the half-German, half-Russian Wilhelm von Lenz (1809–1883) sent him a copy of his just-published analysis of the piano sonatas, *Beethoven et ses trois styles* (Saint Petersburg, 1852), Liszt responded in December 1852 with a long and penetrating letter of simultaneous praise and critique. Certain mythmaking lines deserve our attention but, in observance of the dictum that all roads (seem to) lead to or from Beethoven, let us first hear from Lenz the charming circumstances of his initial encounter with Liszt almost a quarter of a century earlier. The catalyst was Beethoven—in the form of an eye-catching concert poster with thick "monster" letters on a yellow ground:

> In 1828 I had come to Paris, at the age of nineteen, to continue my studies there, and, moreover, as before, to take lessons on the piano; now, however, with Kalkbrenner [Frédéric Kalkbrenner, 1785–1849, a noted international pianist, teacher, and composer]. . . . Already on the way to Kalkbrenner (who plays a note of his now?), I came to the boulevards, and read on the theater bills of the day, which had much attraction for me, the announcement of an extra concert to be given by Liszt at the Conservatoire (it was in November), with the piano concerto of Beethoven, in E-flat, at the head. At that time Beethoven was, and not in Paris only, a Paracelsus in the concert room. I only knew this much of him, that I had been very much afraid of the very black-looking notes in his D-major trio and choral fantasia. . . . From the bill on the boulevards I concluded, however, that anyone who could play a concerto of Beethoven in public must be a very wonderful fellow, and of quite a different breed from Kalkbrenner, the composer of the fantasia, Effusio Musica.[262]

Acting on a spontaneous impulse, Lenz ferreted out the address of Monsieur "Litz," as he was called in Paris, and was admitted into the presence of the pale seventeen-year-old virtuoso who never practiced, "lounging, deep in thought, lost in himself on a broad sofa, and smoking a long Turkish pipe, with three pianos standing around him."[263] It was only "when I explained to him that my family had directed me to Kalkbrenner, but I came to him because he wished to play a concerto by Beethoven in public, he seemed to smile."[264] The word Beethoven had broken the ice and Lenz received a few unforgettable lessons from the Turkish pipesmoker. If in those days Liszt was the Revealer, twenty-four years later Lenz was the one who had respectfully dared to become the Explainer of the Beethoven phenomenon. So respectfully responsible was Lenz's approach to Beethoven that he had even taken extensive notice of what Schindler had to say, as the Original Beethoven Explainer with his usual ill humor smugly publicized: "Few books can have been so freely copied from as my first edition during its general sale. I am sure that Herr Staatsrat Wilhelm von Lenz in Saint Petersburg had no thought of making a disagreeable announcement when, in 1852, after the publication of his book *Beethoven et ses trois styles*, he wrote to me: 'I have quoted you 233 times in my book, for you are and continue to be the source for most of the important details.' "265

Liszt's far more kindly response to Lenz is as opulent in tactful diplomacy as it is grandiose in attempting to seek the spirit, rather than merely the style, of Beethoven. He reveals himself as great souled as the paradigm he would praise. Liszt the Hungarian begins by thoughtfully recognizing the mixed racial heritage that Lenz had brought to his study of Beethoven: "To all the refinement and subtle divination common to Slavic genius, you ally the patient research and learned scruples which characterize the German explorer. You assume alternately the gait of the mole and of the eagle—and everything you do succeeds wonderfully, because amid your subterranean maneuvers and your airy flights you constantly preserve, as your own inalienable property, so much wit and knowledge, good sense and free fancy."266 What author could object to being characterized as a mole under such empyrean conditions? Liszt is put in mind of another Russian music critic, Alexander von Oulibicheff (1794–1858), whose passion for Mozart had recently culminated in a great three-volume biography (Moscow, 1844) that elevated Mozart at the expense of Beethoven.

> It is really curious to observe how the well-known saying "It is from the north that light comes to us today" has been verified lately with regard to musical literature. After Mr. Oulibicheff had endowed us with a Mozart, here comes you with a Beethoven. Without attempting to compare two works which are in so many respects as different and separate as the two heroes chosen by their respective historiographers, it is nevertheless natural that your name should be frequently associated with that of Mr. Oulibicheff—for each is an honor to Art and to his country. This circumstance, however, does not do away with your right to lecture Mr. Oulibicheff very wittily, and with a thorough knowledge of the subject, for having made Mozart a sort of Dalai Lama beyond which there is nothing.267

In criticizing Oulibicheff's partisanship Liszt was stoking the coals of a Beethoven-*versus*-Mozart controversy which was about to ignite into a heated literary conflagration that would spark new definitions of Beethoven's greatness. Lenz attacked his countryman in print and Oulibicheff responded with *Beethoven, ses critiques et ses glossateurs* (Leipzig and Paris, 1857), a vigorous exposition of what he considered the extravagance of Beethoven's later works, caustically quoting Lenz's ecstatic claims that "Beethoven is all things at all times"—a characterization perfectly acceptable to the later Romantics.268

All this was in store for the musical world, but to return to Liszt's letter of 1852, let us observe how a seemingly objective comparison leads to an outburst that is at once a critique of Lenz's limited focus (dealing only with the piano sonatas) and a manifesto of Romantic largesse:

> From a reading of the two works, Mozart and Beethoven, it is evident that, if the studies, predilections, and habits of mind of Mr. Oulibicheff have perfectly predisposed him to accomplish an excellent work in its entirety, yours, my dear Lenz, have led you to a sort of intimacy, the familiarity of which nourished a sort of religious exaltation, with the genius of Beethoven. Mr. Oulibicheff in his method proceeds more as proprietor and professor; you more as poet and lawyer. . . . you really understand Beethoven, and have succeeded in making your imagination adequate to his by your intuitive penetration into the secrets of his genius. . . .
> Were it my place to categorize the different periods of the great master's

219

thought, as manifested in his Sonatas, Symphonies, and Quartets, I should certainly not fix the division into *three styles*, which is now pretty generally adopted and which you have followed; but, simply recording the questions which have been raised hitherto, I should frankly weigh the *great* question which is the axis of criticism and of musical aestheticism at the point to which Beethoven had led us—namely, in how far is traditional or recognized form a necessary determinant for the organism of thought?— The solution of this question, evolved from the works of Beethoven himself, would lead me to divide this work, not into three styles or periods . . . but quite logically into two categories: the first, that in which traditional and recognized form contains and governs the thought of the master; and the second, that in which the thought stretches, breaks, recreates, and fashions the form and style according to its needs and inspirations. Doubtless in proceeding thus we arrive in a direct line at those incessant problems of *authority* and *liberty*. But why should they alarm us? In the region of liberal arts they do not, happily, bring in any of the dangers and disasters which their oscillations occasion in the political and social world; for, in the domain of the Beautiful, Genius alone is the authority, and hence, Dualism disappearing, the notions of authority and liberty are brought back to their original identity [genius].[269]

All in one graceful letter Liszt moves from Slavic-German, mole-eagle, Oulibicheff-Lenz, authority-liberty polarities to the Great Synthesizer, Beethoven. Dualism "disappears" because of Beethoven's rare ability to impose new musical vocabulary onto old musical syntax, simultaneously governing and freeing expressivity, the emotional content of intellectual form. Liszt's image of Beethoven's genius as autonomous and composed of resolved opposites was essential for Romanticism's understanding of Beethoven as the great Revealer who stood at the historic junction of uncharted musical forces. It is in this same letter to Lenz that Liszt introduced the Old Testament simile we have encountered before of obscurity and light, associated with the pillar of cloud and fire that guided the Israelites.

Presumably Liszt sensed that what had begun as a gentle rain of qualified praise might be taken as a thunderous anticlimax by the storm-drenched recipient, for he tacked a postscript to his epistle that was guaranteed to mollify Lenz. It is a postscript that is also of interest for our own collection of links in the revolving chain of Beethoveniana—some of them slightly tarnished by age but still glimmering familiarly: "As Madame Bettina d'Arnim has been passing some weeks at Weimar, I let her know about your book. Feeling sure that the good impression it has made on her would be a pleasure to you to hear, I begged her to confirm it by a few lines, which I enclose herewith."[270]

The indomitable Bettina, now aged sixty-seven, prone to wearing large black hats and cloaked in the permanent aura of her youthful friendships with Goethe and Beethoven, had met Liszt a decade earlier in Berlin, where her pavonian reminiscences of Beethoven entranced Liszt, who prudently wrote her, after safely departing Berlin, that their friendship was a "magnetic force of two natures which will, I believe, increase with distance."[271]

If Liszt cherished old Bettina von Arnim's anecdotal donations to the collective memory of Beethoven, his own contributions to the image of Beethoven formed a veritable legacy. The ambitious undertakings on behalf of his hero were not limited to the concert performances of his *Glanz-Periode* or the thoughtful pedagogy of his Weimar years. The proselytizing dimension of his veneration covered four decades of arranging, transcribing, and editing Beethoven's music. The focus of this activity ranged from simple songs such as "Adelaide" (op. 46; first set by Liszt in 1839) to three piano concertos (opp. 37, 58, 73, arranged by Liszt in versions for two pianos in 1879) to transcribing all nine Beethoven symphonies for piano—a gargantuan task begun by Liszt in 1837 when he was twenty-five and, after exacting revision, completed in 1864. In a century with a large piano-playing public that depended on transcriptions to augment a not-so-easily or universally available experience of orchestral works, Liszt rendered a tremendous service—one almost forgotten in our own century of inexpensive and ubiquitous symphonic recordings and broadcasts. How attentive Liszt was to the instrumental alchemy implied by his piano scores of the Beethoven symphonies is evident in a letter of 1863 sent to Beethoven's former publishers Breitkopf and Härtel, who had commissioned Liszt's revised transcriptions. After remarking on the "aesthetic intelligence" revealed in Beethoven's symphonies, Liszt earnestly explains:

> By the title of Pianoforte score . . . I wish to indicate my intention of associating the spirit of the performer with the orchestral effects, and to render apparent, in the narrow limits of the piano, sonorous sounds and different nuances. With this in view I have frequently noted down the names of the instruments: oboe, clarinet, kettledrums, etc., as well as the contrasts of strings and wind instruments. It would certainly be highly ridiculous to pretend that these designations suffice to transplant the magic of the orchestra to the piano; nevertheless I don't consider them superfluous. . . . pianists of some intelligence may make them a help in accentuating and grouping the subjects, bringing out the chief ones, keeping the secondary ones in the background, and—in a word—regulating themselves by the standard of the orchestra.[272]

In the conclusion of this same letter, in which Liszt asks that Moscheles be shown the work before it is printed in case there are better fingerings to be suggested, the ardent transcriber seems to draw new energy from his almost-completed task. He proposes that he prepare a similar work the following year "on the Quartets, those magnificent jewels in Beethoven's crown which the piano-playing public has not yet appropriated in a measure suitable to its musical culture."[273]

It was not only in private letters to Beethoven publishers that Liszt wrote so reverently of his idol; his pen was also engaged in public avowals and explanations of Beethoven's genius. He contributed numerous articles to musical publications (Liszt's literary work fills six volumes) and in the year 1854 wrote two essays on specific compositions: "Beethoven's Fidelio" and "On Beethoven's Music to Egmont." Finally, even if the music is not so memorable, it should not be forgotten that Liszt composed not one but two *Beethoven Cantatas* for soli, chorus, and orchestra, the first in 1845 (op. 67) for the unveiling of the Beethoven Memorial in Bonn—an event we shall soon witness through the eyes of Moscheles and others—and the second completed twenty-five years later in 1870 (op. 68). Both cantatas pay further homage to Beethoven by including an orchestration of the adagio from the *Archduke* Trio in B-flat, op. 97. Given the lifelong Lisztian devotion to Beethoven's music, it would have been a believable legend had Liszt's last dying word been "Beethoven" (as Mahler is supposed to have uttered the name of Mozart twice just before expiring). But the seventy-four-year-old Liszt, who had outlived his famous son-in-law by three years, had not relinquished the other great and consuming musical passion of his life, Wagner. The one word that his lips formed on the evening he died in July of 1886 was "Tristan."

LUIGI CHERUBINI and FREDERIC CHOPIN

Liszt breathed his last in Bayreuth, permanently fortified citadel of all things Wagnerian. But before we pursue the titanic and self-serving outlines of Wagner's Beethoven, let us consider the no less puissant image of Beethoven held by some of Liszt's contemporaries during those halcyon days in the Paris of the 1820s and 1830s. The Romanticism that deified Beethoven was the stuff of individual dreams in a Germany that knew no national unity but was made up of patchwork kingdoms and modestly competing musical centers; quite the opposite pertained in the vortex of bankers, industrialists, speculators, politicians, newspaper publishers, opera houses, circuses, theaters, and salons that made post-Napoleonic Paris the cultural capital not just of France but of Europe. Here, Romanticism, born of revolution, was a war between the old and the new, one in which every battle was reported with gusto by the feuilletonists and eagerly discussed by society. The pendulum of Beethoven's revolutionary reputation swung between two extremes on Gallic soil: blind (or ''deaf'') acceptance and uneasy tolerance. As an amusing example of the first attitude we have Charles Hallé's citation of a concert given by Liszt in the Salle Erard in 1837 during which the B-flat Trio by Beethoven, which was to begin the program, and Joseph Mayseder's Trio in A-flat, scheduled to lead off the second part, ''were transposed for some reason or other, without the fact being announced to the public. The consequence was that Mayseder's Trio, passing for Beethoven, was received with acclamation, and Beethoven's very coldly, the newspapers also eulogizing the first and criticizing the length and *dryness* of the other severely.''[274]

Recalling Hallé's own fervor as a Beethoven apostle—we met him in the previous chapter as a boy of seven shedding bitter tears at the news of Beethoven's death, and we have seen that he was the first to present all the piano sonatas to the Paris public—his encounters with two auspicious Beethoven ''resisters'' in Paris are of special interest to our mythmaking study. Musicians of the first rank, born exactly fifty years apart, they were Luigi Cherubini (1760–1842) and Frédéric Chopin (1810–1849). For Cherubini (Fig. 81), the ''burnt-out volcano'' of young Mendelssohn's impatient description (Chopin would refer to him as a ''mummy''), who had flourished in the Paris musical world since 1788 and served as head of the Conservatoire since 1822, reluctance to accept Beethoven—ten years his junior—was based on attachment to musical tradition. A musical tradition that the behemoth from Bonn had relentlessly charged and undermined. One Sunday evening in 1838 the nineteen-year-old Hallé was summoned to the Conservatoire where Cherubini, then seventy-eight, lived. Another elderly composer of former operatic fame was also present, Henri Berton (1767–1844)—''les inséparables,'' Paris had dubbed them—and after some general conversation a terse request, repeated on subsequent occasions, was made that Hallé play for them one of Beethoven's piano sonatas. This from the man who had spent time with Beethoven in Vienna and who had attended the first performances of *Fidelio* in 1805 and 1806. Hallé's pianistic revelation of Beethoven met with the same grim reserve that the young Mendelssohn had experienced with Goethe eight years earlier. ''Most of the sonatas I had then the privilege of playing in the presence of Cherubini and Berton were evidently new to them, somewhat to my astonishment, but there could be no doubt about the interest with which they listened to them—an interest demonstrated solely by their silent attention and the requests for repeats, for not once did Cherubini make a remark on the beauty or the character of the works, or criticize them in any way."[275]

It is perhaps just as well that the messianic and gentle Hallé was not present when Cherubini did break his silence to deliver an opinion concerning Beethoven. "It makes me sneeze," he said of Beethoven's later work, according to Mendelssohn.[276] This sneeze that was heard round the Parisian world may actually have been provoked years before in Vienna and by the dust of Beethoven the man rather than by Beethoven the musician. As Schindler was to learn, when he interviewed Cherubini during his sojourns as "ami de Beethoven" in Paris of 1841 and 1842, the Italian musician's total impression of Beethoven revolved upon an idée fixe: "It seemed that Cherubini wished to describe the whole man and everything about him with the one word 'brusque' (moody, impetuous, irritable), for he would conclude every remark about him, every objection to him, with the refrain, 'Mais il était toujours brusque.' "[277] For once Schindler did not spring to Beethoven's defense. By remaining calm there was more Beethoveniana to be wheedled out of the composer whom his idol had esteemed above all living writers for the opera stage. Never mind that he knew Cherubini had told his Paris colleagues that the overture to *Fidelio* was so full of modulations he couldn't tell what key it was written in, or that he had deemed Beethoven so insufficiently schooled in the art of vocal writing that he blithely presented him a copy of the textbook used at the Paris Conservatoire. Cherubini's reminiscences centered on the pre-Schindler Beethoven, illuminating the years before the voracious biographer entered his subject's life. Imagine Schindler's excitement when he learned that Cherubini's wife still had her Vienna diary of 1805–6. Obligingly Madame Cécile produced the tome. "With almost youthful earnestness she would defend Beethoven's conduct, though it was not always praiseworthy, in the face of her husband's sharp criticism, and she would not hesitate to express her sympathy, though it was still half-hearted, for the 'brusque' Beethoven, as Cherubini characterized him."[278] Schindler's fact-finding visits to the Cherubini household were numerous, and in the autumn of 1841, much to his edification, a second Beethoven-Savant joined their conversations. This welcome addition was the German-born English pianist and composer John Cramer (1771–1858), whose acquaintance with Beethoven went back to the winter of 1799. "The opportunity of hearing two such excellent musicians exchange reminiscences and opinions of Beethoven, one of them having but little admiration for him, the other bearing in his heart great love and respect for the master, was of great importance to me," purred Schindler as he attempted to steer the conversation to the nature of Beethoven's piano playing at that time ("rough," opined Cherubini; "inconsistent," recalled Cramer[279]) and to his hero's behavior in public. The legend of lovable bear, so prized by Romanticism, was upheld: "they . . . agreed that in unfamiliar company our composer was reserved, stiff, and seemingly haughty, whereas among friends he would be comical, lively, and sometimes even loquacious. He was fond on such occasions of giving full play to his wit and sarcasm, though he was sometimes indiscreet, especially in expressing his outspoken political and social views. Cramer and Cherubini could also remember many occasions on which he had handled objects such as glasses and coffee cups clumsily, at which point Cherubini would add his refrain, 'toujours brusque.' "[280]

Part of Cherubini's resistance to Beethoven may have been based on the "brusqueness"[281] he perceived in his persona, but Chopin's reservation was due to an innate antipathy towards the very musical qualities that his fellow Romantics so prized and professed to see in Beethoven's music. For the same reasons that the delicate, fastidious, introvert Pole (Fig. 82) was revulsed by the musical athletics and extrovert effusions of his coeval Eastern European, Franz Liszt, Chopin, whose twin gods were Mozart and Bach, was unable to accept Beethoven. Chopin was a Romantic who disliked Romanticism. He waxed sardonic on Liszt's pretentious vacuity as a composer, heartily hated the bombasts of Berlioz, and was mostly indifferent towards Schubert, Schumann (who embarrassed him by hailing his talent in print), and, especially, Mendelssohn. Concerning the progenitor of Romanticism in music, it was the abandonment of "eternal principles"[282] that specifically disturbed Chopin about Beethoven's fulminating legacy. The poised Pole could evoke, but abhorred displaying, passion. Liszt's friend Lenz, of the *Beethoven et ses trois styles* book, reports that after daring to differ with Chopin on his extremely moderate interpretation of Beethoven's Sonata in A-flat Major, op. 26, Chopin snapped back irritably: "I indicate; the hearer must complete the picture," and further, "but must one then always speak so passionately?"[283] Old Cramer's description of Chopin's playing confirms this disinclination to declaim: "I do not understand him, but he plays beautifully and correctly, oh! very correctly, he does not give way to his passion like other young men...."[284] And how did Chopin play Beethoven's sonatas? Lenz, whom Liszt had sent to Chopin as a piano student of great promise, says: "Beautifully, but not so beautifully as his own things, not enthrallingly [*packend*], not *en relief*, not as a romance increasing in interest from variation to variation. He whispered it mezza voce, but it was incomparable in the *cantilena*, infinitely perfect in the phrasing of the structure, ideally beautiful, but *feminine*! Beethoven is a man and never ceases to be one!"[285]

Not gifted with the immense physical prowess of Liszt, Chopin developed a "small" sonority that could nonetheless fill a room with the nuances of gradation from piano to pianissimo. It can be speculated however that Chopin's style of quiet playing was also a partial reaction to the mighty anvil strokes of Beethoven's piano chords as hammered out by his fellow Romantics. Chopin is supposed to have complained that "In his sonatas [Beethoven] is sometimes obviously annoyed because the piano is not an orchestra."[286] The orchestral dimension of the Keyboard Beethoven may indeed have gone against the grain of the more "vocally" inclined Chopin. Hallé is responsible for introducing the epithet "vulgar" into the fabric of Chopin's conception of Beethoven. He writes of playing, at the Polish pianist's request, the Sonata in E-flat Major, op. 31, no. 3, and that after the finale Chopin "said it was the first time he had liked it, that it had always appeared to him very vulgar. I felt flattered, but was much struck by the oddity of the remark."[287]

The person best equipped to understand if not applaud Chopin's defection from the ranks of Beethoven worshipers was Liszt, and it is his analysis that best explains the incompatibility. In the strange potpourri of reflections on Polish national traits ranging from melancholy to mazurka that flavors the meager *Life of Chopin*, published under Liszt's name in 1852, but probably partly written by the Polish Princess Carolyne Sayn-Wittgenstein, we find this revealing passage: "In spite of the high admiration he felt for Beethoven's works, certain parts of them always appeared to him to be too rudely sculptured; their structure was too robust to please him, their wrath was too tempestuous and their passion too overwhelming, the lion marrow which fills Beethoven's every phrase was matter too substantial for the taste of Chopin, and to him the Raphaelic and seraphic profiles wrought into the nervous and powerful creations of that great genius were almost painful from the cutting force of the contrast in which they are so often set."[288]

Familiar as we are with Liszt's literal lionizing of Beethoven, we are not too surprised to come across lion marrow in this hearty broth of Romantic musical criticism. Adolf Gutmann, Chopin's gifted young piano student from Heidelberg, confirmed his teacher's discomfort when confronted with Beethoven's extremes, reporting that Chopin said that Beethoven raised him up one moment to the heavens and the very next moment precipitated him into the mire, as for example the fall to earth Chopin complained he always experienced at the beginning of the last movement of the Fifth Symphony. The first movement of the *Moonlight* Sonata was, on the other hand, quite acceptable to Chopin, who included it in his performing and teaching repertoire.[289]

Before we lay aside Chopin's sharply qualified image of Beethoven, etched in resistance to the hothouse aura of self-indulgent Romanticism that surrounded him, let us add to the scales one anecdote that weighs in on the side of veneration. Chopin, whose great passion was opera (he adored Bellini), seems to have succumbed—unlike Cherubini—uncritically to *Fidelio*. Lenz was on the scene at Maurice Schlesinger's music shop when the boy pianist Karl Filtsch was brought in by his teacher Chopin to receive a special mark of approval: a gift of the score to *Fidelio* along with the words: "Receive, my dear little friend, this great masterwork; read therein as long as you live, and remember me also sometimes."[290] Unfortunately neither pupil nor master was to live much longer. The child prodigy from Transylvania died before his fifteenth birthday in May 1845; four years later Chopin, who had known Beethoven's physician Dr. Malfatti in Vienna, and visited Beethoven's health spa Teplitz four times, would die at the age of thirty-nine, ravaged by Romanticism's most persistent disease, tuberculosis. At his funeral, according to his own request, Mozart's *Requiem* was sung—music that in the Age of Romanticism had not been heard for nine years in Paris, not since the day when Napoleon's ashes had been brought back from Saint Helena.

Part 2   *The Musicians' Musician: Berlioz to Brahms*

"Il se mourait toute sa vie" ["He was dying all his life"] reflected Berlioz about the musical colleague whom he affectionately called "Chopinetto."[291] Whether he forgave his Polish friend his less than all-embracing enthusiasm for Beethoven is not known, but we do know that of all the voices raised on behalf of Beethoven in Paris during the middle decades of the nineteenth century that of Berlioz (Fig. 83) was the most passionate. It was Hector Berlioz (1803–1869) who—conceiving of Beethoven very much in his own image—shaped the lofty, lustrous portrait that would inspire and influence several generations to come in France. For Berlioz the Romantic, Beethoven's transcendent music provided what all Romantics longed for—a link with the infinite. On the wings of Beethoven the initiated listener could glimpse infinity. If Liszt saw Beethoven as a lion, Berlioz's analogy was that of an eagle, who alone among all living creatures could soar to Olympian heights. Nor was Berlioz, who with his small chin, high forehead, and pronounced aquiline nose looked rather like an eagle himself, the only writer to present this ornithological simile to the French public. Even critics who were more befuddled than exhilarated by the sound of Beethoven found themselves reaching for the eagle image. Let us examine the context of Cambini's previously cited 1811 quip concerning the "doves and crocodiles" cohabitating Beethoven's musical terrain: "This composer Beethoven, often bizarre and baroque, sometimes sparkles with extraordinary beauties. Now he takes the majestic flight of the eagle; then he creeps along grotesque paths. After penetrating the soul with a sweet melancholy he soon tears it by a mass of barbaric chords. He seems to harbor doves and crocodiles [*des colombes et des crocodiles*] at the same time."[292]

The music which set loose this mixed menagerie in the mind of the thwarted listener-critic was that contained in Beethoven's first two symphonies. For the ardent thinker-critic Berlioz (discriminating enough to call *The Ruins of Athens* overture unworthy of its creator), contemplation of the Beethoven adagio, sui generis, whether assigned to symphony or solo piano, was sufficient to trigger an unmixed, exclusively eagle metaphor. In the adagio, "those extrahuman meditations into which the Pantheistic genius of Beethoven so loves to plunge itself," Berlioz wrote, the composer is "like those eagles of the Andes who wing through space at heights below in which other creatures would find nothing but asphyxia and death. His glances are directed into space; and he flies towards the suns, singing the praise of infinite nature."[293]

What a superb, or to use the language of Romanticism's second and more extreme generation, *Les Jeunes France*, "ravissant" image. E. T. A. Hoffmann's early Romantic concept of Beethoven's music as the language of the beyond now finds full-fledged corroboration in the idea of Beethoven, the man-eagle, as majestic denizen of Empyrean spheres—that celestial habitat so crudely but presciently suggested by the giant eagle we encountered adorning the frontispiece of the first Beethoven book, Schlosser's hurriedly produced biography of 1827 (see Fig. 54).

Why was it Berlioz—a Frenchman—who would be the one to fashion the most vaulted image yet encountered in Beethoven mythmaking? Was he, figuratively put, a fellow eagle, able to recognize his kind? Many have thought so, including Berlioz himself. (Barbey d'Aurevilly wrote that Berlioz had "the beak of an eagle,"[294] Charles Hallé spoke of his "eagle face,"[295] and Heine called Berlioz "a colossal nightingale, a lark the size of an eagle."[296] In France, where most of his music was never really accepted, Berlioz was called, not always with approval, *"Propagateur de Beethoven"*; in Germany, where enthusiastic reception brought Berlioz the fame and financial success that eluded him at home, he was known admiringly as the "French Beethoven."[297] In his own life and writings, of which the *Memoirs* (begun 1848, completed 1865 and intended for posthumous publication; released 1870) is the most vivid mirror, we repeatedly meet with that alternation of optimism and testy irascibility (the latter provoked by an ignorant musical public) so familiar to the reader of Beethoven's letters. Berlioz's empathic view of Beethoven was based on his own capacity to feel deeply, to be spiritually overwhelmed. The aspirations he held for his own compositions he found realized in those of his great predecessor, whose music hit him like a "thunderbolt" shortly after his twenty-fifth birthday.

Let us glance at the young composer destined to be the "French Beethoven" through the eyes of Ferdinand Hiller, who, we recall, had as a boy of fifteen made several visits to the bedside of the dying Beethoven in the company of his teacher Hummel. From 1828 to 1835 Hiller lived in Paris and his close friendship with Berlioz produced an extensive correspondence that covers a period of almost forty years. When they first met (early in 1829) Berlioz was no longer the reluctant anatomy student whose physician father had half-commanded, half-bribed him to study medicine in Paris in exchange for a new flute. He was a published music critic and ambitious composer-conductor who had given his first orchestral concert while still a student at the Conservatoire. His idols were Shakespeare, Goethe, Gluck, Weber, and Beethoven, though Hiller reported, "he believed in neither God nor Bach."[298] Concerning his comrade's aquiline appearance Hiller wrote: "I do not think that anyone could have met Berlioz without being struck by the extraordinary expression of his face. The high forehead, precipitously overhanging the deep-set eyes, the great curving hawk nose, the thin, firmly cut lips, the rather short chin, the enormous shock of . . . hair . . . whoever had once seen this head could never forget it."[299]

It was to Hiller that this unforgettable-looking young Frenchman felt himself compelled to confess every agony and ecstasy of his worship for yet another idol—a female one. In the early fall of 1827 the Irish actress Harriet Smithson (1800–1854) dazzled Paris with her renditions (in English) of Shakespeare. In the audience for the first performance of *Hamlet* on 11 September were a number of the future Les Jeunes France circle, including Dumas, Hugo, and Delacroix (whose impression of Miss Smithson as Ophelia he would later capture on canvas in his *Death of Ophelia* of 1844). Berlioz was also there, and he was immediately, totally, and irrevocably smitten. Although he did not know a word of English, he pursued the at first unreceptive Miss Smithson off and on for six years until at last they married in October of 1833.[300] Berlioz superimposed his Ophelia on Harriet Smithson with the same urgent single-mindedness that he would impose his perfervid brand of Romanticism upon Ludwig van Beethoven. And in his mind they were linked. Here is an outburst to Hiller (who six years later would be receiving confidences from Mendelssohn concerning *his* intended bride-to-be), vented during the days of desperate courtship:

My dear Ferdinand!

I must write to you again this evening. . . . Can you tell me what is this over-whelming power of emotion, this faculty for suffering which is killing me? . . . Oh, let me not cry out! . . . Always tears, sympathetic tears, I see Ophelia shedding them, I hear her tragic voice, the rays from her sublime eyes consume me. . . . I have spent some time drying the floods that have fallen from my eyes—while I saw Beethoven looking at me with severity. . . . Today it is a year since I saw HER for the last time—oh! . . . Oh! Juliet, Ophelia . . . names that hell repeats unceasingly.

truly:

I am a most unhappy man . . . but I have known some musical geniuses. I have laughed in the gleam of their lightnings. . . . Oh! sublime ones! sublime ones! annihilate me! summon me to your golden clouds! deliver me! . . . Reason says to me

"peace, fool, in a few years there will be no more question of your agonies than of what you call the genius of Beethoven. . . ."[301]

The revelation of Ophelia-Harriet had descended upon the susceptible suitor at the Odéon Theater. Whence did the Gospel of Beethoven reach out to touch him? Not, according to Berlioz, through his own first readings of Beethoven scores. "I had read through two of Beethoven's symphonies and had heard an andante [probably the slow movement of the Seventh Symphony] played, which made me feel dimly that he was a great luminary, but a luminary only faintly discernible through dark clouds."[302] The afflatus unadumbrated hit Berlioz with full force in the hall of his own Conservatoire when, in the early spring of 1828, the violinist-conductor François-Antoine Habeneck (1781–1849) (Fig. 84) led his newly founded Société des Concerts du Conservatoire in the performance of Beethoven's orchestral music. The first concert took place at two o'clock Sunday afternoon, 9 March 1828, and included the Paris premiere of the *Eroica* (Third) Symphony. Later in the season the Fifth Symphony was presented, with most of musical Paris in attendance—some to sneer, more to applaud. Berlioz was *foudroyé* (thunderstruck), to use his own expression. The survivor of the Smithson-Shakespeare tempest described the latest upheaval in his life: "It sometimes happens that in the life of an artist one thunderclap follows another as swiftly as it does in those great storms in the physical world, where the clouds, charged with the electric fluid, seem literally to sport with the thunder, while they hurl it to and fro as if exulting in the effect they produce. I had scarcely recovered from the visions of Shakespeare and Weber when I beheld Beethoven's giant form looming above the horizon. The shock was almost as great as that I had received from Shakespeare, and a new world of music was revealed to me by the musician. . . ."[303]

After acknowledging the foudroyant impression Beethoven had made on his psyche, Berlioz addressed the earthly particulars, crediting Habeneck and his Society with the "glorious success of Beethoven's works in Paris," and asserting (as Schindler did in his *Beethoven in Paris* of 1842) that Habeneck's pioneering activities took place at first in an atmosphere of defiant indifference toward "a class of music which was then chiefly noted for its eccentricity and its difficulty."[304]

The general attitude then prevailing in Paris toward Beethoven's "difficult" music, even among the most well-meaning critics, is best observed in a ver micular obituary published in the influential journal *Le Globe* twelve days after Beethoven's death. On account of his tenebrous intellectuality, the German composer is explained with a crescendo of italicizations as a sort of musical Kant:

"Even those who are not very sensitive to the *abstract* and, so to speak, *metaphysical* beauties of Beethoven's compositions nevertheless cannot forbear admiring in him the greatest modern harmonist. . . . At the bottom of his combinations, apparently all *mathematical*, we always discover I know not what intimate and *concealed poetry* as in the writings, so *logically obscure*, of the philosopher of Königsberg."[305]

It was Berlioz who, with his poetic analyses of the nine symphonies and other Beethoven works, would spearhead the transformation of the French perception of Beethoven as *cerebral* to *passional*. Meanwhile, however, during the final Restoration years before the 1830 July Revolution, the conservative Salon-goers saw Ingres's cool linear neoclassicism challenged by the swashbuckling, painterly style of a Delacroix choosing to illustrate scenes from Shakespeare, Goethe, and Byron, and the traditional holdouts hissed Hugo's *Hernani* for forty-nine nights at the Théâtre Français. Their ranks were increased by the intransigent classicists of the music world who were appalled by Beethoven's musical anarchy—his harsh harmonies, strange modulations, and disregard of proportions. In the face of such awesome musical liberties Berlioz saw through the reservations of some of his colleagues: "Not the least of Habeneck's obstacles lay in the silent opposition, ill-concealed dislike, and ironical reserve of the French and Italian composers, who were but ill-pleased to see an altar erected to a German, whose works they deemed monstrosities, and regarded as fraught with danger to themselves and their school."[306] The fearless Conservatoire student named names, and predictably they included *les inséparables*: Berton, "who regarded the whole of the modern German school with contemptuous pity," and Cherubini, "who dissembled his bile, not daring to vent it on the master whose successes exasperated him and sapped the foundations of all his pet theories. . . ."[307]

Few of the Conservatoire professors were omitted from this indignant litany (written at least twenty years after the fact), and Berlioz's description of the encounter he engineered between his retired teacher Jean-François Lesueur (1760–1837) and Beethoven's music is a charming record, not only of its narrator's contagious ardor but also of the great impact of Habeneck's "orchestral Beethoven."

My master Lesueur, a thoroughly honest man, without malice or jealousy, a lover of his art [he and Berlioz agreed on three heroes—Gluck, Virgil, and Napoleon] . . . persistently absented himself from the Conservatoire concerts, in the face of the fever of enthusiasm with which he saw that all artists in general, and I myself in particular, were possessed. Had he gone he would have been obliged to come to some conclusion about Beethoven . . . he would have been a reluctant witness of the wild enthusiasm which his works had aroused. . . . I left him no peace, however, and insisted so strongly on the necessity for his understanding and appreciating an event of such importance as the introduction of this new style and these colossal forms, that he reluctantly yielded, and allowed himself to be taken to the Conservatoire on a day on which Beethoven's Symphony in C minor [Fifth] was to be performed. He wished to listen to it conscientiously and undisturbed; so he sent me away, and seated himself among strangers in one of the lower boxes. When it was over I went down to find out what effect the marvelous work had produced on him.

I met him striding up and down the passage with flushed cheeks. "Well, dear master?" . . . "Hush! I want air; I must go outside. It is incredible, wonderful! It stirred and affected and disturbed me to such a degree that when I came out of the box and tried to put on my hat I could not find my own head! Do not speak to me till tomorrow."[308]

In this involuntary testimonial to the power of Beethoven's music to stir, affect, and disturb we recognize the quality of *awesomeness* to which the French Romantic imagination, nourished by Berlioz's inspired images as a critic, would so wholeheartedly respond. The *idea* of Beethoven's music, as much as the sound, gained speedy entry into the France of 1828. First had come Shakespeare, then Beethoven. Both breakers of rules. Berlioz was not the only one to succumb to this combination and in this sequence. (And we will recall that E.T.A. Hoffmann—whose *Contes fantastiques* Berlioz discovered in 1829—had coupled the names of Shakespeare and Beethoven in his 1814 defense of the inner unity of Beethoven's music.) Victor Hugo, in his famous preface to *Cromwell* (1827)—an essay that immediately became the literary manifesto of the Romantic movement—advocated a Shakespearean freedom from rules and classical unities in favor of a commingling of the sublime with the grotesque, of tragedy with comedy (features Berlioz would read into Beethoven's scores). Later, in the original version of his *William Shakespeare*, Hugo singled out the contradiction of Beethoven the deaf musician ("crippled body, flying soul"[309]) who "heard the infinite."[310] By the time Berlioz wrote his supposedly autobiographical *Symphonie Fantastique* (1830; dedicated to Liszt) it was second nature to him to combine the Shakespearean principle of violent contrasts with what he believed to be the Beethovenian manner of "life-inspired"[311] music (as with the *Pastoral* and its brief but definite "program"). It is noteworthy that the Shakespeare-Beethoven pairing in connection with Berlioz's music occurred to Schumann towards the end of his long and remarkable review (1835) of the *Symphonie Fantastique* (known to him at that time only from Liszt's published piano transcription of 1834).[312]

Even without invoking the mighty precedent of Shakespeare, the primers fashioned by Berlioz and Hugo on the boundless topic of Beethoven shared much in common. Beethoven's music was "everything" for those sensitive enough to listen well. "The dreamer will recognize his dream, the sailor his storm, Elijah his whirlwind, . . . Erwin von Steinbach his cathedral, and the wolf his forests," proclaimed Hugo in an inspired and inspiring Romantic raptus.[313] The profundity as well as the heights of Beethoven's illimitable music wrested comment from the female members of that circle we have come to know from the celebrated omnium gatherum depicted in Danhauser's *Liszt at the Piano*. Marie d'Agoult described the inner voyage of recollection upon which Beethoven's music launched the listener—"all that you have felt, or experienced, your love, your grief, your reverie"—as permitting access "into the most intimate depths."[314] And George Sand declared the *Pastoral* "more exquisite and more vast than the most beautiful landscapes ever painted."[315]

The contrasts in Beethoven's music did disturb some. Echoing Chopin's "fall-to-earth" sensation, Delacroix complained sadly to his diary after returning home from a performance of the *Eroica*: "All at once you fall down a hundred feet and find yourself amid things that are most singularly commonplace."[316] Although he believed Beethoven's compositions generally demanded a too-prolonged attention ("Painting has this advantage . . . the most gigantic picture is seen in an instant."[317]), Delacroix, like the other French Romantics we have encountered, liked to compare the composer with Shakespeare—both "wild contemplators of human nature."[318] He admitted, almost reluctantly, that Beethoven opened up more horizons than the "celestial" Mozart (by far his favorite composer) and ascribed this to the fact that Beethoven was born later, in fact just in time really to reflect "the modern character of the arts, turned, as he was, to the expression of melancholy and of that which, rightly or wrongly, people call romanticism."[319] The painter communicated this important insight to an author friend: "On returning from the concert with Mme. Sand I said that Beethoven moves us the more because he is the man of our time. He is romantic to the supreme degree."[320] But the reserved, deeply contemplative Delacroix did not always wish to be moved (like other active Romantics he yearned increasingly for repose—that elusive opposite of ravishment) and he approvingly cited a friend's observation that "emotions wear out our lives as much as excesses."[321] Hence we meet with the phenomenon of France's greatest Romantic painter lumping France's greatest Romantic composer with a "sublime" but "uneven" titan of the recent musical past: "Went to hear Berlioz. The Leonore overture produced the same confused impression upon me; I conclude from that that it is bad—full, if you like, of sparkling passages, but disunited. The same thing for Berlioz: the noise he makes is distracting; it is a heroic mess."[322] Despite a shared affinity with Berlioz for Shakespeare, Delacroix, the fastidious Romantic in search of cohesive color combinations, was never able to bring himself wholly to accept the "disunity" he sensed in Beethoven's compositions or in the music of his contemporary whose teachers at the Conservatoire had accused of having "Beethoven on the brain."[323]

Let us return to the Berlioz of Conservatoire years now and observe the Beethoven relevation continue to unfold before the eyes of a young man of great musical talent and unrequited (he was still four years away from marriage) love. A year and a half after encountering Harriet Smithson for the first time, the distraught Berlioz found exactly what he needed most in Beethoven—a fellow *sufferer*: "Yesterday I went to the Conservatoire concert. Beethoven's Symphony in A [Seventh] made a sensation...this inconceivable product of the most sombre and reflective genius is placed exactly among all that the most intoxicating, the most tender and naïvest joy, can offer. It has only two ideas: 'I think, therefore I suffer,' and 'I remember, therefore I suffer more.' Oh, unhappy Beethoven! he too had in his heart an ideal world of happiness into which it was not given him to enter."[324]

Nowhere, not in any of the treasured images of Beethoven projected by the German and Central European musicians we have examined from Weber to Liszt, have we met such extreme self-identification as with this young Frenchman's.[325] This is still the young Berlioz, of course, and the Beethoven image a private one, conjured up for personal solace, but it was upon this capacity to feel emotions he believed Beethoven had felt that Berlioz the mature critic would build his influential musical analyses of Beethoven. And yet Berlioz was very early aware that neither the private nor the public Beethoven was accessible to all. Here he is, three weeks after the "unhappy Beethoven" outburst we have just read, describing to his sister the effect of Beethoven's music on a large audience composed mostly of philistines but harboring a select few who—ravished by the sounds—grimly *understood*. A droll caricature entitled *Upon Hearing a Beethoven Symphony* (Fig. 85), drawn in 1840 by the Parisian artist Eugène Louis Lami (1800–1890), seems almost to be an illustration of the event, although the performance Berlioz attended was of a Beethoven string quartet:

> Ah! you speak to me of the *beautiful*, the *grand*, the *sublime*...but the sublime is not sublime for everybody. What transports some is unintelligible to others, sometimes even ridiculous.... The other day I heard one of the late quartets of Beethoven...there were nearly three hundred persons present, of whom six found ourselves half-dead through the truth of the emotion we had experi-

enced, but we six were the only ones who did not find this composition absurd, incomprehensible, barbarous. He rose to such heights that our breath began to fail us. He was deaf when he wrote this quartet; and for him as for Homer, "the universe was enclosed in his own soul." This is music for him or for those who have followed the incalculable flight of his genius. . . .[326]

Apart from the pleasing circumstance of early Berlioz comprehending late Beethoven, and the vaulted imagery characteristic of Berlioz when writing about Beethoven, we have—central to the elitist and exclusionary tendencies of Les Jeunes France—the important recognition (half boast, half resignation) that Beethoven is not for the crowd. He is not to be profaned by popularity. The notion that Beethoven's music could appeal to the masses would not gain currency until Beethoven's image-makers required a political portrait of their hero. And this necessity would not arise until the Franco-Prussian War and its prolonged aftermath. With Wagner and Romain Rolland waiting in the wings, let us nevertheless persist in seeing young Berlioz through his Conservatoire years.

It would take four attempts before Berlioz, enfant terrible of the Conservatoire, through the sheer force of his talent would break through the reservations of his elders (who included Cherubini) to win the coveted Prix de Rome (with his *Sardanapale* cantata of 1830, during the first performance of which the climaxing Conflagration scene miscued and hence did not take place). After his failure to obtain the prize in August of 1829 (no prize at all was awarded that year, thus neatly circumventing the dilemma) Berlioz plied his journalistic talents for a newly founded weekly, *Le Correspondant*, and as if in defiance of his Beethoven-fearing Conservatoire teachers, published a brief three-part sketch of the composer.[327] Some of the biographical details were obtained from persons who had known the master, such as Hiller and Cherubini, but Berlioz also drew portions of his titanic picture from Beethoven's scores. In the final installment, turning to the Ninth Symphony (which had not yet been performed in Paris), the twenty-six-year-old music critic simultaneously hailed the advanced artistry of the German composer and pilloried the Parisian backwardness that supposed Beethoven's late works to be the products of a deranged mind: "For us, having read attentively this symphony, we do not hesitate to consider it as the culminating point of the genius of its author. Nevertheless one cannot conclude that this is one of his works which will produce most effect in Paris—in two centuries' time, perhaps!"[328]

Actually, Berlioz's Paris did not hesitate nearly that long to accord Beethoven's *Choral* Symphony critical kudos. Fewer than two years after his mocking challenge had been published a determined Habeneck led the fifty-six string and twenty-five wind players of the Conservatoire orchestra (which consisted of past and present pupils) and a chorus in the first Paris production of the Ninth. The date was 27 March 1831 and only one major Beethoven adherent was missing—Berlioz. Unfortunately, as he himself would have said, he had in the meantime won the Prix de Rome, an award which at last reconciled his parents to his musical career but which *obligated*[329] him to quit Paris and take up residence at the French Academy in Rome—to which he reluctantly set off in late February of 1831 for a stay of nearly two years. He therefore not only missed hearing the Ninth, but also the unstinting praise Rossini supposedly accorded the second movement: "I know nothing finer than that Scherzo. *I myself could not make anything to touch it.*"[330] Rossini made this declaration to Hiller (who may well have reported it to his friend Berlioz), and he was overheard to continue, with characteristic Rossinian sweep: "The rest of the work wants charm, and what is music without that?"[331] Whether or not this categorical Rossini coda is canonical, the fiber of such a remark (and there must have been many a Conservatoire listener who left the concert hall that day wondering where indeed the "charm" of music had fled) stands strangely apart from the awesome dimensions required of music—and sounded by Beethoven—by the new Romanticism. Beethoven had revealed that music could wield an ethical force, and he had also given it a new dignity, freeing it—philosophically—from the service of orthodox form (in favor of passional *content*) and—practically—from servitude to court and church.

It was to this Beethoven-indebted new position of music that the prosyletizing players of the Conservatoire orchestra had referred in the *tutti* outburst recorded "verbatim" by Schindler when he interviewed Habeneck's players during his first visit to Paris. The event occurred exactly one decade after the premiere of the Ninth and we should consult the quotation again now in full context: "The musicians who took part in this discovery [of Beethoven's music] still remembered it with noble pride in 1841 when I heard them say: 'Beethoven taught us the poetry of music. His compositions awakened in us the first consciousness of the dignity and significance of our profession, and when we had gained some understanding of him, we recognized our obligation to make his music heard and known. He is our joy, but also our despair, if we hope to emulate him.' "[332]

How exultant the *"ami de Beethoven"* must have been to elicit this pious French image of his beloved master. And he had something to reveal to the devout musicians as well. For lo and behold he had brought with him all the way from Germany his (already "greatly darkened") bust portrait of Beethoven by the amateur painter Ferdinand Schimon, creator of that wild-eyed, windblown im age of genial savagery which through engravings had become so integral to Beethoven mythography. At Habeneck's[333] request, Schindler zestfully tells us, the holy icon was quietly installed in a special room at the Conservatoire on an especially appropriate day, one on which rehearsals for the Seventh Symphony were taking place. At the conclusion of the rehearsals Habeneck informed the assembled musicians of the treat awaiting them in the next room. What followed is best told by our objective German collector of Beethoven data:

(Colorplate 3)

> Already extremely elated by the music, this announcement had the effect of an electric shock on all of them. With impetuousness and shouts of hurrah they all suddenly rushed to that room. And then what a scene there was to behold! Some of the crowd fell to their knees in front of the picture, others sat on tables and stools, and as from many the cry *"Chapeaux bas!"* was heard, there followed a long pause of just pure contemplation during which the countenance of Beethoven seemed to say: "You are all my disciples, I am satisfied with you." It was one of the most moving moments that I have ever experienced in my life; if only a large number of Beethoven admirers could have enjoyed it with me!—After about a quarter of an hour and after a few of the older professors of the Conservatoire had asked a few questions in hushed tones, as one would speak in a church, the group left the room in complete silence, obviously deeply moved by the image of their Ideal.[334]

Enticing as it is to linger over this picture of the Conservatoire orchestra members—not an art connoisseur among them apparently—kneeling in awe with hats doffed before the leonine image of Beethoven, it is even more intriguing to ponder the Lesson the French musicians told Schindler they had learned—"Beethoven taught us the *poetry* of music." For, as literary apologists like Berlioz would confirm, Beethoven's triumphant reentry into France (the first invasion of 1811, that of the "doves and crocodiles" campaign, had not succeeded) was in tandem with an *idea*. It was an idea as far-reaching as Romanticism itself, for it included a new definition of music—as springing from the heart rather than from reason—and it ascribed to music fresh domains such as interiority, extramusical content, sentiment that begets sentience, aspiration, melancholy, fulfillment, and memory. Above all, music was seen to have new powers—the ability to transport, to provide access to the infinite. All this was in Beethoven's music, with its fire, its ecstasy, its images, its inspirations, and especially its proleptic flights towards the sublime. Beethoven's music admitted the listener into the realm of *poetry*.[335]

And so the French love affair with Beethoven began. "A little late," some of the earlier *German* discoverers of Beethoven might have sniffed, and in fact we have heard Friedrich Wieck's superior and slightly suspicious tone in the Paris diary he kept during the unsuccessful attempt to introduce young Clara to the French music world in the spring of 1832. Both father and daughter had been pleased, it will be recalled, to find so much Beethoven included in Habeneck's concerts, including the Third, Fourth, Sixth, and Eighth symphonies. "The French at present affect to love Beethoven above all else; everyone here lives for and demands nothing but Beethoven,"[336] Wieck had noted dryly.

But while this Beethoven brushfire was sweeping Paris, Berlioz, who would have loved the conflagration, was languishing in Italy.[337] "I had left Paris, the center of civilization, and . . . I was suddenly deprived of music, theaters, literature, excitement—in fact, all that made life worth living," he wrote.[338] Nevertheless there were a few compensations, one of them the striking up of a friendship with another composer who also knew and adored Beethoven, the twenty-two-year-old Felix Mendelssohn, who had been in Rome since the first of November the year before. Berlioz—older by almost six years—met him the day after his Rome arrival in mid-March of 1831. The two composers, so different, yet both worshipers at the same shrines of Shakespeare, Goethe, Gluck, and Beethoven, recorded their first impressions of one another. The beautifully brought-up German was slightly scandalized by the self-dramatizing Frenchman:

> Berlioz distorts [*verzerrt*] everything, without a spark of talent, always groping in the dark, but esteeming himself the creator of a new world; writing moreover the most frightful things, and yet dreaming and thinking of nothing but Beethoven, Schiller, and Goethe. . . . I really cannot stand his obtrusive enthusiasm . . . and if he were not a Frenchman (and it is always pleasant to associate with them, as they have invariably something interesting to say), it would be beyond endurance.[339]

Berlioz's few reservations about Mendelssohn were outweighed by his musical appreciation. Reporting back to his and Hiller's circle of friends he wrote:

> I have made the acquaintance of Mendelssohn. He is a wonderful fellow. . . . I am convinced he is one of the greatest musical talents of the age. He has been my cicerone. Every morning I went to his house. He would play me a Beethoven sonata; we would sing from Gluck's *Armide*; then he would take me to see all the famous ruins which, I confess, did not move me very much. He has one of those clear, pure souls that one does not often come across: he believes firmly in his Lutheran creed, and I'm afraid I shocked him terribly by making fun of the Bible. I have to thank him for the only pleasant moments I had during my time in Rome.[340]

A dozen years later in the chronology of his *Memoirs*, Berlioz described at greater length the salutory effect of Mendelssohn's daily doses of Beethoven and Gluck:

> When the sirocco was overpowering I used often to go and interrupt him in his work, for he was an indefatigable producer. [The *Föhn* did not seem to debilitate Mendelssohn!] Then he would lay down his pen with the utmost good humor, and, seeing me bursting with spleen, would try to soothe it by playing anything I chose among such works as we both liked. [Enter a Beethoven sonata.] How often, as I lay there peevishly on his sofa, have I sung the air from [Gluck's] *Iphigénie en Tauride.* . . . [341]

Mendelssohn was not the only fellow adulator at the double altar of Beethoven and Gluck to receive Berlioz's lively approbation. Ingres—an artist as uncomprehending of what Berlioz was exploring in music as he was disapproving of what Delacroix was pursuing in painting—won the following remarkable encomium in a letter Berlioz wrote to Liszt concerning the redeeming feature Ingres had displayed in this regard: "And so you're in Rome. M. Ingres will surely welcome you, especially if you will play him our Adagio in C-sharp minor of Beethoven. . . . I greatly admire the fanaticism of this great painter's musical passion, and you will heartily forgive him for loathing[342] me when you remember that he adores Gluck and Beethoven. . . ."[343]

Seventeen years after voicing these thoughts, Berlioz again expressed his unswerving allegiance to the "two Jupiters": "There are two great superior gods in our art, Beethoven and Gluck. . . ."[344] The "our adagio in C-sharp minor of Beethoven" to which Berlioz refers in his letter to Liszt is of course the adagio of the *Moonlight* Sonata, the schizoid playing of which we have already experienced in Berlioz's two accounts of Liszt's strangely varying renditions.

Indulging in emotional extremes was second nature to Berlioz, especially as a young man (in later life he practiced a tight self-control in public that caused Wagner to consider him "remote"), and it is not surprising to find that the overwhelming elements of "exile" in Italy—loneliness, Beethoven, and Gluck—all coalesced to precipitate an attack of what the composer tenderly called spleen and what we will immediately recognize as that anguished Romantic yearning for the infinite:

> Even in my calmer moods I feel a little of this isolation—for instance on Sunday evenings, when the towns are still and everyone goes away to the country— because there is *happiness in the distance* and people are *absent*. The adagios of Beethoven's symphonies . . . the Elysian fields in [Gluck's] *Orfeo*, bring on fierce fits of the same pain; but these masterpieces contribute their own antidotes; they create tears, and tears bring relief. The adagios of some of Beethoven's sonatas, on the other hand, and Gluck's *Iphigénie en Tauride* pertain wholly to the state of spleen, and induce it; the atmosphere is cold and dark, the sky is gray and cloudy, and the north wind whistles drearily.[345]

The state preceding spleen, as Berlioz with his medical training meticulously analyzes it, is impressively similar to the intense states induced by listening to Beethoven's music, as discussed by Berlioz the critic. Compare these two descriptions, the first about prespleen palpitation, the second about emotional pulsations in Beethoven's Fourth Symphony: "There is a vacuum all round my throbbing breast, and I feel as if under the influence of some irresistible power my heart were evaporating and tending towards dissolution. . . . it is no wish to die—

far from it, it is a yearning for more life, life fuller and completer; one feels an infinite capacity for happiness which is outraged by the want of an adequate object, and which can be satisfied only by the infinite, overpowering *furious* delights proportioned to the incalculable wealth of feeling which one longs to spend upon them."[346] No *malade imaginaire* Berlioz! These attacks were real enough. And now on to the "wealth of feeling" in the Fourth Symphony: "As for the adagio, it seems to elude analysis. Its form is so pure and the expression of its melody so angelic and of such irresistible tenderness that the prodigious art by which this perfection is attained disappears completely. From the very first bars we are overtaken by an emotion which, towards the close, becomes so overpowering in its intensity that only amongst the giants of poetic art can we find anything to compare with this sublime page of the giant of music. . . . This moment seems as if it had been sadly murmured by the Archangel Michael on some day when, overcome by a feeling of melancholy, he contemplated the universe from the threshold of the Empyrean."[347]

Even this brief extract shows that Berlioz, with his passion and literary fire, was every bit Schumann's equal in this new, *poetical* music criticism of Romanticism, born of subjective response to the sensed emotions charging Beethoven's music. Listen to Berlioz's own definition of music as an example of the expanded frontiers assigned the rational discipline by the new criticism. The first seven words ring out like a manifesto: "Music is the art of producing emotion, by means of combinations of sound, upon men both intelligent and gifted with special and cultivated senses. To define music in this way is equivalent to admitting that we do not believe it to be, as some say, *made for everybody*. . . . Music is, at one and the same time, both a sentiment and a science. It exacts from anyone who cultivates it, whether as executant or composer, both a natural inspiration and a range of knowledge only to be acquired by long study and profound meditation. It is this union of knowledge with inspiration which constitutes the art."[348] To *knowledge* must be added *feeling*, Berlioz continues, and like a galvanic current this latter quality can leap from the music containing it to the audience absorbing it: "How often we have seen, at the performance of the *chefs d'œuvre* of our great masters, listeners agitated with dreadful spasms; crying and laughing at the same time, and manifesting all the symptoms of delirium and fever!"[349] With "the burning inspiration and the electric flight of genius"[350] inherent in Beethoven's music, such communicated passion could be physically as well as psychically devastating: "The celebrated singer, Mme. Malibran, hearing for the first time, at the Conservatoire, the C minor Symphony of Beethoven [Fifth], was seized with convulsions to such a degree that she had to be carried from the room. [Publicity stunts were not unknown in the nineteenth century, of course, but we know from all accounts of this famous singer's life that she was indeed "excitable."[351] And we recall that Berlioz's teacher Lesueur, after hearing the same symphony, was so shaken he could not "find his head."] Twenty times have we seen, in similar cases, grave men obliged to withdraw, in order to conceal from the public the violence of their emotions."[352]

It was permissible for even a male Romantic to weep in public, but this music that so perturbed the listener transmitted the full spectrum of the sublime and tears were not always a relief. In contrast to the beautiful (or Rossini's "charm"), the sublime could evoke sensations that were grotesque,[353] even violent—as abrupt in their onslaught and intensity as the dynamic markings in Beethoven's scores. Thus Berlioz, the former medical student, is able to give an "objective" account of the violence wreaked upon him by music of the caliber of Beethoven:

> On hearing certain works my vital strength seems first of all doubled; I feel a delicious pleasure with which the reason has no connection; the habit of analysis then unbidden as it were to engender admiration. Emotion, increasing in direct proportion to the energy or grandeur of the composer's ideas then soon produces a strange agitation in the circulation of the blood; my arteries throb violently; tears which, in a general way, indicate the end of the paroxysm, mark in this case only a *progressive stage* which is liable to be much exceeded. In the latter case, spasmodic contractions of the muscles supervene; the limbs tremble; there is a *total numbness of the face and hands*; a partial paralysis of the nerves of sight and hearing; in short I no longer see or hear perfectly, am seized with giddiness and am half swooning.[354]

This confessional—perhaps more than the reader ever wanted to know about someone else's physical reaction to music—is worth remembering as we turn now to Berlioz the professional critic, for the genuineness of his Beethoven ardor sprang as much from his acute emotional responsiveness as from his nimble intellect.

For four decades—from 1823 to 1863—Berlioz wrote (although he frequently professed irritation and dismay at having to earn his living this way) music criticism for a variety of journals. He was for twenty-eight years a regular contributor to the distinguished *Journal des Débats*[355]—owned by the Bertin of Ingres-portrait fame—and tirelessly addressed himself to the works of that "indefatigable Titan"[356] whose thunderbolt had left him permanently ravished. His commentaries on Beethoven, especially the nine symphonies, charter the moods of the music in unabashedly lyrical terms. These drama synopses are supported by technical observations that brim with admiration and sometimes employ a questioning method that poses alternate solutions, then pounces with redoubled enthusiasm upon the composer's choice. In spite of his belief—made sardonic by experience—that Beethoven's beacon light was not visible to all, he wrote messianically about the music, reading into it the "noble, elevated, firm, bold, expressive, poetical and always *new* style"[357] that so commanded his admiration. And Berlioz's Beethoven writing was largely irresistible. Even Schindler, hawkishly devouring the pages of the *Journal des Débats* in Frankfurt, mentioned Berlioz's criticism without disapproval.[358] The Frenchman had inadvertently found favor with Schindler by disagreeing both in performance and in print with Mendelssohn that two redundant measures printed in the Breitkopf and Härtel orchestral parts of the scherzo of the Fifth Symphony should be deleted. With a rare flash of humor Schindler reported: "Hector Berlioz declared himself for the correctness of the passage in the *Journal des Débats*. Director Habeneck told me he was not going to give up the denounced measures. . . . The most amazing reaction was that the price of cotton in America went up considerably as a result of this international controversy."[359]

 We shall read for ourselves some of the Beethoven analyses that won the hearts of the French public, analyses born during the rapture of a concert-hall performance and enunciated after many preparatory drafts and solitary rewritings. (Berlioz seemed intuitively to follow Winckelmann's dictum: "Sketch with fire; execute with phlegm.") As we peruse Berlioz's literary image of Beethoven, we must remember that the supreme accolade regarding Beethoven's music was to elevate

237

it to the poetical plane, one from which images (that is, *content*) could roll before the mind or memory of the listener. For the French Romantics, Beethoven's music was best experienced through and as a literary form. The finest music was poetry. Hence for Berlioz great musicians like Gluck and Beethoven (and himself, he hoped) were empowered and obligated to rise above the craft of composition to the poetry of creation and revelation. (He prefers not to refer to Beethoven as a musician but as poet.[360])

From this lofty plane Beethoven's First Symphony in C Major (1800) was, obviously, excluded. Berlioz was blunt about it: "In a word this is not Beethoven."[361] And the reason? Because "the poetic idea is completely absent. . . . It is music admirably framed; clear, imbued with life, though but slightly accented; cold and sometimes mean; as for example in the final rondo—a genuine instance of musical childishness."[362] Not yet the real Beethoven then, but, Berlioz assures us, "we are shortly to discover him."[363]

Beethoven's Second Symphony in D Major (1802)—that of the *colombes* and *crocodiles*—seems to have reminded many early reviewers of some sort of fowl or beast. Here is a reaction from Vienna of 1804: "Beethoven's Second Symphony is a crass monster, a hideously writhing wounded dragon [*Lindwurm*], that refuses to expire, and though bleeding in the finale, furiously beats about with its tail erect."[364] Would Berlioz too find a beast of some sort? No. Neither roc nor chimera inhabits the domain reached by Beethoven's music. Berlioz's appreciative prose begins: "In this work everything is noble, energetic and stately; the introductory largo being a *chef-d'œuvre*. The most beautiful effects succeed one another without confusion and always in an unexpected manner; the song being of a touching solemnity, which, from the very first bars, imposes respect and prepares us for emotion."[365] Emotion! Here is a crucial ingredient for our Romantic critic who, we know from his own testimony, is wont to suffer elevated blood pressure under the impact of the energies of genius. But the listener-critic is not unduly agitated, for the emotions discharged are tender, not violent. From characterization of the music's frolicking quality Berlioz moves guilelessly—and with perfect logic it would seem—to presumed states of Beethoven's personality as it was when he wrote the music:

> The andante . . . is the delineation of innocent happiness hardly clouded by a few accents of melancholy occurring at rare intervals. The scherzo is just as frankly gay in its capricious fantasy as the andante was completely happy and calm; for everything in this symphony is genial, even the warlike sallies of the first allegro being exempt from violence, so that one can trace in them no more than the youthful ardor of a noble heart which retains intact the most beautiful illusions of life. The composer still has faith in immortal glory, in love and self-sacrifice. [Is Berlioz writing only about Beethoven or also about himself?] Hence the degree to which he abandons himself to his gaiety, and the felicity of his sallies of wit. To hear the different instruments disputing the possession of some portion of a motive, which no one of them executes entirely [the writhing of the wounded *Lindwurm* of Viennese provenance?], but of which each fragment becomes in this way colored with a thousand different tints in passing from one to the other, one might easily indulge the fancy of being present at the fairy gambols of the graceful spirits of Oberon.[366]

And so it is not the habitat of crocodiles or dragons that Berlioz envisions but the puckish world of *A Midsummer Night's Dream*. Shakespeare had predisposed the French to Beethoven; now Beethoven summons back the whimsical realm of the English poet.

In treating the more sober and far more substantial Third Symphony in E-flat Major (the *Eroica*, 1803–4), Berlioz takes his cue from Beethoven's inscription "to celebrate the memory of a great man," imagining and describing a "hero's *funeral rites*."[367] But he also does something else, something guaranteed to expand French appreciation of the work. It is not the Napoleonic connection that Berlioz takes up but the link with classical antiquity. By demonstrating that the *Eroica* is epic, Berlioz endows it with an impeccable and inspiring pedigree. Both Virgil and Homer figure in his analysis. Here are the relevant passages: ". . . the Funeral March is a drama in itself. We seem to trace it in the translation of those beautiful lines of Virgil on the funeral procession of the young Pallas. . . . The third movement is entitled scherzo, according to custom. . . . At first sight it does not appear obvious how such a style of music can figure in an epic composition. The rhythm and the movement of the scherzo are, indeed, there. There is also play; but it is play of a funereal kind, at every instance clouded by thoughts of mourning—a kind of play, in fact, recalling that which the warriors of the Iliad celebrated round the tombs of their chiefs."[368] The allusion to Homer is one to which Berlioz returns in discussing the *Eroica*,[369] and we observe our critic making use of some facts learned about Beethoven's reading habits as related in Schindler's biography: "In . . . the 'Eroica' . . . the form tends to a greater breadth, it is true; the thought also reaching to a greater height. Notwithstanding all this, however, we cannot fail to recognize therein the influence of one or other of those divine poets to whom, for so long, the great artist had erected a temple in his heart. Beethoven, faithful to the precept of Horace . . . used to read Homer habitually; and, in his magnificent musical epic which, rightly or wrongly, is said to have been inspired by a modern hero, remembrances of the antique 'Iliad' play an admirable and beautiful, but no less evident part."[370]

By directing attention to the symphony's sympathetic vibration with antiquity and by refraining from mentioning the name Napoleon[371] ("modern hero" is as close as he comes), Berlioz keeps his perception of the imagery and emotions of Beethoven's Third Symphony on a vaulted, universal plane. "In this [music] we see that there is no question of battles or triumphal marches . . . but much in the way of grave and profound thought [a first enunciation of the Beethoven-as-Philosopher mystique], of melancholy souvenirs and of ceremonies imposing by their grandeur and sadness. . . ."[372] His final judgment of the work's success embraces all the requirements of Romanticism: "the 'Sinfonia Eroica' possesses such strength of thought and execution, . . . its style is so emotional and consistently elevated besides its form being so poetical, that it is entitled to rank as equal to the highest conceptions of its composer."[373]

Regarding Berlioz's essay on the Fourth Symphony in B-flat Major (1806)—in which he discerned such "irresistible tenderness" and from which we have already quoted—the mercurial nature of Beethoven's scoring is noted as a distinct phenomenon. Berlioz's analysis begins with a general characterization of the music as "either lively, alert and gay or of a celestial sweetness,"[374] but concludes, with cliff-hangerlike suddenness: "The finale . . . is one animated swarm of sparkling notes, presenting a continual babble; interrupted, however, by occasional rough and uncouth chords, in which the angry interspersions, which we have already had occasion to mention as peculiar to this composer, are again mani-fest."[375] Rough, uncouth, angry? Once again we are in the orbit of Beethoven the man, reflected as Beethoven the musician. And indeed Berlioz seems all his life to have mulled over these aspects of Beethoven's character ("*toujours brusque*," Cherubini would have assured him for the hundredth time) which he saw or-chestrated in the symphonies. Five years before his death, ruminating to an old friend on how he wished he might have known Virgil and Shakespeare, he added to the *desiderata* list: "And Beethoven, contemptuous and rude, yet blessed with such profound sensitivity that I think I could have forgiven him all his contempt and his rudeness."[376]

With each symphony Berlioz gets to know and to love Beethoven all the more. He also increasingly identifies with the composer. It is with an almost possessive familiarity that he gives the great Fifth Symphony in C Minor (1805–7) its due: "[It] appears to us to emanate directly and solely from the genius of Beethoven. It is his own intimate thought which is there developed; and his secret sorrows, his pent-up rage, his dreams so full of melancholy oppression, his nocturnal vi-sions and his bursts of enthusiasm furnish its entire subject; whilst the melodic, harmonic, rhythmic and orchestral forms are there delineated with an essential novelty and individuality, endowing them also with considerable power and no-bleness."[377] Each time we consult Berlioz the critic on Beethoven, it is necessary to remind ourselves that we are also consulting the imaginative, innovative com-poser whose great theoretical work *Traité de l'instrumentation et d'orchestration mo-dernes* (1844) demonstrated him to be an extraordinarily gifted and knowledgeable musician-composer in his own right. And yet Berlioz's literary image of Bee-thoven, which does contain numerous analytical breakdowns and theoretical for-ays, never weights the scale in favor of technical arguments to prove Beethoven's genius; the overwhelming evidence for Berlioz is, always, the felt presence of multiple emotions and the ineluctible power of Beethoven's music to transport sensitive listeners in its wake. And so Berlioz, the orchestrator, can and does tell us about the first movement of the Fifth that it "presents a striking example of the effect produced by the excessive doubling of parts under certain circumstances, and of the wild aspect of the chord of the fourth on the second note of the scale; otherwise described as the second inversion of the chord of the dominant,"[378] but—about the same movement—Berlioz, the Romantic, enjoins us: "Listen to those orchestral gasps; to those chords in dialogue between wind and strings, which come and go whilst gradually growing weaker, like the painful respiration of a dying man . . . see that quivering mass; which hesitates for an instant, and then precipitates itself, bodily divided, into two ardent unisons . . . and then, having done this, say whether this passionate style is not both beyond and above anything which had been yet produced in instrumental music."[379] The reader is swept along by this post-Beethoven stream of emotion that seems to relive the composer's hectic life—"the first movement is devoted to the expression of the disordered sentiments which pervade a great soul when a prey to despair,"[380] and the reader rejoices with Berlioz at the finale's "gigantic song of victory; in which the soul of the poet-musician, henceforth free from all hindrance and earthly suf-fering, seems to rise beaming towards the very heavens."[381]

We have just encountered Berlioz's favorite phrase for Beethoven—the poet-musician—and we would be quite correct to anticipate that in assessing the Sixth Symphony in F Major (the *Pastoral*, 1807–8), Berlioz, lover of extramusical content, would see a great deal of specific story in this, the most "programmatic" of the poet-musician's symphonic works. "Pastoral Symphony, or a recollection of coun-try life. More expression of feeling than painting," had been Beethoven's descrip-tion of his Sixth Symphony, we recall. Berlioz paid absolutely no attention to this. His very first sentence happily and self-confidently introduces the simile of paint-ing: "This astonishing landscape seems as if it were the joint work of Poussin and Michel Angelo."[382] The Italian titan's name has previously been linked with the German titan's by French writers (we have taken special note of Stendhal in a pre-vious chapter), but that of Poussin is certainly new! And disappointing, if we ex-pect loyalty in the Romantic ranks—Berlioz could, after all, have mentioned Gé-ricault or Delacroix. Such omission alerts us once again to the fact that not all Romantics cared to label each other or themselves *as* Romantics (Chopin and De-lacroix are examples of this). And not all Romantics recognized their comrades as acceptable cotravelers towards the sublime. We have learned what Delacroix pri-vately thought of Berlioz ("heroic mess"), and we should not be surprised if a confirmed Gluck-lover like Berlioz envisioned serene classical landscapes by Poussin rather than dislocated sweeps by Delacroix while listening to the *Pastoral*.[383]

After assuring his readers that he does not mean the *Pastoral* invokes a land-scape full of "gaily bedecked shepherds,"[384] Berlioz does turn to Beethoven, cit-ing what the composer had entitled the first movement ("awakening of cheerful feelings on arriving in the country") and gingerly continuing with a full-fledged scenario: "The herdsmen begin to appear in the fields. They have their usual careless manner, and the sound of their pipes proceeds from far and near. De-lightful phrases greet you, like the perfumed morning breeze; and swarms of chattering birds in flight pass rustling overhead. From time to time the atmos-phere seems charged with vapor; great clouds appear and hide the sun; then, all at once, they disappear; and there suddenly falls upon both tree and wood the torrent of a dazzling light."[385] We note Berlioz's synesthetic reference to a *perfumed* morning breeze (in his analysis of the *Eroica* he had already spoken of the nuance distinguishing instruments from each other as comparable to "*blue* and *violet*"[386]). The pictorial paragraph now concludes with a sort of disclaimer: "This is the ef-fect, as it appears to me, on hearing this movement; and I believe that, notwith-standing the vagueness of instrumental expression, many listeners have been im-pressed by it in the same way."[387]

Berlioz's sketch of the second movement might have been written while gazing at Lyser's 1833 image of *Beethoven Composing the "Pastoral" by a Brook* (see Fig. 50): "Farther on, there is the 'Scene am Bach'; devoted to contemplation. No doubt the author created this admirable adagio whilst reclining on the grass; gazing up-wards, listening to the wind, and fascinated by the surrounding soft reflections of both light and sound; at one and the same time looking at, and listening to, the tiny white waves as they sparkled along; and, with a slight murmur, broke upon the pebbles of the brink. It is indeed beautiful."[388]

Berlioz avoids being pulled too deeply into the whirlpool of contemporary crit-icism concerning Beethoven's musical portrayals of nightingale, quail, and cuck-oo, and hurries on to question the logic of those who object to imitative bird songs in the symphony but not to the realistic tempest portrayal given to the orchestra. For the *Gewitter-Sturm* movement his admiration knows no bounds:

> I despair of being able to give an idea of this prodigious movement. It must be heard in order to form an idea of the degree of truth and sublimity descriptive music can attain in the hands of a man like Beethoven. Listen!—listen to those

rain-charged squalls of wind; to the dull grumblings of the basses; also to the keen whistling of the piccolo, which announces to us that a horrible tempest is on the point of breaking out. The hurricane approaches and grows in force; an immense chromatic feature, starting from the heights of the instrumentation, pursues its course until it gropes its way to the lowest orchestral depths. There it secures the basses, dragging them with it upwards; the whole shuddering like a whirlwind sweeping everything before it. Then, the trombones burst forth, the thunder of the kettledrums becomes redoubled in violence, it is no longer merely rain and wind, but an awful cataclysm, the universal deluge—the end of the world.

This literally produces giddiness; and many people, when they hear this storm, can scarcely tell whether their emotion is one of pleasure or of pain.[389]

As Beethoven could employ extremes in his musical "depictions," from cuckoo to tempest, Berlioz, prone to similar volatility, could encompass experiencing the universal deluge along with singling out, as Beethoven had musically, the amusing limitations of a rustic bassoon player whose stubborn devotion to duty is cut off only by the storm of the fourth movement. A very concrete and humorous scene had unfolded for Berlioz as he listened to the third movement, marked by Beethoven as a "festive assembly of country people":

They laugh and dance with moderation at first; whilst, from the Musette, there issues a gay refrain, accompanied by a bassoon, which seems only able to entone two notes. Beethoven has probably intended this to represent some good old German peasant, mounted on a barrel and armed with a dilapidated instrument, from which he just succeeds in drawing the two principal notes of the key of F; its tonic and dominant. Every time the oboe gives out its musettelike melody, which seems as simple and gay as a young girl dressed out in her Sunday clothes, the old bassoon brings out his two notes. Should the melodic phrase modulate at all, the bassoon is silent; quietly counting his rests until the return of the principal key permits him to come in again with his imperturbable—'F, C, F.' This effect, so excellently grotesque, seems almost completely to escape the attention of the public.[390]

Juxtaposition of these two extracts, one extolling the universal, the other delighting in the particular, is eloquent proof of why Berlioz's image of Beethoven persuaded his readers to see Beethoven as the German Shakespeare. After admiring the manner in which the concluding movement wondrously conveys Beethoven's explanatory title "Shepherds' song—joyful, grateful feelings after the story," Berlioz, carried away by the potential of modern music in general, ranks Beethoven above even his beloved Virgil and praises the art he shares with the mighty tone-poet:

How the antique poems, however beautiful or admired they may be, pale in significance when compared with this marvel of modern music? Theocritus and Virgil were great in singing the praises of landscape beauty . . . but this poem of Beethoven!—these long periods so richly colored!—these living pictures!—these perfumes!—that light!—that eloquent silence!—that vast horizon! . . . Veil your faces! ye poor, great ancient poets—poor Immortals! Your conventional diction with all its harmonious purity can never engage in contest with the art of sounds. You are glorious, but vanquished! You never knew what we now call melody; harmony; the association of different qualities of tone; instrumental coloring, modulation; the learned conflict of discordant sounds which emerge first in combat, only afterwards to embrace [with this single phrase Berlioz legitimizes Beethoven's—and his own—dissonances]; our musical surprises; and those strange accents which set in vibration the most unex-plored depths of the human soul. . . . The art of sounds, properly so-called and independent of everything, is a birth of yesterday. It is scarcely yet of age, with its adolescence. It is all powerful; it is the Pythian Apollo of the moderns. We are indebted to it for a whole world of feelings and sensations from which you were entirely shut out.[391]

For Berlioz's audience, the implication of living in the nineteenth century, of practicing the arts with resources unknown to the ancients was enthralling. And it was Beethoven, and only Beethoven, who had ushered in this new age of lim-itless possibility.

Almost as if performing some kind of musicological penance for the ecstatic outburst wrung from him by the Sixth Symphony, Berlioz removed his imagerial glasses while writing "analyses" of the Seventh Symphony in A Major (1812) and the Eighth Symphony in F Major (1812) and limited himself to describing and commenting upon the formal elements of the two compositions, especially the rhythms and melodic inventions. Then, somewhat (but not thoroughly) chas-tened, he embarked upon his most ambitious critique—an essay on Beethoven's Ninth Symphony in D Minor (the *Choral*, 1817–23). He begins prudently: "To ana-lyze such a composition is a difficult and dangerous task, and one which we have long hesitated to undertake. It is a hazardous attempt, excuse for which can only lie in persevering efforts to place ourselves at the composer's point of view and thus perceive the inner sense of his work, feel its effect, and study the impres-sions which it has so far produced; both upon privileged organizations and upon the public at large."[392]

The cautious critic then rehearses a variety of judgments already passed on the Ninth Symphony, and ranges from those classifying it as a *"monstrous folly"* or "the parting gleams of an expiring genius," to those, far fewer in number, that rank it as "the most magnificent expression of Beethoven's genius."[393] With this last opinion, Berlioz tells us, he agrees, and then—still exercising unusual re-straint—proposes to explore the motives vindicating this new form of "choral" symphony: "Without prying into what the composer may have wished to ex-press in the way of ideas personal to himself in this vast musical poem, this being a search in favor of which the field of conjecture is equally open to everyone, let us see if the novelty of form is not here justified by an intention altogether inde-pendent of philosophic or religious thought, an intention as reasonable and beau-tiful for the fervent Christian as for the Pantheist or Atheist—an intention, in fact, purely musical and poetical."[394]

What were these musical and poetical intentions? Like Romanticism itself they were the desire to surpass, to transcend: "Beethoven had already written eight symphonies before this. What means were open to him, in the event of his pur-posing to go beyond the point at which he had already arrived, by the unaided resources of instrumentation? *The junction of vocal with instrumental forces.*"[395] Ber-lioz admiringly identifies the new style of mixed music Beethoven employed as his connecting link: "It was the instrumental 'recitative' which thus became the bridge which he ventured to throw out between chorus and orchestra; and over which the instruments passed to attain a junction with the voices."[396] Berlioz sees Beethoven enter into the symphony himself now as the leader of a Greek chorus, using his own words, not Schiller's, to plead for a change of mood: "Then it was that, speaking by the mouth of a Coryphée, he himself cried out, in employing the very notes of the instrumental recitative which he had just employed: *O*

*Freunde, nicht diese Töne! sondern lasst uns angenehmere anstimmen, und freundenvoll-
ere.* In the above lines, so to speak, the 'treaty of alliance' entered into between
chorus and orchestra; the same phrase of recitative pronounced by one and the
other seeming to be the form of an oath mutually taken."[397]

With such persuasive arguments does Berlioz touch the heart of the Philistine
who, even if not previously aware of "instrumental recitatives," was certainly familiar with the efficacy of alliance of powerful forces. Berlioz, the avant-garde
composer and accomplished musical theorist, also has a blunt message for his
fellow writers on music concerning the Ninth: "It is an immense work; and, when
once its powerful charm has been experienced, the only answer for the critic who
reproaches the composer for having violated the law of unity is: *So much the worse
for the law!*"[398]

But not even the discerning Berlioz was able to embrace or explain *all* of the
Ninth. In taking up the presto of the fourth movement, the first rupturing chord
of which we have seen Schumann cite in an attempt to explain the chaos of tones
assulting his inner ear, Berlioz exhibits xenophobia:

> We are now approaching the moment when the vocal and orchestral elements
> are to be united.... The chord of the major sixth (F, A, D) with which this
> presto starts off is intruded upon by an appoggiatura on the B-flat, struck at the
> same time by flutes, oboes and clarinets. This sixth note of the key of D minor
> grates horribly against the dominant and produces an excessive harsh effect.
> This is well expressive of fury and rage; but I still do not quite see what it was
> that excited the composer to this sentiment, unless, before saying ... *Let us turn
> to other tones more pleasant and full of joy,* he wanted, in virtue of some odd whim,
> to calumniate instrumental harmony.[399]

Berlioz's puzzlement is exacerbated when the clamorous chord, also exacerbated,
sounds again just before the vocal recitative: " ... this time the composer [he is
suddenly no longer the 'poet-musician'] is not contented with the appoggiatura
B-flat, for he adds E, G, and C sharp, so that ALL THE NOTES OF THE MINOR
DIATONIC SCALE are played together, and produce the frightful assemblage: F,
A, C sharp, E, G, B-flat, D."[400] The ambitious scope of this simultaneously
sounded scale prompts Berlioz into an amusing tangent about an analogous effect, employing every diatonic, chromatic, and enharmonic interval all at the
same time for the moment of a watery suicide leap in an 1813 opera *Sappho*,[401] but
he then returns seriously and without success to ponder the Beethoven chord conundrum: "I perceive a formal intention—a calculated and thought-out project—
to produce two discords at the two instants which precede the successive appearances of vocal and instrumental recitative. But, though I have sought high
and low for the reason of this idea, I am forced to avow that it is unknown to
me."[402]

In admitting this defeat, Berlioz reveals himself as one Romantic who could not
accept the grotesque implicit in the sublime. (And yet the term "bizarre" would
be leveled at his own music throughout his career.[403]) But if our anxious critic lost
this one Beethoven battle, he certainly did not lose the war. The rest of his Ninth
Symphony analysis traces, technically and descriptively, the complex development of the finale and provides a punctilious translation of Schiller's Ode in order
to give French readers "the key to this multitude of musical combinations, skilled
auxiliaries of a sustained inspiration, docile instruments of a powerful and indefatigable genius."[404] Only at the end of his treatise did Berlioz presume to read the
composer's thoughts—a foray with which admirers of the *Choral* Symphony must

surely have agreed: "Whatever may be said, it is certain that Beethoven, when finishing his work, and when contemplating the majestic dimensions of the monument he had just erected, might very well have said to himself: Let Death come now, my task is accomplished."[405]

Over the years Berlioz continued to study the Ninth and under his baton on 12 May 1852 the symphony created a sensation at the fourth concert of the just-launched New Philharmonic Society[406] in London (founded by, among others, the Cramer of our Schindler-Cherubini-Beethoven conversation). This performance, for which seven rehearsals had been held, and a superb international chorus assembled, created voracious demands for a repetition and so the sixth and final concert of the Society that season, on 9 June, was given over to it (as well as a few fragments from Berlioz's *Faust*). "If only you had been here to hear our second performance of the Choral Symphony," Berlioz wrote his friend and fellow *Débats* contributor, the Liszt biographer Joseph d'Ortigue, raving about the glorious chorus ("Those beautiful women's voices!") and orchestra.[407]

Wilhelm von Lenz's two-volume *Beethoven et ses trois styles* (regarding which we have read Liszt's thoughtful letter of congratulations mixed with criticism) had just come out in print while Berlioz was in London conducting the New Philharmonic Beethoven performances. He found time to write a lengthy and mostly sympathetic review of it (he does take Lenz to task for too many quotes in German and for a tasteless, irrelevant digression on the "Hebraic" element in Mendelssohn's music). This he published later that same year (1852) in his charming and, unlike his music, popular book *Les Soirées de l'Orchestre*—a fanciful potpourri of musical anecdotes, skirmishes, biographies, and discussions all carried on in the form of conversations or recitations by the players in an opera pit during the performance of bad operas.[408] We shall quote extensively from this book in the next chapter when we consult Berlioz's detailed account of the festivities accompanying the unveiling of the Beethoven memorial in Bonn. At this moment another Berlioz essay on Beethoven awaits us—one on Beethoven's "fourth" style, inspired not by Lenz but by the contemporary European mania for table turning, of which we have already had a semiserious glimpse through Robert Schumann's eyes. Berlioz's delicious satire (published in 1862), "Beethoven in the Ring of Saturn (The Medium)," describes the amazing outcome of a medium's successful attempt to make contact with Beethoven:

And thus it came to pass that, on Monday last, a medium who was on extra good terms with the great man, and was not afraid of putting him into a bad humor by making him take such a long voyage for nothing at all, placed his hands on the deal table for the purpose of sending to Beethoven, in Saturn's ring, the order to come and talk with him for a moment.

At once the table began to make indecent movements; to lift its legs and to show—well to show that the spirit was near. The poor spirits, we must admit, are very obedient. Beethoven, whilst he was on earth, would not have put himself out of the way . . . even if the emperor of Austria had sent to beg him urgently to come. And now he quits Saturn's ring, and interrupts his high contemplations to obey the *order* (mark the word) of the very first comer who only happens to be possessed of a deal table. See the effect of death and how that changes your character! . . .

So Beethoven arrives; and, by means of the legs of the table, he says: "Here I am!" The medium, delighted, thereupon gives him a familiar tap. . . . [and] without the least ado, asks the *semi-god* to dictate a new sonata. Beethoven does not wait to be asked twice; so the table begins to frisk about and the sonata is written under the composer's own dictation. This done, Beethoven returns to Saturn; and the medium, surrounded by a dozen wondering spectators, approaches the piano and executes the sonata. . . . Certainly Beethoven, in going to inhabit a superior world, could but perfect himself. His genius could only increase and become more elevated; so that, in dictating a new sonata, he must have intended to give the inhabitants of earth some idea of the new style he has adopted in his new residence; an idea of his

Fourth Period;

an idea of the kind of music they play upon the Erards in Saturn's ring.[409]

Several decades of watching his promising composing career pale in Paris, while his double professions as visiting conductor (Belgium, Germany, Austria, Russia, England, and, sometimes, France) and critic flourished, had calcified Berlioz's natural store of sarcasm. The Beethoven with whom he so identified, especially in the incomprehension and actual hostility initially shown to some of his music, meant more and more to him as each season he witnessed the enthusiastic reception given by his countrymen to the latest musical banalities and bombasts. But there had been one season in Paris, almost a quarter of a century earlier, when the now disillusioned author of ''Beethoven in the Ring of Saturn'' had been singled out and honored as a *composer* in a most remarkable fashion—one that linked him irrevocably with Beethoven and gave international impetus to the Beethoven mythology. This is the episode alluded to in our examination of Paganini's image of Beethoven, when, acting as the catalyst, he joined the names of Beethoven and Berlioz in a way the French public could never forget (and some never forgive). A few weeks after having been in the audience at a performance of Berlioz's *Symphonie Fantastique* (22 December 1833), Paganini, deeply impressed, approached Berlioz with an invitation to write a work for his Stradivari viola. This was the request that engendered the symphony with solo viola *Harold in Italy*, completed and premiered in November 1834. But Paganini was no longer in Paris then and he did not have a chance to hear the music until four years later, when he attended two Berlioz performances in short order, the first a ''massacre'' (Berlioz's word) of the premiere of his opera *Benvenuto Cellini* (10 September 1838) and the second a successful Conservatoire concert, conducted by Berlioz himself, of the *Symphonie Fantastique* and *Harold in Italy* (16 December 1838). With the same clairvoyance that had made him one of the earliest foreign admirers of Beethoven, Paganini now reacted impulsively to the young French composer. We let Berlioz take up the stirring narrative:

> The concert was just over; I was in a profuse perspiration, and trembling with exhaustion, when Paganini, followed by his [thirteen-year-old] son Achilles, came up to me at the orchestra door, gesticulating violently. Owing to the throat infection of which he ultimately died, he had already completely lost his voice.
> . . . He made a sign to the child, who got up on a chair, put his ear close to his father's mouth, and listened attentively. Achilles then got down, and turning to me, said, ''My father desires me to assure you, sir, that he has never in his life been so powerfully impressed at a concert; that your music has quite upset him, and that if he did not restrain himself he should go down on his knees to thank you for it.'' I made a movement of incredulous embarrassment at these strange words, but Paganini, seizing my arm, and rattling out, ''Yes, yes!'' with the little voice he had left, dragged me up on the stage, where there were still a good many of the performers, knelt down, and kissed my hand. I need not describe my stupefaction; I relate the facts, that is all.[410]

But there was more to come. Much more. Berlioz, who had gotten up from a sick bed to conduct the concert, was back in bed having caught a chill. On 18 December, two days after the fateful concert, Berlioz recounts:

> I was alone in my room, when little Achilles entered, and said, "My father will be very sorry to hear that you are still ill, and if he were not so unwell himself, he would have come to see you. Here is a letter he desired me to give you." I would have broken the seal, but the child stopped me, and saying, "There is no answer; my father said you would read it when you were alone," hastily left the room. I supposed it to be a letter of congratulations and compliments and, opening it, read as follows [Fig. 86]:
> " Mio caro amico
> Beethoven spento, non c'era che
> Berlioz che potesse farlo rivivere;
> ed io che ho gustato le vostre divine
> composizioni, degne d'un genio qual
> siete, credo mio dovere di pregarvi
> a voler accettare, in segno del mio
> omaggio, ventimila franchi i quali
> vi saranno remessi dal Sig. Baron
> de Rothschild dopo che gli avrete
> presentato l'acclusa.
> Credetemi sempre
>
> il vostro aff/° amico
> Nicolò Paganini
>
> Parigi il 18 Decembre 1838"[411]

> [My dear friend:
> Beethoven being dead, there is only Berlioz who could revive him; and I who have taken delight in your divine compositions, worthy of a genius such as you are, believe it my duty to beg you to want to accept, as a sign of my homage, twenty thousand francs which will be remitted to you by Sig. Baron de Rothschild after you have presented to him the enclosed.
> Believe me always
> your most affectionate
> Nicolò Paganini
> Paris the 18(th) December 1838][412]

This unprecedented act of generosity, once known by the general public, ignited some grotesque mythmaking gossip about who had really given Berlioz money, and because of the importance of all the circumstances surrounding Paganini's gift, we must allow Berlioz to proceed with his narrative:

> I know enough of Italian to understand a letter like this. The unexpected nature of its contents, however, surprised me so much that I became quite confused in my ideas, and forgot what I was doing. But a note addressed to M. de Rothschild was enclosed, and, without a thought that I was committing an indiscretion, I quickly opened it, and read these few words in French:
> "Sir,
> Be so good as to remit to M. Berlioz the sum of twenty thousand francs which I left with you yesterday.
> Yours, etc., Paganini"
> ... Paganini's noble action soon became known in Paris, and for the next two days my room was the rendezvous of numerous artists, all eager to see the

famous letter, and learn the particulars of so strange an event. . . . Afterwards came out all the remarks, detractions, anger, and falsehoods of my enemies . . . [and] the scandalous insinuations against Paganini. . . . [413]

What "scandalous insinuations" could possibly be made against Paganini we might well wonder as we read these indignant words by Berlioz in his *Memoirs*? The answer is that Paganini was, unfortunately, caught in the web of a myth of his own, one to which he had recently contributed when he refused to play for a Paris charity concert. This bad impression was fortified by French indignation at the high prices tickets to his concerts fetched. Anti-Paganini propaganda had already been afoot for some time—he was reputedly a miser, an ex-convict, a murderer—and this spectacular gift (worth more than twice a normal annual salary) from a theatrical Italian to a controversial French composer whom he dared to link with the genius of Beethoven was simply seen by much of the French press as yet another clever publicity ploy. Very quickly the rumor spread that Armand Bertin of the *Journal des Débats*, in order to promote his friend Berlioz as both a composer and a catch for the *Débats* literary stable, had secretly siphoned the money to him via Paganini. Rossini was ready to believe this theory about the man whose music he disliked so heartily (Berlioz's), and even the gentle and usually judicious Charles Hallé subscribed to the Bertin theory, giving it renewed credence when he divulged "the tale" in his autobiography (published posthumously in 1896), affirming that "the secret was well kept and never divulged to Berlioz."[414] Even Liszt apparently could never bring himself to believe the money had come from Paganini.[415] The Paganini-Beethoven-Berlioz triad was heard about as far as England. Just three months after the episode, Mendelssohn's friend Henry Chorley churlishly wrote in *The Athenaeum* for 23 March 1839: "The rumor of Paganini's benefaction to Berlioz made us anxious to ascertain the real amount of ideas in the compositions of this Beethoven redivivus. We have spent a long morning over his *Sinfonie Fantastique* arranged for the pianoforte by Liszt, and are enabled, without undue haste or presumption, to state our opinion that he stands very low in the scale of composers. . . . This enormous Sinfonie is a Babel, and not a Babylon of music."[416]

Chorley saw Babel, then, where Paganini had seen Beethoven. In a letter to his sister describing his visit to thank Paganini, Berlioz reaffirms this. After a wordless embrace, Paganini, with tears in his eyes, croaked into Berlioz's ear, "You have given me emotions that I had not anticipated; you have advanced the great art of Beethoven."[417] And Berlioz, in his biographical sketch of Paganini, saw a heartrending Beethoven parallel in the pathos of Paganini's loss of voice (he would die of tuberculosis of the larynx): "By putting one's ear up to his mouth, one could just catch one or two of his words. And on the occasions when I went walking with him in Paris . . . I used to take a notebook and pencil. Paganini would write down in a few words the subject on which he wanted the conversation to turn; I would develop it as best I could, and from time to time, taking the pencil again, he interrupted me with reflections that were often highly original in their brevity. Beethoven in his deafness used a notebook in this way to receive his friends' thoughts, while Paganini in his dumbness used it to transmit his thoughts to them."[418]

As for the monetary gift Paganini had transmitted to Berlioz—the grateful recipient immediately set about realizing the musical expectations invested in such a gesture. Clearing his desk of other projects Berlioz began planning an ambitious new work that, like Beethoven's Ninth, would be a choral symphony. Conceived for soloists, chorus, and orchestra, and extending to seven movements, the "program" was a perfect vehicle for Berlioz's brand of Romanticism: Shakespeare's *Romeo and Juliet*.

With no financial worries to distract him, Berlioz's composing advanced quickly and by the first week of September 1839 the "symphonie dramatique" was finished. It was dedicated to Niccolò Paganini. The premiere took place in the Conservatoire hall on 24 November, with two more performances following. Berlioz himself conducted the 160 musicians and 101 vocalists, and all of Les Jeunes France (now middle-aged) turned out. The only notable figure missing was Paganini. He was already in Nice, a shadow of his former self, vainly in search of the sun, and rapidly deteriorating. Death came uneventfully for Europe's greatest showman on 27 May 1840. "Poor dear great friend," mourned Berlioz," . . . to the grief I felt at his death was added that of not knowing whether he would have approved the work undertaken chiefly to please him, and justify him to himself for what he had done to its author."[419] Théophile Gautier's review, in which the Berlioz-Beethoven link is remarked and eulogized, suggests that Paganini would have approved: "[Berlioz] has given a soul to each instrument of the orchestra, an expression to each note; he has wished that every phrase should have a precise sense; this idea, foreshadowed by some masters, used by Beethoven, has been well developed by M. Berlioz. . . ."[420]

Indeed, increasingly, and in spite of their lack of public success in France, Berlioz's works were seen by the critics as proceeding from Beethoven. Of the *Symphonie Fantastique*, the elderly Gaspare Spontini (1774–1851) had already said to Berlioz, concerning the *Marche au supplice*, "There has never been but one man capable of a similar piece, and that is Beethoven. . . ."[421] And from Germany the voice of no less a Beethoven-*Kenner* than Adolf Bernhard Marx would be raised in praise of Berlioz's "légende dramatique," *The Damnation of Faust* (first performed Paris, 6 December 1846). Marx called Berlioz "a disciple of Beethoven."[422] And this was only the latest in a line of similar descriptions. We have already noted that Berlioz was early designated "the French Beethoven" in Germany[423]; so enthusiastic was the young Hans von Bülow upon hearing *Benvenuto Cellini* (1836–8; revised by Berlioz as a three-act opera 1852) during a Berlioz Week staged by Liszt at his Weimar stronghold in November of 1852, that he wrote a series of articles praising the opera and calling its composer "the immediate and most energetic successor of Beethoven."[424] All this fanfare brought a famous German out of seclusion to observe the second Beethoven for herself. She is well known to our study of mythmaking—Bettina Brentano von Arnim, still alive and still possessively watching over her own particular Beethoven legacy, at the age of sixty-eight. The encounter occurred at the end of 1853, when Berlioz visited Hanover and where, as he reported, the worthy lady came "not to see me but to look at me."[425]

In Russia, too, where his conducting and his music were appreciated in equal measure, critics reacted enthusiastically to the Propagateur de Beethoven. The Russian composer César Cui (1835–1918) exclaimed about a Berlioz appearance in Saint Petersburg (end of 1867): "How he understands Beethoven! What serenity, what austerity in the execution! And what effect without tinsel and with no concession to bad taste! I much prefer Berlioz to Wagner as a conductor of Beethoven."[426] Berlioz, for his part delighted at the high quality of the Russian musicians, wrote: "What an orchestra! What precision! What ensemble! I do not know if Beethoven ever heard himself performed in such a way."[427]

If he had been accused as a young man of having Beethoven on the brain, the decades devoted to introducing and performing Beethoven's orchestral works abroad had certainly intensified this condition. Shortly before his fifty-fifth birthday Berlioz wrote down for an old friend, Humbert Ferrand, a "Beethoven dream" he had had (we recall that Moscheles and Schindler also had their Beethoven dreams): "Last night I dreamt of music, this morning I recalled it all and mentally performed the adagio of Beethoven's B-flat symphony [Fourth] just as we did it three years ago at Baden, so that little by little I fell into one of those unearthly ecstasies and wept my eyes out at the sound of that tonal radiance which emanates from angels alone. Believe me, dear friend, the being who wrote such a marvel of inspiration was more than a man. Thus sings the archangel Michael, as he dreamily contemplates the spheres. . . ."[428]

To the same old friend Berlioz sent a description of a never-to-be forgotten Beethoven experience he had had while wide awake. In Vienna for three concerts (November 1845), he entered the Redoutensaal with awe, recalling in indignation the city's petty treatment of its greatest composer (a treatment made more callous by three decades of mythographers at work):

In this vast and beautiful hall Beethoven's masterpieces—now worshipped throughout Europe—when performed some thirty years ago, were received by the Viennese with the most profound contempt. . . . At that time the Viennese were thronging to Salieri's operas! Poor pigmies, to whom a giant had been born! They preferred dwarfs. You may imagine, my dear Humbert, that my legs trembled under me when I stepped for the first time on the platform formerly trodden by his mighty foot. Nothing had changed since Beethoven's time. The conductor's desk of which I made use had once been his; there was the place occupied by the piano on which he used to improvise; he descended those steps leading to the artists' greenroom, when certain far-seeing enthusiasts, after the performance of his immortal poems, gave themselves the delight of recalling him amidst transports of applause, to the utter astonishment of the rest of the audience, who . . . could see nothing in the sublime outbursts of his genius but the convulsive moments and brutal eccentricities of a delirious imagination. Some secretly approved of the enthusiasts, but dared not join them. They did not wish to come into collision with public opinion. [Again, we learn much about Berlioz's own frustrations as he empathizes with those of his hero's.] They must wait. And meanwhile Beethoven suffered. Under how many Pontius Pilates was this Christ thus crucified![429]

How the sufferings of Beethoven, rehearsed thus in the vivid imagination of Berlioz, comforted the present-day victim on the cross of hostile criticism. But always more important for Berlioz the critic was the obligation of sharing with his public not the life trials but the musical greatness of Beethoven. Here is his account, published in *Les Soirées de l'Orchestre* and incorporating the cherished eagle image, of hearing across the hall from his London rooms the sounds of Romanticism's primogenitor:

One evening I heard Beethoven's C Minor trio ringing out . . . I opened my door wide. . . . Come in, come in, and welcome, proud melody . . . God, how fine and noble it is! . . . Wherever did Beethoven find those thousands of phrases, each one more poetic in nature than the last, and all different, all original? . . . And what skillful developments! What unexpected flights! . . . How swiftly that tireless eagle wings his way! How he soars and hovers in his harmonious sky! . . . He plunges into its measureless space, he climbs, swoops down again, vanishes from sight. . . . Then he comes back to his point of departure, more brilliant-eyed, more powerful-winged, impatient of rest, quivering, thirsting for the infinite. . . .[430]

We have come full circle with Berlioz as we listen to this coupling, once again, of Beethoven with the infinite—that persistent siren call of Romanticism. But now it was Berlioz's turn to be inducted into the Romantic hall of fame. He had revealed German music to the French;[431] now a German musician nominated Berlioz as next in line for the throne. Writing from Weimar in 1855 in defense of the new music sweeping Europe, the young Peter Cornelius (1824–1874), friend of Bettina von Arnim, pupil of Liszt, and future confidant of Wagner, summed up what Berlioz meant to the younger, but still very Romantic generation:

> The musicians of Weimar greet him as the master of modern orchestration, the heir of Beethoven, a polyphonist of infinite resource and a polyrhythmist of the highest quality. They admire him as a musician who follows Beethoven and Schubert in sucking the nectar of his compositions only from the noblest flowers, who can fashion original forms out of poetic ideas and can give poetic shape to well-known forms, who is inspired not simply by Palestrina, Bach, Gluck, Mozart, and Beethoven, but also by Shakespeare, Goethe, Byron, Moore, Hugo and Scott. . . . But they acclaim him most as the hero who, out of love of his art, has had the strength to endure discredit, hatred, and calumny in his own country, who has never written a note that was not offered in homage to the ideal of beauty ever present before his eyes . . . and who waits proudly on the heights for the day when the public will rise to meet and greet him there.[432]

This impressive eulogy to Berlioz is of the sort made fashionable by the mythopoeticizing of Beethoven we have been tracking and we quickly perceive just why the "French Beethoven" exerted such appeal: like Beethoven, he too had suffered—worthy credentials for the heir of Beethoven. In fact Cornelius went so far as to propose the following international triad of B's: "On the heights where Bach and Beethoven already dwell, there will the third great B first find recognition . . . the proud and daring hero . . . Berlioz . . . three cheers, now: 'Bach! Beethoven! Berlioz!' "[433] Only later would another Beethoven venerator—Brahms—be substituted for Berlioz to make up the all-German phenomenon displayed to twentieth-century school children as the three B's of music.

Towards the close of his eventful and engaging memoirs, described by Berlioz as "a fairly accurate idea of the principal events in my life, and of the vortex of feeling, labor, and sorrow in which I am destined to revolve, until I shall revolve no longer,"[434] the gray-haired sixty-one-year-old composer who had been *foudroyé* in his youth by Shakespeare and Beethoven, thought of them once again. The context was quintessentially Berliozian: two times a widower, overwhelming memories of his childhood sweetheart drove him to seek out the "aged, saddened, and obscure woman"[435] whom he however saw only verdantly through Thomas Moore's eyes. "I must try to console myself for not having known her sooner, as I console myself for not having known Virgil . . . or Gluck or Beethoven . . . or Shakespeare. . . ."[436] Four years later the Propagateur de Beethoven was dead of intestinal disease at the age of sixty-five.

Berlioz's grandiose conception of Beethoven animated the images fashioned of him by a whole generation of French composers—those born in the 1830s—and it was only with the next generation—that of the 1860s—that, along with an anti-Romantic reaction, Beethoven's stature in France began to diminish for some musicians. Claude Debussy (1862–1918) for example found him a genius without taste, peevishly seeing in the *Pastoral* "a brook where, apparently, the oxen come to drink."[437] Such impish pronouncements—adroitly calculated to shake dust-covered idols—would not have occurred to the generation closer to Berlioz. Charles Gounod (1818–1893), César Franck (1822–1890), and Camille Saint-Saëns (1835–1921) did not chafe under their weighty legacy from the past but, rather, responded to the implications of the late sonatas and quartets of Beethoven. Georges Bizet (1838–1875) (Fig. 87), whose new opera *The Pearl Fishers* was the subject of Berlioz's last (and friendly) article for the *Journal des Débats* (8 October 1863), was awed by the intellect behind Beethoven's creations, while at first shying away from the "dramatic passion"[438] of the music. Nevertheless, under the impress of Berlioz's all-embracing conception, Beethoven won out in Bizet's final estimation. This is the text of his almost unconditional surrender, having survived the temptations of Italian music: "I am German by conviction, heart and soul, but I sometimes get lost in artistic houses of ill fame. And I confess to you under my breath, I find infinite pleasure there. I love Italian music as one loves a courtesan. . . . I put Beethoven at the head of the greatest and most excellent. The *Choral* Symphony is for me the culminating point of our art. Dante, Michelangelo, Shakespeare, Homer, Beethoven, Moses! Neither Mozart, with his heavenly form, nor Weber, with his powerful and colossal originality, nor Meyerbeer, with his mighty dramatic genius, can in my opinion dispute the palm with the Titan, the Prometheus of music."[439]

Here is an interesting emotional allegiance: Bizet, a Frenchman—a *Parisian*—declaring himself heart and soul a German! And earlier Berlioz, responding to the genuineness of German appreciation for his works, had allowed himself to be described as three-quarters German (although he never learned to speak the language). This idea of a fundamental kinship between the two races would be picked up and developed to an unusual pitch by another French cultural personality, whose impact on the image of Beethoven in France during the early twentieth century would be as crucial and far-reaching as that of Berlioz in the nineteenth century. This was Romain Rolland (1866–1944) (Fig. 88). His short, lyrical life of Beethoven (1903), incorporating the idea of joy through suffering (Beethoven's "motto"), was an instant literary and moral success with the public at large—a public who, like Rolland, felt "suffocated" by an "undignified materialism" and who responded to the author's call to "throw open the windows" and "breathe the breath of heroes."[440] And Beethoven was the hero of heroes who, because of his love of liberty and spiritual freedom, transcended nationalities.

We shall return to Rolland's international Beethoven, but for now, having examined at some length France's greatest delineator of the image of Beethoven—Berlioz—it is time to turn our attention to the young Saxon composer, miserably eking out a living at this time in Paris, whose Promethean portrait of Beethoven was shortly to electrify (and glorify) Germany.

RICHARD WAGNER

The new, partisan bearer of the image of Beethoven back to Germany from France was of course Richard Wagner (1813–1883) (Fig. 89). Although the deathly ill Paganini was not in the Paris Conservatoire audience of 1839 to hear the first performances of *Romeo and Juliet*, Wagner was. Only recently arrived in Paris, his response to this new *symphonie dramatique* was admiring (an attitude he would *not* continue to maintain towards Berlioz's music).

"The two enemy brothers descended from Beethoven," as Berlioz and Wagner were dubbed in a marvelous and partly accurate epithet tossed out by a hostile French critic,[441] would never be able to regard each other's music with complete approbation, in spite of their mutual Beethoven "heritage." Two years younger than the Frenchman, whose name, if not universally loved, was certainly known in Paris, the twenty-six-year-old Wagner felt in his own words, "at that time . . . almost like a little schoolboy by the side of Berlioz."[442] A quarter-century later in his autobiography *My Life*, reflecting on his first response to Berlioz's music, he confessed: "But while admiring this genius, absolutely unique in his methods, I could never quite shake off a certain peculiar feeling of anxiety . . . though ravished by his compositions I was at the same time repelled and even wearied by them."[443] Berlioz, on his part, referring admiringly in 1843 to Wagner's operatic success in Dresden with *Rienzi* and *The Flying Dutchman*, summed up with sympathy the Paris period of the young Kapellmeister, who had endured "untold privations in France, and all the mortifications attendant on obscurity."[444] Although their music became more and more mutually unacceptable, the "enemy brothers" shared specific fraternal similarities in their hero worship of Beethoven. We recall Berlioz's lament towards the end of his life at never having met Beethoven or Shakespeare; here is Wagner ruefully exclaiming to the copious note-taker Cosima of 1872: "Oh, to meet someone like B[eethoven]! That was the dream of my early youth; not being able to do it, no longer seeing such men as Shakespeare and B. about, has made me melancholy throughout my life."[445]

This same association—Romanticism's pairing of Shakespeare and Beethoven—had already been made by the fifteen-year-old Wagner as he devoured various portrait likenesses of the composer after hearing his first Beethoven symphony (the Seventh) at the Leipzig Gewandhaus: "The effect on me was indescribable. To this must be added the impression produced on me by Beethoven's features, which I saw in the lithographs that were circulated everywhere at that time, and by the fact that he was deaf, and lived a quiet secluded life. I soon conceived an image of him in my mind as a sublime and unique supernatural being, with whom none could compare. This image was associated in my brain with that of Shakespeare; in ecstatic dreams I met both of them, saw and spoke to them, and on awakening found myself bathed in tears."[446]

Wagner's active musical and theatrical family circle had provided him from earliest childhood with a double stimulus and goal, and if Beethoven was designated poet-musician by Berlioz for purely rhapsodic reasons, Wagner actually *became* a poet-musician—Shakespeare and Beethoven all in one—composing the libretti as well as the music for his dramatic creations. At fifteen he completed a long, spine-chilling Shakespearean tragedy in which no fewer than forty-two characters perished. The ghost-heavy drama was entitled *Leubald und Adelaïde* and Wagner later explained: "As even at that early age I was a great enthusiast for everything really German, I can only account for the obviously un-German name of my heroine by my infatuation for Beethoven's Adelaïde, whose tender refrain seemed to me the symbol of all loving appeals."[447] After finding the music to *Egmont* on his sister's piano and hearing Beethoven's Seventh Symphony (which always remained a favorite) at the Gewandhaus that same year (1828), the ambitious disciple immediately resolved "to set *Leubald und Adelaïde* to music, similar to that which Bee-thoven wrote to Goethe's *Egmont*."[448] Wagner's two musical thunderbolts at this tender age were Weber (a personal acquaintance of his mother's who took an interest in the singing career of one of his sisters) and Beethoven, as represented by *Der Freischütz* (from which Wagner taught himself to play the overture on the piano) and *Fidelio*, respectively. The overture to *Fidelio* in E Major, especially the introduction, "affected me deeply. I asked my sisters about Beethoven, and learned that news of his death had just arrived. Obsessed as I still was by the terrible grief caused by Weber's death [1826], this fresh loss, due to the decease of this great master of melody, who had only just entered my life, filled me with strange anguish, a feeling nearly akin to my childish dread of the ghostly fifths on the violin."[449] (Beethoven's own fifths would soon absorb young Wagner's attention in the opening bars of the Ninth.)

Another revelation was the twenty-five-year-old Wilhelmine Schröder (now married to the actor Karl Devrient)—Beethoven's Leonore at the 1822 revival of *Fidelio*—who appeared in Wagner's hometown in the same role she had made famous as much for her acting abilities as for her vocal prowess (she conveyed a terrible, earnest pathos that left listeners limp and shaken). Here is Wagner's account of his dramatic reaction to Leipzig's great musical event of 1829:

> . . . another miracle . . . suddenly gave a new direction to my artistic feelings and exercised a decisive influence over my whole life. This consisted of a special performance given by Wilhelmine Schröder-Devrient, who at that time was at the zenith of her artistic career, young, beautiful, and ardent, and whose like I have never seen again on the stage. She made her appearance in *Fidelio*. If I look back on my life as a whole, I can find no event that produced so profound an impression upon me. Any one who can remember that wonderful woman at this period of her life must to some extent have experienced the almost satanic ardor which the intensely human art of this incomparable actress poured into his veins. After the performance I rushed to a friend's house and wrote a short note to the singer, in which I briefly told her that from that moment my life had acquired its true significance, and that if in days to come she should ever hear my name praised in the world of Art, she must remember that she had that evening made me what I then swore it was my destiny to become. This note I left at her hotel, and ran out into the night as if I were mad.[450]

Wagner's Beethoven-triggered self-confidence is, even without hindsight, impressive. The note he had written as a sixteen-year-old was kept by the opera singer (who later returned musical favors by singing in three of Wagner's early operas[451]) and recited back to him from memory thirteen years later. Forty-three years after the *Fidelio* thunderbolt Wagner was still thinking of Wilhelmine Schröder-Devrient's impact. He told Cosima, who faithfully included it in that day's entry in the diary devoted to recording for posterity her husband's every act, mood, and pronouncement: "I owe many of my life's impressions solely to her."[452] The role of Leonore also symbolized for Wagner, always comfortably aware of his self-worth, the ultimate sacrifice any wife of his should be willing to make. Writing to his first wife, the actress Minna Planer (their on-again, off-again marriage dragged out for thirty years and was ended not by divorce but by Minna's death at the age of fifty-seven in January of 1866), a few months before their wedding (24 November 1836), Richard holds up this alluring picture of what being his *Weib* could encompass: "Recently I saw *Fidelio*. At the place where Leo-nore has saved her Florestan and embraces him, my eyes filled with tears. . . . I thought: 'Like Leonore your Minna would give up her life for you, or accept any suffering, any hardship to save you, if she knew you were threatened with ruin.' . . . And is it not true, my Minna, that you would do this for me?"[453]

Wagner's overweening self-esteem is not his most endearing trait but the intensity of his confrontation with Beethoven and the lifelong dialogue he held with his worthy predecessor generated positive and fruitful dimensions for the Beethoven image Germany would accept from his hands. As Wagner learned to espouse his own musical cause, he worked to advance the stature—through public exposure—of his hero. What other seventeen-year-old, encountering the orchestral score of Beethoven's Ninth, would have labored with such demonic passion, first to *possess* it—by writing out a full copy for himself—and secondly to *promulgate* on its behalf, by working out a piano transcription? We must marvel at both the audacity and the ambition of the young musician (who had not begun seriously studying the piano until he was twelve) who penned this forceful letter to the publishers of the original edition of the symphony, B. Schott and Sons of Mainz:

Leipzig, 6 October 1830
Honored Sir,
I have long made Beethoven's magnificant last symphony the object of my most attentive study, and the more I realized the greatness of the work the more it saddened me to think that it is still so neglected, so completely unknown to the greater part of the musical public. Now what would make this masterwork more accessible would be an arrangement for the piano, which to my regret I have never yet come across (for the four-handed arrangement by Czerny will obviously not serve this purpose). In my enthusiasm I have therefore dared to attempt myself to produce a version of this symphony for *two hands*, and so far I have succeeded in arranging the first—probably most difficult [an opinion the mature Wagner was to persist in]—movement with the greatest possible clarity and fullness. I therefore apply now to your resp.[ected] publishing company to enquire whether you would be interested in bringing out such an arrangement (for of course I should not be inclined to continue with such a laborious task without this certainty). As soon as I receive your confirmation I shall immediately set to work to complete what I have begun. I should therefore be most grateful for a speedy reply; as for myself, honored Sir, you may be assured of my most earnest diligence.
Your obedient servant Richard Wagner[454]

Only the stilted schoolboy handwriting gave away the age of this extraordinarily self-possessed author. (Liszt, whose piano playing and transcriptive powers left his future son-in-law light years behind, did not take up the challenge of the Ninth until the 1840s, and was still revising his arrangement twenty years later, agonizing over how to instill "into the transitory hammers of the Piano breath and soul, resonance and power, fullness and inspiration; color and accent."[455])

Did Wagner's ploy work? No. Three years after Beethoven's death was too soon for the cautious Schott and Sons to commit themselves to further expenditures on a piece of music that, as we have seen, many in the world of music considered chaotic and unplayable. But let us hear the story from Wagner himself, in less formal language than that used to impress the potential publisher, as he takes up this aspect of his Beethoven veneration in his autobiography. And again, let us admire his precocity in appreciating the *Choral* Symphony while such respected musicians as Weber and Spohr had held back:

Beethoven's Ninth Symphony became the mystical goal of all my strange thoughts and desires about music. I was first attracted to it by the opinion prevalent among musicians, not only in Leipzig, but elsewhere, that this work had been written by Beethoven when he was already half mad. It was considered the *non plus ultra* of all that was fantastic and incomprehensible, and this was quite enough to rouse in me a passionate desire to study this mysterious work. [Richard the rebel? Yes, but also Richard the avid reader of E.T.A. Hoffmann's *Phantasiestücken* and thus drawn to "mysterious" works.[456]] At the very first glance at the score, of which I obtained possession with such difficulty, I felt irresistibly attracted by the long-sustained pure fifths with which the first phrase opens: these chords, which . . . had played such a supernatural part in my childish impressions of music, seemed in this case to form the spiritual keynote of my own life. This, I thought, must surely contain the secret of all secrets, and accordingly the first thing to be done was to make the score my own by a process of laborious copying. I well remember that on one occasion the sudden appearance of the dawn made such an uncanny impression on my excited nerves that I jumped into bed with a scream as though I had seen a ghost. The symphony at that time had not yet been arranged for the piano; it had found so little favor that the publisher did not feel inclined to run the risk of producing it. I set to work at it, and actually composed a complete piano solo, which I tried to play to myself. I sent my work to Schott, the publisher of the score, at Mainz. I received in reply a letter saying "that the publishers had not yet decided to issue the Ninth Symphony for the piano, but they would gladly keep my laborious work," and offered me remuneration in the shape of the score of the great *Missa Solemnis* in D, which I accepted with great pleasure.[457]

This reminiscence differs from the first-movement-only setting Wagner had written the publishers about, but the confusion is dispelled when we realize that he has telescoped events and left out one rejection in *My Life*, as this second letter to Schott and Sons demonstrates—a letter intriguing for Wagner's optimistic obstinancy as well as for his specific Beethoven tastes:

Leipzig, 15 June 1832
Dear Sir!
I am sending you herewith a score for piano, two hands, of Beethoven's Symphony No. 9, which you had last year and sent back to me on account of having too many manuscripts. I am again putting it at your disposal to use as you may see fit, at any time. I ask no fee, but if you would make me a gift of music in return, I should be grateful. May I therefore request through Herr William Härtel, Beethoven's 1/ Missa Solemnis (D major) orchestra and piano score, 2/ Beethoven's Symphony No. 9 full score, 3/ *idem*: 2 quartets, score, and 4/ Beethoven's Symphonies arranged by Hummel? The sooner you could fill this request, the happier I should be.

Your faithful servant Richard Wagner[458]

Still Schott declined to publish the piano arrangement, but this time they kept the manuscript score and Wagner got his free copy of—at least—the *Missa Solemnis*. Schott kept the score for a very long time indeed and we may jump ahead four decades to share Cosima's elation at tracking it down and procuring the return of one more precious artifact pertaining to the genius of her Richard. The diary entry for 15 January 1872 reads triumphantly: "Arrival of the manuscript of the 9th Symphony; infinite joy; this manuscript, well preserved by Schotts', is now more than 40 years old, and now it has come into my hands! R. says jokingly, 'You have stored up my whole life around me—without you I should know nothing of my life.' "[459]

Fig. 109 Otto Böhler, The Musicians' Heaven, *c. 1897, silhouette.*   257

Fig. 110 *William Bradley,*
Sir George Smart, *1829,*
oil on canvas, National
Portrait Gallery, London.

Fig. 112 *Johann Friedrich*
Drake, Model for a Statue
of Beethoven, *1836,*
plaster (now lost).

Fig. 111 *Adolph Menzel,* Presentation Sketch of Johann Friedrich Drake's Beethoven
Memorial Design, *1837, lithograph.*

Fig. 113 *Anonymous artist*, Unveiling of the Beethoven Monument in Bonn with View towards the Cathedral, *12 August 1845, engraving.*

Fig. 114 *Anonymous artist*, Unveiling of the Beethoven Monument in Bonn with View towards Count Fürstenberg's House and the Balcony on which Queen Victoria and Prince Albert Stood, *12 August 1845, engraving.*

259

Fig. 115 Queen Victoria and Prince Albert, calling card photograph of 1861.

Fig. 116 Ernst Julius Hähnel, Beethoven Figure for the Bonn Beethoven Monument, 1845, artist's drawing for the bronze statue.

Fig. 117 Ernst Julius Hähnel, Beethoven Monument, 1845, bronze, Bonn.

DIE FANTASIE

DIE SYMPHONIE

DIE GEISTLICHE MUSIK

DIE DRAMATISCHE MUSIK

Fig. 118 Ernst Julius Hähnel, Bas-Relief
Designs for the Bonn Beethoven
Monument, *1845, artist's drawings.*

Fig. 119 *Joseph Karl*
Stieler, Lola Montez,
1847, oil on canvas,
Schönheitsgalerie,
Nymphenburg Palace,
Munich.

Fig. 120 *Johann Peter Lyser,*
Commemorative Sheet for the Beethoven
Festival at Bonn, *1845, engraving.*

Fig. 121 Antoine Bourdelle,
Beethoven, *1902, bronze,*
Beethoven Halle, Bonn.

Fig. 122 Antoine Bourdelle,
Self-Portrait as a Young Man,
c. 1878, black chalk,
private collection.

Fig. 123 Auguste Rodin, Portrait Medallion of Beethoven, *1871–77,*
facade of the Royal Conservatory of Music, Brussels.

Fig. 124 Beethoven's life mask on the wall of the studio of Rosa Bonheur at By.

Fig. 125 Anonymous artist, Anton Fernkorn's
Beethoven Monument (1860–63)
in Heiligenstadt Park, *1863, engraving.*

Fig. 126 Anton Fernkorn, Beethoven
Monument, *1863, bronze,*
Heiligenstadt Park, Vienna.

Fig. 127 Robert Weigl, Beethoven
Monument, *1902, marble,*
Heiligenstadt Park, Vienna.

Fig. 129 *Johann Nepomuk Schaller,*
Bust of Beethoven, *after 1827,*
plaster, Bodleian Library, Oxford.

Fig. 128 *Anton Fernkorn, Ressel Monument, 1863,*
bronze, Karlsplatz, Ressel Park, Vienna.

Fig. 130 Wilhelm Wolff and Karl Voss, Bust of Beethoven, *c. 1887–96, marble,
Beethovenhaus, Bonn.*

Fig. 131 Aimé de Lemud, Beethoven, *1863, engraving.*

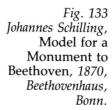

Fig. 132
Carl Kundmann,
Schubert
Monument,
1872, marble
Stadtpark,
Vienna.

Fig. 133
Johannes Schilling,
Model for a
Monument to
Beethoven, 1870,
Beethovenhaus,
Bonn.

Fig. 134 Johannes Schilling, Schiller Monument, 1876, granite and bronze, Schillerplatz, Vienna.

Fig. 135 Kaspar Clemens Zumbusch,
Monument to King Maximilian II,
1866–72, red marble and bronze,
Maximilianstrasse, Munich, photograph
taken year of unveiling, 1875.

Fig. 136 Wilhelm Gause,
Kaspar Clemens Zumbusch Working
on the Maria Theresia
Monument in his Vienna Studio,
3 May 1884, woodcut.

Fig. 137 Ferruccio Busoni, photograph of c. 1900.

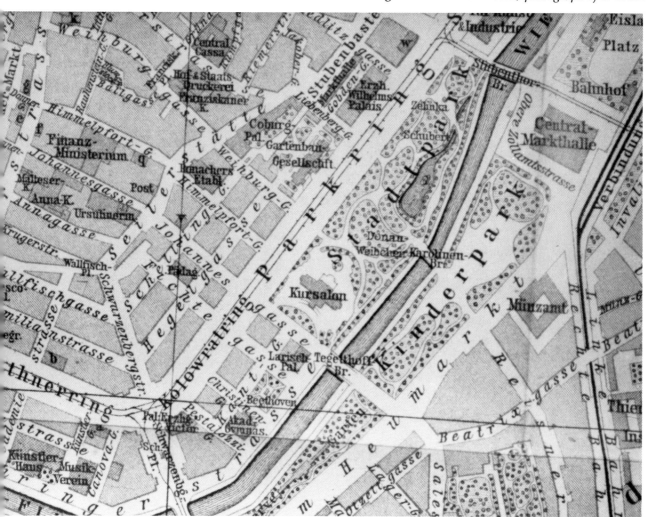

Fig. 138 Map of Vienna's Ringstrasse in 1891 showing the uncovered River Wien and the site of Kaspar Clemens Zumbusch's 1880 Beethoven monument off the (then) Kolowratring.

Thanks to Cosima we do know a great deal about that life (possibly more than some readers might wish to know), but concerning Beethoven's Ninth, Richard was also quite helpful in assembling Wagnerian artifacts for posterity. His surprise Christmas gift to Cosima for the year 1880 was, in the words of her diary entry for 25 December: "The 9th Symphony, copied out by R. 50 years ago—he coaxed it out of Frl. Uhlig for me! Splendidly written, pleasing him, too, with its painstaking thoroughness, which, when I think of all the things that must have been going on in that 17-year-old head, seems incredible to me."[460] Studying the first page of that neatly copied manuscript (Fig. 90) we are afforded a unique glimpse at the impress Beethoven had made upon the young Wagner. This is not a case of musicologically pouncing upon Beethovenian passages in the youthful work of another composer. (Wagner was the first to point out Beethoven influences in his early overtures and the Symphony in C Major.[461]) This is more akin to an art-historical observation of the nuances of emphasis or omission invariably present when one artist makes an "exact" copy of another artist's work (Delacroix's dramatic "copy" of Goya etchings, for example). Twice Wagner has told us about the spooky ("Gespensterhaft," "geisterhaft"[462]) associations excited in him by the sound of open fifths; now he confirms their phenomenological importance visually by the pronounced, imprisoning encirclement he gives the tied whole notes A and E held by the horns—those mysteriously ambiguous sustained fifths (with no key-suggesting third sounded) that begin the first movement of Beethoven's Ninth Symphony in D Minor on the dominant rather than the tonic. "I felt irresistibly attracted by the long-sustained pure fifths with which the first phrase opens,"[463] he had said. His pen fixed the acoustical phantom forever. And Shakespeare's own haunting evocation of the supernatural is also present for Wagner in Beethoven's Ninth: "When the theme in fifths recurs in the middle of the first movement, it always strikes me as a sort of Macbethian witches' cauldron in which disasters are being brewed—it does literally seethe."[464]

Beethoven was the pivotal impetus for Wagner in his first years as an aspiring composer and conductor in regional German theaters, but he served Wagner in other capacities as well during the grim period of Wagner's unsuccessful two-and-a-half-year sojourn in Paris (he arrived there, very poor, with Minna and his huge Newfoundland dog, Robber, on 16 September 1839, barely supported himself with hack work for publishers, agitated in vain to have his works performed, and left in disgust for Dresden on 7 April 1842). For one thing, thanks to an introduction to Habeneck wheedled out of Meyerbeer, he was invited to attend the Conservatoire's rehearsals of the first three movements of the Ninth (1839; Berlioz was also in attendance). A distressing performance of the Ninth that Wagner had suffered through in Leipzig had temporarily dampened his enthusiasm for the complicated symphony, a work he thought perhaps still beyond his comprehension.[465] The Conservatoire rehearsals changed all this: " . . . I listened repeatedly to Beethoven's Ninth Symphony, which, by dint of untiring practice, received such a marvelous interpretation at the hands of this celebrated orchestra, that the picture I had had of it in my mind in the enthusiastic days of my youth [Wagner was now all of twenty-six] now stood before me almost tangibly in brilliant colours. . . . Where formerly I had only seen mystic constellations and weird shapes without meaning, I now found, flowing from innumerable sources, a stream of the most touching and heavenly melodies which delighted my heart."[466]

Wagner was reconverted to the Ninth, and, despite his impecunious situation, his thwarted musical hopes, and grief over the theft of his dog, he experienced a new zest for combat. "I owed the recovery of my old vigor and spirits to the deep impression the rendering of the Ninth Symphony had made on me when performed in a way I had never dreamed of."[467] Furthermore, as a "direct result of this" Wagner felt impelled to compose something that would give him "a similar feeling of satisfaction" and set to work sketching his overture to Goethe's *Faust*[468] (could he have known that this was one of Beethoven's most cherished projects?[469]).

Wagner's creativity was sparked to expression in another vein after the reaffirmation of his Beethoven belief. A further introduction from the always helpful Meyerbeer had brought him into contact with the publisher Maurice Schlesinger (in his youth a personal friend of Beethoven's[470]), who offered the needy musician the onerous job of making various arrangements of Donizetti's *La Favorita*. Wagner accepted with alacrity, but also with mortification, considering he had come to Paris to forward his own music, not that of Italian masters. (This indignity plus Schlesinger's hard business tactics underlie Wagner's description of him as "that monstrous person."[471]) Wagner tells of the unexpected creative outlet in which he indulged while working on the Donizetti scores through a cold Parisian winter: " . . . by the way of counteracting the depression produced by this humiliating occupation, I wrote a short story, *Eine Pilgerfahrt zu Beethoven* (A Pilgrimage to Beethoven), which appeared in the *Gazette Musicale*, under the title *Une Visite à Beethoven*. Schlesinger [publisher of the *Gazette*] told me candidly that this little work had created quite a sensation, and had been received with very marked approval. . . ."[472]

Enduring the hardships of poverty and obscurity in a foreign land, the twenty-seven-year-old Wagner had turned for solace to his noble German predecessor (who *was* known in France) and found comfort in fantasizing an actual visit to the great man. Wagner's story is written with charming self-irony and is full of torturous Hoffmannesque obstacles. Interwoven with the leitmotif of the hero, a penniless young German musician "R," who is walking to Vienna to try to meet Beethoven, is a second strain—a young and wealthy Englishman who is also making the pilgrimage to Beethoven (by private coach) and who embarrasses, then thwarts, and finally has the temerity to accompany "R" when he is at last granted an interview with Beethoven. This is told with such suspenseful adroitness that we can readily imagine readers of the story—strung out over four issues of the *Gazette*—rushing to buy the next week's installment.[473] So much of this Romantic narration, in which Wagner's talents as a librettist are clearly foreshadowed, reflects the image of Beethoven then available, as well as Wagner's particular palette, that it is worth considering certain excerpts. A precedent for this fanciful visit to Beethoven existed in the real visit to Beethoven published in 1809 by the peripatetic young German composer Johann Friedrich Reichardt, whom we have already met and whose not-so *Vertraute Briefe* describing his Beethoven encounter had been read with grudging interest by Beethoven himself. Add to this the fact that Wagner (who was thirteen when Beethoven died) made a pilgrimage to Beethoven's Vienna as soon as he possibly could. It was a trip of six weeks in the summer of 1832, when he was nineteen, "with a fast-growing beard."[474] (Goethe had died that March and there was only one other really "great" German whom Wagner might have met in person—Schopenhauer—but that Revelation had not yet entered into his life.) Let us take a closer look now at Wagner's dream fantasy as realized in his short story of 1840.

The narrator of "A Pilgrimage to Beethoven," R, was born in a medium-size town—"L"—in central Germany, just like the Leipzig-born author; and also just like the author, his first exposure to Beethoven was definitive: "the first time I heard a Beethoven symphony I caught a fever, fell ill, and when I recovered became a musician."[475] This explains why, although Herr R learned about other beautiful music it was Beethoven's above all that he loved and worshiped. "To steep myself in the depths of his genius became my sole delight; so much so, that I came to imagine that his genius had entered into me [this is certainly the real R speaking]."[476] We are not surprised to learn that R is impoverished and leading an exiguous existence. When it dawns on him one day that Beethoven is *still alive*, he becomes consumed with one desire—*to see Beethoven*. Searching for ways to raise the money for such an undertaking, R goes to a publisher with some piano sonatas he has composed modeled on Beethoven's. The publisher ignores the sonatas and advises R that if he wishes to earn money he should make a reputation as a composer of galops and potpourris. "Two years had passed during which I lived in constant fear that Beethoven would die before I made my name as a composer of galops and potpourris."[477] R grew desperate and "the desperation inspired a series of truly excellent galops" for which he received money, enough to make the pilgrimage to Beethoven by foot. After many days of walking, during which the young Englishman's coach leaves him far behind (he refused an offer to ride with the Englishman, feeling it holier to walk, since his desire to see Beethoven was "the product of a deep inner necessity"[478] and incompatible with the whim of his rich rival), R at last arrives within the walls that encircle Beethoven and rents a room on the fifth floor of an inn opposite Beethoven's house. After resting, fasting, and praying for two days, R makes his first attempt to see Beethoven—the master is not at home. Returning after four more attempts to the inn, R is suddenly greeted by the Englishman from his room on the first floor. For him, too, Beethoven has not been at home. Days later, on a tip that Beethoven is usually to be found at a certain Biergarten, R tries to slip there unobserved, but the Englishman has stalked him and sits down beside him. Then the miracle happens—Beethoven strides by with short, swift steps to a table at the farthest corner of the, at that hour, empty Biergarten. "The long blue coat, the ruffled shaggy gray hair—above all, the expression of the face, so like the portrait which had stamped itself upon my memory. . . . I feasted my eyes upon the man whose genius had dominated my thoughts and feelings ever since I had learnt to think and feel."[479] R is appalled as without hesitation the Englishman makes for Beethoven in order to introduce himself. Beside himself with horror, R tries to stop the brash Briton by grabbing his coattails and the fracas attracts Beethoven's attention. He shoots a glance their way and rushes out. Mortified that Beethoven had taken *him* for an Englishman, R unburdens himself in a letter to Beethoven and is wondrously rewarded by a return note curtly inviting him to visit the next day. Ecstatic, R becomes aware of his surroundings: he discovers *Fidelio* will be performed that evening and spends his final funds on a ticket. Shall we guess who was singing? "The Leonore was played by a very young girl—but already in early youth wedded to the spirit of Beethoven. With what ardor, what poetry, what thrilling depth of feeling did she play the extraordinary role. Her name was Wilhelmine Schröder. . . ."[480] The next day R with beating heart appeared before Beethoven's door. Suddenly the Englishman was there too, and despite R's efforts to beat him off, he slipped into the sanctuary at R's side, taking no notice of Beethoven's look of surprise. R's joy was ruined by this embarrassment, "nor was Beethoven's outward appearance calculated to put me at my ease. His clothes were untidy and informal; he wore a red woollen stomach-band;[481] his long dark-gray hair was disheveled; his expression gloomy and unfriendly."[482]

Certainly the contours of Wagner's Beethoven portrait are familiar. We have read many of the same accounts to which, by 1840, he had access. But how effectively Wagner presents the personal impact of dealing with Beethoven's deafness: "At last in a hoarse voice he addressed me: 'You come from L-?' I was about to reply when he interrupted me by picking up a sheet of paper and pencil, which lay to hand. 'Use these,' he said. 'I cannot hear.' Of course I knew all about Beethoven's deafness and had prepared myself. But it smote my heart to hear that hoarse, broken voice say: 'I cannot hear.' To be poor and joyless, one's only solace one's sovereignty in the realm of sound, and have to say: 'I cannot hear.' In a flash I understood why Beethoven looked as he did: why the deeply careworn cheek, the somber angry glance, the tightly drawn defiant mouth."[483]

We see Wagner at his most human (if not most original) here in this lightning appreciation of psychic cause and physical effect. But besides giving the world a portrait of the composer "Pilgrimage to Beethoven" had a second purpose. From Beethoven's lips the world would now hear an explanation of the *Choral* Symphony, an explanation that in retrospect stands as a platform upon which Wagner would later base his own music of the future—the music-drama. The annoying Englishman is dispatched with swiftly—he leaves an elegant piece of music manuscript (his own composition) with Beethoven, calmly requests that the master look it over and put a cross next to any passage that might displease him, and bows himself out of the room. Now the stage is set for the oracle to speak. And the message is a monologue of Wagnerian proportions and precepts:

" . . . why shouldn't vocal music be considered as great and serious as instrumental music? . . . The human voice, a far nobler and more beautiful organ than any orchestral instrument, is *there*, a fact of life. . . . What new results might not be achieved? Develop the very thing which sets the voice apart and you throw open fresh possibilities of combination. Instruments represent the primal organs of Creation and Nature. . . . The genius of the voice is completely different: this represents the human heart, the separate individual sensibility, limited, but clear and definite. Imagine, now, these two elements brought together and united! . . . that second element, the voice, would have a beneficial effect upon the instruments' expression of the struggle of primal feeling in that it would set it within the framework of a definite, unifying course . . . for now its former vague awareness of the Highest would be transferred into a God-like consciousness." Here Beethoven paused for a few moments as though exhausted. [Quite true for the reader at least, since the Wagnerian cart has just been dragged into place before the Beethovenian horse.] "Of course there would be grave difficulties to overcome," he continued with a sigh. "Voices must have words, and where is poetry to be found worthy of such a union?

. . . You will soon be hearing a new composition of mine, a symphony with choruses, which will bring home what I've just been saying. Words had to be found, and the task of finding them was a great problem. In the end I decided to use our Schiller's beautiful "Ode to Joy"—a very noble uplifting poem. . . ."[484]

This double dose of Wagner and Beethoven delivered, the composer draws the interview to a close, enjoining the deeply moved R to defend his new work when it comes out and commanding: "Remember me, when all the pundits think I've gone mad, or at any rate declare that I have. . . . People think I ought to write what *they* consider good and beautiful; they forget that . . . I can only compose as I feel. . . ."[485]

With this last phrase Wagner has fortified the bastion of Romantic music and reminded his readers of the passional imperative motivating the modern artist. "A Pilgrimage to Beethoven" ends with an appropriate and hilarious nemesis for the pushy son of Albion. As the grateful R is taking his leave, Beethoven calls him back, saying he must wait a moment while he deals with the musical Englishman. "He picked up the Briton's manuscript and smiling quickly looked it over. Then he carefully gathered up the pages, threw a sheet of paper over them, seized a thick pen and drew over the folder a single colossal cross."[486]

So successful was Wagner's "Une visite à Beethoven" with the French reading public[487] that Schlesinger asked him to write another story of the same sort. Wagner obliged willingly and "in a sequel entitled 'Das Ende eines Musikers in Paris' ('Un Musicien étranger à Paris') I avenged myself for all the misfortunes I had had to endure."[488] Even more autobiographical than the Beethoven story, the narrative recounts the further adventures of the musician R after meeting Beethoven— his heroic but vain attempts to establish himself in Paris, his abject poverty and isolation, in which his only comfort is a magnificent Newfoundland dog, the disappearance of that same dog under suspicious circumstances (just as had happened with Wagner's dog Robber), and the horrendus Hoffmannesque discovery of the dog at the side of its new master, the same spectral Englishman who had haunted his pilgrimage to Beethoven, and finally a miserable death in Paris from starvation and a broken heart. Before R breathes his last he sends for his friend, the narrator of the story, and gasps out the history of his Paris suffering, culminating in a tear-jerking credo: "I believe in God, Mozart and Beethoven. . . ."[489] A final Romantic irony concludes the sad tale as both the Englishman and the dog show up by chance at the funeral of the good German musician, who had been condemned to die the death of an unknown in Paris. Wagner's heart (and fears?) was really in this story and, as he reported, "Schlesinger was not quite so pleased with this as with my first effort," but "Heinrich Heine praised it by saying that 'Hoffmann would have been incapable of writing such a thing,' " and that "even Berlioz was touched by it, and spoke of the story very favorably in one of his articles in the *Journal des Débats*."[490]

Berlioz's praise encouraged Wagner to try and get to know him better, but the Frenchman's reserve (he had his own Paris career to worry about) put him off and we find Wagner striking out at his French colleague on several levels in a dispatch sent to the Dresden *Abendzeitung* on 5 May 1841, describing an all-Beethoven concert (25 April 1841) given by Liszt, with Berlioz conducting, to raise funds for the Beethoven statue to be erected in Bonn (see chapter 5). Wagner's report begins colorfully (he shows appropriate indignation when the Paris audience calls for Liszt to encore with—in a program devoted exclusively to Beethoven—his famous fantasy on Meyerbeer's *Robert le Diable*) but also a bit crankily: "A wonderful treat! Liszt, Berlioz and . . . Beethoven! . . . Liszt and Berlioz are friends and brothers, both of them know and revere Beethoven, both draw vigor from the miraculous fountain of his wealth, and both know that they could perform no better deed than to give a concert for Beethoven's memorial. But there is a difference between them; Liszt earns money without expenses, whereas Berlioz has expenses but earns nothing."[491] This difference suggested a basic lesson in musical (that is, racial) philosophy:

> Berlioz . . . stands alone. . . . From our Germany the spirit of Beethoven has wafted across to him, and there have certainly been times when Berlioz would have dearly liked to be a German. At such moments his genius urges him to

write as the great master wrote, to express the things he sees expressed in the master's works. But the instant he takes up his pen the national ebullience of his French blood begins to assert itself. . . . Berlioz knew . . . understood [Beethoven's symphonies]. They had thrilled and inspired him, yet he was constantly reminded of the French blood in his veins. He sensed that he could not be like Beethoven . . . so he became Berlioz and wrote his *Fantastic Symphony*, a work at which Beethoven would have laughed . . . but which was able to raise Paganini to the height of ecstasy and win its composer a following which has ears for no other work but this. Berlioz's music is inherently French; were this not so, or were it possible for him to change his nature, one might have been able to regard him as a worthy pupil of Beethoven. But his French characteristics prevent him from ever making direct contact with the genius of Beethoven.[492]

Implicit in this crystalline declaration that if you are French you cannot be German is the further implication that although an Italian (Paganini) might be deceived into thinking Beethoven could be reincarnated on French soil, no kinsman of Beethoven would ever think so. Any "worthy pupil of Beethoven" would, by the logic of chauvinism, simply have to be German. Glaring out between the lines of this carping critique is the inescapable message: Wagner *is* German; Wagner is here; Wagner will continue (and improve upon) Beethoven's musical mission on earth. All this would come to pass when Wagner reorchestrated Beethoven's Ninth and allowed it to preface the musical events at the stone-laying ceremonies at Bayreuth thirty-one years later. But we must not jump too far ahead. For now we may look kindly, if a bit concernedly, at the young Wagner in Paris who was feeling very isolated and very German (as Gertrude Stein, in the next century, would feel intensely American in Paris).

In fact the following year (1842), still with no musical success in Paris but with prospects of seeing two of his operas performed in Germany (*Rienzi* in October, *The Flying Dutchman* in January of 1843, both successfully at Dresden, where their composer was speedily appointed second conductor at the court opera), Wagner quitted that French city "with its sordid spaces and pretensions to greatness,"[493] vowing never to return. He did however, several times, meeting Liszt's sixteen-year-old daughter Cosima there for the first time in 1853. We can gloss over Wagner's fruitful Dresden period (to which we will return for a remarkable Beethoven performance) and ten-year exile in Switzerland for the moment to go back, with Wagner, to Paris and pick up the thread of his Beethoven-predicated relationship with Berlioz. They had spent a friendly enough evening in each other's company as guest conductors passing in the night in London in 1855, and now in Paris again in 1860 it was Wagner who initiated the renewed contact. He sent Berlioz a flatteringly inscribed first copy to the score of *Tristan and Isolde*, called on the ailing composer at home a few days later, and otherwise assured that Berlioz would attend and review the three concerts he was about to give. Although Wagner was able to make journalistic hay out of Berlioz's (generally positive) critique of his music, what concerns us in our Beethoven mythography is the private letter he sent Berlioz, written as he sentimentally points out, "on my birthday" (his forty-seventh; 22 May 1860). The reason for the letter was Beethoven—Wagner's spontaneous reaction to Berlioz's two-part review of a revised performance of *Fidelio*, produced at the Théâtre-Lyrique on 5 May 1860. Here is the letter (written, as Jacques Barzun the Berlioz partisan sniffs, in not quite perfect French):

I have just read your article on *Fidelio*: a thousand thanks to you for it. It is a special kind of joy for me to hear your pure and noble accents of the expression of a soul, of an intelligence which understands so perfectly and takes unto itself the most intimate secrets of a creation by another hero of art. There are times when I am almost more transported by seeing this act of appreciation than by the appreciated work itself, because it bears witness to an uninterrupted chain of intimate relationships binding together the great minds which—thanks to this bond alone—will never fall into misunderstanding.

If I express myself badly, I nevertheless like to think that you will not understand me badly. Your most devoted Richard Wagner

Paris, on my birthday.[494]

Mutual love of Beethoven had brought the "enemy brothers" together again, but only briefly. Despite Liszt's devoted efforts to ease the tension between these two disparate geniuses, their aversion to one another's musical credos (we might say Berlioz's dramatic music versus Wagner's music-drama) made things difficult. On the same day that he wrote Berlioz so warmly about the *Fidelio* review, Wagner gave himself another birthday present by penning the following lines to Liszt: "The article of Berlioz (on *Fidelio*) has made me see clearly once more how lonely the unhappy are . . . I have arrived at the conclusion that today we form a triad exclusive of any other . . . because we are three equals: this triad is composed of you, him, and me. But one must take care not to say so to him. . . ."[495]

Wagner was able to see his not too distorted image in Berlioz's mirror when he read the French composer's *Memoirs* in 1870,[496] an experience which made him more determined than ever never to have anything to do with Paris again. A year later Berlioz was on Wagner's mind in connection with Beethoven again and he canceled out with a terse pronouncement (carefully noted by the constant Cosima) the "perfect understanding" of Beethoven for which he had thanked Berlioz eleven years earlier: "Just as in Hugo there is a blatant misunderstanding of Shakespeare, so in Berlioz there is a misunderstanding of Beethoven; here and there the main object is a garish highlighting of detail."[497] Thus with one blow does the giant Fafner kill his brother Fasolt, severing the tie of Beethovenian brotherhood. Now Wagner is the only son of Beethoven.

Before we turn to a more chronological look at Wagner's Beethoven-related activities and their impact on his and others' images of Beethoven, let us linger a bit longer in the Paris of 1860, for now is the time to look more closely at a visit— briefly touched upon in an earlier chapter—that provided posterity with an intriguing description of the physical Beethoven versus current portrait likenesses. This was Wagner's visit to Rossini in March of 1860, during which the famous conversation about Beethoven took place. The exchange between the two composers was, it will be remembered, jotted down immediately afterwards by the third party present, Edmond Michotte, who published the account in 1906.[498] We shall now avail ourselves of the details of that report to see exactly what image of Beethoven, originally received by Rossini in 1822, was transmitted to the Wagner of 1860. The forty-six-year-old Wagner, who had come to Paris to negotiate a production of *Tannhäuser* (finally staged in March of the following year with disastrous results), was received according to his own testimony[499] with the utmost cordiality by Gioacchino Rossini (1792–1868) (Fig. 91[500]), who was then sixty-eight years old. Rossini inundated the German with a flood of French, assuring him that the malicious remarks wags had attributed to him concerning Wagner's music were not true. Soon he was telling Wagner about his days in Vienna thirty-eight years earlier and his first attendance of a performance of the *Eroica*. Sounding like the author of "A Pilgrimage to Beethoven", Rossini vented his enthusiasm: "That music bowled me over. I had only one thought: to meet that great genius, to see him, even if only once."[501] Wagner encouraged Rossini to go on. He needed no coaxing. With relish he told of the difficulties he was warned surrounded such a project because, as Salieri told him, of Beethoven's "distrustful and fantastic character."[502] Then, after Carpani's successful intervention, he was allowed to present himself. A confirmation of Beethoven's proverbial poverty followed: "As I went up the stairs leading to the poor lodgings in which the great man lived, I had some difficulty in containing my emotion. When the door was opened, I found myself in a sort of hovel, so dirty as to testify to frightening disorder. I remember above all that the ceiling, which was immediately under the roof, was cracked, showing large crevices through which the rain must have come in waves."[503]

After this touch of Italian exaggeration, Rossini made his—to us, familiar—remark about Beethoven's small but piercing eyes, and the look of undefinable sadness that no portrait of the man could express. Beethoven's voice was soft and slightly fogged, and he used it to give Rossini a double-edged compliment: "... raising his head, he said to me brusquely in Italian that was comprehensible enough: 'Ah! Rossini, you are the composer of the Il Barbiere di Siviglia? I congratulate you; it is an excellent *opera buffa*; I read it with pleasure, and it delights me. It will be played as long as Italian opera exists. Never try to do anything but *opera buffa*; wanting to succeed in another genre would be trying to force your destiny.' "[504]

Wagner chivalrously protested this injunction, but Rossini assured him he did indeed feel a greater aptitude for opera buffa. He turned the conversation to German musicians in general, declaring fervently: "If Beethoven is a prodigy of humanity, Bach is a miracle of God!"[505] Bach led Rossini to reminisce about Mendelssohn—not Wagner's favorite—and we find Wagner interrupting the Maestro to ask how his visit to Beethoven ended: "Oh, it was short. You understand that one whole side of the conversation had to be written out. I told him of all my admiration for his genius, all my gratitude for his having allowed me an opportunity to express it to him. He replied with a profound sigh and exactly these words: '*Oh! un infelice!*' "[506]

After a few questions about Italian opera houses and singers Beethoven led Rossini to the door, wishing him success for his *Zelmira* and enjoining him once again to write more *Barbers*. Rossini's final words on his visit to Beethoven accurately reflect the aura of restless isolation the deaf composer had willfully built around himself, and also reveal the narrator in a sympathetic light:

Going down that ramshackle staircase, I felt such a painful impression of my visit to that great man—thinking of that destitution, that privation—that I couldn't hold back my tears. "Ah!" Carpani said, "that's the way he wants it. He is a misanthrope, morose, and doesn't know how to hold on to a single friendship." That very evening I attended a gala dinner given by Prince [Klemens von] Metternich. Still completely upset by that visit, by that lugubrious "*Un infelice!*" which remained in my ears, I... [said] stoutly and without any discretion at all what I thought about the conduct of the court and the aristocracy towards the greatest genius of the epoch, who needed so little and was abandoned to such distress. They gave me the very reply that I had received from Carpani. I demanded to know, however, if Beethoven's deafness didn't deserve the greatest pity . . . I added that it would be easy, by drawing up a very small subscription, to assure him an income large enough to place him beyond all need for the rest of his life. That proposal didn't win the support of a single person. . . . Not having succeeded in my attempts to create an annual income for Beethoven, I didn't lose courage immediately. I wanted to try to get together sufficient funds to buy him a place to live. . . . Generally I got this answer: "You don't know Beethoven well. The day after he became the owner of a house, he would sell it again. He never would know how to adjust himself to a fixed abode; for he feels the need to change his quarters every six months and his servant every six weeks."[507]

Rossini was passing on the Beethoven reality and not the myth in this case. Wagner surely must have agreed with Rossini's idea of a subscription fund to lift the burden of care from a composer's shoulders—throughout his career Wagner was able to attract, often at the brink of financial ruin, stipends, "loans," and allowances from private individuals who believed in his genius. The most extraordinary instance of course was the financial assistance from young King Ludwig II of Bavaria, whose first act practically upon ascending the throne in 1864 was to invite his musical hero to Munich where he was provided with every moral and monetary support, and also promised a new theater in which to produce the *Ring* (a project eventually realized in Bayreuth). Of the combative little Saxon who would all his life have to do battle to spread his musical apostolate, the old Italian composer who had not written an opera for three decades left his own succinct portrait and prophecy: "This Wagner—I must confess—seems to be endowed with first-class faculties. His whole physique—his chin most of all—reveals an iron-willed temperament. It's a great thing to know how to *will*. If he possesses the gift of *being able* in the same degree, as I believe he does, he will get himself talked about."[508]

Wagner succeeded in getting himself talked about (forever after!); he also had plenty of *will*, was *able*, and, we might say so far as his relationship to Beethoven was concerned, *over*-able. Consider him at the age of twenty-one, standing proudly before the provincial Magdeburg orchestra in a "sky-blue dress coat with huge cuffs,"[509] about to conduct a performance of Beethoven's *Battle* Symphony (op. 91) in the small hall of the Hotel Zur Stadt London. In preparation for the event he had doubled the bugles and trumpets of the orchestra and had had specially constructed noise machines rolled into the room to reproduce the artillery effects in the Battle of Victoria. He is the best recounter of what happened: "The orchestra flung itself, so to speak, upon the scanty audience with such an overwhelming superiority of numbers that the latter speedily gave up all thought of resistance and literally took to flight. . . . Everyone rushed out; and Wellington's victory was finally celebrated in a confidential outburst between myself and the orchestra alone."[510]

This lesson in overdoing did not reform Wagner completely. As his conducting powers increased, especially during the six years as a Kapellmeister in Dresden (1843–49), he came to believe that it was not only the right but the obligation of the conductor to "restore" (correct) the scores of certain past masters, especially Beethoven's (since he could not *hear* the instrumental balances or lack thereof), so that intelligible renderings might be obtained. About his careful revision of the Ninth Symphony for a Palm Sunday concert in Dresden in 1846, for example, Wagner wrote: "I never carried my piety to the extent of taking directions absolutely literally, rather than sacrifice the effect really intended by the master to the erroneous indications given. . . ."[511] (Schindler, where are you?) Not only could Beethoven be wrong about Beethoven, so could world-respected interpreters be mistaken, if they were not Wagner. Playing through Liszt's piano transcription of the final movement of the Ninth one evening in the winter of 1878, he complained of this to his faithful audience of one. Cosima dutifully recorded the divine judgment: " . . . he regrets that my father did not take the liberty of giving the accompaniment to the voices, which Beeth. wrote for double basses, to the middle range, like the cellos, for that is how Beethoven had meant it, though he had written it otherwise: 'I should not hesitate to do it,' he says."[512]

It was with this same astonishing self-assurance that Wagner approached his Dresden Palm Sunday performance—the first of several (1846, 1847, 1849) performances of the Ninth by Wagner in that city, so sensationally successful was Beethoven's new Ninth under his baton. One of the reasons for this triumph was the clever campaign Wagner directed: a preconcert educational and publicity blitz that left the public and the performers on tenterhooks. He began with an army of carpenters, and all Dresden buzzed with excitement over what was happening to the old opera house. Wagner tells us:

> I also took care that, by means of the complete reconstruction of the hall, I should obtain good acoustic conditions for the orchestra, which I had arranged according to quite a new system of my own. . . . owing to a totally new construction of the platform, I was able to concentrate the whole of the orchestra towards the centre, and surround it, in amphitheatre fashion, by the throngs of singers who were accommodated on seats very considerably raised. This was not only of great advantage to the powerful effect of the choir, but it also gave great precision and energy to the finely organized orchestra in the purely symphonic movements.[513]

The wily Wagner's next maneuver was to "prepare the public in such a way for the performance . . . and for the work itself, that at least the sensation caused would lead to a full hall. . . ."[514] Before we judge the Conductor Royal of Saxony too severely on this point, it should be noted that two very poor performances of the Ninth in 1838 for a Dresden charity had left a disastrous impression on the collective memory of the city. To counteract the complaints of the local orchestral directors and players (who at first threatened a petition to the king about rescinding the choice of music) Wagner confesses that he "made use of the *Dresden Anzeiger*, by writing all kinds of short and enthusiastic anonymous paragraphs, in order to whet the public taste for a work which hitherto had been in ill repute in Dresden."[515]

Turning to the music itself (the orchestral parts had to be borrowed from Berlin since the Dresden doubters who held Wagner's purse strings refused to buy them), Wagner had, besides the extensive revamping of instrumentation, tempi, and dynamics, two tactics. The first was a demanding schedule of section rehearsals, the likes of which had never been witnessed in Dresden. This time we do not have to take Wagner's word for it; here is an account by the daughter of Wagner's avuncular friend of Dresden days, Ferdinand Heine, costume designer for the Hoftheater. Although she was only fourteen at the time, Marie's memory of the Palm Sunday preparations, written down fifty years later, is vivid and speaks volumes for Wagner's way with an orchestra:

> Never before had there been so many rehearsals for a single work as for the Ninth—and especially the separate rehearsals for the cellos and basses which were held in the rehearsal room of the Hoftheater behind *closed doors*. "No,"

they said with meaningful shakings of the head, "no, there has never been anything like this before! As if our cello and bass players haven't learned long since what to do." But those involved soon found out what Wagner was working toward. They had their rehearsals and only smiled when the other colleagues grumbled, for they were looking forward to the first rehearsal with the whole orchestra. There *they* and *Wagner* with them enjoyed their great triumph. Cellos and basses started the recitativelike passage which introduces the theme of the "Ode to Joy"; they played the theme first with an evenness and tone volume giving the effect of the human voices; the theme itself murmured like an ideal inspiration, surging and fading until at last it joined the full orchestra with violins and violas. Then all of them forgot to continue rehearsing and burst out into an enthusiastic cheer. That was a happy moment for Wagner and probably meant more to him than the public enthusiasm later. He had conquered the whole orchestra![516]

Comparing Wagner's account of these same section rehearsals, we find not only agreement but motivation: "I devoted special attention to that extraordinary passage, resembling a recitative for the 'cellos and basses, which comes at the beginning of the last movement. . . . Thanks to the exceptional excellence of our bass players, I felt certain of attaining to absolute perfection in this passage. After twelve special rehearsals of the instruments alone concerned, I succeeded in getting them to perform in a way which sounded not only perfectly free, but which also expressed the most exquisite tenderness and the greatest energy in a thoroughly impressive manner."[517]

Wagner's aim was to give "as expressive a rendering as possible"[518] to the work which now, at a third crucial period in his life, symbolized as it had twice before for him the enthralling power of music. "Imagine my feelings . . . on now seeing for the first time since my earliest boyhood the mysterious pages of this score . . . [which] I had stayed up for nights together to copy them out. Just as at the time of my uncertainty in Paris, on hearing the rehearsal of the first three movements performed by the incomparable orchestra of the Conservatoire . . . [my] despair . . . was . . . converted into genuine exaltation, thanks entirely to the Ninth Symphony."[519]

Wagner's second tactic concerning the music itself was in keeping with the "more is better" canon that had amplified the cannonade of his Magdeburg *Battle Symphony* production. For the great *Choral* Symphony a giant chorus was essential. Wagner enlisted three hundred singers. Not only should the choir be mammoth, it should be enthusiastic. "In a way quite my own I now tried to get these three hundred singers, who were frequently united for rehearsals, into a state of genuine ecstasy. . . ."[520] Recasting Beethoven's drama to suit his own theater, he explained to the singers that certain passages ("Seid umschlungen, Millionen") could not be sung in the regular manner but had rather to be rapturously proclaimed.[521] "In this I took the lead in a manner so elated that I really think I literally transported them to a world of emotion utterly strange to them for a while; and I did not desist till my voice, which had been heard clearly above all the others . . . was drowned, so to speak, in the warm sea of sound."[522]

The hoarse choir conductor has placed his image of Beethoven underneath the expressive beam of *emotion* once again, for it was an emotional interpretation of Beethoven—his music *and* his life—that gripped him. In one of the anonymous paragraphs to the Dresden newspaper he had written of Beethoven's spiritual "loneliness," explaining the Ninth as an attempt to reach out from the world of solitude to which deafness had condemned him by bringing to his fellow human beings a message of joy.[523]

In addition to the pre-Ninth preparations just examined, from creative carpentry to colossal chorus, Wagner had one more ace up his sleeve and this was saved for the actual day of performance (5 April 1846). Wagner drew up a program—a sort of listener's map through the Ninth—magnanimously providing the audience with selected quotations from Goethe's *Faust* which seemed (to him) to parallel the emotional meaning of the four movements.[524] "I did this in order to provide a guide to the simple understanding of the work, and thereby hoped to appeal not to the critical judgment, but solely to the feelings, of the audience."[525] The meaning of the music was made further explicit by explanations in his own, altiloquent (but purposefully avoiding the technical) Wagnerian prose, wrapped solicitously around the Goethe passages. Just observe the lineup: Beethoven and Schiller, Goethe and Wagner—all Germany was there on that unforgettable Palm Sunday in Dresden!

Let us imagine ourselves in the overcrowded auditorium that day, gazing in anticipation at the strange new disposition of orchestra and chorus on its raised platform, and take a moment to glance through the synopsis of the symphony as drawn up by the thirty-two-year-old conductor whose pecuniary debts are settled with such musical and literary largesse. The preface calls attention to the fact that certain lines of "our" great poet Goethe have been cited which, although in no manner exhausting the meaning of Beethoven's "purely musical creation, yet so sublimely express the higher human moods at bottom of it."[526] The first movement, according to Wagner, appears to be "founded on a titanic struggle of the soul, athirst for Joy, against the veto of that hostile power which rears itself 'twixt us and earthly happiness. The great chief theme, which steps before us at one stride as if disrobing from the spectral shroud [those open fifths still seem apparitional to Wagner], might be translated, without violence to the spirit of the whole tone poem, by Goethe's words: 'Go wanting, shalt thou! Shalt go wanting!' "[527] The phrase "tone poem" is slipped in so effortlessly—after all, the term *Ton-Dichter* was applied in Beethoven's day—that the prominence it will assume in Wagner's iconography of Beethoven is hardly portended. In the passing gleams of orchestral light " . . . force, revolt, defiance, yearning, hope, midway-attainment, fresh loss, new quest, repeated struggle make out the elements of ceaseless motion in this wondrous piece. . . ."[528] At the close of the movement a "gloomy, joyless mood, expanding to colossal form, appears to span the all, in awful majesty to take possession of a world that God had made for—*Joy*."[529]

So far, Wagner's descriptive method is not startlingly different from Berlioz's colorful and committed tracking of musical moods. Both were addressing absolute music with the vocabulary of Romanticism. And in this vein Wagner pursues the elemental storm and stress of the next two instrumental sections. With the beginning of the second movement "a wild excitement seizes us . . . we are swept on to frenzied orgy,"[530] whereas in the third movement the tones of a heavenly strain "calm our wrath, allay the soul's despairing anguish, and turn its turbulence to gentle melancholy."[531] It is the fourth movement that elicits Wagner's most excited associations, however, for here is the bridge from tone poem to music drama that he had already irrevocably crossed in his own music. Finding an appropriate Goethe exclamation ("Aber ach!") to match what Wagner calls the "shriek of horror" with which the final movement begins, he announces soberly:

With this opening... Beethoven's music takes on a more definitely *speaking* character: it quits the mold of purely instrumental music, observed in all three preceding movements, the mode of infinite, indefinite expression; the musical poem is urging toward a crisis, a crisis to be voiced only in human speech. It is wonderful how the Master makes the arrival of a man's voice and tongue a positive necessity, by the awe-inspiring recitative of the bass strings; almost breaking the bounds of absolute music already, it stems the tumult of the other instruments with its virile eloquence, insisting on decision, and passes at last into a songlike theme whose simple, stately flow bears with it, one by one, the other instruments, until it swells into a mighty flood. . . . With these words light breaks on chaos; a sure and definite mode of utterance is won, in which, supported by the conquered element of instrumental music, we may now hear expressed with clearness what boon it is the agonizing quest of Joy shall find as highest, lasting happiness.[532]

"Conquered element of instrumental music"? Beethoven composed one opera; Wagner would compose fourteen. Who else but Wagner, the feisty overarticulator of the *Battle* Symphony, would fashion for himself an image of Beethoven as a composer whose greatest work is that in which one musical force—the vocal—vanquishes another musical force—the instrumental? But this supremacy (of what he would eventually call the "human character" of the voice[533]) was of quintessential importance to Wagner, for it was this concept of Beethoven as "bearer" of the "word" from out the depths of music that became the platform for Wagner's own star performer, the Gesamtkunstwerk—the united work of art. As Wagner put it:

Thus did [Beethoven] urge his course through unheard-of possibilities of absolute tone speech—not by fleetly slipping past them, but by speaking out their utmost syllable from the deepest chambers of his heart—forward to where the mariner begins to sound the sea depth with his plumb. . . . Staunchly he threw his anchor out; and this anchor was *the word*. Yet this word was not that arbitrary and senseless cud which the modish singer chews from side to side, as the gristle of his vocal tone; but the necessary, all-powerful, and all uniting word into which the full torrent of the heart's emotions may pour its stream; the steadfast haven for the restless wanderer; the light that lightens up the night of endless yearning . . . the word which Beethoven set as crown upon the forehead of his tone creation; and this word was—"Freude!" . . . The last symphony of Beethoven is the redemption of Music from out her own peculiar element into the realm of *universal art*. It is the human evangel of the art of the future. Beyond it no forward step is possible; for upon it the perfect artwork of the future alone can follow, the *universal drama* to which Beethoven has forged for us the key.[534]

Dare we guess who is going to turn this key? Putting aside the fact that Wagner has tinted Beethoven's image with his own complexion, drawn his features in his own likeness, it is important to observe the key words that illuminate the programmatic encomium we have just read. For they are key words that echo with harmonic overtones some of the extramusical concepts coloring the image of Beethoven first rehearsed in Grillparzer's funeral oration and since made sacrosanct by the litany of legend. Again we have the image of alienation, of inner necessity and constant striving against all worldly odds (and perils, since Wagner, creator of *The Flying Dutchman*, quite naturally puts Beethoven out to sea in his pungent metaphor). And we have the Faustian-Romantic concept of restless, unfathomed yearning, the eternal seeking for—in Wagner's understanding—*redemption*. Wagner believed this redemption was available to a whole people (*his* people) if they but had the universal art forms and a theater of their own in which ancient myth and modern mimesis could renew humankind's mysterious link with the sublime.[535]

All of this could and would take place in Germany. This Wagner made quite clear during the Franco-Prussian War of 1870–71 by pointing out to the nation in yet another essay brandishing Beethoven as its subject matter that the date was the centenary of a German genius—Beethoven—thus linking artistic right with military (thanks to the new steel cannons of Alfred Krupp) might. This fustian essay of 1870, called quite simply *Beethoven*—a magic word by then—was so convoluted that Wagner's new young friend Friedrich Nietzsche reported a fellow Basel professor had asked him whether the essay was written *against* Beethoven.[536] Nietzsche was a frequent guest at Tribschen (the first house Wagner shared with Cosima, in Switzerland, outside Lucerne), where he and Wagner mutually dazzled each other temporarily, and Cosima, twenty-four years younger than her husband, exerted a distinct charm on him. The impressionable philosopher was enthusiastic about Wagner's *Beethoven* essay, since it seemed to address what he too wanted for Germany's future. We shall return to this younger admirer of the Beethoven-Wagner constellation.

The reason for the weighty tortuosity of Wagner's *Beethoven* essay—so different from the compelling yet charming prose of "A Pilgrimage to Beethoven"—was that in the meanwhile (autumn 1854) Wagner had discovered Arthur Schopenhauer (1788–1860). "Now at last I understand my *Wotan*,"[537] he exclaimed, enchanted at finding in the Frankfurt philosopher's writings a full orchestration for his own developing leitmotifs such as redemption through renunciation and the primacy of the will (of which music was the direct language) over the intellect. "For many years afterwards that book [*The World as Will and Idea*] never left me . . . the effect . . . wrought upon me was extraordinary, and certainly exerted a decisive influence on the whole course of my life,"[538] Wagner acknowledged with enthusiasm, and when he moved into the velvety ambience of his final home, Villa Wahnfried in Bayreuth, the composer proudly hung his friend Franz von Lenbach's (1836–1904) portrait of the philosopher (Fig. 92 and see Fig. 100) who, he said, had translated into wisdom what Beethoven had expressed emotionally.[539]

Wagner's extended *Beethoven* essay of 1870 (the same year in which the house where Beethoven had been born in Bonn was made into a national monument) was written in Tribschen, and the diary of his attentive amanuensis records the exact days on which it was begun (Wednesday, 20 July) and finished (Wednesday, 7 September). In between, Cosima was given previews of some of the essay's contents: "a comparison between Sh[akespeare] and Beethoven; as in Shakespeare the characters, so in Beethoven the melodies—unmistakable, incomparable, an entire, inexplicable world."[540] But the Shakespeare-Beethoven link, already a well-salivated-over chestnut of Romanticism, was only part of the *Beethoven* essay: Schopenhauer—also a German genius—was to be brought in. Not as another comparison[541] but as the articulator of profound aesthetic problems touching upon music in particular. In "A Pilgrimage to Beethoven" Wagner had put his own musical theories into Beethoven's mouth; now he looked at Beethoven's image through Schopenhauer's pince-nez: the musician speaks the highest wisdom in a tongue not understood by his reason. This dictum fit well with Wagner's own earlier characterization of Beethoven's symphonies as revealing another world "whose logic is the logic of feeling."[542]

The exalted state of mind in which Wagner conceived his Schopenhauer-indebted *Beethoven* essay is best followed not in the turgid prose of the final product (Wagner rewrote the end, but it still digests lumpily) but in the special diary—the leather-bound "brown book" given him by Cosima—into which, from 1865 to 1882, the composer wrote intimate notes to Cosima during periods of separation before they were married, some telegraphic diary entries when traveling by himself, and the first drafts of a few essays and poems. Among the latter we find, written between 3 and 19 July 1870, an outline for the *Beethoven*. That nationalism (German cultural greatness) as well as aesthetics was a motivating factor for the work is indicated by the tentative title: "Beethoven and the German Nation." Here are the kernels as Wagner spat them out:

> [Beethoven] Relationship?—to German spirit only? How latter relates to "beauty"? . . . Starting point: Schopenhauer: "World as Will and Conception." . . . Distinction in inwardly and outwardly directed consciousness. This second is what music creates from. Great diversity, dream theory. (Day-side—Goethe. Night-side—Beethoven.) . . . Music the direct dream image. The innermost power on which our poets unconsciously fed . . . in Beethoven directly creative. Terror of inner world basis of sublime. Sublimity. Effect of music always that of sublime: form, however, that of beauty, i.e., in first instance liberation of individual from conception of any causality.—Musical beauty form in which musician plays with sublime. Beeth. = Schopenhauer: his music, translated into concepts, would produce that philosophy. Similarity—to both, German nation.[543]

From these pithy kernels there sprang a mighty tree: its trunk was pure Schopenhauer, its branches ostensibly Beethoven, while from those majestic branches a dense, Wagnerian-formed foliage sprouted. The nourishing soil underneath was pure German. A second tree, Shakespearean in shape, flourished frondiferously nearby. The German tree had long been threatened by French blight. But now, shorn of the deceptively decorous growth of suffocating vines from foreign climes, the pollard was full of promise—it belonged to the forest of the future. If the metaphor (mine, not Wagner's) seems overly arboreal, it at least has the advantage of generic consistency, which Wagner's *Beethoven* essay does not, although the same elements (Schopenhauer, Beethoven, implicit Wagner, Shakespeare, Germany, as well as the dangers of French fashions in dress) are present at much greater length. The first twenty pages of Wagner's published essay deal with and restate Schopenhauer's relationship to music, which alone of all the arts is world-revealing, universal Will, rather than mimetic, particularized Idea. And because the "ecstatic clairvoyance of a musician alternates with an ever-recurring state of individual consciousness" the musician may appear worthier of reverence than other artists "by reason of the sufferings with which he has to compensate for the ecstasy in which he is enabled so inexpressibly to enrapture us all. . . ."[544] This sounds as though we might be getting to Beethoven, but not yet. A detour to Venice, a lofty Alpine meadow, ideas of time and space in music, music's ability to convey the Sublime, Goethe, Palestrina (for Cosima's sake[545]), and ballet intervene. Thirty-five pages into the essay Wagner suggests elucidating what he has just been writing about through an inspection of the "*development of Beethoven's genius.*"[546]

Wagner now happily alludes to the same two Beethoven legends with which we began this chapter on the musicians' musician—Ferdinand Ries's story of Haydn's request that Beethoven put "Pupil of Haydn" on the score of his first two trios, and Ignaz von Seyfried's anecdote of young Beethoven improvising before an astonished Mozart. Concerning the first, Wagner begins as a sober musicologist and waxes into a Beethoven mythologist with Lohengrin-like loyalty:

> Beethoven's earlier works are not incorrectly held to have sprung from Haydn's model. . . . The peculiar nature of this relationship is disclosed by a striking feature in Beethoven's behavior towards Haydn. Beethoven would not recognize Haydn as his teacher, though the latter was generally taken for such, and he even suffered injurious expressions of youthful arrogance to escape him about Haydn. It seems as though he felt himself related to Haydn like one born a man to a childish elder. As regards form he agreed with his teacher, but the unruly daemon [*Dämon*] of his inner music, fettered by that form, impelled him to a disclosure of his power, which, like everything else in the doings of the gigantic musician, could only appear incomprehensibly rough.[547]

It is interesting that Wagner, whose six-months' worth of harmony and counterpoint lessons with the cantor of Leipzig's Thomaskirche, Theodor Weinlig, had ended with happier results than Beethoven's frustrating and brief apprenticeship with the leisurely, distracted Haydn, was attracted to this story, with its implied rejection of what he considered the "Italian euphony" of "fosterers of the sonata" form such as Haydn, in whose "instrumental music it is as though we saw the fettered daemon of music playing before us with the childishness of one born an old man."[548] In other words, both Beethoven and he were endowed with musical visions that far outreached their teachers' earthbound vistas of the art of music.

Wagner's account of the Beethoven-Mozart incident is short, close to the original source, and without elaboration: "Of his meeting with Mozart it is related that he [Beethoven] jumped up from the piano in an ill humor after having played a Sonata to that master, and then, to make himself better known, asked permission to improvise; which, we are informed, he did with such effect upon Mozart, that the latter said to his friends: 'The world will hear something from that young one.' "[549]

From these two character insights Wagner now draws some specific conclusions—an image of the early Beethoven which could serve equally well as an image of the early Wagner (as seen by the fifty-seven-year-old author):

> We see young Beethoven . . . facing the world at once with that defiant temperament which, throughout his life, kept him in almost savage independence: his enormous self-confidence, supported by the haughtiest courage, at all times prompted him to defend himself from the frivolous demands made upon music by a pleasure-seeking world. He had to guard a treasure of immeasurable richness against the importunities of effeminate taste. He was the soothsayer of the innermost world of tones, and he had to act as such in the very forms in which music was displaying itself as a merely diverting art. Thus he ever resembles one truly possessed; for to him may be applied Schopenhauer's saying of the musician in general: "he expresses the highest wisdom in language his reason does not understand."[550]

This is a very serious Beethoven. (Dare anyone mention the twenty-six *Bagatelles*?) The grave image reflected in Wagner's mirror certainly contributed to the aura that has come to be associated with German music in general—an aura of great profundity, of moral forces at work. So intent was Wagner upon accentuating Beethoven's tremendous seriousness of purpose (for a serious purpose of his own) that he—a great lover of puns—overlooked his punster predecessor's darting sense of humor, concluding: "He certainly did not display, even to the most attentive observer, a single trait of wit; and, in spite of Bettina's sentimental fancies about Beethoven, Goethe probably had a hard time of it in his conversations with him."[551] The aside about Bettina's sentimental fancies demonstrates how easy it is for one mythmaker unhesitatingly to discount another mythmaker when the myth doesn't mix.

A curious emphasis in Wagner's wooden image of Beethoven as whittled so far, is that of the composer's combatting "effeminate" taste (Italian as well as French art forms). A weird ad hominem argument is construed by Wagner (who considered himself ugly) in support of this: "A glance at his face and constitution would make it sufficiently clear that beauty and effeminacy were almost synonymous to his mind. The world of phenomena had scanty access to him. His piercing eye [the adjective is straight from Rossini], almost uncanny, perceived in the outer world nothing but vexatious disturbances of his inner life, and to ward them off was almost his sole *rapport* with that world."[552]

Wagner's empathy with his hero is at this point bordering on the autobiographical. The following statement, voiced a few pages later by the author who was notorious for leaving creditors unpaid, is of high octane content, one part Beethoven, one part Wagner: "The surer he felt of his inner wealth, the more confidently did he make his demands outwards; and he actually required from his friends and patrons that they should no longer *pay* him for his works, but so provide for him that he might work for himself regardless of the world."[553]

Wagner had more to say about the physical Beethoven, and his interest extended forensically right into the grave: "So the expression of his face became spasmodic: the spasm of defiance holds this nose, this mouth at a tension that can never relax to smiles, but only expand to enormous laughter. . . . upon the inspection of his remains some years ago [the first exhumation of 1863[554]], we saw, in conformity with the entire skeleton, a skull of altogether unusual thickness and firmness. Thus nature guarded a brain of excessive delicacy, so that it might look inwards, and carry on in undisturbed repose the world contemplation of a great heart."[555]

An inner world of transparent delicacy was protected from the outside world by this robust constitution and massive frame, Wagner tells us, and the more Beethoven lost connection with the vexatious outer world, "the clearer was his inward vision."[556] All this is leading somewhere. Beethoven *needed* to be saved from the outside world. Already he did not see it, as, "enraptured dreamer" that he was, with "fixedly staring, with open eyes, he wandered through the crowded streets of Vienna, solely animated by the working of his inner world of tones."[557] What else was left that might harass the "manly strength of character"[558] as it grappled with shaping the incomprehensible? Wagner has the answer: "The ear was the only organ through which the outer world could still reach and disturb him; it had long since faded to his eye."[559] It takes but a paragraph to smite Beethoven deaf. Abandoning his interest as physician in Beethoven ("after complete deafness had set in, no particular complaints were heard from him"[560]), Wagner gives us the metaphysician's recompense: "A musician without hearing! could a blind painter be imagined? But we know of a blind *Seer*. Tiresias, to whom the phenomenal world was closed, but who, with inward vision, saw the basis of all phenomena,—and the deaf musician who listens to his inner harmonies undisturbed by the noise of life, who speaks from the depths to a world that has nothing more to say to him—now resembles the seer. Thus genius, delivered from the impress of external things exists wholly in and for itself."[561]

Wagner's new myth of adversity-turned-into-good-fortune (he is even able to write happily of the Seventh and Eighth symphonies as having been produced "during the divine period of [Beethoven's] total deafness"[562]) would enchant and inspire a century of future interpreters of Beethoven's life.

But how does all this relate to the greatness of Germany? It relates because Wagner says it relates. What Schopenhauer had said about music in general Wagner has said about Beethoven in particular, and so the twain meet on the Main-Danube tributary of German culture: "Beethoven . . . as he spoke in the purest language to all men, the German spirit has through him redeemed the spirit of humanity from deep ignominy. For inasmuch as he again raised music, that had been degraded to a merely diverting art, to the height of its sublime calling, he has led us to understand the nature of that art, from which the world explains itself to every consciousness as distinctly as the most profound philosopher could explain it to a thinker well versed in abstract conceptions. *And the revelation of the great Beethoven to the German nation is based upon this alone. . . .*"[563]

This fiat taken care of (while Krupp cannons were blasting their French targets), Wagner gives us a Pastoral interlude of sorts by proposing that if "we wish to picture to ourselves a day in the life of our Saint, one of the master's own wonderful pieces may serve as a counterpart."[564] The piece he chooses to illustrate "a genuine 'Beethoven day' by the light of its inmost occurrences"[565] is the String Quartet in C-sharp Minor (op. 131). We have met with earlier mythographers who used Beethoven's music to explain Beethoven's character (and vice versa), but considering that we are now dealing with a major composer and man of genius who identified with Beethoven in many ways, including the process of music creation, what Wagner sees in the "tone-poem"[566] quartet of Beethoven is of particular interest. He had played through the music just a few weeks before starting to write the Beethoven essay and Cosima recorded their "ever-recurring astonishment over this purest piece of Beethoveniana."[567] Here is Wagner's day in the life of Beethoven as encoded in the quartet:

> The longer introductory *Adagio*, than which probably nothing more melancholy has been expressed in tones, I would designate as the awakening on the morn of a day that throughout its tardy course shall fulfill not a single desire: not one. Nonetheless it is a penitential prayer, a conference with God in the faith of the eternally good. . . . And now, in the short transitional *Allegro Moderato*, it is as though the Master, conscious of his strength, puts himself in position to work his spells. . . . We may now (Presto 2/2) fancy him, profoundly happy from within, casting an inexpressibly serene glance upon the outer world. . . . He contemplates Life, and appears to reflect how he is to play a dance for Life itself; (Short Adagio 3/4)—a short, but troubled meditation,—as though he were diving into the deep dream of his soul. . . . he wakens, and strikes the strings for a dance, such as the world has never heard (Allegro Finale). It is the World's own dance: wild delight, cries of anguish, love's ecstasy, highest rapture, misery, rage; voluptuous now, and sorrowful; lightning's quiver, storm's roll; and high above the gigantic musician! banning and compelling all things, proudly and firmly wielding them from whirl to whirlpool, to the abyss. He laughs at himself; for the incantation was, after all, but play to him. Thus night beckons. His day is done.[568]

Aside from identifying the many different passions conjured up by Beethoven, the inference to be drawn from this Berlioz-style of mapping emotions is Romanticism's judgment: the music is the person and the person is the music. Or as Wagner concludes: "It is not possible to consider the man, Beethoven, in any sort of light, without at once having recourse to the wonderful musician, by way of elucidation."[569]

Here are some of the Schopenhauerean accomplishments of Beethoven the musician-man: what he has uttered in his music is "not *his view* of the world, but rather the world itself, wherein weal and woe, grief and joy alternate."[570] The progress which music had made under Beethoven is that it has broken free of the strictures of aesthetical beauty and entered "into the sphere of the Sublime."[571] Furthermore, melody, through Beethoven, "has become emancipated from the influences of fashion and fluctuating taste, and elevated to an ever valid, purely human type."[572] In fact, Beethoven even thoughtfully anticipated Wagner. Concerning *Fidelio*: "that operatic subject embraced so much that is alien and unassimilable to music that, properly speaking, only the great *Overture to Leonore* shows clearly what Beethoven would have us understand by a *drama*. Who can listen to this transporting piece of music without feeling convinced that music also embraces the most perfect drama?"[573] And speaking of great drama, Wagner points out that Shakespeare had remained quite incomparable "until German genius produced in *Beethoven* a being that can only be analogically explained by comparison with him."[574] About the *Choral* Symphony *as* drama, Wagner assures his readers with passion: "It is therefore not Beethoven's particular *work*, but the musician's unheard-of artistic deed contained in it, that we should take as the culminating point in the development of his genius."[575] This hero's feat leads Wagner to greater excitement: "we declare that the work of art entirely formed and quickened by that deed, would also present the most complete *artistic form*."[576] Why the author's excitement at this insight? Because this "then would be the sole new Art-form adequate to the German spirit so powerfully individualized in our great Beethoven; a purely human form, yet indigenous, and originally German, a form that the modern world, in comparison with the antique, has hitherto lacked."[577] The author of *Beethoven* must have gotten goose bumps as he wrote these prophetic lines, for wonder of wonders, this is exactly the art form *he* had been practicing in the *Ring*!

The last fifteen pages of *Beethoven* descend from eternal values and take double aim at the enemy of 1870 and at German women who continue to wear Paris-designed dresses: "Whilst German forces are victoriously penetrating to the center of French civilization, a feeling of shame has of a sudden risen amongst us about our dependence upon that civilization, and it appears publicly in the shape of an appeal [to German womanhood] to lay aside the fashionable costumes of Paris."[578] Having delivered himself of this, dare we say, bête noire, our satin-consuming sartorial stipulator pulls Beethoven, Germany, and the Franco-Prussian War together with a final flourish of his patriotic pen:

> And nothing can more inspiringly stand beside the triumphs of its [the German nation's] bravery in this wonderful year 1870 than the memory of our great *Beethoven*, who just a hundred years ago was born to the German people. There, at the high seat of "insolent fashion," whither our weapons are now penetrating, *his* genius had already begun the noblest conquest. [Schindler would have been pleased.] What our thinkers, our poets, hampered by inadequate translations, have there touched unclearly, as it were with inarticulate sound, Beethoven's symphonies have already roused from the depths; the new religion,

the world-redeeming announcement of sublimest innocence, is already understood there as with us.

Let us then celebrate the great pathfinder in the wilderness of degenerate paradise! But let us celebrate him worthily,—not less worthily than the victories of German bravery: for the world's benefactor takes precedence of the world's conqueror![579]

The day before Wagner began putting down ideas for his *Beethoven* cannonade in the brown book, he and Cosima had been discussing news of the impending war (on 15 July the French had decided to go to war against Prussia, just as Bismarck had secretly hoped). Cosima (Fig. 93), who had grown up in France but adopted the fierce national allegiances of Wagner, consoled her husband with the following declaration: "I tell R. the war is Beethoven's memorial celebration [*der Krieg ist die Beethovenfeier*], on 17 July 1870 the declaration of war was made [actually France declared war on 19 July], on 17 December 1770, Beethoven was born."[580] Richard not only responded to this stimulating idea by composing his *Beethoven* essay over the next two months, he elaborated on it then and there, adding a little Schopenhauer but keeping Beethoven as the centerpiece, in his reply to Cosima: "... war is something noble, it shows the unimportance of the individual; at St. Jakob 2,000 *corpses* defeated the 40,000 feared Armagnacs—a case of an idea proving all-conquering; war is, so to speak, a dance performed with the most dreadful of powers, like a Beethoven finale in which he unleashes all the demons in a magnificent dance."[581] If the formidable Wagners had had their way, the mere sound of Beethoven's Ninth might well have paralyzed the overconfident French army (with its obsolete bronze cannons).

It was of this crowd-enthralling potency that the young Professor Nietzsche (1844–1900) (Fig. 94) was thinking when he described Beethoven's setting of the Schiller poem on the "brotherhood" of man as approaching the Dionysian, when, awestruck, the millions bow down to the dust. Benefiting from provocative discussions held with his Tribschen host and hostess, Nietzsche, an amateur musician himself, invited his readers to transform Beethoven's "Hymn to Joy" into a painting better to understand the Dionysian impulse towards world unity. He spelled out the effect: "Now the slave is a free man; now all the rigid, hostile barriers that ... have fixed between man and man are broken. Now, with the gospel of universal harmony, each one finds himself not only united, reconciled, and fused with his neighbor, but as one with him, as if the veil of *māyā* [Schopenhauer's favorite Sanskrit word = "illusion"] had been torn aside and were now merely fluttering in tatters before the mysterious primordial unity."[582]

These words, in the very first section of *The Birth of Tragedy from the Spirit of Music*, were published early in 1872, and were not, as might appear from the date, a gesture of reconciliation towards the recently defeated French nation. Rather, they were hammering home Nietzsche's new aesthetic notion of the Dionysian, artistic energy of music (intoxication leading to mystical self-abnegation) as opposed to the Apollonian force of sculpture (the individuated image world of dreams). This pithy theory was developed during the period of Nietzsche's discovery of a fellow Schopenhauer fan in Wagner, and, although it was originally concerned with Attic tragedy, Nietzsche's book concluded with a lengthy homage to Wagner and the rebirth of tragedy in his operas. It was also laced with a few references to Wagner's *Beethoven* essay, and it is the latter—the great German Beethoven (-Wagner) connection—that briefly concerns us here.

An initial reference occurs in the "Preface to Richard Wagner" that graced the first edition of Nietzsche's book which, in spite of a disclaimer, fairly glistens with the sharpened sense of nationalism whetted by the recent political hostilities: "You will recall that it was during the same period when your splendid Festschrift on Beethoven came into being, amid the terrors and sublimities of the war that had just broken out, that I collected myself for these reflections."[583] We may wonder, as Nietzsche stakes his claim here to have been hatching his theories simultaneously with Wagner, how war could be "sublime" (Nietzsche had volunteered as a hospital attendant and been laid low not by bullets but by dysentery and diptheria) until we remember that we are dealing with a Romantic of the third wave, and one who had not yet turned skeptic. The twenty-seven-year-old author continues: "Yet anyone would be mistaken if he associated my reflections with the contrast between patriotic excitement and aesthetic enthusiasm . . . if he really read this essay, it would dawn on him, to his surprise, what a seriously German problem is faced here and placed right in the center of German hopes, as a vortex and turning point."[584] How to get from things Greek to issues German in a work exploring the origins of tragedy might have been difficult for the ordinary professor of classical philology, but not for one who had felt the Dionysian waters of *Tristan's* tragic drama close over him. In an extraordinary feat of juggling (Nietzsche later found this first book of his embarrassing), he simply forced past and present to reflect on each other with an eye to the future: a Schopenhauerean blender artificially but effectively mixing Homer and Socrates with Beethoven and Wagner. And thank heaven none of them had been French! "We should also have to regard our German character with sorrowful despair, if it had already become . . . identical with its culture, as we may observe to our horror in the case of civilized France."[585] Nietzsche, who was to become his country's own stringent critic, believed that under the restlessly palpitating cultural life of Germany there was concealed "a glorious, intrinsically healthy, primordial power," the first Dionysian manifestation of which was the "deep, courageous, and spiritual . . . exuberantly good and tender" Lutheran chorale.[586] Although the (desirable) Dionysian spirit in general had mostly disappeared with the "degeneration of Hellenic man," it seemed to Nietzsche that "out of the Dionysian root of the German spirit a power has arisen" and that power was *"German music . . . in its vast solar orbit from Bach to Beethoven, from Beethoven to Wagner."*[587] Wielding the whip of his famous Apollonian versus Dionysian contrast, Nietzsche equates Apollonian thinking in the modern world with science and its insatiable, optimistic quest for knowledge, whereas he represents the Dionysian sphere by the tragic need of art which longs for "the annihilation of the individual" made possible in music.[588] The loss of myth, which so plagues modern times, and to which the consuming desire for knowledge of science speaks, will be restored because of the "capacity of music to give birth to *myth* . . . and particularly the *tragic myth.*"[589] And now comes the good news: Nietzsche has the feeling "that the birth of a tragic age [heralded by Schopenhauer and Wagner] simply means a return to itself of the German spirit, a blessed self-rediscovery. . . ."[590]

Complicated? Less so if we believe with Nietzsche that "music and tragic myth are equally expressive of the Dionysian capacity of a people" and that music, as defined by Schopenhauer (and practiced by Wagner) has "a character and an origin different from all the other arts, because, unlike them, it is not a copy of the phenomenon, but an immediate copy of the will itself," and therefore "represents what is metaphysical, the thing in itself."[591] This is why the fourth movement of Beethoven's Ninth and all of Wagner's *Tristan and Isolde*, being not beautiful but *sublime*, can give Dionysian insight into the "eternal life beyond all phenomenon, and despite all [individual] annihilations."[592] Nietzsche the prophet has spoken, and for added authority (as well as a burning desire to please his adopted family at Tribschen), he cites the high priest: "To this most important insight of aesthetics [that certain music is Dionysian, being will-like] . . . Richard Wagner, by way of confirmation of its eternal truth, affixed his seal, when he asserted in his *Beethoven* that music must be evaluated according to aesthetic principles quite different from those which apply to all plastic [fine] arts, and not, in general, according to the category of beauty."[593]

If the beacon of Wagner's *Beethoven*—as guided by Nietzsche's pen—still does not seem to come from a lighthouse of clarity, there is comfort in the lines Cosima wrote in her diary for 14 November 1870: "Prof. Nietzsche sends back *Beethoven*, remarking that probably few people will be able to follow R."[594] What the bumbling cross-fertilization of Wagner and Nietzsche by the Schopenhauerean bee accomplished is possibly more important to Beethoven mythology than what any one of them actually meant. Romanticism's overworked lexicon had been enriched with several exciting new entries, and Beethoven's music, formerly only "sublime," could now also be "will," "redemption," or "Dionysian." The concept of the universal meaning of Beethoven had been enhanced, and as for his life, the idea of personal suffering leading to joy was emphasized as something desirable, even mandatory for membership in the hall of the gods (Rolland would later latch on to this latter theme with maudlin tenacity).

Membership in Wagner's earthly Valhalla at Villa Wahnfried had been accorded to Schopenhauer via Lenbach's painted image of him. In answer to the obvious question whether Wagner also owned a portrait of Beethoven, the answer is yes. At least three portraits. One of them he did not like; it was a royal gift from the financial underwriter of his Wahnfried paradise, King Ludwig II. It had been sent to his earlier retreat from the world, Tribschen, by the king in October 1869 as a placating gesture for having—against Wagner's wishes—*The Rheingold* produced in Munich. Cosima noted the event and Richard's reaction in the diary: "Arrival of a picture of Beethoven—a present from the king of Bavaria. R. put in a very bad mood by it; first, his behavior, and then this unusable [*ununterbringbare*] gift."[595] Ludwig's Beethoven gift was probably "unusable" not so much for its size or style but because Wagner had already acquired and installed a portrait of Beethoven just three and a half months before the king's white elephant arrived. The lengths to which Wagner went to procure the "right" portrait of his idol were as painstaking and specific as those involving the ordering of the correct weight and color satin that his seamstress industriously turned into the sumptuous dressing gowns needed to put him in the proper state of body and mind for composing.[596] That Wagner—the "real" heir of Beethoven—yearned to possess his own "genuine" portrait of the composer forms one of the keystones of Beethoven mythography.

We have observed that Beethoven's physical appearance and even his facial expression were of such consummate interest to Wagner that he included references to them in "A Pilgrimage to Beethoven" and in *Beethoven*—literary images separated by thirty years. And we know from a letter to Liszt that as early as 1851 Wagner had displayed for his edification a picture—probably an etching or lithograph—of Beethoven in his Zurich apartments (where he also kept a pet parrot, Papo, which was trained to whistle tunes by Wagner's two favorite composers, Beethoven and Wagner[597]). In the letter to Liszt Wagner made the flattering demand that Liszt send him a medallion relief of himself, then added: "If you have a really good portrait, I should like to have that too. You need not be ashamed of hanging on my wall; at present I have there only Beethoven, besides the Nibelung design by Cornelius."[598]

By 1869 Wagner's days of financial hardship and economical living were over; he had the king of Bavaria for his protector, and no longer needed to rely on engravings or medallions for the interior decoration of his home temple. He could have the real thing—a portrait in oil. Already he had tried out the idea in regard to another hero: at his request the Leipzig-based portrait painter Robert Krausse (1834–1903) had made a faithful copy for him of a treasure owned by the Leipzig Schiller Society—Tischbein's 1806 portrait of Friedrich Schiller (Fig. 95).[599] The result, in Wagner's opinion, was a crowning success,[600] and he mentioned this fortuitous experiment in a letter to Hermann Härtel (son of Gottfried Christoph Härtel, of Breitkopf and Härtel, who had commissioned Waldmüller to paint Beethoven's portrait), to whom he wrote on 5 March 1869 asking whether the original of Waldmüller's "quite excellent" portrait of Beethoven, distributed by his firm as a print, was by any chance available "so that an exact copy of it might be made by a really skillful artist."[601] Wagner had received the Leipzig music firm's illustrated publication of a gallery of great Germans (*Bildnisse berühmter Deutschen*[602]) and was smitten by the engraving of the Waldmüller portrait. Herr Härtel answered with justifiable pride: "The portrait of Beethoven which was printed for our collection, is owned by me personally. At my father's request Beethoven let himself be painted for this purpose. The picture was painted alla prima very quickly because Beethoven had little desire to sit for his portrait; it has not always been as favorably judged as by you. If you wish to have a copy made of it, it is at your disposal at any time."[603] Wagner took Härtel up on his offer by return mail, asking that he be allowed to give it to Krausse to copy and assuring Härtel that the rapid execution of the picture was exactly what made it such a real portrait, free from all affectation, and superior to all other Beethoven portraits known to him. By 13 May Härtel was able to inform Wagner that Krausse had that day received not only the Waldmüller picture but also the "death mask, which I also own" (he probably meant the Klein life mask) in order to "control" the portrait results.[604] In not quite so much haste Wagner thanked the thoughtful lender and said he hoped Krausse would not create an ideal portrait but rather a *true* portrait of the man.[605] To Krausse Wagner wrote an encouraging but exacting mandate to fix up—with great discretion—any technical faults that the "al prima" execution of the original might evince, to create the copy in the exact same size as the Waldmüller canvas, and to keep the character of the original without making any essential changes.[606] On the second of July he was able to tell Härtel that the copy pleased him extraordinarily, and to the hard-working copyist he wrote his sincere thanks: "With this artistically executed copy I possess everything that I had wished to possess: an unaffected, real portrait of Beethoven. You comprehended my wish completely and you have known how to comply with it accordingly."[607]

With so much Wagnerian approval expressed on all sides, an exact, perhaps even undifferentiatable, copy is to be expected. Let us follow the Krausse crate into Tribschen through Cosima's diary, take a look at the portrait's final installation at Wahnfried, and then—if we can bear the suspense—compare the copy with the Waldmüller original. Thursday, 1 July 1869: "the joyful moment of the day was the arrival of Beethoven's portrait, which R. has had copied (from the original, in

(Colorplate 6)

Härtel's possession). We receive the great man as a friend and benefactor, and R. says we have pleasures which no others have, we lead a life like few others. . . . Coming back once more to the portrait of Beethoven, R. says to me: 'This pleasure I also owe to you. Without you such an idea would never have occurred to me.'"[608] Saturday, 3 July: "We pass the evening in conversation; he is still delighted with the picture of Beethoven. 'That is how he looked, this poor man who gave us back the language men spoke before they had ideas; it was to recover this language of the birds that Man created the divine art. But this is also the reason why a musician such as he is a being for whom there is absolutely no place in society.'"[609] Friday, 9 July: "Beethoven has now been framed and is hanging on the wall."[610] (Framers were fast in the nineteenth century!)

More diary comments accompany the Krausse-Waldmüller Beethoven portrait to Villa Wahnfried, but now let us look at its installation there (Fig. 96). Our photograph shows us the great *salon*-library in its final stage of sumptuousness, after 1880, with ceiling panels decorated by the coats of arms of cities in which Richard Wagner Societies had been founded. We must wade past five Wagnerian images before coming to the Beethoven portrait. Reading from left to right there is first, Lenbach's famous profile portrait of Wagner in a mammoth beret; second, Lenbach's large "black" (as opposed to a later large "white") three-quarter portrait of Cosima; third, projecting dangerously from above the bookcases, the Russian painter Paul Zhukovski's (1845–1912) immortalization of *The Holy Family* as mimed by the Bülow and Wagner children for Christmas of 1880 (Siegfried, Eva, Isolde, Blandine, and Daniela in a circle, with the painter as Joseph); fourth, Zhukovski's full-length, rather wooden portrait of Cosima; and fifth, on the wall directly above, Ludwig Geyer's (Wagner's stepfather and possibly real father) portrait of Adolf Wagner (Wagner's much-admired uncle) as a young man. Centered between the Adolf Wagner portrait on the left and Krausse's copy of the Tischbein portrait of Schiller on the right is the Beethoven, complete with roving eyes, and disheveled hair.[611] Out of sight on the continuation of this wall, to the right, were portraits of Goethe and Liszt.[612]

Now let us focus, as Wagner did so often and with so much pleasure, on the Krausse (Fig. 97) copy of Waldmüller's Beethoven portrait. Is it an "unaffected, real" portrait of the composer? Has it faithfully preserved the character of the original? Even without the benefit of a color reproduction for Krausse's picture, it is clear that the copy could never be confused for the original. The eyeglasses of Biedermeier objectivity through which Waldmüller had viewed and painted his unidealized model have been exchanged for the subjective spectacles of Romanticism, with which both Krausse and Wagner unconsciously saw their Beethoven. What had originally attracted Wagner to this—the least beloved by commercial mythographers—image of Beethoven was the very fact that it showed Beethoven the aging man, not Beethoven the perpetually youthful hero. But the titanic aspects of that man—his silver-streaked hair, his incipient frown, his compressed lips—have all been, almost involuntarily, enhanced. Krausse clarified, as it were, the impress of suffering and mighty mental activity. The lines of Beethoven's tightly set lips, cheeks, and chin are all just a shade more pronounced. The furrow between the now thicker and longer eyebrows is noticeably more prominent, and a curious feature that usually comes only with aging has actually been added to the eyelids—a slightly hooded aspect has puffed out the originally narrow upper lids, dramatically contributing to the look of grim concentration illuminating Beethoven's features. And, in keeping with the forty-six years that had passed between Waldmüller's and Krausse's portrait efforts, Beethoven's hair has become almost snow white! But no matter. Wagner had never seen the original oil, after all, only the engraving of it (Fig. 98)—a rendering less fierce than the Waldmüller original that also emphasized the contrast between Beethoven's silvering hair and his still dark eyebrows. Krausse's empathic portrait was exactly what Wagner wanted (perhaps the white hair had special appeal for him, since he told Cosima more than once that he rued the fact he was turning gray at the side of his still youthful—and twenty-four years younger—brunette wife). We know that in general Wagner's feeling for the visual arts—which interested him less than music or literature—was characterized by a certain insensitivity to form, but with a simultaneous penchant for expressive or significant content. And so, unconditionally, he welcomed this physical symbol of a spiritual content dear to him since childhood into the final two homes of his adult years. The treasured Beethoven portrait became a frequent touchstone for the bon mots of his declamatory domestic style of life. Here are a few samplings of the Beethoven sparks collected by the ever-attendant Cosima:

22 January 1872 [still at Tribschen]
Hermine [a maid] says she always finds herself looking at the portrait of Beethoven and wishing he could see how well Herr Wagner understands him.[613]

18 January 1875 [Villa Wahnfried]
[As they rearrange the pictures on the wall] 'R. gets very indignant about Beethoven's being pushed into a corner: "Who can be compared to him? What is the equal of a melody, that direct gift from Heaven?' "[614]

12 January 1879
Over coffee he gazes at the wall on which Beeth., Goethe, and Schiller are hanging and says, "There Makart ought to paint a fresco for us, illustrating the Dionysian element in the introduction to the A Major Symphony [Seventh]."[615]

4 January 1881
We . . . delight in the fine winter weather (the sun gladdened us in the *salon*, "and it is always the setting sun," says R., "which gives us this light—like the smile of a god"; the transfigured picture of Beeth. delights him). . . . [616]

Two references to other portraits of Beethoven are of interest for their exposure of Wagner's interior image of Beethoven in relation to himself. A few days before Christmas of 1869 Cosima noted: "The *Illustrierte Zeitung* publishes a portrait of Beethoven in the year 1805 [possibly Fig. 29 in this book, rather than Fig. 6, if either of these]; it is very unattractive, bloated, almost devoid of intellectual expression. 'Well, musicians must be ugly in appearance, in them the heart is everything. . . . The musician does not see people, their movements, and their actions, for him everything is tempo, structure, etc.' "[617] That Wagner, whose own pronounced and irregular features had been subjected to substantial caricature, was sensitive about his (and his spiritual father's) looks is apparent. Concerning a sketch of him in connection with another oil portrait of Wagner on which Lenbach was working a few years later, Richard told Cosima: "I feel really sad that artists see in me only a sharp caricature or a thorough philistine."[618]

A happier impression was made by a second Beethoven likeness that the Wagners chanced upon as houseguests in Mannheim in 1872: "At the Heckels' we see a very interesting picture of Beethoven which captivates R. enormously: 'Yes, that's how he looked; these eyes which see nothing and this mouth, showing all the stubbornness of a man whom nothing in the outside world can influence. [Is this a self-description?] And how wonderfully this man made music!' "[619]

Wagner's persistent image of Beethoven was brought into the bosom of his family when he began noticing that his baby son, Fidi (Siegfried, born 6 June 1869 at Tribschen), *resembled* Beethoven! "R calls Fidi the blond Beethoven, he thinks he looks like him,"[620] Cosima reported indulgently. This was really too much to hope for (and also really wrong), but then Richard had observed Beethoven-like physical characteristics in himself. He remarked to Cosima with wonder one day: "Do you know that sometimes, when I have a musical thought, I catch myself with my mouth set just like Beethoven's in his death mask."[621] (Mirrors were not wanting at Wahnfried.) His attention drawn to mouths, and noticing that as Fidi grew older his mouth frequently seemed to hang open, Wagner reprimanded the boy with a sobering pronouncement: "Beethoven would have composed much more if he had kept his mouth shut."[622] Cosima learned that her husband even thought of Beethoven in the tub. (A bathroom was one of Wahnfried's proud innovations.) "He tells me that the countertheme in the andante of the A Major Symphony [Seventh] came into his mind with particular vividness when he was in his bath, and it affected him like a revelation! 'How divine it is that something like that can suddenly sound in our world, something so beautiful!'—Beethoven melodies and Shakespeare scenes, these are everything to him, he says."[623] A few months after his sixty-sixth birthday, Richard told Cosima solemnly: "I am now already ten years older than Beethoven was,"[624] and they discussed Beethoven's death. Another time he lamented that he was born ten years too late, for he "should have stood in the same relationship to Beethoven as Schubert did."[625] And (like Berlioz) he regretted not having known Beethoven, who, he told Cosima, might have been like Liszt, a contrary but crucial colleague: "If only one had known, had seen a being like that! He would not have put up with us, but what tremendous outbursts there would have been—cries of bliss and ecstasy! [Beethoven admiring the music of the future?] He would then have gone his own way, rather like your father. [A lapsed Wagnerian, Richard frequently thought.] It is quite unimaginable. I have seen both him and Shakespeare in my dreams—towards me always gently consoling."[626] Beethoven the man almost always transported Wagner, however, to Beethoven the musician. He informed Cosima that were he trying to visualize Beethoven "in all his starry glory," he would surely think of the second movement of op. 111, the adagio with variations, for he knows of "nothing more ecstatic," yet at the same time never sentimental.[627]

From the ghost of Ludwig van Beethoven past, in his starry firmament, to the reality of grandnephew Ludwig van Beethoven present, looking for work in Munich, Wagner could reach out with touching solicitude, petitioning Ludwig II to give the impecunious son of Beethoven's nephew, Karl, a post, and referring his monarch for details of the boy to Beethoven's biographer, Ludwig Nohl.[628] (This plethora of Ludwigs did not harmonize: Beethoven's grandnephew was soon in trouble with the Munich police.)

It would be remiss not to inquire what sort of *Götterfunken* arose when the two great image-makers and conductors of Beethoven—Liszt and Wagner—got together. The answer may in this case be contemplated along with not one but two stimulating visual icons of life at Wahnfried when the famous son-in-law played host to his renowned father-in-law. (We get some notion of the underlying tension that was radiated by a Wagner who resented it when his wife paid too much attention to her father—or her children—when we learn that Wagner forbade conversation in French at Wahnfried.) Our first icon is an omnium gatherum of admirers and disciples grouped in the *salon* (this word *was* allowed) (Fig. 99), and featuring, on the right, the portrait presence of King Ludwig II and the pianistic presence of Liszt. Wagner is enthroned at the left, with velvet beret, smoking jacket, and open piano score in hand, along with the pendants of (new) Newfoundland dog, son, and wife on the far left. We have a worthy ensemble, but it would be wrong to expect the sounds of Beethoven here—this is obviously a command performance by the always-obliging Liszt of one of Wagner's operas. Beethoven was for more intimate moments, with just a few guests, such as this after-dinner recital described by Cosima: "In the evening the dean, the mayor, Dr. Landgraf; my father plays the adagio from [op.] 106 [the *Hammerklavier* Sonata] unforgettably, and from time to time R. contributes an explanatory word; our guests, completely unprepared, appear to be utterly overwhelmed."[629]

It is delicious to think of Liszt's Beethoven rendition being overlaid "from time to time" by exegetical gems from the irrepressible Wagner, but a second icon (Fig. 100), set in Cosima's private sittingroom (the "lilac *salon*"), clearly shows the pecking order when visiting Villa Wahnfried. Compositionally and psychologically central, the elegantly attired Wagner stands with his arms acknowledging both sides of the room, listening attentively (and ready to intervene) while the seated Liszt, dressed in his abbé's frock, expounds upon a fine point (of most probably another Wagnerian score) not to his son-in-law but to his spellbound daughter. Once again a protector and a disciple are present—this time King Ludwig listens outdoors, in the form of a huge bronze bust gracing the house's entrance,[630] and indoors, to the far right, sits in reverential attention the young, well brought-up Hans von Wolzogen, energetic editor of Wagner's publicity organ, the *Bayreuther Blätter*. We now learn the location of the final resting place for Lenbach's portrait of Schopenhauer—immediately above Wagner's head, like a halo—and we are treated to a view of Lenbach's second three-quarter-length portrait of Cosima, in white this time.

As for the promulgation of Beethoven, Wagner allowed that Liszt was on a level par with him,[631] and at least once he was totally overwhelmed by Liszt's authority as interpreter of Beethoven. The eyewitness account comes not from Cosima in this case but from a houseguest at Wahnfried in the 1870s, the Hungarian politician, Count Albert Apponyi:

> When the last bars of that mysterious work [the slow movement of the *Hammerklavier* Sonata] had died away, we stood silent and motionless. Suddenly, from the gallery on the first floor, there came a tremendous uproar, and Richard Wagner in his nightshirt came thundering, rather than running, down the stairs. He flung his arms around Liszt's neck, and, sobbing with emotion, thanked him in broken phrases for the wonderful gift he had received. His bedroom led onto the inner gallery, and he had apparently crept out in silence on hearing the first notes and remained there without giving a sign of his presence. Once more, I witnessed the meeting of those three—Beethoven, the great deceased master, and the two best qualified of all living men to guard his tradition. This experience still lives within me, and has confirmed and deepened my innermost conviction that those three great men belonged to one another.[632]

Wagner could on occasion then be overcome by Beethoven's piano music (written by Beethoven for *himself*, he insisted), but his lifelong passion was Beethoven's greatest instrumental-choral masterpiece, the Ninth Symphony—anticipating, as it did, the music of the future. As we conclude our exploration of Wagner's image of Beethoven, let us take the role of the Ninth in Wagner's consciousness as a leitmotif, and do as Wagner did with his "day in the life of Beethoven" speculation and look at a composite day in the life of Wagner. This Beethoven Ninth-oriented "day"—extending over half a century—begins, we remember, as early as 1830, when as a seventeen-year-old Wagner copied out the orchestral score and then set it for piano, continues through the illuminating Habeneck rehearsals of the Ninth in Paris of 1839, and emerges in Wagner's own ambitious productions of the Ninth in Dresden during the mid–1840s. It is taken up again through Wagner's 1855 London performance of the Ninth, his conducting of it by heart in Saint Petersburg in 1863,[633] and culminates but does not terminate in his reinstrumentation of the Ninth for the 1872 Bayreuth dedication, and lingers to within a month of his death in 1883, when he played out the beginning of the Ninth on his piano in Venice. Taking stochastic aim at the sundial marking Wagner's life, we can find him possessed by Beethoven's *Choral* Symphony from dawn to dusk and beyond. Here are some instances culled by Cosima, who "in the early morning" of the first month of their first year together at Tribschen was awakened by Richard "with '*Freude, schöner Götterfunken*' on the piano."[634] Breakfast was a fine time for serving up Beethoven: "When I come down to breakfast, R. greets me in song with the melody from the Ninth Symphony: 'Who has pulled off the great triumph, husband of this wife to be,' etc. 'That is my "Ode to Joy," he says.' "[635] Cosima did not always have to come downstairs to get Beethoven with breakfast: " . . . [Richard] is lively and spirited in the morning, breakfasting beside my bed. A passage in the first movement of the 9th Symphony is occupying his thoughts, the passage in which the tension begins to mount, only to recede again; he sees in this a portrait of the will [a little Schopenhauer in the sausage?], which makes a tremendous effort, only to sink back in impotence."[636] And again: "R. had a good night. He sings the andante theme from the Adagio of [Beethoven's] 9th Symphony and says, 'That is really a dance, a theme for a minuet, and so with this andante the structure of the adagio is nicely variegated.' "[637] But Beethoven was not just for breakfast. The Ninth was shared, albeit somewhat sententiously, with the children: "A lovely moment of the day was that in which—after he had had the children dancing around—R. played them the '*Freude, schöner Götterfunken*' theme. . . . 'All wisdom, all art is forgotten,' says R., 'in the divine nature of this naïve theme, to which, through his noble bass voice, he imparts the whole force of human feeling. Here the naïve and the emotional are combined.' "[638] Undeteterred by this didactic discourse, the little ones appropriated Beethoven's song as one of their own: "We drink our afternoon coffee in the hall [they had just moved into Villa Wahnfried], which is very resonant. Yesterday the children sang . . . '*Freude schöner Götterfunken*' down to us from the gallery as we sat below, with very moving effect."[639]

Wagner too could have fun with the Ninth in spite of his great reverence for it. When Liszt wrote that Weimar's grand duke (Karl August of Sachsen-Weimar-Eisenach) had requested him to perform Beethoven's Ninth as part of his forthcoming wedding celebrations, Cosima recorded that this immediately inspired Richard with the proper irreverence to work out a musical biography of the duke with "the following program: Part I: Rebuff at Oldenburg; II: Scherzo, Travels in the East; III: Meeting at Lake Constance; IV: Joy of the Saxon People! . . . "[640] Such fantasizing however was a rare flash of humor for Wagner concerning the Ninth; usually contemplation of the great work set more serious thoughts in motion.

Here is a more typical Ninth-inspired monologue, delivered to the rententive audience of one who shared his train compartment on a trip from Dresden to Berlin and who wrote it down in her diary that same night: "In the train he began by remarking, 'Just like physicians with their medicines, which they grow more and more to distrust and utilize less, so it was with Beethoven and melodies with cadences; the nearer he came to Nature and its simple motives, the more he avoided as much as he could the dominant (the most striking example of that is the trio of the scherzo in the Ninth Symphony, where he uses it only once); he hated all conventional endings.' "[641]

It is not surprising to find the spinner of drawn-out chromatic webs applauding Beethoven's increasing contempt for diatonic convention. Time and again Wagner's thoughts returned to innovations and devices in the Ninth that excited his admiration. In the evenings, after dinner, was a particularly good time for digesting doses of the symphony, as played through leisurely by the composer on the Wahnfried *salon* piano for his and Cosima's elucidation. Cosima's diary gives several accounts of the revelations that followed such intimate readings. After playing the beginning of the final movement of the Ninth and ending with the andante on one occasion, Wagner got up from the piano exclaiming: " 'What that means—after constructing a whole passionate symphony, to make the double basses softly announce this theme, like something wrapped in cotton wool.' In the whole of art it is unique, he says: 'He heaps one thing on top of another, to give us at the end something like a glimpse into Paradise.' "[642] And again: " . . . in the evening we experience a few happy hours, made unforgettable by the fact that R. plays to us the beginning of the adagio from the 9th. . . . "[643] Beethoven had been on Wagner's mind all day that day, for he had woken up from a dream in which he and Cosima were playing a "new Beethoven composition as a piano duet."[644] But a piano was not necessary to jog appreciation for the Ninth. Another diary entry notes (some nine months before Wagner's death): "In the evening he talks about Beethoven, particularly the first movement of the 9th Symphony, which Beeth. marked *maestoso*—in R.'s opinion very significant for this wild, sorrow-laden piece; what this movement is cannot be expressed in words, he adds, though he had tried to do it."[645] A few evenings later Wagner was back at the piano: "R. plays the Andante from the 9th Symph., better, I think, than he has ever played it before!"[646] And two evenings later Cosima tells her diary: "R. is still very much occupied with the 9th Symphony, the first movement with the marking *maestoso*; he says it is a wonderful piece, though to the shrewd professional musicians of its own time it must have looked like the work of a bungler."[647]

Rounding out this composite "day" of the Ninth Symphony in Wagner's life is the following bedtime entry in Cosima's diary: "A pleasant evening, though we are always left with a strange agitated feeling of exhaustion when other people come between us. When we are alone again upstairs, R. sings *'froh wie seine Sonnen'* ['joyful as his suns'] from the Ninth Symphony and points out that at this point the tenor becomes nothing more than the accompaniment to the march, as if he were becoming absorbed into the procession. But, he says, only a great artist can grasp this and sing it accordingly. . . . "[648]

To sleep is perchance to dream however and occasionally Wagner dreamt not just of Beethoven, but specifically of the Ninth—not always under the best of circumstances, as his dream secretary faithfully added to the permanent log: "R. dreamed that he had to conduct the 9th Symphony, in Dresden or Munich, and passed beforehand through a railroad-station restaurant which had frankfurters; being very hungry, he ordered some; coming back to fetch them, he sees two men eating his portion, the assistant at the buffet maliciously insolent, also the manageress, who refuses him not only the sausages, but beer as well; he is angry, then tries friendly words, all to no avail. In the end he leaves the restaurant, cursing, arrives at the concert hall, walks through the orchestra, is greeted with applause, but has to climb, relies on his agility, but comes to a place which is too steep; when he cannot jump over it, he wakes up!"[649]

While leaving to Freud fanciers an analysis of what being deprived of one's own frankfurters just before conducting the Ninth might mean, the obstacles blocking Wagner's way to the Ninth can be seen as left-over frustrations—shed through the medium of dream disposal—accrued from some real-life activities the year before in connection with conducting Beethoven's Ninth at the dedication consecrating the Bayreuth festival theater (22 May 1872—Wagner's birthday).

The only non-Wagnerian piece of music ever allowed on the same Bayreuth program as Wagner's own work (a phenomenon repeated by Wilhelm Furtwängler in 1951 when postwar resumption of the Bayreuth performances was initiated), Beethoven's Ninth Symphony was, in Wagner's eyes, a symbolic choice dictated by cultural logic—the great *Choral* Symphony (that "salvation of music") was historically crucial as the forerunner to his own music-drama synthesis. But it had taken a mighty effort to pull together the giant orchestra and chorus necessary for Wagner's demanding production of the Ninth at Bayreuth. The privileged Cosima recorded the exciting genesis of Wagner's plan and her part in it:

> Yesterday R. disclosed to me his decision to combine a musical performance with the laying of the foundation stone, and I had to dance for joy, for I had had this very thought myself, but had been scared of expressing it, fearing to cause him yet further excitement and to appear (as it were) to be saying that the laying of the foundation stone was not enough for me. I ask for the Ninth Symphony. And R. intends to put an appeal in the newspapers, saying that he is going to perform the Symphony in Bayreuth, is prepared to pay travel and living expenses, and now invites musicians to come along; he needs 300 singers and 100 orchestral players, and his only condition is that they have to have taken part in a performance of the Symphony before.[650]

Reaction was heartening if at times embarrassing (the mayor of Schweinfurt offered to play the drum). By February of 1872 Cosima was able to write: "News comes from Karlsruhe that almost the entire orchestra wants to play, which means that the performance of the 9th Symphony would be assured,"[651] and by March came the good news that 'Herr Riedel from Leipzig wants to supply more than 300 singers and says people are begging on their knees to take part.' "[652] During the next weeks Cosima's diary makes regular note of Wagner's intensive study of the score, and soon after she joins him in Bayreuth (30 April 1872) they examine the famous Margraves' Opera House where the dedication concert is to take place. She discovers her husband has already been at work, rounding up carpenters as in Dresden days, to reshape the stage for Beethoven: "the proscenium taken out by R., the building revealed in all its original glory; very moved by the knowledge that all these preparations and provisions are being made for the sake of Beethoven's splendid work—its creator could certainly never have dreamed of it!"[653] Wagner is in a rare mood of humility: "R. told me that on my arrival the melody from the first movement [of the Ninth] had come into his mind and he had said to himself, 'You have never done anything like that.' "[654]

The three rehearsals for the Ninth were conducted with mounting success; all the listeners as well as the participants were greatly affected, and Cosima perceived the mighty Beethoven-Wagner link with redundant ecstasy: "At a moment of foreboding Schiller wrote his words to joy, which nobody perhaps understood until Beethoven came along and understood them and made us in moments of foreboding understand them, too, but ununderstood they remained until, in a sublime and foreboding moment, Richard made them resound in words and music."[655] The performance, preceded by Wagner's own *Kaisermarsch*, took place after the stone-laying ceremony (a congratulatory telegram from King Ludwig was enclosed in the capsule buried with the foundation stone), and, in Cosima's words the Ninth Symphony was "quite magnificent, everyone feeling himself freed from the burden of mortal existence."[656]

So intensely, so massively had Wagner rethought Beethoven's Ninth in preparation for conducting it at the Bayreuth dedication, that the cornucopia of Beethovenian fruits harvested by the experience spilled over into an article[657] the following year. Published in April of 1873, the essay was a forcefully argued rationale, buttressed with specific examples, for infusing some Wagnerian will into Beethoven's idea of the Ninth Symphony. "At a performance I lately conducted of this wondrous tone work," began Wagner, "certain reflections touching what I deem the irremissible *distinctness* of its rendering forced themselves so strongly on me that I since have meditated a remedy for the ills I felt. The result I now lay before earnest musicians, if not as an invitation to follow my method, at least as a stimulus to independent study."[658] He lamented that Beethoven had instrumented his orchestral works on exactly the same assumptions of the orchestra's capacities as had Haydn and Mozart before him and asserted that Beethoven, after the advent of his deafness, had lost the aural consciousness of the orchestra with its dynamic values, which would have enabled him to match orchestration with his innovative musical compositions. Wagner's practical solutions for making Beethoven sound more like Beethoven consisted of a number of reinstrumentations and tempo alterations. One of the most interesting "changes" concerns a moment in the Ninth that, as we have seen, had drawn comment from Schumann to Berlioz. It was that moment of (in Wagner's words) "terrifying fanfare of the wind at the beginning of the last movement."[659] Because the tyranny of the three/four beat as sounded intermittently by the trumpets interfered with the distinctness of the unison theme of the woodwinds, Wagner "in a fit of despair quite suited to the character of this terrible passage" took the radical step of having the trumpets join with the woodwinds throughout, with the result that "light was won: the fearsome fanfare stormed across us in all its rhythmic chaos, and we knew at last why the 'Word' must come."[660] The justification for such repairs? Here it is, in grandiose terms, generously granting Beethoven's *Choral* Symphony tone-poem status: " . . . nothing is so worth the utmost study as the attempt to clear the meaning of a phrase, a bar, nay more, a single note in the message handed down to us by a genius such as Beethoven's. For every transformation, however startling, of a being so eternally sincere, arises solely from the godlike ardor to lay bare to us poor mortals the deepest mysteries of its world view. As one should never quit a knotty passage of a great philosopher before one plainly understands it . . . so one should never glide over a single bar of a tone poem such as Beethoven's without having distinctly grasped it. . . ."[661]

And Wagner is the person to comprehend Beethoven, about whom in three sentences he draws the aura of genius-philosopher who has a godlike ardor and is eternally sincere. Wagner's conviction that Beethoven's inspired gropings, without the benefit of a modern orchestra, were worthy of minute study (and occasional assists) was confirmed by the important contribution to the Beethoven myth made by the musicologist Gustav Nottebohm's (1817–1882) publication (1865, 1880) of the Beethoven sketchbooks, which revealed to the general public an inside view of the laborious process of perfecting the creative act. Once again we have the genius who must storm heaven (Beethoven, Wagner) as opposed to the "natural" genius on whom heaven rains its gifts (Mozart). In this favorite dichotomy of the nineteenth century, the former genus of striving genius won the hearts of the Romantics of the first half of the century, but also appealed to Wilhelmenian, Victorian, and Darwinian values of the second half of the century.[662]

As the increasing frequency of heart seizures began to cloud the final months of his and Cosima's life together, the seventy-year-old Wagner retired to Venice with his family in September of 1882, resting from the labors of completing and staging the first performance of *Parsifal* that summer, and pursuing his multiple interests at a calmer but no less intense pace. The piano and Beethoven still attracted him; on 19 January 1883, twenty-five days before he died of a heart attack in Cosima's arms, he played through once again that part of the Ninth, with its spooky pure fifths, which had fascinated him for so many decades—the first movement. Cosima quoted his delighted last judgment: "Such sublime naïveté. How long it takes for one to reach this stage! In the early symphonies he still has scaffolding around him."[663]

Wagner's lifelong meditation on Beethoven, whose successor he genuinely considered himself, was symbolized in the choice of music that marked his final homecoming to Bayreuth: a regimental band played the funeral march from the *Eroica*. The puissant and personal image of Beethoven held by Wagner contributed tremendously to the mystique of a "pure" Beethoven committed to serious, high causes, and also to a perception of *German* music as profound, philosophic, and moral—leading from the divine revelations offered by Beethoven to the redemption of humankind played out in Wagner's music dramas. In Wagner's history of music, Beethoven's promise had been fulfilled by him. Perhaps that is why he was able to repeat to Cosima, without the slightest embarrassment, the following egalitarian dream that visited him exactly three years to the day before his death: "R. dreamed that Beethoven came to invite him to attend the performance of a symphony. 'Good Lord, is he not dead after all? No, this was a dream that he was dead.' He went toward him, each attempted to kneel before the other, and they stood there, arrested in the act of genuflection."[664]

As we take leave of Wagner's Beethoven, each composer kneeling before the other's genius, we might cast a sideways glance at the fanatical worshiper of both Beethoven and Wagner whom we have met several times in these pages—Hans von Bülow (1830–1894) (Fig. 101). Former, and first, husband of Cosima, he had reluctantly but nobly agreed with Cosima that Richard needed her as a wife more than he did. Bülow's earliest image of Beethoven had come from Friedrich Wieck,[665] with whom he began piano lessons at the age of nine. (In later years neither Hans von Bülow nor Clara Wieck Schumann thought much of each other's playing.) More Beethoven perceptions were conveyed to him by his second piano teacher and future father-in-law, Liszt (who praised his great comprehension of the master). Although he was an ardent champion of new music—especially Wagner's—he also devoted himself to Beethoven performances (conducting the Ninth twice in an evening on one occasion, and playing all-Beethoven solo piano recitals) and to Beethoven elucidation, publishing an annotated edition of the piano works from op. 53 to op. 111 in 1871. Cerebral and high strung, his keyboard technique was described as "passionate intellectuality." A schizophrenic chapter in the image of Beethoven story was written when Bülow, in a mad attempt to make himself welcome at Bayreuth, attempted to raise money for a statue of Wagner—whom he venerated as an artist and despised as a man—through a series of Beethoven performances. He explained his ambitious financial plans in a letter of 6 April 1879: "I mean to raise enough money by my Beethoven recitals for a fitting monument [*Denkmal*] to be erected to Wagner in his lifetime, as has been done for his fellow-giant Bismarck."[666] Wagner returned the forty thousand marks raised by Bülow under the banner of Beethoven.

JOHANNES BRAHMS

A photograph of a white-bearded man, skillfully juxtaposed over the view of a music room-sitting room (Fig. 102), draws our attention to one of the later nineteenth-century's most prominent composers—one nominated by Bülow to replace the name Berlioz in the three B's of music—Johannes Brahms (1833–1897). Although physically a "trick" photograph (circulated to raise funds for a Brahms memorial soon after his death), this intriguing image is not misleading from a psychological point of view. The life-size Beethoven bust (an embellished variation on the original Klein bust), gazing out approvingly from the wall bracket over Brahms's head, was a most treasured and long-time icon in the very personal pantheon of idols and images Brahms had assembled in the Vienna Karlsgasse No. 4 apartment where he spent the last twenty-five years of his life. To be sure there were several other images of composers enshrined in Brahms's lodgings. A portrait of Bach hung over the narrow bed in his bedroom, and this room also contained a bisque ceramic bust of Haydn and a photograph of Schumann, while on the walls of the combined sitting-music room there was a large reproduction of Ingres's famous 1842 *Portrait of Luigi Cherubini and the Muse of Lyric Poetry* (see Fig. 81; the fastidious Brahms had placed a permanent homemade curtain over Cherubini's female companion in this portrait[667]), a double medallion print of Clara and Robert Schumann (an etching after the relief by Ernst Rietschel, inscribed affectionately to Brahms), a mezzotint of Hogarth's portrait of Handel, and a reproduction of the drawing Goethe had had made of the boy Mendelssohn playing the piano for him at Weimar. But with the possible exception of the Schumann etching and photograph, none of these inspirational images had been with Brahms as long as the plaster bust of Beethoven. This he had brought with him to Vienna from his parents' house in Hamburg.[668] A drawing dated May 1879 by an amateur artist of Brahms, before he grew his beard, standing by the piano in his Karlsgasse apartment, reveals the music room at an early stage when the only artistic adornment was the Beethoven bust (Fig. 103). In later years Brahms added a second image of Beethoven to his musicians' hall of fame: a replica of the sculptor Kaspar von Zumbusch's Beethoven monument, unveiled in Vienna in 1880 (see chapter 5).

(Colorplate 7)

Brahms had his own three Bs, as attested by the effigies in his apartment, and the lineup agreed with Bülow's only in part. Too modest ever to put himself on a level with Bach or Beethoven, and as fervent a follower of contemporary politics as he was of classical contrapuntalists, Brahms's third B was not a musician at all, but the Iron Chancellor of the newly founded German Empire under Wilhelm I, Otto von Bismarck. (A laurel-wreathed bronze profile of Bismarck hung on the wall just to the left of the Beethoven bust, see Fig. 102.) Although Bach was at the apex of Brahms's all-German pyramid of Bs,[669] the image of Beethoven was a potent force and basic ingredient in Brahms's life. His declaration of musical allegiance to Beethoven had been sounded in the early Piano Sonata in C Major, written when he was twenty, which he later designated as op. 1. Not only the opening bars suggest a direct salute to the *Hammerklavier* Sonata (as noted by all Brahms scholars), but the whole first movement of the sonata is in the spirit of Beethoven. As a boy of ten Brahms had been placed in the hands of Hamburg's respected piano teacher and composer Eduard Marxsen (1806–1887), who had himself studied with Beethoven's friend and early biographer Ignaz Seyfried in Vienna. Marxsen's veneration for Beethoven was so great that he orchestrated the *Kreutzer* Sonata (its rendition in this guise created a sensation in Hamburg in 1835 and was repeated many times) and composed a large orchestral work called *Beethoven's Schatten* (*The Shade of Beethoven*; performed in Hamburg in 1844 and 1845), which was perfervidly reviewed by Seyfried as "a moving dirge on the loss of the immortal singer."[670] Such devotion was not lost on the young Brahms.

Beethoven's music figured in the first public appearance of the boy—a private subscription concert in which the ten-year-old blond Johannes played the piano part in the Quintet in E-flat Major for piano and wind instruments, op. 16. A month before his sixteenth birthday he played the exuberant *Waldstein* Sonata, op. 53, at a public concert in Hamburg in which he also made his debut as a composer, playing a Fantasia of his own. As his career as a pianist progressed he regularly included Beethoven piano concertos on his programs, especially no. 4 in G Major, op. 58. His first concert tour, undertaken in April and May of 1853 (he turned twenty on 7 May) in partnership with the flamboyant young Hungarian violinist Eduard Reményi (1830–1898), put Brahms's talents severely to the test in the service of Beethoven. On two separate occasions, two badly tuned pianos forced him to transpose, at the last moment, the Beethoven C Minor Sonata for piano and violin, op. 30, which he was playing from memory, into C-sharp Minor, and the *Kreutzer* Sonata in A Major, op. 47, which he was also playing from memory, into A sharp. Reményi met him halfway in these crises, tuning his violin accordingly. When the bold violinist introduced his shy accompanist to his celebrated countryman and fellow violinist Joseph Joachim (1831–1907) (Fig. 104) in Hanover at the end of their tour, a friendship was formed which, with one cooling intermezzo, lasted a lifetime and which was largely formed on their mutual appreciation of the classic masters, in particular Beethoven, whose violin concerto Joachim was firmly establishing in the concert repertory of the day. Even before meeting Joachim in person, Brahms had already been captivated by his brilliant performance of the Beethoven work at a Hamburg concert of 11 March 1848 (Brahms was all of fourteen, Joachim sixteen). Joachim hastened to introduce Brahms to his royal patron, the blind, art-loving King George V of Hanover. It was at this king's suggestion that the young woman sculptor Elisabet Ney (1833–1907), who had modeled his portrait bust in 1859, also did one of his court conductor, Joachim. King George was delighted by Brahms's playing and immediately dubbed him the "little Beethoven."[671] A more important introduction was given Brahms by Joachim when he recommended him by letter to Liszt, then holding forth at Weimar among a bevy of students and admirers. Brahms arrived in Weimar with Reményi in early June of 1853. Too overwhelmed to play his own compositions to the great virtuoso and his glittering entourage, Brahms had the awesome experience of listening to Liszt play faultlessly and from sight his first few piano works, including the C Major Sonata, with its appealing spiritual resemblance to the free style of Beethoven's late piano sonatas. Liszt was much taken by the "storm and stress" promise of genius in the reticent twenty-year-old before him at the Altenburg and later wrote a highly approving letter to Bülow about Brahms and the C Major Sonata in particular.[672]

Beethovenian potency in another's music was a supreme virtue that attracted young Brahms's admiration as well, and he used this apparent similarity to praise and encourage Joachim, who had just sent him his op. 10, a set of variations for viola and piano: "Your music affects me just as Beethoven's does. When I got to know a new [Beethoven] symphony or overture, it absorbed me completely for a long time. Everything else just formed arabesques round the beautiful great picture. It is just the same for me with your new works . . . probably nobody has wielded Beethoven's pen so powerfully. . . ."[673] History has proven this jejune judgment erroneous, but Brahms's enthusiasm in trying to bring out the composer in his violinist friend (whose success did continue to be on the virtuoso concert stage) can be forgiven. It was, after all, wholly in the spirit of the times to hope and look for new incarnations of Beethoven.

And that is exactly what Schumann himself saw in Brahms when, acting upon yet another helpful written introduction from the generous Joachim, the young composer-pianist from Hamburg timorously presented himself at the doorstep of the Düsseldorf home of Robert and Clara Schumann on 30 September of that same eventful year of 1853. Here, amid the domestic bliss of one of the century's finest composers and one of Europe's greatest concert pianists, the twenty-year-old Brahms felt no inhibitions. The following day he played to them his Beethovenesque C Major Sonata and their verdict was registered in Robert's diary entry for that date: "Visit from Brahms, a genius."[674] The Schumanns quickly made Brahms feel like a member of the family and Robert introduced the "young eagle"[675] to his disciples, including the congenial composer Albert Dietrich (1829–1908). As a surprise for Joachim, who was due to take part in a concert at Düsseldorf on 27 October, Dietrich, Brahms, and Schumann composed a jointly written violin and piano sonata. On the day of its presentation (Joachim was challenged to guess who had written which movement) in the Schumann home (28 October) a ghost from the past of our Beethoven mythography was very much present: frail and wizened, the sixty-eight-year-old Bettina Brentano von Arnim, wrapped in her sempiternal black. We may picture her as seen in a watercolor of 1854–56, showing her listening to a string quartet in her home and watched over—probably—by the busts of Beethoven and Goethe (Fig. 105). Silently, she observed Schumann's new young Beethovener, Brahms.[676] Schumann actually predicted that Brahms would become "a second Beethoven" in a glowing letter he wrote at that time to his visitor's parents back in Hamburg about their talented son.[677]

Brahms stayed with the Schumanns until early November; three months later the Schumann tragedy began and after his unsuccessful suicide attempt Robert was confined for the last two years of his life in the asylum at Endenich. During this difficult period Johannes was at Clara's side whenever possible and in the early spring of 1854 at Cologne he heard, in her company, Beethoven's *Missa Solemnis* for the first time,[678] and, also for the first time, the Ninth Symphony. The almost devastating impact of this latter work on his own compositions then in progress was acknowledged by the turmoil into which Beethoven's eruptive first movement threw him. Abandoning the idea of a first symphony that he had been sketching (in the same key of D minor as Beethoven's Ninth), he rewrote the work as a sonata for two pianos and only six years later (1860) did it emerge as the emotion-laden Piano Concerto no. 1 in D Minor, op. 15, with its internal references to Robert and Clara Schumann in the first two movements.

"Oh, if only I could teach the important works of Bach, Beethoven, Schumann, Schubert, how pleased I should be,"[679] Johannes wrote Clara wistfully as he took over the lessons of some of her students while she was away on a fund-raising concert tour in Holland. In another report from home to the absent one he told Clara that he was reading Plutarch's *Lives*, as had Shakespeare, and then noted happily, "Beethoven also loved to read Plutarch, and when listening to his music one often imagines that one can see the outline of one of Plutarch's heroes."[680] He could have commented on another similarity in his and Beethoven's reading tastes—Shakespeare. The young bookworm had already bought his own complete set of the English bard, and later he commented on the necessary joys of owning the works of Beethoven and Shakespeare: "For this pair, no youth should have to wait long; but, once he owns them, he need not run rapidly after any others. In these two he has the whole world."[681]

With the greatest excitement Johannes announced to Clara the crowning acquisition in his rapidly growing library: "I have a MS. of Beethoven's!!—a copy of the last A-flat major Sonata (110) with corrections and title written in by his own hand!"[682] This was the germ of what was to become one of Brahms's greatest passions, the acquisition of musical autographs. Exultingly the twenty-two-year-old collector continued in the same letter: "And I also have B.s Eighth Symphony, copied most beautifully, and many things by J. S. Bach and Ph. E. Bach etc."[683] Twenty-one years later he reported to Joachim with no abatement of excitement a very interesting discovery he had just made in connection with Beethoven's Eighth Symphony: "several proofsheets to the oldest score edition (Steiner)," and concluded triumphantly, "Until now nobody knew that Beethoven had corrected this score!"[684]

By the time of his death Brahms's varied and valuable collection of musical holographs and scores (left to the Vienna Gesellschaft der Musikfreunde) included well over a dozen pages from Beethoven's sketchbooks, a page from the conversation booklets with Beethoven's part of the conversation, a letter from Beethoven to the Bonn publisher Simrock, the song "Ich liebe dich," and a copyist's copy of the *Missa Solemnis* with autograph corrections, as well as the collected edition of all of Beethoven's works.[685] To his talented and beautiful former pupil Elisabet von Herzogenberg, Brahms fairly cackled with delight over one of the decade's richest Beethoven finds: "By the way, next to me lie two cantatas by Beethoven [sent to him by Hanslick] which nobody but I knows about (written in 1790 on the death of Josef II. and for Leopold's accession to the throne)."[686] One gloating cackle was not enough for this momentous Beethoven cache; Brahms had also written his adored pupil's husband, the Leipzig-based composer Heinrich von Herzogenberg, about the scores: "Here lying on the table are two cantatas by Beethoven. . . . Certainly no one has set eyes on them for at least 50 years—probably hardly anybody since 1790! Quite recently you could have gotten them at a Leipzig antiquary! The F major theme from the *Leonore* finale comes out of the first one!"[687] The *Cantata on the Death of Emperor Josef II*, discovered for the world in 1884, elicited the following late Romantic musicological judgment from Brahms: "Even if there was no name on the title page none other could be conjectured—it is Beethoven through and through! The beautiful and noble pathos, sublime in its feeling and imagination, the intensity, perhaps violent in its expression, moreover the voice leading and declamation, and in the two outside sections all of the characteristics which we may observe and associate with his later works."[688]

Many of the words Brahms used to characterize Beethoven's music here had been employed by critics to describe his own music—noble, pathos, intensity, violent—and there is little doubt that the younger composer, who would write his own cadenzas to Beethoven's Piano Concertos nos. 3 and 4, identified with his fellow North German. Following in the steps of Beethoven quite literally, and with a deep longing to see the music capital of the world for himself, Brahms had set off for Vienna at the age of twenty-nine in September of 1862. His delighted first impression included an acute awareness of his fellow emigré: "Well this is it! I have established myself here within ten paces of the Prater and can drink my wine where Beethoven drank his."[689] The southern skies and informal manner of the city, so different from his dour, native Hamburg, enchanted him and within a year he had accepted his first post in the city that would become his permanent home. He also quickly made the acquaintance of the musical friends who would form his inner circle for the rest of his life. They in turn sensed a link with Beethoven. "This is Beethoven's heir!"[690] exclaimed the seasoned violinist Joseph Hellmesberger, professor and director of Vienna's Conservatory and leader of a distinguished quartet bearing his name, after rehearsing the two piano quartets Brahms had brought with him from Hamburg (the G Minor Quartet, op. 25, and the A Minor Quartet, op. 26).

Another Conservatory professor whose early acquaintance Brahms made and whom we have already met several times was Gustav Nottebohm, then at work on his first Beethoven sketchbook study (published 1865). With his historical bias and reverence for Beethoven, Brahms was greatly interested in Nottebohm's researches, and helped get them published. But the inveterate prankster in Brahms—a quality not dissimilar to the practical jokester in Beethoven—was not above creating a little Beethoveniana mischief at the expense of the bait-swallowing Nottebohm who was ever on the lookout for new sketchbook pages of the master. Knowing that the professor was in the habit of buying his cold evening meal from a certain cheese and sausage vendor in the Prater, Brahms went to elaborate advance preparations, fabricating a most convincing-looking sheet of old music paper upon which, in Beethoven's unmistakable scrawl, a musical theme was crabbily worked out. The food vendor was brought into the plot, and the portion of cheese destined for Nottebohm's consumption was casually wrapped in the old paper. Brahms and his friends had to keep straight faces as they watched the scholar peer in mounting excitement at the cheese wrapping under a lamppost, then carefully fold and pocket it without a word, bolting down his cheese in convulsive but deathly silent gulps.[691]

A third important friend whom Brahms met soon after his arrival in the Austro-Hungarian capital was that approving reviewer of Clara Schumann's 1856 Beethoven piano performances in Vienna, the almighty defender of musical conservatism and foe of program music and Music of the Future, Eduard Hanslick

(Fig. 107). He had already favorably reviewed a November 1862 performance of Brahms's D Major Serenade for Orchestra op. 11, and by February of the next year he lined up the acquiescent composer-performer as pianist for a lecture he was delivering on Beethoven illustrated by the great Sonata in C Minor, op. 111. If Hanslick associated Brahms as a pianist with Beethoven, this was nothing compared with the great link in the Beethovenian chain that he espied in Brahms as composer in his First Symphony, the Vienna premiere of which (17 December 1876) he reviewed in elated and partisan tones that followed Schumann's prophecy of a second Beethoven coming:

> Seldom, if ever, has the entire musical world awaited a composer's first symphony with such tense anticipation—testimony that the unusual was expected of Brahms in this supreme and ultimately difficult form. . . . Even the layman will immediately recognize it as one of the most individual and magnificent works of the symphonic literature. . . . The fourth movement begins most significantly with an adagio in C minor; from darkening clouds the song of the woodland horn rises clear and sweet above the tremolo of the violins. All hearts tremble with the fiddles in anticipation. The entrance of the Allegro with its simple, beautiful theme, reminiscent of the 'Ode to Joy' in the Ninth Symphony, is overpowering as it rises onward and upward, right to the end.
>
> If I say that no composer has come so close to the style of the late Beethoven as Brahms in this finale, I don't mean it as a paradoxical pronouncement but rather as a simple statement of indisputable fact. . . . He doesn't imitate, but what he creates from his innermost being is similarly felt. Thus Brahms recalls Beethoven's symphonic style not only in his individually spiritual and suprasensual expression, but [in] the beautiful breadth of his melodies, the daring and originality of his modulations, and his sense of polyphonic structure, but also—and above all—in the manly and noble seriousness of the whole.[692]

Here it is again, the virtue of seriousness, so dear to the heart of the latter-day Romantics—fed on Biedermeier propriety—replacing the "sublime" aspect of former interpretation. Beethoven (with Brahms in tow) is advanced along the track from sublimity to seriousness, and the (effeminate) unburdening of earlier, self-confessional Romanticism (Schumann, Berlioz) now gives way to forebearing manliness. All of this leads to Hanslick's next and most important point: "It has been said of Beethoven's music that one of its chief characteristics is an ethical element that would rather convince than charm. . . . This strong ethical character of Beethoven's music, which is serious even in merriment, and betrays a soul dedicated to the eternal, is also decisively evident in Brahms. In the latter's newest works there is even a good deal of the late Beethoven's darker side."[693]

"Beethoven's darker side"? "Serious even in merriment"? Is this really all the Viennese public hoped to see in their Beethoven doppelgänger? No, there was one element missing. Like a true subject of Franz Josef's frivolous realm, Hanslick (who was on "Du" terms with Brahms) delivers one monitory word before his final, jubilant judgment: "Brahms seems to favor too one-sidedly the great and the serious, the difficult and the complex, and at the expense of sensuous beauty. [A capital sin of omission in the capital of wine, women, and song!] . . . The new symphony of Brahms is a possession of which the nation may be proud. . . ."[694]

For one important perception of Brahms's Beethoven, we may briefly take up Hanslick's reviews (of which Brahms read every word) of the next three symphonies composed by the transplanted Hamburg musician, for the manes of Beethoven descends upon each essay.

In addressing Brahms's Second Symphony (premiered 30 December 1877 in Vienna with Hans Richter [1843–1916] conducting), Hanslick, the Beckmesser of Wagner's *Meistersinger* and the man who had in Wagner's stinging words "gracefully hidden [his] Jewish origin,"[695] struck back, laying low the Bayreuth Wagner-Liszt mystique while elevating the Vienna Beethoven–Brahms constellation:

> Richard Wagner and his disciples go so far as to deny not only the possibility of writing symphonies after Beethoven but also the justification for the existence of purely instrumental music altogether. The symphony is alleged to have become superfluous since Wagner transplanted it into the opera. The utmost concession is to admit the contemporary viability of Liszt's "symphonic poems," in one movement and with specific poetic programmes. This nonsensical theory has been cooked up for the domestic requirements of the Wagner-Liszt household. If any further contradiction is needed, there is none more brilliant than the long succession of Brahms's instrumental works, and particularly this Second Symphony.[696]

For the Third Symphony (premiered 2 December 1883 in Vienna) Hanslick takes his cue from an epithet endowed upon it by Richter and makes a nostalgic all-Beethoven comparison with the three Brahms symphonies: "Hans Richter, in a gracious toast, recently christened the new symphony 'Eroica.' Actually, if one were to call Brahms's first symphony the 'Appassionata' and the second the 'Pastoral,' then the new symphony might well be called the 'Eroica.' . . . It repeats neither the unhappy fatalism of the first, nor the cheerful idyll of the second; its foundation is self-confident, rough and ready strength. . . . Its musical characteristics recall the healthy soundness of Beethoven's second period, never the eccentricities of his last."[697]

Finally, in his review of the new Fourth Symphony (first Vienna performance 17 January 1886 under Richter), Hanslick cuts the loose umbilical cord of parallelism with one hand while grafting a tauter, spiritual one with the other: "Manly strength, unbending consistency, an earnestness bordering on acerbity . . . constitute the decisive factors. In the new symphony they create their own form and their own language. Independent of any direct model, they nowhere deny their ideal relation to Beethoven, a factor incomparably more obvious with Brahms than with Mendelssohn and Schumann."[698]

If Brahms was to remain forever tied—somehow—to Beethoven in the stereoscopic vision of Hanslick (the man whom Verdi called the "Bismarck della critica musicale"[699]), this was not the only instance of a critic's continued yoking of the two composers to the same symphonic cart. Back in Brahms's hometown the music critic of the *Hamburger Corespondent*, Josef Sittard, reviewed a 9 April 1886 performance of the Fourth Symphony with Brahms at the podium as follows: "Today we abide by what we have affirmed for years past in musical journals; that Brahms is the greatest instrumental composer since Beethoven. Power, passion, depth of thought, exalted nobility of melody and form, are the qualities which form the artistic sign manual of his creations."[700] Fourteen years before the new century was to begin, then, the Romantic attributes of passion, profundity, and exaltation were still highly valued, whether in Beethoven or Hamburg's surrogate.

The same service Hanslick accorded Brahms by giving him widespread, benign attention in print was extended on a different level by a friend who gave Brahms's musical coinage wide distribution through performances of his orchestral works in Germany and Holland. This was Bülow, in his role as conductor; especially during the years 1880–85, when, as director of the Meiningen court orchestra (whose fame he created), he offered Brahms the chance to try out his new symphonic works. He had met Brahms fleetingly as early as 1854 in Hanover, but became a convert after the publication of the First Symphony in 1877. Recognizing in it the "heir of Luigi [Cherubini] and Ludwig,"[701] he wrote the famous words, repetition of which would haunt Brahms's ascent in the musical world, about his acquaintance with the " 'tenth' symphony, alias the *first* symphony of Johannes Brahms. . . . "[702] There is a sense of Wagnerian rebound in Bülow's immediate ranking of his new discovery: "after Bach and Beethoven he [Brahms] is the greatest, the most exalted of all composers."[703] From this came the insight that inspired Bülow's popular three Bs proposal: "I believe it is not without the intelligence of chance that Bach, Beethoven and Brahms are in alliteration."[704] From now on Brahms's First Symphony was looked upon as the legitimate heir to Beethoven's nine symphonies (much to the dismay of Bruckner fans), and "Bs" in music meant Bach, Beethoven, and Brahms, not Berlioz or Bruckner.

The general public had no doubt about which of the three great Bs it would be hearing at the September 1895 music festival in Meiningen (under the direction of Fritz Steinbach), which had taken Bülow's motto as its title. Brahms's First Symphony and his Double Concerto were performed on the same program as Beethoven's Piano Concerto no. 5; his *Song of Triumph* with Bach's *Saint Matthew Passion* and Beethoven's *Missa Solemnis*. Even Johann Strauss, Jr. (1825–1899) (Fig. 106), felt the invisible "link" between Beethoven and his good friend Brahms. He responded musically and completely characteristically by dedicating to Brahms his op. 443 (1892), a waltz inspired by Beethoven's use of Schiller's "Ode to Joy" and entitled *Seid umschlungen, Millionen* (*Be Embraced, Ye Millions*). (Bülow in turn "sensed" Beethovenian illumination in Strauss: "From his performances one can learn things for the Ninth Symphony and for the *Pathétique*.")[705]

Brahms's own modesty prevented him from making the same Beethoven associations as the enthusiastic Bülow, but the two things he most admired about his famous North German predecessor were qualities of which one he possessed in full and the other he relentlessly pursued. Responding to a question put to him as to whom he considered the perfect type of creative genius, his unhesitating answer was: "Beethoven. He had lofty inspirations, and at the same time he was an indefatigable worker."[706] This essential assessment could have been derived solely from Beethoven's music, of course, especially since through Nottebohm's studies Brahms became more and more familiar with the labored sketchbook processes, but we know that Brahms took steps to acquaint himself with Beethoven the man, his character, his habits, his sayings. As early as 1856 he was already discussing the biographical *Notizen* on Beethoven by Wegeler and Ries with Clara Schumann, responding to an apparent comment from her that Beethoven's two friends should have been more discreet about his foibles (Schindler's old complaint): " . . . but what would become of all historical research and biographies if undertaken with an eye to the susceptibilities of the subject?"[707] Commenting possibly on Beethoven as the rule-breaker of music, Brahms is supposed to have said with approval, "It would have been possible for Beethoven to become a great criminal."[708] He frequently *did* quote Beethoven's supposed slogan "The contrary is probably just as true," in contented explanation of his own—unpopular with his friends—instinctive habit of contradiction.[709]

Certainly on one unusual occasion Brahms briefly experienced not the hope, but the fear that he might become like Beethoven. Not the musician but the man beset by deafness! Summering at his beloved Bad Ischl retreat in July of 1880, during a period of heavy rain storms, he was afflicted with a mild ear inflammation that affected his hearing. Extremely worried, and obviously with the image of the stricken Beethoven before him, he sent an urgent telegram to his doctor friend in Vienna, Theodor Billroth (1829–1894), the eminent North German surgeon and active amateur musician with whom he was on intimate terms, and then precipitously showed up at his house while the family was still at their noonday meal. So great was the composer's agitation that Billroth personally escorted him to an ear specialist, who diagnosed the trouble for what it was, promising no dread aftereffects. Mythmakers got hold of the incident however and a short notice about the Beethoven-fate scare appeared in the newspapers, forcing Brahms to reassure his friends that all was well.[710]

A more joyous image of Beethoven came for both Brahms and Billroth when the latter found out that his house was once owned by the physician Johann Peter Frank (1745–1821), director of Vienna's General Hospital and professor of medicine at Vienna University, to whom Beethoven had once come for advice concerning his progressive deafness. This happy discovery had special relevance, as Billroth explained: ''Beethoven came into the house where there were often musical affairs. . . . The interesting thing to me, however, is that Johann Peter Frank and Beethoven developed a friendship in my home and that such a friendship—let us for once be arrogant—is carried on in this house between you and myself, almost a hundred years later.''[711] How ready the latter-day Frank was to believe in this Beethoven story with its appealing parallel to his own friendship with Brahms! They would have both been disappointed to read Beethoven's own words on the subject, penned in the famous letter to Wegeler in which he revealed his deafness to his old physician friend from Bonn days: ''Frank tried to *tone up* my constitution with strengthening medicines and my hearing with almond oil, but much good did it do me! His treatment had no effect, my deafness became even worse and my abdomen continued to be in the same state as before.''[712]

That Billroth was irresistibly drawn to making comparisons between Beethoven and Brahms—not always to Brahms's advantage—was inadvertently revealed to Brahms by Hanslick, who in a pre-Freudian slip included the indiscreet statement along with a packet of letters to him from Billroth about Brahms's music to the composer. ''He is often offensively rough to his friends like Beethoven, and is as little able as Beethoven was to free himself entirely from the effects of a neglected education.''[713] These were the words Brahms's eyes gazed upon in the bundle of Billroth letters. The one-sided chill during the last few years of their relationship was never explained by Brahms to Billroth, and yet there were many points of legitimate comparison besides the unstable environment of their youth that Billroth and other friends of Brahms made about Beethoven and Brahms, occasionally to Brahms's face. Both did indeed have a bearish side (Bülow actually called Brahms a ''bear''), were blunt, even wounding in conversation, were great walkers, receiving musical inspiration on their long, isolated walks, and both never married. Such parallels (even their mutual love for strong coffee) were common talk, almost a point of pride with the Viennese, and from similarities in conduct arose the unlikely but fixed notion of similarity in looks. Brahms's later biographer Florence May,[714] who as a young girl went to Baden-Baden in 1871 to study with Clara Schumann, frequently met the still clean-shaven Brahms in her teacher's home and wrote that the impression of intense mental concentration he conveyed was ''accentuated by a constant habit he had of thrusting the rather thick underlip over the upper, and keeping it compressed there, reminding one of the mouth in some of the portraits of Beethoven."[715] May was not the only one to think of the physical image of Beethoven in connection with Brahms. The singer-composer-conductor Georg Henschel (1850–1934), who became closely acquainted with Brahms in 1875, described him on vacation in the island of Rügen (Billroth's birthplace): "He walks about here just as he pleases, generally with his waistcoat unbuttoned and his hat in his hand, always with clean linen, but without collar or necktie. These he dons at the *table d'hôte* only. His whole appearance vividly recalls some of the portraits of Beethoven."[716]

Whether or not Brahms himself subscribed to any of these look-alike Beethoven impressions purveyed by his friends, he did once react with great emotion at the unexpected sight of his own painted effigy next to that of Beethoven. The occasion was the opening concert (October 1895) of the recently built Tonhalle in Zurich, in which his *Song of Triumph* was coupled on the program with Beethoven's Ninth. Seated in the new concert hall, the sixty-two-year-old composer was observed to weep silently as, glancing up at the ceiling painting, he saw the image of himself looking respectfully over the shoulder of Beethoven (Fig. 108). Wagner stood to Beethoven's left, facing Bach and other composers of the classical past. It is tempting to think that at least one of the three Bs was pleased. Upon Brahms's death two years later, the city of Vienna created its own permanent juxtaposition of Beethoven and Brahms: across from the graves of Beethoven and Schubert, the final remains of Johannes Brahms—that latter-day Beethoven—were laid to rest in the musician's part of the great Central Cemetery's Honor Graves.[717]

Chapter Five

THE THREE-DIMENSIONAL BEETHOVEN

Soon after the death of Brahms in April 1897, an engaging silhouette fantasy depicting the special heaven reserved for musicians (Fig. 109) was published. It was an instant sentimental success. In the upper level, where joyous putti romp, we see Brahms's two musical Bs, with Bach holding forth at the organ while to his left Beethoven holds up a titanic fist in approving response. Next to Beethoven is the slight figure of Mozart and to Bach's right are Wagner (characteristically diverting Bach's attention to himself), a dignified Weber, and, playing a toy kettle drum held up to him by a cherub, Haydn. Far below, on the lower left, the newest heavenly arrival—Brahms—is being greeted by his old friend Robert Schumann (this musicians' paradise seems to be reserved for males), who in turn looks back towards a row of already established inhabitants with, in ascending order, Bruckner, Mendelssohn, Schubert, Liszt, Bülow, Berlioz, Gluck, and Handel. Several members of this celestial ensemble were actually present at the earthly festivity accompanying the unveiling of the first major sculptural monument dedicated to Beethoven—Bonn's Beethoven memorial of 1845—and it is to the three-dimensional Beethoven that our mythmaking study now takes us. The Tone Hero had become larger than life, and so the art of sculpture was called in to endow the monumental proportions proper to the mighty image of Beethoven.

The decade of the 1840s had begun auspiciously for the erection of monuments honoring musicians: in 1842 the Mozart memorial in Salzburg's Mozartplatz was unveiled, and the very next year, due largely to Mendelssohn's persistence, the Bach monument outside the Thomaskirche in Leipzig was dedicated in an impressive ceremony. Plans for a Beethoven memorial in Bonn had been under way for a number of years, but had progressed only slowly and with interruptions, attended by the usual amount of human error, intrigue, and gaffes that such projects seem to attract. A musicologist-composer of indifferent talent but burning Beethoven fever, Heinrich Carl Breidenstein (1796–1876)—music director at the University of Bonn—had proposed that the city honor its native son as early as

1828, a year after Beethoven's death. A rampant outbreak of cholera postponed public attention temporarily, but a few years later a Beethoven monument committee was formed, with the respected August Wilhelm Schlegel[1] of Shakespearean translation fame as president (a position Breidenstein took over upon Schlegel's death in Bonn on 12 May 1845). By 17 December 1835 an international appeal for funds was circulated with the backing of the future king of Prussia, Friedrich Wilhelm IV (who succeeded to the throne in 1840), and the art-loving King Ludwig I of Bavaria. Considering that ten more years were to slip by before the Bonn campaign bore fruit, the city of Vienna had ample time to beat its rival to the monumental punch, but, as Schindler had scornfully remarked, neither a museum nor a good oil portrait of Beethoven was to be found in the city of his master's death. In the snails' race for a Beethoven Denkmal it would be a victory for the North Germans over the Austrians, for Vienna did not come up with a major monument until 1880—a brooding Michelangelesque image to which we shall return.

The illustrious name of Liszt was joined to the Bonn committee's flagging efforts, with gratifying material results, in the fall of 1839, but Schumann was apparently the first to link music with money on behalf of the memorial when, as we have seen, he informed his publisher in 1836 that all copies of his *Phantasie*, op. 17, were to be sold in aid of the Bonn memorial. That same year Charles Hallé attended two all-Beethoven summer concerts on behalf of the monument given by the Court Orchestra at Darmstadt. The next year, 1837, Sir George Smart (1776–1867) (Fig. 110), Beethoven's loyal English promoter, who had visited the composer in person in 1825 to confer about the tempi of the Ninth, participated in a concert given in London on 19 July in aid of the Beethoven momument.[2] The diary he kept of his attendance at the Bonn unveiling ceremonies is a wonderfully Victorian as well as informative document of the event and we shall take up Sir George's account shortly.

The twenty-seven-year-old Liszt's attention was drawn to the plight of the Bonn committee by a newspaper report in which the paltry sums raised by each country so far were given. France had only contributed 424 francs and 90 centimes (Liszt would later personally contribute 10,000 francs towards the monument, pay for the foreign press passes out of his own pocket when the Bonn committee "overlooked" this cost, and underwrite the construction of a special auditorium for the event). Shocked at the shabby French showing—"such a niggardly almsgiving,"[3] he wrote Berlioz indignantly—he became obsessed with the idea of saving the campaign. After prudently checking out the going rate for marble monuments with his friend the Tuscan sculptor Lorenzo Bartolini (1777–1850), who had done a fine, almost wartless bust of him the year before and whose fame in Italy was second only to that of the late Canova, Liszt wrote the Bonn committee, magnanimously offering to supply the funds still needed for the monument. Only one condition was stipulated: that the commission go to Bartolini. Here is the letter that took the despairing committee by such delightful surprise:

Pisa, 3 October 1839

Gentlemen:
    As the subscription for Beethoven's monument is only getting on slowly, and as the carrying out of this undertaking seems to be rather distant, I venture to make a proposal to you, the acceptance of which would make me very happy. I offer myself to make up, from my own means, the sum still wanting for the erection of the monument, and ask no other privilege than that of naming the

artist who shall execute the work. That artist is Bartolini of Florence, who is universally considered the first sculptor in Italy.

I have spoken to him about the matter provisionally, and he assures me that a monument in marble (which would cost about fifty to sixty thousand francs) could be finished in two years, and he is ready to begin the work at once. I have the honor to be, etc.,

Franz Liszt[4]

Bartolini's name was not unknown to the Bonn organizers. In fact it was too well known as being associated exclusively with Italy and France (as a young man Bartolini had been discovered by Napoleon and sent to Carrara in 1808 to establish a school for sculptors). True, he had sculpted marble busts of musicians and other notables (Cherubini and Rossini; also Byron, Madame de Staël, Napoleon, and Ingres), but how did that qualify him for approaching the countenance of the Great German? In other words, Bartolini was a foreigner. That Liszt was also a foreigner did not seem to trouble the committee by one centime as they affixed their signatures to a wily response, which evidently took two months to concoct (it is dated December 1839) and which, while graciously accepting Liszt's financial aid and *appearing* to accept the marble maestro Bartolini, ingeniously threw up two irksome roadblocks, one of metal, the other of competitive reputation:

> But, sir, we are compelled to point out to you that very serious considerations have determined us to prefer, for the construction of the statue, bronze to marble . . . forced as we are to erect the monument in one of the public squares of this town, where we could not shelter it from the weather and other damage. We do not doubt that you, sir, as well as M. Bartolini, will share our opinion about this, all the more so as M. Bartolini is taking charge not only of the making of the model (in connection with which we reserve only our approval) [*only*?] but also of the casting and every other aspect of the construction. It is also in this way that, recently, M. Thorvaldsen [the Danish-born sculptor had been one of Eusebius-Schumann's candidates for a Beethoven monument] enriched Germany with several bronze monuments, among others the town of Mainz with that of Gutenberg, and as, according to the opinion of experts, the cost of a monument in bronze is not greater than that of a similar work in marble . . . we are persuaded, sir, that in every respect you will approve our reflections.[5]

Bonn's cunning committee guessed correctly that the busy Bartolini would not care to spend months in a foundry, and no more was heard about the Italian intervention. In the meantime Liszt had already impetuously initiated his series of six fund-raising Beethoven memorial concerts in Vienna, given in November and early December 1839, for which he earned the approving epithet Protector of Beethoven already noted. The time gap and news of Liszt's activities enabled the Bonn committee to add an astonishing paragraph to their belated December letter of acceptance: ''The sum that we have at our disposal at the moment amounts to about 40,000 francs, and would no doubt be further augmented if your generous proposition had not been known so early and so widely.''[6] Liszt, with characteristic mildness, seems to have ignored the insulting boners of the Bonn burghers who seemed constitutionally inclined to bite the hand that fed them. While they went on to appoint a consulting committee of (German) experts, including the highly respected artist Wilhelm von Schadow (1788–1862), son of the sculptor Gottfried Schadow (1764–1850) and director of the Düsseldorf Academy, Liszt, after pausing to pose for Danhauser's portrayal of him playing Beethoven, carried his Beethoven campaign to Paris and London. On 26 April 1841 he joined forces with Berlioz at the Conservatoire to give a fund-raising concert (the one attended by Wagner) for the Bonn memorial. He reflected on the success of his "commentary" coda ("almost as long") to Beethoven's *Adelaïde*: "I played it all without being hissed [by the Beethoven purists] at the concert given at the Paris Conservatoire for the Beethoven monument, and I intend to play it in London, and in Germany and Russia."[7] In an honest, if not modest self-assessment, he concluded: "My two concerts *alone*, and especially the third at the Conservatoire, for the Beethoven monument, are concerts out of the ordinary run, such as *I only* can give in Europe at the present moment."[8] He was right.

The year 1841, which brought the two-volume large-print translation of Schindler's Beethoven biography to the English-reading public, saw a plea for funds at the end of the book by its famous editor, Moscheles, on behalf of the Bonn Beethoven monument. After alluding to a concert in aid of the monument held in Drury Lane Theater on 19 July 1837, and to the "generous donation of 10,000 francs from Liszt,"[9] Moscheles announced exciting news from Bonn: "The Committee has already [October 1840] issued an address to artists, inviting them to send designs for the Monument before the 1st of March, 1841. From among the designs or sketches that shall be received, the three best will be selected by competent judges.... The competition is open to artists of all countries [except Italy?].... It is decided that the Monument, or rather the statue, which is to form the most essential part of it, shall be executed, not in marble, but in bronze."[10]

One of the designs that came in as a result of this international call was by the popular Berlin sculptor Johann Friedrich Drake (1805–1882), a favorite of the new king, Friedrich Wilhelm IV, and creator of the recent (1836) colossal statue of the German historian and political figure Justus Möser (1720–1794) for Osnabrück. Drake's design (Fig. 111), handsomely converted into a presentation lithograph by his friend the artist Adolph Menzel (1815–1905), envisioned another colossal effigy. Dressed in a nondescript garment stretching tightly across the upper body and falling in togalike folds across the knees, a giant Beethoven sits holding a giant open score, his head literally and ludicrously cocked to the heavens, while his left leg slips off the circular pedestal. Below, life-size female figures holding musical objects (a long pipe or recorder, a curved horn, a music scroll, and a violin and bow) stand on their own hexagonal pedestal, which is raised aloft by a solid four-stepped plinth. The static ensemble has been placed in situ by the helpful Menzel, who provides a broad view of the Rhine, in accordance with one of the sites proposed for the memorial, an area in front of Bonn's old customs house overlooking the Rhine.

Drake's seated Beethoven project had been designed as early as 1837. Even earlier, in 1836, the sculptor had exhibited two designs for a standing statue of Beethoven at Berlin's Royal Academy of Arts. The small plaster model for one of the versions is known through an old photograph (Fig. 112). A meaty-looking Beethoven, with pendant jowels, looks up alertly from a thick score upon which he lightly rests the outspread fingers of his right hand. Drake has attempted to avoid the age-old quandary of whether to show a historical figure in correct contemporary dress and surround or in a timeless sphere of nonspecific (hence frequently neoclassical) garb and ground. His standing Beethoven is an awkward mix of an almost involuntarily indicated frock coat and trousers with a providential massive mantel that does its serpentine best to swaddle its bearer in classical folds.

Neither a beefy standing burgher nor a seated classical-scholar type with Rhine maidens in tow was what the Bonn committee was looking for, however, and Drake's entries were passed over. The competition results were announced on 10 February 1842. The winner was almost an unknown: Ernst Julius Hähnel (1811–1891) of Dresden. Not quite thirty-one, he had made the obligatory Italian study sojourn and had found some initial success in Munich, where he was befriended by Moritz von Schwind,[11] future creator of the Beethoven-studded *Lachner Roll* (see Fig. 60), and the architect Gottfried Semper (1803–1879), destined to be commissioned by Ludwig II to design a festival theater for the performance of Wagner operas in Munich (1864; project not carried out). Hähnel had only a few sculptures to his credit—an effigy of Homer for Munich's state library, standing figures of Perugino and Poussin for the Alte Pinakothek there, and for the facade of the new Hoftheater in Dresden the niche busts of Aristophanes, Sophocles, Shakespeare, and Molière. Certainly not the track record of a Bartolini, but he was *German*. We shall have the opportunity to examine his winning Beethoven conception when we attend, through several eyewitness accounts, the unveiling of the monument—a date the Bonn committee proposed as 6 August 1843 (portentously coinciding with what would be the celebration of the Thousand Year Reich), but which young Hähnel in his contract prudently postponed for another two years to August 1845.

In the meantime, as a consolation prize and heavy-handed compliment to Liszt, the Bonn committee invited the Protector of Beethoven to compose a special work for the musical offerings that would accompany the festival marking the monument's unveiling, and Breidenstein, who had extended the invitation, resolved to do likewise—a decision that would later provide one of the low moments of the ceremony. Liszt began to wax enthusiastically over the idea of contributing music as well as money to the Bonn event and settled on the idea of a cantata.[12] The text, supplied by one O. L. B. Wolff, inspired Liszt to score his first large-scale work for soloists, chorus, and orchestra, and by April 1845 he announced with satisfaction: "I expect to go to Bonn in the month of July, for the inauguration of the Beethoven Monument, and to have a Cantata performed there which I have written for this occasion. The text, at any rate, is tolerably new; it is a sort of Magnificat of human Genius conquered by God in the eternal revelation through time and space,—a text which might apply equally well to Goethe or Raphael or Columbus, as to Beethoven."[13]

Liszt did indeed go to the Rhineland in July and began holding weekly rehearsals of his cantata, commuting from the home of friends in Cologne, and conveniently missing a number of Breidenstein's tedious committee meetings. The English contingent started arriving early in the second week of August and included some Beethoven admirers met with earlier in this mythography, such as George Hogarth (critic for *Harmonicon*), Henry Chorley (critic for the *Athenaeum* who had cited Beethoven and Shakespeare in the same breath), Ignaz Moscheles (now fifty-one and a director of the London Philharmonic, which he had conducted in rousing performances of the Ninth in 1837 and 1838[14]), and, most important for our eyewitness account of the events, Sir George Smart. One more most auspicious visitor from England was expected for the day of the unveiling: Queen Victoria. The twenty-six-year-old monarch would be making her first trip to the continent since her accession to the throne, and she was bringing her beloved consort with her. It was a sentimental journey for Prince Albert of Saxe-Coburg and Gotha, for he was going to be able to show his wife all the sites of his childhood and youth, including Bonn, where he had briefly studied. The dedication of the Beethoven memorial was but one item on their agenda, but they would attend the event with their hosts, King Friedrich Wilhelm IV of Prussia and his wife, Queen Elisabeth.

The prospect of ogling two sets of royal couples had filled Bonn's modest hotel resources to the limit, and many foreigners who arrived at the last minute found no lodgings. During the three official days of the festival (which began on 10 August 1845, a Sunday) a number of notables from the music world were observed to be present, of which a partial list was compiled by Berlioz, his reporter's eye alert to the task.[15] Names familiar to us from our mythopoetic researches are: from Berlin, Giacomo Meyerbeer, Ludwig Rellstab (he who upon meeting Beethoven in 1825 had asked himself, "Yet why should Beethoven's features look like his scores?"), and Jenny Lind; from Vienna, Karl Holz (Schindler's rival for Beethoven's affections from 1825); from Kassel, Ludwig Spohr; from Aachen, Anton Schindler himself; from Paris, Charles Hallé (who made the trip with Berlioz), François Joseph Fétis (Berlioz's persecutor in print for many years), and Maurice Schlesinger (publisher of Wagner's *A Pilgrimage to Beethoven* fantasy); from Brussels, Marie Pleyel (Berlioz's former inamorata); and "from everywhere," as Berlioz charmingly put it, "Franz Liszt, the soul of the celebration."[16]

Commenting on this "nearly Europe-wide meeting," Berlioz explained his use of a qualifier: "I say nearly, because of the predictable and understandable absence of musicians from Italy"[17]—an accurate indication of the lack of any emergence of a Beethoven cult in that country still attuned to bel canto. Berlioz's attention focused next on those conspicuous by their *absence* (we may already have wondered about a few of them ourselves) as he wrote tactfully but specifically: "Among the composers and leading conductors whose absence from Bonn astonished everyone, and whom surely only serious reasons can have kept away, are: Messrs Spontini . . . Auber, Ambroise Thomas, Habeneck, Benedict, Mendelssohn, Marschner . . . R. Wagner . . . Ferdinand Hiller, Schumann[18] . . . Louis Schlösser [the man who remembered Beethoven's "snow-white teeth" sixty-three years after encountering them] . . . Glinka . . . Nicolai . . . the brothers Lachner. . . ."[19]

The noticeable absence of members of what some saw as the Leipzig clique—Mendelssohn, Schumann, and Hiller—seemed to express the discomfort felt at that aspect of Liszt the showman about which they had indeed expressed private reservations. Berlioz neglected to mention that Chopin was not present and it is certainly true that Liszt's tendency to self-dramatize and assume center stage irked the Polish-French musician. Here are some rather sullen, long-distance observations about the Beethoven festival written to Chopin's family that year both before and after the event:

[20 July 1845] Also I have received an invitation from the committee which is to put up a monument to Beethoven (at Bonn on the Rhine), to come for the inauguration. You can guess how likely I am to go. . . . Franchomme [Chopin's cellist friend] writes that Habenek [sic] is going to Bonn for that inauguration, that Liszt has written a cantata, which will be sung, with Liszt conducting. Spohr will conduct a big concert, which will be given in the evening; three days' music.[20]

[1 October 1845] Liszt is to call out the hurrahs in Bonn, where the Beethoven monument is to be placed, and where also the crowned heads are expected. In

Bonn they are selling cigars; véritables cigarres à la Beethoven, who probably smoked nothing but Viennese pipes; and there has already been such a sale of old bureaus and old desks which belonged to Beethoven, that the poor composer *de la symphonie pastorale* would have had to drive a huge trade in furniture.[21]

Chopin's sarcastic remarks on the commercial aspects of mythmaking found corroboration in Sir George Smart's experiences in Bonn during the festivities. With veiled disapproval he reported of Karl Holz (whom he had already met in Vienna in the company of Beethoven): "He has a MS. work of Beethoven's called *The Dervishes* [from *The Ruins of Athens*, op. 113], and wishes to sell Beethoven's violin & viola which he gave to Mr. Holz."[22] It would be interesting to know how many "Beethoven manuscripts" and "Beethoven violins" were sold at Bonn during the month of August that year!

Another Beethoven-related celebrity about whose absence Berlioz forgot to wonder was Carl Czerny—Beethoven's pupil and the teacher of Liszt. In August 1845 Czerny would only have been fifty-four, but his general physical frailty and aversion to excitement would not have inclined him to leave Vienna for anything so crowd-jostling as the Bonn ceremonies were bound to be. (Professional pickpockets from France and England attended the affair, doing extremely well according to the complaints registered by their victims.)

Berlioz *had* noted that Wagner was missing from the ceremonies honoring the hero of *A Pilgrimage to Beethoven*. This strange nonattendance is explained not so much by Wagner's sometimes shaky relationship with Spohr, who had been given such a prominent role as principal conductor of the Bonn concerts,[23] as, probably, simply by his exhaustion and the need to recuperate from a strenuous Dresden musical season. His doctor had ordered him to rest and to take the waters. In July and August 1845 he was following the second half of this prescription at Marienbad, while also feverishly sketching out the libretto to *Die Meistersinger* in order to escape the compulsion to write another serious work that had him in its thrall—*Lohengrin*. That he knew however exactly what was going on at Bonn, and even precisely when (Chopin had been vague about the actual date, as we have just seen), can be demonstrated by a remarkable letter he wrote to Liszt—whom at that time he barely knew—from Marienbad on 5 August 1845 while the recipient was in the thick of rehearsing his Beethoven cantata and averting the daily disasters besetting the somnambulistic committee of Breidenstein, who had suddenly realized that an influx of some five thousand people was about to descend upon drowsy Bonn. Given the pressure of last-minute preparations—something about which Kapellmeister Wagner did have some knowledge—Wagner's letter to Liszt is truly presumptuous:

Dear Sir,

At last you are within safe reach of me, and I take this long-desired opportunity to gain you, as far as is in my power, for our scheme of celebrating Weber's memory by a worthy monument to be erected in Dresden. You are just on the point of crowning your important participation in the erection of the Beethoven monument; you are for that purpose surrounded by the most important musicians of our time, and in consequence are in the very element most favorable to the enterprise which of late has been resumed chiefly through my means. As no doubt you heard at the time, we have transferred Weber's remains to the earth of his German home. [Weber, wasted by tuberculosis, had died during the night of 4–5 June 1826 in London at the home of Sir George

Smart. Eighteen years later his body was brought back to German soil; at Hamburg the Funeral March from the *Eroica* was played as his remains were placed in a small boat for the trip up the Elbe to Dresden, where Wagner was waiting with a band of wind instruments to lead a torchlight procession to the cemetery.] We have had a site for the intended monument assigned to us close to our beautiful Dresden theater, and a commencement towards the necessary funds has been made. . . . These funds, however, I need scarcely mention, have to be increased considerably if something worthy is to be achieved. . . . *A good deal of this care I should like to leave to you* [italics mine], not, you may believe me, from idleness, but because I feel convinced that the voice of a poor German composer of operas . . . is much too feeble to be counted of importance for anything in the world.[24]

The mind reels at Wagner's excessive and uncharacteristic humility and even more so at the gross insensitivity of his timing. Liszt had in fact no spare time to devote to extracurricular mythmaking just then. Four weeks before the Beethoven Festival was to begin, Breidenstein and his inept committee had noticed that Bonn lacked a proper auditorium for the announced three days of gala concerts. All seemed lost until Liszt proposed that a special Beethoven Hall be constructed immediately; still the torpid committee did not move. Liszt declared himself ready to bear the costs; the committee acquiesced. The same architect who was engaged to complete Cologne Cathedral was consulted and, filled with nationalist enthusiasm for the linking of Beethoven and Bonn, he and a team of builders working round the clock improvised a three-thousand-seat, three-hundred-foot-long, oblong auditorium in eleven days—possibly the greatest accomplishment of the entire festival. The wooden building was ready on 9 August, one day before the opening concert (the rehearsals for which had been held in the arena of the local riding school).

Fortunately Breidenstein had given advance thought to assembling the musical performers. A choir of 343 singers and an orchestra of 162 players were brought together for the occasion. (This, after Liszt vetoed the committee's penny-pinching suggestion that they not hire any woodwind or brass players.) Prominent instrumentalists from England, Belgium, Holland, and France joined the orchestral ranks and leading the thirteen double-bass section was the fabled Domenico Dragonetti (1763–1846) from London, then eighty-two years old and still considered the greatest player of his instrument the world had ever known. In his youth he had become friends with both Haydn and Beethoven: the Venetian-born musician was in Vienna in 1799 and again in 1808–9 (Napoleon dreamed of taking him to Paris by force). The following Beethoven-Dragonetti anecdote had long since entered into the Beethoven myth repertoire, and here it is, as it must have been reverently circulated during the Bonn festival: "Beethoven had been told that his new friend could execute violoncello music upon his huge instrument, and one morning, when Dragonetti called at his room, he expressed his desire to hear a sonata. The contrabass was sent for, and the Sonata, No. 2, of Op. 5, was selected. Beethoven played his part, with his eyes immovably fixed upon his companion, and, in the finale, where the arpeggios occur, was so delighted and excited that at the close he sprang up and threw his arms around both player and instrument."[25]

Berlioz would not neglect to mention old Dragonetti's forceful leading of the double-bass section in his *Débats* report: "I have rarely heard the figure in the Scherzo of the C-minor Symphony [Fifth] so energetically and cleanly played . . .

Beethoven was worth being treated to the luxury of bringing Dragonetti from London. . . ."[26]

It had been known for quite awhile that Liszt had been asked to take part in the festival not only as composer, but also as pianist (he was to play the *Emperor* Concerto) and as conductor (he was to conduct Beethoven's Fifth Symphony). Two months before the Bonn event Schindler made his move. Choosing not a local Bonn rag but the widely read *Kölnische Zeitung*, he published a protest at the choice of Liszt to conduct a Beethoven symphony, since, being a mere pianoforte player, he did not have the requisite experience.[27] An anonymous rebuttal immediately appeared, hotly informing Schindler that Liszt had already conducted two Beethoven symphonies, the Fifth and the Seventh, at Weimar.[28]

Schindler seems to have suffered in silence through the actual performance, which was described in approving terms by Berlioz with a delicious dig at the prominently absent Habeneck: "Then Liszt moved to the podium and conducted the C-minor Symphony, the Scherzo of which he gave us just as Beethoven wrote it—not cutting out the double basses at the beginning, as was done for so long at the Paris Conservatoire, and playing the finale with the repeat indicated by Beethoven, a repeat that is still audaciously left out even today at the concerts of the said Conservatoire. I have always had so much confidence in the taste of those who improve the great masters that I was quite surprised to find the Symphony in C minor still more beautiful when executed entire than when corrected. I had to go to Bonn to make this discovery."[29]

Just prior to mounting the podium Liszt had performed his duties as solo pianist in a manner, perhaps chastened by the knowledge of Schindler's forbidding presence, that met with—astonishingly—Schindler's printed approval fifteen years later in the final edition of his Beethoven biography: "Liszt's feeling for [Beethoven's] works was not devoid of a poetic sense, and there were moments when his playing, though far from Beethoven's, was still in the master's spirit. . . . He even had occasional times of tranquillity, and even reverence, when he might have completely satisfied the great composer himself—for instance, his performance of the concerto in E-flat major at the ceremony in Bonn in 1845 for the unveiling of the Beethoven monument."[30]

Berlioz, overwhelmed, agreed with this assessment: "To say that Liszt played it, and that he played it in a superb, exquisite, poetical, and yet ever-faithful manner, is mere tautology. It brought forth a hurricane of applause and orchestral fanfares that must have been heard outside the hall."[31] A diary comment from Sir George Smart rounds out this particular episode in the group homage to Beethoven and gives us a glimpse of that ostentatious side of the young, still unbridled Liszt that offended some music lovers: "It was curious to see Liszt get up after the first part of the concerto and walk about the orchestra, bowing to the applause. Spohr shook hands with him, then he sat down and finished the concerto."[32] The two prime participants—Spohr, aged sixty-one, and Liszt, not quite thirty-four—also received (and accepted) too many tributes for Sir George's reserved English taste: "After Spohr had conducted the 1st Act [of the concert] he came and sat with us to be near his wife. By the bye there was rather too much Drumming and Trumpeting to Spohr & Liszt, who had some Bouquets thrown to them by the Chorus Girls (very good looking, all dressed in White) for the Festival was in honor of Beethoven *not* of Spohr and Liszt. . . ."[33]

From Smart's diary we learn that two of Beethoven's oldest Bonn acquaintances were present for the festival. They were Beethoven's physician friend Franz

Wegeler—now eighty years old—who quickly published an appendix to his and Ferdinand Ries's *Biographische Notizen*,[34] and Franz Anton Ries (1755–1846; father of Ferdinand)—now ninety years old and enjoying the festival to the hilt—who had been Beethoven's violin teacher. Ries also savored the sudden attention paid to him and responded richly with some Beethoven mythology of his own, as Smart learned: "After coming from the inspection of the Regiment we called upon Mr. Ries. He is a very fine, agreeable old man and upwards of ninety. He seemed to enjoy our conversation. He had been to one Rehearsal, too infirm to go to the concerts—said that Beethoven's Grand Father was a Chapel Master, but his Father was only a Tenor Chorus Singer, and so little was thought of young Beethoven that no one can say in which house in Bonn he was born, tho' 2 houses claim that honor, but what is more extraordinary, old Mr. Ries said, tho' it was known that Beethoven died in Vienna, no one could say *where* he was *buried.*"[35]

It was quite true that two different houses were being pointed out to Bonn's devout visitors in 1845 as the site of Beethoven's birth: Bonngasse No. 515 (now No. 20; Beethoven's actual birthplace) and Rheingasse No. 934 (where Beethoven spent much of his boyhood). Schindler, in the 1860 edition of his Beethoven biography, referred to the dispute with disdain: "Jealousy and ambition claimed as Beethoven's birthplace No. 934 Rheingasse, a house that the Beethoven family did indeed occupy in the 1780s. Even Wegeler's *Nachtrag zu den biographischen Notizen*, which came out in the same year [as the Bonn Beethoven unveiling], declaring that Beethoven was beyond a doubt born in the house on Bonngasse, did not silence the clamorous opponents."[36] The evidence was overwhelming for the Bonngasse house, but nothing was really done about it for preservation of the Beethoven mystique (except for a memorial plaque put over the front door in 1870) until 1889, when newspapers announced that the house, which dated from the beginning of the eighteenth century, was to be sold and demolished. Local music lovers sprang into action, an international appeal (signed by Bismarck, Brahms, Billroth, Joachim, Lachner, Rubinstein, Clara Schumann, and Verdi among others) was responded to with donations and gifts of Beethoven memorabilia, and the Beethovenhaus was rescued. Bought by the Beethovenhaus Society that came into being for this purpose, it was henceforth restored and run by the Society as a Beethoven museum. A first exhibition and music festival were held in the spring of 1890; in 1892 Rubinstein played a concert in Bonn for the restoration of the house, and in 1903 Joachim's Quartet performed all sixteen of Beethoven's string quartets in five days at the Beethovenhaus's sixth festival of chamber music. All this lay ahead, but in 1845 the house at Bonngasse No. 515 was a shabby and uncared-for sight. Liszt could not be everywhere! The city did honor Beethoven and Liszt in another way, however, that kept costs at a minimum but attracted free publicity from the newspapers. On 14 August 1845 two new streets were inaugurated in Bonn: one named Beethovenstrasse; the other, Lisztstrasse. This was to be all the thanks that Liszt received for his monumental part in making the Bonn Beethoven monument a reality.

Meanwhile, Schindler was compensating for the painful silence he had maintained during Liszt's conducting of Beethoven's Fifth Symphony. He told any and everyone he met about the terrible injustice done to him by another famous Beethoven personality present at the festival, Ignaz Moscheles. Smart, to whom Schindler had written a few days after Beethoven's death, thanking him in Beethoven's name for the London Philharmonic Society's gift of one thousand thaler (and, incidentally, telling him exactly where the composer had been buried), reports two encounters with Schindler on the streets of Bonn: [12 August]" . . . I was introduced to Herr Schindler, who wrote Beethoven's Life. I gave him my address in London. I believe he lives in Cologne. He was pleased to say that my name is well known in Germany. . . . He laid it into Moscheles, who is, as he states, shown up in the twelfth edition of his work, that is Beethoven's Life. [13 August] . . . I was glad to hear from Herr Schindler, who wrote Beethoven's Life (which Moscheles *said* he translated[37]), that Mr. Ries had that day been made a Doctor in consequence of his own worth, and having been the intimate friend of Beethoven and the father of the talented F. Ries."[38]

Had Sir George been at all inclined to believe Schindler about Moscheles's supposedly deceitful ways on 12 and 13 August, his farewell visit to old Ries on 14 August gave him a totally different perspective:

> During our visit to Mr. Ries this Morning, who gave me 2 Kisses On Parting, he told me an extraordinary anecdote of the King of Prussia having given a large sum to, and settled a Pension of about £60 English, on Mr. Schindler for some Ms. Music of Beethoven sold to the King by Mr. S.—but Mr. Holz told Mr. Ries, and showed him a paper signed by a dozen Persons stating that Mr. S. had taken this Music and a Trunk containing other things from Beethoven's house immediately after his death without permission from his Nephew or anyone else. Mr. Ries says this affair will be made public; if so, and the assertion against Mr. Schindler should be proved, Mr. Moscheles will be sufficiently revenged for all that Mr. Schindler has said against him for pirating his book of Beethoven's Life.[39]

Schindler's own, not so secret, relentless anti-Semitism, along with his invidious inability to share Beethoven with anyone else, was at the bottom of his anti-Moscheles campaign, but it was also, like that of Wagner's, unfortunately in tune with the times. A clearer instance of this will soon emerge in Smart's diary.

Let us now attend the festival concerts and ceremonies through the eyes of this dignified sixty-nine-year-old English advocate of Beethoven who had relatively few axes to grind and was refreshingly unaware of German musical politics. With his traveling companion, Henry Robertson, treasurer of the Covent Garden Theatre, Sir George Smart made the crossing from Dover to Ostend on 5 August, stayed overnight in Ghent, and proceeded on to Cologne by train the next day. The following morning, 7 August, they paid their respects to the great cathedral, which, Smart observed, had been much built up since his previous visit of 1825. (In 1845 Cologne Cathedral was just three years away from its consecration; Schumann would honor it in the fourth movement of his *Rhenish* Symphony in 1850, and by 1880 the monumental edifice—abandoned in 1560—would be complete.) They left Cologne at 10:20 A.M. and arrived in Bonn one hour and ten minutes later. Although most of the musical Great Guns (as Smart called them) were staying at the Goldener Stern (favorite stopping place of the English royal family), Smart and Robertson went to the nearby Hotel de Trêves, whose owner was the son of Beethoven's Bonn publisher, Nikolaus Simrock. That afternoon on their way to the first general rehearsal, held in the riding school, they walked to the post office on the Münsterplatz, where they passed by "Beethoven's *covered* Statue."[40] At the rehearsal, which began an hour late at four in the afternoon, "the pieces rehearsed were Beethoven's Mass in D, conducted by Spohr, and a new cantata by Liszt, conducted (with plenty of twisting of the person) by himself."[41] The next morning Smart skipped the second general rehearsal (the *Missa Solemnis* again and the Ninth Symphony), but in the afternoon he attended a rehearsal in the late Romanesque cathedral dominating the Münsterplatz of Beethoven's Mass in C, op. 86. "Many parts of this beautiful Mass were unsteady, the fault seemed to be the worthy Conductor [Breidenstein, spreading himself thin] who may not have had sufficient experience . . . Spohr . . . left his seat to go up into the Orchestra, probably to speak to the conductor about the wrong times."[42] Some excitement of a different nature was created after that by the arrival of the king and queen of Prussia at the Bonn railroad station, where their carriage was taken off the track and a team of six post horses hitched up to whisk them away to Stolzenfels castle. Smart likewise treated himself to an excursion (by omnibus) to the castle at Godesburg, where he heard the praises of Prince Albert sung.

The next morning was Sunday, the first official day of the Beethoven Festival, and Bonn's citizens had decorated their houses with German and English flags in anticipation of the arrival of Queen Victoria and her German husband. Wreaths and flags were piled up around the base of the still-veiled statue in the Münsterplatz. Smart duly attended "part" of mass in the cathedral, and after lunch went over to the Goldener Stern to take a look at a "MS. copy belonging to Oury of a Cantata by Beethoven which Oury doubts if he will give it to the King of Prussia or to Prince Albert. *Doubtless* he will fix on the latter."[43] From admiring Beethoven in manuscript Sir George turned to admiring Beethoven in performance: the opening concert was scheduled for six in the afternoon in the recently finished Beethoven Hall. As Smart and Robertson entered they read a proud sign over the doorway: "Through the union and enthusiasm of the Citizens of Bonn erected in eleven Days, from the 27th of July to the 7th of August 1845"[44] (the sign was a bit exaggerated; finishing touches had taken up to the night before the first concert). Smart made a sketch of the long wooden auditorium with its trimmed fir-tree pillars and pale red wallpaper and described the decoration with relish: "It is curious that in the Tablets round the room relative to Beethoven the one close to where we sat was the Mount of Olives—and the one over the Royal Box was appropriately . . . 'The Battle of Victoria.' "[45] These shields culminated in a "good portrait"[46] of Beethoven and although Smart gives no more than his aesthetic judgment of the work, we can deduce which one (or copy thereof) of the familiar famous images of Beethoven stared out over the first night audience of some eighteen hundred rapt souls. The London music critic and editor of the *Musical World*, James William Davison (1813–1885), left a more detailed account: "At the furthermost end of the room is a very equivocal portrait of Beethoven, 'in doubtful oil' [this suggests a copy], at either side of which are two figures, supported by two angels, who are placing a wreath on the brow of the great composer, while he is writing the Mass in D."[47] There is only one picture specifically showing Beethoven writing his *Missa Solemnis* in D and that is Stieler's portrait of 1819. So far we have two pronouncements on its quality—Smart deemed it "good," Davison thought it "equivocal"—and it is therefore most interesting to learn what adjective the Romantic reviewer Berlioz accorded this festooned image of his idol. "Melancholy" was Berlioz's empathic word choice.[48]

The ambitious opening concert consisted of two giant works: the *Missa Solemnis* (making the choice of Stieler's image most appropriate) and the Ninth Symphony, both led by that powerhouse of a conductor, Spohr. Smart, as a fellow conductor always alert to the mechanics of things, tells us: "The Audience was most attentive. Great applause to Spohr when the Band saluted him with Drums & Trumpets as I have before described. In order to make silence before the *Sinfonia* began there was a short roll of a Drum—good idea, as it made the audience sit down in

(Colorplate 4)

expectation of the commencement."[49] Smart's pleased if somewhat laconic comments on the *music* had preceded these practical observations: "The Mass in D is too complicated in parts but was well performed, particularly by the Chorus & Band, and well conducted, so was the Sinfonia The Ode to Joy, which went famously. The P's & F's so well attended to that I never heard this Sinfonia so well performed before, but the Trumpets had a bad tone . . . the Principal Singers in this Ode infinitely more effective than ours, but the German words seem to suit better (I was delighted to see how orderly the Performers were in obeying the Conductor.)"[50]

Schindler, for once, approved. Erroneously (or stubbornly) believing that this was the first complete performance of the *Missa Solemnis*,[51] and switching the kudos from Cassel's Spohr to Cologne's organist and chorus master Franz Weber (1805–1876; no relation to Carl Maria von Weber), the "*ami de Beethoven*" fairly bubbled over: "It is principally to the royal music director in Cologne, Franz Weber, that we owe thanks for his faith that a performance of the *Missa* was not only possible but (and this is of far greater significance) that its performance could be perfect in every respect. With unflagging zeal he spent months rehearsing all the participating choral societies of the Rhine Province in their respective towns, thereby achieving a sureness and unity that was a source of wonder to the thousands of listeners who came from all parts of Europe."[52]

Berlioz, put off by the "high notes with which Beethoven has unfortunately studded the soprano parts in all his works,"[53] chose to give greater press to the second item on the program: "The effect produced by the 'Choral' Symphony was marked by depth and grandeur. The first movement, with its gigantic proportions and the tragic accent of its style, the Adagio, so poetically expressive of nostalgia, the Scherzo, sparkling with such lively colors and scented with such sweet rustic odors, successively astonished, moved, and enraptured the audience. . . . But the religious chorus: 'Bow, ye millions,' burst forth, strong and awe-inspiring as the voice of a whole people in a cathedral. It was of a stupendous majesty."[54]

With this trio of responses to the opening concert of the Beethoven Festival, we move from British benevolence to German self-gratulation to French fervor, and certainly—given the noble purpose of the occasion and the internationalism of the event (we are only three years away from the revolutions of 1848)—all were in order. What Beethoven worshiper could *not* have failed to thrill to the ensemble of freshly hewn concert hall and mammoth music in the town of Beethoven's birth? Berlioz wrote for all visitors on that August Sunday of 1845 when he described the impression received upon first entering the new Beethoven Hall:

This collection of celebrated names, great artists who had come of their own accord from all parts of Germany, France, England, Scotland, Belgium, and the Netherlands; the expectation of the divers sensations all were about to experience; the respectful passion felt by the whole assembly for the hero of the occasion; his melancholy portrait seen above the platform through the lights of a thousand candles; the huge hall, decorated with foliage and shields bearing the names of Beethoven's various works; the imposing dignity conferred by the age and talent of Spohr, who was to conduct the performances; the youthful and inspired fervor of Liszt, who went through the ranks prodding the lukewarm, rebuking the indifferent, and imparting to all a little of his fire; the triple row of young women in white; and above all, the shouts across the hall between friends who were seeing one another after three or four years' separation and were now meeting almost unexpectedly in such a place and for the realization of such a dream—all this was enough to create the fine intoxication that art and poetry and the noble passions that are their daughters sometimes excite in us. And when the concert began, when the sheaf of lovely, well-trained, and confident voices raised its harmonious clamor, I assure you it took a certain amount of willpower to keep one's emotions within bounds.[55]

What could follow these emotional pyrotechnics except an exterior display of fireworks over the Rhine that night? Those not too exhausted attended the colorful display, and that second international team of visitors—the pickpockets—assiduously set about practicing their craft.

The next day, Monday, 11 August, no musical events were scheduled and instead a nautical homage to Beethoven—son of the Rhine—took place. A brand-new steamer was christened *Ludwig van Beethoven* with great ceremony and amid cannon salvos from ship and shore. This latest member of the Kölner Dampf-schiffahrts-Gesellschaft, which now owned a fleet of twenty-four steamships, then made its maiden voyage to Liszt's beloved island of Nonnenwerth, with such Beethoven-adherents as Spohr, Smart, Moscheles, and Karl Holz (avoiding Schindler?) aboard. Sir George was, by his own report, almost crushed to death while attempting to board; only later was there enough calm on the S.S. *Beethoven* for Moscheles to pass on to him some gossip "about Madame Pleyel who has left her husband for 100 others."[56] The arrival of two other notable women in Bonn the next day would however leave Marie Pleyel's extramarital affairs quite forgotten. One of the women was Queen Victoria, future Empress of India; the other was Lola Montez, current reigning femme fatale of all Europe. Both would leave their imprint on the Beethoven festivities.

Tuesday, 12 August, was the day all Bonn had been awaiting—the day Beethoven's statue, standing mysteriously shrouded in the cathedral square, would be unveiled. As a prelude that morning, Beethoven's Mass in C—conducted by Breidenstein—was performed in the Münster, towards which the image of Beethoven was facing (Fig. 113). While most of musical Bonn was in the cathedral listening to Beethoven (and Smart noted in his diary that the performance went well, much better than the rehearsal), the royal party was slated to pull in at the train station and proceed to the house of a fortunate Count von Fürstenberg, whose balconied home (now a post office) fronted the Münsterplatz opposite the draped monument. The royal visitors would include the cousins Queen Victoria of England and King Friedrich Wilhelm IV of Prussia, Prince Albert, Queen Elisabeth of Prussia, the princess of Prussia, and the archduke Friedrich of Austria. But the royal party was late. In the square below a band began to play excerpts from Beethoven symphonies and overtures. The distinguished visiting musicians were left to fend for themselves, as Berlioz ironically tells us, revealing unknown pugilistic talents:

> Immediately after Beethoven's Mass came the inauguration of the statue in the adjoining square. It was then especially that I had to make persevering use of my fists. Thanks to them, and to my bravely climbing a fence, I managed to get a place in the reserved enclosure. Taking all in all, the invitation I received from the committee in charge of the Bonn festival did not positively prevent me from witnessing it. We stood there packed close together for an hour, awaiting the arrival of the King and Queen of Prussia, the Queen of England, and Prince Albert, who were to behold the ceremony from the top of a balcony fitted out

to receive them. Their Majesties having arrived, guns and bells began their racket once more, while in another corner of the square a military band struggled to gain a hearing for a few scraps of the *Egmont* and *Fidelio* overtures.[57]

Sir George felt a patriotic tug at his heart as he described the same event (he had had the foresight to get to a reserved seat earlier):

A most beautiful morning during the Ceremony. Our Queen, with the King & Queen of Prussia with Prince Albert, arrived soon after 11, ½ an hour later than was appointed. They came in 4 or 5 Carriages from Brühl. There was a delay in the Royal Party coming into the balcony at Count Somebody's house, the People were impatient, but when they appeared (our Queen in a Pink Bonnet) the cheering was great. The Ceremony began with a Speech (from a Paper) by Dr. Breidenstein without his hat. At the end of it the Statue was suddenly uncovered, the Sun broke forth at the moment. The Shouts of the immense number of People, the Beating of Drums, the ringing of Bells and Cannons at a distance, the loud reports, all had a grand effect.[58]

Smart, the perfect Victorian, had been kind to Herr Breidenstein, noting only his lack of head covering. Berlioz was . . . Berlioz: "Silence having been nearly restored, the president of the committee, M. Breidenstein, delivered a speech the effect of which on the audience might be compared to that of Sophocles reciting his tragedies at the Olympic games."[59]

For all his delightful sarcasm, Berlioz missed the greatest irony of the day: the planning committee's biggest blunder. When it was unveiled, the statue of Beethoven was discovered to be standing with its *back* to the balcony on which the royal party stood (Fig. 114)! This was a case of art inadvertently aping "life"—just as the mythology of Beethoven had lovingly preserved the Teplitz Incident, when Beethoven supposedly turned his back on Archduke Rudolf. Now a bronze Beethoven ignored the visiting Austrian Archduke Friedrich. Charles Hallé and Queen Victoria noticed the Bonn boner. Here are their separate accounts, first Hallé's: "The Beethoven festival at Bonn . . . to which Berlioz and I journeyed together from Paris, drew together a large number of the most notable musicians from all countries, all anxious to do homage to the memory of that incomparable genius. It was graced by the presence of the King of Prussia and his guests, Queen Victoria and the Prince Consort, who witnessed from a royal box built purposely in the square the unveiling of the statue, which, to the astonishment of the multitude that surrounded it, was found when the veil fell to turn its back upon the Royalties."[60] The journal entry made by Queen Victoria (Fig. 115) notes the faux pas merely as unlucky, not insulting: "We stepped onto the balcony to see the unveiling of Beethoven's Statue, in honour of which great festivities took place, concerts, etc. But, unfortunately, when the statue was uncovered, its back was turned to us. The *Freischützen* fired a *feu de joie*, and a chorale was sung. The people cheered us, and dear Albert most particularly, who is beloved here; and the band played a 'Dusch' at the same time, which is a flourish of trumpets, and is always given in Germany, when healths are drunk, etc."[61]

As the band saluted the presence of Queen Victoria with Thomas Arne's "Rule Britannia" (on which Beethoven had written a series of five piano variations in 1803), and the Queen gazed at the enigmatic verso of the Beethoven statue, her thoughts may have wandered to the time she played duets with the great composer's former pupil Czerny in London some eight years earlier. If she mused about what lay ahead after the Beethoven inauguration events were over, she may also have anticipated with pleasure an itinerary that was to take her deeper into Germany, to the Franconian part of Saxony and the seat of the little dukedom from which Albert had inherited his title, Coburg, where the hilly Thuringian landscape would remind them both of Scotland. On the twenty-sixth of August her beloved husband's twenty-sixth birthday would be celebrated in his hometown. Little could she have imagined that twenty years later to the day she would be back in Coburg as deeply grieving widow attending yet another inauguration, the unveiling of the memorial statue of Albert. Bonn and the Beethoven monument would always mean to her the carefree, happy time she had witnessed the canonization of a national hero with her own hero-husband at her side.

"A chorale was sung," the Queen had written in her report of the Beethoven unveiling. Before we walk with Liszt, Spohr, and others around to the front of the Beethoven statue to see what it looked like, let us give a brief hearing to this "chorale," which was, after all, composed in honor of Beethoven and destined for at least four pairs of royal eardrums. Actually, it was an ode, written for the occasion by a poet from Aachen, and the text was charged with patriotic partisanship, concluding smugly:

> Denn hier bei uns am deutschen Rhein,
> Ob jedes Land dich nenne sein
> Gewalt'ger, ist dein Vaterland.[62]
> (For here with us on the German Rhine,
> though every land may claim you
> as its Mighty One, is your fatherland.)

What Beethoven-worshiping composer could fail to be inspired by such stirring words? The answer is Bonn's own Breidenstein. This excellent and ubiquitous gentleman had conscientiously assigned himself the task of setting the text to music, scoring it for male voices and wind instruments—a somewhat hazardous combination under the best of circumstances, but especially so in a public square crowded with several thousand people. How went the music and the acoustics? We have four reports, two English, two French. The kindest was Smart's: "Then followed a dull piece of music, composed & conducted by Dr. Breidenstein, accompanied by Wind Instruments only, and sung by Male Voices only, tho' all the Female Chorus singers were seated in front of the Statue [lucky female choristers; they at least could see the statue when it was unveiled!]. . . . I am sure that the Royal Party were too far off to hear one word of Dr. B's speech, or any of the Music, perhaps they might have heard the Drums when the music ended."[63] Sir George's countryman Davison was blunter, delivering himself of the opinion that, unlike the parchment signed by all the visiting dignitaries, which was to be entombed in the Beethoven monument in a small leaden casket, Breidenstein's Beethoven ode "did not need lead to weigh it down, its own weight being sufficient."[64] Berlioz, the great orchestrator of unusual effects, was interested from a practical point of view, although his mordant wit caught up with him. Having just compared Breidenstein's efforts at public oratory to the effect of Sophocles reciting his tragedies at the Olympic games, he continued mischievously: "I beg M. Breidenstein's pardon for likening him to the Greek poet, but the fact remains that only his immediate neighbors heard a word he said. . . . It was the same with his cantata. Even had the atmosphere been calm, I should certainly not have taken in much of that composition; the futility of vocal music in the open air is notorious; but the wind blew violently towards the choristers, and my portion of M. Breidenstein's harmony was unjustly conveyed in its entirety to the listeners at the other end of the square; and gluttons that they were, they still thought it small rations."[65] Berlioz's fellow critic Léon Kreutzer (1817–1868; nephew of the violinist Rodolphe Kreutzer so admired by Beethoven) was hotly indignant: fulminating to his readers in the *Gazette Musicale*, he cited the "ridiculous musician coming to inflict on Beethoven's statue the martyrdom of such loathsome music that it must have shuddered even though it was made of bronze."[66]

Turning our attention now to the bronze effigy that "shuddered" through the first (and last) performance of Breidenstein's Beethoven ode, we may seek out firsthand reactions as to the aptness of the image (Fig. 116). We have three, all from persons who had known Beethoven personally. Smart, who had met, talked, and dined with him a couple of times in September 1825, declared simply that the statue was "a good likeness."[67] Moscheles, whose friendly acquaintanceship with Beethoven had begun as early as 1810, knew the physical Beethoven well. We recall the Seelekarikatur in which he indulged for the benefit of the players of the London Philharmonic, imitating Beethoven's manner of conducting in order to convey the composer's musical intentions; he even possessed a lock of the composer's hair, sent to him by the once friendly Schindler after Beethoven's death. Moscheles's response to the bronze Beethoven was brief but approving: "I was deeply moved when I saw the statue unveiled, the more so because Hähnel has obtained an admirable likeness of the immortal composer."[68] This from the man who so understood the sometimes jarring conduct of Beethoven that, pleading rhetorically with future Beethoven mythographers, he wrote: "If we were to take the external manner for the internal man, what egregious mistakes should we often make!"[69] Our final consultant is Schindler. Need there be any suspense as to the judgment of this *Schutzengel* of the Beethoven Image according to Schimon? Sniffed Schindler contemptuously: "... one would do well to avoid the statue in Bonn made after Hähnel's model, for there is nothing to be seen there that conforms to reality."[70]

What was it about Hähnel's Beethoven that satisfied two Beethoven cognoscenti yet provoked the disdain of a third? Beethoven is shown standing, legs apart with both feet planted firmly on the ground, holding a pen in his lowered right hand and a notebook in his left hand, his arm bent at the elbow and held close to the waist. His bearing is upright and he stares ahead, his features concentrating in the well-known frown upon an inner vision, while his thick hair waves energetically about his high brow. Sir George Smart must also have observed that the figure, although dressed in street clothes, was hatless. Hidden in Gerhard von Breuning's description of Beethoven walking is perhaps the answer to Schindler's objection that the Bonn Beethoven displayed nothing that matched reality:

> He was powerful looking, of medium height; his walk as well as his very lively movements were energetic; his dress was not elegant but rather that of a plain townsman.... The two unbuttoned coat-fronts, especially those of the blue frock coat with brass buttons, turned outward and flapped about his arms, especially when he was walking against the wind. In the same manner the two long ends of the white neckerchief knotted about his broad, turned-down shirt collar streamed out. The double lorgnette, which he wore because of his nearsightedness, hung loosely down. His coattails, however, were rather heavily burdened ... the weight of [his] notebooks considerably extended the length

(Colorplate 8)

of the coattail containing them. . . . Beethoven's outward appearance, owing to that indifference to dress peculiar to him, made him uncommonly noticeable on the street.[71]

This is the "uncommonly noticeable," preoccupied pedestrian of the images by Böhm (see Figs. 14 and 15) and Lyser (see Figs. 45, 46, 47). But the Hähnel image avoids any hint of windblown disarray or sartorial shabbiness. This *should* have appealed to Schindler, who in 1860 went out of his way to instruct future image makers how to go about treating the person of Beethoven:

In selecting the clothing for the portrait of a historical person, one has much to consider—whether it should be everyday dress or Sunday best, and even the time of year. A man like Beethoven, who always dressed well for the street or the salon, requires the utmost attention. In this connection one must say of the master that right up to the last days of his life he liked to dress with care, and would always choose garments that went well together. A coat of a fine blue material (the favourite color of that day) with metal buttons was very becoming to him.[72]

The better groomed Beethoven of Schindler's laundered memory at least agrees with Breuning's "plain townsman" opening statement emphasizing the composer's energetic and lively walk. And it was exactly the "real" Beethoven, the earthling with his metal-buttoned frock coat, that seems to have embarrassed the sculptor, presenting him with the problem confronting all icon makers, that of transforming the temporal into the eternal. Weighted-down coattails would have been anathema to the earnest artist who was striving for contemporary accuracy (the buttons and cravat *are* there, after all) while attempting heroic universality. Perhaps taking to heart Carlyle's belief in the power of "brazen and other images" to influence passersby, Hähnel clutched at the cliché of a voluminous mantle, which he wrapped around the plain town clothes, neutralizing, if not altogether hiding them, and creating the desirable impression of a classical—and therefore timeless—cloak. This static hybrid—half-god, half-pedestrian—must have been what, with some justification, so irked Schindler, whose god needed no classical artifacts. Perhaps Hähnel himself felt a bit defensive about his artistic compromise; an interesting comment by Clara Schumann describes the Dresden artist a few years later as given to holding forth defiantly.[73]

Classical allegories were much less controversial in regard to Beethoven, and not even Schindler left any protest concerning the four bas-relief panels referring to various aspects of the Ninth Symphony, which Hähnel had designed to adorn the sides of the giant pedestal supporting the bronze figure (Figs. 117 and 118). Below Beethoven (whose projecting right foot the final bronze version has placed a step lower than the left, enhancing the "walking" aspect of the statue) on the front side of the pedestal is the figure of a female musician playing her harp while riding astride a springing, sphinxlike creature that is part animal, part woman. This wingless but floating duo symbolizes "Phantasy." On the verso a lute-wafting, pagan version of the Sistine Madonna (which had resided in Hähnel's Dresden since 1754) represents "Symphony," while on the sides a modestly garbed woman playing the organ (left side) stands for "Sacred Music" and her counterpart, equipped with two theatrical masks (one on her head), a small horn, and a lute, represents "Dramatic Music." Wagner would have approved. In fact, he was given a chance to, even though he had not attended the Bonn unveiling, for as a friend of the sculptor and a coinhabitant of the old Marcolini palace in Dresden

(Hähnel too liked luxury) he was given "as a mark of friendship an ornament in the shape of a perfect plaster cast of one of the bas-reliefs from Beethoven's monument representing the Ninth Symphony."[74]

Of all the witnesses to the unveiling of the three-dimensional image of Beethoven in bronze that day in Bonn, only Berlioz—a foreigner—seems to have given much thought to the larger dimensions of the event, the universal impact of Beethoven's music. It is worthwhile reading this arch-Romantic's eloquent report just as a compendium of the Beethoven mystique and the multiple dimensions it invoked, seventy-five years after the composer's birth:

> When the monument was uncovered, applause, cheers, trumpet fanfares, drum-rolls, volleys of gunfire, and the pealing of bells—in fact all the noises expressing admiration that constitute the voice of fame among civilized nations, burst forth anew and paid respect to the statue of the great composer. Today, then, the thousands of men and women, young and old, who have spent so many sweet hours with his works, whom he has so often carried away on the wings of his thought to the highest regions of poetry; the enthusiasts whom he has excited to the point of delirium; the humorists whom he has diverted by so many witty and unexpected turns; the thinkers to whose reveries he has opened immeasurable realms; the lovers whom he has moved by reawakening the memory of their first tender affection; the hearts, wrung by an unjust fate, to which his energetic accents have given strength for a momentary revolt, and who, rising in their indignation, have found a voice to mingle their screams of fury and grief with the furious accents of his orchestra; the religious souls to whom he has spoken of God; the nature-lovers for whom he has so faithfully depicted the carefree contemplative life of the countryside in the beautiful summer days, the terror of the hurricane, and the consoling ray threading its way through the tattered clouds to smile on the anxious shepherd and restore hope to the terrified tiller of the soil—today all these intelligent and sensitive souls, on whom his genius has shed its radiance, turned to him as toward a benefactor and a friend.[75]

Abruptly, these lofty sentiments of Berlioz's turned from the prospect of what Beethoven had done for others to what so many others had *not* done for him: "But it was too late; this Beethoven in bronze is unconscious of all this homage. And it is sad to think that the living Beethoven whose memory is thus honored might perhaps not have obtained from his native town in his days of suffering and destitution—of which there were so many during his difficult career—the ten-thousandth part of the sums lavishly spent on him after his death."[76]

That afternoon, at four o'clock, a second all-Beethoven concert took place in the Beethoven Hall and was attended by some 2,100 persons (but not by the royal party, which had gone on to Brühl). The first part consisted of the *Coriolanus* Overture, the canon from *Fidelio*, the *Emperor* Concerto, with Liszt as soloist (winning, as we have seen, Schindler's rare approbation fifteen years after the fact), and parts of the first section of *The Mount of Olives*. Spohr had conducted the first half of the program; for the second part Liszt took up the baton to direct Beethoven's Fifth Symphony (executed "entire," as Berlioz had happily pointed out), then instrumentalists from Cologne played a String Quartet in E-flat (probably op. 74), and the finale from *Fidelio* closed the concert. A spectacular fireworks display was given that evening by the city of Cologne, and the royal guests observed it from a steamer on the Rhine before returning to Brühl for the night. They were due to attend the festival's closing Artists' Concert the next morning back in Bonn.

At nine in the morning on Wednesday, 13 August, before an audience of 2,350, Liszt—the prime mover of the festival—faced his four soloists, choir, and orchestra in the Beethoven Hall and waited. The royal guests were late again. The composer stalled for over an hour, then began his Beethoven cantata. Just after the first movement finished the royal party arrived, with several distinguished visitors, including the explorer Alexander von Humboldt. Liszt saluted them with the Prussian national anthem, "Heil Dir im Siegerkranz" (which served to greet the English royal couple as well, since the tune was the same as "God Save the Queen") and then, without a moment's hesitation, began his cantata over again. Hallé considered Liszt's daring repeat performance "an unpardonable trick," for it was a work "of considerable length [forty-five minutes], devoid of interest."[77] Berlioz could not help but admire Liszt's presence of mind. "He had made a lightning calculation which the event proved correct: 'The public will think that I am starting over again by the King's command, and I shall now be better performed, better listened to, and better understood.' "[78] The musical quotations from the *Archduke* Trio within the work also sparked Berlioz's admiration: " . . . the adagio variations from Beethoven's B-flat Trio, which Liszt has had the happy idea of introducing at the end of his own cantata, to make of it a sort of hymn of praise glorifying the master. This hymn, presented first in its original character of sad grandeur, finally bursts forth with the majesty of an apotheosis. . . ."[79] Queen Victoria, although misidentifying the work, also noticed this nice quotation in her brief journal entry on the concert: "Unfortunately, though very well executed, there was but very little of Beethoven;—only part of one of the Symphonies, brought into a Cantata by Liszt, and the Overture to Egmont, directed by Spohr."[80]

After the extended concert was over (the royal party had had to leave before it finished) came what should have been the culminating social event in Bonn's three-day homage to Beethoven. This was a banquet, held in the brand-new dining-room annex of the Hotel Goldener Stern. Even though it had been grandly named the Beethoven Room, the high and nourishing purpose of the locus did not prevent what Moscheles called "a series of disgraceful scenes"[81] from happening. Since some of the ire was directed at Liszt, his supporter Berlioz tactfully left the unpleasant episode out of his *Débats* report, but Sir George Smart, with his customary terse thoroughness, left us a tantalizing outline as well as a taste of the prevalent anti-Semitism in evidence:

> Not very long after we began eating [the Beethoven Room held five hundred], Toasts were given by Wolf [*sic*; the poet Wolff, who had written the words to Liszt's Beethoven cantata], Liszt, Dr. Breidenstein, and others. It seems that Liszt in his 1st speech complimented *all* nations except the French, in his 2nd speech, having been privately told of his omission, he praised the French from whom he had received such kindness. However, this omission caused dissatisfaction among the French, who, with the Jews, are not popular here. . . . Then began a row caused by Wolf the poet (who they say was also a Jew) who would speak (after having given 2 or 3 toasts) and they would not hear him but called for Spohr who got up and sat down again, he being not inclined to speak. . . . This row was noisy, and fearing we might get into a scrape we left the Room. . . . We saw Moscheles going up to his Room from the Dinner Table, he said, "I am ashamed of my Countrymen!" I conclude he did not like the remarks about the Jews which he must have heard. It seems that the Germans are very angry with us for *emancipating* the Jews as they term it.[82]

One disruptive personality Smart had not noticed (but Moscheles had) in the crowded banquet hall before he prudently left it was Lola Montez (1818?–1861) (Fig. 119). As the evening wore on she suddenly indulged in the sort of daring public display that would soon bring her to the mesmerized attention of Ludwig I, contributing to the loss of his throne in 1848. Here in Bonn she seemed determined to unseat Liszt, insisting at the Goldener Stern banquet hall entrance (the hotel had already refused her lodgings) that she was his guest. Pushing her way through the packed room she managed to take a seat opposite the highly embarrassed Liszt, and after the *"Vous avez oublié les français"* ruckus broke out, the self-declared Spanish dancer from Limerick, Ireland, jumped on top of the main dining table and executed a bit of fandango to "quiet" the room so that the poet Wolff could speak. After that the international debacle was in full swing. Beethoven was forgotten as the failures of Liszt, the Bonn committee, and the festival in general were hotly debated in several languages. What was not forgotten was the scandalous link the appearance of Lola Montez had forged with Liszt in the collective memory of Bonn's citizenry. Twenty-five years later, when the one-hundredth anniversary of Beethoven's birth was celebrated in Bonn, the city fathers did not even send him an invitation to attend.

"Beethoven Festival in Honor of Franz Liszt" ran the headline of one newspaper report after the event.[83] Challenging the anti-Liszt feeling—which the spectacular antics of Lola Montez had not helped—Berlioz sadly chided the world at large for the human failings he had seen paraded at the festival:

> It may be asked why and how there could be any ill will against Liszt, the eminent musician whose eminence is unquestionable and moreover Germanic, whose fame is widespread and generosity proverbial, who is rightly credited with being the instigator of everything that has been successful at the Bonn Festival, who has scoured Europe in all directions giving benefit concerts to cover the expenses of this festival, and who has even offered to make good the deficit if there is one.[84] What feelings could subsist in the crowd other than those which meritorious deeds such as this should naturally inspire? Alas, the crowd is ever the same, especially in small towns. It was precisely these noble and meritorious deeds that gave offense. Some had a grudge against Liszt because of his extraordinary talent and exceptional success, others because he is witty, still others because he is generous, because he has written too fine a cantata, because the works composed for the festival and given the previous day were not a success, because he has hair and not a wig, because he speaks French too well, because he knows German too thoroughly, because he has too many friends, and doubtless also because he hasn't enough enemies.[85]

Certainly there resided only goodwill in the heart of that deaf painter Lyser, whose identification with his tone hero had resulted in the earnest spate of Beethoven-standing, Beethoven-walking, Beethoven-sitting-by-the-Brook images of the 1830s (see Figs. 44–47, 50). Now, newly inspired by the Bonn celebrations, he created his most ambitious (and also most awkward) Beethoven image yet, a whole commemorative sheet printed in honor of the Beethoven Festival (Fig. 120). Unabashedly imitating Schwind's multiple register style, Lyser surrounds his large central scene—the crowning of Beethoven—with nine smaller panels offering a mixture of religious, Romantic, and musical imagery. The panels seem to refer to specific works of Beethoven, reflecting no doubt Lyser's own preferences but also telling us something most intriguing about the taste of Beethoven's mid-nineteenth-century admirers. Not all the scenes in this compound image of the composer's animus and oeuvre are specific enough for secure identification, but let us attempt to describe the general program and see what conclusions can be drawn.

Reading clockwise round the sheet from the top right, we have Christ kneeling in prayer (probably a reference to Beethoven's oratorio *Christ on the Mount of Olives* op. 85), and a striding pilgrim with staff whose cloak does not hide the fact that his feet are encased in armor (possibly signifying the sixteenth-century Flemish general and statesman Egmont and Beethoven's incidental music to Goethe's eponymous drama, the *Egmont* Overture, op. 84). Next is a domestic scene in which a young woman pours something into a glass while a man, his hands clasped to his face and his back turned to her, strides out of the room. This third, "bourgeois" panel is the most enigmatic. Does it symbolize Beethoven having to turn away in anguish from marital and domestic happiness (a knowing reference to *An die ferne Geliebte*, op. 98)? Or is the literal-minded Lyser referring to another of the many Lieder—none of which quite seem to fit the strange circumstances of the scene? Below this perplexing panel a fairy-winged girl figure displays a scroll with the words "Fantasia für Piano," representing Beethoven's keyboard music. In the predella area underneath the main "altar" scene is a readily recognizable and dramatic moment from *Fidelio*: "Fidelio" reveals herself as Leonore, her husband's wife and rescuer, and points her pistol at a quite terrified Don Pizarro. To the left of this scene, and across from the personification of Beethoven's keyboard music, a young boy holds a large sheaf of music announcing "Qurtett [*sic*] von L. v. Beethoven," representing Beethoven's chamber music. Immediately above, between two halves of a fallen column, stands and strums a young musician of indeterminate sex who holds a long-necked mandolin or cittern, suggesting *The Ruins of Athens*, op. 113. Above this scene in the eighth panel we find a young pipe-playing peasant boy in close communion with his girl and dog—surely a reference to the *Pastoral* Symphony as subtitled "Recollections of Country Life." Just as the effigy for string music was positioned opposite that for piano music, so the Sixth Symphony allusion is placed as a complementary image opposite the second panel, pairing pastoral and heroic concepts in the best iconographic tradition of contrasting counterparts. (Notably missing in Lyser's Biedermeier Beethoven ensemble is the Beethoven of Prometheus, or the Beethoven of the *Appassionata* and *Pathétique* sonatas.) A reference to the Ninth Symphony makes its appearance in the topmost figure to the left—not by accident numbering as panel nine in our clockwise reading. Sharing the *Mount of Olives* plane, a female figure floats and opens her arms for an "Ode to Joy" type of cosmic embrace ("Seid umschlungen Millionen! Diesen Kuss der ganzen Welt!"), raising her arms against a starry sky ("... uber'm Sternenzelt"). Directly above the central panel two child-angels adore a radiant cross-revealing monstrance (an allusion to the *Missa Solemnis*?).[86]

How Christ and Beethoven fit liturgically into this sampling of sinners and saints was best understood by mid-nineteenth-century believers in Beethoven, but Berlioz's enumeration of those who have been touched by Beethoven's music, from nature lovers, lovers, and shepherds to rebels and religious souls, does not seem too different in spirit from Lyser's ecumenical Denkblatt. The central scene is Romanticism turned into pure Biedermeier Sentimentalism. Standing at the edge of a (German) forest, where he had been scribbling down music on a conveniently table-high tree stump, Beethoven, his pen still in his hand, but his worn top hat cast to the ground, receives laurel crowns from two (competing) spirits—a floating young Christ type on the right with well-laced sandals, and a levitating female figure on the left, who crowns the still meditating composer and holds a goblet aloft as if to announce that the mortal Beethoven need drink no more from the cup of sorrow, for this day (Bonn inauguration day) he will be received into the bliss of paradise.

We have encountered Beethoven's abandoned head gear before in Lyser's presentations, but this elaborate and "authentically" detailed coronation image brings yet one more mythic Beethoven feature into the public domain. So humble and apparently inconsequential is the iconographic addition that only one who, like Lyser, devoured every detail of Beethoven's eccentricities of dress and deportment would seize upon it. Another sentence from Gerhard von Breuning's description of Beethoven's clothing gives us the clue. Having commented on the extended length of the composer's heavily burdened coattails, the pockets of which were weighed down by his quarto sketchbooks, thick carpenter's pen, and octavo-format conversation book, Breuning further explained: "... and, in addition, the pocket itself because of its own frequent pulling out and that of the notebooks, hung down visibly on the same side, turned outwards."[87] It is this detail that Lyser lovingly admitted into his laureation of 1845.

Berlioz felt a wave of melancholy sweep over him as he prepared to take leave of Bonn's bronze Beethoven that August. Moved by his ability to be moved, and filled with a nostalgia for his own bygone *les Jeunes France* days, as well as for the lost Beethoven, the forty-one-year-old "French Beethoven" wrote:

> The impression the Bonn festival made on me was so deep and vivid! I feel sunk in sadness merely from telling you about it. Beethoven is no more! Our poetic world is a desert! We shall never again experience the upheavals, the conflagration of the soul caused by the first hearing of his symphonies! The glorious realities of our youth now seem to be vanished dreams, vanished forever. Did spring and summer really exist? The cold, stormy wind blows day and night with such cruel persistence! No more green meadows, bubbling brooks, mysterious woods; no more azure in the sky; the grass is scorched, the water frozen, the forest bare; leaves, flowers, and fruit have fallen, the cold earth has gathered them, and we—soon—shall follow them.[88]

In an outburst of autumnal tristesse, he bade the three-dimensional image farewell: "The festival is over. Beethoven stands in the main square of Bonn, and already the children, heedless of the great, play around the base of the statue. His noble head is at the mercy of wind and rain, while the mighty head that wrote so many masterpieces serves as a perch for common birds."[89]

How gratified Berlioz would have been had he known that ten years hence the mere sight of the silent effigy would cheer Schumann's spirits on his daily walks from the asylum at Endenich into Bonn. In 1880, twenty-four years after Schumann's death, the city of Bonn unveiled a second mythmaking image—a monument to Schumann placed over his grave in the Alter Friedhof, where lay also the body of Beethoven's mother. Present for that occasion were the original mourners, all venerators of Beethoven as well as Schumann—Clara Schumann, Dietrich, Joachim, and Brahms. During the graveside ceremony (at which Brahms conducted the music), the mayor of Bonn was handed a telegram that linked the two departed German composers together. It read: "The Society of Music-lovers and the Conservatoire of Vienna congratulate Bonn on the honor of having today erected the first memorial to Schumann as previously that to Beethoven."[90] Once

337

again Vienna, city of mythmaking talk, had by a comfortable margin missed its chance to initiate a permanent memorial to one of the world's musical greats.

As we follow Berlioz and the worn-out Liszt back to France briefly, it is pleasant to think that Liszt too might have been gratified to know that despite Bonn's pointed ignoring of him at the Beethoven centennial celebration of 1870, his other gift to that city—the hastily but handily constructed Beethoven Hall (all visitors had been in agreement about the fine acoustics of the wooden auditorium)—would be given permanent, concrete form well over a century later when the new Bonn Beethoven Halle (1957–59) was erected. In it is a Beethoven bust (Fig. 121)—one of more than forty-five sculpted and drawn images of Beethoven made by a latter-day Lyser type, the Beethoven-obsessed French sculptor Antoine Bourdelle (1861–1929). As a boy in his native Montauban (Ingres's hometown), he had chanced upon a bust of Beethoven in a local bookstore and was struck not only by the tragic mien and agitated hair of the unknown idol, but even more by what he fancied to be a marked resemblance to his own looks (Fig. 122). This dramatic introduction to Beethoven, whose sonatas and symphonies he then eagerly devoured, inspired a lifelong fixation with the image of Beethoven—an elusive goal that Bourdelle pursued in various media from oil to marble, red chalk to bronze, throughout his career. He modeled his first Beethoven image, *Beethoven with His Head Resting on His Hand*, at the age of twenty-six in 1887; his last one, *La Pathétique* (Beethoven against a cross), in the year of his death, forty-two years later. In all his three-dimensional images of Beethoven, Bourdelle applied a Rodin-derived technique of pitted and puffed surfaces, equating a ragged exterior with the tumult of his hero's inner life.[91] Like Christ, Beethoven was for Bourdelle both man and god (Rolland's conception of Beethoven as suffering hero whose mightiness of soul overcame all obstacles was quick to take root). How firmly embedded in Beethoven mythography the words ascribed to him by Bettina von Arnim had become is evident in the colorful "Beethoven quotation" with which Bourdelle reverently embellished the pedestal of his over life-size Beethoven head of 1902 (see Fig. 121): "I am the Bacchus who presses out delicious nectar for humanity."[92] This disembodied, early twentieth-century craggy countenance is far removed from the "traditional" three-dimensional devotional image of Beethoven as handed down through the previous century. Even Bourdelle's teacher, Auguste Rodin (1840–1917), stayed within conventional boundaries when he sculpted a large portrait medallion of the composer (Fig. 123) for the facade of the Royal Conservatory of Music in Brussels in the mid-1870s. Rodin's grimacing Beethoven is old and frazzled looking; vitality has passed from the long, limp hair to the cloak that arches about the shoulders of this still realistic if remote image. Yet both Rodin's and Bourdelle's Beethovens are partially the product of that French perception of absolute values in Beethoven transmitted so eloquently and with such frequency by the apostle Berlioz.

For Berlioz, it was Beethoven's *music*, with its link to infinity, that served as a betterment for the human race; for the later explicateurs, whose readings would also shape the more personal renderings of Rodin and Bourdelle, it was Beethoven the *man*, mighty in his suffering and triumph, yet also great in his heart, that provided consolation and inspiration. The culminating voice to articulate this French line of thought was that of Romain Rolland, whose international Beethoven we have already briefly considered. The subject of Beethoven occupied Rolland, as it did Bourdelle, all his life. After the sweeping success of his 1903 life of Beethoven, when a France in need of spiritual regeneration responded to his call to breathe the breath of heroes, he constructed two more broad avenues to Beethoven, both of them the lengthy results of decades of writing. They were also diametrically opposed in format. One was a scholarly, seven-volume study (uncompleted) of Beethoven's creativity (*Beethoven: les grandes époques créatrices* [Paris, 1928–45]); the other was a ten-volume *roman-fleuve* (*Jean-Christophe* [Paris, 1904–12]), a work generally read and highly regarded for many years. The novel's hero, Jean-Christophe Krafft, a musical genius who rises to fame despite many tribulations and reversals, is pointedly like Beethoven in his heritage—born in a small Rhineland town to a family troubled by poverty and drunkenness. Unlike his real-life counterpart, however, he gravitates not east to Vienna but west to Paris, where his artistic and spiritual development take place. In appropriating Beethoven for France, Rolland knitted the best qualities of the two races in whose spiritual kinship he believed and posited a supranational hero with tremendous popular appeal. The novel was widely translated. In addition to these two serialized monuments to Beethoven, Rolland created a word "Portrait of Beethoven in His Thirtieth Year" (originally published in the first volume of his Beethoven studies) that pulsates with a three-dimensionality of its own. Parts of this "portrait" may be inserted here, between the carved and cast effigies of Beethoven we are examining, as an engrossing example of empathy, vibrant writing, and mythopoesis legitimized. We will recognize many of Rolland's sources in fact and fiction as we peruse his composite image of an all-too-human, god-like Beethoven:

> [Beethoven] is the masculine[93] sculptor who dominates his matter and bends it to his hand; the master-builder, with Nature for his yard. For anyone who can survey these campaigns of the soul from which stand out the victories of the *Eroica* and the *Appassionata*, the most striking thing is not the vastness of the armies, the floods of tone, the masses flung into the assault, but the spirit in command, the imperial reason. . . .
>
> He is built of solid stuff well cemented; the mind of Beethoven has strength for its base. The musculature is powerful, the body athletic; we see the short, stocky body with its great shoulders, the swarthy red face, tanned by sun and wind, the stiff black mane, the bushy eyebrows, the beard running up to the eyes, the broad and lofty forehead and cranium, "like the vault of a temple," powerful jaws "that can grind nuts," the muzzle and the voice of a lion. . . . He sustains this strength of his by means of vigorous ablutions with cold water, a scrupulous regard for personal cleanliness, and daily walks immediately after the midday meal, walks that lasted the entire afternoon and often extended into the night. . . . Like a good Rhinelander he loved wine, but he never abused it—except for a short period (1825–26) with Holz, when he was badly shaken. . . .[94]
>
> As he grows older, the demon that possesses him brings more and more disorder into his way of living. He needs a woman to look after him, or he will forget to eat. . . . But though his avid nature cries out for love . . . he is on his guard against them, on guard against himself. . . . his conception of love is too lofty for him to be able, without a sense of shame, to degrade it in these—to

use his own word—bestial [*viehisch*] unions. He ended by banishing the sensual from his own passional life. . . . he guards his art, his deity, against contamination: "If I had been willing thus to sacrifice my vital force," he said to Schindler, "what would have remained for the nobler, the better thing?"[95]

Having delivered himself of the almost Victorian sentiment that Beethoven had "ended by banishing the sensual from his own passional life," Rolland turned to another crucial aspect of his portrait of Beethoven, his deafness. He comes to the subject fresh from a discussion of Beethoven's "faults": "The prime condition for the free man is strength. Beethoven exalts it; he is even inclined to overesteem it. Kraft über alles! There is something in him of Nietzsche's superman, long before Nietzsche. . . . He is rich in scorn. . . . But we must recognize that the two currents, vast love, vast scorn, often came to a clash in him, and that in the full flush of his youth, when victory broke down all the floodgates, the scorn poured out in torrents."[96] Now—apparently—comes divine retribution: "But it is here we become conscious of the antique sublimity of the destiny that smites him, like Oedipus, in his pride, his strength, just where he is most sensitive—in his hearing, the very instrument of his superiority. . . . We who, at a century's distance, can see that tragedy for what it was, let us prostrate ourselves and say, 'Holy! holy! Blessed is the misfortune that has come upon thee! Blessed the sealing up of thine ears!' "[97]

Were Beethoven alive to learn of Rolland's ecstatic invitation to bless the deafness that descended on him in service of "the nobler, the better thing," it is not likely that he would have taken much comfort in Rolland's praise of him as an excellent victim of fate:

The hammer is not all: the anvil also is necessary. Had destiny descended only upon some weakling, or on an imitation great man, and bent his back under this burden, there would have been no tragedy in it, only an everyday affair. But here destiny meets one of its own stature, who "seizes it by the throat" [Rolland is quoting Beethoven's 16 November 1801 letter to Wegeler here], who is at savage grips with it all the night till the dawn—the last dawn of all—and who, dead at last, dies with his two shoulders touching the earth, but in his death is carried victorious on his shield; one who out of his wretchedness has created a richness, out of his infirmity the magic wand that opens the rock.[98]

Relishing the moment, Rolland extends it and even manages deftly to enlist Beethoven as a Jacobinic heir of the French revolutionary spirit acting out his egalitarian principles in Viennese drawing rooms:

Let us return to the portrait of him in this decisive hour when destiny is about to enter; let us savor deliberately the cruel joy of the combat in the arena between the Force without a name and the man with the muzzle of a lion! This superman over whose head the storm is gathering (for the peaks attract the thunderbolt) is marked, as with smallpox, with the moral characteristics of his time—the spirit of revolt, the torch of the Revolution. . . . This proud profession of republican faith is arrogantly carried by the young Jacobin—whose political convictions will indeed change in time, but never his moral convictions— into the upper-class salons of Vienna, in which, from the days of his first successes, he behaves without ceremony towards the aristocrats who entertain him.[99]

Rolland's mythic monument to Beethoven (with its Tolstoy-derived doctrine of joy through suffering) needs but a few more blows on the literary chisel to round it out. The spirit of proud revolt breaks out not only against class but against rules—the rules of music. Obeying his own internal laws—"What I have in my heart must out: that is why I write"[100]—he demonstrates a remarkable *intensity* (Goethe's observation), a terrific fixity of idea (causing his inner ear to congest?), an inward monologue that is constantly *à deux*, "of two souls in one, wedded and opposed, discussing, warring, body locked with body, whether for war or in an embrace, who can say? But one of them is the voice of the Master: no one can mistake it."[101]

Beethoven is proud, Beethoven is rebellious, Beethoven is alone, without love yet filled with love; an ill-mannered humanitarian, the very metal of whose talents tempts Vulcan's anvil, while his furious concentration pits him against contending forces in a divine arena. All of this mounts relentlessly in Rolland's portrayal to the inevitable denouement: "Beethoven is felled to the ground; never has a more heartrending cry of despair than this testamentary letter (which was never dispatched) been torn from a human breast. He measures his length on the ground,—but, like the Titan of the fable, only to raise himself again at a bound, his strength multiplied by ten. 'No, I will not endure it!' . . . He seizes destiny by the throat. . . . 'You will not succeed in bowing me utterly down.' "[102]

The moral of Rolland's Beethoven monument? It is a message to the France that has twice been locked in the embrace of war (1870–71 and 1914–18) with the very land that produced Beethoven. Rolland's Beethoven is larger than Jean-Christophe Krafft, larger than Europe. He belongs to all peoples. That is why Rolland offers his portrait of Beethoven to the world. Its example provides universal inspiration: "In natures such as this," concludes the "Portrait of Beethoven in His Thirtieth Year," "the excess of suffering determines the salutary reaction; the strength increases with that of the enemy. And when the prostrated one finds himself on his feet again, he is no longer merely one man: he is the army of the *Eroica* on the march."[103]

The religious aspect of the French Beethoven cult, initiated by Rolland in his first Beethoven biography of 1903, would be countered by Vincent d'Indy (1851–1931)—for whom Catholicism was religion enough—in a life of Beethoven (Paris, 1911) that gave short shrift to tragedy, suffering, love, struggle, triumph, liberty, humanity, and destiny and instead concentrated on the musical greatness of the composer, especially the Ninth Symphony.[104]

Whether the deification of Beethoven in France stemmed from emphasis on the music, as with the Berlioz–Bizet–d'Indy camp, or from the presumed moral might of the man, as with Rolland, the second half of the nineteenth century witnessed not only the widespread public familiarity with the composer's works but also the rise of a Beethoven religion that caused his effigy, be it in plaster or in bronze, to become a common and, even, de rigueur house god. A wall in the studio of the artist Rosa Bonheur (1822–1899) at By (preserved today as a museum) (Fig. 124) gives characteristic testimony to the ubiquitous image of Beethoven in late nineteenth-century France, which, if it did not honor him with public monuments in marble, did so in the sanctuary of countless individual homes.[105]

It is now time to return to Vienna and see how Beethoven's adopted home—the city to whose musical fame he had so substantially contributed—responded to Bonn's achievement in erecting the first major monument to the composer. The imperial city on the Danube responded by *not* responding. Although the Austrian archduke Friedrich had been present at the Bonn ceremonies of 1845, he apparently brought no urgent message back to Vienna about doing likewise. (Perhaps the bronze back Beethoven had turned upon the royal party at the unveiling was more of an affront than anyone realized?) There was talk in a few quarters of doing something, but only talk. The centennial year of 1870 was eyed with torpid gaze—it was still twenty-five years away. Still there was talk and hopeful rumors surfaced and circulated, gliding even beyond the Vienna *glacis*. Thus we find Eduard Hanslick chagrined by the widespread belief—*abroad*—that Vienna was building a monument to Beethoven. This was brought home to him when, on the occasion of his second visit to Rossini in Paris,[106] in July 1867, the seventy-five-year-old composer suddenly asked him whether or not the Beethoven monument in Vienna had been finished. "We three Austrians looked rather embarrassed," confessed Hanslick.[107]

A three-dimensional Beethoven image (the word monument is barely applicable) about which Hanslick *could* have told Rossini, had he regained his aplomb if not his pride, was the over-life-size bronze bust recently created for, well, not the city of Vienna, but for the village just outside Vienna where the composer had been staying when he wrote his despairing testament of 1802—Heiligenstadt (Fig. 125). Our contemporary engraving shows a modest "monument," with a tall, rectangular pedestal supporting the classical-looking, idealized (beyond recognition!) bust of Beethoven. This herm is set in a small, fenced enclosure and surrounded by a little grove of newly planted trees. A pamphlet published for the dedication ceremony on 15 June 1863 informs us that the marble pedestal was carved by Robert Streschnak (c. 1827–1897), and that the bronze head, cast in the late fall of 1862, is the work of Anton Fernkorn (1813–1878). Although it is hardly likely that the name of Streschnak, whose major accomplishment as a city stonemason was his protracted work on Kaiser Franz Josef's Votivkirche—then abuilding (1856–79)—was known outside Vienna, it is possible that the reputation of Fernkorn, knighted by the emperor in 1860 for his bronze equestrian monument to the archduke Karl, the first to deal a defeat to Napoleon, had traveled abroad. Nevertheless, the listless, prosaic ensemble (Fig. 126) rendered more homage to a favored Beethoven site—Heiligenstadt—than it did to Beethoven the musician. Starting higher up from the Kahlenberger Strasse is, in fact, the brook-lined promenade so frequently traversed by the composer that it was already known as Beethoven's Walk ("Beethovengang"; also "Beethovenruhe"). The image of Beethoven out walking in a *Pastoral*-inspiring environment was taken up in the dedication pamphlet of 1863 (a poem entitled "Beethoven und Goethe" nostalgically paces through the Teplitz Incident once again[108]), and the logical step of placing a three-dimensional image of the *walking* Beethoven in Heiligenstadt Park was achieved in 1902 with the unveiling of a frock-coated monument in marble[109] (Fig. 127) that, pedestrian in both pastime and execution, earnestly perpetuates the myth-inspiring picture released by Schindler of Beethoven's own description of how and where he composed the second movement of the *Pastoral*. This is the place to savor Schindler's seductive word-painting for ourselves:

> One day in the latter half of April 1823, a time of many troubles and reverses, Beethoven decided to take a respite by returning north to Heiligenstadt and its lovely surroundings. It was a place where he had put many musical works on paper and where, too, he had conducted his studies of nature; but he had not been there for ten years. The sun shone warmly and the landscape was already

arrayed in its most beautiful spring finery. . . . we turned our steps towards the Kahlenberg in the direction of [Nussdorf]. Between Heiligenstadt and [Nussdorf] there lies the pleasant, grassy valley of a gently murmuring brook [the Schreiberbach] that rushes down from a nearby mountainside. While crossing this valley, overhung here and there by tall elm trees, Beethoven would frequently pause and let his enraptured gaze wander over the spectacular scene before him. Once he sat down on the grass and, leaning against an elm, asked me if there was a yellowhammer singing in the topmost branches of the trees. But all was quiet. Then he said, "It was here that I composed the Scene at the Brook, and the yellowhammers up there, the quails, the nightingales, and the cuckoos composed along with me."[110]

Before we leave Fernkorn's Heiligenstadt bust in search of a more imposing Austrian monument to Beethoven, we might ask why this particular image of the composer was so idealized by the sculptor (enough to elicit a disapproving reference from Thayer[111]). Fernkorn, after all, was a capable portraitist in bronze: his Karlsplatz monument to the recently deceased Josef Ressel (1793–1857), inventor of the screw propeller, was unveiled in the exact same year (18 January 1863) as the Beethoven bust and exhibited realism to the point of a miniature ship stern with projecting, workable screw propeller (Fig. 128). (The pedestal plaque does an admirable job of getting this accomplishment into Latin: "Josepho Ressel patria Austriaco, qui omnium prior rotam cochlidem [sic] pyroscaphis propellendis adplicuit anno 1827.") Ressel, who, we note, had demonstrated his invention to the world in the year of Beethoven's death, had simply not yet rotated to the feature-tampering fame of the tone poet. And then there was the sculptural precedent for idealizing Beethoven's features set by Anton Dietrich in 1822 in his second, classicizing bust of Beethoven à l'antique, with short hair (see Fig. 19). Fernkorn's "non-Beethoven" image has another antecedent as well: the idealized bust modeled after Beethoven's death by the Viennese sculptor and engraver Johann Nepomuk Schaller (1777–1842) for the London Philharmonic Society (Fig. 129). The well-groomed curly locks, sloping forehead, and drooping drapery of the plaster cast have little to do with the Beethoven remembered by Sir George Smart. Only the grimace is familiar. The exaggeration of the compressed, downward-pulling lips and cleft chin would be repeated in a three-dimensional image of the composer fashioned for the Beethovenhaus at the end of the century. This carved marble bust, the work of two North German sculptors,[112] substitutes "contemporary" for the classical garb and keeps solitary watch in the room of Beethoven's birth (Fig. 130).

A Beethoven idealized was not exclusively the property of Germanic artists. A few months after Fernkorn's bronze bust was dedicated in the Heiligenstadt Park, an engraving titled simply *Beethoven* (Fig. 131) received a medal at the Paris Salon of 1863. The artist was Aimé de Lemud (1816–1887) and this was not the first time he had created a successful print from a fantasy portrait of a departed hero. In 1839 he had painted the image of a fellow Beethoven admirer, E.T.A. Hoffmann. The painting from which he derived his Beethoven print was called *Beethoven's Dream*, and indeed some Hoffmannesque characters seem to have invaded the dream world of the slumbering musical genius who is surrounded by cello, square pianoforte, and crumpled scores. The "power" of Beethoven's music sheds its blinding light over a discouraged, confused, and fleeting knot of humanity whose various national costumes almost distract attention from the unusually elegant, bob-haired, long-nosed, redolently Gallic Beethoven.

But to return to Vienna. Surely the centennial year of Beethoven's birth would find the city of Vienna about to unveil a proper monument to its most famous former resident. If an outlying village (not yet annexed by Vienna as part of the nineteenth-district suburb of Döbling) like Heiligenstadt, with its limited resources, could erect a public memorial, certainly the *kaiserlich und königlich* ("imperial and royal") capital of the Habsburg Empire could come up with an appropriately majestic monument to its great citizen. But the centenary year came and went in *k. u. k.* Vienna and no three-dimensional image of Beethoven rose to receive the grateful salutations of the Viennese inhabitants of what Robert Musil would later (1931) call *Kakania*—his delightfully transparent pseudonym for an Austria-Hungary in which every institution of state was preceded by either one (for Hungary only *königlich* applied) or two k's.[113] The person who was to be a driving force to build a Beethoven monument—one that would be worthy of its subject and positioned handsomely in the heart of Vienna—had his mind elsewhere in the year 1870. Nikolaus Dumba (1830–1900), the wealthy industrialist whose new palatial home stood on the Ringstrasse (Parkring 4; completed 1865), was indeed involved in strenuous efforts to raise a memorial, but the intended honoree was Schubert. As a young man Dumba had been an excellent performer of Schubert songs and he had since become an avid and important collector of Schubert autographs. For the past eight years his financial acumen had been at the service of the Vienna Men's Choral Society in an ambitious project to create a Schubert monument. This was finally accomplished in 1872 and the genial effigy carved from Carrara marble by Hähnel's former student Carl Kundmann (1838–1919) (Fig. 132) was unveiled on 15 May.[114] In the meantime upstart Heiligenstadt jumped into the Beethoven breach again, and Richard Wagner was there. Cosima's diary pinpoints the event: "Yesterday [Richard] told me of a ceremony he had attended in Heiligenstadt near Vienna, when a plaque was fixed to the house in which Beethoven had lived, stating that here B. had composed the *Pastoral*."[115] (There are today thirty-one different memorial plaques to Beethoven in the city of Vienna.)

While Vienna did nothing for a Beethoven monument in 1870 (although it did hold a Beethoven festival concert at which Liszt played), Wagner's former home of Dresden, now attuned to Beethoven's greatness—partly because of Wagner's revelatory performances of the Ninth there in the 1840s—decided to erect a three-dimensional image of Beethoven to honor the centenary. Although the project was not realized, posterity has inherited one of the proposals for a Saxon tribute to Beethoven. It is the model for a colossal statue of Beethoven (Fig. 133) submitted by the Dresden sculptor Johannes Schilling (1828–1910). Schilling had been the pupil of Ernst Rietschel (creator of Dresden's 1860 Weber monument[116]), Johann Friedrich Drake (see Fig. 112), and Ernst Hähnel (see Figs. 116–118). And it showed. The would-be monumental sculptor's enthusiastic design borrows Drake's circular pedestal with freestanding figures and tops it off with Hähnel's conception of an over-life-size, standing figure of Beethoven. Only now there is no attempt at portraying the historical Beethoven. Schilling's mythicizing contribution is to present Beethoven as a modern-day Apollo. The enormous lyre and full-length Classical garb belong to the gods; only the billowing haircut is remotely Beethovenian. Perhaps Dresden's coffers and will had been drained by Wagner's campaign for the Weber monument (a much less pretentious, single-figure bronze on a simple pedestal placed near the Zwinger Museum); at any rate Schilling's monster monument came to naught, and he arrived in Vienna with

(Colorplate 8)

unrequited dreams of multistepped, figurated granite pedestals crowned by huge bronze effigies. The City of Dreams blessed him with one come true, and on 10 November 1876 Schilling's four-tiered monument to the poet Schiller, surrounded by the four ages of humanity, was unveiled (Fig. 134). Once again, Vienna had honored a "foreign" hero before acknowledging one of its own.

Kakania, Land of Procrastination, had not of course been oblivious of the Beethoven centennial or of the homage rendered Beethoven in other countries. Wagner's 1870 monograph *Beethoven*, linking artistic right with military might in relation to the Franco-Prussian War, the designation that year of the house where Beethoven was born as a national monument, and Ludwig Nohl's publication the following year on the Beethoven festivities and modern art—all these left their mark on the more thoughtful caretakers of Vienna's cultural heritage, and finally on 7 February 1871 a committee for a Beethoven monument was set up by the Gesellschaft der Musikfreunde (Society of the Friends of Music). The leading member and president of the committee was Nikolaus Dumba, whose efforts on behalf of the Schubert memorial were about to be crowned with corporeal success. Dumba took on his new assignment with typical verve. Through a mutual friend, the dramatist and librettist Salomon Mosenthal (1821–1877), he had the committee contact the most eminent and successful Beethoven fund raiser of all time—Liszt. But this was a Liszt grown twenty-seven years older and wiser than the impulsive young impresario of Bonn days. Now sixty-one years old and tired of musical politics, he voiced his feelings about the project to his adored "stepdaughter" Marie zu Sayn-Wittgenstein (daughter of his lover, Carolyne), who lived in Vienna, in a frank letter dated 28 November 1872:

> [Mosenthal] wrote me eloquently, in July, that they were counting on me to furnish the pedestal for the new statue. I replied that I had done at Bonn in 1845 what they were now asking me to do again in Vienna; and to take the opportunity for such a repetition seemed to me dubious, in the light of my age and of the circumstances. In all truth, for more than 40 years Beethoven's Symphonies have been performed unceasingly in every country. The same is true for his piano works: these were played a short while back in Vienna by Bülow and Rubinstein in such an admirable manner, that I could merely pick up the pieces they left behind. Furthermore, the hundredth anniversary of the birth of the Sublime Master was celebrated everywhere, in December 1870, by musical festivals lasting several days; to continue these festivals for the occasion of M. von Mosenthal's *local* project, would be perhaps to risk too much the enthusiasm of the public,—a risk in which I prefer not to participate at all, for fear of succumbing myself. . . .
>
> To conclude, if already they are thinking of honoring the Art by another embellishment of one of Vienna's public squares, wouldn't there be a better way to do it than to erect a statue of Beethoven, in the style of the town of Bonn and 30 years later?[117]

The interesting thumbnail sketch of the rise of Beethoven's popularity over the past forty years given by Liszt in this letter is followed by a spontaneous suggestion for a different kind of musician's monument that reveals Liszt as unconscious subscriber to the myth that Beethoven was born in *Vienna*! Without noticing his mistake he proposed: "Why not raise a collective monument joining together the five great musicians, *born in Austria* [Liszt's underlining]: Gluck, Haydn, Mozart, Beethoven, Schubert?"[118] Had he written "died in Austria," Liszt would have been correct; as it stood, he had by uncaught ukase gratuitously moved the birthplaces of Gluck from the Upper Palatinate and of Beethoven from the Rhineland to within the boundaries of Franz Josef's empire—so powerful was the seductive mystique that linked musicians with the City of Music in birth as well as in life and death.

Instead of siding with Liszt, Marie, who had married the former aide-de-camp to Franz Josef, Prince Konstantin von Hohenlohe-Schillingsfürst, seems to have sided with Dumba's Beethoven committee camp, urging them to even greater efforts of persuasion and flattery. Liszt's next letter to Marie mentions in a pleased tone that the committee had written him "an extremely nice letter covered with signatures"[119] but that he had nevertheless declined their invitation to be associated with the fund-raising drive. Princess Marie proved to be quite a diplomat: while holding out hope to Dumba she made an epistolary advance on Liszt that comforted and appealed to him on several fronts. Obviously willing to reconsider, he wrote back immediately: "Your kind words concerning my answer to the Beethoven Committee calmed me. In stopping myself at the preamble to what I wrote Mosenthal in July, I do not claim to exclude myself completely from the affair; it is only that I feel neither the age nor the inclination to draw my sword."[120] Turning to what must have been a complimentary response to his pentaploid musical monument idea, he purred contentedly:

> As for the collective monument of the five Austrian Musician-Geniuses [Marie seems to have been equally taken in by Liszt's newly assigned nationalities], I dared risk the *idea* only in very humble confidence to Your Highness. If you don't altogether reject it, perhaps some day it too will have its happy moment. Schubert's very successful statue, in the *Stadt-Park*, doesn't seem to me to be a definite obstacle against the quintuple monument; the chief difficulty rests in the composition of the group. To my way of thinking the place in the center belongs to Mozart, due to the universality of his genius; but how should the others be grouped and shown?[121]

Little could Liszt have known that, with the exception of Haydn (whose body was removed to Eisenstadt in 1820), his description of an honorary ensemble of Austria-related musicians, with Mozart in the center, would find necropolitan realization in the Graves of Honor section of Vienna's Central Cemetery, where since the late 1880s, after the reburial of Beethoven and Schubert, just such an arrangement has existed, with the centrally placed Mozart memorial, flanked on either side by the graves of Beethoven and Schubert, facing the grave of Gluck.

Something that Liszt would live to see, however, in connection with a Beethoven monument in Vienna was the selection of that sculptor whose name first came to his mind in connection with the project (unlike his unsuccessful promotion of Bartolini for the Bonn monument). Answering his own question about how the composition of his quintuple monument should be solved, he had continued in his letter to Marie: "May Zumbusch be able to 'Eureka'! When I have the pleasure of meeting him again at Your Highness's, I'll ask him to sketch secretly the group, and I'm counting on his design to get me your indulgence."[122] The Zumbusch in whom Liszt had so much ready confidence was Kaspar Clemens Eduard (Ritter von) Zumbusch (1830–1915), whose large bronze bust of Ludwig II we have already observed in place in front of Wagner's Villa Wahnfried (see Fig. 100 and chapter 4, note 607). Zumbusch, creator of several marble portrait busts of both Wagner and Liszt[123] and future portrayer of Brahms's surgeon friend Billroth (1897), had just been enticed to Vienna with the offer of a professorship at the Academy after winning universal admiration for his recently completed (1866–72) monument in Munich to King Maximilian II (Fig. 135). The model for this quadruple figured monument with putti was shown in the World Exposition held in Vienna in 1873, and the city fathers expected great things from their Bavarian import. They were not to be disappointed. The fifteen years that Zumbusch devoted to the sixty-six-foot-high, multifigurated Maria Theresia monument (Fig. 136; unveiled 1888), with high-relief images of the empress's three greatest musicians—Gluck, Haydn, and the six-year-old Wunderkind Mozart—resulted in a landmark for the city (between the Museums of Fine Arts and of Natural History, facing the Ringstrasse) and a knighthood for the sculptor.

While Liszt was being wooed into lending his prestigious name and pianistic fingers to the fund-raising aspect of Vienna's projected Beethoven monument, Dumba's committee was able to proclaim on 5 May 1873 that a competition for worthy designs had been opened to four sculptors—Anton Paul Wagner, Johannes Benk, Carl Kundmann (the latter two, former students of the creator of the Bonn Beethoven monument), and Kaspar Clemens Zumbusch (who was not a Hähnel product). Shortly after the closing date for entries (1 February 1874), three models (all three feet four inches in height) submitted by Benk, Wagner, and Zumbusch were put on public exhibition and a lively discussion of their respective merits took place in the press, with most of the votes going to Zumbusch. By 18 February 1874 the eight-member jury, which included Dumba and and the neoclassical painter Anselm Feuerbach (1829–1880; a friend and favorite painter of Brahms), announced its decision. The choice went to Zumbusch, Feuerbach's fellow professor at the Vienna Academy,[124] and the phrase *Professorenplastik* ("professorial sculpture") entered the critics' vocabulary. Princess Marie must have been in on the deliberations, for two days before the jury's official announcement Liszt was writing her: "I am delighted by your approbation of Zumbusch's *Beethoven Monument*, and I sincerely wish it continuing successes in a growing *crescendo*."[125] With a crew of six helpers, Zumbusch went to work on the twelve figures and one swan planned for the monument, which would take several years to model and cast in bronze, and the pedestal, which was to be carved in porphyry, was awarded to a stone cutter.

Liszt's final resistance melted away with the selection of his admired friend Zumbusch and he threw himself generously, if not really enthusiastically, into plans for a gala benefit concert, scheduled for March 1877, the fiftieth anniversary of Beethoven's death. He wrote Dumba's committee that, "rejoiced to be able to help you, I will work with you with a full heart and both hands in the concert for the Beethoven Monument."[126] He further specified that he wished to play only music "absolutely" by Beethoven, gracefully sidestepping the committee's idea of a performance of one of his own Beethoven cantatas.[127] The concert took place on 18 March 1877 in Vienna with, as Liszt had requested, an all-Beethoven program that included the *Emperor* Concerto, the Fantasia for Piano, Chorus, and Orchestra (op. 80), and Caroline Bettelheim singing some of Beethoven's Scottish Songs arrangements (op. 108). Liszt was either soloist or accompanist in all three works,[128] but he was able to donate only nine instead of the ten piano-playing fingers he had promised. An injury to his left hand forced him to play without using the fourth finger of that hand—rather a remarkable and typically Lisztian feat—and although most of the audience did not notice, one young listener was "bitterly disappointed"[129] by Liszt's subdued performance. This severe judge was the eleven-year-old Ferruccio Busoni (1866–1924) (Fig. 137), who later became the best performer of Liszt after Liszt himself. Although Liszt did not fulfill Busoni's expectations on this occasion, he was subsequently elevated by Busoni to the apex of his holy trinity of great composers, the base of which consisted of Bach and Beethoven. It may have been the memory of the elderly Liszt performing to raise money for the erection of a memorial to Beethoven that inspired Busoni to describe his own idea for a Beethoven monument. We may cite the description here, noting how the Italian musician's notable penchant for form carries over into his visual concretization:

> I have a beautiful idea for a Beethoven monument, and would not like to have this idea lost, so I tell it to you. The uppermost group shows Beethoven on a thronelike chariot, drawn by four horses. These horses symbolize the Third, Fifth, Seventh, and Ninth symphonies. The first horse (Eroica) is all in armor; the second one (Fifth Symphony) is bare, very vigorous, with uplifted head; the third horse (Seventh Symphony) is slender and passes on with a dancelike gait; the fourth one (Ninth Symphony) is entirely covered with cloth, including the head, though holes are cut in for the eyes.
>
> The middle group shows the Ideal in the center, connecting art with the Heavenly; at the right side a boy worshiping, at the left side a girl in worship. The lower group, high relief full of figures and motion. In the center Florestan and Leonore, or the rescue of the man by the Love of his wife; at the right, among other figures, Josef Haydn and Friedrich von Schiller; at the left Napoleon as a young general; all around workmen, soldiers, revolutionaries. The two great front statues: at the right, love of mankind; at the left, independence, freedom. At the back facade: beautiful columned architecture. Below in three (corners): music, lyric poetry, drama. Is this not very beautiful?[130]

Busoni's grandiose quadriga idea (perhaps inspired by the proud example atop the Brandenburg Gate in Berlin—the composer's home from 1894 on) with its attendant symbols of the *social* implications of Beethoven ("workmen, soldiers, revolutionaries"), is the natural extension of the later nineteenth-century conception of Beethoven as the property of not just the aristocratic or musical elite but the common citizen. The first expression of this enfranchisement of Beethoven for the masses (or of the masses for Beethoven) had taken place in the final site selection for the Bonn monument: Hähnel's Beethoven had been placed in the middle of the town's busiest and most central square, the Münsterplatz, watched over by cathedral and post office alike.

A far more subtle declaration of the "people's Beethoven" would occur with the choice of site for Zumbusch's projected Beethoven monument in Vienna. Likely spots would have been in front of any of the numerous houses where Beethoven spent more than a few months' residence, and most especially the Schwarzspanierhaus (torn down in 1902) on the Alserstädter glacis where he died. But it was the decade of the 1870s, and the very core of Vienna was undergoing a remarkable physical change that had important social and political ramifications. This was the creation, through private funds, of the Ringstrasse—that great boulevard of large apartment houses, palatial private residences,[131] and monumental public buildings rising up on the stretch of flat ground encircling the inner city—Beethoven's beloved *glacis*. The broad *glacis* with its cliff like fortifications that had once been Vienna's defense against Turkish invaders had already been given over in part to the people as a recreational area by Josef II; nine months after assuming the throne in 1848 the young Kaiser Franz Josef, acting against the recommendations of the military, declared this vast belt of undeveloped land separating Vienna's growing suburbs from the old inner city open for civilian and public purposes. A City Expansion Commission and fund were established, most of the city ramparts were demolished, and the first "public" building to go up was a "monument of patriotism and of devotion of the people of Austria to the Imperial House,"[132] the Gothic Revival Votivkirche—financed by public subscription in thanks for the emperor's narrow escape from an assassin's bullet in 1853. (Liszt was later asked to play a concert for the Kaiser Franz Josef Foundation.[133]) The edict opening up the way for conversion of Vienna's glacis into the broad tree-lined avenue ringing the inner city we know today was issued at the end of 1857 (20 December). Eight years later Dumba moved into his new palais on the Ringstrasse (corner of Zedlitzgasse on the Parkring), opposite the northern tip of the Stadtpark (laid out 1861–67), which ran along the left, or outer side of the Ring as it proceeded southwards towards the culminating musical point of the inner city, the *kaiserlich-königlich* Opera House (1861–69). The following year (1866) a handsome Gothic Revival building, the Academic Gymnasium, was finished on the southwest side of a pleasant arbor lying just off the outer edge of the Ringstrasse. This grove, bordered on two sides by wooden trellised arcades thick with vines, was situated five blocks south of Dumba's residence and one block from the southern edge of the Stadtpark. It was this already popular and "public" pocket park in the (then) Kolowratring[134] that was procured by Dumba's committee for the Beethoven monument site (Fig. 138). That Beethoven, the ordinary citizen made noble by his gift of music, would be honored here, amid the new communal Prachtbauten ("buildings of splendor"), was a declaration of possession by the prosperous bourgeois elite to whom the city of Vienna would owe its final shape and appearance.

Prefigured by Carlyle's pragmatic hero concept (he admired Bismarck, did not care however for Beethoven), the desire of ordinary citizens to "now praise famous men" (and sometimes women) grew in converse proportion to the decline of the first and second estates, especially after the revolutions of 1848. Monarchs, popes, and princely generals still commanded painted effigies and three-dimensional memorials, but self-made politicians, scientists, philosophers, physicians, and artists appealed to the third estate, which was developing its commercial talents and tasting the success of power. Dynastic monuments, such as Zumbusch's Maximilian II in Munich (see Fig. 135) or his Maria Theresia in Vienna, began to share public space with bronze burghers who, by virtue of some heroic or world-changing accomplishment, also deserved immortality. The erection as early as 1863 of a monument to celebrate the inventor of a ship's screw propeller (see Fig. 128) was certainly a precocious indication of this new civic pride. Josef Ressel, wrestling with problems of world-wide importance, had seemingly earned his pedestal in front of Vienna's (then) Polytechnisches Institut.[135]

Such monuments were clearly statements of national self-consciousness as well. On behalf of Germany, Bonn had proclaimed itself the birthplace and nurturer of Beethoven. But as soon as Vienna came up with a proper marmorean or bronze response, Austria would very probably, in the eyes of the world, convincingly claim the larger share of the Beethoven legacy. The city's experience with raising funds for Johannes Schilling's Vienna Schiller monument (see Fig. 134) was an intriguing if sobering example of thwarted nationalism. The German-speaking inhabitants of Franz Josef's multinational empire had originally responded to the plan of a public monument to Schiller as an expression of the idea of the unity of all Germanic states. But after Austria's humbling withdrawal from the Confederation (1866; Bismarck had provoked Austria into the Seven Weeks'

War, which it lost), the citizenry was caught up in conflicting emotions of resentment towards Bismarck's Germany and hunger for spiritual ties with German classical culture. "Where two Germans are, there is Schiller among them," ran one emotional headline[136] of the day. But the provincial capitals did not share this uplifting sentiment. Prague's fund-raising committee was immediately dissolved; Budapest sent word that it would gladly support a Schiller memorial in Weimar, but that it would not send a kreuzer to Vienna; and Lemberg announced peevishly: "The Poles consider Vienna's Schiller Memorial to be pig's meat."[137] Stubbornly the German faction continued on alone. The terrible stock market crash of 1873 delayed but did not deter efforts to complete the giant ensemble. A large square was cleared for it in 1874 in front of Theophil Hansen's new Academy of Fine Arts, then under construction (1872–76). Ten years after the Austrians' humiliating defeat by their Prussian brethren at Königgrätz, Schilling's monumental Schiller monument was unveiled on 10 November 1876. The extraordinary number of police prudently but visibly deployed to discourage anti-German demonstrations became the butt of a newspaper caricature (Fig. 139) that showed Schiller rising from his casket to observe the cordoned-off scene. He remarks in bewilderment: "I must really have been a very dangerous threat to the state if, after so many years, such an army of police is commandeered for the unveiling of my monument."

Would such a fate await the Rhinelander Beethoven when his monument was unveiled in Vienna four years later? Perhaps musicians, because of the frequently imputed universality of their language, were exempt from political disputes such as those that surrounded the erection of the Schiller monument. The 1872 unveiling of the monument to that most Viennese of all Austrian composers, Schubert (see Fig. 132), in the south section of the Stadtpark (almost opposite Dumba's palais, see Fig. 138) provoked no mass protests from Czech, Hungarian, or Polish nationalists. And Kundmann's kindly conception was hardly geared to incite anything but empathy. A very nonthreatening Schubert, Biedermeier in details of dress, sits on an "outdoor" bench, leaning against a tree stump with a pen in his upraised right hand and an open notebook on his lap, his mild, inspired glance directed heavenwards. He is barely taller than his pedestal, which, with its front bas-relief panel of a lute-holding female on the back of a springing sphinx, reminds us that Kundmann was a most observant Hähnel student (compare Fig. 118). On either side of Kundmann's allegory of Musical Fantasy are scenes representing, on the left, Instrumental Music, and, on the right, Vocal Music—again similar to Hähnel's Bonn pedestal reliefs of Sacred and Dramatic Music.

Given the instant popularity of the Schubert monument (another three-dimensional homage to a thoroughly Viennese artist would be created by Kundmann in 1889 for Beethoven's friend Grillparzer[138]), it might be wondered whether Zumbusch's prize-winning design had also essayed a "man-of-the-people" approach. Absolutely not. The titan was not to be tampered with. Mythopoesis had made too much headway not to be materialized, quite literally, on a mighty pedestal and with heroic mien. Hähnel[139] and his students might produce accessible, period-bound personages in bronze, but Zumbusch, creator of Munich's multi-figured, larger-than-life Maximilian II monument, and since 1874 hard at work on a truly architectonic in scale monument to Maria Theresia (see Fig. 136), had no such intention. *His* Beethoven was awesome (Fig. 141). Grave, formidable, and imposing was this genius who did not walk with notebook and pen in hand as did Hähnel's, but who sat, as though on a throne, wrapped in frowning and solitary concentration. But not only was Zumbusch's Beethoven a man of contemplation, he was also, by implication, a man of action. Every muscle of his powerful body is tensed, ready to respond. The figure seems to swivel on its low seat, the left leg projects forward, the right pushes inward, and the contrapposto is continued in the arms as the left arm—elbow thrust out—grasps and checks the fist-clenched right arm that stretches across the turning torso.

Is this the historical Beethoven? To be sure a contemporary jacket, vest, up-turned shirt collar, and neck ruffle are shown, but the shirt is spread open at the neck and the ruffle ripples and projects with the same energy as the abundant, twisting locks of hair. The potentially distracting detail of a buckle shoe is circumvented by the elegant and eye-catching cloaking of the lap and legs with an unabashed and literal mantle of fame (compare the somewhat awkward attempt at this in the Schubert memorial). How different from Hähnel's burgher-of-Bonn conception (see Fig. 116 especially). And how reminiscent of one of Michelangelo's greatest figural statements of "action in repose," the *Moses* for the tomb of Julius II (Fig. 140). The similarity is not by chance. We know that Zumbusch owned and treasured several photographs[140] of the marble masterpiece in front of which he had stood in reverence during his student sojourn in Rome (1857–58). It was this Michelangelesque bronze Beethoven, cast before the other figures intended for the monument, that Zumbusch sent to the Paris world exposition of 1878. Entranced viewers there shivered before the same terribilità that the judges of the exposition had felt: the towering titan (over eight feet high) was awarded a gold medal.[141]

The Beethoven figure that commanded a gold medal in the Parisian metropolis was not quite the same Beethoven figure Zumbusch had submitted to the city of Vienna in his model of 1874 (Fig. 142). The bronzed plaster model shows a gentler, more earthbound Beethoven, his thoughtful expression one of musing rather than fierce cogitation, his legs closer to each other, not yet thrust apart in swiveling restlessness. Shirt collar and cravat are in place, as are the luxuriant locks of hair. It is a tamer and younger Beethoven we see. The great eagle-composer has not yet spread its feathers, nor stretched to full, majestic height. And yet even this more domesticated (the jacket has neat wide cuffs here, abandoned in the bronze realization) Beethoven had elicited most favorable commentary from the Vienna press. A critic for the *Allgemeine Zeitung* of 10 February 1874 praised Zumbusch's conception unreservedly: "Seldom have I seen a sculpted work of such gripping simplicity, so vigorous in mood and so powerfully effective through its clarity of conception. . . . Beethoven sits on . . . a boulder, alone, like his genius. The history of the genesis of an entire symphony can be read in the deeply ground features, how he suffered as he created. This face tells us this, this face upon the forehead of which is unmistakably imprinted the mark of suffering genius."[142]

Zumbusch's reworking of the face for the bronze version—intensifying the contracted brow and downward-turning lips—reflected his continuing ambition to capture the psychological as well as the physical Beethoven. He had embarked upon a zealous hunt for contemporary likenesses of the composer, collecting pictures and engravings, and procuring a copy of Klein's 1812 life mask. But, he later revealed, the greatest help had been a small Beethoven plaque handed to him by a total stranger one day as he was leaving the Academy.[143] Perhaps too his growing friendship with Franz Brentano (1833–1917), newly appointed (1874) professor of philosophy at Vienna University, whose aunt was the famous Bettina, played a role in the recasting of Beethoven's features along more grandiose lines.[144] The two men may have discussed Bettina's lofty Beethoven, but also Franz Brentano's namesake, Beethoven's own good friend Franz Brentano (1765–1844; Bettina's half-brother) of Frankfurt.

(Colorplate 7)

Zumbusch stood by his original, ambitious scheme—as presented in the competition model—of placing the colossal figure of Beethoven high up "in open nature" on top of a smooth granite porphyry pedestal, alone, but presiding over the twelve giant figures below (Fig. 143)—a two-sphered ensemble not unlike his Munich Maximilian II monument. The Vienna jury was particularly impressed by the sculptor's decision to posit a solitary Beethoven, unaccompanied by any allegories of music; not even physically surrounded by his seat-support (as is Kundmann's Schubert, who leans against his companionable tree stump). As confirmation of Zumbusch's felicitous inspiration to distance the figure of Beethoven from the other figures planned for the lower zone of the monument, some critics quoted Beethoven's own words, written to Archduke Rudolf in 1823: "There is nothing higher than to approach the Godhead more nearly than other mortals and by means of that contact to spread the rays of the Godhead through the human race."[145] It was this deity-approaching Beethoven of Zumbusch's compelling conception that Brahms elected to add, in replica form, to his collection of idols and images. So highly did the city of Vienna think of Zumbusch's Beethoven figure, and so impatiently did the Viennese await the monument's far-off unveiling day, that a full-size plaster cast of the statue was set up in a place of honor within the lobby of the new Vienna Academy where its creator taught. Rudolf von Alt's (1812–1905) detailed watercolor recording the opening festivities of the Academy in 1877 (Fig. 144) shows the distinguished participants dwarfed by the great white Beethoven effigy in the left-hand corner. Vienna would still have three years to wait before the entire monument was cast and ready.

The twenty-two-foot-high ensemble design invites titanic associations not only because of the height of the pedestal, which contributes to the superhuman impression of the Beethoven figure, but also because of the real titan—Prometheus—placed to Beethoven's lower right. It is Prometheus bound, languishing under the vulture's daily attack, and he faces away from the wreath-bearing Nike, who offers her victory crown to the mortal titan who brought not fire but music to humankind. Beethoven's achievement would seem to be the greater of the two. Together, the two noble (larger-than-life) pediment figures—Prometheus and Nike—represent the supposed poles of Beethoven's music and of Beethoven's life: struggle and triumph, suffering and victory. Analogy and message were unmistakable. The composer's gift to the world is symbolized by a ring of nine putti, five in front (Fig. 145) and four in back (Fig. 146), who represent—on one level—the nine symphonies. They may also stand for the different aspects of Beethoven's music: heroic, elegiac, tragic, idyllic, painful, and pastoral.[146] The (left-handed!) lute player in the center (the only putto with wings) of the front group is balanced by the figure of a swan on the verso of the monument—possibly a literal reference to Beethoven's swan song of the Ninth Symphony (so alluded to by Grillparzer in his funeral oration).[147] Beethoven, a Prometheus unbound and restored to lofty heights, looks down towards his earthbound, second self and upon his incarnate children born in pain, the symphonies. How different these nine three-dimensional personifications of music are from the allegorical panels on the Hähnel Beethoven and the Kundmann Schubert. "The monument will be

Fig. 139 Newspaper caricature of the unveiling of the Schiller monument in Vienna,
10 November 1876.

Fig. 140 Michelangelo Buonarroti, Moses, c. 1513–16, marble, from the tomb of Pope Julius II, San Pietro in Vincoli, Rome.

Figure 141 Kaspar Clemens Zumbusch, Beethoven Figure for the Vienna Beethoven Monument, 1878, bronze, Vienna.

Fig. 142 Kaspar Clemens Zumbusch, Model for the Figure of Beethoven for the Vienna Beethoven Monument, 1874, bronzed plaster, present whereabouts unknown.

Fig. 143 Kaspar Clemens Zumbusch, Beethoven Monument, 1880, bronze and granite porphyry, Beethovenplatz, Vienna.

Fig. 144 Rudolf von Alt, Opening of the New Vienna Academy, 1877, watercolor, present whereabouts unknown.

Fig. 145 Kaspar Clemens Zumbusch, Five Putti on the Front of the Beethoven Monument, *1880, bronze, Beethovenplatz, Vienna.*

Fig. 146 Kaspar Clemens Zumbusch, Four Putti and Swan on the Back of the Beethoven Monument, *1880, bronze, Beethovenplatz, Vienna*

Fig. 147 *Alfred Rethel*, Compositional study for an "Eroica Symphony," *c. 1852, pencil drawing, Kupferstichkabinett, Hamburg.*

Fig. 148 *Moritz von Schwind*, Scenes from Beethoven's *Fidelio*, *1865–67, fresco lunette in the foyer of the Vienna Opera House.*

Fig. 149 *The sculptor Kaspar Clemens Zumbusch in his studio with plaster casts of the putti, Beethoven figure, and ensemble model for the Vienna Beethoven monument, photograph of c. 1900.*

Fig. 150 Vinzenz Katzler, Unveiling of the Beethoven Monument in Vienna, *1 May 1880, lithograph.*

Fig. 151 Kaspar Clemens Zumbusch, Beethoven Monument, *1880, bronze and granite porphyry, Beethovenplatz, Vienna. Photograph of the monument in its second installation after being turned 180° around.*

Fig. 152 Gustav Mahler, photograph of 1907.

Fig. 153 Gustav Klimt, photograph of 1902.

359

Fig. 154 Max Klinger, photograph of c. 1900.

Fig. 155 Julius Langbehn, photograph of c. 1890.

Fig. 156 Max Klinger, Christ in Olympus, *1897, oil on canvas, marble, and mahogany, Kunsthistorisches Museum, Vienna, on loan to the Museum der bildenden Künste, Leipzig.*

Fig. 157 Gustav Klimt, Schubert at the Piano, *1899, oil on canvas, destroyed 1945.*

Fig. 158 Lionello Balestrieri, Beethoven (Kreutzer Sonata), *1900, oil on canvas, Museo Revoltella, Trieste.*

Fig. 159 *Vienna Secession artists at the Max Klinger Beethoven Exhibition of 1902, left to right: Anton Stark, Gustav Klimt (seated on the throne), Koloman Moser (seated in front of Klimt), Adolf Böhm, Maximilian Lenz (lying down), Ernst Stöhr (with hat), Wilhelm List, Emil Orlik (seated), Maximilian Kurzweil (with cap), Leopold Stolba, Carl Moll (lying down), and Rudolf Bacher.*

Fig. 160
*Felecian
von Myrbach,*
The Beethoven
Monument in
Heiligenstadt,
1902, woodcut.

Fig. 161
Carl Moll,
Beethoven's
House in the
Eroica-Gasse,
*1902,
woodcut.*

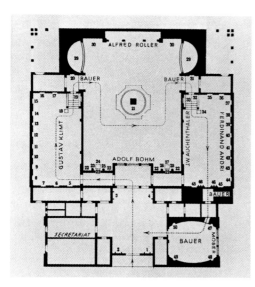

Fig. 162 Joseph Hoffmann,
Orientation Plan of the Secession
Building for the Max Klinger
Beethoven Exhibition, *1902, Vienna.*

Fig. 163 Installation photograph of the Klimt (left) room of the Max Klinger
Beethoven Exhibition, 1902, Secession building, Vienna.

Fig. 164 Gustav Klimt, "The Longing for Happiness," detail from the Beethoven Frieze *for the Max Klinger Beethoven Exhibition, 1902, casein colors on stucco with gold and semiprecious stone inlay. Installation photograph of 1902.*

Fig. 165 Gustav Klimt, "The Knight-Hero," detail from the Beethoven Frieze.

Fig.166 Gustav Mahler, photograph of 1897. For Klimt, Mahler was a modern-day knight-hero, and the visual analogy between his painted "Knight-Hero" and Mahler's profile was intentional.

Fig. 167 Gustav Klimt, "The Hostile Powers," detail from the Beethoven Frieze *for the Max Klinger Beethoven Exhibition, 1902, casein colors on stucco with gold and semi-precious stone inlay.*

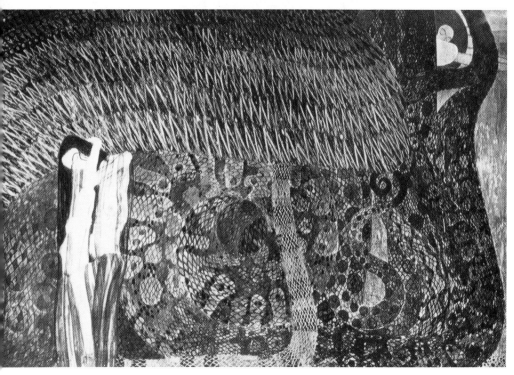

Fig. 168 Gustav Klimt, "Gnawing Worry," detail from the Beethoven Frieze *for the Max Klinger Beethoven Exhibition, 1902, casein colors on stucco with gold and semiprecious stone inlay.*

Fig. 169 Gustav Klimt, ''Poetry,'' detail from the Beethoven Frieze for the Max Klinger Beethoven Exhibition, 1902, casein colors on stucco with gold and semiprecious stone inlay.

Fig. 170 Gustav Klimt, ''Choir of the Angels of Paradise'' (''Joy, Beautiful Spark of the Gods,'' ''This Kiss for All the World!''), detail from the Beethoven Frieze for the Max Klinger Beethoven Exhibition, 1902, casein colors on stucco with gold and semiprecious stone inlay.

Fig. 171 *Photograph of Max Klinger's Leipzig studio taken c. 1900 showing various parts of the* Beethoven Monument. *Left to right: the marble torso, plasticine throne model, onyx mantle, and painted plaster ensemble.*

Fig. 172 *Max Klinger,* The New Salome, *1893, various colored marbles and amber, Museum der bildenden Künste, Leipzig.*

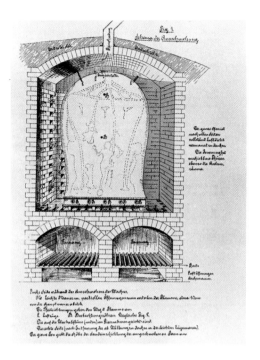

Fig. 173 Max Klinger, design for the special kiln and firing process to be used for the bronze casting of the Beethoven Monument *throne, 1901.*

Fig. 174 Max Klinger, throne for the Beethoven Monument, *1902, bronze, polished gold, ivory, antique glass, and precious stones, Gewandhaus, Leipzig.*

Fig. 175 Max Klinger, design for title page to Goethe's
Faust II, 1880, drawing, private collection, Leipzig.

Fig. 176 Michelangelo Buonarroti, The Erythrean Sibyl from
the Sistine Chapel Ceiling, 1508–12, fresco, Vatican, Rome.

Fig. 177 Michelangelo Buonarroti, The Prophet Jeremiah from
the Sistine Chapel Ceiling, 1508–12, fresco, Vatican, Rome.

Fig. 178 (below) Max Klinger, Herod, from On Death, I,
Opus XI, 1889, etching and aquatint.

Fig. 179 *Max Klinger*, Misery [The Oppressed], *from* On Death, *II, Opus XIII, 1892, etching and engraving.*

Fig. 180 *Max Klinger*, Integer Vitae Scelerisque Purus *("Blameless in life and free of evil"), from* On Death, *II, Opus XIII, 1895, 1900, engraving.*

Fig. 181 Max Klinger, *view of left side of the throne for the* Beethoven Monument, *1901, bronze, Gewandhaus, Leipzig.*

Fig. 182 Max Klinger, *view of right side of the throne for the* Beethoven Monument, *1901, bronze, Gewandhaus, Leipzig.*

Fig. 183 Max Klinger, *view of back of the throne for the* Beethoven Monument, *1901, bronze, Gewandhaus, Leipzig.*

Fig. 184 Max Klinger, "Tantalus" group, left side relief of the Beethoven Monument throne, 1901, bronze, Gewandhaus. Leipzig.

Fig. 185 Max Klinger, "Adam and Eve," right side relief of the Beethoven Monument throne, 1901, bronze, Gewandhaus, Leipzig.

Fig. 186 Max Klinger, back of the Beethoven Monument throne, 1901, bronze, Gewandhaus, Leipzig.

Fig. 187 Max Klinger, Beethoven Monument, *1902, various colored marbles, ivory, precious stones, polished gold, and bronze, Gewandhaus, Leipzig. Photograph of c. 1906.*

Fig. 188 Socrates,
c. 320 B.C.,
Roman copy of a
work by Lysippos
(the head is a
reconstruction),
Ny Carlsberg
Glyptotek,
Copenhagen.

Fig. 189 Auguste
Rodin, The Thinker,
1880, bronze,
Rodin Museum,
Paris.

Fig. 190 Eugène Delacroix,
Michelangelo in His Studio,
1850, oil on canvas, Montpellier.

Fig. 191 Max Klinger, Beethoven figure and eagle from the Beethoven Monument *seen from the left side, 1902, various colored marbles, Gewandhaus, Leipzig.*

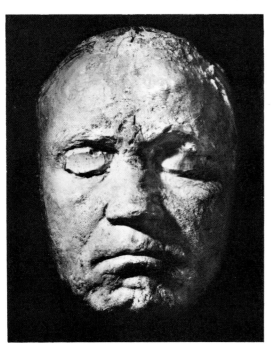

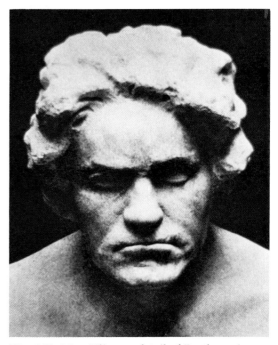

Fig. 192 Franz Klein, Life Mask of Beethoven, *1812, plaster, Beethovenhaus, Bonn.*

Fig. 193 Max Klinger, detail of Beethoven's face from the Beethoven Monument, *1902, marble, Gewandhaus, Leipzig.*

Fig. 194 Max Klinger, painted plaster model for the Beethoven Monument, 1886. *From a photograph of Klinger's Leipzig studio taken in 1920.*

Fig. 195 Max Klinger, Beethoven ex libris plate for the Musikbibliothek Peters, *c. 1894, etching and engraving.*

Fig. 196 Max Klinger, Crucifixion, 1890, oil, Museum of Fine Arts, Leipzig.

Fig. 197 Max Klinger, Beethoven
(copy after Carel Lodewijk Dake),
1892, pen and ink drawing, private
collection, Dallas.

Fig. 198 Carel Lodewijk Dake,
Beethoven, c. 1890, etching.

378

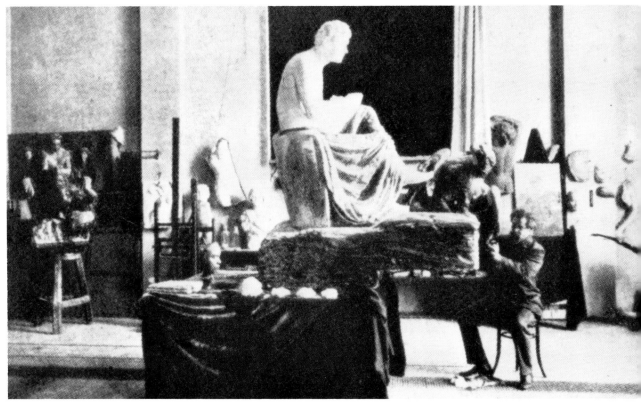

Fig. 199 Photograph of Max Klinger in his Leipzig studio putting the finishing touches on the marble part of his Beethoven Monument, 1901.

Fig. 200 Max Klinger, Pietà, 1890, oil, destroyed.

379

Fig. 201 Max Klinger, Bust of Franz Liszt, *1904, marble, Hochschule für Musik, Leipzig.*

Fig. 202 (far right) Max Klinger, Bust of Richard Wagner, *1904, marble, formerly Wallraf-Richartz-Museum, Cologne.*

Fig. 203 Max Klinger, design for a Leipzig. Wagner Monument (not completed), 1904–20.

Fig. 204 Max Klinger,
Brahms Monument, *1905–9,*
marble, Musikhalle,
Hamburg.

Fig. 205 Photograph of Max Klinger's Beethoven Monument *from the back as installed in the Vienna Secession Beethoven Exhibition of 1902 with mural decoration* Dawning Day *by Adolf Böhm.*

Fig. 206 Photograph of Max Klinger's Beethoven Monument *from the front as installed in the Vienna Secession Beethoven Exhibition of 1902 with mural decoration* Sinking Night *by Alfred Roller.*

Unangenehmes Abenteuer Mahler's in der Secession.

Beethoven: Hab ich Dich endlich! Na wart', Du Symphonieverhunzer!

Kikeriki bei Klinger's Beethoven.

Dem Manne kann geholfen werden!

Fig. 207 Caricature from Kikeriki, *1902, no. 33, last page.* Unpleasant Adventure of Mahler in the Secession: "At last I have you! Just wait, you symphony botcher!"

Fig. 208 Caricature from Kikeriki, *1902, no. 36, title page.* Kikeriki at Klinger's Beethoven: "The man can be helped."

Fig. 209 Christian Horneman,
Beethoven, 1803, miniature on ivory,
Collection Dr. H. C. Bodmer,
Beethovenhaus, Bonn.

Fig. 210 Max Klinger, detail
of Beethoven's face from the
Beethoven Monument, 1902, marble,
Gewandhaus, Leipzig.

Fig. 211 Photograph of overflow
crowd listening to loudspeaker
relay of Beethoven's Fidelio
outside the just reopened Vienna
Opera House, 5 November 1955.

rather grand," Zumbusch had written his mother, " . . . I have proposed a completely new approach."[148]

A precedent for Zumbusch's "symphony-children" did exist, although it is unlikely that the sculptor was aware of it. This was the compositional sketch of about 1852 for an "Eroica Symphony" (Fig. 147) by the German mural painter and graphic artist Alfred Rethel (1816–1859).[149] Instead of musicians or musical instruments, a cloaked female figure, her head illuminated like a candle by the light of musical inspiration, embodies the symphonic art form, specifically Beethoven's Third Symphony. She cradles a baby (evanescent Fourth Symphony?) in her left arm and parts her copious mantle with her right to reveal four active children—the four movements of the *Eroica*—paired in combative (left) and harmonious (right) motions signaling the familiar polarity of struggle and victory sensed by so many of our nineteenth-century interpreters of Beethoven in the *Eroica*. Closer to home, in the recently decorated Vienna Opera House, was another precedent-setting example of the dualism animating the drama of Beethoven's music. While Hähnel had been adorning the loggia balustrade with bronze personifications,[150] the painter Moritz von Schwind, creator of the Beethoven-studded Lachner Roll (see Figs. 60 and 61), was at work on fourteen frescoes for the foyer lunettes which would display various scenes from famous operas (1865–67[151]). One of these was devoted to a tripartite invocation of *Fidelio*, with an emotional progression from suffering despair to heaven-sent hope to victorious rescue (Fig. 148).

With such pictorial responses to the dichotomies of Beethoven's music in mind, a closer look at the pairings and attributes of the putti on Zumbusch's Beethoven monument is rewarding. The symphony-children seem to divide into groups with symbols relating either to warfare (the helmet, sword, and lowered torch of the pair on the left front) or pastoral tranquility (the fruit and flower garland and panpipes of the pair on the left back). We note also the presence of other items, such as a tragic mask in possession of the putti pair closest to Prometheus's vulture (right back); a bundle of thunder bolts, a lyre, and a flute—all attributes of the gods of antiquity—hence the edifying implication that Beethoven is not only a modern-day Prometheus, but also an Orpheus or Apollo. Such classical cross-references would have been fresh in Zumbusch's mind since he was also involved, during the casting of the Beethoven pieces, in the most interesting work of restoring statuary and objects uncovered in the recent archaeological digs at Samothrace (he restored the head and arms of the famed Nike of Samothrace for the Louvre in 1879).

A photograph taken around 1900 of the elderly Zumbusch standing among the plaster models of his various creations (Fig. 149) shows the complete miniature model for the Beethoven monument (far right), a life-size plaster cast of the seated Beethoven (center left in the back), and the two most distinctive putti groupings from the pedestal (left front), the *Pastoral* and the *Eroica* pairs (the martial couple is repeated in smaller size just to the left of Zumbusch) from the back and front of the monument respectively. The sculptor was happy to have these silent souvenirs of his first Vienna success, one which, with the devoted help of his Academy students, had slowly but steadily taken final bronze shape by the beginning of 1880. "The Beethoven-Monument is now ready to be erected," he jubilantly reported to his mother, "the pedestal is already in the square where the garden layout has been completed. The figures, all placed together at the bronze foundry, were recently inspected in my presence by the emperor, who expressed great pleasure. . . ."[152]

The unveiling (Fig. 150) came at long last on the morning of the first day of May 1880. Strings of garlands and banners filled the square and decorated the house towards which the monument was to face, the (then) Palais Gutmann, backing the outer side of the built-up Kolowratring (see Fig. 138). The River Wien (not yet routed into the mostly subterranean canal of the city's massive regulation project begun in 1891) formed a watery backdrop to the newly named Beethovenplatz. In spite of heavy rain that day, many thousands attended the ceremony, the overflow crowd being practically forced into the river. In our print documenting the occasion (and reproducing the sculptural ensemble fairly accurately) the houses lining the far side of the river can be made out and the black-bearded figure of the forty-nine-year-old Zumbusch can be seen standing stiffly to the far right, facing the master of ceremonies, Dumba. Seated in the front row of chairs directly behind Dumba are the figures of two women. Let us take up the account of the *Wiener Allgemeine Zeitung* at this point:

> Committee President von Dumba demonstrated untiring zeal in accommodating the guests streaming into the vicinity, and to the wonderment of the guests of honor he showed two unknown women to the best seats—they were however Beethoven's niece and grandniece—and at ten o'clock he received the Archdukes Carl Ludwig and Rainer representing the Kaiser who had come down with a cold. The people's hymn rang out inspiringly . . . a signal . . . and the monument stood unveiled. All eyes turned upon it with amazement and admiration, then sought the creator, who was keeping modestly in the background. From a reverent silence there pealed aloft after awhile Beethoven's "Praise God" [*Ehre Gottes*; op. 48/4?]. As it evaporated President Dumba began his address. He thanked all who had made the realization of the Monument possible (the Kaiser, the municipality, artists, and art institutes at home and abroad, etc.) and then continued: "Carried along by genuine enthusiasm, Master Zumbusch pledged his full artistic strength and the costs of this work did not have to be obtained by begging . . . no! To the sounds of immortal Beethoven music the ore gushed into the form of this Memorial which is and shall remain a token of the grateful admiration of our song-and-music-rich imperial city for its great citizen van Beethoven [*Bürger van Beethoven*]."[153]

The changing image of Beethoven had now reached a milestone in its mythography. With the alliterative approval of the *Wiener Allgemeine Zeitung* Beethoven had become a citizen-hero: he was both bourgeois and Promethean. He belonged to humanity but came from and had returned to heaven. None of Austria-Hungary's nationalist groups had any problems with this, it would seem, for no police escort of the sort that had accompanied the unveiling of the "German" Schiller monument just four years earlier was required for installation of Zumbusch's "universal" Beethoven. Music proved itself to be beyond politics or race, at least this time. Adolf Schicklgruber would not be born as a humble subject of Kaiser Franz Josef's realm for another nine years, and the Mendelssohn monument (by Werner Stein; unveiled in front of the Leipzig Gewandhaus, 1892) would not become the object of Nazi displeasure and removal "for racial reasons" until 1936.

As for the exciting, unheralded attendance of "Beethoven's niece and grandniece," the *Allgemeine Zeitung* had been a little too *allgemein* in its identification of the mystery women who got to sit in the best seats. It was not Beethoven's niece who was present at the Zumbusch unveiling, but the widow of Beethoven's nephew, Karl, Caroline van Beethoven (née Naska). And actually Dumba had escorted *five* mysterious ladies to their seats in the front row of the honored guest section, for the aged Caroline had brought her four daughters with her (Beethoven's grandnieces all). A heartfelt thank-you note written to Zumbusch a few days-after the event is signed by the Beethoven contingent as follows: "Caroline van Beethoven, widow of Karl v. B, Caroline Weidinger born v. B, Marie Weidinger born v. B., Gabriele Heimler born v. B., Hermine Axmann born v. B."[154] Not noted by the *Wiener Allgemeine Zeitung* was the absence from the ceremony of Caroline's only son, the troublesome Ludwig whom Wagner had attempted to aid with an introduction to Ludwig II. *He* had since served the Beethoven mythology in such a way that in 1872 he was sent to prison for four years for embezzlement: his lesser crimes included passing himself off as the grandson of the composer, calling himself Baron *von* Beethoven, and selling counterfeit Beethoven memorabilia. Ludwig exited from the documentable scene in 1889 (myth says he went to America); his mother, who received financial support from a pension fund set up by Viennese Beethoven lovers, lived until 1891.

About one thing the *Wiener Allgemeine Zeitung* was not wrong: Vienna's new monument had proved itself worthy of the Beethoven myth: Zumbusch's citizen-hero presentation had eclipsed Bonn's pedestrian native-son image. "The city of Vienna has not become richer just because of a monument; it has become richer because of a fitting and authentic work of art, something worth seeing."[155]

Liszt was in complete agreement. Eleven days after the unveiling he wrote: "Speaking of monuments designed for great Artists, I don't know any comparable to that of Beethoven in Vienna. The City and the Sculptor, Zumbusch, can legitimately be proud of it."[156] Liszt was in a good position to know the effect of Zumbusch's monument: in 1877 Dumba's committee had commissioned the sculptor to make a bronze reduction of the ensemble for presentation to Liszt in thanks for his enormously successful fund-raising concert on behalf of the monument.[157] His single performance, for which the highest ticket prices had been charged, had added ten thousand florins to the committee's coffers of seventy-four thousand florins.[158]

The final positioning of Zumbusch's Beethoven monument contributes an interesting footnote to the history of urban development, a force to which even mythmaking must often bow. In 1901, after the covering over of the River Wien had begun, the entire ensemble of bronze figures was given a 180-degree turn. From now on burgher Beethoven would sit with his back to the old inner city and face out towards the environs he had so loved in life and that were now being so swiftly transformed by his industrious fellow citizens. One touch of the old square and earlier garden setting was preserved (until recently). The wooden trelliswork of the original vine arbor still framed the titan as he looked down from his self-earned height upon his latter-day admirers (Fig. 151).

Chapter Six

VIENNA'S BEETHOVEN OF 1902: APOTHEOSIS AND REDEMPTION

Among the musicians besides Busoni present in the vast audience that turned out to hear Liszt's gala Beethoven concert of 18 March 1877 was the sixteen-year-old Gustav Mahler (1860–1911) (Fig. 152), then in his first year at the Vienna Conservatory.[1] The two artists who were to cross Mahler's path a quarter of a century later in a collective apotheosis of Beethoven—the fourteenth Vienna Secession exhibit of 1902—were Gustav Klimt (1862–1918) (Fig. 153) and Max Klinger (1857–1920) (Fig. 154). Their routes to Beethoven led from emphatically different backgrounds: Mahler, the Moravian Jew, rigid, brittle, and brilliant; Klimt, the stocky, laconic Viennese of Lucullan sensibilities; and Klinger, the ultra-German bourgeois (he was the son of a wealthy Leipzig soap manufacturer) who nonetheless was visited by and communicated visions of suprareal intensity. But the three disparate artists breathed in the same cultural atmosphere that, during the last two decades of the nineteenth century, hung heavy with disillusionment at the materialistic present and was stifled by a nostalgia for the past. Bismarck's force-fed industrial revolution with its dehumanizing applications of mass technology, Franz Josef's stultifying Kakania, with its bureaucratic mazes and merry-go-round ceremonial of manners and mores, left the seemingly soulless societies of Germany and Austria yearning for something that success and security were not providing.

This vague discontent of modern life tended to put a premium on the irrational just as science was promulgating the rational. A subliminal longing for deliverance from modernity coupled with remembrances of German greatness predisposed people for a cultural hero from the past rather than a political or military hero (Bismarck, Moltke) of the present. A corresponding *redemption through art*—that Germanic aspiration first formulated by Schopenhauer—had been offered by Wagner not only in his heroizing of Beethoven, but also in his later operas when he discarded history for myth and intuitively provided Germany with an intoxicating national answer to the still bitterly remembered Napoleon in the person of Siegfried. And now, a decade before the close of the century, the widespread readiness to enshrine other manifestations of national genius received sudden confirmation in the appearance and phenomenal success of a wild, incoherent book with the messianic title *Rembrandt as Educator* (*Rembrandt als Erzieher*). Published in January of 1890 at Leipzig, the book was brought out anonymously as simply "By a German" ("Von einem Deutschen"). In two years it went through thirty-nine editions. The general public loved it and even the Rembrandt scholar Wilhelm von Bode gave it a serious review. Why was it such a success? Vehemently nationalistic, purportedly programmatic (according to its table of contents), the book was a babbling stream-of-consciousness attack on modern science and intellectualism; a strident, high-sounding bid for a revival of the great German past in which art, individuality, and the irrational energies of the folk would reign freely. Wagner's and Nietzsche's views of Beethoven had fertilized the soil from which this thornbush had sprung. Personifying the great German past was Rembrandt—the Northerner—an individualistic, anticlassical artist whose mysterious chiaroscuro appeared to be a somnambulistic intuition of the primordial life spirit, a spirit that the pace of modern life, enslaved to science and industry, had almost obliterated. German culture could only be renewed through the mystic and mythic forces of art. If Rembrandt's chiaroscuro communications were essentially "North German," Beethoven's moody messages were the Germanic spirit personified. Here is a sampling of the best-seller's leapfrogging logic and grand girth: "Richard Wagner has correctly observed that the Adagio is 'the foundation of all musical tempi'; and in so far as the Germans are the most musical of all peoples, one may call it the special German tempo; what is after all more German than an Adagio by Beethoven? Here we recognize our souls. In the same manner Rembrandt's pictures are expressed in Adagio form . . . it is a North German music and a North German melancholy that lives in his pictures. . . . But they are this also interiorly; a bitterness resolved into harmony fills them—like the works of Beethoven."[2]

So appealing was this metaphysical salt-and-pepper mixture of hysterical nationalism and moral sense of purpose that an intrigued Bismarck invited the no longer anonymous "German" writer to his estate for a visit. Julius Langbehn (1851–1907) (Fig. 155) was the author's name. He was a bizarre, slightly mad, former student of art history who had delivered himself of a dissertation on early Greek Nike statues at the University of Munich and then attempted to deliver the truly mad Nietzsche by walking and talking with him for two weeks at the Jena asylum where he was confined. He was unsuccessful in this attempt—Nietzsche momentarily recovered his reason and threw a table his way. Undaunted, Langbehn borrowed the philosopher's *Schopenhauer as Educator* title, substituted the name Rembrandt, and brought out his own sensationalist critique of German culture, offering a science-hating update on the Wagner-Nietzsche popularization of Schopenhauer's formula for redemption through art.[3]

Apotheosis and redemption were in the air. The worship of heroes was exhilarating, and in such an ambience Beethoven's credentials were even more impeccable than Rembrandt's since, Dutch and Flemish claims aside, Beethoven was *really* a German. Following so closely upon Langbehn's identification of the German ideological crisis and need for a cultural hero, the course of the opening years of twentieth-century mythmaking, as it concerned the three-dimensional Beethoven, was clear: to promote him from the Promethean hero of Zumbusch's conception to a demigod of Zeus-like proportions and powers. This Max Klinger,

Gustav Klimt, and Gustav Mahler would accomplish in the great Vienna Secession Beethoven "happening" of 1902.

How did the sculptor, the painter, and the musician come to focus on Beethoven? For Klinger, the talented amateur pianist and passionate music lover whose veneration of his coeval Brahms would inspire the homage of an entire graphic suite entitled *A Brahms Phantasy*,[4] the rendering of a three-dimensional image of the great tone hero of the past was a suddenly conceived, complete vision that had beckoned to him for many years; for Klimt, it was the plenitude of world imagery in Schiller's Ode as used by Beethoven that ignited the opulent, yet recondite pictorial response of frescoes he contributed as introductory icons in the temporary temple to Beethoven prepared by the Secession; and for Mahler, Beethoven was, with Wagner, one of the only two gods of music. "Now I stick to Beethoven. There are only he and Richard—and after them, nobody. Mark that!," Mahler wrote his young wife Alma (1879–1964) in the summer of 1904.[5]

Although it was as a conductor and not as a pianist that the mature Mahler would convey his—at times vigorously contested—radiant image of Beethoven to both the Old and the New Worlds, it was the fifteen-year-old Mahler's playing of the composer's *Les Adieux* Sonata no. 26, op. 81a, that brought him from the obscurity of his parents' home at Iglau to the illustrious halls of the Vienna Conservatory, where Brahms's violinist friend Hellmesberger was director, in September of 1875. Thirty-five years later Mahler wove a loving reference to this "farewell" leitmotif of Beethoven's into the principal melody of the long first movement of his own Ninth Symphony. So superstitious was he about meeting the same fate that had awaited Beethoven after completing the Ninth, that Mahler resorted to intricate subterfuge to deceive the jealous destiny that had reached out again for Bruckner before he could complete *his* Ninth. Alma lucidly observed her husband's evasive stratagems: "At first he wrote *Das Lied von der Erde* as the Ninth, but then crossed the number out. When later he was writing his next symphony which he called the Ninth, he said to me: 'Actually, of course, it's the Tenth, because *Das Lied von der Erde* was really the Ninth.' Finally when he was composing the Tenth he said, 'Now the danger is past.' "[6]

If Mahler empathized with Beethoven to the point of fearing death after the completion of a Ninth Symphony, the example of Beethoven's nine symphonies was also a siren call that he willingly heeded. Beethoven's spirit seemed to hover over his own composing with particular vividness at times. Bogged down by an especially bothersome passage in his grandiose Third Symphony, which he was at work on during the summer of 1896, Mahler's mind continued to ponder the problem one night while he slept and the next day he joyfully recalled the dream solution that had descended upon him: "a voice called out to me as I slept (it was Beethoven's or Wagner's—I don't keep such bad company at night, do I?): 'Let the horns come in three measures later!' "[7] And reminiscences of the slow movement of Beethoven's final quartet in F Major, op. 135, of which he had heard a memorable performance in Hamburg, crept into the final movement of the Third Symphony as he completed it that summer.[8]

Like Beethoven, Mahler had frequent recourse to the sketchbooks he always carried with him during the frequent and strenuous nature walks that—again like Beethoven—were constitutionally so necessary to his composing processes. Gravely aware of the parallel, and irritated that his doctors had counseled avoiding exertion after diagnosing a valvular defect in his heart (1907), Mahler wrote his protégé Bruno Walter: "I cannot work at my desk. My mental activity must be complemented by physical activity. . . . Now imagine Beethoven having to have his legs amputated after an accident. If you know his mode of life, do you believe he could then have drafted even one movement of a quartet?"[9] During his first summer of enforced leisure after the doctors' discovery, Mahler requested Alma to bring him his "bicycling suit" (to Mahler's mind bicycling was preferable to the "moderate" pace of walking he had been commanded to adopt) and "Beethoven's Letters."[10] The solace or distraction he may have found in the letters of a fellow sufferer seemed to strengthen his sense of identification with the composer whose loss of hearing he had occasionally declared, vis-à-vis his critics, to envy. Now he too had a physical flaw that contrived to remove him from the world of frenetic activity that had hitherto comprised his way of life. "He had taken to saying 'Spitting on the floor doesn't help you to be Beethoven,' " Alma reported of those later years.[11]

Identification with Beethoven, not only in musical deeds but in individual traits or sayings, had long been Mahler's delight. Wanting to compliment a writer friend on his translation of the Polish national poet Adam Mickiewicz, Mahler wrote him: "*Adam* 'stands as solid as a house' (a remark of Beethoven's about *Der Freischutz*), and even if you write no more of it, it is one of the finest things in the world."[12] Interestingly, Mahler had already used Beethoven's remark without modification or parenthetical explanation in an earlier congratulatory letter of a year before to the same correspondent about the same topic: "I really can't tell you what pleasure [*Adam*] has been giving me. 'Kaspar stands as solid as a house!' "[13]

In a strange sense Mahler did resemble Beethoven and more than he realized. The composite Beethoven of mounting fact and crescent legend possessed the same vacillating humors and obsessive intensity that all acquaintances observed in Mahler. The genus Beethovenis described by so many witnesses in the pages of this book is instantly recognizable in young Bruno Walter's (1876–1962) awe-struck impression of the Gustav Mahler of 1894:

> Never before had I seen such an intense person. . . . I was fascinated to observe how the same intensity, the same spiritual tenseness, that had previously filled his rehearsing, was now manifested in his conversation. The vehemence with which he objected when I said something that was unsatisfactory to him . . . his sudden submersion in pensive silence, the kind glance with which he would receive an understanding word on my part, an unexpected, convulsive expression of secret sorrow and, added to all this, the strange irregularity of his walk: his stamping of the feet, sudden halting, rushing ahead again—everything confirmed and strengthened the impression of demoniac obsession.[14]

Bruno Walter (then Bruno Schlesinger) was only eighteen years old when he met Mahler, and just as the seventeen-year-old Wilhelmine Schröder had felt she was watching one of Hoffmann's fantastic figures as the violently gesticulating Beethoven attempted to rehearse her in *Fidelio*, so the impressionable Bruno Walter saw in Mahler the conductor "the incarnation of Kreisler, the arresting, alarming, demoniac conductor . . . of E.T.A. Hoffmann's fantastic tales."[15] As Walter got to know him better (he worked as coach and chorus director under Mahler for two years at the Hamburg Opera from 1894 to 1896), his original Hoffmannesque impression was "replaced by one more just and comprehensive," which revealed, to Walter at least, "his spiritual kinship with the real Beethoven. He had within him his thunderstorms, his power, his love."[16] Like Alma he was introduced to Mahler's machinations to avoid numbering a Ninth Symphony. "When he first spoke to me of *Das Lied von der Erde*, he called it a 'Symphony in Songs.' It was planned to be his Ninth. Then he changed his mind. He thought of how, for Beethoven and for Bruckner, a ninth symphony had written *finis*; he hesitated to challenge fate."[17]

From his close vantage point Walter was privy to how the image of Beethoven hovered in the mind and music of his mentor. He heard Mahler's story of how, at the audacious conclusion of the first movement of his First Symphony in D Major (1888), "he saw Beethoven before him, breaking out into peals of laughter and running off."[18] This acute consciousness of Beethoven in regard to his First Symphony, as reported by Walter, is a telling contradiction of the explanation occasionally found in Mahler scholarship that the name Mahler initially gave this work and later decided to suppress—*The Titan*—is a reference to Jean Paul's novel of the same name. Mahler may have been thinking of the *Eroica* or of the titan Beethoven himself as hero, or even of Mahler as hero (the symphony was, after all, like Berlioz's *Symphonie Fantastique*, the inspired aftermath of a passionate love affair[19]), or an association of all three,[20] but the bacillus was Beethovenian in origin. It spilled over into the first movement of the Second Symphony in the form of a *Totenfeier* (Funeral Rite) for the hero of the First Symphony. Mahler confirmed this in an explanatory remark about his new Symphony in C Minor: "I called the first movement 'Totenfeier.' It may interest you to know that it is the hero of my D-Major symphony who is being borne to his grave. . . ."[21]

Mahler's image of Beethoven was obsessive enough, he admitted, to create qualms about adding voices to his Second Symphony (1888–94, scored for soprano, alto, mixed chorus, and orchestra): "I had long contemplated bringing in the choir in the last movement, and only the fear that it would be taken as a formal imitation of Beethoven made me hesitate again and again. Then Bülow died, and I went to the memorial service.—The mood in which I sat and pondered on the departed was utterly in the spirit of what I was working on at the time.—Then the choir, up in the organ-loft, intoned Klopstock's *Resurrection* chorale.—It flashed on me like lightning, and everywhere became clear in my mind! It was the flash that all creative artists wait for. . . ."[22] After the removal of the powerful Beethoven interpreter Bülow from the scene (Bülow had admired Mahler as a conductor but *not* as a composer) Mahler seemingly felt secure about not being accused of emulating Beethoven on a superficial level, for the block about adding voices to his symphonies vanished. Vocal parts would appear not only in the Second but in the Third, Fourth (soprano solo only), and Eighth symphonies, as well as in the "secret" Ninth, *Das Lied von der Erde*. Each of Mahler's symphonies revolved around a fundamental philosophy, whether signaled by words or not, and it is in this context that a purported favorite remark of Mahler's can be understood—Beethoven, he said, had composed only one Ninth, but every one of *his* symphonies was a "Ninth."[23]

In 1897, musing on the textual solution he had found for his Second (*Resurrection*) Symphony, Mahler referred again to Beethoven and also to Wagner's Beethoven: "Whenever I plan a large musical structure, I always come to a point where I have to resort to 'the word' as a vehicle for my musical idea.—It must have been pretty much the same for Beethoven in his Ninth, except that the right materials were not yet available in his day.—For Schiller's poem is, in the last resort, inadequate; it cannot express the wholly new, unique idea he had in mind. Incidentally, I recall R. Wagner's somewhere saying the same thing quite badly."[24]

During these early years Mahler was involved not only with the ever-haunting image of Beethoven that he carried within him, but with at least once an actual physical image of the composer. Or so he thought. A letter to a Hamburg physicist-friend written in September of 1895 opens briskly with the line: "First and foremost, the Beethoven portrait herewith enclosed."[25] The enclosure must have been a photographic print or graphic copy of the original Beethoven portrait mentioned, for in his next letter to the same correspondent Mahler wrote that he was hastening to send two more "pictures" for mutual friends, but "I should add, to you privately, that there is none left for *myself*, for I only had six made—I shall now order a further six. . . . On principle I shall *not have any more* copies made, so that the pictures will retain rarity value. Incidentally, I have strictly forbidden further copying."[26] Had Mahler come across a portrait unknown to official Beethoven iconography? He must have believed so at the time, but after his death Alma Mahler, in her editorial capacity as supervisor of the publication of her husband's letters, added the following note: "The supposed portrait of Beethoven was in fact that of an unknown Viennese got up *à la* Beethoven."[27] It is fascinating (if perhaps merely fanciful) to imagine Alma, daughter of Austria's greatly respected landscape painter Emil Jacob Schindler—of whom a lifesize marble effigy had been erected in Vienna's Stadtpark in 1895—brushing aside her husband's treasured "Beethoven" icon with the self-assurance of a painter's daughter when she took over Mahler's household as a young bride in 1902. Or perhaps the discovery of the "false" Beethoven was made only years later? At any rate what matters is that Mahler, at the age of thirty-five, thought he owned a genuine portrait of Beethoven and that he shared the precious image, through copies, with a few close friends.

Mahler's appreciation for the visual arts blossomed only tardily and was mainly prompted by his association with Alma and her circle (her stepfather was the painter Carl Moll and Gustav Klimt was an ardent admirer of Alma's beauty). He might therefore not have wondered about the authenticity of a painted image of his hero, but he could indeed entertain doubts when it came to a question of the acoustical correctness of Beethoven's musical intentions. Like Wagner before him, Mahler felt obligated to make some changes in Beethoven's orchestral scores in the interests of clarity and in practical observance of the new sort of concert halls in which Beethoven's music now sounded. His orchestral modifications of the *Eroica* and of the *Coriolanus* Overture provoked indignant charges of Beethoven "tampering" during his first season as conductor of the Nicolai-Richter–trained Vienna Philharmonic in 1898 (a tension-ridden association that only lasted three years). More controversy broke out when, following Bülow's precedent, he conducted the entire string section of the same orchestra in a performance of one of Beethoven's string quartets. Things came to a violent head when he dared to conduct his revised version of Beethoven's Ninth for the Viennese on 18 February 1900. Unlike Wagner, Mahler had not thought to "prepare" his listeners for the alterations by advance benign publicity or printed explanations. The public loved the performance but the critics, poised for attack, leapt swiftly into the arena. With characteristic indignation the *Neue Freie Press* lamented happily: "In contemporary music there is a tendency to adopt the thoroughly reprehensible system of 'overpainting' the works of our great classical composers. What was proffered yesterday as 'Beethoven's Ninth Symphony' is a deplorable example of this aberration, this barbarism. A vast number of passages were completely reorchestrated, altered in sound and therefore in sense, against the clearly expressed intention of Beethoven, whose genius rose to unprecedented heights in this very Symphony."[28]

This complaint was nothing compared to the pure venom rushed into print by Robert Hirschfeld, implacable enemy of Mahler's later years in Vienna. Sounding more like Nietzsche contra Wagner, Hirschfeld let fly some spiteful barbs at the, to him, excruciating clarity of Mahler's interpretation, which left nothing to the imagination:

> Great surges of sound or subtle nuances draw attention to every minute detail of the *melos*; a ritardando or an accelerando alerts the audience to what is coming for fear it should miss anything. This *Ninth Symphony* is a triumph of lucidity. . . . With it, Mahler has asserted himself as a modernist, at least in so far as this modern age impels the ship of art toward the reefs of science. . . . Instead of silencing him, the grandeur of the *Ninth Symphony* aroused his intellect . . . and he has scaled its heights with clever interpretations and pretty details. . . . Instead of trying to understand Beethoven, Mahler should simply believe in him, as Richter did.[29]

Mahler despaired over the tone of such attacks and made the, probably unfortunate as far as fueling critical fire was concerned, decision to publish a defense of his Beethoven interpretation. His explanation was hurriedly printed as a leaflet and distributed to the concertgoers for the 22 February repetition of the oversubscribed event. As an insight into Mahler's interior image of Beethoven, the document is worth some scrutiny, for certainly Mahler's allegiance to aural over textural Beethoven would have far-reaching effect on twentieth-century approaches to the composer. Signed and dated "Vienna, February 1900," the somewhat wordy leaflet began with an oblique acknowledgment of the press's hostility:

> As a result of certain public utterances, a part of the audience might form the opinion that in tonight's performance the conductor has arbitrarily changed details of Beethoven's symphonies, especially of the Ninth. Therefore it seems necessary to issue a statement clarifying this matter. As his ear complaint grew into actual deafness, Beethoven lost that indispensable inner contact with reality, with the world of physical sound, just at a time when his conceptions were developing most powerfully and moving him to find new means of expression, to use the orchestra in such a drastic manner as had been unimaginable before. It is also well known that the quality of brass instruments in his time completely precluded certain tone sequences necessary to the melody. This very shortcoming ultimately led to the perfection of these instruments, and it would seem outrageous not to use them now to achieve as perfect a performance of Beethoven's works as possible.[30]

The harassed apologist next turned to an awesome precedent in retouching Beethoven's Ninth:

> Throughout his life Richard Wagner sought to rescue Beethoven's works from intolerably negligent performance. In his essay 'On the performance of Beethoven's Ninth Symphony' (*Collected Works*, vol. 9) he has shown how to present this symphony so as to get closest to the composer's intention. All modern conductors have followed his lead. Fully convinced of the rightness of this by his personal experience of the work, tonight's conductor has taken the same course, without materially overstepping the limits of interpretation indicated by Wagner. *There can be absolutely no question of reorchestration, alteration, let alone 'improvement' of Beethoven's work.* The long-established augmentation of the string instruments resulted, also long ago, in a corresponding augmentation of

the wind instruments, purely with the object of strengthening their volume *and without assigning to them a new orchestral role*. In this . . . it can readily be shown by reference to the score . . . that the conductor, neither indulging in arbitrary willfulness nor blinded by regard for so-called tradition, has made it his sole aim to pursue Beethoven's will down to its minutest manifestations, not to sacrifice one iota of the master's intentions in the execution, nor let them be submerged in a confusion of sounds.[31]

Mahler's revisions of the Ninth had actually been initiated five years earlier when, after a long study of all the available Beethoven literature, including the performance accounts of contemporaries, especially those of Schindler, he presented the symphony for Hamburg audiences on 11 March 1895. Eight years earlier, in Prague, he had amazed his listeners by conducting the (unrevised) Ninth from memory, inspiring a letter of thanks signed by a group of university professors that included the Austrian musicologist Guido Adler (1855–1941), who would later (1916) publish a study of Mahler. That Mahler was musicologically steeped in Beethoven's Ninth was not the point with his Viennese critics of the turn of the century however. What bothered them was an interpretation that, as the unremitting Hirschfeld wrote when Mahler presumed to conduct the symphony a third time (27 January 1901), "moved farther away from Beethoven as it drew nearer to Mahler."[32] And in truth, Mahler's Beethoven *was* inescapably Mahler's Beethoven. Or, as he bluntly put it to a well-meaning friend who had chided him for the unfamiliar rendition, "Your Beethoven is not my Beethoven."[33]

It was the intensity of his own musical experience of Beethoven that gave Mahler the adamantine conviction of possessing the "right" Beethoven image. Supreme self-confidence illuminates the words he used to justify his revolutionary conception of the *Pastoral* (the tempi of which had shocked his Hamburg listeners and astonished the Viennese critics):

In order to understand it, one must have a *feeling for nature*, which most people lack. From the very start of the piece, one must be able to share Beethoven's somewhat naive thoughts on the subject: the pleasure of breathing fresh air and admiring the sunlight breaking through a forest, or the open sky above an open field. In particular, no one seems able to render the scene by the brook, which is taken either too fast (in four beats), or too slowly (in twelve beats). The former is usually the case, because of Beethoven's joke at the end of it: surprised by the rain, the nature lovers run for shelter and the tempo accelerates.[34]

Not even Berlioz, with all his effusive empathy, had injected himself so corporeally into the symphony that he had had to run for cover at the approaching musical storm! Real rushing waters versus the *Pastoral* were the subject of a comparison Mahler made in America in the winter of 1910. It was a comparison in which the symphony's power won out over Niagara Falls. On tour with the New York Philharmonic in upstate New York, he and Alma had taken advantage of the opportunity to visit the great natural spectacle. That evening, in Buffalo, he conducted the *Pastoral* and when he returned to the hotel he discussed the two phenomena with Alma, concluding that Beethoven's symphony was more tremendous than all the Niagara Falls: "I have realized today that articulate art is greater than inarticulate nature."[35]

Mahler's image of Beethoven was most enduringly impressed upon his production of *Fidelio*. In the same city where Mahler the music student had been passed over for the newly instituted Beethoven Prize (Brahms, Hanslick, and Richter were on the jury that considered his 1881 entry *Das Klagende Lied*), Mahler the Imperial Opera-House conductor created what he hoped would be his permanent monument as an opera conductor. The Secession painter Alfred Roller (1864–1935), whom Mahler had gotten to know and admire through Alma's agency, was in charge of the new stage designs and it was a practical request from him that he be allowed more time for change of scene from dungeon to courtyard before the last scene that gave Mahler the inspired idea—in practice almost universally since—of having the *Leonore* Overture no. 3 in C Major introduce the finale.[36] Previously it had been the custom in Vienna to play this long overture, itself an orchestral description of the drama, at the beginning of the opera. The short E-Major Overture—the one finally intended by Beethoven to open the opera—was reinstated by Mahler and the longer symphonic recapitulation of events in its new place before the final scene allowed the tradition-loving Viennese to have their cake and eat it too. The new sequence, premiered on 7 October 1904, was a musical (and technical!) success, and was repeated in New York for the Metropolitan Opera revival of March 1908.

If Mahler's image of Beethoven received sanctification beyond the borders of Austria through his *Fidelio* reforms, his association with the apotheosis of Beethoven staged by the Vienna Secession in the spring of 1902 brought him—temporarily at least—local approval and acclaim. Founded five years earlier, the Secession was a group of internationally minded painters, sculptors, and architects who had resigned from the imperial city's conservative and xenophobic artists' association, the Künstlerhaus, to create an independent entity that would have its own modern exhibition building (the "cabbage"-domed Secession, constructed by the brilliant young architect Joseph Maria Olbrich [1867–1908] in six months). Here would be shown the best of foreign as well as local art in a series of artistically mounted exhibitions in which interior design and applied arts were to be given equal prominence with the fine arts. It was also planned from the outset that some of the proceeds from the shows would be used to acquire major art works for the city. Klimt was a founding member in 1897 and the Secession's first president. The first exhibit took place almost a year later, after wide-ranging preparation and contact with foreign artists. Klinger, whose Beethoven monument was already taking definitive shape, was represented by some drawings for his print cycle *Eros and Psyche* (1880). As a painter and well-known graphic artist—his *Brahms Phantasy* cycle had excited much favorable comment—he was vastly admired in Vienna and, as in the case of Zumbusch before him, attempts were made to lure him to the city by offers of a professorship in 1895. But Klinger, happily ensconced in his native Leipzig and about to move into a spacious studio, declined the honor. He remained however on cordial terms with Vienna's artistic community.

In fact, for their third exhibition (January–February 1899) the Secession devoted its central room to Klinger's enormous, mixed-media 1897 triptych *Christ in Olympus* (Fig. 156). Raised on a pedestal of multiveined gray marble, and divided into three sections by carved mahogany shafts representing palm trees, the ambitious allegory presents the confrontation of two great cultures, the classical and the Christian. An advancing, self-confident Christ faces the startled king of the gods, while below, in the painted predella, the battle of the titans in Hades is depicted with rhythmical animation. To either side, facing in towards the picture, are the marble pedestal figures of Remorse (left) and Hope (right). Because of the importance of this pagan-versus-Christian concept to the allegorical reliefs with which Klinger would embellish the great throne of his Beethoven monument, we might take note of the exhibition catalogue's description of this earlier Gesamtkunstwerk by Klinger:

> Into the brightly colored, cheerful world of the senses inhabited by the Olympians, there has suddenly erupted a strange, stern apparition. With measured tread, dressed in a bright yellow robe, the founder of Christianity approaches Zeus, father of the gods, who is seated on a marble throne. Faced with this apparition, the hilarity of the gods is silenced as if by magic. In a flash, the realization has come upon Zeus that his dominion is at an end. Recoiled in stiff horror, he looks upon Christ, while Ganymede clings to him in fright. Eros turns with a gesture of distaste away from the earnest stranger, while Psyche sinks to her knees at the feet of Christ, with a gesture of humility laying her hands in his. Dionysus offers him a cup of nectar, which he solemnly rejects.[37]

It was not only the awesomeness in Klinger's message that impressed his Austrian admirers but also the multiplicity of his media—a unification of the arts dear to the hearts of the Secession artists who wished to dissolve the barriers between fine and applied arts. Theirs was a characteristic aim of the whole Art Nouveau movement then sweeping Europe, and an attitude that would later find resurgence and respectability in the Bauhaus—the influential school of design founded by Alma Schindler Mahler's second husband, Walter Gropius, in 1919.

A painting by Klimt devoted specifically to the image of one musician was a featured and much-beloved item in the next and fourth Secession exhibition (March–May 1899). There was only one world in *Schubert at the Piano* (Fig. 157)— the world of music. And it was a particularly Viennese one, conjured up with flickering delicacy, beguiling intimacy, and poetic tenderness. One Viennese artist portraying in the final year of the Romantic century another Viennese artist from the beginning of that century. The work had been commissioned by an art patron associated with erecting the city's memorials to Schubert and Beethoven, Nikolaus Dumba. He had seen both these ambitious sculptural projects through to their public unveilings. He had also done something for himself. Design and decoration of the study, dining room, and music salon of his Parkring palais were entrusted to painters (rather than architects), and to Klimt, fellow lover of Schubert, went the honor of creating the layout and pictoral decoration for the music room.[38] Thus at the same time that Klinger was working on his grandiose three-dimensional Beethoven ensemble, Klimt was also actively engaged in paying homage to a cult figure from the musical past. How radically Klimt's style and thematic emphasis would change in response to the self-assumed task of providing a painted Introit to Klinger's sculpted Sanctus will soon become apparent.

Klinger tirelessly searched out the marble quarries of Europe in answer to an inner command—a compulsion to realize the haunting image of Beethoven that had come to him unsolicited one evening while playing the piano. The power of the past, especially of the nonpolitical, cultural past, held tremendous appeal for those who, like Klimt and Klinger, were appalled by the cynical worldliness of the present. As the old century came to a close, cult figures from the "unblemished," heroic past assumed extraordinary importance. The image of Beethoven, the man-god who had known suffering, was particularly apostrophized time and again. And this phenomenon was not limited to German-speaking lands. One of the most instantly popular images invoking the spirit of Beethoven was produced by an unknown Italian and introduced with wild success in Paris at the 1900 world exposition. The artist was Lionello Balestrieri (1874–?), and the title of his over-night sensation was *Beethoven (Kreutzer Sonata)* (Fig. 158). Strikingly composed, with its empty front space on the right and swiftly receding diagonal of five intense listeners on the left, the picture quickly directs attention to two focal points—the musical performers on the right and the life mask of Beethoven on the wall to their left. The viewer has deftly been brought inside the humble studio of impoverished artists—la vie bohème—and may share with them the shattering experience of hearing the *Kreutzer* Sonata as devoutly rendered by the young woman at the upright piano and the stocky violinist with rumpled hair—his unkempt figure suggestively similar to the fabled figure of Beethoven himself as seen from the back. White highlights touch with varying emphasis the upraised violin bow, outstretched pianist's hand, the Beethoven mask, and heads of the introspective listeners, culminating in the face of the rapt young girl who leans lightly against her serious companion on the left. The spirit of Beethoven has transfixed and transported these suffering young artists of the present and all Paris empathized and applauded. Puccini's *La Bohème* of 1896 seemed to live again in Balestrieri's earnest tearjerker. The painting was awarded a gold medal, and after being exhibited in Venice in 1901, went on tour through Europe and America. Its fame was spread through lithographs (still to be found today in flea markets) and its creator became a favorite painter of the Bohemian life.[39] For his sentimental, turn-of-the-century age, the obscure artist had touched upon what Beethoven could mean universally to the spiritually hungry. Transcendence.

It was with a similar longing to celebrate the uplifting power of music, and of Beethoven in particular, that the artists of the Vienna Secession made the unusual decision to dedicate their fourteenth exhibition (15 April–15 June 1902) to one single work of art, Max Klinger's *Beethoven*. True to their penchant for uniting major and minor art forms into one cohesive Gesamtkunstwerk, Klimt and his colleagues (Fig. 159) resolved to provide a collective "frame" for the Klinger monument. The Secession building would be turned into a temple in which the supreme, transcendental mission of art could be voiced and enacted. Individuality would be subordinated to the whole; only monograms, not signatures, would be used to identify each artist's ephemeral contribution. Different genres would be welded together—stucco with colored concrete, mosaic with ceramic, oil paint with metal and glass; and water in the form of fountains would merge with marble and live music. The elegant catalogue was crafted with the care of an incunabulum; original woodcuts graced the 102 pages of the small, almost square (six by seven inches), golden yellow bound booklet. Two of the sixteen full-page woodcuts dealt with specific Beethoveniana. Felecian von Myrbach (1853–1940), director of Vienna's Arts and Crafts School (where Oskar Kokoschka would study), contributed a dramatic profile view of Fernkorn's brooding Beethoven bust in the Heiligenstadt Park (Fig. 160; compare with Figs. 125 and 126). Carl Moll (1861–1945) produced a vibrantly gouged close-focus vista of the composer's house in the Eroica-Gasse (Fig. 161), the thematic intensity and rushing perspective of which anticipates the intentionally rough-hewn dynamism of Die Brücke, first cell of German Expressionism.

The groundplan of Olbrich's Secession building had been envisioned from the start as a radically simple arrangement of three capacious exhibition rooms, all laid out on the same level around a central core, which could either be left spaciously intact or partitioned into numerous subdivisions according to the demands of individual shows. For this purpose the roof of the building rested on only six supports, with even lighting provided by large glass skylights. Such functional flexibility made conversion of the Secession into a Beethoven temple that much easier for the distinguished young architect in charge of the installation—Josef Hoffmann (1870–1956). (A year later he would collaborate in the founding of the arts-and-crafts-oriented organization known as the Wiener Werkstätte.) Hoffmann's tripartite division of the Secession building into nave and side aisles echoed the actual structural layout but introduced a definite orientation according to which visitors to the Beethoven exhibit were directed through a screening entrance foyer into a long left side room (Fig. 162). It was only after the pictorial initiation provided by the Klimt frieze occupying the top third of the niche-perforated walls of this room that the visitor-worshiper could proceed into the central "throne" room where the three-dimensional Beethoven reigned in isolated splendor. Three large openings in the inner wall of the Klimt room offered enticing glimpses of the polychromatic climax to come (Fig. 163), and a matching side room to the right, also discreetly decorated with frescoes and figurated niches, gently led the visitor away from the inner sanctuary and back into the secular world. The interior decoration, alternating great spans of rough white wall with painted, polished, and shiny surfaces, and contrasting the silent monotone of space before the throne with the cheerful chromatic splash of two fountains in the background, was intended as *visible music*. The catalogue introduction explained this high aim and the purposeful subordination of frame to central image:

> The guiding idea that was to give our undertaking both the inspiration and the binding element came to us in the hope that we might be able to make an outstanding work of art the focal piece of our exhibition. The Beethoven Monument of Max Klinger was nearing completion. This single hope, to create a worthy setting for the fervent and magnificent reverence for the great Beethoven that Klinger brings to his monument, sufficed to call forth that joy in labor [*Arbeitsfreude*] which, in spite of the awareness that we were creating for only a few days, elicited lasting devotion to the problem we had set ourselves. And so there came into being this exhibition which should not bear the stigma of mere transitory existence. . . . Hoffmann, to whom the entire artistic integration was entrusted, had to sound this great chord out of the simplest means and yet at the same time endeavor to prepare ahead for that wealth which in Klinger's Monument shines forth like a jewel. So may this exhibition do homage to Max Klinger, who through his creative activity as well as through his writing has brought clarity into the way we look at art.[40]

The "writing" to which the catalogue referred was Klinger's much admired pamphlet on *Painting and Drawing* (*Malerei und Zeichnung*, 1891) in which he contrasted different evocative capacities of color versus black and white (awarding to graphic arts the darker subject matter of life—a thesis that would confirm Käthe Kollwitz in her discovery of the puissance of black and white). As further homage to Klinger a few choice extracts from his treatise concerning a Wagnerian-derived Gesamtkunstwerk relation of the visual arts were reprinted in the Beethoven exhibition catalogue.[41]

The catalogue also furnished a brief guide to the puzzling thematic program of Klimt's *Beethoven Frieze*. The composition, divided into separate compartments painted in casein colors on a stucco base and decorated with gold and semiprecious stone inlay, wound along the long left outer wall of the room, across the short end wall opposite the entrance, and back down the inner long right wall. The human condition ("The Longing for Happiness"), its pitfalls and encumbrances ("The Hostile Powers"), and its sublime goal ("Joy") were the three Beethoven-inspired themes that covered the three walls, with the human and angelic "good" protagonists facing each other on the long walls and the supernatural or underworld "evil" protagonists dominating the short wall (Fig. 163). Two separate lines from Schiller's "Ode to Joy" closed the catalogue description:

> The three painted walls constitute a coherent sequence. First long wall, opposite the entrance: the Longing for Happiness. The sufferings of weak humanity: their pleas to the powerful knight in armor as external, to pity and ambition as internal, driving forces which move him to take up the struggle for happiness. Narrow wall: the Hostile Powers. The giant Typhon, against whom even the gods fought in vain; his daughters, the three Gorgons. Disease, insanity, death. Debauchery and unchastity, intemperance. Gnawing Worry. The longings and desires of humankind fly away over these. Second long wall: the longing for happiness finds appeasement in poetry. The arts lead across into the ideal kingdom where alone we can find pure joy, pure happiness, pure love. Choir of angels of paradise. *"Freude, schöner Götterfunke [sic]." "Diesen Kuss der ganzen Welt!"*[42]

Klimt's program thus takes its philosophical points of departure and return from the fourth movement of Beethoven's Ninth, but the intervening saga of resolute hero versus ghoulish hostile powers is quite his own invention—at once personal and universal in implication. Beethoven had rejected from his setting of *An die Freude* those Schiller verses that smacked too literally of the Dionysian joys of drinking, but Klimt seems to have gone out of his way to invoke the very conditions that can attend intoxication—"debauchery," "unchastity," and "intemperance." As with so much late nineteenth-century artistic expression (once Baudelaire had strewn his seductive "fleurs du mal" over the path of cultural consciousness), the spectacle of evil exerted as great, if not greater, a fascination as did the sight of good. In the first two of Klimt's three ceiling paintings for the great hall of the University of Vienna—allegorical panels representing *Philosophy* (exhibited at the Secession in 1900) and *Medicine* (shown at the Secession in 1901)—the artist had already juxtaposed what scandalized critics identified as evil, ugly, and outrageous figures with the abstract concepts of good encountered by his floating knots of despairing humanity. In the new Beethoven frieze, hostile *critics* could and would say that the repulsive hostile *powers* concentrated on the narrow end wall opposite the entrance were not only the physical focal point of the room but the disconcerting psychological focus as well. "And this is the Klimtian way that is supposed to lead us to Beethoven?"[43] asked a Frankfurt reviewer in indignation.

During the course of the exhibition critics tried to outdo each other in interpreting not only Klinger's Beethoven monument, but also Klimt's quixotic, startling *Beethoven Frieze*. Let us take a closer look at the individual panels which were to present such an enigma (if not insult!) to many of the exhibition visitors in spite of the official catalogue explanation. If we follow the intended orientation, moving from left to right, we first come upon an ensemble of six figures, including the knight in armor, that represent "The Longing for Happiness" (Fig. 164). Three naked figures to the left—a standing young girl and a kneeling man and woman—clasp their hands in supplication, signifying the "sufferings of weak humanity." The object of their pleas is the hero, dressed in a suit of pale golden armor, who like his fellow humans, is presented in profile. He stares ahead with noble resolve, his helmet still on the ground but his left hand firmly grasping a sword of Wagnerian weight. Behind and above him, encased in a decorative embryo of gold leaf, are the personifications of those inner forces that will impell the knight to take up the struggle for happiness—pity on the right, looking down with concern and clasped hands at the hero, and ambition on the left, staring fixedly and frontally ahead, with a victory wreath held invitingly aloft in her right hand.

That the knight-hero might also symbolize a modern-day musician-hero—Gustav Mahler (Figs. 165 and 166)—was a visual implication instantly appreciated and enthusiastically accepted.[44] Klimt's personal friendship with the conductor (he had been present at the fateful dinner party where Alma and Gustav had met) and his own parallel position as controversial artist subject to vicious public attacks were such that he could sincerely emphathize with Mahler's role as isolated cultural combatant. Beethoven was the artist-messiah, and Mahler, through his intrepid interpretation of Beethoven, was the artist-warrior who would lead his listeners into an aesthetic kingdom secured through the agency of music, highest of all the arts.

Before that kingdom could be reached however a truly frightening array of Hostile Powers (Fig. 167) waited to intercept the hero, either by temptation or terror. Typhon, the monstrous giant, is shown as a kind of winged black ape, with fanged jaws (the teeth were mother-of-pearl insets) and far-reaching shadowy wings. This was he who had dared to attack the gods on Mount Olympus. The apelike appearance of this primeval defier of Zeus signals that greatest barrier in the ascent to pure joy—bestiality. On the left are Typhon's terrifying daughters, the three Gorgons, with the demonic, pale faces of vampires hauntingly painted by Vienna's most famous depicter of modern femmes fatales. Their serpentine locks of long black hair are decorated by live coils of black-and-gold speckled snakes who also obligingly form themselves into sinuous bracelets and anklets. The efforts of a gasping anthropomorphic (Freud would have pronounced it phallic) blob are kept firmly underfoot by the frontmost Gorgon, while on the same level farther along to the right two bleached human skulls are crushed within the hairy fist of Typhon. The horrible genealogy (or offspring) of this subhuman world is seen above the Gorgons in the wildly staring countenances of "disease, insanity, and death."[45] Balancing the Gorgons on the right is the trio of sins, "debauchery," "unchastity," and "intemperance"—the latter bloated figure an ingenious tribute to Aubrey Beardsley.[46] Farther along to the right is a contorted image that might certainly have invited Freud's attention: "Gnawing Worry," an eloquent personification of psychic suffering (Fig. 168). At the extreme upper right of this short wall a floating female figure with closed eyes and outstretched arms again represents humanity's longing to fly over these encumbrances.

The comfort of "Poetry," with its great decorative lyre (Fig. 169), awaits the somnambulistic knot of floating figures who now enter the happier realm pictured on the long right wall. The dark powers have been left behind. Art has triumphed and the divine music of Beethoven affords entry into Elysium, "the ideal kingdom where alone we can find pure joy." A look-alike choir of angels bursts into *Freude, schöner Götterfunken* while, under the comet-tailed symbols of sun and moon, human longing finds realization in a naked kiss of "pure love" (Fig. 170). Klimt's depiction of the victory of joy here purposefully echoes the

401

matic apotheosis of the *Freude* theme at the end of the fourth movement of Beethoven's Ninth Symphony. Redemption through art has again been achieved and the two supposed poles of Beethoven's music—struggle and triumph—have found their counterparts in the serialized "story" of Klimt's apparently arcane yet accessible *Beethoven Frieze.*

Each of the three walls contained one of the vital elements of the Beethoven mythology: suffering, obstacles, and victory. For the contemporary viewer this dramatic sequence applied to Beethoven's life as much as it did to the presumed musical content of the—almost autobiographical—Ninth Symphony. And just as the themes of the first three movements of the Ninth are reviewed and then impatiently dismissed in the beginning of the finale before the fresh motif of the *Freude* theme steals in with the wind instruments, so Klimt's central motifs of terror and temptation are repudiated by the floating forms with outstretched arms— the one element common to all three walls—who fly over them and on to the climax of pure joy. But the forty-year-old Klimt's pictorial response to Beethoven and the Ninth Symphony was essentially one of fantasy rather than of deep intellectuality. The depiction of the Hostile Powers titillated his imagination and the greatest originality, time, and care were lavished by the artist on this "lascivious" chapter of the epic narrative. It would be left to others—well-meaning and friendly critics like Hermann Bahr, Ludwig Hevesi, Joseph August Lux, and Berta Zuckerkandl—to construct the superstructures of interpretation that saw Klimt's *Beethoven Frieze* as painted philosophy.[47] Other writers saw the *Beethoven Frieze* as painted pornography. The easily offended reviewer from Frankfurt was one of the shrillest voices: "Klimt's frescoes would be appropriate for a Krafft-Ebing Temple.... The representation of unchastity... belongs to the most extreme of what the field of obscene art has ever produced."[48] A Victorian Viennese raged: "What should one say to this painted pornography?... for an underground locale in which hedonistic orgies are celebrated, these paintings might be appropriate, but for rooms to which artists have been bold enough to invite honorable women and young maidens, no."[49]

Olbrich's stark, utilitarian Secession building had been nicknamed the "Assyrian convenience" by a scatologically minded local pundit. Now the charge of "Assyrian" was leveled at Klimt's frankly stylized, two-dimensional frieze (one critic called the style "Egyptian"), but not even the novel flat style could long deflect unfriendly critics from what most irked them about Klimt's work: the apparently immoral *content* of the frieze. By personifying the Hostile Powers as Medusa-like, bloodthirsty (and startlingly contemporary) femmes fatales against whom the golden knight must battle in order to achieve pure love, Klimt had actually done nothing more than reexpress in explicit pictorial terms that favorite late nineteenth-century theme of an opposition between sex and intellect. In a simplistic alignment of woman with sensuality and the irrational, and of man with civilization and the rational—an alignment generally subscribed to by both art and science—the two sexes had again been pitted against each other. This modern revival of a presumed polarity between the sexes (it was also one of the themes in Langbehn's *Rembrandt as Educator*) was obsessed by the notion of a creative "male" spirit and intellect open to sensual, Dionysian, "female" onslaughts. What did all this have to do with Klimt's conception of his *Beethoven Frieze*? Everything. Eros was to him primarily a female principle: it could drain and destroy if not properly channeled by its historical victim, man. Beethoven had not been willing to sacrifice his "vital force" to the pitfalls of sensual love; he had striven for the "nobler, the better thing"—pure love. It was this simple mythology—the subduing of the sensual—to which Klimt gave voice in his 1902 *Beethoven Frieze*, essaying a pictorial voyage from earth into the infernal regions of sexuality before reaching the safety of a celestial haven. "If I can not budge the gods, then I will move Acheron," was the line from Virgil's *Aeneid* with which Freud had prefaced his *Interpretation of Dreams* of 1900. Concurrently, and in the same city, the founder of psychoanalysis was developing an implicitly misogynist psychology based upon his unquestioned acceptance of a conflict between sex and intellect. His ultimate message was that sexuality must not be denied but mastered. Or, as suggested in Klimt's *Beethoven Frieze*, it could be sublimated in art. An updated consequence of the Schopenhauer-Wagner redemption through art credo. Only now it was a sexual imperative that yearned for the nirvana of resolution. How differently charged was the aura surrounding Vienna's Beethoven of 1902 from that of Bonn's Beethoven of 1845! In 1845 it sufficed that Beethoven had conquered the mighty realm of music; in 1902 Beethoven must triumph over a far vaster realm—that of the self. Would Klinger's effigy partake of this distinctly modern reading or was the ambitious Klimt "frame" purely a local Viennese phenomenon?

Before we transfer our attention to this last three-dimensional image of Beethoven to command the interest of our mythmaking study, let us note that the homage to Beethoven offered by Klimt and the Secession was gravely appreciated by a famous foreign visitor who made a three-hour tour of the exhibition. The guest was Auguste Rodin. After the tour, seated next to Klimt at an afternoon coffee gathering in the Prater, the French sculptor turned to the Austrian artist and said earnestly: "I have never before experienced such an atmosphere—your tragic and magnificent Beethoven fresco; your unforgettable, templelike exhibition. . . ."[50] The sixty-two-year-old Rodin, who three decades earlier had himself created an image of Beethoven (see Fig. 123), did not consider Klimt's frieze prurient. He who had endowed the halting procession of *The Burghers of Calais* with edifying pathos, who had infused the cosmic stream of struggling humanity in *The Gates of Hell* with ennobling melancholy saw with clear eyes the pessimistic sexual determinism with which Klimt's vision of everyman's passage through the cycle of life was colored. He saw it and understood.

The pictorial prelude improvised by Klimt for Klinger's three-dimensional Beethoven was not intended as a permanent work of art; its life was to be only as long as the exhibition itself.[51] Quite the contrary was true for Klinger's monumental sculptural ensemble. Seventeen years of thought and labor had gone into the work, the conception of which, as we have noted, came to Klinger in 1885 in a sudden flash of inspiration. He had spent the intervening years hunting down the different types of marble required for his polychromatic vision and experimenting with bronzecasting techniques for the huge, figured throne. For many years his Leipzig studio housed a frustrating if intriguing array of disparate parts of the intended whole (Fig. 171): the marble torso of Beethoven, a plasticine model of the throne with its allegorical reliefs, the separately carved onyx mantle and pedestal-cliff, the marble eagle (not visible in our photograph), and the painted plaster model of the ensemble (about two-thirds the size of the final work). The artist left a reminiscence of the initial vision that was to occupy him so centrally for so long a time. Since childhood he had passionately loved and admired Beethoven, to whose works he had been introduced by his musically gifted father. As an adult he delighted in performing Beethoven for himself on the piano and it may well be that he was playing through something by the com-

(Colorplate 10)

poser when the compelling image of a Beethoven monument occurred: "Bee-thoven came into being exactly as it now is, in all of its details, only in different proportions and in another material, as early as 1885. . . . The idea came to me one beautiful evening at the piano in Paris. It was as clear and the colors as pro-nounced as are very few things: the pose, the clenched hand, the red [sic] mantle, the eagle, the throne, the drapery folds—even the gold throne arms."[52]

The next year, while still living in Paris, Klinger created a plaster model of what he had seen in his mind's eye. He applied gold to certain parts and painted other areas, giving the face and hands a flesh tonality. In the same year he also conceived the idea for a polychromatic and frighteningly realistic figure of a modern femme fatale with the severed heads of two male victims beneath the folds of her robe, *The New Salome* (completed 1893) (Fig. 172). This seemingly remote-from-Beethoven marble effigy would play an important if mundane role in the realization of the Beethoven monument and would also, as with Klimt's dialectical concept, leave its imprint on Klinger's interpretation of the Beethoven mystique. The practical service rendered by the modern Salome to Klinger's eternal Beethoven was that of being sold to the Leipzig Museum for a handsome sum of money, the plenitude of which enabled Klinger to embark on a long marble-acquiring Odyssey through the Greek isles and peninsula in 1894. In Athens he met the members of a German archaeological team whose most recent dig had unearthed remnants of colored sculpture, thus reinforcing Klinger's own interest in merging modern sculptural techniques with antique traditions. He returned with what would be Beethoven's torso and feet—a block of shim-mering white marble (with a propensity to develop a natural light golden-brown patina of its own) from the island of Syros. That same year (end of April) he visited Brahms in Vienna and presumably saw Zumbusch's mighty Beethoven monument for himself. The next year, 1895, he was able to inspect Hähnel's effigy in Bonn. Neither the Bonn nor the Vienna Beethoven had a throne and, more firmly wedded to his vision than ever before, Klinger began work on his majestic adjunct, designed from the outset to be cast in bronze as a contrast to the marble figure of Beethoven. By the end of 1898 the model for the Beethoven figure had been translated into marble: in time the left foot, which was carved a year before the torso, would begin to show a first hint of the famous ocher Syros patina. A trip to the French Pyrenees (Bagnères-de-Bigorre) at the begin-ning of 1899 yielded two more crucial blocks of marble, one of deep blue-purple coloring for the cliff-pedestal, the other of white-flecked black with a single prominent white veining for the eagle. And the renowned marble quarry of the village of Laas in South Tyrol surrendered a beautiful yellow-brown banded slab of onyx for the drapery. Bronze foundries in Germany and Italy were approached and found wanting, so by 1900 the plaster cast for the throne was shipped to Paris where the reputable firm of Pierre Bingen was willing to attempt the casting, through the *cire-perdue* method, of the throne in one piece. The eagle's claws were cast first as an experiment, and a year and a half passed while Klinger worked with the founder on refining and preparing, with cuts and mountings, the plaster model for application of the sheathing mold. The correct ratio of tin to brass also had to be worked out. A special kiln and firing process were developed to accommodate the complicated throne shape and varying density of relief decoration (Fig. 173).

In the meanwhile Klinger worked on fashioning models for the five angel heads (to be cast in bronze then carved by an expert from African ivory) that would adorn the inner face of the throne at the top (Fig. 174). At last, with much bated breath and suspenseful supervision, the throne was cast on 2 December 1901 in a continuous process that began at seven in the morning and lasted until two the following morning. The outcome exceeded all expectations and by mid-March, 1902, the entire ensemble, complete with gold, mosaic, and precious-stone inlay, stood on public display in Klinger's Leipzig studio, awaiting shipment to Vienna and exciting tremendous local admiration. Klinger's seventeen-year labor of love was meant not only to endure but to offer German monumental sculpture an authoritative direction: the employment of precious, mixed, and contrasting media and the use of polychromy (a practice traced back to Phidias) to create a single—overwhelming in effect and tactilely sensuous—Gesamtkunstwerk. What Wagner had done with opera, Klinger proposed to achieve for sculpture. Beethoven's introduction of voices into a symphony had been an innovation of far-reaching consequence; Klinger's combining of marble and bronze would constitute a knowledgeable and provocative salute to the composer's daring departure.

For the sculptor the effectiveness of his three-dimensional Beethoven image depended upon the inherent natural beauty of the polychromatic instrumentation he had introduced of marble, ivory, precious stones, and bronze. An "art-technical" discussion of these four media constituted the four main chapters of a handsome monograph devoted to Klinger's Beethoven monument that appeared in Leipzig the same year as the 1902 Vienna Secession Beethoven Exhibition: *Max Klingers Beethoven: Eine Kunst-technische Studie*. Lavishly produced, with eight heliograveur plates and twenty-three text illustrations, the book created a minor artistic sensation of its own, even receiving an approving press review from the formidable turn-of-the-century connoisseur of Beethoven imagery, Theodor von Frimmel (1853–1928). An unpublicized but widely known bonus feature of the book was that its author was Klinger's part-time model and full-time lover (a child, Désirée, was born to them in 1900), Elsa Asenijeff (1868–1941). Exotic and ambitious, Asenijeff was a red-haired Viennese who passed herself off as a Slav of mysterious origin. She had married and divorced a Bulgarian diplomatic official, had published a feminist *Tagebuchblätter einer Emancipierten (Diary Pages of an Emancipated Woman)*, and was earning her living as a writer in Leipzig when she met Klinger at a literary event early in 1898. The painfully shy but equally red-haired Klinger was smitten and for the next fifteen years they lived together in a stormy but productive relationship. She was his real-life Salome and she accompanied him on all his marble-gathering trips for the Beethoven monument, her effusiveness offsetting his reticence, and her reporter's eye absorbing all aspects of the Beethoven-birthing. It was this first-hand experience of the arduous progress and complicated realization of Klinger's monument that Asenijeff brought to her monograph, and her blow-by-blow description of the final throne casting process not only kept her readers on tenterhooks but contributed to public enthusiasm for the sculptor's polychromatic pulchritude. Asenijeff was herself immortalized as part of the three-dimensional Beethoven ensemble: the center ivory angel head bears the features of her own childhood portrait, as she tells us in her otherwise rather impersonal "art-technical" study of the monument (see Fig. 174).[53] Thus, in the guise of angelic inspiration, Klinger endowed his Beethoven with a younger, more innocent replica of the woman who was at the time his own life companion (they split up later). The darker, femme-fatale aspect of such a presence would be taken up by the sculptor on the allegorical reliefs assigned by him to the three outer surfaces of the composer's throne.

Klinger's Beethoven throne played as important a role as did Klimt's *Beethoven Frieze* in presenting a modern commentary on the Beethoven-as-hero concept. The mighty throne served as Olympian environment for its deified occupant but also as field of commentary. The *complete* meaning of Klinger's marble Beethoven figure could only be grasped in conjunction with its narrative frame. Thrones and the symbolism of thrones were themes that had fascinated Klinger for several decades. The handsome design for a projected title page to Goethe's *Faust II* (Fig. 175), drawn as early as 1880, demonstrates admiration for Michelangelo's Sistine ceiling frescoes,[54] where sibyls and prophets sit pensively in niches framed by figurated piers (Figs. 176 and 177). Klinger's drawing also addresses the ratio and relation of figure to throne. In this early sketch the artist hit upon two devices that he would carry over to his Beethoven ensemble: the sandaled feet and the projection of head above curving throne back. A literary allusion to Goethe's *Faust II* had also originally been planned by Klinger for his Beethoven monument: inscribed on the cliff-pedestal of the plaster model were the opening words of act 4, scene 1, which takes place in a high mountainous region characterized by jagged peaks: *"Der Einsamkeiten tiefste schauend unter meinem Fuss"* ("Gazing down on the most lonely depths beneath my feet"). This motto linking two contemporary German geniuses was left off the final marble carving, but its presence for so many years on the plaster model in Klinger's studio confirms the vaulting sense of isolation from humankind that the sculptor intended to convey with his rocky setting, the clouded violet colors of which suggested a storm-visited mountain peak.

A poignantly empty "pagan" throne at the summit of a four-stepped pedestal was the haunting motif of one of the plates in Klinger's first (1889) of two cycles on the theme of death (Fig. 178). Entitled *Herod*, the print shows the king toppled from his throne by the sudden whim of death, his final convulsive agony incuriously watched by distant spectators in an amphitheater. Two ferociously snarling lions form the arm rests of the phantasmagorical throne, the curving single-banded back of which would recur in the Beethoven throne. The idea of a relief-decorated throne appeared in a picture entitled *Misery [The Oppressed]*, of 1892, from Klinger's second cycle dealing with death (Fig. 179). Ram heads project from the upper corners of the throne, at the level where angel heads would adorn the Beethoven throne, and a large butterfly with wings extended dominates the top of the throne at the center—paralleling in placement and motif the mosaic butterfly wings that connect the five angel heads on the Beethoven throne (see Fig. 174). Finally, the idea of a brooding titanic figure ensconced above a landscape that includes references to both ancient and modern civilizations—an idea central to the allegorical reliefs on the Beethoven throne—was independently essayed by Klinger in the most apparitional of his second death series prints, the *Integer Vitae Scelerisque Purus* ("Blameless in life and free of evil") (Fig. 180). The giant figure of Time sits in meditation on a natural throne of mountains and clouds, his left hand clasping an hourglass and his right hand capping an erupting volcano. About to plunge into the abyss that opens up under the hourglass on the right are Moses, Christ, Buddha (?), and—already plummeting—Zeus. Before the architectural ruins of Greek and Roman civilizations a naked youth, symbolizing the present, approaches the abyss with trepidation. The philosophical consequences of Neitzsche's assertion that God is dead seem to underlie the theme of innocent humanity's spiritual groping if deprived of religious belief, whether in old or newer gods.

That antiquity and Christianity were obsessive parallel themes in Klinger has already been noted. A confrontation between the two world views had been the curious subject matter of the artist's large triptych painting *Christ in Olympus* (see Fig. 156). Now the great bronze throne surrounding Beethoven would serve as Klinger's ultimate meditation on the great dichotomy—a dichotomy that had exerted its influence on Beethoven and over which, by virtue of the sensuous beauty and spiritual power of his music, he reigned. As with the division of scenes in *Christ in Olympus*, large palm trees—symbols of majesty[55]—set off the three scenes from each other (Figs. 181, 182, 183). The two side reliefs show the longing and desire of humanity as personified in three basic drives: thirst, hunger, and love. Each need is symbolized through an ancient legend. On the left side (Fig. 184) a couple called the Tantaliden by Klinger portray eternal thirst and hunger: the female figure stooping to fill her shallow bowl at a stream is one of the Danaidae,[56] doomed forever to draw water with a sieve in Hades; the arching figure of the man on the cliff behind her who strains to reach the fruit on a tree the branches of which perpetually elude his grasp is Tantalus. One of the crimes for which he was meted this cruel punishment was that of stealing nectar and ambrosia from the table of the gods—an action applicable to Beethoven as well, in Klinger's sympathetic symbolism. The right side of the throne leads us from the nether world of Greek mythology to the biblical Paradise of Adam and Eve (Fig. 185). Love and the traditional relationship between the sexes are here represented by the story of original sin. The moment of temptation is shown, as Eve offers the receptive Adam an apple and the beholder a full view of her buxom form.

The old myth—still subscribed to in Klinger's day—of woman as sensuality incarnate, ever luring man who partakes of it but is not likewise defined by it, is given inescapable prominence on the back of the Beethoven throne in a figurated panel that covers twice the area of the side reliefs (Fig. 186). The lower half of the throne back is given over to the pagan world, represented on the right in high relief by Venus Anadyomene, rising from the sea on a scallop shell. Goddess of love, beauty, and sexual rapture, she exposes her voluptuous nudity to the viewer's gaze by her gesture, as she throws up her arms in surprise or defense. An attack is indeed being launched against her by the draped and passionately animated figure of John of the Apocalypse, who, situated on a cliff in the mid-distance on the left, wheels towards Venus with a pointing, accusatory finger. Defiantly, a sea nymph emerging from the water beneath him cups her hands and shouts back a retort. The world she challenges is that of Christianity. Golgotha spreads across the upper register of the throne back: in low relief the Crucifixion takes place while to the right the sun sinks below the horizon. Between the two thieves Christ faces out front and is flanked by the mourning figure of his mother in profile on the left and two grieving women on the right (Mary Magdalene collapsing on the lap of Mary of Cleophas), one of whom looks towards the setting sun. The birth of Venus is countered by the death of Christ. Christ's suffering and death on the cross promise redemption for those inheritors of original sin who have continued that sin from race to race. And yet it is not without resistance that this new spiritual belief takes hold, for it seems that the antique

pagan world of unfettered passions and innocent sexual enjoyment will also celebrate its triumph again in the future. The love goddess in her splendid nudity
personifies the relentless drives of the flesh.[57]

Klinger did not by any means intend to signify a victory of the Christian over
the classical world in his Beethoven throne reliefs. Rather, his intention in both
the Beethoven monument and in *Christ in Olympus* was to project an eventual
third world, in which the old dualism between flesh and spirit, between the
irrational and the rational, would be fused into a higher entity. This as yet
unresolved battle between the two worlds that formed Beethoven's psychic
pedigree was patently expressive of the contemporary Zeitgeist, which yearned
for the redemption of pure joy and yet was anchored in an apparently contradictory sensuality. As in Beethoven's music, so in Beethoven's throne the themes
of suffering and beauty had been united. Surely a sublime harmony would result.
The future beneficiaries of such a resolution are shown on the upper rim of the
throne as small, recumbent, dreamy figures of both sexes who float expectantly
within the ambience of Beethoven's powerful shoulders.[58] The apotheosis of
Beethoven implicit in the godlike throne promises a solution to the age-old
dilemma enunciated by Klinger in his allegorical reliefs.

(Colorplate 10)

For Klinger's Beethoven is indeed deified (Fig. 187). Presentation and pose con-
spire to promote the tone hero from Promethean striver to Zeus-like creator. This
is no longer Beethoven the man, not even Beethoven the musician. This is Beethoven the enthroned genius. The empyrean eagle, attribute and companion of
the king of the gods, who alone can ascend to Olympian heights, scarcely dares
to land on the cloud-piercing cliff that supports the throne of ideas upon which
such a godlike creator sits. Removed from the world, Beethoven is occupied in
the divine work of creative thought. Gone are the pen and notebook of Hähnel's
Bonn statue; absent is the historicizing clothing of Zumbusch's Vienna monument. Klinger's Beethoven is stripped to the waist in heroic and timeless nudity.
Like Venus and Christ, whose realms on the throne back represent the undying
urges of the flesh and the spirit, Beethoven too is now presented as an *immortal*.
Klinger's Beethoven, though stocky and strong, is not an athlete; he is a man of
middle age, with sleeping muscles, purposefully reminiscent in physique and
pose of Greek and Roman representations of philosophers (Fig. 188).

The German sculptor has invented an effective and original pose for his thinker
figure. Although contemporaneous with Rodin's *The Thinker*[59] (Fig. 189), who
also meditates atop a rocky pedestal, the Beethoven figure has little in common
with the French work. Rodin's primeval naked man reflects the muscular stress
of abstract thought: his right fist presses against his teeth (Rodin's description)
and his toes curl inward, unconsciously digging into the ground beneath them.
He is literally plunged into thought. *What* the figure is thinking of is not conveyed; it is rather the mood of intense concentration that is expressed in this
general and universal symbol that traces its mighty torsion back to Michelangelo's brooding Jeremiah (see Fig. 177). Klinger's Beethoven is, by contrast, not
bowed down by cogitation but buoyed up by it. Like a great white ship coursing
a straight line through the waves, the Beethoven figure inclines forward, his
head raised and gazing ahead in the direction vectored by the thrust of his right
leg. The leg is raised high over the left one and it extends forward in a kicklike
motion similar to but more pronounced than the crossed-leg pose of Michelangelo's Erythrean sibyl (see Fig. 176). The balled fists of Klinger's Beethoven
support his body while his eyes fix on an inner vision. Asenijeff, Klinger's official

apologist, suggests the subject of Beethoven's contemplation: "His face expresses and reflects all that is narrated on the throne, the entire human Odyssey."[60]

The emphatically positive aspect of Klinger's cogitating Beethoven differs significantly from Rodin's pessimistic, *Gates of Hell*-derived thinker with its "I think, therefore I am damned" aura,[61] but also from earlier Romantic imagery of genius engrossed in thought. Delacroix's empathic portrayal of *Michelangelo in His Studio* (Fig. 190) of 1850 is an instructive example. The portrait is an autoscopic study of melancholia—that temperament most likely to dominant in the type of personality disposed to genius. The great artist whose meditation leads to masterpieces is also, at times, incapacitated by that very propensity for contemplation—his vivid inner visions outstripping practical realization, his full-blown fantasies defying corporealization. Despairing not of artistic inspiration but of the human means to render that inspiration palpable, the creator sinks into inactivity—in Michelangelo's case the hammer and chisel are cast aside and the slumping body echoes the mental depression generated by this impasse between thought and action. Not so with Klinger's Beethoven! Along with the vision he spies the solution; his hands literally enact the grasping of ideas. A celestial accompaniment of five angels greets the spectacle with approving glances; the angel to the right points to the creant deity. Down below the amber-eyed eagle—life-size incarnation of the soaring eagle of Schlosser's Beethoven biography (see Fig. 54)—starts back in awe at the new Zeus (Fig. 191).

The concentrated psychic energy that flows through the statue's powerful arms into the involuntarily clenched fists has its fountainhead in Beethoven's face, and it is to this face that the beholder's attention, directed by the pointing angel, returns time and again. It is clearly and carefully based on Klein's life mask (Figs. 192 and 193). And yet, in spite of the striking resemblance, the marble features have undergone a subtle metamorphosis. The change is from individual to *type*, and we can observe the shift in Klinger's conception if we compare the painted plaster model of earlier origin with the final execution in marble. In the earlier version (Fig. 194) the cheeks are fuller (as in the Klein mask), the lips more firmly pressed together as if responding to the difficulty of comprehending an idea, and the eyes have been painted a water blue color. Klinger obviously began to think the effect too specific, too pronouncedly a portrait effigy and not sufficiently an image of genius. He had already experimented with reproducing the "flesh and blood" Beethoven for Max Abraham (1831–1900), a Leipzig lawyer who since 1880 had been the sole owner of the famed music publishing firm of C. F. Peters and who in 1894 founded a library for the furtherance of musical studies—the Musikbibliothek Peters—that was open free of charge to the public. Klinger had been asked to create the collection's ex libris plate and his design (Fig. 195) shows the historical Beethoven, wrapped in a cloak against the elements, clutching his battered hat in one hand and leaning in scowling meditation against a brick wall. The physical specificity of both bookplate and plaster model were ultimately rejected by Klinger in hopes of achieving a more spiritual impression for his monument. The sculptor had first wanted to set Beethoven's eyes with amber or opals, but the effect was too individual and too distracting, he found. For the same reason Klinger left the angel faces in white, including the eyes (their hair and eyes had been painted different colors on the plaster model). Only the blue mosaic band of opals and antique glass fragments uniting the ocher-, brown-, and black-studded butterfly wings of agate and jasper with gold leaf underlay intervened to set a celestial color note behind the white marmorean Beethoven. In the end Beethoven's eyes were left blank; not even pupil holes were drilled. The result was enormously effective. It "spiritualized" the face and avoided the staring explicitness of the artist's earlier three-dimensional effigy *The New Salome* (see Fig. 172), whose fleshy challenge so pervades the Beethoven monument's allegorical reliefs. Possibly obeying the dictates of the new spirituality thus achieved, Klinger also omitted any indication of straps on Beethoven's sandaled feet.

Although apotheosis of Beethoven removed him from the world, the desire to convey the composer's compassion for that world, to suggest his great humanity as expressed in his music, was an important factor in Klinger's final conception of the marble face.[62] The rumpled hair seems to reverberate to a throbbing behind the high forehead, and the downward pull of Beethoven's lips imparts an expression that is tinged with pain as well as fixed in concentration. That Klinger specifically equated Beethoven's countenance with some of the noblest and earliest manifestations of Christianity finds intriguing corroboration in two large religious works by the artist painted in Rome in 1890. Both pictures were originally conceived of in Paris, during the period of Klinger's Beethoven inspiration, and both unmistakably introduce the composer's facial features through the medium of the figure of Saint John, the beloved disciple. In Klinger's monumental and controversial *Crucifixion* (Fig. 196) (controversial because of the completely naked Christ), the central figure is not Christ, but John. He stands just to the left of the good thief, in the compositional axis of the picture, and looks down with dignified sympathy at the swooning figure of Mary Magdalene. To the left Mary the Virgin stands frozen in profile, silently returning the gaze of her son who perishes on the cross. The beholder is brought into this private communion by the frontal figure of John, who reaches out with his right hand to support the fainting Magdalene. His long blond hair parts to reveal the high Beethovenian forehead, the lips are pressed tightly together in mute suffering, and the downcast eyes are reminiscent of the composer's death mask. Klinger's *Pietà* (Fig. 200) is an even more conspicuous statement of the Saint John-Beethoven association. The dramatis personae are reduced to an intense life-size ensemble of three—the dead Christ, his mother, and John. With unspeakable tenderness John holds the hand of Mary between his own hands while she despairingly lifts her son's lifeless fingers to her heart. The grieving countenance of John-Beethoven (even the cheek line from the life mask is indicated here) gazes stalwartly past the recumbent figure of his master and focuses upon an interior world of solemn determination. In the Beethoven monument a new Zeus takes up the act of creation; in the *Pietà* a second Christ, in the conflation of John-Beethoven, resolves to bring the message of redemption once more to humanity. To explain why he had given Beethoven's features to John, Klinger declared that, as the man looked who created the Ninth Symphony, so may have looked the man to whom popular belief ascribed the incomprehensible fantasies of the Revelation.[63]

Two years after casting Beethoven as a witness to the life and death of Christ, Klinger returned to the historical Beethoven in a somber pen-and-ink drawing (Fig. 197). The sketch is of considerable interest in establishing *which* of all the available two-dimensional images of the composer held the most appeal for him. For the drawing is a meticulous copy of an etching produced by one of Klinger's contemporaries, the Dutch artist Carel Lodewijk Dake (1859–?) (Fig. 198). The original bust-length portrait by Dake shows Beethoven with a white collar and cravat (the only features of which Schindler would probably have approved), his gloomily brooding face in three-quarter view, and a mane of short-cropped, wavy hair falling down the back of the neck. The cheeks are full and the girth of the face is broad—in fact it is the Klein life mask seen in a quarter turn to the left. Dake's scrupulous reproduction of all of the life mask's facial pockmarks (especially the area above the eyebrows, the single pit mark beside the cheek line, and the chin) affirms the three-dimensional source. The Klinger "copy"— while at first glance seemingly identical—differs in one telling respect: all blemishes are gone. Beethoven's complexion, like his persona, is idealized. A further aspect of Klinger's drawing also attracts the attention of the experienced Beethoven watcher. Contrary to the established raised or roving-eye iconography affirmed by contemporary verbal and pictorial descriptions, Klinger's historical Beethoven gazes ahead with a level stare; the large pupils fill the eyeballs. This is in decided and conscious contrast to the Dake original, where the white of each eyeball shows underneath the slightly raised and smaller pupils. Rejecting the remoteness conveyed by Dake's Beethoven, Klinger has redone it and in the process created for himself a leaner, less formidable, and more personal Beethoven. The sculptor in him had dismissed the graphic impressions done from life—engravings of which were ubiquitous—and instead he had been drawn to a modern but to all extents more "authentic" image, one painstakingly based on the Klein life mask. It would be the life mask to which Klinger would now return as he attempted to transform the letter of physical imperfections into the spirit of the creative paragon.

A photograph taken in 1901 (Fig. 199), before the bronze throne had been cast, shows Klinger putting the finishing touches on the marble portions of his Beethoven monument. In a corner to the left is the two-thirds-size gilt and tinted plaster model, complete with throne. On the draped pedestal supporting the marble ensemble stands Klinger's Beethoven life-mask copy. Its slightly snub-nosed profile differs noticeably from the somewhat more elongated and pronounced nose of the marble silhouette. The "spirituality" for which Klinger was striving is already evident without the ennobling frame of the heavenly throne. That Klinger, while doing homage to Beethoven, was in fact also endeavoring to shape a monument to the *idea* of genius, is made clear when we compare his effigies of other musicians with the Beethoven monument. The artist sculpted images of Liszt, Wagner, Brahms, and Richard Strauss. (He also did busts of Schiller, Nietzsche, and Georg Brandes.) With one exception these images can be considered as physical rather than spiritual portraits. They are partly idealized, as in the case of Liszt (Fig. 201) and Wagner (Fig. 202), but highly responsive to the particular physiognomy of the sitter. Klinger's never completely realized project for a Leipzig monument to its native son Wagner (Fig. 203) envisioned the mantle-enveloped composer standing lost in thought on a low plinth into which two steps have been cut—accessible and yet remote in his classical simplicity and severity.[64] An homage to one man's indomitable willpower perhaps, but not an evocation of genius. Only in the Hamburg monument to his beloved Brahms (Fig. 204) did Klinger again attempt to elevate his subject from the level of portrait verisimilitude to that of inspired creator. The influence of Rodin's drapery-wrapped *Balzac* (1897) permeates the rippling, columnar monument. Brahms's body is concealed beneath a massive cloak; only his bearded face and hands are visible, sharing the sculptural summit with a female muse who puts her arm protectively around him. Two more female spirits cling dreamily to his side while, below, the partially indicated figure of a man clasps at the hem of his robe (how Brahms would have cringed at all this symbolic accompaniment!). Klinger's *idea* of genius is here sadly overwrought, the intended loftiness anchored down by four allegorical weights. Begun in 1905, three years after completion of the Beethoven monument, and carved entirely of Seravezza marble, its monochromatic severity was thought of by Klinger as a purposeful renunciation of the polychromatic splendor previously so integral to his conception of sculpture. The reason for this change was a 1904 retrospective of Rodin (with whom he was in friendly correspondence) that included a bronze cast of *The Thinker*. "Next to it my Beethoven seems terribly playful to me,"[65] announced Klinger dejectedly. The creator of the—seventeen years in the making—Beethoven monument was already seeing it with twentieth-century eyes.

And certainly the Beethoven monument and its Vienna enshrinement were crepuscular expressions of the preceding century. It was the Romantic century's ability—and need—to believe in heroes that was the single refrain of the multiple orchestration provided by the Secession for Klinger's three-dimensional Beethoven. The temple atmosphere, especially of the central room where the monument was displayed, was altogether appropriate for Klinger's cabalistic sanctification. From almost the beginning the sculptor had envisioned his Beethoven image not as an outdoor monument to be displayed in a public square but as a materially precious work of art to be housed in an especially conceived interior. The Vienna exhibition of 1902 offered one such artistic environment and when the city of Leipzig bought the monument shortly after the show's closing (Viennese public opinion was violently divided over the question of whether to acquire it), Klinger planned and paid for its final installation (1906) in a specially built, uniquely lit room at the Leipzig Museum.[66]

In Vienna's presentation the enthroned musical deity was placed between two large mood-evoking, semiabstract, star-studded murals. Surrounded by a low circular rail guard the three-dimensional Beethoven sat facing a representation of Adolf Böhm's *Dawning Day* (Fig. 205) while behind him arched Alfred Roller's depiction of *Sinking Night* (Fig. 206). No other major art works intervened. To either side of the monument, hidden inside two grottoes, the melodious sprinkling of two fountains provided continuous background accompaniment. Truly this cosmic sanctuary *was* a temple fit for a god. Illumined as it was by its Gesamtkunst setting, the polychromatic presence of Klinger's Beethoven was overwhelming. Hevesi rhapsodized: "This is the work of a sculptor who is a painter, as was Phidias. A painter-sculptor who is completely drenched through by highest music. The Beethoven is Max Klinger's Ninth Symphony."[67] Hermann Bahr thought it all to be the most beautiful thing he had ever experienced, and furthermore could not conceive of Klinger's Beethoven without the Klimt pictures.[68] But not everyone was of like mind. The Hungarian writer Felix Salten (1869–1945) would recall much later that reaction was sharply split—the statue and setting were simultaneously labeled "scheusslich" ("horrible") and "himmlisch" ("heavenly").[69] One of the most stinging indictments was this review, entitled *The Assyrian Swimming School*: " . . . the Secession . . . could think of no greater honor for Beethoven than to place him as the focal point in an old Assyrian bathhouse. . . . At any rate one has to blame it on the setting if the first thought of so many visitors upon seeing the Beethoven statue is simply that the tone-hero has just stepped out of the bathtub. Certainly everything that they have seen since entering the building only prepares them for the therapeutic ablutions in the center room . . . which is thought of as the common bathing room for both sexes."[70]

This lampooning with balneatory bathos of Beethoven's Secession sanctuary was an extreme reaction (and yet not so inaccurate if applied to the historic Beethoven, who in his final years kept his bathing apparatus in the anteroom of his Schwarzspanierhaus apartment[71]). But it was one easily invited by the startling nudity of Beethoven's torso, the ceaseless splashing of the fountains, and the flat "Assyrian" stylization given by Klimt to the conspicuously naked— not nude—figures of his *Beethoven Frieze*.

None of these possible distractions marred the enjoyment of those who attended the lavish private opening of the Beethoven exhibit gotten up by the Secession artists in honor of their esteemed guest from Leipzig. Mahler, through his close connection with his wife's artist father-in-law, Carl Moll, had been brought into the preparations. He chose the closing section for quartet and chorus from the finale of the Ninth and set to work rescoring it for brass and wind instruments only. The Schiller passage he had chosen to recast was one that pointed to astral heights—very much in keeping with the Secession setting and Klinger's Olympian conception:

> Ihr stürzt nieder, Millionen?
> Ahnest Du den Schöpfer, Welt?
> Such' ihn über'm Sternezelt.
> Über Sternen muss er wohnen.
>
> Do you fall down, ye millions?
> Do you sense the creator O World?
> Seek him above the starry canopy.
> He must reside above the stars.

The new arrangement was enthusiastically rehearsed in the Klimt room with players and chorus members from the Opera and, in Alma Mahler's words, "it rang out as starkly as granite."[72] On the day of the opening Mahler conducted his powerful ensemble and his wife proudly noted the effect: "Klinger, who was a very shy man, came in just as the first note clanged out above his head. He was so moved that tears ran slowly down his cheeks."[73]

Elsa Asenijeff had of course accompanied Klinger to the event, which was followed by an artists' banquet at the Grand Hotel. Alma Mahler had few kind words to say about the author of the *Kunst-technische Studie*: "[Klinger] was entirely dominated by Assenjeff [*sic*], a red-headed Russian woman, who had him completely under her thumb. She was hysterical, and on one occasion suddenly burst into tears at table, because she had once had a jaguar she loved and it died. Klinger tried to control her by glances of despair, but it was no use. Some scene or other broke out at every moment, and we felt sorry for him."[74]

Felix Salten was also a guest at the Klinger Banquet and he remembered only the accord not the acrimony of the evening as he drank in the sight of two famous artists united by their veneration for Beethoven:

> On the evening of the opening the artists and friends of the Secession assembled at a banquet for Max Klinger and Gustav Klimt. The two masters sat next to each other. Two wonderful heads, which bore upon their expressive faces the stamp of powerful personalities. Klinger's face, surrounded by a blaze of white hair and beard, had a fiery, youthful glow, and his small narrow eyes

sparkled. Gustav Klimt, with his brown face, dark beard and somewhat lighter hair, presented the picture of blooming health and teeming strength. A peaceful, happy enjoyment flowed from his being, the peace of a man who works hard and who for once enjoys relaxation from all his efforts. . . . Here, in this room, was true understanding, true harmony. . . .[75]

An intuitive harmony was indeed discernible in the joint homage rendered Beethoven by the turn-of-the-century trio of Mahler, Klimt, and Klinger. Klinger's polychromatic three-dimensional conceptualization of the man turned myth was partly in response to the synaesthetic multicolored impressions the *sound* of Beethoven's Ninth afforded him.[76] Klimt's *Beethoven Frieze* was more than a symbolic paraphrase of the Ninth; structurally, perhaps just because of its uncompromising two-dimensionality, it "sounded" a marked rhythmic principle that was inherently musical, with its long, drawn-out articulation of empty spaces on the two side walls—visual "silences"—punctuated by the syncopated entries of groups or individual figures, much as in Beethoven's symphony.[77] And as for Mahler's innovative reinstrumentation in the interest of patterning sound in space, the Ninth had long intrigued him in this regard. Bruno Walter has described this daring experiment with the Ninth conducted by Mahler while still in Hamburg: "He had the B-flat major march in the finale played by an off-stage orchestra, while the tenor and the male chorus sang on the rostrum, the main orchestra reentering with the start of the subsequent fugato. This was no mere whim. He thought he had discovered Beethoven's intention, as prefigured in Schiller's text: namely, that the winged progress of the young man should, from the hesitant pianissimo of its start, through the crescendo to the ultimate fortissimo, make its way as though from a vast distance into a victorious presence."[78]

The Zeitgeist that linked this last generation of nineteenth-century Beethoven mythmakers in apotheosizing a German culture hero was also one that could poke fun at itself. Among the cartoons and caricatures that, along with the praise and condemnation, filled contemporary press coverage of the Secession events, two stand out. One responds to Mahler's remodeling of the Ninth—an accumulated sin. Entitled *Unpleasant Adventure of Mahler in the Secession*, it shows Klinger's Beethoven swatting the surprised conductor with his lap robe (revealing a pair of polka-dot shorts) while the angel faces jeer and the eagle squawks approvingly (Fig. 207). "At last I have you! Just wait, you symphony botcher!" cries Beethoven in broad Viennese dialect. The other caricature seizes upon the strained position of Beethoven on his throne to suggest another kind of throne—common to bathhouses and private homes alike—a different problem from that of creative cogitation, and a remedy (Fig. 208). The rooster title figure of the satirical magazine *Kikeriki* solicitously advances upon the constipated creator with a large bottle of tonic—"Hunyady's Bitter Water"—announcing firmly, "The man can be helped." Such parodying of Klinger's three-dimensional Beethoven monument actually helped to make it, within a few weeks of its exhibition in Beethoven's Vienna, the most widely discussed work of art in Europe.[79]

In the halcyon summer of 1902, then, just a dozen years before the outbreak of a war that would involve all of the European countries where the name of Beethoven was hallowed, three artists had collaborated in response to a century of mythmaking. Over the years since the death of Beethoven the musician, the question about his image had changed. Changed from "What does Beethoven *mean*?" to "What does Beethoven mean to *us*?" At the Vienna Secession exhibit of 1902 Gustav Mahler, Gustav Klimt, and Max Klinger attempted to answer that question for their generation. Together they presented not the portrait of a man who had lived from 1770 to 1827 (Figs. 209 and 210), but the deified hero in whom the present could express, and yes, perhaps even redeem, itself.

On 5 November 1955 the rebuilt Vienna Opera House, almost completely destroyed in World War II bombings, reopened. Cultural logic dictated only one opera appropriate for the great occasion, *Fidelio*. For those who could not be accommodated inside, loudspeakers carried Beethoven's message of redemption to a collective audience of thousands (Fig. 211). What Beethoven will mean to us in another hundred years can only be awaited. Mythmaking continues as civilization's autobiography. The gods are innocent of the uses to which humans put their lavish gifts. Beethoven, if not a god, is also innocent.

NOTES

CHAPTER ONE:
INTRODUCTION: MYTHMAKING AS CULTURAL
HISTORY

1. Almost all biographers of Beethoven have taken-account of the metamorphosis of "van" into "von" in the composer's name soon after his second arrival in Vienna, but the most recent and also most ambitious examination of Beethoven's reasons for allowing the story of his supposed noble ancestry to circulate is in Maynard Solomon's psychobiography, *Beethoven* (New York, 1977). Although chained to a classical Freudian framework, Solomon's analysis of the composer's "nobility pretense" is stimulating and plausibly sustained. An interesting earlier—even more Freudian—interpretation of Beethoven vis-à-vis his nephew, Karl, was published by Editha and Richard Sterba, *Beethoven and His Nephew* (New York, 1954), but the latent homosexuality hinted at in their book is certainly not the thesis of Solomon's more comprehensive study, which reads Beethoven's psychological motivations as dominated by the need of an emotionally blocked person to create a loving family triad, in which frequently he played the roles of both parents in regard to Karl.

For anyone exploring the subject matter covered in the first two chapters of the present book—Beethoven's life and the images produced of him during his lifetime—the bibliography cited below is indispensable. The first two items are 19th-century biographies by Beethoven's self-serving former secretary, Anton Felix Schindler (1795–1864) (see chapter 2, n. 7) and the American scholar who set out exhaustively to right Schindler's wrongs, Alexander Wheelock Thayer (1817–1897) (see chapter 2, n. 39). Both biographies were originally published in German and have been reissued in modern English editions with scrupulous editorial notes and these are the editions consulted for this book: Anton Felix Schindler, *Beethoven As I Knew Him*, ed. Donald W. MacArdle (New York, 1972) 1840; rev. and enlarged eds. 1845 and 1860); Thayer-Forbes, *Thayer's Life of Beethoven*, ed. Elliot Forbes (Princeton, 1970) (orig. vols. taking Beethoven's life up to 1817 by Alexander Wheelock Thayer published 1866–79).

Descriptions of Beethoven by contemporaries are available in several anthologies. Very useful are: Friedrich Kerst, ed., *Die Erinnerungen an Beethoven*, 2 vols. (Stuttgart, 1913); O. G. Sonneck, ed., *Beethoven: Impressions by His Contemporaries* (1926; New York, 1967).

Beethoven's letters can be consulted in English translations in the following: D. W. MacArdle and Ludwig Misch, eds. and trans., *New Beethoven Letters* (Norman [Okla.], 1957); Emily Anderson, ed. and trans., *The Letters of Beethoven*, 3 vols. (London, 1961).

There is not yet an English edition of Beethoven's conversation books; in German a complete and annotated edition is in progress and the first eight volumes have been published: Karl-Heinz Köhler, Grita Herre, and Dagmar Beck, eds., *Ludwig van Beethovens Konversationshefte* (Leipzig, 1972–81); unfortunately the falsified entries of Schindler, who at one time owned 400 of the conversation books but only passed 136 (by his count; 137 by modern count) onto posterity (see chapter 2, n. 70), are included. Helpful excerpts from the conversation books are to be found in most of the works cited here.

For the iconography of Beethoven—portrayals by contemporary artists—the following sources are available, but caution must be used in consulting the first two items since the author's rambling discussions are sometimes contradictory and include references that are now out-of-date: Theodor von Frimmel, *Beethoven-Studien I: Beethovens äussere Erscheinung. Seine Bildnisse* (Munich and Leipzig, 1905); idem, *Beethoven im zeitgenössischen Bildnis* (Vienna, 1923); Robert Bory, ed., *Ludwig van Beethoven: His Life and His Work in Pictures* (London, 1966); H. C. Robbins Landon, *Beethoven: A Documentary Study* (New York, 1970); Joseph Schmidt-Görg and Hans Schmidt, *Ludwig van Beethoven* (Hamburg, 1970).

Other sources are given throughout the notes but three major articles contributing to Beethoven iconography should be cited here: Franz Glück, "W. J. Mählers Beethovenbildnisse und seine Porträte andere Persönlichkeiten," *Alte und Moderne Kunst*, 6, no. 45 (Vienna, 1961); 11–16; idem, "Prolegomena zu einer neuen Beethoven-Ikonographie," *Festschrift Otto Erich Deutsch zum 80. Geburtstag am 5 September 1963*, eds. Walter Gerstenberg, Jan LaRue, and Wolfgang Rehm (Kassel, 1963), pp. 203–12.

2. Robert Schumann, *On Music and Musicians*, ed. Konrad Wolff, trans. Paul Rosenfeld (New York, 1969), p. 99.

3. Ibid., p. 101. Schumann is speaking here in the voice of the emotional Eusebius, one of the three alter egos (Eusebius, Florestan, and Master Raro) whose pen names appear after articles contributed by Schumann to his journal, *Neue Zeitschrift für Musik*. The stormy Flo-

restan immediately reproaches Eusebius for joining the mindless praise of pop-eyed ''Beethovenians,'' and introduces the topos of Beethoven's personal struggle: ''Do they believe they understand him when they smile and applaud him who fought so hard in innumerable battles?''

A 20th-century update of the Schumann-Eusebius ''Beethoven'' sigh can be found in the touching hero-worship of Schroeder, Charlie Brown's little sidekick, in the *Peanuts* cartoon strips of Charles Schulz.

4. Thayer-Forbes, *Thayer's Life of Beethoven*, pp. 777–78.

5. In January of 1839, after the deaths of both Beethoven and Goethe, Bettina Brentano von Arnim published what purported to be three letters to her from Beethoven, dating from the years 1810, 1811, and 1812 (*Athenaeum für Wissenschaft, Kunst und Leben*, Nuremberg). Only the second letter (10 February 1811) is considered to be genuine, as the autograph exists and has not been challenged. Autographs have not been discovered for the other two letters, however, and convincing stylistic evidence suggests that they were written by Bettina von Arnim herself in the desire to transcribe comments made to her by Beethoven for posterity. See chapter 3 for a fuller discussion of this and of Schindler's visit and vain attempt to persuade Frau von Arnimto show him the autographs of the two doubtful Beethoven letters. See also Thayer-Forbes, *Thayer's Life of Beethoven*, pp. 497–99, 505. A sympathetic hearing is given Bettina von Arnimby Romain Rolland, who is inclined to accept much of the substance of the two doubtful letters, if not their autographic authentication; see his *Goethe and Beethoven*, trans. G. A. Pfister and E. S. Kemp (New York, 1931), pp. 216–17, n. 61.

6. Concerning the doubtful authenticity, see above, n. 5 and chapter 3. A full English translation is given in Schindler, *Beethoven As I Knew Him*, pp. 492–93.

7. Ibid., p. 492.

8. How pleased these revolutionaries of 1848 would have been to know that among the some forty-four books found in Beethoven's estate at the time of his death were several that, in the Vienna of Franz I, were subject to confiscation because of their liberal, masonic, or antiroyalist sympathies. A partial listing of the confiscated authors and titles is given in Paul Nettl, *Beethoven Encyclopedia* (New York, 1956), p.186; included is the controversial writer and playwright August Kotzebue (1761–assassinated 1819), considered ''a dramatic genius'' by Beethoven, who wrote to him on 28 January 1812 expressing his interest in composing music to a libretto by him and suggesting Attila as a subject (ibid., p. 114). Nettl's helpful handbook—an alphabetized discussion of topics, persons, and places relating to Beethoven—is based on the extensive and pioneering two-volume work by Theodor Frimmel, *Beethoven-Handbuch* (Leipzig, 1926).

9. Letter to Prince Hermann von Pückler-Moskau (published as part of his correspondence and diaries in 1873), as given in Sonneck, *Beethoven: Impressions by His Contemporaries*, p. 87.

10. Letter dated 2 September 1812, ibid., p. 88.

11. Letter dated 9 August 1812, Anderson, *The Letters of Beethoven*, 1:384.

12. Ibid., letter dated 17 July 1812, p. 379 (''Goethe Is Here'') and letter dated 24 July [1812], pp. 382–83.

13. Letter to Anton Bihler, dated 9 July 1810, Sonneck, *Beethoven: Impressions by His Contemporaries*, p. 77.

14. Hugo Leichtentritt, *Music, History, and Ideas* (Cambridge, 1941), p. 190.

15. As reported in the *New York Times*, 15 January 1974. Schubert was also scorned as an ''Austrian capitalist.''

16. Nettl, *Beethoven Encyclopedia*, p. 205.

17. Hitler's outburst was occasioned by the timid attempt of Austrian Chancellor Schuschnigg to remonstrate with him that Austria's contribution to German culture could not be summarily dismissed in the fateful conversation at Berchtesgaden on 12 February 1938, see William L. Shirer, *The Rise and Fall of the Third Reich* (New York, 1962), p. 446.

18. Otto Friedrich, *Before the Deluge* (New York, 1972), p. 384.

19. A similar outraged wonderment at the incongruity of turning from Beethoven to mundane activities was expressed by the great Viennese architect Adolf Loos (1870–1933), who, like Beethoven, suffered from advancing deafness. ''But whoever goes to the Ninth Symphony and then sits down to design a wallpaper pattern is either a rogue or a degenerate,'' from his famous speech ''Ornament and Crime'' (1908), Ludwig Münz and Gustav Künstler, *Adolf Loos: Pioneer of Modern Architecture* (New York, 1966), p. 231.

20. *The Works of Leo Tolstoi* (New York, 1928), ''The Kreutzer Sonata,'' pp. 395–458.

21. Ludwig Weininger's strange inscription for his son's tomb is given in David Abrahamsen, *The Mind and Death of a Genius* (New York, 1946), p. 147. Abrahamsen's penetrating study of Otto Weininger is an important source for that disturbed author's peculiar family history and includes interesting letters from August Strindberg, a great admirer of Weininger's book and, like Weininger, a devout fan of Beethoven. The Schwarzspanierhaus—site of the deaths of both Beethoven and Weininger—was razed in 1904.

22. For fantasy see Marie Hrussoczy [Mariam Tenger], *Beethovens Unsterbliche Geliebte, Nach persönlichen Erinnerungen* (Bonn, 1890); for five years of devoted research but impossible conclusion (Countess Marie Erdody), Dana Steichen, *Beethoven's Beloved* (New York, 1959), and for psychobiographical and apparently conclusive identification of the ''Immortal Beloved'' as Antoine Brentano, see Solomon, *Beethoven*, pp. 158–89. Solomon first published his startling (and persuasive) identification in an article in the *New York Times*, 21 May 1972.

CHAPTER TWO:
BEETHOVEN ALIVE: EYEWITNESS ACCOUNTS AND CONTEMPORARY LIKENESSES

1. Sonneck, *Beethoven: Impressions by His Contemporaries*, p. 180.

2. Heinrich Friedrich Ludwig Rellstab, *Aus meinem Leben*, (Berlin, 1861), 2: 224ff.

3. About 1797, first of two letters written by Beethoven to the amateur singer Christine Gerhardi, see Anderson, *The Letters of Beethoven*, 1:29.

4. Sonneck, *Beethoven: Impressions by His Contemporaries*, p. 151.

5. Ibid., p. 153.

6. In his old age, Höfel recounted his memories of

the Artaria commission to Thayer, who visited him in Salzburg on 23 June 1860, see Thayer-Forbes, *Thayer's Life of Beethoven*, p. 589.

7. Schindler published his *Biographie von Ludwig van Beethoven* in 1840. The 296-page volume was published at Münster (Aschendorff) and was set in roman type. The book contained two facsimiles and an engraved portrait of Beethoven executed by the Berlin artist Friedrich Eduard Eichens (1804–1877) after the oil portrait of Beethoven painted by Ferdinand Schimon (see Color pl. 3 and text below). The following year, an English translation of Schindler's biography was—with his permission—brought out in London by the publisher Henry Colburn in two volumes. The title page reads: *"The Life of Beethoven including his Correspondence with his Friends, Numerous Characteristic Traits and Remarks on his Musical Works* edited by Ignace Moscheles, Esq. Pianist to his Royal Highness Prince Albert, London, 1841.'' In an extraordinary omission the name of Schindler does not appear on the title page—an oversight never to be forgotten by the already anti-Semitic Schindler (who blamed the Jewish Moscheles for the blunder), and a circumstance that has misled countless Beethoven scholars into presuming that the Prague-born Ignaz Moscheles, who lived almost continuously in London from 1821 to 1845, was the actual translator of Schindler's book (see Donald MacArdle's foreword, Schindler, *Beethoven As I Knew Him*, p. 19, and *The New Grove Dictionary of Music and Musicians* [ed. Stanley Sadie, London, 20 vols., 1980; 1981], 12:599). Moschele's own editor's preface to the London publication makes the actual situation quite clear and the relevant parts are worth quoting here: ''In acceding to Mr. Colburn's request that I would add to the English translation of Schindler's Biography of Beethoven which he was about to publish, such explanatory notes, characteristics, and letters as might tend more fully to illustrate and complete the whole, I had to subscribe to one clause in the agreement between Mr. Schindler and the publisher, namely, that the work should be given as he wrote it, without omission or alteration. The Notes bearing my signature, then, are all that belong to me in these volumes. The Appendix is, however, of my collection . . . '' (p.iv).

In 1845 Schindler brought out a second edition of his *Biographie*, printed again at Münster (Ashendorff) and set once again in roman type. The reproduction of Schimon's Beethoven portrait as copied and engraved by Eichens for the 1840 edition was repeated and a third facsimile was added. Excerpts from the conversation books were furnished in an Appendix (pp. 277–92), and a second Appendix entitled ''Beethoven in Paris'' (paginated separately as pp. 1–102) was included. This second Appendix was based on observations Schindler had made during two recent trips to Paris concerning the growing French acceptance and performance of Beethoven's music; see further chapter 5. During the last few years of his life Schindler prepared a thoroughly revised and richly annotated third edition of his life of Beethoven (denouncing Moscheles in footnotes and text alike and taking indignant swipes at other persons who had dared to write about Beethoven; see chapter 3). This 373-page final effort of Schindler's was published at Münster (Aschendorff) in 1860 and, possibly in response to the newest wave of nationalist feeling swelling in Germany, was set in gothic type. The

same Eichens portrait engraving after Schimon was used for the 1860 edition as for the first edition of twenty years before (MacArdle is thus in error in stating that ''for the 1860 edition of the *Biographie*, Schindler had a reproduction of the Schimon painting prepared by Eduard Eichens,'' Schindler, *Beethoven As I Knew Him*, p. 453, editor's asterisked note) and two facsimiles were provided.

For Schindler's *reliability*, especially concerning his entries in the Beethoven conversation books, see below, n. 71.

8. Schindler, *Beethoven As I Knew Him*, p. 451.

9. Beethoven described most of these recurrent problems in a letter of 29 June 1801 to his friend back in Bonn, Franz Gerhard Wegeler, full text in Anderson, *The Letters of Beethoven*, 1:57–62. Wegeler, who became a distinguished physician in the Rhineland, was born in Bonn in 1765 and died at Koblenz in 1848. He became acquainted with Beethoven as early as 1782 and was also on intimate terms with the von Breuning family to whom he introduced Beethoven; he married Eleanore von Breuning in 1802. During his medical studies in Vienna from 1787 to 1789 he was in close contact with the composer and as a result of the French invasion of Bonn he returned to Vienna from 1794 to 1796, maintaining his close friendship with Beethoven. Although they did not see each other again the men remained on affectionate terms and after Beethoven's death Wegeler published in 1838 with Ferdinand Ries (also of Bonn and briefly a student of Beethoven's in 1801) an invaluable account of Beethoven, especially of his earlier years. Beethoven did not hesitate to mention his physical problems to nonphysicians, however. In a letter to no less a person than Archduke Rudolf written in September 1814, he expresses his condolences regardng the archduke's ill health and then turns to his own ''inflammation of my intestines.'' Ibid., p. 467.

10. Ibid., p. 60.

11. Ibid.

12. Schindler wrote these lines in reference to a shattering incident during a rehearsal for a November 1822 performance of *Fidelio* that Beethoven had attempted to conduct himself and, because of his inability to hear the singers, had twice ground to a full halt. When Beethoven realized he was responsible for the confusion he rushed home with Schindler following anxiously, threw himself on the sofa, covered his face with both hands and remained so until they went to dinner, during which ''he did not say a word; his whole demeanor bespoke depression and defeat.'' Schindler wrote that this giving way to despair was unique—that always before (and after) Beethoven quickly mastered his melancholia. Schindler, *Beethoven As I Knew Him*, p. 237.

13. One of these friends was Antoine Brentano, Maynard Solomon's candidate for the ''Immortal Beloved,'' see chapter 1, n. 22.

14. Schindler, *Beethoven As I Knew Him*, p. 451 (Supplement A: Beethoven's Portraits).

15. Ibid.

16. Ibid.

17. Sonneck, *Beethoven: Impressions by His Contemporaries*, p. 165.

18. Ibid.

19. Ibid.

20. Ibid., pp. 165–66.

21. Ibid., p. 180. Yet both Schindler and Rellstab agreed on Beethoven's complexion: brown with a yellowish tone—sure signal to a physician's eye of jaundice.

22. *The Musical Journeys of Louis Spohr*, trans. and ed. Henry Pleasants (Norman [Okla.], 1961), p. 210.

23. Ibid., p. 101.

24. Sonneck, *Beethoven: Impressions by His Contemporaries*, p. 160.

25. Ibid., p. 135. An example of the ease with which the reporting of facts can inadvertently be inflated while ostensibly simply transcribing events springs from this charming confession by Schlösser. The young man only shadowed Beethoven once, by his own confession, but George Marek in his very readable *Beethoven, Biography of a Genius* (New York, 1969), p. 572, recasts Schlösser's narrative as follows: ''He used to follow Beethoven on his walks, 'until darkness hid him from sight.' '' This pluralizing of Schlösser's one-time act of innocent espionage, although welcome at the mythmaking level, demonstrates the ever-present danger of paraphrasing quotations.

26. Sonneck, *Beethoven: Impressions by His Contemporaries*, p. 138.

27. Ibid., p. 139. A similar complaint about his reputed antisocialness was voiced by Beethoven to the young composer Ignaz Moscheles. Moscheles and his brother had concocted an intricate plan by which the brother might meet the composer, which involved the brother's waiting half an hour outside the composer's apartment while Moscheles talked with him within and suddenly ''remembered'' an appointment with his brother waiting on the landing. ''And is it possible that you, too, could think me such a bear as not to receive your brother with kindness?'' Beethoven reprimanded Moscheles after dragging the terrified brother inside. Ibid., pp. 91–92.

28. Ibid., p. 140.

29. Ibid., p. 144. Moscheles made a similar plea on Beethoven's behalf: ''If we were to take the external manner for the internal man, what egregious mistakes should we often make!'' Ibid., p. 92.

30. Ibid., pp. 8–9. Fischer began to set down the family reminiscences around 1840 at the urgings of Beethoven fans who visited Bonn and showed up at the Rheingasse house, where Fischer still lived, in the belief that it was the composer's birth house.

31. Ibid., p. 20.

32. It must have been the stipple pattern—a painterly convention used by Horneman to show facial shadow on the forehead and lower cheeks—that misled the usually reliable H. C. Robbins Landon into believing he saw a face pitted by scars. His description of the Horneman miniature says that the artist ''accurately represented Beethoven's facial features and proportions—even to the disfiguring pockmarks. . . .'' Robbins Landon, *Beethoven: A Documentary Study*, p. 10. The author may have been working from a black-and-white reproduction of the portrait ivory (although it is reproduced as a color plate—103—in his book) in which case the stipling, spreading in a mosslike pattern, does seem to disfigure the composer's face. (Another color reproduction of the Horneman portrait, lighter in tonality and hence not so misleading, is given in Hans Conrad Fischer and Erich Kock, *Ludwig van Beethoven* (Salzburg, 1970), p. 44. Nor does Theodor von Frimmel, who stud-

ied the miniature while it was still in the von Breuning collection in Vienna, discuss any depiction of pockmarks in the Horneman image.

33. Sonneck, *Beethoven: Impressions by His Contemporaries*, p. 26. The Campe *Robinson Crusoe* referred to by Czerny was actually titled *Robinson der Jüngere* (1779–80), a widely read children's book written by the former tutor to the Humboldt family, Joachim Heinrich Campe (1746–1818), who based his book on Daniel Defoe's *Robinson Crusoe* of 1719. Translated into several languages, Campe's narrative of the resourceful shipwrecked sailor was accompanied by fanciful illustrations showing Crusoe in a makeshift shaggy tunic and with wild, very long hair—a perfect visual preparation for Czerny's childhood encounter with the unshaven, disheveled Beethoven!

34. Ibid.

35. Ibid., pp. 196–207. Gerhard von Breuning later became a distinguished physician in Vienna. In 1874 he published his delightful and moving reminiscences of Beethoven in a book titled *Aus dem Schwarzspanierhause*. His father, Stephan von Breuning, outlived their friend Beethoven by only two months.

36. Ibid., p. 179.

37. Ibid., p. 180.

38. Schindler, *Beethoven As I Knew Him*, p. 455.

39. It is interesting to come across a note of Yankee impatience with Rellstab's soul searching concerning the impression made on him by the physical Beethoven. Thayer's reference to the date and motive of Rellstab's visit to Vienna (primarily to meet Beethoven) concludes with this remark: ''His account of the meeting is like many others except that it is written with literary elegance, albeit with that excessive fervor, that *Überschwänglichkeit*, which is characteristic of German heroworshipers. Thayer-Forbes, *Thayer's Life of Beethoven*, p. 947.

We in turn note something about the American Thayer's brand of hero worship. A Harvard graduate (1843) and employed as a librarian at his alma mater, Thayer decided after reading Moscheles's English translation of the Schindler biography of Beethoven that an absolutely definitive life of the composer was needed—having noted the many inconsistencies in the former secretary's account of his master's life. Thayer spent the next two decades of his life hacking out a literary living in Europe and America, and, despite poverty and bouts of illness, managed to research his subject with incredible thoroughness, interviewing any and all persons even remotely connected with Beethoven's life, and consulting the conversation books to establish a firm chronology. In 1862 Thayer was employed at the American Legation in Vienna—a dream come true as far as his research was concerned—and three years later he was appointed the American consul at Trieste, where he lived until his death at the age of eighty in 1897. His exhaustively detailed and scrupulously objective life of Beethoven was published serially in German in three volumes (1866, 1872, and 1879), but only covered the composer's life up to 1817. ''An ounce of historical accuracy is worth a pound of rhetorical flourish'' was his motto. Nevertheless, since his interest in Beethoven did not diminish over the next fifteen years, we must ask why the final volumes of Thayer's biography—for which he left voluminous notes—were never completed. (They were finished by Hermann Deiters and

Hugo Riemann and published as the fourth and fifth volumes in the series.) Thayer began to develop severe headaches that lasted all day whenever he worked on the biography, even though he was able to publish two other scholarly books during the same period. Why did he renounce the Beethoven? The Sterbas and Solomon have suggested the answer: like Schindler before him, even the objective Thayer fell prey to hero worship. His Victorian scruples simply could not come to grips with some of Beethoven's love-affair choices and with the personality traits revealed during the long litigation for legal guardianship of his nephew. Writer's paralysis was Thayer's unconscious method of avoiding having to deal with the complete Beethoven, the only too mortal man.

40. Edward Larkin, "Beethoven's Medical History," in the Appendix to Martin Cooper, *Beethoven: The Last Decade 1817–1827* (London, 1970), p. 449, n. 1. For an unconvincing but interesting modern medical response to Beethoven's large-sized forehead and leonine looks, see V. S. Naiken, "Did Beethoven Have Paget's Disease of Bone?" *Annals of Internal Medicine*, 74, no. 6 (June 1971): 995–99.

41. The sight of Beethoven's life mask on display in a Parisian shop excited one of Rainer Maria Rilke's most passionate monologues in the journal of his "other" self, *The Notebooks of Malte Laurids Brigge* (1910). Here are some excepts: "The mouleur, whose shop I pass every day, has hung two masks beside his door. The face of the young drowned woman, a cast of which was taken in the Morgue because it was beautiful, because it smiled, smiled so deceptively, as though it knew. And beneath it, *his* face, which did know. That hard knot of senses tightly drawn together. That relentless self-condensing of a music continually seeking to evaporate. The countenance of one whose ear a god had closed so that there might be no tones but his own. . . . For who will now fetch you out again from ears that are covetous? Who will drive them from the concert halls, the venal ones with their sterile hearing that fornicates and never conceives?" Rainer Maria Rilke, *The Notebooks of Malte Laurids Brigge*, trans. M. D. Herter Norton (New York, 1949; 1964), pp. 70–71.

42. Reminiscences of Willibrord Joseph Mähler, given in his old age to Thayer, Thayer-Forbes, *Thayer's Life of Beethoven*, p. 134. For more on the painter, see Glück, "W. J. Mählers Beethovenbildnisse und seine Porträte anderer Persönlichkeiten," pp. 11–16. I am most grateful to the late Dr. Glück for his thoughtful generosity and sustained interest in helping me with this Beethoven iconography.

43. Thayer-Forbes, *Thayer's Life of Beethoven*, p. 337.

44. Ibid.

45. Letter of c. 1804, Anderson, *The Letters of Beethoven*, 1: 125. We do not know whether Mähler's painterly magic worked for Beethoven with this particular candidate, but we do know that Beethoven, the eternal bachelor, could be successful with women without having to resort to an idealized doppelgänger. Gerhard von Breuning cites the following exchange between his parents: "Once my father told my mother, when she had incidentally said to him that she could not quite understand how Beethoven, since he was neither handsome nor elegant, but looked positively unkept and unkempt, could have been such a favorite with the ladies: 'And yet he always has been fortunate with women.' "

Sonneck, *Beethoven: Impressions by His Contemporaries*, p. 198. Both the Sterbas and Solomon, among modern commentators, explore Beethoven's pattern of developing erotic interest only in women who were—usually because of marriage—beyond his reach and therefore "safe." The Sterbas point out that after the composer won possession of his nephew he evinced no further signs of any erotic interest in women. They make this interesting comparison of Beethoven's life with his opera: "In his only opera, *Fidelio*, composed in 1809 and subtitled 'Conjugal Love,' the principal part is played by a woman, Leonore, who, disguised as a man, saves her husband Florestan from prison. . . . It is unmistakable that, years later, when he saved his nephew from destruction—Johanna [Karl's mother, loathed and defamed by Beethoven]—Ludwig assumed the role of Leonore himself. And in doing so, he too was a woman in man's clothing. . . . His masculine love of woman was transformed into maternal love of his nephew." Editha and Richard Sterba, *Beethoven and His Nephew*, pp. 110–11. Whatever we may think of this analogy between the man and his music, it is abundantly clear that future explorers of the Beethoven myth will have to disentangle the man from his twentieth-century psychoanalysts.

46. See comments on Thayer, above, n. 39. Solomon cites Thayer's selection of Therese von Brunsvik for the "Immortal Beloved" as an illustrative example of his puritanical choices on behalf of Beethoven's love objects. Solomon, *Beethoven*, pp. 161–62.

47. See the fascinating introduction to Anderson, *The Letters of Beethoven*, 7: xi–xxii.

48. This summary is based on the interesting discussion in Nettl, *Beethoven Encyclopedia*, pp. 81–83.

49. Schindler, *Beethoven As I Knew Him*, p. 451.

50. We can not succumb to the temptation of a textual exegesis on Schindleriana in this book, but see above, ns. 7 and 39 concerning Schindler's injustices to Moscheles and Thayer's problems with Schindler's veracity.

51. The drawing was made in an album belonging to the Malfatti family. Underneath it, in an unknown hand, is the following identification: "*Ludwig van Beethoven*. By the old Director Schnorr von Carolsfeld from Dresden in the year 1808 or 1809 in a sketchbook of the Malfatti. . . ." (See Robbins Landon, *Beethoven: A Documentary Study*, p. 229.) This reference to the "old Director Schnorr von Carolsfeld from Dresden" indicates that the writer has confused Ludwig with his more famous brother Julius (1794–1872), who did indeed in later life become the director of the Dresden Picture Gallery. Ludwig Schnorr von Carolsfeld remained in Vienna as a successful artist and in 1834 was appointed first custodian of the Belvedere Gallery. The suggestion of Otto Erich Deutsch in his article "Beethovens Leben in Bildern," *Österreichische Musikzeitschrift*, vol. 16, no. 3 (March 1961), that the painter brothers' father, the artist Johann Veit von Carolsfeld (1764–1841), was the author of this portrait sketch is hardly tenable since from 1803 until his death he was resident in Leipzig, first as teacher of drawing at the Academy there, and then in 1816, as professor and director. Frimmel did not question the attribution to Ludwig Schnorr von Carolsfeld of "Dresden."

52. See Thayer's piecing together of the story of Beethoven's ill-fated hope of marriage with Therese Mal-

fatti, along with pertinent letters, in Thayer-Forbes, *Thayer's Life of Beethoven*, pp. 486–91.

53. The mirror-rich cellist was Nikolaus Zmeskall von Domanovecz (1759–1833). See Beethoven's notes to him, one of which was endorsed by Zmeskall as being received on 18 April 1810. Idem, pp. 487–88.

54. Idem, p. 439.

55. Beethoven did not yet look old in the two oil portraits painted of him by the Viennese artist Isidor Neugass (c.1780–after 1847) around 1806, but he also did not look even remotely like Beethoven. Even Frimmel was forced to call Neugass a "weak" painter, see *Beethoven im zeitgenössischen Bildnis*, p. 23. Comparison of the inept Neugass portraits (for black-and-white reproduction side by side, see Bory, *Ludwig van Beethoven, His Life and His Work in Pictures*, p. 119; for color reproduction of the signed version see Robbins Landon, *Beethoven: A Documentary Study*, p. 235) with the Klein life mask mythometer demonstrates that they are insignificant in so far as documenting Beethoven's physiognomy. But they are not completely irrelevant for as both Frimmel and Robbins Landon point out the artist documented the fact that at this period in his life Beethoven wore a gold chain around his neck from which he suspended the double lorgnette he used to correct his shortsightedness; see chapter 3 and ns. 112, 113.

It is not my aim in this book to reproduce every single portrait of Beethoven created during his lifetime. This Herculean (and cumulative) task has been assumed by Frimmel, Bory, Robbins Landon, and others (see chapter 1, n. 1). Imagerial remoteness or public inaccessibility have been the criteria for omission. Nevertheless three portraits merit acknowledgment:

1. *Beethoven at the Age of Thirteen*, an anonymous oil painting discovered in 1972 (reproduced in color in H. C. Robbins Landon, *Beethoven: A Documentary Study*, abridged ed. [New York, 1975], Ill. 4, p. 6. This small (17 x 22 cm.) picture, recently restored and found to have had changes made around the mouth and chin, is identified on the back as a gift of Beethoven to Baron von Smeskal (Zmeskall, see above, n. 53). Beethovenesque features are the narrow eyelids, broad nose, pronounced philtrum, and rosy cheeks. Nevertheless, this authentic 18th-century canvas could be the portrait of many another thirteen-year-old boy, artfully doctored at a later date to look the way the child Beethoven "ought" to have looked. (The prominent red—rash—of Beethoven's cheeks seems to have come into existence only *after* his serious illness at age fifteen–sixteen.

2. Johann Christoph Heckel (1792–1858), *Beethoven*, 1815, oil portrait, Library of Congress, Washington, D.C. (reproduced in color, ibid., Ill, 10, p. 14). Supposedly Beethoven sat for this artist at the piano salon of his friend Andreas Streicher, but the result is not piano: the composer's hair looks like a black helmet, creating a ludicrous effect. The upper part of the face is misleading (by comparison with the Klein life mask) but the peculiar configuration of the chin is accurately rendered. The portrait was in private hands for many years. (See Bory, *Ludwig van Beethoven, His Life and his Work in Pictures*, p. 62, for a second version of the Heckel portrait and a lithograph of the original portrait.)

3. Gustav Adolph Hippius (1792–1856), *Beethoven*, c. 1814–16, pencil sketch. Formerly private collection, Russia (reproduced in Robbins Landon, *Beethoven: A Docu-*

mentary Study, abridged ed., Ill. 7, p. 13). The converse of the Heckel "helmet" oil, this portrait sketch—presumably done from life—is more accurate regarding the upper half of Beethoven's face: although the proportions of the forehead are off (too low), the composer's characteristic "roving" glance, broken frontal hairs, and lumpy skin at the root of the nose are all depicted. The philtrum and cleft chin are also distinctly indicated; nevertheless, the ensemble simply does not spell Beethoven.

56. The version reproduced here, with red cravat, belongs to the Gesellschaft der Musikfreunde in Vienna, which owns at least ten other portraits from Mähler's famous *Tonkünstler-Galerie*, including those of Salieri and Hummel. A second version, with white neck piece, is in the possession of Wolfgang von Karajan, Salzburg, and a third copy, apparently also with colored cravat (for black-and-white reproductions of all three see Bory, *Ludwig van Beethoven, His Life and His Work in Pictures*, p. 163), made for Beethoven's friend Baron Ignaz von Gleichenstein, was sent to Germany and is still in the Gleichenstein Collection.

57. Cited by Glück, "W. J. Mählers Beethovenbildnisse und seine Porträte anderer Persönlichkeiten," p. 14, n. 1, translation mine.

58. They were the composers Joseph von Eybler (1764–1846), Adalbert Gyrowetz (1763–1850), Johann Nepomuk Hummel (1778–1837), Ignaz von Seyfried (1776–1841), and Joseph Weigl (1766–1846). According to the reminiscences of the tenor Luigi Cramolini, another musician in Mähler's portrait gallery was also in attendance at Beethoven's funeral, Michael Umlauf (1781–1842), but this is not substantiated by either Schindler or Thayer.

59. *Wiener Zeitschrift für Kunst, Literatur und Mode* (Vienna, 1818), p. 1134.

60. Klöber's reminiscences, written in a letter of 26 November, 1863, were published in the last year of his life, some forty-six years after the event, in the *Allgemeine musikalische Zeitung*, no. 18, 4 May 1864, p. 324. The translation used here is from Robbins Landon, *Beethoven: A Documentary Study*, pp. 296–97.

61. Ibid., p. 296.

62. Ibid.

63. Ibid., p. 297.

64. Ibid., pp. 296–97.

65. Ibid., p. 297.

66. The lithographer was Klöber's Berlin student Theodor Neu (1810–?) and Klöber makes reference to the lithograph as smaller than the oil painting in his reminiscence. Ibid.

67. Ibid.

68. Schindler, *Beethoven As I Knew Him*, p. 452.

69. Ibid., pp. 452, 456.

70. Ibid., p. 452.

71. Ibid., p. 451. During the 1840s, while he was living and teaching privately in Aachen, his worsening financial conditions forced Schindler to offer up his collection of Beethoven documents and memorabilia for sale to the highest bidder. In the summer of 1845 he received an irresistible offer from the king of Prussia for a lump sum plus a life annuity, and it must have been at this time, just before handing over his collection, that Schindler commissioned the "considerably improved" copy of his precious Schimon portrait to be made. The most valuable items in Schindler's (largely pilfered) col-

lection of Beethoveniana were, of course, the conversation books. Traditional Beethoven scholarship from Thayer to MacArdle has held that Schindler originally possessed about 400 of these, allowing approximately only 137 to survive and committing the other volumes to flames. But recent research has now cast doubt on this long-accepted story and focused attention instead on the large number of forged entries—some 240 of them—added by Schindler after Beethoven's death to the extant conversation books. By inserting numerous entries (all of them now proved spurious) into the conversation books of 1819 and 1820 in particular Schindler attempted to establish that he had been Beethoven's intimate some three and a half years earlier than in fact was the case, see Dagmar Beck and Gritta Herre, "Anton Schindlers fingierte Eintragungen in den Konversationsheften," in Harry Goldschmidt, ed., *Zu Beethoven: Aufsätze und Annotationen* (Berlin, 1979), pp. 11–89.

72. Ibid., p. 452.

73. Sonneck, *Beethoven: Impressions by His Contemporaries*, p. 117.

74. Schindler, *Beethoven As I Knew Him*, p. 452.

75. Anderson, *The Letters of Beethoven*, 2: 866.

76. Sonneck, *Beethoven: Impressions by His Contemporaries*, pp. 114–16. Taken from the 1828 edition of Sir John's book.

77. Pointed out in Robbins Landon, *Beethoven: A Documentary Study*, p. 14. Böhm also made a small portrait medallion of Beethoven with his head turned to the right, and his comment to Beethoven on its progress appears in a conversation book of January 1820: "I am glad to see you, because my medallion is nearing completion. I want to do the hair this way in the middle, somewhat less and shorter than it is now; I will let you see it before I finish it—goodby." Ibid, p. 325.

78. Very early in his Vienna career Beethoven had apparently been the unwitting subject for an unflattering portrait sketch that made the rounds of the circle of friends he had met through the soprano Christine Gerhardi. In a letter of 1797 to her about getting the portrait out of circulation, Beethoven cautions the singer to proceed discreetly, then laments: "I assure you that after this experience I will appeal in the Press to all painters not to paint me again without my knowledge. I really did not think that this face of mine would ever cause me embarrassment." Anderson, *The Letters of Beethoven*, 1: 29.

79. Anderson, *The Letters of Beethoven*, 2: 901. Anderson's suggested dating of "summer 1820" has, with the discovery of pertinent exhibition reviews of 6 and 8 June 1820, been fixed more precisely by Glück as "spring 1820," "Prolegomena zu einer neuen Beethoven-Ikonographie," pp. 206–7. Glück's article presents a persuasive argument for identification of Dietrich (and not a painter) as the interlocutor who wrote in Beethoven's conversation book of mid-July 1820 reporting on a current art exhibition in which Beethoven's "head" was on display, and my text makes use of Glück's valuable data, which includes a transcript of the entire "conversation" just mentioned.

Dietrich's birth date has traditionally been given as 1799 but recently (1980) convincing evidence has been published showing that Dietrich was sixteen in 1813, hence making his date of birth 1796 or 1797, see Badura-Skoda, "Der Bildhauer Anton Dietrich. Ein Beitrag zur Ikonographie Beethovens und Schuberts," pp. 30–31.

80. An example of the "contemporary," long-haired type belongs to the Historisches Museum der Stadt Wien and is kept on permanent display in Room I of the Beethoven Memorial ("Pasqualati") House at Mölkerbastei 8 in Vienna. An example of the "classical," short-haired version, identified as being made out of ivory, is reproduced by Bory in *Ludwig van Beethoven, His Life and His Work in Pictures*, p. 176. For the whereabouts and history of other copies (most of them not known to Glück) see Badura-Skoda, "Der Bildhauer Anton Dietrich. Ein Beitrag zur Ikonographie Beethovens und Schuberts," pp. 39, 48. Frimmel was apparently so put off by the nonresemblance of either Dietrich type that he did not deem them worthy of reproduction; see his discussion in *Beethoven im zeitgenössischen Bildnis*, pp. 49–52.

81. Beethoven conversation book of mid-July 1820, see Köhler and Herre (with, in this volume, Günter Brosch), *Ludwig van Beethovens Konversations-hefte*, 2 (Notebook is, c. 6 July–19 August 1820), pp. 180–81, translation mine. See also above, n. 79.

82. This study was actually Beethoven's bedroom and the room in which he died. Although Hoechle made this intriguing document only three days after Beethoven's death, things were already slightly changed: the Konrad Graf piano, which stood end to end, interwinged with the famous Broadwood piano shown in the drawing, had already been removed.

83. Schindler, *Beethoven As I Knew Him*, p. 456.

84. Ibid., p. 507. This cupid candlestick with shade is now in the Beethovenhaus, Bonn. It is reproduced in black and white in Bory, *Ludwig van Beethoven, His Life and His Work in Pictures*, p. 204, and in color in David Jacobs, *Beethoven* (New York, 1970), p. 6.

85. Schindler, *Beethoven As I Knew Him*, p. 453.

86. Ibid., p. 451.

87. Thayer-Forbes, *Thayer's Life of Beethoven*, p. 760.

88. Now in the Beethovenhaus, Bonn; reproduced in color in Schmidt-Görg and Schmidt, *Ludwig van Beethoven*, p. 255.

89. Schindler, *Beethoven As I Knew Him*, p. 453.

90. Ibid., p. 456.

91. Kriehuber also made "copies" of the Mähler portrait of 1804–5 and of the Dietrich ("classical" version) bust, see Fig. 19.

92. See Glück, "Prolegomena zu einer neuen Beethoven-Ikonographie," p. 206, n. 8.

93. Schindler, *Beethoven As I Knew Him*, p. 455.

94. The first lithographic reproduction of Stieler's Beethoven portrait was issued during Beethoven's lifetime and was made by Stieler's seventeen-year-old nephew, Friedrich Dürck (1809–1884). It was commissioned and published by Artaria sometime during the second half (probably early summer) of 1826. Ibid., p. 358, n. 249. Kriehuber's copy was apparently made after Beethoven's death, but the artist did not escape the misdirected indignation of Schindler who, mistaking yet another lithographer's copy of the Stieler Beethoven portrait for one by Kriehuber, wrote: "This lithograph shows Beethoven with a black cravat. With no thought whatsoever, Kriehuber included this article of modern dress. The white cravat, which had been in vogue for a full century, and which our Beethoven always wore, apparently was to the lithographer an affront to aesthetic propriety of dress." Ibid, p. 456. Schindler does not

seem to have been offended by the red ascot bestowed on the composer by Stieler in the original oil portrait.

95. See Beethoven's memorandum to Matthias Artaria (summer 1826) requesting ''three selected reproductions of the portrait of L. van Beethoven,'' in MacArdle and Misch, *New Beethoven Letters*, p. 518. Two recipients of the print were Beethoven's old physician friend from Bonn, Franz Wegeler, and Stephan von Breuning. Schindler, *Beethoven As I Knew Him*, p. 358, n. 249.

96. Rochlitz's letter of 9 July 1822 to his wife and Gottfried Christoph Härtel at Leipzig, as quoted in Schindler, *Beethoven As I Knew Him*, p. 454. For Rochlitz's encounter with Schubert, see chapter 4 and n. 22.

97. Dagobert D. Runes, *Pictorial History of Philosophy* (New York, 1959), p. 289.

98. Schindler, *Beethoven As I Knew Him*, pp. 454–55.

99. Sonneck, *Beethoven: Impressions by His Contemporaries*, pp. 111–12.

100. The painting—unacknowledged in previous studies of Beethoven iconography—first appeared in London at a sale held by Christie's in 1911, when it was bought by a Swedish banker named Poulsen who, after 1930, gave the portait to his son. The son sold the portrait to Howard Moorepark of Los Angeles and the picture then passed through several more hands and was last (1985) known to be in the collection of the former Mrs. Walter (Jo Beth) Garrard (now Mrs. Robert [Jo Beth] Milton) of Atlanta, Georgia. Mrs. Garrard kindly furnished me with photographs of the work.

101. Another ''contemporary'' icon to surface recently from an American private collection is now (1985) on display at the Kennedy Center for the Performing Arts in Washington, D.C. (gift of Mr. and Mrs. Robert W. Levy of New Orleans). It shows the composer emaciated and sickly looking, seated next to, but turned away from, his piano, his right elbow resting on a musical score, and his eyes raised to heaven in a prolonged moment of concentration and inspiration. The nose is long and thin; the hair quite white (a wig?). Although the work is not dated, it is signed. The painter is Theodor Matthias von Holst (1810–1844), grand uncle of the composer Gustav Holst. Born in London (on 3 September) to a musical family who had migrated to England from Riga, he studied with Henry Fuseli at the Royal Academy where, from 1827 on, he exhibited yearly. The date of his first European visit is not certain but by 1839 he had painted Bettina von Arnim in Berlin. He would only have been sixteen years old during Beethoven's last year of life and it is highly unlikely that the ailing composer would have posed for him. The portrait does respond, however, to the suffering image of Beethoven as condoned and articulated by the myth-making process even before the year of Beethoven's death. I am grateful to Christopher Minnes for providing me with color photographs of this fanciful icon.

102. The black cravat worn by Waldmüller's sitter of 1834 reflects the new modern fashion commented upon by Schindler in his blast at anachronistic imagery, see above, n. 94.

103. For a discussion of Waldmüller's unique contribution to Austrian Biedermeier see my *The Fantastic Art of Vienna* (New York, 1978), pp. 7–8. The definitive study of this important artist is still awaited, but two useful monographs are Arthur Roessler, *Ferdinand Georg Waldmüller* (Vienna, 1907), Bruno Grimschitz,

Ferdinand Georg Waldmüller: Leben und Werk (Vienna, 1945), and Maria Buchsbaum, *Ferdinand Georg Waldmüller* (Salzburg, 1976).

104. Schindler, writing in 1860, was in error about the chronology of Waldmüller's career: the painter was not named a professor at the Vienna Academy until 1830. In 1822, a year before the commission from Beethoven's publishers, Waldmüller had exhibited five portraits at the Academy with great success and this is probably why—as Vienna's most prominent portraitist—he received the order from Leipzig for a Beethoven portrait. Waldmüller's fortunes changed and he died impoverished and forgotten, a bitter man with bitter memories of his once beloved Academy whose conservative methods he had fought against unsuccessfully.

105. Schindler, *Beethoven As I Knew Him*, pp. 453–54.

106. Ibid., p. 454.

107. Sonneck, *Beethoven: Impressions by His Contemporaries*, p. 161. Waldmüller's portrait of Beethoven was completed by May 1823; Benedict's visit to the composer occurred on 5 October 1823. Weber's son, Max Maria von Weber, presented Benedict's remarks in a three-volume biography of his father, *Carl Maria von Weber: Ein Lebensbild*, published in Leipzig in 1864–66 (vol. 2, pp. 510–12). Benedict published his own account of Weber in a book bearing the composer's name in 1881.

108. Sonneck, *Beethoven: Impressions by His Contemporaries*, pp. 130-31.

109. Schindler, *Beethoven As I Knew Him*, p. 455.

110. Ibid., p. 510, n. 354. Joseph Kriehuber, who as we have seen, had made lithographic copies of the 1804–5 Mähler portrait and the Dietrich bust, also made a copy of the Decker portrait drawing.

111. Anderson, *The Letters of Beethoven*, 3: 1322.

112. The recipient was Maurice (Moritz) Adolf Schlesinger, oldest son of Adolf Martin Schlesinger, who had founded a music publishing business in Berlin in 1795. The Paris branch of the firm was started by Maurice in 1822. Three years earlier young Maurice had forever won Beethoven's heart by sending him as a surprise the roast veal dinner he had complained of not being able to get at his local restaurant. Sonneck, *Beethoven: Impressions by His Contemporaries*, pp. 112–13 and chapter 3 in this book. Beethoven's dedication on the Decker lithograph is dated 4 September 1825.

113. *Odyssey* 9.441; as quoted by Schindler, *Beethoven As I Knew Him*, p. 315.

114. Anderson, *The Letters of Beethoven*, 1: 61. The print was published in 1800 by Giovanni Cappi (a former apprentice at Artaria; it is not clear whether he was still with Artaria when the print was issued—Beethoven apparently thought so). The engraving was done by Johann Josef Neidl (1776–1832), who also engraved a portrait of Haydn, from a now lost portrait drawing of the composer made by Gandolph Ernst Stainhauser von Treuberg (1766–1805). Stainhauser's drawing served as the model for another engraving by an unknown artist and issued in Leipzig in 1801 by Beethoven's friend the music publisher Franz Anton Hoffmeister (1754–1812). A third artist, C. F. Riedl (dates unknown) also made an engraving in 1801 based on the Stainhauser drawing.

115. Anderson, *The Letters of Beethoven*, 3: 1321–22 (letter of 7 December 1826). We see from this letter to

his old friend Wegeler that, after letting the nobility myth have its way for some thirty-three years, Beethoven was at last ready to set the record straight, or at least let a future biographer do so. In an interesting analysis of this letter, Solomon points out Beethoven's continuing reluctance to renounce the legend of noble birth: he delayed mailing the letter until mid-February 1827, literally just a few weeks before his death, and in it he "unconsciously restated his lingering adherence to the Family Romance by means of a long recital of his medals and honors, and especially by stressing his dedication of the Ninth Symphony to Friedrich Wilhelm III, the scion of his supposed father." Solomon, *Beethoven*, pp. 287–88.

116. Sonneck, *Beethoven: Impressions by His Contemporaries*, pp. 225–26.

117. Thayer-Forbes, *Thayer's Life of Beethoven*, p. 1050.

118. Ibid.

119. Teltscher's intimate documents, which also included a drawing of just the bed, remained in private hands and could not have influenced 19th-century Beethoven imagery. They were first published by Frimmel in 1909 (*Blättern für Gemäldekunde* [Leipzig], 5:3) and again in his *Beethoven im zeitgenössischen Bildnis*, Figs. 26 and 27. Later the deathbed drawings passed into the collection of a fervent Beethoven fan, Stefan Zweig.

120. Thayer-Forbes, *Thayer's Life of Beethoven*, pp. 1050–51.

121. Ibid. From a medical point of view, the defiant fistclenching gesture of the dying Beethoven described with such awe by Hüttenbrenner is perfectly consistent with the irrational responses to disturbing stimuli (in Beethoven's case the bolt of lightning and clap of thunder) manifested by many a comatose patient suffering hepatic death throes. See for example S. J. London, "Beethoven: Case Report of a Titan's Last Crisis," *Archives of Internal Medicine* 113 (March 1964):448.

122. Nettl, *Beethoven Encyclopedia*, p. 43. Wawruth's reminiscence of Beethoven's final illness and death was written on 20 May 1827 and first published after his death in the *Wiener Zeitschrift*, 30 April 1842.

123. Schindler, *Beethoven As I Knew Him*, p. 325.

124. Ibid., p. 332. Delighted with this acknowledgment of his indispensable judgment and advice, Schindler went to the trouble of reproducing a facsimile of Breuning's letter to him in his Beethoven biography: Ibid., pp. 330–31.

125. Ibid., p. 332. Schindler was incorrect about Danhauser's becoming renowned as a sculptor; he became a painter—see Fig. 71, Color pl. 5, and discussion of his portrait of *Liszt at the Piano* in chapter 4.

126. The autopsy was conducted in the presence of Dr. Wawruth by a then twenty-six-year-old "master of the art of dissection," Dr. Johann Wagner (1800–1832), assistant in pathological anatomy at the Vienna Medical School. The findings confirmed cirrhosis of the liver as cause of death. Dr. Wagner's detailed autopsy report (given in full in Thayer-Forbes, *Thayer's Life of Beethoven*, Appendix B, pp. 1059–60), with all its grisly observations, was particularly concerned with establishing the irregular configuration, shrunken state, and advanced vascularity of the hearing apparatus.

127. Carl Danhauser's memoirs of 1891 set the date as the morning of 26 March, but clearly 28 March is meant. From the letter of 27 March quoted in the text

above written by Breuning to Schindler asking his advice on whether to permit Danhauser's request to take a plaster cast "tomorrow morning" it is obvious that the twentyeighth was the day in question. Also Beethoven had not died in the morning of the twenty-sixth—the time of day at which Carl Danhauser's account is fixed—but in the early evening of the twenty-sixth of March. See Glück, "Prolegomena zu einer neuen Beethoven-Ikonographie," pp. 210–12 for complete citation of the document. The monograph on Josef Danhauser written by Arthur Roessler (Vienna, n.d., c. 1910) gives a similar account of the events related by Carl Danhauser and begins: "As news of the death of the great tone master spread through Vienna and was rushed to Danhauser, he reacted to the news in true artist's fashion, namely with the request to be allowed to take a plaster cast of the dead man's face." Roessler, *Josef Danhauser*, p. 14, translation mine.

128. Glück, "Prolegomena zu einer neuen BeethovenIkonographie," p. 211, translation mine.

129. Ibid., pp. 211–12, translation mine.

CHAPTER THREE:
BEETHOVEN DEAD: SHAPING THE
POSTHUMOUS PORTRAIT

1. Charles Hallé, *The Autobiography of Charles Hallé*, ed. Michael Kennedy (1896; New York, 1973), p. 28.

2. Some of them painted by Mähler for his Musicians Gallery, see chapter 2, n. 58. Beethoven's nephew, Karl, did not get back from his army post in Moravia in time for the funeral.

3. Sonneck, *Beethoven: Impressions by His Contemporaries*, p. 154; Grillparzer as quoted by Philip Gordon.

4. Thayer-Forbes, *Thayer's Life of Beethoven*, Appendix A. pp. 1057–58.

5. Ibid., pp. 304–5. Beethoven's Heiligenstadt Testament is cited in full as an example of the "Outsider" in the age of Romanticism by Howard E. Hugo, *The Portable Romantic Reader*, (1957; New York, 1972), pp. 192–96. See Solomon, *Beethoven*, pp. 116–25 for a discussion of Beethoven's inability to name his brother Johann in the Heiligenstadt Testament and for an analysis of the complex motives that inspired this carefully redrafted document Beethoven kept all his life.

6. With the new information gained, and at a time when the ancestry of Ludwig "van" Beethoven was a matter of increasing interest, "science" was utilized to make some extraordinary claims. Thus a certain Dr. Schaaffhausen, giving an address at the Eighth Congress of the German Anthropological Society in 1887, was able to announce: "There is still another explanation of the flatness of Beethoven's skull... that is the Dutch origin of the master. Now there is no country in Europe where the flat skull is so ancient a national type as Holland." See the *Mitteilungen der anthropologischen Gesellschaft in Wien*, Sitzungsbericht for 19 April 1887. Offsetting claims that Beethoven's ancestry was of Dutch origin were those made by the Belgian musicologist Ernest Closson (1870–1950), who summoned up equally impressive "psychological" (as opposed to phrenological) evidence that Beethoven was Flemish, see Closson, *L'élément flamand dans Beethoven* (1928; Brussels, 1946). With the aid of a compelling syllogism, Closson (a self-confessed Walloon) demonstrates that (a) all Flemings are "stiff," dull, and plebeian; (b) Bee-

thoven, in his tastes, his habits, his essential simplicity, his frequent lack of tact, his "stiff" manner, was both inwardly and outwardly dull and ple beian; and (c) therefore Beethoven was Flemish.

For a summary of the two exhumations of Beethoven's body and their largely inconclusive results (the skull had already collapsed into nine separate fragments by the time of the first exhumation, see Frimmel, *BeethovenStudien I: Beethovens äussere Erscheinung*, pp. 153–57; drawings of the reconstructed skull on pp. 151, 168 (same as p. 151 but larger and half the actual size), 169, and 170. The profile view (p. 168) shows Beethoven's protruding upper and lower teeth quite clearly and confirms the impression of powerful jaw bones noted by contemporaries. In modern dental terms, Beethoven had what is called a double protrusion with both upper and lower jaws and lips forward. The low lower jaw angle contributed to his "stern" look and short lower facial height. What young Julius Benedict remembered in his memoirs of Beethoven as "jawbones which seemed meant to crack the hardest nuts" (see chapter 2 and n. 107) is substantiated in a 1982 orthodontic analysis of the Frimmel profile drawing: "Beethoven could probably have bitten through a nail with his back teeth." Letter to the author from William J. Wise, D.D.S., M.S.D. of Dallas, 21 June 1982.

7. Thayer-Forbes, *Thayer's Life of Beethoven*, p. 759.

8. See Köhler and Herre (with, in this volume, Günter Brosche), *Ludwig van Beethovens Konversationshefte*, 1 (Notebook 8, c. 23 February–c. 12 March 1820), p. 318, and Thayer-Forbes, *Thayer's Life of Beethoven*, p. 759. Probably in continuing response to E.T.A. Hoffmann punning possibilities, Beethoven also composed a canon that year on the words: "Hoffman, sei ja Kein Hofmann," Ibid., p. 772.

9. Ibid., p. 759. See Anderson, *The Letters of Beethoven*, 2: 884–85, for a translation that is more polished but less literal and hence less reflective of the simple, unaffected style used by Beethoven to address this influential music critic.

10. Oliver Strunk, *Source Readings in Music History: The Romantic Era* (New York, 1950), p. 35.

11. Ibid.

12. Ibid., pp. 35–37.

13. Friedrich Kerst and Henry Edward Krehbiel, *Beethoven: The Man and the Artist, as Revealed in His Own Words* (New York, 1964), pp. 23–24; letter of 13 February 1814. This translation is given in preference to Anderson's (*The Letters of Beethoven*, 1: 445) for the same reasons as those expressed above in n. 9.

14. Strunk, *Source Readings in Music History: The Romantic Era*, pp. 37–38.

15. Anonymous critic (Johann Nepomuk Möser?) writing for the 11 September 1806 issue of the Berlin-based *Der Freimüthige*, as cited by Max Graf, *Composer and Critic: Two Hundred Years of Musical Criticism* (1946; New York, 1971), p. 155.

16. For a helpful tour through Beethoven's sketchbooks, see Alan Tyson, "Sketches and Autographs," in Davis Arnold and Nigel Fortune, eds., *The Beethoven Reader* (New York, 1971), pp. 443–58. For an enlightening discussion of the *Pastoral* sketches, see the same author's article "A Reconstruction of the Pastoral Symphony Sketchbook," in Alan Tyson, ed., *Beethoven Studies* (New York, 1973), pp. 67–96.

17. Sonneck, *Beethoven: Impressions by His Contemporaries*, pp. 146–47.

18. Schindler, *Beethoven As I Knew Him*, p. 385.

19. Strunk, *Source Readings in Music History: The Romantic Era*, p. 38.

20. In his Vienna lectures of 1807–8 (*Über dramatische Kunst und Literatur*, published 1809–11) August Schlegel introduced the idea of aesthetic relativism by citing the Pantheon in conjunction with Saint Stephen's Cathedral, and Sophocles in the same breath as Skakespeare, asking whether admiration of one compels depreciation of the other. A superb discussion of some of the sources for German Romanticism is to be found in W. D. RobsonScott, *The Literary Background of the Gothic Revival in Germany* (Oxford, 1965).

21. Strunk, *Source Readings in Music History: The Romantic Era*, p. 38.

22. Ibid.

23. Ibid., pp. 38–39.

24. Harvey W. Hewett-Thayer, *Hoffmann: Author of the Tales* (Princeton, 1948), p. 285.

25. Ibid.

26. Hoffmann's half-mad Kreisler is thought to be modeled upon a real-life peripatetic musician, Johann Ludwig Böhner (1787–1860), whose immense talents were almost invalidated by his bizarre behavior and who ended his life as a destitute alcoholic. This pathetic figure was encountered not only by Hoffmann but by Goethe and Schumann.

Concerning the rumors of Beethoven's supposed insanity even during his lifetime (rumors upon which Beethoven occasionally remarked), see the entry and bibliographical references on "Insanity" in Nettl, *Beethoven Encyclopedia*, pp. 99–100, and the discussion of the composer's neurotic conduct in Solomon, *Beethoven*, pp. 256–57. Perhaps Goethe's remark to Zelter (chapter 1 and n. 10) about Beethoven after the Teplitz meeting best hits the mark: "an utterly untamed personality." Goethe gave a pithy and oft-quoted summary of the "untamed" genius in a letter written to his wife from Teplitz on 19 July 1812: "More concentrated, more energetic, more inward I have never yet seen an artist." ("Zusammengefasster, energetischer, inniger habe ich noch keinen Künstler gesehen.") Rolland, *Beethoven and Goethe*, pp. 89, 216.

27. This according to Lyser's—not always trustworthy—testimony, see Geraldine I. C. de Courcy, *Paganini the Genoese*, 2 vols. (Norman [Okla.] 1957), 1: 398, n. 57. A biography of this strange man was written by Friedrich Hirth, *J. P. Lyser, der Dichter, Maler, und Musiker* (Munich, 1911).

28. Frederic Ewen, ed. and trans., *Heinrich Heine: SelfPortrait and Other Prose Writings* (Secaucus [N.J.] 1948), p. 366. The great German expatriate, writing in the person of a certain Maximilian, gives a fascinating (and extravagantly Romantic) description of Paganini as he appeared on the street and as he appeared in concert. Ibid., pp. 366–73. According to Heine, he and Lyser only observed Paganini; there is no mention of drinking punch with him.

29. " . . . treu nach der Natur gezeichnet, wie er in den letzten Jahren seines Lebens durch die Strassen Wiens mehr sprang und lief denn ging," as cited by Frimmel, *Beethoven-Studien I: Beethovens äussere Erscheinung*, p. 124; see also Frimmel, *Beethoven im zeitgenössischen Bildnis*, p. 54.

30. Frimmel, *Beethoven-Studien I: Beethovens äussere Erscheinung*, pp. 120–21.

31. The printed "signature" in the *Cäcilia* drawing is not by Lyser but probably supplied by a former owner of the drawing, C. F. Pohl, Ibid., pp. 122–23.

32. So successful and "authoritative" in fact that it had been reproduced in the long entry on Beethoven in *Grove's Dictionary of Music and Musicians* (1878–90), as noted by Frimmel in 1905 (*Beethoven-Studien I: Beethovens äussere Erscheinung*, p. 121, n. 1). The Lyser drawing is reproduced in the latest edition of Grove's as well (6th ed., 1980, vol. 2, p. 391).

33. One of Lyser's many given names was in fact also Ludwig. The hero worship and identification of the deaf, music-loving Lyser with his deaf music-producing idol is so obvious that I find it difficult to understand why such a knowledgeable Beethoven scholar as Robbins Landon would state: "It is something of a mystery why the talented Danish artist Johann Peter Theodor Lyser made so many sketches of Beethoven, for according to Lyser experts it appears that the two men were never in the same place at the same time" (Robbins Landon, *Beethoven*, p. 14). Possibly it escaped Robbins Landon's attention that Lyser, the former hopeful musician and later active music critic who reviewed Beethoven's work, was deaf.

34. Ewen, *Heinrich Heine: Self-Portrait and Other Prose Writings*, pp. 366–67. Lyser goes on to comment that Paganini "has signed over his body and soul to the devil in order to become the best violinist in the world...." (p. 367).

35. See Frimmel, *Beethoven-Studien I: Beethovens äussere Erscheinung*, pp. 124–27.

36. Thayer-Forbes, *Thayer's Life of Beethoven*, p. 436.

37. Irving Kolodin, *The Interior Beethoven* (New York, 1975), p. 172; see further Gustav Nottebohm, *Ein Skizzenbuch von Beethoven aus dem Jahre, 1803* (1880; New York, 1970), p. 55.

38. See Schindler's rhapsodic and also quite instructive description of his April 1823 visit in the company of the reminiscing composer to the site of *Pastoral* inspiration, Schindler, *Beethoven As I Knew Him*, pp. 144–47 (see also chapter 5 of this book and n. 110). Thayer could do no better than to reprint Schindler's account in his own book.

39. For the latest (only slightly Freudian), see Solomon, *Beethoven*, chapter 13, "Bonaparte: The Crisis of Belief," pp. 132–42. A recent link in the Beethoven-Napoleon *Eroica* legend was fashioned by Anthony Burgess in his novel *Napoleon Symphony* (New York, 1974). At the conclusion of his raunchy exposition of a theme nominally Napoleonic, a rhyming "Epistle to the Reader" (ibid., p. 365) directs attention to the following:

The symphony was there—Third, in E-flat,
The Eroica. This novel, then is that:
Napoleon's career, unteased, rewoven
Into a pattern borrowed from Beethoven.
The story is well-known: Count Bernadotte
Met Beethoven and said to him: "Why not
A *Sinfonia Buonaparte*?"—"Yes:
This great First Consul merits nothing less,"
Said Beethoven, and so he wrote the work.
But certain ogreish traits began to irk,
Then deeplier disturb, then fire to rage
Ludwig, who ripped the dedication page

To ribbons, crying: "Hero of the age?
Ach, nein—another tyrant." He was right . . .

40. This account was given by Ries in the joint *Biographische Notizen über Ludwig van Beethoven* coauthored with Franz Wegeler and published in 1838 (see text below) and is given here as cited in Thayer-Forbes, *Thayer's Life of Beethoven*, pp. 348–49.

41. Schindler, *Beethoven As I Knew Him*, pp. 115–16.

42. Ibid., p. 116.

43. Ibid., pp. 116–17.

44. As cited by Marek, *Beethoven: Biography of a Genius*, p. 345, asterisked note; to my knowledge Marek was the first modern Beethoven scholar to publish this amusing analysis of the *Eroica*.

45. Thomas Carlyle's lectures of 1840, "On Heroes, Hero-Worship, and the Heroic in History," became one of the two focal points (Nietzsche is the other) of Eric Bentley's *A Century of Hero-Worship* (Philadelphia, 1944). Beethoven was not one of Carlyle's heroes (nor was Carlyle to his long-suffering, neglected wife of forty years, Jane Welsh).

46. George Grove, *Beethoven and His Nine Symphonies* (1896; 3rd. ed., 1898; New York, 1962), p. 73.

47. Philip G. Downs, "Beethoven's 'New Way' and the *Eroica*," in Paul Henry Lang, ed., *The Creative World of Beethoven* (New York, 1971), p. 101.

48. Ibid., pp. 101–2.

49. Ibid., p. 102.

50. Sonneck, *Beethoven: Impressions by His Contemporaries*, p. 117.

51. Francis Toye, *Rossini: A Study in Tragi-Comedy* (1934; New York, 1947), p. 85.

52. Thayer-Forbes, *Thayer's Life of Beethoven*, p. 805.

53. Schindler wrongly interpreted Beethoven's anger at the fact that such a story was common coinage, reporting what he believed to be Rossini's failure to meet the composer (he knew only of Rossini's two attempts to meet Beethoven through Artaria, which had indeed come to nothing), and commenting that "Beethoven would not tolerate any mention of this incident among his friends, and he never spoke of it to anyone." Schindler, *Beethoven As I Knew Him*, p. 377.

54. Ferdinand Hiller (1811–1885), the young musician who with his teacher Hummel visited the dying Beethoven three times during March 1827 and who later published a description of those visits (*Neue Folge*, pp. 169ff, vol. 3 of his collected writings, *Aus dem Tonleben unserer Zeit* [Leipzig, 1868–71]), was told by Rossini in 1856: "During my sojourn in Vienna I had myself introduced to him by old Calpani [Carpani]; but between his deafness and my ignorance of German, conversation was impossible. But I am glad that I saw him, at least." Thayer-Forbes, *Thayer's Life of Beethoven*, p. 805.

55. Schindler, *Beethoven As I Knew Him*, pp. 376–77.

56. Toye, *Rossini: A Study in Tragi-Comedy*, pp. 182–85.

57. Hanslick had first paid a visit to Rossini in 1860; Rossini was seventy-five years old when Hanslick visited him for a second time in 1867. He reported their conversation:

"I remember Beethoven well," continued Rossini after a pause, "although it is nearly half a century ago. On my visit to Vienna I hastened to look him up."

"And he did not receive you, as Schindler and other biographers assure us."

"On the contrary," said Rossini, correcting me: "I had Carpani, the Italian poet . . . introduce me, and he received me at once and very politely. True, the visit did not last very long, for conversation with Beethoven was nothing less than painful. His hearing was particularly bad on that day and in spite of my loudest shoutings he could not understand me; his little practice in Italian may have made conversation more difficult." Thayer-Forbes, *Thayer's Life of Beethoven*, p. 805.

58. Richard Wagner, "Erinnerungen an Rossini," *Allgemeine Zeitung*, Augsburg, 17 December 1868.

59. Edmond Michotte, *Souvenirs Personnels: La Visite de R. Wagner a Rossini* (Brussels, 1906). Translated into English with an introduction and appendix by Herbert Weinstock, *Richard Wagner's Visit to Rossini and An Evening at Rossini's in Beau-Sejour* (Chicago, 1968).

60. Marie Henri Beyle [Stendhal], *Life of Rossini*, trans. and annotated by Richard N. Coe (New York, 1970), p. 53. Stendhal obviously knew nothing about Rossini's visit to Beethoven during his Vienna sojourn.

61. Ibid., p. 63.

62. See chapter 2, n. 107.

63. As given in Schindler, *Beethoven As I Knew Him*, Appendix F (pp. 479–83), pp. 481–82. This parody, chapter 4 from Weber's unfinished and partly autobiographical novel *Tonkünstlersleben* (*A Composer's Life*), was published in the 27 December 1809 issue of the Stuttgart *Morgenblatt für gebildete Stände*, see John Warrack, *Carl Maria von Weber* (New York, 1968), pp. 89–95. Although the satire is usually identified as referring to the Fourth Symphony (which had been completed the year before and published in 1809) Warrack believes Weber was attacking the composite Beethoven, rather than the *Pastoral* specifically, since Weber's description does not really fit the music. Ibid., pp. 94–95. The entire text of Weber's *Tonkünstlersleben* is now available in John Warrack, ed., and Martin Cooper, trans., *Carl Maria von Weber: Writings on Music*, (Cambridge, 1981), pp. 312–64.

64. Letter of 21 May 1810, as given in Warrack, *Carl Maria von Weber*, p. 95.

65. Ibid., letter of 1 December 1814, p. 157.

66. Letter of 17 July 1823 to the Dresden court theater director Hans Wilhelm Traugott von Könneritz, Anderson, *The Letters of Beethoven*, 3: 1065.

67. Draft of 28 January 1823, as cited in *Grove's Dictionary of Music and Musicians*, 3rd ed. (New York, 1938), 5: 670.

68. Sonneck, *Beethoven: Impressions by His Contemporaries*, p. 160.

69. As quoted in *Grove's Dictionary of Music and Musicians*, 5: 651.

70. Warrack, *Carl Maria von Weber*, p. 93.

71. Ibid., pp. 93–94, published, Warrack states, by Schindler in the *Blätter für literarische nterhaltung*.

72. "Published by August Hitzschold of Zürich in the 20th issue of the *Niederrheinische Musik Zeitung* [Cologne] for 1853," Schindler crowingly tells us, Schindler, *Beethoven As I Knew Him*, p. 479.

73. Ibid., pp. 482–83.

74. Ibid., p. 482. Anticipating his reviewers' protestations, Schindler the Unshakeable immediately goes on to say, "This evaluation, too, appeared in print, and sooner or later it will turn up as the others have." Ibid. At the time of this writing, 1985, it still has not turned up, despite the thorough searches of Weber experts.

75. See ibid., Appendix B, "Beethoven and His Last Physician, Dr. Wawruth," whose article on Beethoven's final days Schindler characterizes as one "in which our master was made out to be a drunkard," p. 457 (disputed by the modern-day editor of Schindler's book, Donald MacArdle, ibid., p. 355, n. 237). Clumsily compounding matters, Schindler includes a second musician in his next rebuttal: "It was very disconcerting to me to be asked so often in Paris if it was true that Beethoven and Schubert were given to drink and found their inspiration in strong liquors." Ibid., pp. 458–59.

76. Schindler denounced the authenticity of the publication as early as 1835 and was delighted to include in his 1860 edition of the biography (Appendix D, pp. 468–72) every word of a thoroughly convincing and scholarly article refuting the "textbook" (most of which was material taken from the 1797 treatise on rules of composition written by Johann Joseph Fux, *Gradus ad Parnassum*—some rococo examples of which Beethoven had copied down in a notebook still in his possession at the time of his death). The article was by a Cologne musician, Franz Derckum, and originally published in the *Rheinische Mujsik-Zeitung*, 2: 572, of 1852.

77. Schindler, *Beethoven As I Knew Him*, p. 465.

78. The bust portrait—a half profile facing left—is discussed but not reproduced by Frimmel, *Beethoven-Studien I: Beethovens äussere Erscheinung*, p. 140, n. 1. Schindler kept up his indignant sniping at Kriehuber: "In issue No. 2 of the *Allgemeine musikalische Zeitung* [Leipzig] for 1835 there was a flowery advertisement for a lithographed 'head of Beethoven, only one inch high,' made by Kriehuber of Vienna and available at Haslinger's. It was proclaimed the 'best likeness of Beethoven.' This lithographer, who was a clever artist otherwise, had only seen the master in the street, and had not made this drawing until seven years after the composer's death. One may then imagine how accurate the likeness was!" Schindler, *Beethoven As I Knew Him*, p. 466.

79. The entire incident of *Cäcilia's* publication of Beethoven's "joking" biography of the Viennese publisher Tobias Haslinger is given in Thayer-Forbes, *Thayer's Life of Beethoven*, pp. 934–36. It is an ironic twist of fate that Haslinger, who seemed to bear Beethoven no real grudge concerning the matter while the composer was alive, should have been involved in publishing Seyfried's falsification of the so-called *Beethovens Studien*, see text above.

80. I have limited this listing to journals published in England and found previous to the year 1840. But mention should be made that the second great 19-century biographer of Beethoven, Thayer the Harvard graduate, contributed important pieces on the composer, along with lives of his contemporaries, to the Boston periodical *Journal of Music* (1852–81). For the critical reception of Beethoven in America see Ann Chan, "Beethoven in the United States to 1865," unpublished Ph.D. dissertation, University of North Carolina at Chapel Hill, 1976.

81. The full title is *Vertraute Briefe, geschrieben auf einer Reise nach Wien und den österreichischen Staaten zu Ende 1808 und zu Anfang 1809* (Amsterdam, 1809; 1810).

82. Albert Leitzmann, ed., *Ludwig van Beethoven: Berichte der Zeitgenossen, Briefe und persönliche Aufzei-*

chnungen, 2 vols. (Leipzig, 1921), 1: 99–100, letter of 30 November 1808, translation mine.

83. Ibid., letter of 10 December 1808, pp. 102–3, translation mine.

84. Anderson, *The Letters of Beethoven*, 1: 250, letter of December 1809 to Breitkopf and Härtel.

85. Sonneck, *Beethoven: Impressions by His Contemporaries*, pp. 150–51.

86. Ibid., pp. 151–52.

87. Ibid., p. 152.

88. Ibid., p. 114.

89. *Quarterly Musical Magazine and Review*, 7 (1852); 80ff., as given in Arnold and Fortune, *The Beethoven Reader*, pp. 498–99.

90. The conductor Sir George Smart, Beethoven's great promoter in London through his performances of Beethoven symphonies with the Philharmonic Society (he premiered the Ninth on 21 March 1825), visited the composer in 1825 but the diary he kept of this memorable and cordial encounter was not published until the beginning of the twentieth century. H. Bertram Cox and C.L.E. Cox, eds., *Leaves from the Journals of Sir George Smart* (London, 1907). For more on Sir George see chapter 5 of this book.

91. Charles Burney, *General History of Music*, 4 vols. (London, 1776–89). The legal inventory of Beethoven's estate was published in the *Harmonicon* issue of April 1828 and reprinted in Moscheles's 1841 English edition of Schindler's Beethoven biography 2:373–76. This inventory is given in Thayer-Forbes, *Thayer's Life of Beethoven*, Appendix C, pp. 1061–70. See Nettl, *Beethoven Encyclopedia*, p. 186, for a listing of some of the forty-four books left over for the 5 November 1827 auction (including Burney's 4-volume *General History of Music*) after Schindler's plundering (he took Beethoven's Homer and Shakespeare translations, his well-thumbed Latin, French, and Italian dictionaries, and a 6-volume edition of Schiller). See also chapter 1, n. 8, concerning confiscated books in the composer's library.

92. Thayer-Forbes, *Thayer's Life of Beethoven*, pp. 956–57. See also O.E. Albrecht, *A Census of Autograph Music Manuscripts of European Composers in America* (Philadelphia, 1953), p. 30.

93. Sarah Burney Payne's account was republished as Appendix No. VI ("Extract from a letter written by an English lady, dated Vienna, October, 1825") in the English translation of Schindler's life of Beethoven edited by Moscheles (1841). The quotation and summary given above are taken from this source, pp. 295–98. It might be hoped that the great Burney's daughter would not be a target for Schindler's darts, but her very Englishness seems to have incited Schindler's wrath. In her report she observed: "Beethoven speaks good French, at least by comparison with most other Germans" (p. 297) and this was enough to threaten Schindler's chauvinistic credos: "Ein solches Urtheil von einer Britin zu hören klingt doch gar zu possierlich" ("To hear such a judgment from a Briton sounds absolutely too affected") he thundered in the second edition (1845) of his biography (p. 176). Asterisking the "Briton's" emotional phrase "such handfuls of notes," he further fulminated: "What monstrous musical mind speaks from out of the words of the lady!" Finally he relented: "But she means it well" (p. 178; translation mine).

94. Sir George Smart, of whom we shall make a more prolonged acquaintance in chapter 5, had introduced Beethoven's *The Mount of Olives* to England as early as 1814. Over the next few years he led the Philharmonic Society of London in performances of Beethoven's *Eroica* (1820), the Sixth and Seventh symphonies (1821), the Fourth Symphony (1824), and, on 21 March 1825, the first English production of the Ninth Symphony. Not satisfied with his reading of the score, he decided to visit the continent and consult with Beethoven about the tempi in person. Although Sir George kept diaries of his experiences all his life, his memoirs were not published until forty years after his death (*Leaves from the Journals of Sir George Smart* [London, 1907]) and were therefore unavailable to mythographers during Beethoven's lifetime. Sir George's description of his 16 September 1825 visit to Beethoven in Baden, where he noticed the composer's four rooms were furnished "*à la genius*," is given in Sonneck, *Beethoven: Impressions by His Contemporaries*, pp. 192–96; for conversation books entries pertaining to their discussion, see Thayer-Forbes, *Thayer's Life of Beethoven*, pp. 964–65.

95. *Harmonicon*, 7 (February 1829). This self-congratulatory expression of British superiority at having discovered Beethoven earlier than the French was pointed out by Elsie and Denis Arnold, eds., "The View of Posterity: an Anthology," in Arnold and Fortune, *The Beethoven Reader*, p. 494, from where this quotation of the *Harmonicon* is taken.

96. Sonneck, *Beethoven: Impressions by His Contemporaries*, pp. 209–10.

97. Ibid., 211.

98. Ibid., pp. 211-12.

99. This incident, related by Holz to Fanny Linzbauer, was first cited by Ludwig Nohl in his *Beethovens Leben* (3 vols. in 4, 1864; 2nd. ed., 4 vols., Vienna, 1909–13) and is given in most lives of Beethoven since Nohl. The quotations here are taken from Solomon, *Beethoven*, pp. 288–89.

For the complete letter exchange between Beethoven ("since I am also so fortunate to count myself a citizen of Bonn and therefore one of your subjects") and King Friedrich Wilhelm III ("I thank you . . . and hand you the accompanying diamond ring as a token of my sincere appreciation"), see Thayer-Forbes, *Thayer's Life of Beethoven*, p. 1002.

100. The exchange, which included Rochlitz's two separate and reluctant but firm declinations, is given in Schindler, *Beethoven As I Knew Him*, pp. 31–33, and Thayer-Forbes, *Thayer's Life of Beethoven*, pp. 1086–87. We must be wary of this exchange as reported by Schindler, however. Modern Beethoven scholarship of the 1970s has demonstrated that Thayer (who had indeed suspected and even identified some Schindler distortions of facts) was misled by Schindler's account that Beethoven, on his deathbed, had designated Rochlitz as his official biographer. It now seems that Schindler, knowing Rochlitz would be unable to take on the task, was preparing the way for himself to become—by distinguished default—Beethoven's official biographer, see Goldschmidt, *Zu Beethoven: Aufsätze und Annotationen*, pp. 95–101.

101. Johann Aloys Schlosser, *Ludwig van Beethoven: Eine Biographie* (Prague, 1827), p. v; this and the following Schlosser translations in this note are mine. The book had a less formal title on its frontispiece (Fig. 54— *Ludwig van Beethoven's Biographie*—but the full entry on

the title page runs as follows:"Ludwig van Beethoven. Eine Biographie deselben, verbunden mit Urtheilen über seine Werke. Herausgegeben zur Erwirkung eines Monuments für dessen Lehrer, Joseph Haydn, von Joh. Aloys Schlosser, mit einem lithographirten Briefe Beethovens."

Schlosser's foreword concludes with the designation: "Wien, im Junius 1827" ("Vienna, in June of 1827") (p. xiv), confirming the impression that the book was quickly written and the Prague publishing firm seems to have included the author: Stephani und Schlosser. Folded inside the back of the book was a lithographic facsimile, as promised on the title page, of the composer's interjesting letter of 6 February 1826 to his musical priest friend, the Abbot Maximilian Stadler (1748–1833), concerning the latter's just-published monograph (1826) defending the authenticity of Mozart's *Requiem* (see Anderson, *The Letters of Beethoven*, 3: 1275–77 for full citation of the letter and musical examples provided by Beethoven in his approving response). A second embellishment was the inclusion of a Beethoven portrait (see Fig. 24) that, in the author's words, "is the most successful" of all: "it is by Kriehuber's master hand, executed after the most excellent among the two busts which the famous sculptor Anton Dietrich prepared during sittings with Beethoven" (p. xii). Schindler must have sputtered over this praise of Kriehuber, whose "legitimacy" as a portrayer of Beethoven he would soon sarcastically contest, see above, n. 78.

One of the most extraordinary statements in Schlosser's naive but well-intended (for Haydn's sake) life of Beethoven is the following: "When, in Beethoven's biography, not so much of interest is to be found as in Haydn's and Mozart's, that is not my fault but rather it is the result of a life impoverished in contact with other people and in travel. He also ranks behind both in influence, but not in will or in suffering" (pp. xi–xii). The shadowy Schlosser seems at least to have observed Beethoven in person: he describes his eyes as proclaiming "unfathomable depth of feeling" and his "glorious" forehead as "a true seat of majestic creativity" (p. 46).

102. Thayer-Forbes, *Thayer's Life of Beethoven*, pp. 1085, 64. Actually Beethoven himself labored for years under the delusion that he was born in 1772 and not 1770; for psychological implications see Solomon, *Beethoven*, pp. 3–4, 21, 23, 155, 276–77. Beethoven was the second child born to his parents; the first had also been a son and was also named Ludwig. He was born on 12 November 1767 and lived only six days. An interesting parallel to this aspect of Beethoven's early family history can be found in Vincent Van Gogh, who was preceded one year to the day of his birth by a previous Vincent, who was stillborn.

103. As Schindler's 20th-century editor MacArdle notes, the spider story had already appeared in the Leipzig *Allgemeine musikalische Zeitung* in 1880 and Schlosser's service to scholarship was to explain that the story was true but about another musician whose name sounded like Beethoven's, Berthaume; see Schindler, *Beethoven As I Knew Him*, pp. 38–39, and p. 81, n. 12.

104. Sonneck, Beethoven: *Impressions by His Contemporaries*, pp. 124–28.

105. Schindler, *Beethoven As I Knew Him*, p. 243.

106. Ibid., p. 244. Another "foreigner" (meaning a North German unfamiliar with the intricacies of the Austrian political situation) had recently published a

description of Beethoven's unrestrained political monologues, delivered to any and all in public restaurants, in the May 1827 issue of the *Allgemeine musikalische Zeitung*. This was a certain W.C. Müller who met Beethoven briefly in 1820 and who is also scornfully cited by Schindler as an instructive example of the miscomprehension of Beethoven, who "was wise enough to know better than to expose his most secret thoughts before strangers," Schindler, *Beethoven As I Knew Him*, pp. 243, 244. Schindler, incidentally, *was* a subject of the Habsburg Empire—he was born in Moravia (present-day Czechoslovakia) in the little town of Meedl, near Olmütz, and arrived in Vienna in 1813. He did not die under Habsburg rule however: in 1831 he left Vienna to become director of the Münster Musikverein and his later sojourns took him to other German cities (Aachen and Frankfurt am Main) and he died in Bockenheim near Frankfurt.

107. Sometimes such misinterpretations—as in the cases of Wagner and Berlioz—were of a more creative rather than deliberately misrepresentative nature. I have attempted to portray some of the mistaken but stunningly fruitful miscomprehensions of the works of Schopenhauer (who saw in Beethoven's symphonies a *rerum concordia discors*—the discordant concord of things) in an article "In Praise of Creative Misinterpretation, or 'How a Little Bit of Schopenhauer Changed My Life,' " *Arts Magazine* 52, no. 11 (March 1978): 118–23.

108. Sonneck, *Beethoven: Impressions by His Contemporaries*, p. 128. Rochlitz later published his *Allgemeine musikalische Zeitung* letters on Beethoven in the fourth volume of his widely read essays, *Für Freunde der Tonkunst* (Leipzig, 1832). The anecdotes passed on by Rochlitz about Mozart, prefacing the first issue of the *Allgemeine musikalische Zeitung*, were later thoroughly disqualified by Otto Jahn.

109. Sonneck, *Beethoven: Impressions by His Contemporaries*, p. 125.

110. Thayer-Forbes, *Thayer's Life of Beethoven*, p. 370.

111. Ibid., pp. 370–71.

112. The strength of Beethoven's concave lenses is given as -4.O D. in Patrick Trevor-Roper's fascinating book, *The World Through Blunted Sight* (London, 1970), p. 31.

113. Grillparzer reminisced: "I first saw Beethoven in my boyhood years [1804 or 1805]. . . . He wore glasses, which I noticed in particular, because at a later period he ceased to avail himself of this aid to his shortsightedness." Sonneck, *Beethoven: Impressions by His Contemporaries*, p. 154. Frimmel maintains that Beethoven did avail himself of this aid for distance viewing at least part of the time up until the year 1817. *Beethoven-Studien I: Beethovens äussere Erscheinung*, p. 27, n. 3. Frimmel cites another testimonial to Beethoven's use of glasses in 1805 (at the premiere of *Fidelio*). Ibid., p. 35.

114. Sonneck, *Beethoven: Impressions by His Contemporaries*, p. 54.

115. The artist in question was Isidor Neugass, see chapter 2, n. 55.

116. Schindler, *Beethoven As I Knew Him*, p. 270.

117. Sonneck, *Beethoven: Impressions by His Contemporaries*, p. 201.

118. A continuous narrative sketch shows, in three different sequences, the thin, bespectacled figure of Weber conducting at Covent Garden (engraved by F.

Hayter [1826?]); for reproduction see Warrack, *Carl Maria von Weber*, opp. p. 336. A formal oil portrait by John Cawse, painted between 14 March and 5 June 1826, shows the pale-eyed Weber with his glasses on (opposed to Schimon's idealizing portrait of Weber, see Fig. 52); for reproduction see ibid., opp. p. 240. Sir George Smart, in an oil portrait by William Bradley (National Portrait Gallery, London), looks no less smart in his circular glasses. Schubert was shown several times with his glasses on by Moritz von Schwind and by W. A. Rieder and this was an iconographical feature picked up by Klimt in his 1899 fantasy portrait of the composer (for reproduction of the latter see my book, *Gustav Klimt* [New York, 1975], pl. 52). By the time Mahler appeared on the scene, his flashing glasses were an integral part of the mystique captured by caricaturists.

119. A charming image of Beethoven was concocted recently (1982) by the Rowohlt Tauschenbuch Press of Hamburg in regard to a campaign soliciting suggestions for more historical personages to be the subjects of individual "Rororo" monographs. A flyer announcing the event was published showing the Klein bust of Beethoven, a pince-nez in place, peering into the open Rororo monograph on him. Two "real" hands hold the book up to Beethoven's face, and the three-dimensional effect is startling (if misleading, since Beethoven only used his glasses for distance).

120. Sonneck, *Beethoven: Impressions by His Contemporar*, pp. 38, 42–43. Schindler did not object to Seyfried's account of a Beethoven in need of corrective lenses but he did explode in print at Seyfried's folksy claim that the composer visited the market place himself, selecting, bargaining, and paying for his own food. "Oh! Oh! Oh! Herr von Seyfried! Quousque tandem!" exclaims a scandalized, Latin-loving Schindler in the 1845 edition of his Beethoven biography (p. 267). (The full expression is: "Quousque tandem abutere patientia nostra?" ["How long will you abuse our patience?"])

121. Ibid., p. 44. The thematic attraction for the visual arts of an absentminded and obsessive promenade through the city streets was by no means limited to the figure of Beethoven. Mahler's rigid schedule of walking to and from the Vienna Opera House (so punctual to the minute that people claimed they could set their watches by him) became the favorite sport of caricaturists. Brahms, who walked to the same restaurant for the last fourteen years of his life, was also a treat for caricaturists (see my article, "The Visual Brahms: Idols and Images," *Arts Magazine* 54; no. 2 (October 1979): 123–39).

122. Sonneck, *Beethoven: Impressions by His Contemporaries*, pp. 45–46. See Beethoven's two letters of January 1817 with instructions to his publisher Haslinger that the German equivalent (he was not sure what was the correct term) for pianoforte be used on his latest piano sonata: "In regard to the title, a linguist should be consulted as to whether *Hammer* or *Hämmer-Klavier* or, possibly, *Hämmer-flügel* should be inserted," Anderson, *The Letters of Beethoven*, 2:660; and his (incorrect) assertion to Haslinger that the pianoforte—"Hämmer-Klavier"—was a "German invention," ibid., p. 657.

123. Sonneck, *Beethoven: Impressions by His Contemporaries*, p. 36.

124. Schindler triumphantly reprinted the whole of Franz Derckum's 1852 article in the third edition of his

life of Beethoven, see text above and Schindler, *Beethoven As I Knew Him*, pp. 468–72.

125. As quoted in Arnold and Fortune, *The Beethoven Reader*, p. 502.

126. Letter of 5 March 1818 from Beethoven to Ferdinand Ries in London. Anderson, *The Letters of Beethoven*, 2: 759.

127. Sonneck, *Beethoven: Impressions by His Contemporar*, pp. 108–9.

128. Schindler, *Beethoven As I Knew Him*, p. 26. For Schindler's full account of the failed project to write a tripartite Beethoven biography (Wegeler, Ries, Schindler) see ibid., pp. 26–27, 34. For a Schindler hot on the trail of Riesian Wrongs, see ibid., pp. 120–21, 427–31. For Riesian Rights see Alan Tyson, "Ferdinand Ries (1784–1838): The History of His Contribution to Beethoven Biography," *19th Century Music* 7 (1984): 211–12.

129. Sonneck, Beethoven: *Impressions by His Contemporaries*, pp. 18–19.

130. One of the strangest moments in Hollywood's contribution to Beethoven iconography occurs in Rupert Julian's silent screen classic *The Phantom of the Opera* (1925) when Lon Chaney, his face grotesquely made up to look like a living skull, pauses and poses with defiantly folded arms next to a large bronzed plaster statue of Beethoven standing with crossed arms and wrapped in a heroic mantle, his "handsome" (by contrast!) face looking down sadly on his demented modern-day brother composer. A still from this good-versus-evil-genius juxtaposition is reproduced in S.S. Prawer, *Caligari's Children: The Film as Tale of Terror* (Oxford, 1908), plate insert between pp. 86 and 87.

131. Schindler, *Beethoven As I Knew Him*, p. 56.

132. For more Ries information on Beethoven and the casual women in his life, see his account of breaking in on the composer in his Baden retreat and finding him with an attractive woman whose identity he afterwards claimed not to know (she was the "mistress of a foreign prince" Ries later determined). Sonneck, *Beethoven: Impressions by His Contemporaries*, p. 55.

133. The account of how Beethoven cruelly punished Ries by refusing to let him stay in the presence of Prince Lichnowsky and a number of other people who had come to his house to hear his *Fidelio* music played through on the piano is given in Thayer-Forbes, *Thayer's Life of Beethoven*, p. 382.

134. Sonneck, *Beethoven: Impressions by His Contemporar*, pp. 56–57.

135. Ibid., p. 58.

136. Ibid., p. 57.

137. Pleasants, *The Musical Journeys of Louis Spohr* pp. 213–15.

138. Sonneck, *Beethoven: Impressions by His Contemporar*, p. 59. This gallant conclusion of Ries's attempt to present a fair but frank picture of the Beethoven he had known did not lenify Schindler's sense of outrage. Not even Ries's death in 1838 softened Schindler's heart for, just after sending his manuscript on the composer's life to the printer's, he learned that Beethoven's Paris publisher, Moritz Schlesinger, had brought out a French translation (1840) of the Wegeler-Ries book. Schindler's dismay knew no bounds. It was too late to comment fully on the travesty, but a footnote could be and was added to the final page of the first edition of Schindler's life of Beethoven (1840). Although his *terribilità* had to be confined to a few sentences, he managed to suggest

just what he thought of the Ries memoir: "It is the most criminally botched piece of work that has perhaps ever been sent out into the world about so great a man. Is it possible to win sympathy for Beethoven if one takes for truth what Herr Ries published about him? The reader must first comprehend what a grotesque view of character, way of conducting business affairs, and manner of life [is presented] when encountering that wild, hairy, forest man . . ." (p. 296, translation mine).

Schindler's diatribe concludes by lamenting the fact that whole pages of arbitrary postscripts containing utterances, anecdotes, and data are now included in the French version of the Wegeler-Ries book and will now also pass, via their authority as "genuine sources," into the characterization of Beethoven. The mythmaker's territorial claim is at stake!

139. See chapter 1 and ns. 5 and 9. Bettina Brentano von Arnim published the "three" Beethoven letters again in her book *Ilius Pamphilius und die Ambrosia* (Berlin, 1857), vol. 2.

140. Anderson, *The Letters of Beethoven*, 1:312–13. It is unfortunate that Anderson, usually such a sensitive translator and so alert to linguistic nuances, does not give her English-language readers any indication that Beethoven, in this one authentic letter to Bettina, changes his form of address from the formal *Sie* to the intimate *Du* and back again to *Sie* at the end of his letter, see discussion in text.

141. All three "Beethoven" letters to Bettina are given in A.C. Kalischer and Theodor Frimmel, eds., *Beethoven sämtliche Briefe*, 5 vols. (2nd. ed., Berlin, 1908–11); for the unauthenticated letter of 11 August 1810 (in which only the formal form of address is used), see ibid, 1:321–23, no. 220; for the authenticated letter of 10 February 1811 (employing both formal and intimate forms of address), see ibid, 2:1–2, no. 228; and for the unauthenticated and final letter from Teplitz of August 1812 (in which both forms of address are used; see below, n. 144), see ibid., 2:94–95, no. 309. The German quoted in the text above is as given in Karl Kobald, *Beethoven: Seine Beziehungen zu Wiens Kunst und Kultur, Gesellschaft und Landschaft* (Vienna, 1946), pp. 214–15. Slight variations from the Kalischer-Frimmel decoding of Beethoven's handwriting exist in the Kobald citation: "lebe wohl" (instead of "leb wohl" in Kalischer-Frimmel) and "Freundin" (instead of "B." ["Bettine"] in Kalischer-Frimmel). The later German version (Kobald) reads more smoothly, but it will probably never be possible definitively to determine whether Beethoven's abbreviation is an "F." (Freundin) or a "B." (Bettine). Adding to these problems is Schindler's second edition of his Beethoven biography (1845) in which the three "Beethoven" letters to Bettina are quoted in full (pp. 157–63) but with their source punctiliously designated as "Aus dem Supplement der englischen Uebersetzung von Beethoven's [sic] Biographie" (p. 157), thus implying a reverse translation from English to German!

142. This crucial information—not mentioned by Anderson—is given in another English translation of the letter, see A.C. Kalischer, ed., and J.S. Shedlock, trans., *The Letters of Ludwig van Beethoven*, 2 vols. (London, 1909), 1:209. See also Schindler, *Beethoven As I Knew Him*, supplement 1, p. 492, "illegible word." Dana Steichen, whose whole book is devoted to solving the riddle of the identity of Beethoven's Immortal Beloved (see chapter 1, n. 22), is the only English-lan-

guage author I have found who goes to the pains of pointing out Beethoven's deletion of the original words after "I kiss you"; see Steichen, *Beethoven's Beloved*, p. 196. The latest identifier of the Immortal Beloved, Maynard Solomon, while not deigning to mention Steichen's book in his bibliography, does not—in spite of his acute attention to all facts pertaining to the Brentano family (since his choice for the Immortal Beloved is Bettina's Viennese sister-in-law, Antonie Brentano)—make note of the vigorous scratching out in this single authentic letter of Beethoven's to Bettina, whom he dismisses as a flirt (which she was, but also an original blithe spirit who managed, temporarily, to turn even the head of Goethe). A thorough study of Bettina Brentano von Arnim's "three" Beethoven letters appeared in the *Zeitschrift für Musik* for 1927, 943:154–59, written by R. Gottschalk and entitled "Die drei Beethovenbriefe Bettinas." For Romain Rolland's treatment of the letters, covered in his book *Goethe and Beethoven* (translated into German in 1928 and into English in 1931) see chapter 1, n. 5. The myth of Bettina's "close" friendship with Beethoven is repeated in *The New Grove Dictionary of Music and Musicians*, 3:259.

143. Anderson, *The Letters of Beethoven*, 3:1355–56.

144. Ibid., 3: 1357–59. The specific passages in German involving change of address from the formal to the intimate, then back to the formal in closing are: " . . . wir hatten gerade von Ihnen gesprochen Gott! hätte ich solche Zeit mit Ihnen. . . . Was kam mir nicht alles in den Sinn, wie ich dich kennen lernte . . . muss ich Dich wiejdersehen. . . . In Wien hoffe ich einen Brief von Ihnen, schreiben Sie bald—Adieu, Adieu Beste, dein letzten Brief. . . . Musikanten erlauben sich alles. Gott wie liebe ich Sie! Dein treuster Freund und tauber Bruder   Beethoven" (As given in Kalischer and Frimmel, *Beethovens sämtliche Briefe*, 2:95–96.)

145. During her long life (1785–1859) Bettina Brentano von Arnim also produced one literary monument to a woman: her 1840 *Die Günderode* is a life of the poet Karoline von Günderode, who committed suicide in 1806. In 1849 Frau von Arnim took up her pen in the cause of social reform, writing about the oppresive conditions of the Silesian weavers (a topic that later caught the attention of Gerhart Hauptmann and Käthe Kollwitz) in a book laying the problem—and its solution—before the king, *Dies Buch gehört dem König*.

146. Anderson, *The Letters of Beethoven*, 3:1357. It is really a wonder that a carefully forged "autograph" of this third "Beethoven" letter to Bettina has not yet appeared on the world market. So many facsimile reproductions of Beethoven letters are available, beginning with early 19th-century examples in obscure publications, that counterfeits have become a major problem for Beethoven scholars. Anderson, commenting on the phenomenon, reports the startling case in which the great Swiss collector of Beethoveniana, H.C. Bodmer (whose holdings are now at the Beethovenhaus, Bonn), was offered a "Beethoven" autograph that faithfully reproduced a (geniune) Beethoven letter he already owned! Ibid., 1: xvii.

147. Nettl, *Beethoven Encyclopedia*, p. 19. Recounted in almost all biographies of Beethoven.

148. Schindler, *Beethoven As I Knew Him*, p. 158. The Teplitz comment and other criticisms were added by Schindler to his 1860 edition of the *Biographie*, and his vigorous attack on Bettina's "first" Beethoven letter

printed in his 1840 edition was deliciously resavored by him when he repeated the entire text of this earlier diatribe in his third edition.

149. Ibid., p. 158.

150. Bell Gale Chevigny, *The Woman and the Myth: Margaret Fuller's Life and Writings* (Old Westbury [N.Y.], 1976), p. 60.

151. Ibid., pp. 61–62. Later, during the "Roman years" of Margaret Fuller, the still-living Italian hero Giuseppe Mazzini (1805–1872) would replace Beethoven in her heart and galvanize her into a woman of action on behalf of his efforts to create a united Italy. She, her Italian husband, and their new-born child were all lost at sea, within sight of land, in a shipwreck off Long Island on their way home to America in 1850.

152. It will be recalled that Moscheles neglected to place Schindler's name on the title page, see chapter 2, n. 7. Three decades and one year later, Moscheles's diary references to Beethoven were made public in the posthumously published *Aus Ignaz Moscheles Leben*, edited by his wife, Leipzig 1872.

153. See chapter 2, n. 27 for the story of Moscheles's successful attempt to slip his brother inside the Beethoven fortress.

154. Reported by Ries (1838) as follows: "It was Haydn's wish that Beethoven place on his earliest works: 'Pupil of Haydn.' This Beethoven refused to do because, as he said, though he had taken a few lessons from Haydn, he never had learned anything from him," as given in Sonneck, *Beethoven: Impressions by His Contemporaries*, p. 49.

155. Ibid., p. 93.

156. Ibid. Moscheles, who was fourteen at the time, did in fact become Salieri's pupil and according to his own account was his assistant for three years.

157. This incident was reported to Thayer, whose thoroughness took him to Beethoven's "Land-Owner" brother's godforsaken estate at Gneixendorf, where Beethoven visited with Karl after Karl's suicide attempt, and the story was published in the *Deutsche Musikzeitung* in 1862. See Thayer-Forbes, *Thayer's Life of Beethoven*, p. 1007 and n. 42.

158. Schindler, *Beethoven As I Knew Him*, Appendix N, p. 503.

159. As early as 1806 this division between the beautiful and the sublime had been brought up in regard to Beethoven's music. The Viennese correspondent for *Der Freimüthige* ("The Candid," edited by playwright August Friedrich Ferdinand von Kotzebue in Berlin) wrote ironically in the issue of 11 September 1806: "[Beethoven's friends] want to build an altar to Beethoven on the ruins of other composers. They want to include all that most definitely cannot be called beautiful in Beethoven's work under the wider sphere of the great and the sublime, as if real greatness and sublimity were not simple and unpretentious." As quoted in Graf, *Composer and Critic*, p. 155.

160. As translated in Thayer-Forbes, *Thayer's Life of Beethoven*, p. 494.

161. Ibid.

162. Ibid.

163. Ibid., pp. 495–96.

164. Schindler, *Beethoven As I Knew Him*, p. 158.

165. As translated in Thayer-Forbes, *Thayer's Life of Beethoven*, pp. 496–97. For a compelling analysis of the personalities of Goethe, Bettina Brentano, and Bee-

thoven and their complicated responses to one another, see Rolland's 254-page study, *Goethe and Beethoven*.

166. In this third and final edition of his life of Beethoven, Schindler was able to respond to some but not all the publications on Beethoven that had appeared since his 1840 edition and which had been authored by persons acquainted with the composer. Some of the eyewitness items added a few more Beethoven features to the century's posthumous portrait. The main contributors were, chronologically:

1. Johann Wenzel Tomaschek (1774–1850), composer, organist, and teacher from Bohemia who heard Beethoven play three times in Prague in 1798 and visited him in Vienna on 10 October and 24 November 1814. His autobiography, published in 1845 in a periodical called *Libussa*, contained a description of Beethoven's piano playing and manner of improvising, and reported Beethoven's (and Tomaschek's) opinion of Meyerbeer (agile but superficial). Tomaschek found Beethoven's reception room "as disordered as was his hair," Sonneck, *Beethoven: Impressions by His Contemporaries*, p. 100.

2. Karl von Bursy (1791–1850), a physician who visited the composer on 1 June and 27 July 1816 and published his diary entries from that time in 1854 in the Saint Petersburg *Zeitung*. His description of Beethoven confirms all previous reports: "Short, somewhat stout, his hair swept back, much of it already grey, a rather ruddy complexion, fiery eyes, which, though small, are deep set and full of extraordinary energy." About his personality and tendency towards violence: "Gall and venom rage in him. He scorns everyone, is dissatisfied with everyone and everything, and curses a great deal, especially about Austria and more especially about Vienna. He speaks quickly and with the greatest vivacity. Often he struck the piano so violently with his fist that the whole room resounded with the blow. . . . 'Only the artist and the independent scholar carry their happiness within them.' . . . As soon as he was quiet, he wrinkled his brow and took on a sinister appearance, so that one could easily become afraid of him if one did not know that such an exalted artist's soul must be fundamentally good." As translated by Michael Hamburger, *Beethoven: Letters, Journals and Conversations* (New York, 1960), pp. 141–43.

3. Fanny Giannatasio del Rio (1790–1868), twenty-sixyear-old daughter of the owner of the boarding school where Beethoven put his nephew, Karl, in 1816: she saw a great deal of the composer during 1816–18 and confided her growing secret, but hopeless, love for him to her diary (a complete transcript of which was found among the confidence-inspiring Thayer's papers after his death). Her memoirs with recollections of Beethoven were published on 3 April 1857 in *Grenzboten*, Leipzig. One remark she quotes Beethoven making fixes the date of his serious childhood illness: "It's a bad man who doesn't know how to die! Ever since I was a boy of fifteen I have known how to die." As given in Hamburger, *Beethoven: Letters, Journals and Conversations*, p. 146. All his life Beethoven stubbornly held on to the idea that he had been born in December 1772, and that it was his older brother Ludwig Maria—who lived only six days—who had been born in December 1770 (despite the fact that at his repeated requests over the years his Bonn friends sent him copies of his baptismal certificate showing the date 17 December 1770). Thus

when Beethoven said he had known how to die ever since he was a boy of fifteen, he did not realize—or would not accept—that he was actually seventeen years old at the time of his early illness. For more on this, but from a Freudian point of view, see Solomon, *Beethoven*, pp. 3–4, 21, 23, 155, 276–77.

CHAPTER FOUR:
BEETHOVEN INTERPRETED

1. Sonneck, *Beethoven: Impressions by His Contemporaries*, p. 49. For early discussions of the teaching role played by Haydn and the "secret" instruction provided by the helpful Johann Schenk (who caught the blatant mistakes in Beethoven's counterpoint exercises that were overlooked by the preoccupied Haydn), see Schindler, *Beethoven As I Knew Him*, pp. 52–55 and Thayer-Forbes, *Thayer's Life of Beethoven*, pp. 138–46.

2. For a charming description of this important event (during which the seventy-five-year-old Haydn "thought he felt a little draft," causing the women present to smother him in shawls), see the account given by the landscape painter Albert Christoph Dies (1755–1822), published in 1810, as translated and reproduced by Vernon Gotwals, ed., in *Joseph Haydn: Eighteenth-Century Gentleman of Genius* (Madison [Wis.], 1963), pp. 177–78. A color reproduction of Wigand's box-cover scene of the homage to Haydn is in H. C. Robbins Landon, *Haydn: A Documentary Study* (New York, 1981), p. 168.

3. This incident was written about by Seyfried and also reported by the early Mozart biographer Otto Jahn (see chapter 3, n. 108). Jahn's account of the 1850s was quoted by Thayer, from which the text citation here is taken, with the comment: "The oft-repeated anecdote of Beethoven's introduction to Mozart is stripped by Professor Jahn of Seyfried's superlatives," Thayer-Forbes, *Thayer's Life of Beethoven*, p. 87. Ries did not mention this incident but did make the following brief allusion to the principals of our print (Fig. 56): "During his first stay in Vienna Beethoven took some lessons from Mozart, but complained that Mozart never played for him." Sonneck, *Beethoven: Impressions by His Contemporaries*, p. 49. Schindler also makes guarded reference to the story, admitting that the exact occasion and time of Mozart's prophetic remark were not certain. Schindler, *Beethoven As I Knew Him*, p. 46.

4. A reproduction of this print is in the collection of the Library and Museum of the Performing Arts at Lincoln Center, New York.

5. Wilhelm Dilthey, *Gesammelte Schriften*, 4 vols. (Leipzig, 1925), 4: 528–54. For Dilthey Beethoven's symphonies were the highest possible musical accomplishment.

6. Herman Nohl, *Die Weltanschauungen der Malerei* (Jena, 1908). Some of Nohl's and Dilthey's candidates for the three types of *Weltanschauung* discussed above are given in René Wellek and Austin Warren, *Theory of Literature* (1949; 3rd ed., New York, 1962–63), p. 117.

7. Schindler, *Beethoven As I Knew Him*, "Musical Section," especially p. 397, 405–26.

8. Ibid., pp. 426–27.

9. Ibid., p. 427.

10. Ibid.

11. Ibid., p. 415. Having just reluctantly lauded Czerny, Schindler swiftly rights the balance by observing: "He deserves our praise up to the point where he began his attempts to impose upon Beethoven's music with the elaborations of the modern virtuosi; from that point on he deserves nothing but censure." Ibid. But we needn't take Schindler's words for this: the constant biographer has an ace in his deck and chooses this moment (1860) to flash it: "A letter from Beethoven to Czerny written in 1812 and published in 1857, after Czerny's death, speaks of the latter's aspirations towards virtuosity even then. The letter reads: 'Dear Czerny: I cannot see you today, but tomorrow I shall come to you myself to have a talk with you. I burst out yesterday with that remark, but afterwards I was very sorry to have done so. But you must forgive a composer who would rather hear his work just as he had written it, however beautifully you played it otherwise. . . . ' " Ibid.

The Argus-eyed Schindler sleepily attests not to have noticed that Czerny had himself published this reprimand by Beethoven, quoting the letter in full, in the *Allgemeine Wiener Musik-Zeitung* for 20 September 1845 (see Thayer-Forbes, *Thayer's Life of Beethoven*, pp. 641–42 and n. 13). Czerny reproduced Beethoven's letter in full and then commented stalwartly: "This letter did more than anything else to cure me of the desire to make changes in the performance of his works, and I wish that it might have the same influence on all pianists." Ibid., p. 641. See further, MacArdle's objective comments on Czerny's interpretation of Beethoven. Schindler, *Beethoven As I Knew Him*, p. 447, n. 328.

12. Ibid., p. 416.

13. See chapter 3, n. 54.

14. Even Schindler, usually so jealous of anyone else's possible intimacy with *his* master, was moved by the sight of the reconciliation between Beethoven and Hummel. On 14 March 1827 he wrote Moscheles in London: "Hummel and his wife are here; he came in haste to see Beethoven once again alive, for it is generally reported in Germany that he is on his deathbed. It was a most touching sight last Thursday to see these two friends meet again," Thayer-Forbes, *Thayer's Life of Beethoven*, p. 1044.

15. Ibid., pp. 1045–47.

16. A short essay with just this title, dealing with conscious or possibly unconscious quotations from Beethoven in Schubert's music, written by Edward T. Cone, is included in Lang, ed., *The Creative World of Beethoven*, pp. 277–91. For some Beethoven connections in Schubert's songs, see Dietrich Fischer-Dieskau, *Schubert's Songs: A Biographical Study* (New York, 1977).

17. Otto Erich Deutsch, *The Schubert Reader*, trans. Eric Blom (New York, 1947). p. 64. I have quoted the first sentence from Schubert's diary entry out of sequence (it begins the second paragraph of that date's entry) in order to give the setting—Salieri's jubilee—that occasioned this anti-Beethoven outburst. Deutsch affirms that Schubert's reference to "one of our greatest German artists" is clearly to Beethoven and points out that the word "eccentric" ("*bizarr*") was the label used by Amadäus Wendt for the "Beethoven manner" in an 1815 issue of the Leipzig *Allgemeine musikalische Zeitung*. Ibid.

18. A facsimile of the title page of the first edition of Schubert's op. 10 is given by Deutsch in ibid., p. 255; see also the announcement of publication and its dedica-

tion to Beethoven as printed in the *Wiener Zeitung* of 19 April 1822, ibid., p. 221.

19. Schindler, *Beethoven As I Knew Him*, p. 375.

20. Josef Hüttenbrenner's account (written in May 1861) was cited by Schubert's early biographer Heinrich Kreissle von Hellborn (*Franz Schubert* [Vienna, 1865]) and repeated by Thayer in an attempt to clarify "Schindler's improbable story," Thayer-Forbes, *Thayer's Life of Beethoven*, p. 806 and n. 41. See also Deutsch, *The Schubert Reader*, p. 222. For further speculation concerning the reliability of the Schindler account and whether Schubert might not have omitted recounting such a humiliating incident to Hüttenbrenner, see Arthur Hutchings, *Schubert* (rev. ed., London, 1973), pp. 47–48.

21. For doubts strongly expressed, see Deutsch, *The Schubert Reader*, p. 229.

22. As given in Thayer-Forbes, *Thayer's Life of Beethoven*, p. 800. Rochlitz's letter, first printed in the Leipzig *Allgemeine musikalische Zeitung* in September 1828, was reprinted in his book *Für Freunde der Tonkunst* (Leipzig, 1832), 4:352, (see also p. 350).

23. Deutsch, *The Schubert Reader*, p. 288.

24. The Teltscher portrait of "Schubert lithographed" is mentioned twice in the diary of the popular young Burgtheater actress Sophie Müller (1803–1830), at whose home Schubert was a frequent visitor. See entries for 11 and 24 January 1826, as given in Deutsch, *The Schubert Reader*, pp. 503, 505. The Schubert iconography also boasts a sculptor in common with Beethoven: both composers were the subjects of portrait busts by Anton Dietrich (see chapter 2 and Figs. 18–25 for Dietrich's Beethoven, and Badura-Skoda, "Der Bildhauer Anton Dietrich. Ein Beitrag zur Ikonographie Beethovens und Schuberts," pp. 42–52 for Dietrich's—probably posthumous—Schubert). Until recently it was also thought that Willibrord Joseph Mähler, whose 1804 and 1815 portraits of Beethoven we have examined (see Color pl. 1 and Fig. 10), was the painter of a bust-length oil portrait showing Schubert without glasses commissioned by Josef Sonnleithner around 1827 for his collection of musicians' portraits. The picture is reproduced and attributed to Mähler by Deutsch, *The Schubert Reader*, p. 800, but recent (1981) scholarship no longer accepts the work as by Mähler (see Badura-Skoda, "Der Bildhauer Anton Dietrich. Ein Beitrag zur Ikonographie Beethovens und Schuberts," p. 49).

25. This statement is cited frequently by Schubert biographers; for one of the latest see Fischer-Dieskau, *Schubert's Songs: A Biographical Study*, p. 242.

26. This remark was circulated by Vogl's widow, Kunigunde; as quoted in Joseph Wechsberg, *Schubert: His Life, His Work, His Time* (New York, 1977), p. 80.

27. Entry in Vogl's diary, as given in *Grove's Dictionary of Music and Musicians*, 3rd ed. (London, 1927), 5:559. Vogl's diary is lost, but was quoted by Schubert's friend Eduard von Bauernfeld (1802–1890) in his obituary on Vogl of 1841. Vogl died 19 November 1840, the same day his friend Schubert had died twelve years before.

28. John Reed, *Schubert: The Final Years* (New York, 1972), p. 113.

29. As given in Thayer-Forbes, *Thayer's Life of Beethoven*, p. 1043, and cited from an amplified account of the event by Schindler in an article published in the 3 May 1831 issue of the Vienna *Theaterzeitung*. Schindler also referred to his having laid Schubert's songs before the dying composer in all three editions of his Beethoven biography; for the 1860 version, see Schindler, *Beethoven As I Knew Him*, p. 321.

30. Related in a letter of 21 February 1858, as cited in Thayer-Forbes, *Thayer's Life of Beethoven*, p. 1044.

31. Ibid. Schindler—unaccountably—makes absolutely no reference to this incident. Seekers after the facts (if there are facts) in the personal encounter(s?) between Beethoven and Schubert must conclude, as one great Schubert interpreter recently did, that "the relations between the men . . . are as obscure and unexplained as they were shortly after their deaths." Fischer-Dieskau, *Schubert's Songs: A Biographical Study*, p. 243.

32. As (cautiously) recounted in *Grove's Dictionary of Music and Musicians*, 3rd ed., 4: 611. A single visit is cited by Deutsch, who speculates that both Hüttenbrenner brothers were present and that the date was around 19 March. See Deutsch, *The Schubert Reader*, p. 618. On the day that Danhauser arrived at the Schwarzspanierhaus to take Beethoven's death mask, one of Schubert's young friends Franz von Hartmann (1808–1875) recorded in his diary that he had visited and viewed "the body of the divine Beethoven." Like Hüttenbrenner and Danhauser before him, he could not resist appropriating a lock of the dead man's hair! See Deutsch, *The Schubert Reader*, p. 621. In the same diary entry for 28 March, Hartmann comments: "In the Kohlmarkt we looked at the latest portrait that has appeared of him and found that his corpse still resembled it very much." Ibid. Deutsch, in his annotation, theorizes: "The portrait, evidently in the shop of Artaria & Co., was probably Danhauser's drawing of the dead man's head, made on 28th March." Ibid., p. 622. I doubt that Danhauser would have let the precious original drawing out of his hands before it was lithographed for distribution or that he would have had time to take it by Artaria's on the very day he drew it, considering that his main preoccupation that day was the safe transport home of the death mask he had just taken. It seems much more probable that the portrait young Hartmann saw on the Kohlmarkt was a lithographed copy of the Decker grayhaired "titan" portrait (see Fig. 33), which Beethoven's corpse did indeed still resemble. Two separate visits to Beethoven by Schubert are accepted by Hutchings, *Schubert*, p. 75.

33. Diary entry for 29 March 1827 by Fritz von Hartmann (1805–1850; Franz's older brother, see above, n. 32), as cited in Deutsch, *The Schubert Reader*, p. 623.

34. Ibid. Deutsch points out the disparity between these two accounts.

35. Ibid., p. 825.

36. Ibid., p. 831, No. IX. Schubert's Beethoven was given a posthumous boost by the French press at this time when the Paris *La Revue musicale* of January 1829 published the news of his death and announced "A subscription was opened to erect a monument to him next to Beethoven, whose friend he was." Ibid, p. 850, No. XXIV.

37. In Schwind's handwriting on the *Figaro* sketch book is the comment: "This book was kept by Beethoven during his last days, and returned to me after his death." Nettl, *Beethoven Encyclopedia*, p. 228, and Deutsch, *The Schubert Reader*, p. 618.

38. Schwind's famous and much-beloved sepia drawing, *A Schubert Evening at Josef von Spaun's* (Schu-

bert Museum of the City of Vienna), was not done until 1868; the only contemporaneous drawing he made of Schubert that has been preserved is the small staffage figure of Schubert sitting on the ground in his shirt sleeves with his long pipe—an image drawn into the foreground of Franz von Schober's amateur scene, *Game of Ball at Atzenbrugg,* c. 1820 (reproduced in Deutsch, *The Schubert Reader,* p. 448). As for Beethoven, whom Schwind certainly had had occasion to observe, only a few posthumous sketches (exaggerating, as in the *Lachner Roll,* his leonine hair and flat nose) are known. See Frimmel, *Beethoven-Studien: Beethovens äussere Erscheinung,* pp. 142–43.

39. Spohr discusses his interest in art and refers specifically to the self-portrait reproduced here in his autobiography: ''The periods between practicing I spent in painting. From my earliest childhood, I had drawn and worked with watercolors and, with no instruction to speak of, had become quite good at it. Indeed, there was a time when I was undecided about which of the two arts to adopt as a profession. I now [1802] made my first attempt at portraiture. According to the diary, under the date of May 12: 'Sunday I began a miniature portrait, and finished it this morning. It is a self-portrait, and I am quite pleased with it.' '' Pleasants, *The Musical Journeys of Louis Spohr,* p. 11.

40. See Schindler's praise of the *Missa Solemnis* performance in particular—''perfect in every respect''—in Schindler, *Beethoven As I Knew Him,* p. 289.

41. Pleasants, *The Musical Journeys of Louis Spohr,* pp. 105–6. Early in his autobiography, while discussing the impact of having heard a Mozart opera for the first time at the age of fifteen, Spohr confessed: ''From that time onward and for the rest of my life, Mozart was my idol and my ideal.'' Ibid., p. 6.

42. Opinion expressed by Beethoven in July 1825 to the young organist Karl Gottfried Freudenberg. See ThayerForbes, *Thayer's Life of Beethoven,* pp. 955–56.

43. Franz Grillparzer, *Gesammelte Werke,* 20 vols. (Vienna, 1923), 2:46, translation mine.

44. This judgment with Wagner's music, as with those concerning Beethoven, was apparently kept within the confines of Spohr's autobiographical writings. See *Grove's Dictionary of Music and Musicians,* 3rd ed., 5:100.

45. Proudly quoted by Spohr as the album's ''most treasured'' entry, along with the short three-voiced canon to words by Schiller which Beethoven neatly wrote out for him. Pleasants, *The Musical Journeys of Louis Spohr,* pp. 115–16. Beethoven's entry is dated Vienna, 3 March 1815.

46. As reported by an eyewitness and published in the *Wiener Theaterzeitung* on 20 May 1828. See de Courcy, *Paganini the Genoese,* 1:273. While Paganini was in Vienna the portrait lithographer Josef Kriehuber (of Schindler scorn) drew his portrait (reproduced in ibid., illus. 1, opposite p. 80); this was reproduced and widely distributed as a lithograph, see Fig. 75 in this book.

47. The friend who requested Paganini's autobiographical sketch was Peter Lichtenthal (1780–1853), a Hungarian musician who had been living in Milan since 1810. Lichtenthal sent a copy of this 1828 essay to the Leipzig *Allgemeine musikalische Zeitung,* which published it in the original Italian in April 1830. English translation in de Courcy, *Paganini the Genoese,* vol. 2, appendix 2, pp. 366–68.

48. Schottky's 1830 ''mosaic'' life of Paganini was published in Prague under the title *Paganinis Leben und Treiben als Künstler und als Mensch;* English translation of Paganini's autobiographical contribution in de Courcy, *Paganini the Genoese,* vol. 2, appendix 3, pp. 368–73. Paganini's disclosure of his father's despotic conduct goes so far as to report his threat to kill his son if he did not hand over to him the entire sum of his savings. Ibid., p. 373. The Italian prodigy thus outstrips the German one as far as harsh fathers are concerned. De Courcy points out the impact that familiarity with Beethoven's life story had upon Paganini and his sudden willingness to reveal his joyless childhood. Ibid., 1:13–14.

49. As cited in ibid., 1:263. Paganini continued the practice of framing his music with Beethoven's in several other Vienna performances: the concert of 16 May opened and closed with Beethoven, beginning with the first movement of the Seventh Symphony (which Paganini heard for the first time at the 1 May Augarten performance that had reduced him to tears) and ending with the second movement of the Seventh. The concert of 22 May included two movements from Beethoven's Second Symphony. Ibid., 1:277.

50. The phrase used by Schubert's friend Eduard von Bauernfeld in his diary notation on hearing Paganini play. Ibid., 1:266.

51. As cited in Wilfrid Blunt, *On Wings of Song: A Biography of Felix Mendelssohn* (New York, 1974), p. 34.

52. From the 1866 reminiscence of the Weimar court musician Johann Christian Lobe (1797–1881), who had tried without success to demonstrate to Goethe how antiquated Zelter's compositions were in comparison with Beethoven's, and who was one of the players present at this extraordinary scene; as cited in Heinrich Eduard Jacob, *Felix Mendelssohn and His Times* (Englewood Cliffs [New Jersey], 1963), p. 33, see also ibid., p. 34.

53. Account given by Ludwig Rellstab in *Aus meinem Leben* (Berlin, 1862) as cited in W. A. Lampadius, *The Life of Felix Mendelssohn-Bartholdy,* trans. W. L. Gage (Boston, 1887), p. 21.

54. Rellstab, as cited in ibid, pp. 21–22. The song may have been the manuscript of *Wonne der Wehmut.* See Rolland, *Goethe and Beethoven,* p. 224, n. 92.

55. Exactly how news of the ''twelve''-year-old Mendelssohn reached Beethoven is still to be determined; Rellstab could not have told Beethoven about the Weimar events in person until his visit to Vienna to meet the composer in 1825. For the conversation-book entry concerning Mendelssohn, see Köhler and Herre (with, in this volume, Günter Brosche), *Ludwig von Beethovens Konversationshefte,* 3 (Notebook 35, 29 June–mid-July 1823), p. 377. Mendelssohn was actually fourteen years old in July 1823.

56. Eric Werner, *Mendelssohn: A New Image of the Composer and His Age* (New York, 1963), p. 25.

57. Letter from Rome of 22 November 1830, as quoted in George R. Marek, *Gentle Genius: The Story of Felix Mendelssohn* (New York, 1972), p. 81.

58. ''For him [Felix] music may become a profession. For you it has to remain a decoration. It can and should never be the be-all and end-all of your life.'' Ibid, p. 83. Fanny was ever the obedient daughter: in 1829 she married her long-time courter, the unassuming but attractive painter Wilhelm Hensel (1794–1861) to whom we are indebted for so many portrait sketches of the Mendelssohn family, and by whom she had one

child, Sebastian, before her untimely death—six months before that of Felix—from the Mendelssohn family curse, apoplexy.

59. This previously unpublished letter by the sixteenyear-old Mendelssohn, posing as Beethoven, was made available to Eric Werner, who published portions of it with perceptive commentary in his *Mendelssohn: A New Image of the Composer and His Age*, pp. 108–9.

60. Letter to Karl Klingemann dated Berlin, 4 July 1832; in G. Selden-Goth, ed., *Felix Mendelssohn: Letters* (New York, 1973), pp. 201–2.

61. Jacob, *Felix Mendelssohn and His Times*, p. 47. As a very real token of his affection, Goethe also presented Mendelssohn with a copy of Stieler's portrait of himself.

62. Selden-Goth, *Felix Mendelssohn: Letters*, p. 72, letter of 25 May 1830.

63. Robson-Scott, *The Literary Background of the Gothic Revival in Germany*, pp. 178–79.

64. My interpretation follows Rolland's learned and loving presentation and reassessment of the facts and psychological factors surrounding the two principals in *Goethe and Beethoven*, see chapter 1, n. 5.

65. Ibid., especially pp. 75–93 concerning the frequency of performance of Beethoven's music in Weimar, either at concerts or at the theater, and even at Goethe's own house.

66. Letter dated 22 October 1826, formerly in the possession of Romain Rolland, ibid., p. 68, and cited by Rolland to illustrate this self-protective aspect of Goethe's character.

67. Selden-Goth, *Felix Mendelssohn: Letters*, p. 81, letter dated Munich, 22 June 1830. As for Beethoven's image in the Bavarian capital, Mendelssohn reported further to Zelter: "Here in Munich . . . even the best pianists . . . had just the faintest notion of Beethoven. . . . Recently, at a soirée given by a countess, who is supposed to lead in fashion, I had an outbreak. . . . and started right out with the C-sharp minor sonata of Beethoven. When I finished, I noticed that the impression had been enormous; the ladies were weeping, the gentlemen hotly discussing the importance of the work. I had to write down a number of Beethoven sonatas for the female pianists who wanted to study them." Ibid., p. 82.

68. Marek, *Gentle Genius: The Story of Felix Mendelssohn*, pp. 126–27, letter dated Weimar, 3 June 1830.

69. After reporting his vivid impression of Beethoven at Teplitz in July 1812 in letters to his wife Christine and to Zelter, Goethe's pen never again formed the word Beethoven during the composer's lifetime. Only a year after Beethoven's death did Goethe ever refer, in writing, to Beethoven—and this only incidentally because he was reporting on Tomaschek's new Requiem. See Rolland, *Goethe and Beethoven*, p. 87 and n. 116.

70. Letter of 14 July 1831, as given in Marek, *Gentle Genius: The Story of Felix Mendelssohn*, pp. 190–91.

71. This incident related in *Grove's Dictionary of Music and Musicians*, 3rd ed., 3:413.

72. As quoted in Werner, *Mendelssohn: A New Image of the Composer and His Age*, p. 321.

73. Ibid., pp. 321–22.

74. Ibid., p. 233 and n. 24 concerning unpublished letters by Mendelssohn of 7 and 13 May 1833.

75. Ibid., p. 295, letter of 14 December 1837 to the historian Johann Gustav Droysen.

76. Schindler, *Beethoven As I Knew Him*, p. 437.

77. Ibid., pp. 436–37.

78. They were the overture to *A Midsummer Night's Dream* and the Second Concerto for Two Pianos in A-flat.

79. Schindler, *Beethoven As I Knew Him*, p. 437.

80. Ibid., p. 423, asterisked note. Schindler still wasn't through persecuting Mendelssohn; in the third edition of his life of Beethoven he treats Mendelssohn's analysis of two measures in the Scherzo of the Fifth Symphony to a full blast of his inimitable sarcasm and holy indignation. See ibid., Appendix G, pp. 483–86. Eric Werner has pointed out that Schindler and Mendelssohn may well have been rival candidates for the same position in Düsseldorf in 1833. See Werner, *Mendelssohn: A New Image of the Composer and His Age*, p. 240. Since Mendelssohn was the successful (if short-lived) choice, Schindler may have harbored a further secret grudge against the young and wealthy genius to whom all things came—apparently—so easily. What might the self-righteous Schindler have found to say had he been present at Mendelssohn's 1847 London performance as soloist in Beethoven's Fourth Piano Concerto (Mendelssohn's favorite) when, to the astonishment of the conductor, Michael Costa, Mendelssohn extended the cadenza far beyond the usual time because, as he admitted afterwards, two great women were in the audience—Jenny Lind and Queen Victoria.

81. Letter of 25 February 1847 to his former assistant conductor at Düsseldorf, Julius Rietz, as quoted in Werner, *Mendelssohn: A New Image of the Composer and His Age*, p. 484.

82. Ignaz Moscheles, *Recent Music and Musicians* (New York, 1874), pp. 343–44.

83. Charlotte Moscheles enriched her husband's material with extracts from the many letters written home by Moscheles while concertizing abroad: the resulting ensemble was published in two volumes under the title *Aus Moscheles Leben* (Leipzig, 1872) and translated into English by A. D. Coleridge under the title *Recent Music and Musicians* (New York, 1873). In 1888 the rich trove of Mendelssohn letters to Ignaz and Charlotte Moscheles was also published.

84. Moscheles, *Recent Music and Musicians*, p. 15.

85. Ibid., p. 3.

86. Sonneck, *Beethoven: Impressions By His Contemporaries*, p. 89.

87. Moscheles, *Recent Music and Musicians*, p. 10.

88. Ibid.

89. Ibid., p. 409.

90. Not that Moscheles was completely uncritical of Beethoven's compositions. In 1845, shortly after the loss of his brother—the same one he had clumsily contrived to introduce to Beethoven so many years earlier (see chapter 2, n. 27)—he discovered some upsetting aspects in one of the piano sonatas: "The thought of my loss is interwoven with everything I undertake . . . they made me play four of Beethoven's sonatas. . . . In the Adagio in F-sharp minor my feelings were most powerfully moved, but in the fugue it pained me to find so many extravagances. It contains more discords than concords, and Beethoven seems to me all the while to be saying, 'I intend working up a subject in a learned manner, it may sound well or not.' " Ibid., p. 313.

91. Ibid., p. 314.

92. A number of eyewitness accounts of Beethoven's conducting mannerisms, all of which agree with or even surpass in reported eccentricities Moscheles's "imitation," exist. See especially Spohr and Wilhelmine Schröder-Devrient, but also the description given in the *Autobiography* (1860) of the singer Franz Wild, as given in Thayer-Forbes, *Thayer's Life of Beethoven*, p. 570.

93. Moscheles, *Recent Music and Musicians*, p. 238.

94. Ibid.

95. Ibid., p. 245.

96. The London *Times*, 4 May 1841, as quoted in ibid., pp. 280–81.

97. Ibid., p. 337.

98. Ibid., p. 251. Moscheles continues: "What a pity it is that his last letters are not complete, for they end with those written to Ries, after which his correspondence with me began." Ibid. This may have been the seed that germinated into Moscheles's desire to see his own Beethoven letters published, a project realized when he appended them to the 1841 English translation of Schindler's Beethoven biography.

99. This sentimental act is not admitted to by Schindler in any of the three editions of his Beethoven biography. Instead, before quoting part of the letter of 14 March 1827 Beethoven dictated to him to be sent to Moscheles, Schindler declares in a truly extraordinary footnote: "Beethoven himself was never in the least acquainted with Moscheles," Schindler, *Beethoven As I Knew Him*, p. 322. This statement was allowed to pass even though elsewhere in the same edition Schindler mentions eating in Vienna during November 1823 with Beethoven and Moscheles, claiming full credit for the culinary event: "I took him to see the master and we three dined together." Ibid., Appendix 2, p. 372. We learn about the lock of hair only from Moscheles's posthumous memoirs, in which is printed the entire text of Schindler's own letter to him of 24 March 1827. The letter concludes: "I have just left Beethoven: he is actually dying, and before this letter is beyond the precincts of the city the great light will be extinguished forever. . . . The enclosed lock of hair I have just cut from his head, and sent it you [*sic*]. God be with you! Your most devoted Friend, Ant. Schindler." Moscheles, *Recent Music and Musicians*, p. 107.

100. Ibid., p. 120.

101. Ibid., pp. 270–71.

102. Ignaz Moscheles, ed., *The Life of Beethoven* (London, 1841), p. iv. See chapter 2, n. 7 for the full quotation and a discussion of the historical confusion concerning the assumption that Moscheles was also the translator of Schindler's book—an assumption still held as previously discussed (see chapter 2, n. 7) in the latest edition of *The New Grove Dictionary of Music and Musicians*, Stanley Sadie, ed., 12:599.

103. Schindler, *Beethoven As I Knew Him*, Appendix 2, p. 371.

104. Ibid.

105. Ibid., p. 372. When we read Moscheles's journal and letters home for the year 1823 we learn that while he was in Vienna (mid-October to the end of December) he was quite ill for a time after his arrival so that, once on the road to recovery, "having to return some visits," he began with Beethoven. Moscheles, *Recent Music and Musicians*, p. 58. (This was the visit when Moscheles managed to introduce his brother "who was burning with anxiety to see the great man" to Beethoven, see chapter two, n. 27). Concerning the loan of the English piano, Charlotte Moscheles sums up the circumstances and reason for the request: "In November and December, Moscheles gave a second and third concert in the Kärntnerthor Theatre, and for the last occasion Beethoven lent him with the greatest readiness his Broadwood piano. Moscheles wished, by using alternately at one and the same concert a Graf and an English piano, to bring out the good qualities of both. . . . 'I tried,' says Moscheles, 'in my Fantasia to show the value of the broad, full, although somewhat muffled tone of the Broadwood piano; but in vain. My Vienna public remained loyal to their countryman—the clear, ringing tones of the Graf were more pleasing to their ears.'" Ibid., pp. 59–60. What sort of "financial speculation" could Schindler-Beethoven have had in mind? Was Moscheles perceived as a secret traveling salesperson for the firm of Broadwood?

106. Schindler, *Beethoven As I Knew Him*, p. 373. With an eye to the "children of Israel" in his reading public, Schindler grandly adds the following comment to this last statement in an asterisked editorial footnote: "In recent times, Christians have had no grounds for reproaching Jews for anything in musical matters." Ibid. MacArdle, the modern-day editor of Schindler, felt compelled to make his own editorial comment at this point: "While Beethoven and his associates used the word 'Jew' as a term of opprobrium, the present editor knows of no documented basis for a charge of antisemitism against Beethoven." *This* present writer agrees with MacArdle in his restrained conclusion that "Schindler's charge probably reflects his own attitude more accurately than that of Beethoven." Ibid., p. 391, n. 297. Schindler had already attacked Moscheles in the supplement to the second edition of his book, "Beethoven in Paris"—a fact that he helpfully brought to the attention of eleven reporters from the "London papers present at the Beethoven Festival in Bonn in 1845 [who] invited me to an interview." Ibid., p. 373. Moscheles, who usually followed the policy of ignoring the attacks of jealous colleagues, and who demonstrates a good-natured equanimity throughout his memoirs and letters, finally discussed the Schindler problem with wry amusement in a letter of 1854 concerning some rude attacks made in the Leipzig papers against his colleague, the virtuoso violinist Ferdinand David: "I have a fellow-feeling for him in this matter, and when we discussed the subject yesterday, I handed him Schindler's lately published pamphlet, 'On the Development of Pianoforte playing since Clementi,' in which I am very roughly handled. His egotism is the chief feature throughout; it is 'I' perpetually; 'Clementi, Cramer, Beethoven, and I' worked together for the promotion and welfare of art. 'Hummel and Moscheles have perverted pianoforte playing.' The latter (says he) has actually had the 'audacity to set to metronome Tempi works of Beethoven, *whom he never heard play*'—he, Schindler, has already paid him out properly for this." Moscheles, *Recent Music and Musicians*, p. 385. A few lines later, in the same letter, Moscheles also reports a delicious counterattack: "Ferdinand Hiller published a letter to Schindler in reply, in which he showed to demonstration the absurdity of his pretending to be the intimate friend of Beethoven, and asked him, 'if he ever

got so far in his whole life, as to be able to play Cramer's first Study? Can he show him a single trace anywhere of any one composition by Schindler? or has he, as a conductor, a past history only known to himself? What are his claims to the position of Beethoven's Stadtholder and alter ego?' '' Ibid., pp. 385–86.

107. Anderson, *The Letters of Beethoven*, 3:1124, letter written shortly after the 7 May 1824 "Grand" concert of Beethoven's latest music, which, although a musical triumph, was financially disappointing for the composer, thus causing his chronic distrust to focus upon the luckless Schindler.

108. Moscheles, *Recent Music and Musicians*, p. 350.

109. Ibid., p. 349.

110. Ibid., p. 350. Moscheles's travel accounts from these later years are an interesting barometer of the taste for German music in other climes. On a trip through North Italy in the summer of 1853, he reports sadly about the Milan Conservatory: "The Professors show me great respect, my 'Studies' are adopted, that is all they know of my music, of Beethoven or Mendelssohn they know absolutely nothing." Ibid., p. 379.

111. Ibid., p. 381; written in 1853 when Brahms was all of twenty years old. Not all promising musicians got the benefit of this sort of comparison with Beethoven. Writing about the "stormy" overture to *The Flying Dutchman*, which he found full of "Geist" but "distracting and joyless," Moscheles concluded with a touch of irony, "and yet the papers will maintain that, just as Beethoven's latest works were not immediately understood, so it will take time to become familiar with Wagner." Ibid., p. 389 (year 1854–55).

112. At the end of a successful but strenuous concert tour of the United States in 1872–73, Rubinstein informed his startled American manager, Maurice Grau, that he wished to give seven farewell recitals in New York—historical-music recitals in which he would teach the public what real piano music meant. The program for the second recital consisted exclusively of Beethoven piano sonatas, six of them. Sixteen years later, after resuming directorship of the Saint Petersburg Conservatory, he held a series of thirty-two Historical Lectures (September 1888–May 1889) of which seven were devoted to Beethoven. Echoing E.T.A. Hoffmann's thoughts on the superiority of instrumental music, Rubinstein asked his rapt audience after performing the Sonata in A-flat, op. 110: "Can you not see, here, how instrumental music stands higher than vocal music? The deepest feeling, the greatest grief, the most excellent rapture can find expression only in tones, not words." As cited in Catherine Drinker Bowen, *"Free Artist": The Story of Anton and Nicholas Rubinstein* (New York, 1939), p. 315. Rubinstein's veneration for Beethoven once prompted him to give a distinguished guest a public tongue lashing. *The Kreutzer Sonata* had recently been published and Rubinstein had read and reread it with disapproval. Now he expressed himself to his dinner guest: "Count Tolstoi, in your book you missed entirely the meaning of Beethoven's music . . . no matter how great you may be in your own line, that does not give you the right to distort the work of another artist." Ibid., p. 333.

113. Moscheles, *Recent Music and Musicians*, p. 398 (year 1854–55).

114. Ibid., pp. 419–20, diary entry for Tuesday, 20 December 1869. Moscheles's dream emphasis on the fact that Beethoven would appear only to those with whom he had been personally acquainted during his lifetime might be construed as a subconscious refutation of Schindler's incredible claim that "Beethoven himself was never in the least acquainted with Moscheles" (see n. 99), but can also be seen as an interesting dream transformation of an actual incident that took place during Moscheles's personal acquaintance—the ruse he practiced to get his brother into Beethoven's presence (see chapter 2, n. 27). It was Schindler himself who had informed Moscheles by letter (24 March 1827) of Beethoven's deathbed (but not last) words: "He feels that his end is near, for yesterday he said to Breuning and me: 'Plaudite, amici, comoedia finita est.' " Schindler, *Beethoven As I Knew Him*, p. 324; Moscheles, *Recent Music and Musicians*, p. 106. See also Thayer's discussion of these words in connection with Dr. Wawruch and Hüttenbrenner, Thayer-Forbes, *Thayer's Life of Beethoven*, pp. 1048–49 and ns. 52, 53.

115. Moscheles, *Recent Music and Musicians*, p. 352, letter of 2 January 1849.

116. May Herbert, ed. and trans., *The Life of Robert Schumann Told in His Letters*, 2 vols. (London, 1890), 1:211. Schumann was responding to a musical admirer in Belgium, Simonin de Sire, who had apparently ranked Schumann with Beethoven and Weber. Schumann's letter of 15 March 1839 begs: "But don't [place me] between Beethoven and Weber, though somewhere near them, so that I may go on learning from them all my life." Ibid.

117. Schumann, *On Music and Musicians*, p. 107; published in 1840 (see Robert Schumann, *Gesammelte Schriften über Musik und Musiker*, 4 vols. [Leipzig, 1854], 3: 195ff.). This is the beginning of the famous article in which Schumann gave an account of his discovery at the house of Schubert's brother Ferdinand of the score to Schubert's Symphony no. 7 in C Major (now numbered no. 9, the *Great* C Major). He persuaded Mendelssohn to give it a first performance at the Gewandhaus back in Leipzig the following year (March 1839).

118. Herbert, *The Life of Robert Schumann Told in His Letters*, 1:184–85, letter of 10 October 1838. Schumann also refers to the finding of the steel pen on Beethoven's grave in his article on the Schubert Symphony in C Major (above, n. 117), reverently declaring: "I never use it save on festal occasions like this one; may inspiration have flowed from it!" Schumann, *On Music and Musicians*, p. 112. Another "festal" occasion for which Schumann allowed himself use of this special Beethoven talisman was for the writing out of his own first symphonic attempt, the Symphony no. 1 in B-flat Major (*Spring*).

119. Schumann, *On Music and Musicians*, pp. 109–10.

120. As quoted by Robert Haven Schauffler, *Florestan: The Life and Work of Robert Schumann* (1945; New York, 1963), p. 132. By 10 March 1839 Schumann knew that the Vienna venture was a distinct failure. In a letter of that date to one of the *Neue Zeitschrift* contributors, the critic and folklorist Anton Wilhelm Florentin von Zuccalmaglio, Schumann wrote frankly: "Neither the paper nor I shall remain in Vienna. The fact is, we are out of place here. After mature consideration from every point of view, the affair has not proved a success. The chief obstacle is the Censure." Herbert, *The Life of Robert Schumann Told in His Letters*, 1: 203. By mid-April

Schumann was back in Leipzig, with new courage to fight for his marriage to Clara Wieck.

121. Sonneck, *Beethoven: Impressions by His Contemporaries*, pp. 208–9. Wieck's recollections of his visit to Beethoven put the date as May 1826 (1824 has been suggested as more likely, see ibid., p. 207) and were written down long after the event in a letter to his second wife. This account originally appeared in the *Dresdener Nachrichten*, and was reprinted in the *Signale*, no. 57, in December 1837—the year of old Wieck's death. See Thayer-Forbes, *Thayer's Life of Beethoven*, p. 989.

122. Gerald Abraham, ed., *Schumann: A Symposium* (London, 1952), p. 9.

123. Fanny Raymond Ritter, trans. and ed., *Music and Musicians. Essays and Criticisms by Robert Schumann* (London, 1877), pp. 17–18.

124. Ibid., pp. 18–19, free translation of Goethe's lines mine.

125. The talented pianist and promising composer Ludwig Schunke, whose long face reminded Schumann of Thorvaldsen's sculpture of Schiller, was born the same year as Schumann (1810) but died just short of his twentyfourth birthday in 1834.

126. Ritter, *Music and Musicians. Essays and Criticisms by Robert Schumann*, p. 20. Jonathan's contribution continues with an interesting borrowing from Goethe's *Von deutscher Baukunst*: as Goethe laments not being able to find the tombstone for Erwin von Steinbach, architect of mighty Strassburg Cathedral, so Jonathan complains in his Beethoven commentary of not being able to locate the grave of J S. Bach in Leipzig's churchyard, and that when he asked the sexton he received the reply: "There have been so many Bachs." Ibid., pp. 20–21.

127. Ibid., pp. 21–22.

128. Ibid., pp. 22–23.

129. Ibid., p. 24.

130. Ibid., pp. 24–25. The name of Liszt, who would later be the prime mover in raising funds for Bonn's Beethoven monument (see chapter 5), is not included in this list, which singles out sixteen more musicians and towns, but which was compiled prior to Liszt's series of fund-raising concerts (begun in 1839) on behalf of the Bonn monument.

131. André Boucourechliev, *Schumann* (London, 1959), p. 73. Later Schumann came to associate his opus 17 with the despair and longing he had felt for Clara—his single "Tone"—during the separation forced on them by Papa Wieck in the difficult year 1836.

132. Herbert, *The Life of Robert Schumann Told in His Letters*, 1: 180, letter of 7 September 1838 to Hermann Hirschbach of Berlin.

133. Ibid., 1: 159, letter of 13 June 1838 to Hermann Hirschbach.

134. Ritter, *Music and Musicians. Essays and Criticisms by Robert Schumann*, p. 333; this "credo" was written in 1835 when Schumann was only twenty-five as part of his long, laudatory review of Ferdinand Hiller's recently published op. 15.

135. Ibid.

136. Ibid.

137. Schumann, *On Music and Musicians*, pp. 101–2.

138. Ibid., p. 102.

139. Ibid., p. 103. Schumann, editing his collected writings in 1854, was able to comment in a footnote to this plea for a collective edition of Beethoven's four overtures that his wish had since been fulfilled.

140. Herbert, *The Life of Robert Schumann Told in His Letters*, 1: 162, letter of 15 June 1838.

141. Ibid. One of the contributors to the *Neue Zeitschrift*, Wolfgang Robert Griepenkerl (1810–1868) of Brunswick, had written a novel called *Das Musikfest, oder die Beethovener* (Leipzig, 1838). Referring to the second edition (1841), which contained an introduction by Meyerbeer (one of the few composers whom Schumann was unable to review kindly), Schumann wrote the author: "I have always considered your book a very loveable creation. But I should like it still better—may I speak openly?—without the dedication. I wonder whether you were fascinated by his personality? I expect you know my opinion of Meyerbeer, so will say no more about it." Letter of 31 October 1841, Herbert, *The Life of Robert Schumann Told in His Letters*, 1: 279.

142. Ibid., p. 105.

143. The autograph of Beethoven's op. 129 was discovered by Otto Albrecht, and its original title, as supplied by Beethoven, was simply "Alla ingharese quasi un capriccio," see Thayer-Forbes, *Thayer's Life of Beethoven*, p. 176. See also Otto Albrecht, "Adventures and Discoveries of a Manuscript Hunter," *Musical Quarterly* 31 (1945): 495, concerning Diabelli's part in obscuring the fact that the work was unfinished, and, concerning the authenticity of the "Rage over the Lost Penny" title, Erich Hertzmann, "The Newly Discovered Autograph of Beethoven's *Rondo à Capriccio*, Op. 129," *Musical Quarterly*, 32 (1946):182.

144. This is in fact the opening line of the essay, Schumann, *On Music and Musicians*, p. 105.

145. Ibid.

146. Herbert, *The Life of Robert Schumann Told in His Letters*, 1:223, letter of 14 June 1839 to the composer Eduard Krüger, who would later (1847) dedicate a piano quartet to Schumann.

147. Schumann, *On Music and Musicians*, p. 260, letter of 13 April 1838.

148. Ibid., p. 96. Written in 1835 in a review of the Leipzig premiere of Spohr's Fourth Symphony, "The Consecration of Sound." Schumann continues: "When Beethoven conceived and carried out his idea for the *Pastoral* Symphony, it was not a single short spring day that inspired him to utter his cry of joy, but the dark commingling of lofty songs above us (as Heine, I believe, somewhere says). The manifold voices of creation stirred within him." Ibid. At the end of the century similar arguments would be advanced to describe Cézanne's timeless, nonimpressionist *The Bay from L'Estaque* (1883–85, The Metropolitan Museum of Art)—a view derived from the sum total of many viewings, and one that is *represented* rather than reproduced.

149. Schumann chattily revealed the identity of "Vater Doles" to *Neue Zeitschrift* contributor Theodor Töpkin in a letter of 18 August 1834, commenting that he "can do much better than 'B' in the last numbers" and that "he is going to give us two more similar pictures, Haydn and Handel." Herbert, *The Life of Robert Schumann Told in His Letters*, 1:57. In an article on Schubert's *German Dances*, Florestan shouts "in the ear of Fritz Friedrich (the deaf painter)" to fetch his magic lantern for the amusement of the reveling Davidites, a request the "bovine-eyed painter" speedily granted, filling the room with shadow figures "of which a few spider-legged ones" ran up the wall to the ceiling in true Hoff-

mannesque fashion. Schumann, *On Music and Musicians*, p. 125.

150. Schumann, *On Music and Musicians*, pp. 56–57. Schumann was certainly aware of the boldness of his suggestion and had in fact a specific precedent in mind, one in which the "correction" did not turn out well for the corrector: "Ries tells us how enraged Beethoven became over a passage in the *Eroica* Symphony which Ries had altered with the best intentions." Ibid., p. 57. On Schumann's reaction to the just-published Wegeler-Ries *Notizen* on the life of Beethoven, see his letter to Henriette Voigt, cited above in n. 140.

151. Herbert, *The Life of Robert Schumann Told in His Letters*, 1:100, letter of 14 September 1836 to *Neue Zeitschrift* contributor Heinrich Dorn of Riga.

152. Schumann, *On Music and Musicians*, pp. 98–99.

153. Ibid., p. 99.

154. Ibid.

155. Ibid.

156. Herbert, *The Life of Robert Schumann Told in His Letters*, 1:57, letter of 18 August 1834 to *Neue Zeitschrift* contributor Theodor Töpken of Bremen.

157. Schumann, *On Music and Musicians*, pp. 96–97.

158. Ibid., p. 96.

159. Ibid., p. 97. Beethoven had preserved his own example of a ludicrous interpretation of the Seventh Symphony. A description of it in terms of a political uprising was published by the overly zealous Beethoven admirer Karl Iken, editor of the *Bremer Zeitung*, and Schindler found a copy of this and three other "programmes" by Iken among the composer's papers after his death. See Thayer-Forbes, *Thayer's Life of Beethoven*, pp. 765–66.

160. Schumann, *On Music and Musicians*, p. 100.

161. Ibid., pp. 100–101.

162. Ibid., p. 101. In this review of 11 February 1841 Schumann has shed one of his last coats of Jean Paulism.

163. Herbert, *The Life of Robert Schumann Told in His Letters*, 1:224, letter of 30 June 1839, to *Neue Zeitschrift* contributor Hermann Hirschbach of Berlin. Hirschbach had sent Schumann a review of Beethoven's Ninth Symphony the year before and although Schumann approved of the "morality and strictness" of Hirschbach's opinions, he gracefully rejected the review for publication, writing: "What is cannot be changed; and in our opinion the Ninth Symphony is still, in spite of everything, the mightiest work in recent orchestral music" (letter of 5 June 1838, ibid., p. 158).

164. Quoted from the diary of the pianist Amalie Rieffel who, with her father, visited Schumann in his rented rooms on 6 August 1840, in Schauffler, *Florestan: the Life and Work of Robert Schumann*, p. 154. The deathbed drawing of Schunke is reproduced in ibid., opp. p. 80.

165. Berthold Litzmann, *Clara Schumann: Ein Künstlerleben*, 3 vols. (Leipzig, 1902–8); 1: 7, all translations mine.

166. Ibid., 1: 18.

167. Ibid., 1: 29.

168. John N. Burk, *Clara Schumann: A Romantic Biography* (New York, 1940), p. 68. (See below, n. 187.)

169. The virtuoso pianist Sigismond Thalberg (1812–1871) was one of the first to give concerts in which the services of an assisting orchestra were dispensed with and the piano alone stood on the stage. Liszt and Hallé soon adopted this practice.

170. Burk, *Clara Schumann: A Romantic Biography*, p. 116.

171. Ibid., p. 118.

172. Ibid.

173. Ibid., p. 119.

174. Litzmann, *Clara Schumann: Ein Künstlerleben*, 1:170–71.

175. Ibid., 1: 171, letter of 11 January 1838.

176. Ibid., 1: 172, letter begun on 18 January 1838; the private recital took place on 14 January and was attended by almost thirty persons including "die grösste Dichter Wiens," of which one was Grillparzer.

177. Burk, *Clara Schumann: A Romantic Biography*, p. 207.

178. Litzmann, *Clara Schumann: Ein Künstlerleben*, 2: 19, entry of August 1841.

179. Ibid., 2: 17, entry of July 1841.

180. Schindler, *Beethoven As I Knew Him*, p. 435.

181. Ibid.

182. Eduard Hanslick, *Music Criticisms 1846–99*, trans. and ed. Henry Pleasants (Baltimore, 1950), pp. 48, 51, review of 1856. Clara Schumann did suffer from one irreparable handicap in Hanslick's opinion however: "She could be called the greatest living pianist rather than merely the greatest female pianist, were the range of her physical strength not limited by her sex." Ibid., p. 49. In spite of this awesome defect she does as well as she does, Hanslick helpfully explains in one of those unquestioned clichés with which the nineteenth century felt so at home, because of "the masculinity of her playing." Ibid., p. 50.

183. Schindler, *Beethoven As I Knew Him*, pp. 433–34.

184. Ibid., p. 434.

185. Ibid.

186. Ibid.

187. Hanslick, *Music Criticisms 1846–99*, p. 50. In his life of Clara Schumann, largely and frequently too literally lifted from the three-volume Litzmann biography not to merit specific and continuous acknowledgment, Burk (see above, n. 168) inexplicably quotes, without giving his source, what he calls "the pontifical Hanslick—a purring voice this time" on Clara Wieck's December 1837–April 1838 concert series in Vienna (Burk, *Clara Schumann: A Romantic Biography*, p. 48). Had Hanslick indeed written the 1838 review ascribed to him by Burk, he would have been music history's most precocious critic: born on 11 September 1825, he would have been twelve years old at the time (and commuting from his hometown Prague). Hanslick's first review was written in December 1844 and published in the Prague review *Ost und West*.

188. Litzmann, *Clara Schumann: Ein Künstlerleben*, 1: 155; concert of 3 December 1837. Father Wieck's instant solution for the slumbering state of music in Vienna was, as he told his diary, that "Mendelssohn should come here" (ibid.)—Mendelssohn, that man of action whose predilection for rapid tempi characterized his life as well as his music.

189. That Schumann, in two of his works marked *presto possibile*, then indicates *piu presto* has been pointed out by Donald Francis Tovey, *Essays in Musical Analysis* 6 vols. (London, 1939), 6: 166.

190. Schindler, *Beethoven As I Knew Him*, pp. 435–36.

191. Ibid., p. 436.

192. Eduard Hüffer, "Anton Felix Schindler," Ph.D. dissertation (Münster, 1909), p. 45 (translation mine). Hüffer had access to Schindler's estate which, after his death on 16 January 1864, had passed into the hands of his sister Marie, an actress, who died in 1882. The author is uncritically attached to his thesis subject ("Schindler war ein durchaus eherenwerter Mann," ibid., p. 76) and seems to have been a relative (grandson?) of Ed. Hüffer, the Münster publisher who brought out the various editions of Schindler's Beethoven biography.

193. Burk, *Clara Schumann: A Romantic Biography*, p. 336.

194. It does not however excuse his final, most callous attack on Clara Schumann in which, switching from charges of Beethoven desecration, Schindler quotes Hanslick's 1859 review criticizing the *presto* tempo at which she played the first piece of the *Kreisleriana*, and acidly concludes: "These words show that Frau Schumann abused even the music of her late husband." Schindler, *Beethoven As I Knew Him*, p. 438.

195. Letter of 25 April 1853 to Schumann's friend Ferdinand Hiller, the man responsible for bringing the Schumanns to Düsseldorf and the same Hiller whom we met as a boy visiting, with his teacher Hummel, Beethoven on his deathbed; as quoted by Schauffler, *Florestan: the Life and Work of Robert Schumann*, p. 240.

196. Letter of 12 February 1854 from Schumann to Julius Stern, ibid., p. 248.

197. Berthold Litzmann, ed., *Letters of Clara Schumann and Johannes Brahms, 1853–1896*, 2 vols. (1927; New York, 1973) 1: 28–31, letter of 23 and 24 February 1855.

198. Ibid., p. 16, letter dated Endenich, 27 November 1854.

199. Burk, *Clara Schumann: A Romantic Biography*, p. 311. Brahms was describing the arrival of Schumann's letter at the Düsseldorf household on 15 September 1854, just three days after the fourteenth anniversary of the Schumann marriage—and their first one spent apart.

200. Litzmann, *Clara Schumann: Ein Künstlerleben*, 2: 414, entry describing the sad events on 27 July 1856.

201. La Mara (Marie Lipsius), ed., and Constance Bache, trans., *Letters of Franz Liszt*, 2 vols. (London, 1894), 1: 151, letter of 2 December 1852 to Wilhelm von Lenz (1809–1883)—by profession, imperial Russian councilor of state at Saint Petersburg; by avocation, tremendously prolific writer on musical matters, especially Beethoven, see text below.

202. Sonneck, *Beethoven: Impressions by His Contemporaries*, pp. 162–63. This account was recorded by Liszt's student, Ilka Horowitz-Barnay, to whom in 1875 Liszt related the event in a "tone of deepest emotion, with tears in his eyes" (ibid., p. 163). Liszt's erroneous reference to having visited the composer in his Schwarzspanierhaus quarters (Beethoven did not move into the Schwarzspanierhaus until 15 October 1825) is quite understandable in view of the fame that this last residence of Beethoven had acquired over the decades in literature and legend.

203. Thayer-Forbes, *Thayer's Life of Beethoven*, p. 847.

204. Ibid.

205. Ibid.

206. Ibid.

207. Schindler, *Beethoven As I Knew Him*, p. 376. The question of who (if anyone) did provide young Liszt with a theme for his concluding "free improvisation" continues to intrigue and baffle Liszt scholars. The original handbill for this farewell concert (a copy of which is in the Historisches Museum der Stadt Wien) lists the final number expectantly as *Freie Fantasie auf dem Pianoforte von dem Concertgeber, wozu er sich zum Sujet von Jemand der Zuhörer ein schriftliches Thema unterhängist erbittet* ("Free fantasy on the pianoforte by the concert giver for which purpose he most humbly begs a written theme from someone in the audience"). For the latest discussion (in which the question is still unresolved), see Alan Walker, *Franz Liszt: The Virtuoso Years 1811–1847* (New York, 1983) (vol. 1 of a projected 3-volume biography of Liszt), p. 80. Walker considers only the possibility of Beethoven (negative) and does not take up Schindler's provocative references to the emperor and the archduke. A far more interesting drama of omission takes place throughout Walker's book, however, concerning modern Lisztian research. Nowhere in the 481 pages of his otherwise hugely complete and informative investigation does Walker make mention of the previous "massive" Liszt study of modern times, Eleanor Perényi, *Liszt: The Artist as Romantic Hero* (Boston, 1974) (a book nominated for the 1975 American National Book Award). The reason for this scholarly slight would seem to lie in the pages of Perényi's book, where several times Walker's previously published thoughts on aspects of Liszt are not only dismissed but caviled in the grossest of terms (see especially p. 65, asterisked note proposing that Walker consult the English housewife Rosemary Brown, whose claims of receiving daily visitations and musical dictation from Liszt, Beethoven, and others amused the musical world in the early 1970s). Walker apparently has decided not to dignify Perényi in any form whatsoever, not even bibliographical! On the other hand Walker's prose debt to one of the earliest and most beautifully written Liszt studies in English deserves greater acknowledgment: Sacheverell Sitwell, *Liszt* (1934; rev. ed., London, 1967). Compare for example their passages on Ingres and Liszt: Sitwell, p. 51, Walker, p. 266. For further critical comment on Walker, see the recent review by Allan Keiler, "Liszt Research and Walker's Liszt," *Musical Quarterly* 3, no. 4 (Fall 1984): 374–403; concerning the *Weihekuss*, see especially pp. 381–96.

208. Schindler, *Beethoven As I Knew Him*, p. 416.

209. Quite the contrary is true of the formalist and almost procrustean pedagogy to which Czerny forced the inadequately trained Liszt to submit.

210. Schindler, *Beethoven As I Knew Him*, pp. 432–33.

211. La Mara, *Letters of Franz Liszt*, 1: 410, letter of 1 December 1859. Liszt was discussing Beethoven's circumvention of Albrechtsberger's rigid codification of counterpoint.

212. Ibid., 1: 299, letter of 2 January 1857 concerning recently deceased composers who, now that they are *dead* are considered classics ("Schumann, the Romanticist" is also cited by Liszt).

213. Thayer-Forbes, *Thayer's Life of Beethoven*, p. 847.

214. As pointed out by Forbes, ibid., p. 847, n. 57.

215. Schindler, *Beethoven As I Knew Him*, p. 376. We do know that Beethoven attended at least three performances of his own music after 1816—the first two in his professional capacity as conductor on 25 December 1817 and 17 January 1819 (as well as the aborted at-

tempt to conduct a rehearsal of *Fidelio* for its revival in the fall of 1822)—and that he was present, sitting with Schindler and von Breuning in a box in the front tier of the theater, for the second performance of *Fidelio* on 4 November 1822. See Thayer-Forbes, *Thayer's Life of Beethoven*, p. 691, p. 733, 812. The inconsistencies of Schindler's statements concerning Beethoven's presence at a concert by Liszt and the version transmitted by Ludwig Nohl (who heard the story from Liszt himself) that Beethoven did indeed attend the concert might be resolved if we entertain the possibility of a private concert by Liszt at the home of Czerny's parents, where, every Sunday from 1816 to 1823, Czerny regularly presented his best pupils in recital and where Beethoven was often in attendance. Ferdinand Hiller's version of the event is that it happened in Beethoven's lodgings, as pointed out by Sitwell, *Liszt*, p. 11. Perényi, in her *Liszt: The Artist as Romantic Hero*, relies heavily on Sitwell for her surprisingly uninformed account of the event; some of the problems she piquantly poses (ibid., p. 15) could have been solved had she consulted the Beethoven conversation books, Schindler, or Thayer. But this is the same author who breezily asserts that Lola Montez "graduated from Liszt to Bavaria's mad King" (ibid., p. 232), confusing the quite sane Ludwig I with his grandson, the insane Ludwig II.

216. Walker bravely and amusingly takes up the challenge of the *Weihekuss* (see Walker, *Franz Liszt: The Virtuoso Years 1811–1847*, pp. 81–85), remarking how later prints commemorating the occasion have been used by biographers as "proof" of the event. He points out that there is only one instance of any written reference to the Beethoven "kiss" by Liszt. This is an interesting letter of 1862 to the grand duke of Weimar describing a mystical experience Liszt once underwent while contemplating Michelangelo's *Last Judgment* in the Sistine Chapel, when "there emerged . . . slowly unutterably great, another shadow. Full of inspiration I recognized it at once; for while he was still bound to this earth he had consecrated my brow with a kiss" (ibid., p. 84, n. 36).

217. La Mara, *Letters of Franz Liszt*, 1: 8–9, letter written 2 May 1832. Upon rereading these lines the nineteen-year-old author decided they were a bit much and penned the following addendum, dated six days later: "My good friend, it was in a paroxysm of madness that I wrote you the above lines . . . in a word I was delirious." Ibid., p. 10.

218. Schumann's op. 3, printed 1833, and op. 10, published 1835—both sets of six studies after the Paganini Capricci; Brahms's set of twenty-eight variations on one of the Capriccio themes, op. 35, published 1866. The final version of Liszt's six *Paganini Études* appeared in 1851. During the first decade of his work on transcribing Paganini for piano, Liszt was on excellent terms with the Schumanns as we see in a letter of 25 December 1839 to Clara (then still Wieck) in which he refers to the " 'Studies after Paganini,' which are dedicated to you." La Mara, *Letters of Franz Liszt*, 1: 41.

219. As quoted in Perényi, *Liszt: The Artist as Romantic Hero*, p. 176; of interest is this author's discussion (pp. 175ff.) of the possible role Liszt's lover, Marie d'Agoult, may have had in the creation of Liszt's reports on Italian life, art, and music (*Lettres d'un bachelier-ès-musique*, 1835–1840) as published in the Paris *Gazette Musicale*. The most recent discussion of Liszt's literary col-

laborations is to be found in Walker, *Franz Liszt: The Virtuoso Years 1811–1847*, pp. 17, 20–23.

220. Blandine was born 18 December 1835; Cosima, 24 December 1837; Daniel (in Rome), 9 May 1839. Ingres drew a handsome double portrait of Marie d'Agoult with the eleven-year-old Cosima in 1849; the Ingres portrait drawing of Liszt passed into the possession of Wagner's descendants at Bayreuth.

221. As quoted in Walter Friedlaender, *David to Delacroix* (1930; Cambridge [Mass.], 1952), p. 74.

222. It was under this title that "Danhauser's latest picture" was reviewed with effusive enthusiasm in the *Wiener Zeitung* for 13 May 1840 by J. F. Castelli. See Roessler, *Josef Danhauser*, p. 34.

223. The actual piano is today in the musical instrument collection of the Kunsthistorisches Museum in Vienna (Inventory No. 38). The same, or very similar, Graf piano model (*Hammerflügel*) is seen in another painting by Danhauser, his *Woman Playing the Piano* of 1844, reproduced in Roessler, *Josef Danhauser* (ills. not paginated), listed on p. 74. Compare also with the slightly less ornate model presented to Beethoven by Graf in 1825—a four-string instrument now on display at the Beethovenhaus in Bonn. Piano-maker to the imperial and royal court, Conrad Graf also made a piano (1839) as a gift to Clara Wieck upon her marriage to Robert Schumann (this piano passed into the possession of Brahms and is now in the Kunsthistorisches Museum in Vienna).

224. Glück, "Prolegomena zu einer neuen Beethoven-Ikonographie," p. 212 (translation mine).

225. Earlier scholars (Frimmel, Glück, Badura-Skoda) have remarked on the similarities of the Danhauser bust *not* to the death mask that the young painter had taken, but rather to the Klein life mask and to the Dietrich portrait busts. See further the exhaustive consideration given the possibility of a Danhauser-Dietrich collaboration, Badura-Skoda, "Der Bildhauer Anton Dietrich. Ein Beitrag zur Ikonographie Beethovens und Schuberts," pp. 35–38.

Considering the pronounced differences between the Danhauser Beethoven bust, with its drilled pupils and individually articulated, multiple locks of short curly hair, and the Dietrich "contemporary" Beethoven bust, characterized by eyes left blank and a cascade of undifferentiated long strands of hair that bob out at the ear, it is hard to understand how scholars can confuse the two. And yet as recently as 1983 this occurred in an exhibition dedicated to Danhauser's paintings and drawings in his native city of Vienna. In the exhibition catalogue (*Josef Danhauser, Gemälde und Zeichnungen*, Graphische Sammlung Albertina, Vienna, March–May 1983), Veronika Birke claims the bust unequivocally for Dietrich and takes earlier art historians to task ("Wiederholt wurde die Meinung geäubert, auch die Büste sei ein Werk Danhausers. Sie stammt jedoch von Anton Dietrich. . . ." ibid., p. 78). One needs only to compare copies of the Dietrich busts (Birke does not distinguish between the "classical" and the "contemporary" versions) with the Danhauser bust, copies of all of which are available in Vienna, to come down fearlessly on the side of Danhauser.

226. I was recently (October 1983) made frustratingly aware of this ambiguity while trying to match up the painted piano keyboard of Danhauser's *Liszt at the Piano* with a real Graf piano that the staff of the Musical In-

strument Museum in West Berlin allowed me to place next to Danhauser's large painting.

227. This most appropriate detail is provided by the 1840 reviewer of Danhauser's painting, see above, n. 222, and Roessler, *Josef Danhauser*, p. 38. Danhauser painted Conrad Graf's portrait in the same year as his Liszt picture (1840) and also used a wood panel—presumably furnished again by the obliging piano manufacturer, see ibid., p. 73. In this portrait (collection of the Vienna Academy of Art), Graf sits placidly before his small wooden desk, not a piano in sight, leaning his left arm on a partially opened roll of drawing paper covered with notations of various measurements and piano specifications. From atop the desk, gazing approvingly at this dedicated servant of art, is a bust, not of Beethoven or Liszt, but of the piano maker's own former imperial and royal patron, Kaiser Franz I (1786–1835).

228. After Josef's death at the age of thirty-nine in 1845, his original Beethoven death mask passed into his brother Carl's possession, and as we learn from the explanatory statement of 19 May 1891 (see chapter 2, n. 127) the eighty-year-old Carl later presented this original death mask, a copy of the Klein life mask, and the precious strands of Beethoven's hair to the "gnädige Frau" addressed in his notarized document. From the final paragraph of this statement we discover that there was still one Beethoven relic the sentimental old author was unable to part with—the razor used to shave Beethoven's face before the plaster cast was taken. See Glück, "Prolegomena zu einer neuen Beethoven Ikonographie," p. 212. Glück speculates that the recipient of these Beethoven trophies was probably Frau Ella Lang, daughter of Auguste Littrow-Bischoff. Ibid.

229. To the right of the death mask is one of the two white medallion portraits Liszt owned of Wagner and of Berlioz. The medallion profile looks like that of Wagner's but it is difficult to ascertain with certainty which portrait medallion is in our photograph. When I visited the Hofgärtnerei in 1975 neither medallion was in evidence and Beethoven's death mask had long since left Weimar: Liszt gave it to Marie, the daughter of Princess Carolyne SaynWittgenstein, from whom it passed into the possession of the Historisches Museum der Stadt Wien in Vienna. This Vienna example is considered to be a more faithful copy of Beethoven's death mask than the one owned by the Beethovenhaus at Bonn (acquired in 1890).

230. The complications included the facts that apparently the proceeds of the 1840 sale were to benefit not Johann Beethoven, who lived on until 1848, but the ten-year-old son of Amalie Waldmann-Stölzle, the deceased (1831) illegitimate daughter of his wife Therese, and that Beethoven's other sister-in-law, Johanna—"Queen-of-theNight" (Beethoven's phrase) wife of Caspar Carl Beethoven (who had died in 1815) and mother of Beethoven's beloved nephew, Karl, to whose guardian the Heiligenstadt Testament had originally been given—also got into the act and wrote Liszt about the other half of the family's decision to put the document up for sale (this may be one reason why Liszt—even if so tempted—did not buy the autograph himself). See George Kinsky, "Zu Beethovens Heiligenstädter Testament," *Schweizerische Musikzeitung und Sängerblatt*, vols. 14/15 (1934), pp. 519–20.

231. Schindler, *Beethoven As I Knew Him*, p. 96, asterisked note.

232. In 1890 Otto Goldschmidt, pianist-conductor husband of Jenny Lind (who had died in 1887), presented the Heiligenstadt Testament to the library of his native city, Hamburg.

233. George Eliot's amiable reminiscences of Liszt are quoted in James Huneker, *Franz Liszt* (New York, 1927), pp. 258–62. "In the music salon stand Beethoven's and Mozart's pianos. Beethoven's was a present from Broadwood, and has a Latin inscription intimating that it was presented as a tribute to his illustrious genius." Ibid., p. 262.

234. After Liszt's death at Bayreuth in August 1866 Beethoven's Broadwood piano, which was then in the Hofgärtnerei house at Weimar, became, like the Beethoven death mask, the possession of Marie, daughter of Princess Carolyne Sayn-Wittgenstein, who died in Rome seven months after Liszt's death in March 1877. Marie, by then also a princess (she married Prince Konstantine von Hohenlohe-Schillingsfürst in 1859), promptly (1877) gave the Beethoven Broadwood to the Hungarian national museum in Budapest, as Liszt had directed. Liszt also owned a spinet reputed to be that of Mozart's, see above, n. 233.

235. Kriehuber's original portrait drawing of Paganini (in the Albertina, Vienna), from which the direction-reversing lithograph was made, faces to the left and shows the violinist with a *black* cravat, the latest fashion in 1828, as we know from Schindler's indignant reaction to Kriehuber's substitution of a black cravat for the white one "which our Beethoven always wore" in his lithograph portrait of Beethoven, see chapter 2 and n. 94.

236. Grevedon's flattering portrait lithograph of Rossini was skillfully copied and distributed as a print (in which the features are slightly harsher) by the English engraver Albert Henry Payne (1812–1902), who from 1838 made his fame and fortune in Leipzig.

237. Although Danhauser obviously was able to work directly from the model in the case of his friend Liszt, it is still permissible to wonder, I think, whether the final proportions of the pianist's finely chiseled profile and jaw-bone length haircut did not perhaps get an *aide mémoire* boost from Kriehuber's handsome (and remarkably similar) profile portrait of Liszt, shown seated in a chair, done in 1838, two years before Danhauser's ambitious group portrait. For a reproduction of the Kriehuber portrait (showing Liszt with a *black* cravat, Schindler would have been quick to note) see Zsigmond László and Béla Mátéka, *Franz Liszt par l' image* (Budapest, 1978); ill. 104. (This all-embracing, slightly non-discriminatory picture album is the belated Hungarian answer to Robert Bory's fine *La vie de Franz Liszt par l' image* [Geneva, 1936].)

238. Walker, *Franz Liszt: The Virtuoso Years 1811–1847*, p. 151.

239. Not infrequently Dumas *père* is identified in books of recent vintage as Alfred de Musset underneath reproductions of Danhauser's *Liszt at the Piano* (the latest author to do so is Karl Schumann, who also misidentifies Hugo as Berlioz, see *Das Kleine Liszt-Buch* [Hamburg, 1981], Color pl. 3). George Sand's affair with Musset had expired in Italy in 1834.

Devéria also executed a handsome frontal portrait lithograph of Liszt (1832) and a charming portrait of

Paganini's son (c. 1831–32), whose first name, Achille, he shared.

240. Following Liszt's opening concert of 18 November 1839, where he played for the first time his Nohant-produced transcription of Beethoven's *Pastoral* Symphony. See Walker, *Franz Liszt: The Virtuoso Years 1811–1847*, p. 280.

241. As cited in Huneker, *Franz Liszt*, p. 214.

242. Ibid., p. 215. For a second eyewitness of this moonlit event in which a dying fire plays a part see Ernest Legouvé, *Soixante Ans de souvenirs*, 4 vols. (Paris, 1887); : 144–45.

243. Walker, *Franz Liszt: The Virtuoso Years 1811–1847*, p. 316 and n. 35.

244. Ibid., p. 358.

245. Ibid., p. 359.

246. As quoted in Perényi, *Liszt: The Artist as Romantic Hero*, p. 319.

247. Pointed out by Walker, *Franz Liszt: The Virtuoso Years 1811–1847*, p. 317 and n. 39.

248. See Walker's far-reaching discussion of Liszt as interpreter, ibid., pp. 316–18.

249. Given in Huneker, *Franz Liszt*, pp. 217–18.

250. One of Beethoven's later conversation books records that the "new English poets," Byron and Thomas Moore, were the subject of a visit with his friend the poet Christoph Kuffner. See Marek, *Beethoven: Biography of a Genius*, p. 585.

251. Walker, *Franz Liszt: The Virtuoso Years 1811–1847*, p. 280.

252. Liszt's every word and action during this Hungarian Return were observed and carefully noted down for posterity by his Austrian friend Franz Ritter von Schober in *Briefe über F. Liszt's Aufenthalt in Ungarn* (Berlin, 1843). For the narrative covered in my text, see Walker, *Franz Liszt: The Virtuoso Years 1811–1847*, pp. 60, 333–34.

253. La Mara, *Letters of Franz Liszt*, 1: 266 (written 17 March 1856, a year before Czerny's death).

254. Sonneck, *Beethoven: Impressions by his Contemporaries*, p. 27.

255. Ibid., p. 29. Czerny was contrasting Beethoven's playing to that of Hummel.

256. There is one exception to Kriehuber's wholesale mirror imagery: in the Danhauser original the featured musical composition—Beethoven's A-flat Major piano sonata—is the folded piece of music; in the (reversed) Kriehuber copy the Beethoven title has been switched to the upright music cover centered directly above Liszt's hands. The artist's intervention here confirms that we the viewers are to understand that Beethoven, not Paganini allà Liszt, is being performed.

257. Since Kriehuber's picture dates from 1846, the Paganini "Fantasia" must refer to Liszt's *Grande Fantaisie sur La Clochette de Paganini* of 1831–32.

258. La Mara, *Letters of Franz Liszt*, 1: 66, letter of 26 March 1845.

259. As quoted in Perényi, *Liszt: The Artist as Romantic Hero*, p. 61.

260. La Mara, *Letters of Franz Liszt*, 2: 369, letter of 11 November 1880 to the widow and author Anna Benfey-Schuppe, who had written Liszt with a list of questions about his Weimar career in preparation for bringing out a pamphlet (originally contemplated by her husband) to be called *Beethoven and Liszt*.

261. Ibid., 2: 299, letter of 21 June 1876. Both Beethoven and Liszt had been guests at these remote estates in Prussian and Austrian Silesia respectively.

262. Huneker, *Franz Liszt*, pp. 201–3.

263. Ibid., p. 204.

264. Ibid.

265. Schindler, *Beethoven As I Knew Him*, p. 28. Further anger is vented against Lenz, "the great virtuoso of conjectural criticism," ibid., p. 463.

266. La Mara, *Letters of Franz Liszt*, 1: 149–50, letter of 2 December 1852.

267. Ibid., 7: 150.

268. Schindler deals even more harshly with Oulibicheff than with Lenz, recognizing in the Mozart worshiper a "bitter, prejudiced adversary." Schindler, *Beethoven As I Knew Him*, p. 29.

269. La Mara, *Letters of Franz Liszt*, 1: 151–52.

270. Ibid., 1: 153.

271. Letter of 15 March 1842, as quoted in Walker, *Franz Liszt: The Virtuoso Years 1811–1847*, p. 374, n. 29. That Bettina was almost thirty years older than Liszt at the time of their first meeting did not allay the suspicions of Marie d'Agoult, who sensed (sometimes quite rightly) a rival in any woman whom Liszt found interesting. She took revenge by publishing under her brand new pseudonym, Daniel Stern, a biting critique of Bettina's writings. Bettina had come to Weimar in the fall of 1852 to help her friend Princess Carolyne Sayn-Wittgenstein arrange Liszt's rooms at the Altenburg.

272. La Mara, *Letters of Franz Liszt*, 2: 57, letter of 28 August 1863, written from Rome.

273. Ibid., p. 59.

274. Hallé, *The Autobiography of Charles Hallé*, p. 58.

275. Ibid., p. 61.

276. As cited by Frederick Niecks, *Frédérick Chopin as a Man and Musician*, 2 vols. (London, 1888), 1: 226.

277. Schindler, *Beethoven As I Knew Him*, pp. 119–20.

278. Ibid., p. 119.

279. Ibid., p. 413.

280. Ibid., p. 120.

281. The thoughtful Mozart worshiper Delacroix uses the same adjective "brusque" in referring to the "brusque novelty which we find today in Beethoven," Eugène Delacroix, *The Journal of Eugène Delacroix*, trans. Walter Pach (New York, 1937), p. 296, entry of 21 April 1853.

282. Delacroix reported the following observation by Chopin on the difference between Mozart and Beethoven: "Where the latter is obscure and seems lacking in unity, the cause is not to be sought in what people look upon as a rather wild originality, the thing they honor him for; the reason is that he turns his back on eternal principles; Mozart never." Ibid., p. 195, entry of 7 April 1849.

283. Niecks, *Frédérick Chopin as a Man and Musician*, 2: 104.

284. Ibid.

285. Ibid.

286. As cited in Casimir Wierzynski, *The Life and Death of Chopin* (New York, 1949), p. 182, letter to Delphine Potocka. We must be wary of this and other opinions purportedly expressed by Chopin in "letters" to the Countess Delphine Potocka however. A latter-day Bettina seems to have invaded the musicological scene of the mid–1940s in the person of Pauline Czernicka, who announced from Poland that she had chanced across a trove of letters from Chopin to Countess Po-

tocka—letters that revealed a surprisingly licentious and boastful Chopin, with peevish things to say about Liszt and with Freudiansounding analyses of his own musical sublimation. The "originals" of these highly suspect letters are, inexplicably, all torn into fragments and experts have not been able to authenticate them. For a full and witty discussion of this intriguing problem see Bernard Gavoty, *Frédéric Chopin* (New York, 1977), pp. 167–77.

287. Hallé, *The Autobiography of Charles Hallé*, p. 55. Op. 30 is inadvertently cited in Hallé's text, but since this comprises three sonatas for violin and piano and none is in the key of E-flat, Beethoven's opus 31—three piano sonatas with the last in E-flat Major—must have been what Hallé had in mind. This is confirmed in Niecks, *Frédérick Chopin as a Man and Musician*, 2: 110.

288. Franz Liszt, *Life of Chopin*, trans. John Broadhouse (London, 1879), pp. 179–80.

289. Gutmann's reminiscences of Chopin's Beethoven likes and dislikes were passed on to Niecks, *Frédérick Chopin as a Man and Musician*, 2: 110. Chopin played and taught Beethoven's piano sonatas up to op. 57 (the *Appassionata*) but not beyond.

290. Ibid., 2: 140.

291. As quoted in W. J. Turner, *Berlioz: The Man and His Work* (London, 1934), p. 183. Turner contests the idea that this remark was intended as a sneer.

292. Giovanni Giuseppi Cambini in the March 1811 issue of *Les Tablettes de Polymnie* (pp. 310f), as cited in Leo Schrade, *Beethoven in France* (New Haven, 1942), p. 3; see also chapter 3 of this book.

293. Hector Berlioz (*A travers chants*, Paris, 1862) *A Critical Study of Beethoven's Nine Symphonies*, trans. Edwin Evans, Sr. (1913; London, 1958), p. 123. (Cited hereafter as *Beethoven's Nine Symphonies*.)

294. As cited by Jacques Barzun, *Berlioz and the Romantic Century*, 2 vols. (1950; 3rd ed., New York, 1969), 2: ill. opposite p. 230.

295. Hallé, *The Autobiography of Charles Hallé*, p. 86.

296. As cited in Hugh Macdonald, *Berlioz* (London, 1982), p. 244.

297. Schumann's *Neue Zeitschrift* contributor from Brunswick, Wolfgang Robert Griepenkerl (see above, n. 141), was among the first to wax enthusiastic over Berlioz as the "French Beethoven." His *Das Musikfest, oder die Beethovener* of 1838 (reprinted in 1841) was followed in 1843 by a pamphlet, *Ritter Berlioz in Braunschweig, zur Charakteristik dieses Tondichter*, written in enthusiastic response to Berlioz's music and personality. We note in passing that it was no longer unusual (as it had been in Beethoven's day) for a composer to be called a *Tondichter*.

298. Hector Berlioz, *Memoirs*, trans. Rachel and Eleanor Holmes, annotated and revised trans. Ernest Newman, (1932; New York, 1966), p. 103.

299. Ibid.

300. It was a marriage doomed to failure, Berlioz's passion being, as Hiller aptly characterized, more a matter of his imagination than of his heart. Hector and Harriet (whom he always called Henriette) separated in 1844; their only child, Louis, died two years before Berlioz of yellow fever in Havana.

301. Hector Berlioz, *Berlioz: A Selection from His Letters*, ed. and trans. Humphrey Searle (1966; New York, 1973), pp. 26–28, written in March 1830.

302. Berlioz, *Memoirs*, pp. 49–50. The slow movement of Beethoven's Seventh Symphony was first inserted into the Second Symphony "in order to help to *pass off the remainder*" at the Concerts Spirituels of the Paris Opera, Berlioz tells us with disdain in *Beethoven's Nine Symphonies*, p. 25; see further p. 83.

303. Berlioz, *Memoirs*, pp. 75–76.

304. Ibid., p. 76. Habeneck was director of the Société des Concerts du Conservatoire from its foundation in 1828 until his death in 1849.

305. As cited by Schrade, *Beethoven in France*, p. 25 (obituary published 7 April 1827).

306. Berlioz, *Memoirs*, p. 76.

307. Ibid., p. 77.

308. Ibid., pp. 76–77. When Berlioz eagerly rushed off to see Lesueur the next day he found "a quite different being from the man of the day before. . . . But I persisted until Lesueur, after again admitting how deeply the symphony had affected him, shook his head with a curious smile, and said, 'All the same, such music ought not to be written.'" Ibid., p. 78.

309. As quoted by Schrade, *Beethoven in France*, p. 84.

310. Ibid., p. 83; see also p. 257, n. 15 concerning the fact that an important section of the Beethoven references in the original version of *William Shakespeare* has been left out of the complete edition of Hugo's *Oeuvres*.

311. Jacques Barzun's useful phrase; see Barzun, *Berlioz and the Romantic Century*, 1: 165. See also Barzun's persuasive discussion of how unliterally programmatic Berlioz's "programmatic" *Symphonie Fantastique* really is, ibid., 1: 152–67.

312. Schumann, *On Music and Musicians*, pp. 164–88; see especially p. 181.

313. As quoted by Schrade, *Beethoven in France*, p. 57.

314. Ibid., p. 65 (from Marie d'Agoult, *Mémoires 1833–1854* [Paris, 1927], p. 92). Berlioz agreed with this acknowledgment of the capacity of music to evoke interior memories. An interesting passage from the year 1847 reads: "Music is the sole art that has this retroactive power; no other, not even that of Shakespeare, can thus poetize the past it recalls. For music alone speaks at once to the imagination, the mind, the heart, and the senses. . . ." Berlioz, *Memoirs*, p. 443.

315. From Sand's *Lettres d'un voyageur*, as cited and translated by Schrade, *Beethoven in France*, p. 48.

316. Delacroix, *The Journal of Eugène Delacroix*, p. 194, entry of Friday evening, 6 April 1849.

317. Ibid., p. 190, entry of Sunday, 11 March 1849 (after hearing the *Pastoral*).

318. Ibid., p. 150, entry for 27 February 1847.

319. Ibid. This statement is almost autobiographical in its parallels with Delacroix's own personality; see chapter 6 and discussion of Delacroix's painting *Michelangelo in His Studio*, Fig. 190.

320. Ibid., p. 156, entry for 7 March 1847.

321. Ibid., p. 157, entry for 11 March 1847; written as he was approaching the age of fifty.

322. Ibid., p. 210, entry of Tuesday, 19 February 1850.

323. This epithet gleefully recorded by Berlioz himself, see *Memoirs*, p. 89. Delacroix does manifest a rare knowledge and precocious appreciation for Beethoven's laborious method of composing, however. A dozen years before Nottebohm published the first of his pioneering studies of Beethoven's creative process (*Ein Skizzenbuch von Beethoven*, 1865), Delacroix mused to himself in a diary entry of 26 October 1853: "In the case

of singular geniuses, one must not too greatly spare what are called their negligences, and what ought rather to be called the breaks in their work; they could not have done other than what they did do. Often they have sweated heavily over very weak or very disturbing passages. This state does not seem to be at all rare with Beethoven, whose manuscripts are often as full of corrections as those of Ariosto." Delacroix, *The Journal of Eugène Delacroix*, p. 341.

324. Letter of 2 March 1829 to his friend Albert Du Boys, as given in Turner, *Berlioz: The Man and His Work*, p. 110.

325. Perhaps even more overwhelmed by Beethoven's life trials was Berlioz's viola playing friend Chrétien Urhan (1790–1845), who in an article in *Le Temps* of 25 January 1838 discussed the Ninth Symphony of Beethoven as a "moral biography"; for an illuminating presentation of Urhan, one of the founders of the Société des Concerts du Conservatoire, see Schrade, *Beethoven in France*, pp. 59–60.

326. Letter to his sister Nanci, dated Paris, 29 March 1829, as given in Turner, *Berlioz: The Man and His Work*, p. 111.

327. Berlioz's serial biography of Beethoven appeared in the issues of 4 and 11 August and 8 October 1829.

328. As quoted in Turner, *Berlioz: The Man and His Work*, p. 118.

329. The coveted Prix de Rome came, ironically, at the very worst time for Berlioz from a personal and professional point of view. Temporarily giving up Harriet Smithson, he was assiduously courting a teenage pianist, Camille (Marie) Moke (who married the forty-two-year-old head of the Pleyel piano manufacturing firm a few weeks after Berlioz left for Italy), and he was tasting his first musical success in Paris (Habeneck conducted the premier of his *Symphonie Fantastique* on 5 December 1830, and such notables as Spontini, Meyerbeer, and the nineteen-year-old Liszt were in the audience). Realizing that he should stay in Paris to capitalize on his success he petitioned the Minister of the Interior to exempt him from the Roman sojourn, but neither this nor the attached doctor's certificate attesting his poor health and the supplications of his old teacher Lesueur, Spontini, and Meyerbeer had any effect! The winner of the Rome prize was ordered to get himself hence. A few weeks after his arrival in the Eternal City the eternal Ninth Symphony was played for the first time in a Berlioz-less Paris.

330. This anecdote was related by Antoine Elwart, first a pupil, then a professor at the Conservatoire, in his useful *Histoire de la Société des Concerts* (Paris, 1860) and picked up by Grove, *Beethoven and His Nine Symphonies*, p. 362, from where I have quoted it here.

331. Ibid.

332. Schindler, *Beethoven As I Knew Him*, p. 503.

333. Although Habeneck's father was from Mannheim, Schindler goes out of his way to tell us that Habeneck himself, having been born in Paris, "did not know a word of German." Ibid., p. 502, asterisked footnote. Schindler's life of Beethoven was translated into French and published in 1865, with a list of prominent subscribers at the front and a reversed (including the signature) engraved, "signed" portrait of Beethoven.

334. Anton Felix Schindler, *Biographie von Ludwig van Beethoven (Zweite, mit zwei Nachträgen vermehrte Ausgabe)*

(Münster [Aschendorff], 1845), Appendix No. 2, pp. 22–23 (long footnote taking up the body of the two pages; translation mine). Concerning the multiplication of Beethoven's portrait image in France, what Schindler next tells us not only is amusing but gets in a dig at Viennese veneration for Beethoven: "When, a few days later the Gazette musicale gave the news of this scene, whole processions of pilgrimages to the Beethoven picture started up, and even though this pleased me it also soon became a nuisance, because I lost so much time with it. The further consequences of that scene were that, yielding to the petition of the Comité of the Société des Concerts, I allowed a lithograph of large size to be made of Beethoven's portrait. There were as many copies printed of it as there were members of the Society. One feared a restrike.—I also have to note that a great number of Parisian artists were dissatisfied with the proceedings of the Society, calling it pure egotism, and reproaching me bitterly because of it. Everybody wanted prints of the portrait and to contribute to the costs. Since this wasn't possible, however, they sought comfort in deriding the incident, and one of the smaller papers found consolation in the fact 'that at the Museum in Vienna five very good portraits of Beethoven could be found of which one could have lithographs.' That however in Vienna neither a [Beethoven] museum nor a good portrait in oil of Beethoven exists, the Viennese know better than the Parisians." Ibid., p. 23.

335. The term "poetical," used so frequently by Berlioz in acknowledgment of the supreme achievements of Beethoven's music, is discussed at length with informative applications by Schrade, *Beethoven in France*, pp. 39–69. Schrade also perceives Beethoven's musical entry into France as "accompanied by an idea," pp. 36ff.

336. Burk, *Clara Schumann: A Romantic Biography*, p. 68.

337. Recalling this enforced period of residence in Italy, Berlioz the physically active Romantic weighed the good and the bad: "If we include some sport and riding, we get a clear idea of the agreeable routine in which my mental and physical existence was spent during my stay in Rome. If, on the other hand, you include the paralyzing effect of the sirocco, the ever increasing longing for musical pleasures, the sad recollections, the trial of finding myself exiled for two years from the musical world, and the actual, though perhaps inexplicable, impossibility of doing any work at the Academy, you will have some idea of the dejection from which I suffered." Berlioz, *Memoirs*, p. 142.

338. Ibid., p. 139.

339. Felix Mendelssohn Bartholdy, *Letters From Italy and Switzerland*, trans. Lady Wallace (London, 1862), pp. 125–26, letter to his mother of 29 March 1831.

340. Berlioz, *Berlioz: A Selection from His Letters*, p. 37, letter written to Hiller and others of 6 May 1831 from Nice (then still an Italian possession) where he had cut short his impetuous plan to return to Paris and confront (with pistols!) his fiancée upon learning of her engagement to Camille Pleyel.

341. Berlioz, *Memoirs*, p. 279; for a full account of this Roman period of Berlioz's friendship with Mendelssohn as well as the later renewed acquaintance in Leipzig, where at Berlioz's request the two "brother" musicians exchanged batons, see ibid., pp. 277–86. To this

section Berlioz added this slightly disillusioned foot-note, dated 25 May 1864: "I have just seen, in Felix Mendelssohn's letters recently published by his brother, in what his Roman friendship for me really consisted." Ibid., p. 277, n. 1.

342. Ingres, as a jury member, did at least protest the superficial basis on which Berlioz's musical composition was juried during his third attempt to win the Prix de Rome; see Berlioz's letter to his father of 2 August 1829 as given in Turner, *Berlioz: The Man and His Work*, p. 115.

343. Berlioz, *Berlioz: A Selection from His Letters*, pp. 75–76, letter dated 22 January 1839. We hear some news of other interesting friends in this same letter: "Heine is 'not happy'. Chopin is ill, in the Balearic Islands. Dumas drags his chain, which feels heavier every day. Mme Sand has a sick child. Hugo alone stands calm and strong." Ibid., p. 76.

344. Letter to his protégé, the pianist Theodore Ritter, dated 12 January 1856, as given in Turner, *Berlioz: The Man and His Work*, p. 284. See also Barzun, *Berlioz and the Romantic Century*, 2: 123, n. 67 for Berlioz's fervid pronouncement concerning "these two Jupiters [who] make but one god."

345. Berlioz, *Memoirs*, p. 164.

346. *Ibid.*, pp. 163–64.

347. Berlioz, *Beethoven's Nine Symphonies*, pp. 55–56.

348. Ibid., pp. 1–2.

349. Ibid., p. 7. As a former medical student, Berlioz's penchant for medical analogies is understandable, but one sometimes wonders how many pseudo-illnesses this pathology-prone Romantic might have diagnosed, had he followed a career in medicine.

350. Ibid., p. 151: this phrase was lavished by Berlioz on *Fidelio*.

351. Maria Felicita Malibran (1808–1836) recovered from her Beethoven convulsions and performed in an English version of *Fidelio* given in London in June of 1835.

352. Berlioz, *Beethoven's Nine Symphonies*, pp. 7–8.

353. In his forty-five-page essay on Beethoven's Ninth, Tovey approvingly cites Thomas Hardy's observation on astronomy "that when we come to such dimensions the sublime ceases and ghastliness begins." Tovey, *Essays in Musical Analysis*, 2: 41.

354. Berlioz, *Beethoven's Nine Symphonies*, pp. 8–9.

355. Berlioz's debut "débat" was an article on Beethoven's *Missa Solemnis*, published 25 January 1835.

356. Berlioz, *Beethoven's Nine Symphonies*, p. 121.

357. Ibid., p. 122.

358. We shall not deprive ourselves of the sentences—few but uncritical—that Schindler set down about the French Beethoven. Here they are (intended to discredit Czerny and his claim that he had found living traces of the Beethoven tradition in Vienna): "Hector Berlioz, who was well acquainted with all the European capitals, gives us an account of the general understanding of Beethoven's music at that time [1830s] throughout the world of art in an article published in the *Journal des Débats* of 11 August 1852. He confesses there that among all the virtuosi he has heard, he is hardly able to name six capable of playing Beethoven's music with true understanding of its spirit. We know from his travel diary how accurately he evaluated matters in the Austrian capital." Schindler, *Beethoven As I Knew Him*, pp. 408–9.

359. Ibid., p. 484, Supplement G; this relates to events in the year 1846 when, at the Lower Rhine Musical Festival held in Aachen, Mendelssohn announced the discovery of a letter from Beethoven to his publisher calling the two measures in question "a great blunder," meaning, Schindler asserted, the fact that the notes were erroneously printed as half notes rather than as separated quarter notes, as in the succeeding two "correct" measures. From Berlioz we learn the not so astonishing news that he had actually received a letter from Schindler about this matter in 1850: "M. Schindler's purpose was to thank me for *not* having made the correction. M. Schindler, who spent his life with Beethoven [Berlioz had swallowed the Schindler myth whole], does not believe in an engraver's mistake, and he assured me that he had heard the two famous bars in every performance of the symphony that had taken place *under Beethoven himself*." Berlioz, in *Berlioz: Evenings with the Orchestra*, trans. Jacques Barzun (New York, 1956), p. 321 (Second Epilogue). For more 19th-century discussion on this subject, see Grove, *Beethoven and His Nine Symphonies*, pp. 174–76.

360. Schrade was the first to point this out, see Schrade, *Beethoven in France*, p. 51, and n. 644.

361. Berlioz, *Beethoven's Nine Symphonies*, p. 31. (The analytical studies of all nine Beethoven symphonies were collected and published by Berlioz in *Voyage musicale en Allemagne et en Italie* [Paris, 1844].) Berlioz does point out the "only real novelty" of the still Mozart-like First Symphony: "the scherzo is the first born of that family of charming humorous pieces of which Beethoven invented the form, and determined the movement; and which he substituted in nearly all his instrumental works for the minuet of Mozart and Haydn. . . ." Ibid., p. 30.

362. Ibid., pp. 30–31. We recall that Berlioz was also put out with Beethoven's *The Ruins of Athens* overture. French taste could differ: it was just this piece and this piece exclusively that Toulouse-Lautrec would request his friend Misia, wife of the *Revue blanche* editor, Thadée Natanson, to play on the piano for him (see Maria Cionini Visani, *Toulouse-Lautrec* [New York, 1971], p. 2).

363. Ibid., p. 31.

364. Printed in Vienna's *Zeitung für die Elegante Welt*, May 1804, as quoted and translated in Nicolas Slonimsky, *Lexicon of Musical Invective* (1953; Seattle, 1972), p. 42.

365. Berlioz, *Beethoven's Nine Symphonies*, p. 35.

366. Ibid., pp. 36–37. Berlioz imputes a far happier state of mind to Beethoven during the time he completed the Second Symphony than the year indicates—1802 was the date of the Heiligenstadt Testament.

367. Ibid., p. 41.

368. Ibid., pp. 44–45.

369. Curiously not in the essay entitled "Symphony No. 3 in E Flat"—the last paragraphs of which are devoted to recording absurd opinions on the Ninth Symphony—but in Berlioz's essay devoted, titularly at least, to Beethoven's "Symphony No. 5 in C Minor." See ibid., pp. 61–68, especially pp. 61–62.

370. Ibid., pp. 61–62. Concerning Beethoven's own preferences in Homer, Schindler in his 1860 edition of the biography (written after Berlioz's Beethoven essays) remarked: "It is interesting that in Beethoven's

447

estimation the *Iliad* was far inferior to the *Odyssey*." Schindler, *Beethoven As I Knew Him*, p. 378.

371. This might be the place to insert a famous example of the purist point of view concerning the *Eroica*. After the first few moments of a rehearsal of Beethoven's Third Symphony at Queen's Hall, London, in 1937, Arturo Toscanini stopped the orchestra and admonished the players: "No! No! Nein! Is-a not Napoleon! Is-a not 'Itler! Isa not Mussolini! Is Allegro con brio!" As lovingly quoted by a witness to the event, Spike Hughes, *The Toscanini Legacy* (1959; New York, 1969), p. 39.

372. Berlioz, *Beethoven's Nine Symphonies*, p. 41.

373. Ibid., p. 46.

374. Ibid., p. 53.

375. Ibid., pp. 56–57.

376. Berlioz, *Berlioz: A Selection from His Letters*, p. 192, letter to Humbert Ferrand of 10 November 1864.

377. Berlioz, *Beethoven's Nine Symphonies*, p. 62.

378. Ibid., p. 63.

379. Ibid., pp. 62–63.

380. Ibid., p. 62.

381. Ibid., p. 67.

382. Ibid., p. 71.

383. Of Théophile Gautier's (1811–1872) "trinity of Romanticism" (Hugo, Delacroix, and Berlioz), the great painter and the superb musician, so alike in many ways, simply did not appeal to each other. Berlioz does allude appreciatively to Delacroix's painting of *Ophelia* (based on *his* Miss Smithson) in his *Memoirs* (pp. 470–71), and he held no malice towards the painter professionally—in fact it was Berlioz who would help effect Delacroix's election (10 January 1857) to the French Academy.

384. Berlioz, *Beethoven's Nine Symphonies*, p. 71.

385. Ibid., pp. 71–72.

386. Ibid., p. 45. Wagner and Kandinsky were also notably synesthetic.

387. Ibid., p. 72.

388. Ibid. In contrast to this "immediate" or proto-Impressionist concept of Berlioz, is Schumann's "cumulative" reading: "When Beethoven conceived and carried out his idea for the *Pastoral* Symphony, it was not a single short spring day that inspired him to utter his cry of joy, but the dark commingling of lofty songs above us...." Schumann, *On Music and Musicians* p. 96; see also text above in the discussion of Schumann's image of Beethoven.

389. Berlioz, *Beethoven's Nine Symphonies*, p. 75.

390. Ibid., p. 74.

391. Ibid., pp. 77–79.

392. Ibid., p. 103.

393. Ibid., pp. 103–4.

394. Ibid., p. 104.

395. Ibid.

396. Ibid., p. 105.

397. Ibid. Tovey tells us that Hans von Bülow once mischievously played the "Oh, friends, not these sounds" exhortation theme on the piano after having to follow a particularly poor singer. Tovey, *Essays in Musical Analysis*, 2:39, n. 1.

398. Berlioz, *Beethoven's Nine Symphonies*, p. 110. Beethoven would certainly have been in complete agreement with Berlioz here!

399. Ibid., pp. 110–11.

400. Ibid., p. 111.

401. By Désiré Martin-Beaulieu (1791–1863).

402. Berlioz, *Beethoven's Nine Symphonies*, p. 112.

403. The term "bizarre" had already been hurled at Berlioz by his bête noir, the learned (but conservative) musical littérateur François Joseph Fétis (1784–1871), in his *Biographie Universelle des Musiciens* (Brussels, 1837). Fétis was once Berlioz's supporter at the Conservatoire, but after the "corrections" he had proposed for a French edition of Beethoven had been indignantly revealed to the public by Berlioz (see Berlioz, *Memoirs*, pp. 192–95) hostilities ensued. (The beautiful *L'Enfance du Christ* oratorio of 1854 reconciled Fétis to Berlioz.) Schindler was none too happy about Fétis's designation of his hero as a "skinflint and a miser." See Schindler, *Beethoven As I Knew Him*, p. 304.

404. Berlioz, *Beethoven's Nine Symphonies*, p. 115. See p. 116 for Berlioz's French version of the Schiller words. The phrase "celui qui possède une femme aimable" (ibid., p. 116) must have struck home with particular irony for Berlioz since by now his marriage to the once coveted Harriet Smithson had become one of mutual misery. By 1841 Berlioz had found comfort with the singer Marie Recio (1814–1862) with whom he set up a second and separate household. After Harriet died in March 1854 Hector and Marie were married, but he was to outlive his second wife as well. The death of his son in 1867 (see above, n. 300) was another crushing blow.

405. Ibid., p. 117. Berlioz gives a further medley of vastly differing reactions to Beethoven's Ninth at the end of his essay on the *Eroica*. Ibid., pp. 49–50. His conclusion, after parading his cast of mostly ludicrous critiques, is to "prefer the foolish view of beauty being absolute." Ibid., p. 50.

406. The New Philharmonic Society lasted fifteen years and its final concert (20 March 1867) featured Clara Schumann as the solo pianist in Beethoven's *Choral Fantasia*.

407. Berlioz, *Berlioz: A Selection from His Letters*, p. 121, letter dated London, Saturday, 12 June [1852]. Berlioz's informed conducting of Beethoven did not need the sort of showmanship with which a fellow French conductor had dazzled London a few years earlier. This was Louis Antoine Jullien (1812–1860), who, *Punch* reported, conducted all pieces by Beethoven with a jewelled baton, and wearing a pair of kid gloves (see Berlioz, *Memoirs*, p. 456, editor's note). Berlioz recounts his own dramatic experiences with the "mad" Jullien (he actually did die in a lunatic asylum) during his first stay in London (1847–48), see *Memoirs*, pp. 454–56.

408. This is Berlioz's own description of his book, see his letter to Joseph d' Ortigue dated London, 5 May [1852] in Berlioz, *Berlioz: A Selection from His Letters*, p. 120. Berlioz's review of the Lenz book originally appeared in the *Journal des Débats* on 11 August 1852.

409. Berlioz's *Beethoven's Nine Symphonies*, pp. 162–65. The essay records the listeners' dismay and disappointment in this new style, "for there is no mistake about the sonata in the sense that it is *no semi-piece of nonsense*. It is, on the contrary, a fine full-blown piece of nonsense...." Ibid., p. 164.

410. Berlioz, *Memoirs*, p. 226.

411. Ibid., p. 227. Berlioz gives Paganini's note in the original Italian and I have done the same, spacing the lines as the great violinist wrote them, placing the name "Berlioz" directly under the name "Beethoven" (see

Fig. 86). As to his signature, Paganini signed his Christian name, according to mood, with three variant spellings: Niccolò, Nicola, and—as here—Nicolò.

412. Translation mine.

413. Berlioz, *Memoirs*, pp. 227–29. Berlioz immediately penned an ("inadequate") letter of thanks to Paganini, dated the same day as his benefactor's, 18 December 1838: "Great and worthy artist: How can I express my gratitude? I am not rich; but, believe me, the approbation of a man of such genius as yours touches me a thousand times more deeply than the royal generosity of your gift. Words fail me; I will hasten to embrace you as soon as I can leave my bed, to which I am still confined today. H. Berlioz." Ibid., p. 228, n. 1.

414. Hallé, *The Autobiography of Charles Hallé*, p. 90.

415. But it *had*. Modern scholarship has turned up two letters written by Paganini, both dated 17 December 1838, the first to his Genoa banker Migone requesting him to pay a sight draft for twenty thousand francs which he had that morning received against the draft from Rothschild, and the second to his Genoa lawyer of many years Germi, notifying him of the double transaction so that it would go through without any complications, see de Courcy, *Paganini the Genoese*, 2:289 and reproductions of the two letters opposite pp. 184, 185. The originals are now in the Liceo Musicale Nicolò Paganini in Genoa.

416. As cited in Slonimsky, *Lexicon of Musical Invective*, p. 57.

417. Letter dated 20 December 1838 to his sister Adèle, as given in Turner, *Berlioz: The Man and His Work*, p. 214.

418. Berlioz, *Evenings in the Orchestra*, trans. C. R. Fortescue (Harmondsworth [Middlesex], 1963), pp. 166–67 (Sixteenth Evening). I agree with Barzun that a better translation for the English title of this book would be "Evenings with the Orchestra," as this more clearly conveys the notion that the narrator (Berlioz) is down in the pit with the chatty musicians, rather than sitting as a passive listener in the auditorium. See Barzun, *Berlioz and the Romantic Century*, 2:54, n. 1, and his own translation of *Les Soirées de l' Orchestre*, cited above in n. 359.

419. Berlioz, *Memoirs*, pp. 230–31.

420. Article in the *Presse* of 11 December 1839, as given in Turner, *Berlioz: The Man and His Work*, p. 220.

421. Spontini's remark is quoted by Berlioz in a letter to his father of 5 December 1830, as given in ibid., p. 144. Berlioz devoted the Thirteenth Evening of his Soirées to a sympathetic biography of Spontini, who, like Beethoven, became deaf, but only at the end of a long life.

422. As quoted in Barzun, *Berlioz and the Romantic Century*, 1:97, n. 35. Barzun is mistaken when he says that Marx "then" (1846 or afterwards) invited Berlioz to contribute to the "Berlin *Musikalische Zeitung*" (ibid.), because that periodical only had a run of seven years, from 1824 to 1830. Berlioz's contribution to Marx's *Berliner allgemeine musikalische Zeitung* was in the year 1829.

423. See above, n. 297.

424. As quoted by Barzun, ibid., 2:47 and n. 58.

425. As cited in Turner, *Berlioz: The Man and His Work*, p. 265, n. 3. (Her age is incorrectly given by Turner as seventy-two.) If Bettina only came to look, another distinguished person—blind since childhood—had come expressly to listen. Berlioz reported

with pride: "My chief claquer is the king himself. He and the queen have insisted on coming to all my rehearsals. 'I cannot see you conducting, but I can sense it,' he said." Letter to his sister Adèle, dated Hanover, 17 November 1853, in Berlioz, *Berlioz: A Selection from His Letters*, p. 124.

426. As given in Turner, *Berlioz: The Man and His Work*, p. 344.

427. Ibid., letter of 15 December 1867 to Edouard Alexandre.

428. Berlioz, *Berlioz: A Selection from His Letters*, p. 157, letter to Humbert Ferrand, dated 26 November 1858.

429. Berlioz, *Memoirs*, pp. 373–74.

430. Berlioz, *Evenings in the Orchestra*, p. 217. Berlioz's most felicitous use of the eagle simile to convey the uplifting character of Beethoven's music is the following: " . . . one of those superhuman adagios where Beethoven's genius soars upwards, immense and solitary as the colossal bird of the snowy heights of Chimborazo." Berlioz, *Memoirs*, p. 338. We have seen how willingly Berlioz turned not just his phrases but his energies to the service and promotion of Beethoven, and indeed we find him in the 1850s helping the singer Louis Paulin establish the curriculum for a private Beethoven Music School in Paris.

431. Gluck, Weber, and Beethoven were not the only Germanic composers cherished by Berlioz. He used his pen to express admiration for a contemporary musician from Vienna who, with his twenty-eight-man orchestra, had taken Paris by storm in the fall of 1837, Johann Strauss, Sr. (1804–1849). Of him Berlioz wrote the following, his thoughts turning to Beethoven in a discerning comparison: "The influence [Strauss] has already exercised over musical feeling throughout Europe in introducing cross rhythms into waltzes is not sufficiently appreciated. . . . If, out of Germany, the public at large can be induced to understand the singular charm frequently resulting from contrary rhythms, it will be entirely owing to Strauss. Beethoven's marvels in this style are too far above them, and act at present only upon exceptional hearers; Strauss had addressed himself to the masses. . . ." Berlioz, *Memoirs*, p. 376. As for Strauss's own feeling for Beethoven, perhaps the most telling example is the fact that for several years he nursed a grudge against one of the members of his orchestra because he had failed to come in on cue during the prelude to *Fidelio* ("Beethoven is sacred!"). See H. E. Jacob, *Johann Strauss, Father and Son: A Century of Light Music* (Richmond [Virginia], 1940), p. 75.

432. Published in *Revue et gazette musicale*, 27 May 1855, as given in Macdonald, *Berlioz*, pp. 205–6.

433. As pointed out and cited by Barzun, *Berlioz and the Romantic Century*, 2:76. The article from which Barzun quotes was written by Cornelius in 1854.

434. Berlioz, *Memoirs*, p. 467.

435. Ibid., p. 518.

436. Ibid., p. 530.

437. Claude Debussy, *Debussy on Music*, trans. Richard Langham Smith (New York, 1977), p. 117. (Published in *Gil Blas*, 16 February 1903.)

438. Bizet, letter of 31 December 1858 as cited in Winton Dean, *Bizet* (1948; London, 1975), p. 240. At this point in his career (he had won a Prix de Rome) Bizet felt that "while adoring Beethoven . . . with all my faculties, I feel my nature brings me to love art that is pure

and fluent [like that of Mozart and Rossini] rather than dramatic passion." Ibid.

439. Ibid., p. 241, written in March 1867 to his pupil Paul Lacombe. It is not generally remembered that Bizet was an unusually talented pianist (even Liszt was impressed by him). One of his favorite keyboard compositions, which he played extremely well according to all reports, was Beethoven's Thirty-Two Variations in C Minor (WoO 80). At the time of his death from a heart attack at the age of thirty-six Bizet's musical library boasted almost the complete works of Beethoven.

440. Romain Rolland, *Beethoven* (1903), trans. B. Constance Hull (London, 1927), p. v., from Rolland's fervid and soon famous preface, an address to the French nation to emulate Beethoven, who conquered against all adversity. The preface quotes Beethoven's injunction: "O man, help thyself" taken out of Moscheles's context (see chapter 2), and ends: "May we be inspired by his noble words. Animated by the example of this man's faith in life and his giant confidence in himself, let us again take heart." Ibid., p. viii. For other French writers on the image of Beethoven after Berlioz, especially Edgar Quinet and his annexation of Beethoven to the socialist cause (about the *Freude* theme in the Ninth, Quinet wrote that it was the Marseillaise of humanity), see Schrade, *Beethoven in France*, pp. 134–36, and chapters 4 and 5.

441. The influential and extremely conservative critic P. (Pierre, Paul) Scudo (1806–1864), the "Beckmesser" of Paris, whose hatred of the whole modern school caused him to revile Wagner and Liszt and actively to hamper the success of Berlioz's work; as quoted in Barzun, *Berlioz and the Romantic Century*, 1:338.

442. Richard Wagner, *My Life*, 2 vols. (New York, 1911), 1:235. At the request of King Ludwig II, Wagner composed and dictated the story of his life to Cosima during the years 1865–70. The lengthy results were privately printed in an edition of eighteen in 1870. The first public edition (supervised by Cosima) was *Mein Leben*, 2 vols. (Munich, 1911) and the first authentic edition was published in Munich in 1963.

443. Wagner, *My Life*, 1:235.

444. Berlioz, *Memoirs*, p. 289 (letter to Ernst).

445. Cosima Wagner, *Cosima Wagner's Diaries*, trans. Geoffrey Skelton, 2 vols. (New York, 1978 and 1980) (original ed., Cosima Wagner, *Die Tagebücher*, ed. Martin Gregory-Dellin and Dietrich Mack, 2 vols. [Munich, 1976–77]), 1:527, entry of 23 August 1872. The sad monologue faithfully taken down by Liszt's daughter continues: "And none of my contemporaries has ever given me the impression of being truly great . . . Schopenhauer? Him I missed meeting . . . your father looked as though he would become great, but—!" ibid. We may presume that Cosima did not even blink at this dismissal of her father from the halls of genius, so complete was her devotion to Wagner.

446. Wagner, *My Life*, 1:36.

447. Ibid., 1:30. How different Debussy's opinion: " . . . a song by Beethoven bearing the somewhat old-fashioned title of 'Adelaïde.' I think the old man must have forgotten to burn this piece, and we must put the blame for its execution on his greedy heirs." Debussy, *Debussy on Music*, pp. 95–96.

448. Wagner, *My Life*, 1:36.

449. Ibid., 1:35–36.

450. Ibid., 1:44. Comparison of Wagner with his "en-emy brother descended from Beethoven" now ends: Wilhelmine Schröder-Devrient did not become Wagner's Harriet Smithson; she was exclusively his musical muse. In her own right, Schröder-Devrient deserves a place in our Beethoven mythography. It was her creation of the Leonore role that at last brought the revival of *Fidelio* to its just success (Beethoven had been present at the first performance of the revival on 3 November 1822 and afterwards thanked her, patted her cheek, and promised to write an opera for her), but she also considered it her life mission to further the works of her countrymen. In 1830 she traveled to Paris (dropping in at Weimar to sing for Goethe) to join a German opera company with this messianic motivation: "I had to think not only of my own reputation but to establish German music. *My* failure would have been injurious to the music of Beethoven, Mozart, and Weber." (From C. von Glümer, *Erinnerungen an Wilhelmine Schröder-Devrient* [Leipzig, 1862], as quoted in *Grove's Dictionary of Music and Musicians*, 3rd ed., 4:578). We know that she converted Goethe to Schubert's setting of his *Erlkönig*; perhaps she also sang Beethoven's *Adelaïde* for the old man—it was one of her specialties and Mendelssohn has described the furor raised by her impromptu rendition of it, dressed in ordinary traveling clothes, at the Gewandhaus concert of 11 February 1841. Ibid. Schumann said of her that she was the only singer who could last out a song with Liszt as accompanist!

451. She sang the roles of Adriano Colonna in *Rienzi*, Senta in *The Flying Dutchman*, and Venus in *Tannhäuser*.

452. Wagner, *Cosima Wagner's Diaries*, 1:475, entry of 7 April 1872. Wagner's mind was very much on Beethoven at the time: he was preparing to conduct the Ninth Symphony at the stone-laying ceremony in Bayreuth (22 May 1872).

453. John N. Burk, ed., *Letters of Richard Wagner: The Burrell Collection* (New York, 1972), p. 46, letter dated Berlin, 23 May 1836 to Minna in Königsberg. It was true. Time and time again Minna suffered privation to sustain the impoverished Richard or to revive a freshly financially ruined Richard; in the end her obsession with security was matched only by her bitterness at her husband's many infidelities. They saw each other for the last time in 1862; Richard did not attend her funeral (28 June 1866). On August 1870 Richard (aged fifty-seven) and Cosima (aged thirty-three) married (Cosima's divorce from Hans von Bülow came through on 18 July 1870). For Cosima their marriage was not dissolved by death. After Richard died on 13 February 1883, the rest of her exceptionally long life was spent in the thrall and promotion of the Wagner myth. She died on 1 April 1930 at the age of ninety-two.

454. Herbert Barth, Dietrich Mack, Egon Voss, eds., *Wagner, A Documentary Study* (New York, 1975), p. 152. The handsomely penned letter is reproduced on p. 153.

455. La Mara, *Letters of Franz Liszt*, 2:42–43, letter to Brietkopf and Härtel of 26 March 1863, written in Rome.

456. Wagner calls Hoffmann his favorite author at that time and described this period when he "really lived and breathed in Hoffmann's artistic atmosphere of ghosts and spirits." See Wagner, *My Life*, 1:38. Modern scholarship has unearthed a Hoffmann-Wagner connection that Wagner never knew: entries of 17 June and 31 December of 1813 in Hoffmann's diary mention meeting and liking Wagner's father (Karl Friedrich Wilhelm Wagner, who died at the age of forty-three, just

six months after Richard was born)—"an exotic fellow"—and Wagner's uncle (Adolf Wagner, 1774–1835, a formative influence on his young nephew)—"a learned man—speaks 1,700 languages." See Barth, Mack, Voss, *Wagner, A Documentary Study*, p. 149.

457. Wagner, *My Life*, 1:42–43.

458. Burk, *Letters of Richard Wagner: The Burrell Collection*, pp. 452–53.

459. Wagner, *Cosima Wagner's Diaries*, 1:449. Ernest Newman, whose extensive biography of Wagner, *The Life of Richard Wagner*, 4 vols. (1933–47; London, 1976), was written without the benefit of Cosima Wagner's diaries, made an understandable error in presuming that the Christmas gift of 1880 given by Richard to Cosima (see text below) was the 1830 piano arrangement of Beethoven's Ninth. See ibid., 4:633. The Christmas gift was in fact Wagner's careful copy of the orchestra score to the Ninth, also made in his youth. See text below and n. 460.

460. Wagner, *Cosima Wagner's Diaries*, 2:582. In 1849 Wagner had given this youthful exercise of fearful dimension to his good friend from Dresden years Theodor Uhlig (1822–1853). The loyal Uhlig, who made the piano transcription of *Lohengrin*, died young of tuberculosis, and remained a beloved memory for Wagner. "I believe my copies of the C minor Symphony [Fifth] and the Ninth Symphony by Beethoven are still preserved as souvenirs," Wagner the modest autohistorian had said in *My Life* (1:42), completed in 1870. Ten years later he obviously remembered exactly where his copy of the Ninth was being preserved and he successfully talked Uhlig's heir into returning the manuscript to him.

461. About the 1830 *Paukenschlag* Overture in B-flat Major (that of the famous, irretractable kettledrum bang on the second beat of every fifth bar; see Wagner, *My Life*, 1:63–65), Wagner said it was the "outcome of my study of Beethoven's Ninth Symphony" (ibid., p. 63); "My D minor Overture [1831] . . . clearly showed the influence of Beethoven's *Coriolanus* Overture" (ibid., p. 70). Concerning his overture to *König Enzio* (1832) he wrote, "again Beethoven's influence made itself even more strongly felt" (ibid.), and of the big Symphony in C Major (1832) he reminisced: "in this work I showed what I had learnt by using the influence of my study of Beethoven . . . the passionate and bold element of the *Sinfonia Eroica* was distinctly discernible, especially in the first movement" (ibid., p. 71).

462. Wagner, *Mein Leben*, 1:40, p. 47.

463. Wagner, *My Life*, 1:42.

464. Wagner, *Cosima Wagner's Diaries*, 1:450, entry of 17 January 1872. Wagner was again preoccupied with performing the Ninth at the stone-laying ceremonies for Bayreuth.

465. For Wagner's description of the slaughter of Beethoven's Ninth at the hands of one Christian August Pohlenz (1790–1843; Mendelssohn's predecessor at the Gewandhaus), see his amusing account in *My Life*, 1:69–70.

466. Ibid., 1:214–15.

467. Ibid., 1:215.

468. Ibid.

469. Schindler quotes Beethoven as saying in 1823: "Once this period is over [of writing to earn money], I hope to write the thing closest to my heart, the most sublime work of art: *Faust.*" *Beethoven As I Knew Him*, p. 252, see also p. 455.

470. See chapter 2, n. 112, and chapter 3 concerning the story of the roast veal dinner young Schlesinger once provided Beethoven.

471. Wagner, *My Life*; 1:213; see further pp. 227–28, 229, 232–33.

472. Ibid., 1:233.

473. The story, for which Wagner had to pay a hefty translation fee to Schlesinger, was published serially on 19, 22, 29 November, and 3 December 1840.

474. Wagner, *My Life*, 1:77; see pp. 75–77. Curiously, Wagner makes no mention in his autobiography of seeking out Beethoven's house(s) or grave. Also, he seems to have had no opportunity to hear music by Beethoven, but rather that of Gluck, Cherubini; a great deal of "the magic violinist" Johann Strauss (ibid., p. 77); and the new French opera *Zampa*, by Ferdinand Hérold (1791–1833). On his second trip to Vienna (July 1848) Wagner "received a very nice impression of Herr Grillparzer, the poet, whose name was like a fable to me . . ." (ibid., p. 446). Wagner was in Beethoven's Vienna again in the early 1860s, hoping to make it a base for his musical activities (1861; 1862—his first concert at the Theater an der Wien; 1863; 1864—had to flee the city because of debts), and once again with Cosima in May 1872, where she reported "the country around Vienna pleases him, he can imagine Beethoven in it and recognize the atmosphere of many of the sonatas. . . ." Wagner, *Cosima Wagner's Diaries*, 1:483, entry of 6 May 1872.

475. Robert L. Jacobs and Geoffrey Skelton, eds. and trans., *Wagner Writes from Paris* . . . (New York, 1973), p. 65.

476. Ibid.

477. Ibid., p. 66.

478. Ibid., p. 69. Wagner's actual words are "als das tiefe, innige Bedürfnis einer enthusiastischen Seele." Richard Wagner, *Dichtungen und Schriften*, 10 vols. (Frankfurt, 1983), 5:93.

479. Jacobs and Skelton, *Wagner Writes from Paris* . . . , pp. 72–73.

480. Ibid., p. 76.

481. Wagner's imagination seems to have furnished this red stomach band; no such item appears in the meticulous inventory of Beethoven's clothing and personal linen (see Thayer-Forbes, *Thayer's Life of Beethoven*, p. 1074) although the famous blue overcoat is indeed accounted for.

482. Jacobs and Skelton, *Wagner Writes from Paris* . . . , p. 77.

483. Ibid., p. 78.

484. Ibid., p. 81.

485. Ibid.

486. Ibid., p. 82. This delightful revenge may not have been just an invention on Wagner's part. There is a second-hand Schindler connection confirming the story. Cosima's diary entry of 2 October 1878—thirty-eight years after publication of "A Pilgrimage to Beethoven"—reads: "After supper we come to talk about his Beethoven story and he recalls in amusement that his sister O[ttile] had known Reichardt, and the anecdote about the X had been told him by Schindler's sister, a singer in Magdeburg." Wagner, *Cosima Wagner's Diaries*, 2:162.

487. The first German publication of Wagner's story, *Eine Pilgerfahrt zu Beethoven*, was also in 1840, in the

Dresdener Abendzeitung. Another literary project of Wagner's Paris years went unrealized but deserves mention as an example of his unflagging—almost psychologically necessary—devotion to his fellow German composer while still a struggling unknown himself. Early in his Paris stay Wagner made the acquaintance of Gottfried Engelbert Anders (1795–1866), an eccentric, impoverished musicologist of mysterious origins—as his pseudonym Anders (Other) suggested—who worked in the Bibliothèque Royale and who had for years been collecting data for a Beethoven biography. Wagner suggested they collaborate and that they present their subject in the form of a *Künstlerroman.* No publisher for their intended Beethoven novel was found however. For more on this, see Klaus Kropfinger, *Wagner und Beethoven* (Regensburg, 1975), pp. 72–79.

488. Wagner, *My Life,* 1:233.

489. Jacobs and Skelton, *Wagner Writes from Paris . . . ,* p. 101. (The English title of Wagner's sequel has been nicely shortened by the translators to "Death in Paris.")

490. Wagner, *My Life,* 1:233. Wagner had recently met Heine in Paris at the home of his friend the writer Heinrich Laube (1806–84). "Death in Paris" remained one of Wagner's favorite stories and as late as 1878 we find him reading it aloud to Cosima (Wagner, *Cosima Wagner's Diaries,* 2:173, entry of 17 October). Two years later, in honor of Beethoven's birthday, they were reading "reminiscences of him by a Herr Louis Schlösser, which reminds us of R.'s short story. . . ." Ibid., 2:577, entry of 17 December 1880.

491. Jacobs and Skelton, *Wagner Writes from Paris . . . ,* p. 133.

492. Ibid., pp. 130–31.

493. Wagner, *My Life,* 1:268.

494. As impeccably translated from the "somewhat im perfect French" by Barzun, *Berlioz and the Romantic Century,* 2:174. There could certainly be a second meaning to Wagner's concluding line hoping that if he expresses himself badly, Berlioz will not understand him badly. Wagner had just attacked Berlioz's review of his concerts in a letter to the press in which he pretended not to understand Berlioz's remarks, and this phrase could be a signal that the public Wagner is not to be taken too literally. Berlioz's answer to Wagner's letter, written the following day, is a fine example of the tired "remove" which so irked Wagner, who was accustomed to sucking all acquaintances into the vortex of his enthusiasms:

"Paris, 23 May 1860

I am very glad that you liked my articles on *Fidelio.* I worked on them with care, but without any hope that they would be of the least use to anybody. . . . I do not know if you still have illusions; for my part, for many years now I have seen things as they are. You at least are full of ardor and ready for the struggle; I am only ready to sleep and to die. All the same I still feel a kind of feverish joy whenever my love for the beautiful finds an answering echo. . . . So I thank you for your letter: it has done me good. . . . So it was your birthday yesterday? You Germans are very punctilious about such occasions. . . . [Wagner had insisted on pointing out in print that Berlioz, being French, could never truly be the inheritor of the Beethoven mantle; was Berlioz having his private revenge here, one wonders?] Farewell, good day, courage, and don't call me 'dear master' any more: it annoys me. Kindest regards." Berlioz, *Berlioz:*

A Selection From His Letters, p. 167. Barzun points out that the *Fidelio* revival came at an opportune time for Berlioz, pulling him out of a deep depression and reawakening his own creative vitality. Barzun, *Berlioz and the Romantic Century,* 2:175.

495. As quoted in Turner, *Berlioz: the Man and His Work,* p. 289.

496. Berlioz's only comments on Wagner include the already cited sympathetic summary of his first Paris period (see text above and n. 444) and some hot and cold remarks on *Rienzi* and *The Flying Dutchman,* both of which he heard in Dresden in 1843, where Wagner, only just installed as a conductor there, assisted Berlioz with rehearsals of his own music "with both zeal and goodwill." Berlioz, *Memoirs,* p. 289. An entry by Cosima for 7 May 1870 makes two references to Richard's reading the Berlioz *Memoirs.* Wagner, *Cosima Wagner's Diaries,* 1:217.

497. Wagner, *Cosima Wagner's Diaries,* 1:373.

498. See text in chapter 2 and chapter 3, n. 59.

499. Oddly enough, Wagner dedicated only one sentence to this visit in his autobiography (Wagner, *My Life,* 2:734) and gave no details when he published his obituary on Rossini, see chapter 3, n. 58.

500. The photographs of Rossini (Fig. 91) and Wagner (see Fig. 89) reproduced in this book are taken from photograph cards given to Michotte in the year of their interview, 1860. The photograph of Wagner is by P. Petit; that of Rossini by Numa Blanc: see Weinstock, *Richard Wagner's Visit to Rossini and an Evening at Rossini's in BeauSejour,* opposite p. ix.

501. Ibid., p. 39.

502. Ibid., p. 40.

503. Ibid., p. 42.

504. Ibid., p. 44.

505. Ibid., p. 49.

506. Ibid., p. 52.

507. Ibid., pp. 52–54. Schumann was aware of Rossini's visit to Beethoven and has Eusebius declare: "The butterfly crossed the path of the eagle, but the latter turned aside in order not to crush it with the beating of his wings." Schumann, *On Music and Musicians,* p. 235.

508. Weinstock, *Richard Wagner's Visit to Rossini and an Evening at Rossini's in Beau-Sejour,* pp. 85–86.

509. Wagner's own description as he reminisced about the event on a return visit to Magdeburg thirty-seven years later with Cosima. Wagner, *Cosima Wagner's Diaries,* 1:569, entry of 10 December 1872.

510. Wagner, *My Life,* 1:121.

511. Ibid., 1:400.

512. Wagner, *Cosima Wagner's Diaries,* 2:204, entry of 18 November 1878.

513. Wagner, *My Life,* 1:402. The old opera house was burned to the ground during the 1849 uprisings in Dresden, a few weeks after Wagner had conducted his third Palm Sunday concert of the Ninth Symphony there. A militia man shouted to Wagner that one of Beethoven's "schöner Götterfunken" had sparked off the conflagration! See Hans Gall, *Richard Wagner* (1963; New York, 1976), p. 46.

514. Wagner, *My Life,* 1:398.

515. Ibid., 1:399. Wagner's Beethoven-whetting comments were printed on 24 and 31 March and 2 April 1846. Mendelssohn had given a successful performance of the Ninth at the Gewandhaus in Leipzig (11 February 1836) a decade before Wagner's Dresden debut.

516. Burk, *Letters of Richard Wagner: the Burrell Collection*, p. 129. This is part of the reminiscences written in 1895 and early 1896 by Marie Schmole, née Heine, who was ten years old when Wagner first began visiting, with Minna, her family home. The enterprising Mary Burrell, Wagner's English fan and would-be biographer (she died in 1898, her elaborately detailed manuscript advanced only so far as Wagner's twenty-first year) discovered Frau Schmole still living in Dresden in 1895 and persuaded her to write down for her all her memories of Wagner's years in Dresden. See ibid, p. 118.

517. Wagner, *My Life*, 1:401.

518. Ibid., 1:399.

519. Ibid., 1:398–99.

520. Ibid., 1:401.

521. Did Schönberg, with his *Sprechgesang*, know of Wagner's interpretation? For Schönberg the painter's own mythmaking contributions to the protean theme of musicians and imagery see my article, "Through a Viennese Looking Glass Darkly: Images of Arnold Schönberg and His Circle," *Arts Magazine* 58, no. 9 (May 1984):107–19.

522. Wagner, *My Life*, 1:402.

523. See Wagner, *Dichtungen und Schriften*, 9:9–11. Newman points this out and that the longing to escape from loneliness by bringing a message of beauty to people was fermenting at that time in the formulation of his own *Lohengrin*. See Newman, *The Life of Richard Wagner*, 1:423, n. 2.

524. In a rare display of independence Cosima wrote the following in her diary entry for 26 September 1879: "I admit to R. that in this work [Beethoven's Ninth] I feel no need for a program, and I even put his, based on *Faust*, right out of my mind." Wagner, *Cosima Wagner's Diaries*, 2:370.

525. Wagner, *My Life*, 1:399.

526. Albert Goldman, ed., Evert Spinchorn, intro., and H. Ashton Ellis, trans., *Wagner on Music and Drama* (New York, 1964), p. 167.

527. Ibid.

528. Ibid.

529. Ibid., p. 168.

530. Ibid.

531. Ibid., p. 169.

532. Ibid., pp. 171–72.

533. Later, in his long essay on Beethoven of 1870 (see text below), Wagner would repudiate the "meaning" of the word in favor of the "human character" of the voice. To this end Wagner, in his editor's role as he supervised publication of the first edition of his collected writings (Leipzig, 1871–73, 1883), inserted a footnote to that effect for this 1846 discussion of the Ninth, as pointed out in ibid., p. 172. This change came about after exposure to the ideas of Schopenhauer, whose writings Wagner had come across—with ecstatic approval—at the end of 1854; see text below.

534. Ibid., pp. 159–60.

535. For a full dose of this grandiose, germane, and exclusively Germanic line of thought, see Wagner's *The Artwork of the Future*, ibid., pp. 179–235.

536. Wagner, *Cosima Wagner's Diaries*, 1:308, entry of 16 December 1870. Cosima's entry for the following day, 17 December (Beethoven's birthday), begins: "Beethoven Day! How to celebrate this unique occasion?" ibid.

537. Wagner, *My Life*, 2:616; see also pp. 614–17 for Wagner's description of his first encounter with *Die Welt als Wille und Vorstellung*. For Schopenhauer's opinion of Wagner, see my article "In Praise of Creative Misinterpretation, Or, 'How a Little Bit of Schopenhauer Changed My Life,'" pp. 118–19.

538. Wagner, *My Life*, 2: 616.

539. Cosima and Richard were both painted by Lenbach, Munich's most illustrious portrait painter, and they acquired his bust portrait of Schopenhauer (done from a photograph) for Wahnfried in 1875. A diary entry for 16 January of that year announces with pleasure that "Schopenhauer is now to be hung," Wagner, *Cosima Wagner's Diaries*, 1:819. Two days later Cosima reported at greater length: "Decision to take Schopenhauer down from the wall 'because he does not belong with Goethe, Schiller, Beethoven; the philosopher must stand alone [for where, see Fig. 100 and text below]—translating into wisdom everything the others express emotionally.'" Ibid, 1:820.

540. Ibid., 1:250, entry for 31 July 1870; see also entry for 2 August: "R. reads me his continuation of the Beethoven essay: 'To please you I have mentioned Palestrina.'" Ibid., 1:251.

541. On 18 September 1870 Cosima read parts of the *Beethoven* manuscript and was "filled with admiration for its depth of thought and clarity. R. says to me: 'I regret after all not having compared Beethoven with Schopenhauer. There would have been a fuss, and yet in Beethoven's world he does represent *reason*.'" Ibid., 1:272.

542. From *The Artwork of the Future*, in Goldman and Sprinchorn, *Wagner on Music and Drama*, p. 187. Much of Wagner's 1870 essay however is at odds with the theories expressed in his earlier writings.

543. Joachim Bergfeld, ed., and George Bird, trans., *The Diary of Richard Wagner 1865–1882: The Brown Book* (London, 1980), pp. 176–77.

544. Richard Wagner, *Beethoven*, trans. Edward Dannreuther, 3rd ed. (London [n. d., 1880's?]), p. 21.

545. See above, n. 540.

546. Wagner, *Beethoven*, p. 35.

547. Ibid., pp. 37–38.

548. Ibid., p. 37.

549. Ibid., p. 38.

550. Ibid., p. 39.

551. Ibid., p. 57.

552. Ibid., p. 49.

553. Ibid., p. 52.

554. Wagner had been in and out of Vienna during the years Beethoven's remains were exhumed and inexpertly analyzed, and the "findings" were much discussed at the time. Nevertheless, in spite of his Beethoven veneration, Wagner did not resort to the fanatical grave-side conduct of another Beethoven worshiper. This was Anton Bruckner (1824–1896), whom Wagner designated somewhat enigmatically in 1882 as the only living composer who "reached out to Beethoven" (not really saying whether he made it or not), see Newman, *The Life of Richard Wagner*, 4:403, n. 24. Bruckner (who admired Wagner thereby incurring, like Wagner, Hanslick's powerful disapproval), when he heard that Beethoven's body was being dug up a second time (1888) for reinterment in Vienna's great Central Cemetery, pulled all the strings he could to insure that he might be present at the exhumation. For Bruckner's morbid fascination with death (he also wanted to see

Emperor Maximilian's body when it was returned to Vienna from Mexico) see Hans-Hubert Schönzeler, *Bruckner* (London, 1970), p. 113. Bruckner is perhaps the best example of post-Beethoven composers obsessed by the Ninth Symphony, and Bruckner's own Ninth Symphony (unfinished, see discussion of Mahler, chapter 6) is, like Beethoven's, in D Minor.

555. Wagner, *Beethoven*, pp. 49–50.

556. Ibid., p. 52.

557. Ibid., p. 53.

558. Ibid., p. 46.

559. Ibid., p. 53.

560. Ibid.

561. Ibid., p. 54.

562. Ibid., p. 55.

563. Ibid., p. 41.

564. Ibid., p. 61. Wagner adds the caveat "without ever identifying the one with the other." Ibid.

565. Ibid.

566. Ibid.

567. Wagner, *Cosima Wagner's Diaries*, 1:240, entry of 30 June 1870. That Wagner wove the emotions of his own life into his music-dramas is well known, and it is quite in character that he would perceive similar rises and falls of moods in Beethoven's music. Here is an interesting specific example of Wagner's attitude in this regard as recorded by Cosima: "After lunch the musicians played us the *Idyll* [*Siegfried's Idyll*] in an arrangement by Richter, much emotion! R. said how curious it seemed to him: all he had set out to do was to work the theme which had come to him in the Starnberg (when we were living there together) . . . into a moving serenade, and then he had unconsciously woven our whole life into it—Fidi's [Siegfried's] birth, my recuperation, Fidi's bird, etc." Wagner, *Cosima Wagner's Diaries*, 1:330, entry of 30 January 1871. Cosima had learned her Schopenhauer well through Wagner's explications; her next sentence is: "As Schopenhauer said, this is the way a musician works, he expresses life in a language which reason does not understand." Ibid.

568. Wagner, *Beethoven*, pp. 62–64.

569. Ibid., p. 64. Certainly Wagner believed this practice should be applied by history to himself!

570. Ibid., p. 69.

571. Ibid., p. 71.

572. Ibid., p. 72.

573. Ibid., p. 77.

574. Ibid., p. 79.

575. Ibid., p. 89.

576. Ibid.

577. Ibid.

578. Ibid., p. 91.

579. Ibid., p. 112–13. It is too bad Hitler did not read *all* of Wagner.

580. Wagner, *Die Tagebücher*, 1:259, entry of 17 July 1870, translation mine. The translation for this phrase has been given as "the war is Beethoven's jubilee" in Wagner, *Cosima Wagner's Diaries*, 1:246. I think the "memorial" aspect of this date was uppermost in Cosima's mind here, and I can not go as far as the delightful Robert Gutman, who translates the phrase somewhat outrageously (for the benefit of those allergic to Cosima) as a congratulatory "the war is a Beethoven festival"; Robert Gutman, *Wagner: The Man, His Mind, and His Music* (New York, 1968), p. 314. Gutman does point out that, because of Cosima's close French connections

(her dead sister had been married to the man who headed one of France's ministries when war was declared), she may have been led in self-defense to "an almost lunatic jingoism." Ibid., n. 8. Ludwig Nohl's book of 1871 (which he sent to Wagner) entitled *Die Beethoven-Feier und die Kunst der Gegenwart* was, like Wagner's essay, inspired by the idea of honoring the one hundredth anniversary of Beethoven's birth, and should be translated as *The Beethoven-Centennial and the Art of the Future*.

581. Wagner, *Cosima Wagner's Diaries*, 1:246.

582. Friedrich Neitzsche, *The Birth of Tragedy and The Case of Wagner*, trans. Walter Kaufmann (New York, 1976), p. 37.

583. Ibid., p. 31.

584. Ibid.

585. Ibid., p. 136. As Kaufmann has pointed out this anti-French, pro-German passage is an echo of Wagner; after the rupture of their friendship (1878) Nietzsche's writing contained numerous approving references to French culture.

586. Ibid., pp. 118, 119.

587. Ibid., p. 119.

588. Ibid., p. 104.

589. Ibid., p. 103. Wagner's influence on his disciple—thirty-one years his junior—is quite evident here.

590. Ibid., p. 121.

591. Ibid., p. 100.

592. Ibid., p. 104.

593. Ibid., p. 100.

594. Wagner, *Cosima Wagner's Diaries*, 1:296.

595. Ibid., 1:154, entry of 12 October 1869. See also p. 157, entry of 25 October for reference to Ludwig II's follow-up letter concerning his production of *The Rhinegold*.

596. Wagner's letters (over fifty) to Bertha Goldwag, the Viennese seamstress who executed his scrupulous and hefty orders and patiently awaited deferred payments from 1863 to 1871, were obtained and published, with maliciously funny comments, by Daniel Spritzer in Vienna's *Neue Freie Presse* in 1877, see Leonard Liebling, *Richard Wagner and the Seamstress* (New York, 1941).

597. For instance, Wagner tells us: "the great march in the finale of the Symphony in C Minor [Fifth], the beginning of the Eighth Symphony in F major, or even a bright bit out of the *Rienzi* Overture." Wagner, *My Life*, 2:546.

598. Francis Hueffer, trans., *Correspondence of Wagner and Liszt*, 2 vols. 2nd ed., rev., (1897; New York, 1973), 1:182, letter dated 14 December 1851. The Nibelung designs by the Nazarine painter Peter Cornelius (1783–1867; not to be confused with Wagner's friend, the composer Peter Cornelius) were a series of seven drawings executed in 1812–17 and engraved as a composite title page for the Nibelung in 1817. Liszt did send his medallion portrait and three years later Wagner returned the favor: "Has Eugène [Wittgenstein] sent you my medallion? It is not bad, only a little sickly." Ibid., 2:23, letter from Wagner to Liszt dated 9 April 1854. (See Liszt's acknowledgment, ibid., 2:33, letter of 20 May 1854.) See also Wagner's letter to Liszt of 15 January 1852 concerning the medallion and a portrait he promises to send Liszt. Ibid., 1:185. Later Liszt kept a small portrait bust of Wagner on his writing desk as "*unicum*," and wrote Wagner that "Beethoven, Weber, Schubert, and others of that stamp keep company to your portrait

(that with the motto, 'Du weisst wie das wird') in the ante-room.'' Ibid., 2:314–15, letter dated Weimar, 31 May 1860; concerning this ''motto'' portrait, see Wagner's letter to Liszt of 15 January 1854. Ibid., 2:8. Another reference to the Wagner bust by Liszt occurs in a letter of 22 August 1859: ''You are of course without the company of any other celebrities—no Mozart, no Beethoven, no Goethe. . . . '' Ibid., 2:306. Liszt knew Wagner's jealous nature exceedingly well.

599. Johann Friedrich August Tischbein (1750–1812), cousin of the so-called Goethe-Tischbein. A copy of this portrait is in the Schillerhaus at Weimar. Tischbein shows Schiller in a Roman toga. He made a preparatory study of the poet from life in February 1805, and completed the oil portrait in 1806 after Schiller's death in May 1805.

600. On 11 November 1869 when Cosima told Richard that they had neglected to mark Schiller's birthday the day before, he replied: ''Well, yesterday was the very day on which, while I was working, I felt inwardly pleased by Schiller's picture opposite me, and I pictured to myself his whole essence.'' Wagner, *Cosima Wagner's Diaries*, 1:163.

601. This and other pertinent letters in the exchange between Wagner and Härtel are given in Ludwig Volkmann, ''Das Beethoven-Bild im Haus Wahnfried und seine Entstehung,'' *Allgemeine Musikzeitung* 66, no. 17 (28 April 1939):271–75; letter of 5 March 1869, p. 272 (translation mine).

602. Other portraits included Haydn, Gluck, Mozart, Kant, and Lessing. Ibid., p. 271.

603. Ibid., p. 272, letter of 16 March 1869.

604. Ibid.

605. Ibid., letter of 15 June 1869.

606. Ibid., p. 273, letter of 4 May 1869.

607. Ibid., pp. 272, 274. So pleased was Wagner with Krausse's work that soon after moving to Bayreuth (April 1872), he commissioned Krausse to come to Bayreuth to discuss adorning the facade of his future home, the Villa Wahnfried, with a *sgraffito* panel (to be paid for by Ludwig). The negotiations were begun on 31 July 1872, continued on 12 September 1873, and on 13 September 1874 Krausse arrived with the whole completed cartoon. On 3 October of that year he moved into the house with the Wagners (his effusive dinner conversation annoyed Richard, who forbade the painter to use the word ''colossal'' one more time) and by 29 October the *sgraffito* was all but completed, according to Cosima's diary entries. The allegorical *sgraffito* (often mistaken for a relief by writers on Villa Wahnfried) shows a typically Wagnerian iconography: the union of classical tragedy, Germanic myth, music, and the future, through depictions of Ludwig Schnorr von Carolsfeld (nephew of the Schnorr von Carolsfeld who sketched Beethoven, see Fig. 9) as Wotan in the center, Wilhelmine Schröder-Devrient as antique drama on the left, and Cosima with their son Siegfried as music and the future on the right. Kaspar Clemens Zumbusch's (see next chapter) large bronze bust of King Ludwig II was sent to complete the ensemble in July of 1875 (see Fig. 100). The *salon* and one third of the house (now restored and a museum) were destroyed during a bombing raid on 5 April 1945.

608. Wagner, *Cosima Wagner's Diaries*, 7:117–18.

609. Ibid., p. 119.

610. Ibid., p. 122.

611. The usually reliable Geoffrey Skelton, admirable translator of the Cosima Wagner diaries, has mistakenly identified Krausse's copy of Waldmüller's *Beethoven* as ''Lenbach's portrait of Schopenhauer,'' see Skelton, *Richard and Cosima Wagner: Biography of a Marriage* (Boston, 1982), verso of unnumbered illustration page following p. 176. Aside from the visual evidence we have Cosima's diary notation of the decision to take Schopenhauer down from the wall because Richard said he did not belong with Goethe, Schiller, and Beethoven, see above, n. 539.

612. A photograph of the whole *salon* wall is reproduced in Gutman, *Richard Wagner: The Man, His Mind, and His Music*, illustration section between pp. 330–31. The Liszt portrait, also by Lenbach, is in the center of its group of three to the right, matching the placement of the Beethoven portrait in the center of its group of three to the left. Originally the three Lenbach portraits hung as a holy trinity above the bookcases of the wall dedicated to ''The Holy Family'' in this order: Liszt (complete with warts), with gaze directed to the right, Cosima, in a frontal stance, and Wagner, with ''sharp and energetic'' (Cosima's description) profile looking left. The frames for all three were initially less extravagant than the floreate surrounds visible in our illustration (Fig. 96). For a photograph of the three Lenbach portraits in their first installation, see Martin Gregor-Dellin, *Richard Wagner: Eine Biographie in Bildern* (Munich, 1982), p. 164. Scattered Cosima diary entries record the arrival and framing of these important future family heirlooms (see especially the years 1869–72). The Goethe portrait was less valuable, being merely a copy of a portrait of the young Goethe obligingly dashed off by Lenbach (apparently at Cosima's request), but it was equally cherished by Wagner: ''I enter this room and look at the Goethe portrait in its fine frame, presented to me in love, and I feel happy and believe in happiness here on earth.'' Wagner, *Cosima Wagner's Diaries*, 1:276, entry of 25 September 1870.

613. Wagner, *Cosima Wagner's Diaries*, 1:326.

614. Ibid., 1:820.

615. Ibid., 2:252–53. Relations with Nietzsche may have cooled but Wagner still liked the Dionysian definitions the philosopher had left in his wake. On another occasion he told Cosima that she was Apollonian, he Dionysian. Ibid., 1:445, entry of 3 January 1872. The Austrian painter Hans Makart (1840–1884), a popular depicter of lavish history and mythological scenes, had been a friend of the Wagners since they met in Vienna in 1875.

616. Ibid., 2:590.

617. Ibid., 1:174, entry of 20 December 1869.

618. Ibid., 1:456, entry of 8 February 1872.

619. Ibid., 1:558, entry of 19 November 1872. This was Wagner's lucky day. Not only did he see an intriguing portrait of Beethoven, he received from a member of the Mannheim orchestra a Beethoven autograph that day as well, notes Cosima's next sentence.

620. Ibid., 1:318, entry of 4 January 1871.

621. Ibid., 2:116, entry of 18 July 1878.

622. Ibid., 2:537, entry of 9 September 1880. Fidi was eleven years old.

623. Ibid., 2:568, entry of 4 December 1880.

624. Ibid., 2:351, entry of 8 August 1879. Wagner was reading Nohl's biography of Beethoven at this time (see ibid., p. 353, entry of 12 August 1879).

625. Ibid., 2:291, entry of 12 April 1879.

626. Ibid., 2:614, entry of 4 February 1881.

627. Ibid., 1:983–84, entry of 25 September 1877.

628. Wagner wrote Ludwig on behalf of Beethoven's grandnephew on 25 August 1868; see Newman, *The Life of Richard Wagner*, 4:157–58. For more on the ill-fated Ludwig van Beethoven II (1839–?), see chapter 5 and n. 154 and below, n. 710.

629. Wagner, *Cosima Wagner's Diaries*, 7:661, entry of 31 July 1873.

630. See above, n. 607.

631. "He is of the opinion that he and my father have done much towards disseminating Beeth.'s last works, and he tells us how they were regarded 'in olden times,' " reports Cosima. Ibid., 2:611, entry of 30 January 1881.

632. Albert Apponyi, *The Memoirs of Count Apponyi* (New York, 1935), p. 101. There are also numerous references in Cosima's diaries to times when either her father or Josef Rubinstein (1847–1884; their "resident" Russian Jewish pianist friend who committed suicide after Wagner's death) played Beethoven's *Hammerklavier* Sonata to their rapturous joy. Very occasionally Wagner experienced an anti-Beethoven reaction: "In Beeth. everything is dramatic. I sometimes feel I don't want to hear anything more by Beeth." Wagner, *Cosima Wagner's Diaries*, 2:198, entry of 11 November 1878.

633. "Several times Wagner had to conduct symphonies by Beethoven, including even the *Ninth*, at a time when he had no opportunity to look at the score beforehand, but he knows all Beethoven's symphonies *by heart*, as well as he knows his own music, so that he was able to conduct even the *Ninth Symphony*, in rehearsal and before the public, *without the score, from memory*." From the article "Richard Wagner in St Petersburg" by the composercritic Alexander Nikolayevich Serov (1820–1871), who described himself as "Wagnermad," as translated in Barth, Mack, and Voss, *Wagner: A Documentary Study*, p. 202.

634. Wagner, *Cosima Wagner's Diaries*, 1:37, entry of 13 January 1869.

635. Ibid., 1:266–27, entry of 1 June 1870. They were expecting final word on Cosima's divorce from Bülow; this came on 18 July 1870.

636. Ibid., 1:602, entry of 7 March 1873.

637. Ibid., 2:89, entry of 8 June 1878.

638. Ibid., 1:86, entry of 14 April 1869.

639. Ibid., 1:754, entry of 4 May 1874.

640. Ibid., 1:669, entry of 30 August 1873. Grand Duke Karl August was to marry the daughter of Prince Hermann, Duke of Saxony, hence the "Joy of the Saxon People."

641. Ibid., 1:584, entry of 15 January 1873.

642. Ibid., 2:406, entry of 30 November 1879.

643. Ibid., 2:529, entry of 28 August 1880.

644. Ibid., 2:528, entry of 28 August 1880.

645. Ibid., 2:855, entry of 10 May 1882.

646. Ibid., 2:856, entry of 17 May 1882.

647. Ibid., 2:857, entry of 19 May 1882.

648. Ibid., 2:208, entry of 22 November 1878.

649. Ibid., 1:886, entry of 6 January 1876. Two months earlier Beethoven's Ninth Symphony appeared in another Wagner dream: "R. dreamed that I was conducting [Beethoven's] A Major Symphony [Seventh] at a concert . . . after it he was supposed to conduct the 9th, but I was doing so well that he asked himself whether he could possibly perform the same office!" Ibid, 1:695, entry of 8 November 1873.

650. Ibid., 1:448, entry of 10 January 1872. The Wagners were still living at Tribschen.

651. Ibid., 1:461, entry of 25 February 1872.

652. Ibid., 1:468, entry of 16 March 1872.

653. Ibid., 1:481–82, entry of 2 May 1872.

654. Ibid., 1:482, entry of 2 May 1872.

655. Ibid., 1:487, entry of 21 May 1872.

656. Ibid., 1:488, entry of 22 May 1872.

657. The article was entitled "Zum Vortrag der neunten Symphonie Beethovens" ("On the Rendering of Beethoven's Ninth Symphony").

658. Goldman and Sprinchorn, *Wagner on Music and Drama*, p. 309.

659. Ibid., p. 316.

660. Ibid., pp. 317, 318.

661. Ibid., p. 324.

662. Wagner himself noted a similarity between his and Beethoven's working methods in this respect. Cosima's diary entry for 15 May 1875 reads: "We occupy ourselves with Beethoven's sketches for the Ninth Symphony, edited by Nottebohm–very strange how trivial almost, how commonplace the most significant themes when first written down; R. says it is like that with him—what he first writes down he can hardly ever use just in that way. . . ." Wagner, *Cosima Wagner's Diaries*, 1:846.

663. Ibid., 2:994.

664. Ibid., 2:425, entry of 14 January 1880. Concerning the Beethoven-Wagner link as perceived by others, Ludwig Nohl, a great admirer of Wagner, whose edition of Beethoven's letters had been published in 1865 with a dedication to Wagner, later quoted Wagner's emotional letter of thanks to him about the special significance Nohl's coupling of their names had for him, see the *Bayreuther Festblaetter in Wort und Bild* for 1884 (March) and the article by Nohl, "Wagner und Beethoven," p. 18. In America, after Liszt's death, the Hungarian-born journalist Joseph Pulitzer donated seven hundred fifty thousand dollars to the New York Philharmonic with the mandate that the music of Liszt, Wagner, and Beethoven be featured.

665. Wieck's published description of his meeting with Beethoven had come to the attention of the Wagners in 1876: "We read a report of a visit to Beethoven by old Wieck, and a letter from Czerny about the first performance of the 9th Symphony; very affecting, as everything one hears about a genius always is . . . ," Wagner, *Cosima Wagner's Diaries*, 1:885, entry of 3 January 1876.

666. Letter to his future second wife, the actress Marie Schanzer, as given in Newman, *The Life of Richard Wagner*, 4:644. In an excess of nationalism Bülow once declared (1892, in Berlin) that Bismarck was "Beethoven's twin, the Beethoven of German politics," as quoted in Jacques Barzun, ed., *The Pleasures of Music* (1952; London, 1977), p. 354.

667. "Dieses Frauenzimmer *mag* ich nicht!" ("I don't *like* this hussy!") said Brahms—the steadfast bachelor and habitual brothel visitor—about her; see my article "The Visual Brahms: Idols and Images," p. 128 and n. 12.

668. The Englishwoman Florence May (1845–1923), pupil of both Clara Schumann and, later, Brahms, and one of Brahms's earliest biographers, places the Bee-

thoven bust in Brahms's possession as early as 1858. It was in the room set aside for Brahms by his parents in their new and more spacious quarters at Fuhlentwiethle 74, where it stood on top of a large bookcase, see Florence May, *The Life of Johannes Brahms*, 2 vols. (1905; enl. and illustrated ed., Neptune City [N.J.], 1981), 1:232.

669. Brahms liked to say that the two most important events in his lifetime were the creation of the German Empire by Bismarck and the completion of the Bachgesellschaft Edition, to which he was an early and enthusiastic subscriber. Bach's music was usually to be found open on Brahms's piano, and Brahms's final work, the eleven chorale-preludes for organ completed in 1896, pays indisputable homage to Germany's master contrapuntalist.

670. As cited in Walter Niemann, *Brahms*, trans. Catherine Alison Phillips (1920; reprint, New York, 1969), p. 19. Fourteen days before his death at the age of eightyone, Marxsen attended his last concert—a performance of Beethoven's Ninth by the Hamburg Philharmonic Society.

671. Ibid., p. 31.

672. Ibid., p. 35.

673. Karl Geiringer, *Brahms: His Life and Work* (1935; 2nd ed., rev. and enl., New York, 1947), p. 347, letter dated 13 February 1855.

674. Entry of 1 October 1853 as given in May, *The Life of Johannes Brahms*, 1:122. To Joachim a few days later Schumann wrote simply: "This is he that should come." Ibid., 1:123.

675. Schumann's favorite phrase for Brahms, when writing about him to others, see ibid., 1:128. In the famous "New Paths" article, published in the *Neue Zeitschrift für Musik* on 28 October 1853, Schumann (who had not written for the magazine in ten years) introduced Brahms to the world as having sprung from the head of Jove, fully armed, like Minerva.

676. Bettina's daughter Gisela was also present and attracted the admiration of the not altogether music-concentrating Joachim, see May, *The Life of Johannes Brahms*, 1:129–30. (Joachim *was* able however to identify correctly the authors of the various movements of the sonata composed in his honor.)

677. See Robert Haven Schauffler (enthusiastic author of a two-volume life of Beethoven, published New York, 1929, and entitled *Beethoven: The Man Who Freed Music*), *The Unknown Brahms* (New York, 1933), p. 45. The author zestfully reproduces the broad Low German (*PlattDeutsch*) accent of Brahms's father as he proudly announced the contents of Schumann's letter: "Schumann hett seggt, min Hannes . . . ward noch mal 'en tweeten Beethoven!" Ibid.

678. In a letter to Clara Schumann of 9 November 1859 Brahms asked her to order a copy of the score to Beethoven's *Missa Solemnis* so that he might send it as a Christmas present to his revered teacher Marxsen; letter given in Richard Litterscheid, *Johannes Brahms in seinen Schriften und Briefen* (Berlin, 1943), p. 182.

679. Litzmann, *Letters of Clara Schumann and Johannes Brahms 1853–1896*, 1:23, letter dated Düsseldorf, 25 January 1855.

680. Ibid., 1:44, letter of 14 August 1855.

681. As quoted by Schauffler, *The Unknown Brahms*, p. 216. In later years Brahms indeed kept an engraved portrait of Shakespeare on top of the linen cabinet in

the bedroom of his Karlsgasse apartment, next to his photograph of Schumann.

682. Litzmann, *Letters of Clara Schumann and Johannes Brahms*, 1:57, letter dated 4 December 1855.

683. Ibid.

684. Litterscheid, *Johannes Brahms in Seinen Schriften und Briefen*, p. 333, letter dated Vienna, 24 May 1876, translation mine.

685. Brahms also owned the collected editions of all of the works of Mozart, Schubert, Bach (his greatest joy), Handel, Schütz, Chopin, and Schumann (he had helped edit the latter). For a complete listing of the Beethoven items in Brahms's collection, see Alfred Orel, "Johannes Brahms' Musikbibliothek" (*Simrock-Jahrbuch*, 3, Leipzig, 1930–34) as reprinted in Kurt Hofmann, *Die Bibliothek von Johannes Brahms: Bücher- und Musikalienverzeichnis* (Schriftenreihe zur Music, Hamburg, 1974), pp. 147–48. Karl Geiringer's most recent reference to the matter repeats the claim he previously made in 1933 of "more than sixty sheets of sketches by Beethoven," see Geiringer, "Brahms as a Musicologist," *Musical Quarterly* 64, no. 4 (fall 1983):465. As for the visual arts, Brahms had collected over 200 prints by Daniel Chodowiecki, as well as engravings by Jacques Callot, and drawings and prints by Anselm Feuerbach and Adolph Menzel, to say nothing of the stunning gift of prints entitled *A Brahms Phantasy* sent to him in 1894 by his admirer, the artist Max Klinger (see chapter 6 of this book and also my article, "The Visual Brahms: Idols and Images," pp. 128, 129, n. 16).

686. Hans Gall, ed., *Johannes Brahms Briefe* (Frankfurt, 1979), p. 132, letter dated Vienna, 24 April 1884, translation mine.

687. Litterscheid, *Johannes Brahms in seinen Schriften und Briefen*, p. 388, letter dated Vienna, 28 March 1884, translation mine.

688. Letter to Hanslick of May 1884, as quoted in ThayerForbes, *Thayer's Life of Beethoven*, p. 120.

689. Hans Gall, *Johannes Brahms: His Work and Personality*, trans. Joseph Stein (New York, 1971), p. 14, letter of November 1862 to Julius Otto Grimm.

690. As quoted in Richard Specht, *Johannes Brahms*, trans. Eric Blom (London, 1930), p. 128. The Hellmesberger Quartet (founded 1849) featured Beethoven's late quartets in its annual concert series. Joseph Hellmesberger edited Beethoven's fragmentary C Major Violin Concerto, published in Vienna in 1879.

691. See Schauffler, *The Unknown Brahms*, pp. 139–40. Brahms's meticulous future biographer Max Kalbeck (*Johannes Brahms*, 8 vols., Berlin, 1904–14) was the first to relate this amusing story. Brahms played a similar joke on Kalbeck, but in reverse, slipping the original manuscript sketches to Beethoven's C-sharp Minor Quartet into a roll of popular music he presented to Kalbeck as a gift, see Schauffler, *The Unknown Brahms*, pp. 140–41.

692. Hanslick, *Music Criticisms 1846–99*, pp. 125–27. As mythmaking grew up around Brahms, the incident of Schumann's finding the steel pen on Beethoven's grave (the pen he reserved to write only his most ambitious musical compositions) was transferred to Brahms, who, legend had it, picked up a pen from Beethoven's grave in 1862 with the intention of using it to write his First Symphony, see Maryvonne de Saint-Pulgent, "Brahms et Beethoven: pour en finir avec une lég-

457

ende," in *L'AvantScène*, no. 53 (June, 1983 [*Johannes Brahms* issue]), p. 91.

693. Hanslick, *Music Criticisms 1846–99*, p. 127.

694. Ibid., pp. 127–28.

695. When in 1869 Wagner brought out a new edition of his anonymously published essay of 1850 *The Jew in Music* [*Das Judentum in der Musik*] under his own name, he added a postscript referring to Hanslick's "zierlich verdeckte jüdische Abkunft," and labeled him the incarnation of anti-German, Semitic art criticism.

696. Hanslick, *Music Criticisms 1846–99*, pp. 157–58.

697. Ibid., pp. 210–11.

698. Ibid., p. 244.

699. As quoted in Erwin Doernberg, *The Life and Symphonies of Anton Bruckner* (Toronto, 1960), p. 74. Verdi's image of Beethoven, while extremely respectful (in later life he took a pocket edition of the Beethoven quartets with him on his trips), is not a fruitful one for our mythmaking study, since the great Italian in no way shaped the image of Beethoven as perceived in his own or any other country. We do have these words of Verdi's concerning Beethoven, however, written in May 1889, in answer to an invitation from Joachim, the honorary president, to become an honorary member of the recently founded Musical Society of the Beethovenhaus in Bonn. Asserting that to participate in such ceremonies was against his principles, the seventy-five-year-old composer interjected [but] "Beethoven is in question and before his name we all bow in reverence." As cited in Francis Toye, *Giuseppe Verdi: His Life and Works* (New York, 1946), p. 195. Thus Verdi, along with Brahms, Clara Schumann, and Joachim (among others) added his name to the appeal to save Beethoven's birth house, after it was announced early in 1889 that the building would be put up for sale and demolished. The house was saved (see next chapter). Verdi's opinion of Beethoven's Ninth was that the first three movements were "sublime," the last movement, however, "bad as a structure," letter of April 1878, see Aldo Oberdorfer, ed., *Giuseppe Verdi: Autobiografia dalle Lettere* (Milan, 1941), p. 325.

700. May, *The Life of Johannes Brahms*, 2:585.

701. As quoted by Niemann, *Brahms*, p. 131.

702. May, *The Life of Johannes Brahms*, p. 2:528, extract from Bülow's writing dated October and November 1877.

703. Gall, *Johannes Brahms: His Work and Personality*, p. 69, letter to Marie Schanzer, see above, n. 666.

704. May, *The Life of Johannes Brahms*, 2:529, extract from Bülow's writing dated October and November 1877.

705. As quoted by Joseph Wechsberg, *The Waltz Emperors: The Life and Times and Music of the Strauss Family* (New York, 1973), p. 240.

706. As cited in Schauffler, *The Unknown Brahms*, p. 179. This question was put to Brahms a year before he died by the American violinist Arthur M. Abell.

707. Litzmann, *Letters of Clara Schumann and Johannes Brahms 1853–1896*, 1:70, letter dated Düsseldorf, 16 May 1856. Nevertheless, Brahms did not make his own biographers' tasks any easier when he requested the return of all his letters to Clara Schumann. Here is what happened, according to Clara's daughter Marie Schumann: ". . . in 1886 the friends agreed to return each other's letters, and Brahms gave back my mother's letters to her without reading them again. . . . Brahms also got his let-

ters back, but he told us later on that as he went to Rüdesheim on the very day they arrived, he availed himself of the opportunity to throw them overboard into the Rhine. The fact that, in spite of this, so many of his letters have survived is due to my mother's having begged him to allow her to keep back a number of them which were among her particular favorites." Ibid., pp. v–vi. Clara Schumann did not think as highly of her own letters to Brahms. Marie tells us that soon after she received them back from Brahms she began destroying them (June, 1887), "but fortunately I was able to stop her in the middle of it, and she yielded to my urgent entreaty to preserve them for us her children." Ibid., p. v.

708. As quoted by Graf, *Composer and Critic: Two Hundred Years of Music Criticism*, p. 151.

709. As quoted and discussed by Schauffler, *The Unknown Brahms*, p. 145.

710. See his letter to Billroth from Ischl of 21 July 1880 and the commentary following in Hans Barkan, trans. and ed., *Johannes Brahms and Theodor Billroth: Letters from a Musical Friendship* (Norman [Oklahoma], 1957), p. 95.

711. Ibid., p. 135, letter to Brahms dated Vienna, 27 July 1883.

712. Anderson, *The Letters of Beethoven*, 1:59, letter dated Vienna, 29 June [1801]. The autograph was still in the possession of Wegeler's heir, Julius Wegeler, when Anderson published it in 1961.

713. May, *The Life of Johannes Brahms*, 2:654.

714. See above, n. 668.

715. May, *The Life of Johannes Brahms*, 1:3.

716. As given in Gall, *Johannes Brahms: His Work and Personality*, p. 40. After three years as director of the newly founded Boston Symphony Orchestra, Henschel settled in England in 1884 (where he was later knighted) and established the London Symphony Concerts through which medium in 1895 he performed almost the complete orchestral works of Beethoven.

717. Billroth already lay nearby, and two years later Johann Strauss, Jr., whose funeral Mahler attended, was laid to rest next to his friend Brahms.

CHAPTER FIVE:
THE THREE-DIMENSIONAL BEETHOVEN

1. Originator of the idea of aesthetic relevance, see chapter 3, n. 20.

2. Of which he felt obligated to remind Breidenstein in a wounded note he wrote to him after having in vain twice called upon the busy impresario upon his arrival in Bonn for the unveiling festivities; Smart's own copy of his 11 August 1845 letter is given in Percy M. Young, *Beethoven: A Victorian Tribute Based on the Papers of Sir George Smart* (London, 1976), p. 61. (Henceforth referred to as *Beethoven: A Victorian Tribute*.)

3. As quoted in Walker, *Franz Liszt: The Virtuoso Years 1811–1847*, p. 270.

4. Ibid.

5. Ibid., p. 271.

6. Ibid.

7. La Mara, *Letters of Franz Liszt*, 1:52, letter to Breitkopf and Härtel dated London, 7 May 1841.

8. Ibid., 1:53, letter to Simon Löwy in Vienna dated London, 20 May 1841.

9. Moscheles, ed., *The Life of Beethoven Including the Biography by Schindler, Beethoven's Correspondence with His*

Friends, Numerous Characteristic Traits, and Remarks on His Musical Works, 2:371.

10. Ibid, 2:371–72. Volkmar Essers, in his excellent monograph on the Berlin sculptor *Johann Friedrich Drake* (Munich, 1976), was not aware, obviously, of this international aspect of the competition for a Beethoven monument when referring to the Bonn invitation as being sent out only to the sculptors of Germany. Ibid., p. 36.

11. To whom Hähnel created a memorial in Munich, 1890.

12. An early reference shows him thinking of "a Cantata for Beethoven, which I should like to set to music and to have it given at the great Festival which we expect to organize in 1842 for the inauguration of the Statue at Bonn." La Mara, *Letters of Franz Liszt*, 1:48, letter dated 29 August 1840, to Franz von Schober.

13. Ibid., 1:68–69, letter dated Marseilles, 28 April 1845, to the Abbé Félicité de Lamennais.

14. In London as late as 9 March 1845 Moscheles performed a demanding program of Beethoven piano sonatas to raise money for the Bonn monument.

15. Berlioz was sent to cover the festival by the *Journal des Débats*. In a letter dated 2 August 1845 to the cellist George Hainl (1807–1873) Berlioz wrote with some excitement: "I am getting ready to leave for Bonn, where everybody is going. It's a regular exodus of artists, men of letters, and the inquisitive. I don't know where we shall be able to stay. I expect they will have to put up tents on the banks of the Rhine and sleep in the barges." Berlioz, *Berlioz: A Selection From His Letters*, p. 90. The excitement was contagious: Hainl also attended the Bonn ceremonies.

16. Berlioz, *Berlioz: Evenings with the Orchestra*, p. 328.

17. Ibid., p. 327. Berlioz's explanation is of mythometric interest. "The reason is patent: in Italian eyes Beethoven is an enemy. Wherever his genius has sway or his inspiration has a hold on hearts and minds, the Italian muse is bound to consider herself humbled and seeks safety in flight. Italy, moreover, is aware of its national fanaticism and consequently dreads the opposing fanaticism of the German school." Ibid., p. 328. Berlioz was of course speaking from his own first-hand observations as a former Prix de Rome visitor in Italy. It must be added that—if the long-time expatriate can still be considered a representative of Italy—Cherubini had at least been very much in favor of the Bonn monument. Rossini, in poor health, indolent except for his honorary consultancy with the Bologna Liceo Musicale, was not heard from. (He would not rejoin the Parisian musical world until 1855.)

18. Young, in his commentary to Sir George Smart's diary, says that both Clara and Robert Schumann were present with Berlioz at the Hotel Goldener Stern's table d'hôte on the first day of the festival, but I have not found evidence to corroborate this (no mention, for example, during August 1845 of any travel to Bonn in the household account books of the Schumann family, see Gerd Nauhaus, ed., *Robert Schumann: Tagebücher: Haushaltbücher*, 3, part 1 [covering years 1837–47] [Leipzig, 1982]:396–97); and it seems strange that Berlioz would have deliberately cited Schumann's absence if they had eaten together, see Young, *Beethoven: A Victorian Tribute*, p. 53.

19. Berlioz, *Berlioz: Evenings with the Orchestra*, p. 329.

20. E. L. Voynich, trans., and Henryk Opieński, coll., *Chopin's Letters* (1931; New York, 1973), pp. 285, 288.

21. Ibid., p. 295. Chopin still thought of the Bonn events as about to happen.

22. Young, *Beethoven: A Victorian Tribute*, p. 64.

23. Spohr admired Wagner's early operas (with some reservations): he had given *The Flying Dutchman* in Kassel in June 1843 and was, in 1845, wondering why his young colleague was not pushing to produce his own new opera, *Die Kreuzfahrer*, which he had sent to Dresden that year. The score was kept a full year before it was returned to him in poor condition with a brusque note of rejection. In his not wholly-to-be-trusted autobiography, Wagner maintains that he did indeed recommend production of Spohr's opera and that the general management was to blame (Wagner, *My Life*, 1:405–6).

24. Hueffer, *Correspondence of Wagner and Liszt*, 1:2–3. Beethoven fever mounted throughout Germany after the Bonn unveiling, and it is noteworthy that Wagner's own Beethoven unveiling—the great Palm Sunday performance of the Ninth at Dresden—took place the following year. Wagner would have been one of many at the Bonn festivities; his Dresden Beethoven triumph belonged solely to him. All his life he seems to have preferred the company of admirers to that of his peers. The Weber monument had to wait another fifteen years before enough funds were raised, a large part of them through the devoted efforts of Sir George Smart in England. Dresden neglected to thank this foreign benefactor or even to invite him to the unveiling (1860; see below, n. 73), and the eighty-five-year-old Smart, in whose house Weber had died, was quite hurt, as his letter to Weber's son, dated 28 November 1861, makes quite plain, pointing out that he *had* after all, as a subscriber, been invited to the inauguration of the Beethoven monument in Bonn, see Young, *Beethoven: A Victorian Tribute*, pp. 113–14.

25. Thayer-Forbes, *Thayer's Life of Beethoven*, p. 208; the year was 1799. A somewhat miffed-sounding letter written by Dragonetti to the London Philharmonic Society on 21 January 1825 (preserved in the British Museum) gives an interesting insight into what he considered the arduous task of playing the instrumental recitatives (performed as solos on the double bass) in the final movement of Beethoven's Ninth: "I will accept the engagement for the ensuing Season at 10 Guineas per night, and play all the Solo's [sic] in Beethoven's new Symphony . . . I beg to leave to add, that I saw the score of Beethoven's last Sunday, and had I seen it before I sent in my terms I would have asked double." See Pamela J. Willetts, *Beethoven and England: An Account of Sources in the British Museum* (London, 1970), p. 52. The name of Beethoven was linked once again with that of Dragonetti at the end of the Italian's long life. Less than a year after the Bonn festival, as he lay dying in his room, he was visited by Johann Andreas Stumpff (1769–1846), the well-known harp maker and virtuoso who had befriended Beethoven in 1824 and who had sent the edition of Handel's works that gave Beethoven so much comfort in his last days. Taking Dragonetti's great callused hand into his own, Stumpff exclaimed, "This is the hand which Beethoven our great friend, whose

spirit now dwells in purer regions, bade me press." As given in *Grove's Dictionary of Music and Musicians*, 3rd ed., (1972) 2:92.

26. Berlioz, *Berlioz: Evenings with the Orchestra*, p. 331.

27. *Kölnische Zeitung*, no. 179 (June 1845), as cited in Walker, *Franz Liszt: The Virtuoso Years 1811–1847*, pp. 420–21 and n. 9.

28. Ibid., p. 421, n. 10: "Ad Vocem Beethoven-Fest," Bonn, 29 June 1845. Walker is in error, however, when he states that Liszt yielded the baton to Spohr for Beethoven's Fifth (ibid.), as Berlioz's review of Liszt's conducting of that symphony (see text below) shows.

29. Berlioz, *Berlioz: Evenings with the Orchestra*, pp. 333–34.

30. Schindler, *Beethoven As I Knew Him*, p. 433. Schindler was being too kind. He snapped back to his venomous self in the next sentence: "About ten years ago Liszt exchanged the life of a virtuoso for that of a conductor and composer, so that he need occupy us no further here, and since as a teacher of piano he adheres firmly to the 'old-fashioned principles,' it appears that even classical music has little or nothing more to fear from him and his pupils. The Fates be praised!" Ibid.

31. Berlioz, *Berlioz: Evenings with the Orchestra*, p. 333.

32. Young, *Beethoven: A Victorian Tribute*, p. 75.

33. Ibid., p. 74.

34. Entitled *Nachtrag zu den biographischen Notizen über Ludwig van Beethoven*; published in 1845.

35. Young, *Beethoven: A Victorian Tribute*, p. 54. Mozart's fate seems to have been grafted on to the Beethoven myth here!

36. Schindler, *Beethoven As I Knew Him*, p. 37.

37. It is difficult to tell from Sir George's wording *who* is reporting the translation claim here, Schindler or Moscheles. Probably Sir George was paraphrasing Schindler, since Moscheles in his capacity as editor of the English edition of Schindler's Beethoven biography never made any such claim, see chapter 2, n. 27.

38. Young, *Beethoven: A Victorian Tribute*, pp. 73, 84.

39. Ibid., pp. 91–92. Old Ries's King of Prussia story was accurate: in the summer of 1845 Schindler had received and accepted King Friedrich Wilhelm's offer of a lump payment of two thousand thalers and an annuity of four hundred thalers a year for life. He turned over his (decimated) Beethoven material to the King's Royal Library in January of the following year.

40. Ibid., p. 44.

41. Ibid. Smart goes on to give his opinion of Beethoven's *Missa Solemnis*: "As a whole the Mass is too difficult in many parts—to me—non-effective." Ibid.

42. Ibid., p. 47.

43. Ibid., p. 53. Antonio James Oury (1800–1883), a violinist at the King's Theatre in London, was married to the pianist Anna Caroline de Belleville who, as Czerny's student in Vienna, had met Beethoven numerous times.

44. Ibid., p. 54.

45. Ibid., p. 55.

46. Ibid., p. 76.

47. As quoted by Young, ibid., pp. 57–58 (no primary source cited). A friend of Mendelssohn and always conservative in his views, Davison became the music critic of the *Times* in 1846, a post he held for thirty-three years.

48. Berlioz, *Berlioz: Evenings with the Orchestra*, p. 329.

49. Young, *Beethoven: A Victorian Tribute*, p. 58.

50. Ibid.

51. If Schindler knew about Moscheles's London debut of the *Missa Solemnis* in 1832, he chose to ignore it. See Schindler, *Beethoven As I Knew Him*, p. 289, and editor's n. 213 (p. 351) for other early performances unknown to Schindler. The first full performance was on 7 April 1824 in Saint Petersburg (Schindler and Beethoven had quarreled that year and Schindler was temporarily no longer privy to Beethoven's life and letters).

52. Ibid., p. 289.

53. Berlioz, *Berlioz: Evenings with the Orchestra*, p. 332.

54. Ibid.

55. Ibid., pp. 329–30.

56. Young, *Beethoven: A Victorian Tribute*, p. 65.

57. Berlioz, *Berlioz: Evenings with the Orchestra*, p. 336.

58. Young, *Beethoven: A Victorian Tribute*, pp. 70–71.

59. Berlioz, *Berlioz: Evenings with the Orchestra*, p. 336. The tenor of Breidenstein's scintillating speech ran thus: "No mourning wife, no son, no daughter wept at his grave. But a world wept at it!" As quoted in Ann M. Lingg, *Mephisto Waltz: The Story of Franz Liszt* (New York, 1951), p. 140; see also Breidenstein's pamphlet documenting the Bonn events, *Festgabe zu der am 11. August 1845 Stattfindenden Inauguration des Beethoven-Monuments* (Bonn, 1845). The pamphlet, printed in advance, does not reflect that the inauguration was postponed by one day at the request of the Prussian monarchs, who were running late in their feting of the royal English visitors.

60. Hallé, *The Autobiography of Charles Hallé*, p. 103. Hallé had experienced a more positive Beethoven revelation at the two 1836 fund-raising concerts he had attended in Darmstadt: "I now clearly see that Beethoven's works are not, as it is usually considered, only capable of being appreciated by connoisseurs, but, when thus interpreted, even the musically uneducated who have minds in the least susceptible, must be impressed by them, as by every work of the highest art." Ibid., p. 50, letter of 23 September 1836.

61. As quoted in Young, *Beethoven: A Victorian Tribute*, pp. 71–72.

62. Ibid., p. 72.

63. Ibid., p. 71.

64. As paraphrased in ibid., p. 73.

65. Berlioz, *Berlioz: Evenings with the Orchestra*, p. 336.

66. As given in Walker, *Franz Liszt: The Virtuoso Years 1811–1847*, p. 420; article published 17 August 1845.

67. Young, *Beethoven: A Victorian Tribute*, p. 71.

68. Moscheles, *Recent Music and Musicians*, p. 316.

69. Sonneck, *Beethoven: Impressions by his Contemporaries*, p. 92.

70. Schindler, *Beethoven As I Knew Him*, p. 457. Schindler had just been describing "the master's light step, erect bearing, and graceful movements" (ibid.)—none of which *he* saw reflected in Hähnel's effigy.

71. Sonneck, *Beethoven: Impressions by his Contemporaries*, pp. 197, 200, 201.

72. Schindler, *Beethoven As I Knew Him*, p. 456.

73. As paraphrased in Burk, *Clara Schumann: A Romantic Biography*, p. 253, expressed during the Schu-

manns' almost six-year residency in Dresden (after 13 December 1844), where they also had social contact with Wagner and the future sculptor of Wagner's and Sir George Smart's much desired Weber monument (unveiled 1860), Ernst Rietschel (1804–1861), who would found the Dres den Sculpture School with his colleague Hähnel.

74. Wagner, *My Life*, 1:413.

75. Berlioz, *Berlioz: Evenings with the Orchestra*, p. 337.

76. Ibid., pp. 337–38.

77. Hallé, *The Autobiography of Charles Hallé*, p. 103. He continued: "...Liszt, to our dismay, began the whole cantata over again, inflicting it a second time on the im mense audience, who, out of respect for the crowned heads, had to endure it, though probably not without inward grumbling." Ibid., pp. 103–4.

78. Berlioz, *Berlioz: Evenings with the Orchestra*, p. 338.

79. Ibid., p. 340, Liszt himself thought highly of this first Beethoven cantata. In 1848 he wrote: "Since my Beethoven Cantata I have written nothing so striking and so spontaneous." La Mara, *Letters of Franz Liszt*, 1:88. Nevertheless, the manuscript remains unpublished at Weimar.

80. As quoted in Young, *Beethoven: A Victorian Tribute*, p. 81. Actually there was more music by Beethoven—an aria from *Fidelio* and *Adelaïde*, with Liszt accompanying at the piano (Moscheles had been invited to do the slight honors by the blundering Breidenstein, but declined with hurt dignity).

81. Moscheles, *Recent Music and Musicians*, p. 317.

82. Young, *Beethoven: A Victorian Tribute*, pp. 82–85. England was a little ahead of Germany in lessening the political and social restrictions on Jews at that time. Here is Moscheles's account of the disastrous banquet: "Immediately after the King's health had been proposed, Wolff, the Improvisatore, gave a toast which he called the 'Trefoil.' It was to represent the perfect chord, Spohr, the keynote, Liszt, the connecting link between all parties, the third—Professor Breidenstein, the Dominant, leading all things to a happy solution. Universal applause. Spohr proposes the health of the Queen of England, Dr. Wolff that of the Professor Hähnel, the sculptor of the monument, and also that of the brass founder. Liszt proposes Prince Albert; a professor with a stentorian voice is laughed and coughed down, people will not listen to him, and then ensued a series of most disgraceful scenes which originated thus: Liszt spoke rather abstrusely upon the subject of the festival. 'Here all nations are met to pay honor to the master. May they live and prosper, the Dutch, the English, the Viennese who have made a pilgrimage hither!' Upon this Chelard gets up in a passion and screams out to Liszt, '*Vous avez oublié les Français.*' Many voices break in, a regular tumult ensues, some for, some against the speaker. At last Liszt makes himself heard, but, in trying to exculpate himself, seems to get entangled deeper and deeper in a labyrinth of words, seeking to convince his hearers that he has lived fifteen years among Frenchmen, and would certainly not intentionally speak slightingly of them. The contending parties, however, become more uproarious, many leave their seats, the din becomes deafening, and the ladies pale with fright. The fete is interrupted for a full hour." Moscheles, *Recent Music and Musicians*, pp. 317–18.

83. As cited by Lingg, *Mephisto Waltz: The Story of Franz Liszt*, p. 142.

84. Although the festival brought in 12,900 thaler, there was a deficit of 2,893 thaler, which was defrayed by the king of Prussia (800 thaler) and the members of the Bonn committee (see Young, *Beethoven: A Victorian Tribute*, p. 88). Walker, taking Liszt's word for it, is in error when he states that there was no loss, see Walker, *Franz Liszt: The Virtuoso Years 1811–1847*, p. 417, n. 2. Until the accounts for the festival were closed, Liszt's Beethoven Hall money was tied up in escrow, with the result that he almost went bankrupt immediately following the festival.

85. Berlioz, *Berlioz: Evenings with the Orchestra*, p. 339. Inspired by the events at Bonn, Berlioz completed the score to his *Damnation of Faust* the following year.

86. Such speculative conclusions concerning Lyser's enthusiastic iconography did not come to me without considerable consultation with musicologist friends and colleagues. I gladly acknowledge their aid and thank the following in particular for taking the time to muse, sometimes in great detail, on the layers of Lyser's labyrinth: Philip Gossett, David B. Greene, Robert Gutman, Virginia Hancock, Joseph Kerman, Donald Mitchell, Claudio Spies, Leonard Stein, William Weaver, Christoph Wolff, and Elizabeth Wood. The art historian Julius Held drew my attention to important details in panels two and seven. I have not been able to agree with all my colleagues' helpful suggestions and should like to point out two alternative readings: Joseph Kerman sees panel seven (*Ruins of Athens*) as a likely candidate for *An die ferne Geliebte*, and Richard Strawn points out that the pine trees in panel two (*Egmont*) suggest the idea of Coriolanus returning to Rome, hence a reference to Beethoven's *Coriolanus* Overture, op. 62.

87. Sonneck, *Beethoven: Impressions by his Contemporaries*, p. 201.

88. Berlioz, *Berlioz: Evenings with the Orchestra*, pp. 343–44.

89. Ibid., p. 326. Berlioz's two-part report on the Bonn festival was originally published in the *Journal des Débats* on 22 August and 3 September 1845.

90. As cited in May, *The Life of Johannes Brahms*, 2:552. The Schumann monument was created by the wellknown Weimar sculptor Adolf Dorndorf (1835–1916). In 1896 Clara Schumann was laid to rest beside the body of her husband in Bonn and the forty-year separation was ended.

91. In January 1903 Bourdelle wrote of the Beethoven heads he had sculpted: "As a child, then as a boy, an adolescent, and a man, I have harvested the harmonious words of Beethoven; it is they that give life to the brow in the faces of him that I construct, it is they that determine their gazes, they that bring order to his hair." As quoted in Michel Dufet, *Das Drama Beethoven Erlebt von Bourdelle* (Paris, [1970]), p. 7, translation mine.

92. "*Moi je suis Bachus qui pressure pour les hommes le nectar delicieux.*" Not even Bourdelle the believer felt compelled to affix the entire heady line, which ends the wine metaphor, as reported by Bettina, with the results for humanity of musical wine imbibing: "...and makes them spiritually drunken." (See chapter 3 and n. 160.) A replica of this particular Beethoven head, known as the "Metropolitan," is at The Metropolitan

Museum of Art in New York (in the reading library); another copy is at the Kranner Art Center, University of Illinois, Urbana.

93. Although Rolland was interested in the emancipation of women, this did not extend to their participating in his aesthetic enjoyment of Beethoven. He makes this fascinating, frank statement after referring to Beethoven as the most virile of musicians: ''I must confess that, a very few works excepted, I do not care to hear him played by women.'' See Romain Rolland, *Beethoven the Creator* (1927; trans. Ernest Newman, New York, 1929; 1964), p. 295, n. 3.

94. At this juncture Rolland in a footnote to his readers warns: ''But we must mistrust here the testimony of Schindler, who hated Holz for having ousted him.'' Ibid., p. 297, n. 10.

95. Ibid., pp. 3–6. This self-protective maxim is quoted from the same Schindler against whom Rolland had just warned his readers (see Schindler, *Beethoven As I Knew Him*, p. 105, for quotation of the text Rolland consulted). Beethoven's remark was however actually written down in a conversation book of February 1823; see ThayerForbes, *Thayer's Life of Beethoven*, p. 290, where explanatory additions to these remarks inserted later by Schindler are indicated in brackets. See also MacArdle's editorial remark in Schindler, *Beethoven As I Knew Him*, p. 190, . 71. Ludwig Nohl, in his biography of Beethoven (1864–77) interpreted Beethoven's remark for his audience: ''Beethoven had said of himself that he had something to do in the world beside marrying. His ideal was not to live in such cramped circumstances. He knew of 'nobler and better things.' '' See John J. Lalor, trans., *Life of Beethoven by Louis Nohl* (Chicago, 1896), p. 66.

96. Rolland, *Beethoven the Creator*, pp. 8–9.

97. Ibid., p. 10.

98. Ibid., pp. 10–11.

99. Ibid., pp. 11–12.

100. Ibid., p. 17. Rolland is paraphrasing Beethoven's pun-motto with which we have met before: ''I do not write notes, I write out of necessity.''

101. Ibid., pp. 22–23. Delacroix's heroic mural of *Jacob Wrestling with the Angel* in Saint-Sulpice makes a fine visual counterpart (and perhaps inspired Rolland, who was also an art historian) to this motif of ''body locked with body, whether for war or in an embrace.''

102. Ibid., p. 34.

103. Ibid. The implied shift from Beethoven the Creator, of Rolland's conception, to Beethoven the Conqueror, occurred with Emil Ludwig (1881–1948), who first approached the composer as one of three cultural giants in his *Three Titans* (1927; [New York, 1930]; the other two were Michelangelo and Rembrandt), then devoted an entire book to the composer, *Beethoven: Life of a Conqueror* (New York, 1943). Beethoven veneration ran in this German author's family: his grandfather was so enamored of him that he gave each of his three sons the middle name of Ludwig; his father legally changed the family name from Cohn to Ludwig in 1883. Emil discovered Beethoven for himself as a boy of twelve when, recuperating from an operation, he listened to his mother read him a short biography of the composer. Rolland's emphasis on Beethoven, the musical rule breaker, had been taken up by Robert Haven Schauffler in his long book *Beethoven: The Man Who Freed Music*, see chapter 4, n. 677.

104. D'Indy had actually served in the Franco-Prussian War of 1870–71; perhaps this sobered him somewhat as to the political regenerative force of music. Nevertheless, a pilgrimage to Bayreuth in 1876 made him a Wagnerite for life—he was writing about *Parsifal* on the day he died, fifty-five years later. For more on the French Beethoven fallout, especially after World War I, see the ever alert and informative Schrade, *Beethoven in France*, pp. 200–51.

105. In Italy even the author and daring World War I aviator Gabriele d'Annunzio (1863–1938) kept a replica of Beethoven's life mask (along with one of Liszt) enshrined on the wall of his crowded music room at his Vittoriale villa in Gardone on Lake Garda.

106. See chapter 3, n. 57.

107. Reported by Hanslick in one of his ''Musical Letters from Paris'' in the 21 July 1867 issue of the *Neue Freie Presse*; see Thayer-Forbes, *Thayer's Life of Beethoven*, p. 805 and n. 37. Rossini also queried his visitor about a Vienna monument to Mozart. Mozart was not honored with a monument until 1896—a marble ''Rococo'' standing figure by Victor Tilgner (1844–1896), now in the Burggarten off the Ring (see below, n. 138).

108. The poem, the best virtue of which is that it rhymes, concludes with a pious invocation of Beethoven's reputed nongreeting of the royal family:

> Sie wandern wieder in Waldalleen
> Entwickeln und fassen Weltideen
> Und links und rechts bleibt Alles steh'n
> Lässzt ungegrüsst nicht vorübergeh'n.
> (Once again they walk through forest lanes
> Solving and grappling with world ideas
> And left and right the people stand still,
> Left once more ungreeted.)

From the pamphlet *Beethoven-Monument in Heiligenstadt bei Wien* (Vienna, 1863), pp. 21–22.

109. The artist was Robert Weigl (1851[52?]–1902), the Viennese sculptor also responsible for a Schubert bust and bronze statuette of Schubert (Schubert Museum, Vienna). In honor of the two-hundredth performance of *The Gypsy Baron*, Weigl's silver statuette of a waltzing couple was presented to Johann Strauss, Jr.

110. Schindler, *Beethoven As I Knew Him*, pp. 144–45. Schindler, who had not been back to Vienna for thirty years when he wrote this reminiscence, mistakenly wrote ''Grinzing'' for ''Nussdorf,'' as Thayer points out, see Thayer-Forbes, *Thayer's Life of Beethoven*, p. 437 and n. 16; see also chapter 3 in this book and n. 38.

111. ''An excessively idealized bust of the composer'' is Thayer's description, Thayer-Forbes, *Thayer's Life of Beethoven*, p. 437, n. 16.

112. The bust was begun by the Berlin sculptor Wilhelm Wolff (1816–1887) and completed by his student, the Bonn sculptor Karl Voss (1825–1896).

113. The arrangement of the two k's was even more complicated. 'All in all, how many remarkable things might be said about that vanished Kakania! For instance, it was *kaiserlich-königlich* (imperial-royal) and it was *kaiserlich und königlich* (imperial and royal); one of the two abbreviations, *k. k.* or *k. & k.*, applied to everything and person, but esoteric love was nevertheless required in order to be sure of distinguishing which institutions and persons were to be referred to as *k. k.* and which as *k. & k.*'' See Robert Musil, *The Man Without Qualities* (New York, 1953), 1:32–33.

114. Kundmann also did the tombstone (1888) erected over Schubert's new grave at the Vienna Central Cemetery. Beethoven's friend and eulogist Grillparzer would also be honored with a memorial by Kundmann (see below, n. 138).

115. Wagner, *Cosima Wagner's Diaries*, 1:446, entry of 4 January 1872. Wagner was apparently reminiscing about his Penzing period in Vienna (1863) and the event he refers to may have taken place at the same time as the June unveiling of Fernkorn's bust in Heiligenstadt Park. Beethoven "houses" in Vienna's nineteenth district are at Silbergasse No. 4 (1815), Pfarrplatz No. 2 (1817, where he did indeed compose the *Pastoral* Symphony), and Pykergasse No. 13 (1822). Wagner's next comment to Cosima in regard to Beethoven's Heiligenstadt surroundings is an interesting if unconscious denial of Schindler's brookinspired Beethoven description: "Well, you have only to see that place, its barren nature, to see what the relationship is between the work of genius and its creator's life." Ibid.

116. See above, n. 73.

117. Howard E. Hugo, trans., *The Letters of Franz Liszt to Marie zu Sayn-Wittgenstein* (Cambridge [Massachusetts], 1953), pp. 150–51.

118. Ibid., p. 151.

119. Ibid., pp. 151–152, letter written from Budapest dated 3 December 1872.

120. Ibid., p. 152, letter written from Budapest dated 10 December 1872.

121. Ibid., pp. 152–53.

122. Ibid., p. 153.

123. See chapter 4, n. 607. Zumbusch also took the death mask of Johann Strauss, Jr.

124. As an insider Feuerbach, who taught at the Vienna Academy from 1873 to 1876, was able to give a dry report on Zumbusch's self-promotion to his stepmother in a letter of 1874: "The Ministry received a hint from Zumbusch that was served up with a pitch fork." In O. J. Kern and Hermann Uhde-Bernays, eds., *Anselm Feuerbachs Briefe an seine Mutter*, 2 vols. (Berlin, 1911), 2:304.

125. Hugo, *The Letters of Franz Liszt to Marie zu Sayn-Wittgenstein*, p. 166, letter of 16 February 1874.

126. La Mara, *Letters of Franz Liszt*, 2:311, letter dated 10 December 1876. How Liszt really felt about it is reflected in this line from a letter he wrote Princess Marie from Budapest on 20 November 1876: "In mid-March it would be hard for me to avoid the boring chore of a Concert for the Vienna Beethoven Monument...." Hugo, *The Letters of Franz Liszt to Marie zu Sayn-Wittgenstein*, p. 205.

127. As early as his 28 November 1872 letter to Princess Marie (see above, n. 117) Liszt had expressed his reluctance to include his new Beethoven cantata (op. 68, written in 1869–70 for the occasion of a Musicians' Convention in Weimar in May 1870): "Confidentially, I may add that, while being really grateful for the idea of placing my Beethoven cantata on the program, I hesitate to follow this path." See Hugo, *The Letters of Franz Liszt to Marie zu Sayn-Wittgenstein*, p. 150. Liszt seemed genuinely to consider his cantata homage to Beethoven not worthy for scheduling in a Beethoven fund-raising concert. He wrote Hans Richter, thanking him for his intention to give the Beethoven cantata in a performance at the Opera House, and declared that Beethoven's andante from the *Archduke* Trio, which he had again

quoted in his new cantata, "shines like a guiding star, above my insignificant work." La Mara, *Letters of Franz Liszt*, 2:303, letter of 10 November 1876.

128. A week later Liszt was visiting the Wagners in Wahnfried and Cosima reported "much pleasurable chat, mostly concerning Vienna, where my father played for the Beethoven memorial." Wagner, *Cosima Wagner's Diaries*, 1:954, entry of 24 March 1877; see also p. 1148.

129. As quoted by Sitwell, *Liszt*, p. 293.

130. Letter of Busoni to his wife from Basel, 15 May 1912, as quoted by Hugo Leichtentritt (author of the earliest monograph on Busoni, 1916) in *Music, History and Ideas* (Cambridge [Massachusetts], 1941), p. 191.

131. The intricacies of whether a residential building on the Ringstrasse was a *Palast* (or palais, as in Dumba's new Parkring mansion), an *Adelspalais* ("aristocratic palace"), a *Wohnpalast* ("apartment palace") or *Mietpalast* ("rent palace"), or, from the view of the owner-renter, a *Zinspalast* ("interest-bearing palace") are amusingly clarified for the English reader by Carl E. Schorske in *Fin-de-Siècle Vienna: Politics and Culture* (New York, 1980), p. 47; see also Renate Wagner-Rieger, *Wiens Architecktur im 19. Jahrhundert* (Vienna, 1970).

132. As cited in Schorske, *Fin-de-Siècle Vienna: Politics and Culture*, p. 30.

133. The occasion was the celebration of the twenty-fifth anniversary of the reign of Franz Josef, and the Votivkirche was still six years from completion; see Liszt's two letters of 1873 concerning this in Hugo, *The Letters of Franz Liszt to Marie zu Sayn-Wittgenstein*, pp. 161–62.

134. The Kolowratring (now subsumed into the Schubertring) was named after Count Kolowrat (d. 1862), whose private palais was in this spot before expansion of the Ring began; see Eugen Guglia, ed., *Wien: Ein Führer durch Stadt und Umgebung* (Vienna, 1908), p. 103.

135. The Polytechnisches Institut became the Technische Hochschule around the turn of the century and is now called the Technische Universität. The city of Trieste, where Ressel had tried out his invention on the thirtythree-ton steamer *Civetta* in 1829, and for which the Ressel monument was originally intended, declined the honor. Not because the far-away Habsburg provincial capital was excessively anti-Austrian on this occasion, but because the city town council had been advised by its Academy of Science faculty that Ressel might not be remembered by history as the acknowledged inventordeveloper of the screw propeller. They were right. Ressel's model was not perfected and his invention remained unworkable.

136. As cited in Hans-Ernst Mittig and Volker Plagermann, eds., *Denkmäler im 19. Jahrhundert* (Munich, 1972), p. 13.

137. Ibid., pp. 13–14.

138. Unveiled 23 May 1889 and located in the Volksgarten opposite Theophil Hansen's neoclassical Parliament building (1873–83) on the then Franzensring (now Dr.-Karl-Renner-Ring). A bronze bust of Grillparzer had been set up in the Baden Kurpark as early as 1874. Other noncontroversial (from a political if not always aesthetic standpoint) "citizen" musician and writer monuments followed: Mozart, by Victor Tilgner in 1896 (originally opposite the Albertina Museum in the Albrechtsplatz; since 1953 in the Burggarten off the Op-

ernring; see above, n. 107); Bruckner, also by Tilgner, in 1899 (in the Stadtpark); Goethe, by Edmund Hellmer in 1900 (on the edge of the Burggarten facing the Schiller monument across the Ring); Strauss-Lanner, by Robert Örley and Franz Seifert, in 1905 (Rathauspark); Brahms, by Rudolf Weyr, in 1908 (originally in the Ressel Park of the Karlsplatz; recently moved closer to the Musikverein building on the Lothringer-Strasse side of the Karlsplatz); and Strauss, Jr., by Hellmer, in 1921 (Stadtpark).

139. It is interesting that Hähnel, whose bronze equestrian statue of Field Marshal Prince Karl of Schwarzenberg had graced the large Schwarzenbergplatz since 1867, was not invited to compete by Dumba's committee. This was not Hähnel's only work for Vienna. During the mid-1860s he had produced for the balustrade of the loggia of the opera house five much admired bronze figures representing Heroism, Drama, Fantasy, Comedy, and Love. Hähnel, who had cofounded the Dresden Sculpture School in 1860 (see above, n. 73), was a robust sixty-two when the committee announced the Vienna Beethoven competition in May 1873—perhaps it was intended to be kept an ''Austrian'' affair (Zumbusch had just moved to Vienna that month to assume his professorship at the Academy; Kundmann, Benk, and Wagner had all been born within the confines of the AustroHungarian Empire). If, on the other hand, Zumbusch fared well in southern Germany and Austria, he did not do so in Bonn: his 1862 entry model for a world competition held by Bonn for a monument to the North German patriot Ernst Moritz Arndt (1769–1860) was rejected.

140. The latest scholar to report this is Hans-Ernst Mittig in ''Das Wiener Beethoven-Denkmal von Zumbusch und die Wende der Beethoven-Darstellung,'' *Alte und Moderne Kunst* 14, no. 104 (May–June, 1969):25–33, p. 27, n. 32.

141. ''The colossal Beethoven in bronze,'' it was designated. Soon after, Zumbusch was made a corresponding member of the French Academy in honor of his Beethoven achievement.

142. Carl von Vincenti, as quoted by Maria Kolisko (friend and biographer of Zumbusch) in *Caspar von Zumbusch* (Vienna, 1931), p. 54, n. 1.

143. Ibid., p. 56. Zumbusch already had had experience in sculpting the busts of well-known historical personages. In 1864, for Baron Stiglitz of Saint Petersburg, he did bronze busts of Shakespeare, Dante, Goethe, Schiller, Cervantes, Voltaire, and Byron, among others.

144. Franz Brentano was a frequent and welcome visitor to Zumbusch's busy atelier on the Arsenalweg, high above the Belvedere, with its excellent view of Vienna and its surroundings.

145. Anderson, *The Letters of Beethoven*, 3:1095.

146. Carl von Vincenti's suggestion, as reported by Mittig, ''Das Wiener Beethoven-Denkmal von Zumbusch und die Wende der Beethoven-Darstellung,'' p. 32. Mittig himself thinks the nine putti may also refer to Beethoven's *Creatures of Prometheus* ballet (op. 43) in a free paraphrase of the different scenes, ibid.

147. Mittig points out that together, the lute-playing putto and the swan are the symbol of Vienna's Gesellschaft der Musikfreunde. Ibid., pp. 32–33.

148. Kolisko, *Caspar von Zumbusch*, p. 54; this was written before the sculptor knew that his design had been selected by the jury.

149. This precedent is presented by Mittig, ''Das Wiener Beethoven-Denkmal von Zumbusch und die Wende des Beethoven-Darstellung,'' pp. 28–29. He also illustrates Schwind's *Fidelio*, see text below.

150. See above, n. 139.

151. Schwind had already begun the commission (1863) to do fresco scenes from Mozart's *The Magic Flute* for the loggia of the Vienna Opera House (completed 1866–67).

152. As quoted in Kolisko, *Caspar von Zumbusch*, p. 63.

153. Ibid., pp. 63–64, translation mine.

154. The Beethoven clan's letter to Zumbusch is given in ibid., pp. 63–64. Karl and Caroline had married in 1832. The birth dates of Beethoven's grandnieces and grandnephew are: Karoline, 1833; Marie, 1835; Ludwig, 1839; Gabriele, 1844; Hermine, 1852. Hermine became a pianist. The only person who could have claimed to be Beethoven's ''niece'' was Amalie, daughter from another liaison of the wife of Beethoven's brother Johann, but she had died in 1831. Beethoven's sister-in-law Johanna, mother of his beloved nephew, later (1820) had an illegitimate daughter whom she named, somewhat pointedly, Ludovica (Beethoven had taken her Karl; she would have her strange revenge).

155. *Wiener Allgemeine Zeitung*, as quoted in ibid., p. 64.

156. Hugo, *The Letters of Franz Liszt to Marie zu Sayn-Wittgenstein*, p. 245, letter dated Weimar, 12 May 1880. Liszt had just been speaking of the new Schumann monument in Bonn.

157. Zumbusch made a second bronze reduction in 1894 for a Utrecht musician, and another one in 1897 for the general music director in Dresden, see Kolisko, *Caspar von Zumbusch*, p. 133. In 1877 Zumbusch had also carved a marble colossal bust of Beethoven for a certain H. Nowotny of Dresden, ibid.

158. Ibid., p. 59.

CHAPTER SIX:
VIENNA'S BEETHOVEN OF 1902:
APOTHEOSIS AND REDEMPTION

1. Henry-Louis de La Grange, in his continuing biography of the composer, tells us in *Mahler*, vol. 1 (New York, 1973), pp. 40–41, that one morning in November of 1876 when the new student arrived two hours late to class and was about to be admonished, Mahler escaped punishment by declaring to the professor that he had been attending the unveiling of the new Schiller monument. La Grange gives the date of the Liszt fund-raising concert as 16 March (ibid., p. 42), but Liszt sources give the date as 18 March. Around the same time Mahler also heard Anton Rubinstein play the complete cycle of the Beethoven piano sonatas, performed especially for the Conservatory students. Busoni and Mahler, the two youthful witnesses of Liszt's 1877 homage to Beethoven, would join forces more than once in their later careers: the pianist was soloist under Mahler in Beethoven's Piano Concerto no. 5 at a concert of the Vienna Philharmonic on 26 February 1899, and appeared under Mahler's baton again in Beethoven's Piano Concerto no. 4 at an allBeethoven performance in Strassburg on 22 May 1905.

2. Julius Langbehn, *Rembrandt als Erzieher, Von einem Deutschen* (1890; 39th ed. [Leipzig, 1891]), p. 22 (translation mine). For a readable presentation and discussion of Langbehn's book and impact see Fritz Stern, *The Politics of Cultural Despair: A Study in the Rise of the Germanic Ideology* (Berkeley, 1961).

3. Langbehn's commercial success and pell-mell prose invited a bevy of parodies. One of these, written "Also by a German," and satanically entitled *Höllenbreughel als Erzieher* (Leipzig, 1890, published in the same size and format as the Langbehn original), has a delightfully nonsequitur "analysis" of Beethoven's Ninth Symphony, pp. 85–85.

4. Brahms, who had met the artist briefly in 1880, received Klinger's *Brahmsphantasie* (op. 12, 1894)—a suite of forty-one etchings and lithographs—quite unexpectedly one day in the mail in 1894. The notes of his *Schicksalslied* had been meticulously engraved on the copper plates that bore Klinger's fantastic pictorial response to the composer's setting of Hölderlin's fatalistic poem on human destiny. After initial reservations Brahms was quite won over, sent them to Joachim to admire, and in an eloquent return gesture during the summer of 1896 published his penultimate work, the *Four Serious Songs* (op. 121), with a dedication to Klinger. Later (1905–9) Klinger created a marble Brahms monument for the Hamburg Musikhalle (see Fig. 204). Klinger also made a bronze mask of Brahms, and sculpted images of other musicians (see Figs. 201–203). He was friends with the composer Max Reger (who moved to Leipzig in 1907) and sketched him on his deathbed in 1916.

5. Alma Mahler, *Gustav Mahler: Memories and Letters* (1946; rev. ed., Seattle, 1971), p. 239.

6. Ibid., p. 115. And yet, as Alma points out, Gustav did not live to finish his Tenth Symphony, nor to hear the Ninth performed.

7. As told to his close friend the violinist Natalie BauerLechner, who recorded Mahler's conversations with her in a journal (*Erinnerungen an Gustav Mahler* [Leipzig, 1923]), as given in Dika Newlin, *Bruckner, Mahler, Schoenberg* (London, 1978), p. 164.

8. This specific late Beethoven evocation has been pointed out by Kolodin, *The Interior Beethoven*, p. 311.

9. Knud Martner, ed., *Selected Letters of Gustav Mahler* (New York, 1979), p. 324, letter dated Toblach, 18 July 1908.

10. Mahler, *Gustav Mahler: Memories and Letters*, p. 291, letter written in July 1907.

11. Ibid., p. 183.

12. Martner, *Selected Letters of Gustav Mahler*, p. 244, letter of 19 August 1900 to Siegfried Lipiner (1856–1911).

13. Ibid., p. 237, letter to Lipiner of July 1899. Repeating himself in this way was highly characteristic of Mahler as Alma noted: "It was a habit of his to repeat for days and weeks, even months together, some thought which particularly pleased him, turning it over in his mind and introducing variations." Mahler, *Gustav Mahler: Memories and Letters*, p. 184.

14. As quoted by Michael Kennedy, *Mahler* (London, 1974), p. 25. See also the less satisfying translation in Bruno Walter, *Gustav Mahler* (1957; New York, 1974), pp. 5, 7.

15. Walter, *Gustav Mahler*, p. 4.

16. Ibid., pp. 19, 93.

17. Ibid., p. 67.

18. Ibid., p. 125.

19. During his tenure at the Leipzig Opera House (August 1886–May 1888) Mahler had fallen in love with Marion von Weber (wife of Weber's grandson) while editing Weber's uncompleted comic opera *Die drei Pintos*, presented at Leipzig on 20 January 1888. The First Symphony took sudden shape in what Mahler mysteriously referred to as "this trilogy of the passions and whirlwind of life" in a letter of 4 January 1888 to his archaeologist friend Friedrich Löhr (1859–1924) in Vienna, see Martner, *Gustav Mahler: Selected Letters*, p. 109. By midMarch 1888 Mahler joyously reported to Löhr about the genesis of the just completed First Symphony: "It has turned out so overwhelming it came gushing out of me like a mountain torrent! This summer you shall hear it. All of a sudden all the sluice-gates in me opened! Perhaps one of these days I shall tell you how it all happened!" Ibid., p. 112. Goethe-reader Bruno Walter characterized the work thus: "[Mahler's] First Symphony might be called his *Werther*. There a heart-rending experience finds artistic release." Walter, *Gustav Mahler*, p. 120. Mahler himself wrote of the First Symphony eight years later that it began "at a point beyond the *love affair*," and that "the real-life experience was the *reason* for the work, not its content." Letter dated Hamburg, 26 March 1896, to the music critic Max Marschalk (1863–1940), whose proposed interpretation of the symphony had greatly pleased Mahler. Martner, *Gustav Mahler: Selected Letters*, p. 179. Martner believes the "love affair" mentioned refers to an earlier infatuation of Mahler's for Johanna Richter, a theater singer at Kassel with whom he became embroiled at the end of 1884.

20. Natalie Bauer-Lechner (see above, n. 7) wrote that Mahler intended in the First Symphony to portray the life, sufferings, struggle, and defeat of a vigorous, heroic man; as paraphrased in Kurt Blaukopf, *Mahler* (London, 1969), p. 76.

21. Letter dated Hamburg, 26 March 1896, to Max Marschalk in Berlin (see above, n. 19), in Martner, *Gustav Mahler: Selected Letters*, p. 180.

22. Martner, *Gustav Mahler: Selected Letters*, p. 212, letter dated Hamburg, 17 February 1897, to the Dessau critic and professor of music history, Arthur Seidl (1863–1928). Seidl wrote books on Wagner and Richard Strauss and was a lifelong admirer of Mahler. See Theodor Reik, *The Haunting Melody* (New York, 1953) for a Freudian interpretation of how the death of Bülow "liberated" Mahler from his composing block on the Second Symphony.

23. This is pointed out and elaborated upon in Blaukopf, *Mahler*, pp. 76–77. "*From Beethoven onwards* there is no modern music that has not its inner programme," Mahler wrote in a letter of January 1902 to Brahms's friend and biographer Max Kalbeck. Martner, *Gustav Mahler: Selected Letters*, p. 262.

24. Martner, *Gustav Mahler: Selected Letters*, p. 212, letter of 17 February 1897 to Seidl (see above, n. 22). In 1897 Mahler had not of course yet written his other purely instrumental symphonies besides the First (Fifth, Sixth, Seventh, and—avoiding the Beethoven comparison—Ninth).

25. Ibid., p. 165, letter to Arnold Berliner (1865–1942).

26. Ibid., p. 166, letter to Arnold Berliner, undated (Hamburg, September 1895).

465

27. Ibid., n. 3.

28. As quoted in Blaukopf, *Mahler*, p. 152. The agitated critic was Hanslick's successor, Richard Heuberger (1850–1914), a musician who had given up vocal conducting for music criticism in 1881. At least Hanslick's hope, expressed in 1861, that Beethoven's Ninth Symphony would be loved was fulfilled by the protective protests of Vienna's critics against Mahler's version of the symphony. The Vienna Philharmonic Concerts were founded by Carl Otto Nicolai (1810–1849) in 1842 for the express purpose of offering the public first-rate performances of Beethoven's symphonies. In 1843, after thirteen separate rehearsals of the Ninth, Nicolai reintroduced it to Viennese concertgoers with great success.

29. As given in La Grange, *Mahler*, 1:556–57.

30. As quoted in Blaukopf, *Mahler*, p. 154. Mahler's Polish translator friend Siegfried Lipiner (see above, n. 12) had lent a hand in the writing of this pamphlet and this may explain its rather awkward verbosity.

31. Ibid., pp. 154–55.

32. La Grange, *Mahler*, 1:609. Mahler's published defense of his Beethoven interpretation provided a regular field day for the clever Hirschfeld, who wittily berated him for lack of logic as well as style: "Herr Mahler is not obliged to write intelligible German, but neither is he obliged to demonstrate this fact to the public. . . ." Ibid., p. 558.

33. As recorded by Walter, *Gustav Mahler*, p. 93.

34. Quoted in La Grange, *Mahler*, 1:542.

35. As given in Mahler, *Gustav Mahler: Memories and Letters*, p. 184.

36. Mahler had already tried interpolating the *Leonore* Overture no. 3 at the beginning of the last act for his Drury Lane Theatre performance in London on 2 July 1892.

37. The description is not by Klinger but by a bold contributor to the exhibition catalogue, Paul Kühn. I have followed the translation provided in Peter Vergo, *Art in Vienna 1898–1918* (London, 1975), p. 44. An earlier mixedmedia work of Klinger's, *The Judgment of Paris* of 1885–87—a large oil painting laid out in triptych format and provided with a colored wood and plaster sculpture border—had been received by the public with wild acclaim and was acquired for the Austrian state in 1901.

38. The project had begun in the early 1870s with Hans Makart's sumptuous wall and ceiling paintings in the study (1872–73). This was followed by a commission for decorating the dining room, carried out by Klimt's colleague Franz Matsch (1861–1942) during 1893–99. Klimt began work on the music salon in 1897, busying himself with every aspect of the interior design, in true Gesamtkunstwerk spirit. His figural contributions were the two supraporte panels *Music* of 1898 and *Schubert at the Piano* of 1899 (see Fig. 157). For excellent discussion and reproductions of the Dumba decorations, see Christian M. Nebehay, *Gustav Klimt Dokumentation* (Vienna, 1969), pp. 170–78. After the death of Dumba's widow in 1937 the contents of the palais were scattered.

39. Balestrieri had a second myth-perpetuating success in 1905 with a Venice showing of his *Chopin Triptychon*. The following year the Algierian-born artist Lucien LévyDhurmer (1865–1953) produced a Beethoven "Symbolist" triptych in pastel featuring in the center panel the head of Beethoven floating frontally in close focus against a nondefined, "mystic" background (the lateral "panels" were entitled *The Appassionata* and *Hymn to Joy*). This artist also produced Symbolist "responses" to the music of Fauré and Debussy.

40. From Ernst Stöhr's foreword to the Beethoven exhibition catalogue of the fourteenth Secession exhibition (*XIV. Kunstaustellung der Vereinigung Bildender Künstler Österreichs Secession*, Vienna, April–June, 1902), pp. 11–12, translation mine.

41. Ibid., pp. 15–20.

42. Ibid., pp. 25–26, translation mine.

43. Review of 20 April 1902 as collected by Hermann Bahr in his book *Gegen Klimt* (Vienna, 1903) and quoted in Nebehay, *Gustav Klimt Dokumentation*, p. 297.

44. Klimt's Mahler-as-knight figure was reproduced in an early tribute to Mahler by the critic Paul Stefan (1879–1943) in *Gustav Mahler—Ein Bild seiner Persönlichkeit in Widmung* (Munich, 1910). The once widespread presumption of this tantalizing analogy was first pointed out to me in 1962 by a friend and patron of Klimt, Frau Friedericke Beer-Monti, see my books *Egon Schiele's Portraits* (Berkeley, 1974), pp. viii, 127–32, and *Gustav Klimt* (New York, 1975), p. 24 and n. 27.

45. This interpretation follows that of Joseph August Lux in his 1902 review article "Klinger's Beethoven und die Moderne Raum-Kunst," *Deutsche Kunst und Dekoration* 10 (1902):475–517, especially p. 480.

46. And to Albrecht Dürer, see my *Gustav Klimt*, p. 24 and Figs. 38 and 39.

47. "I often had to laugh when critics saw profound philosophical problems secretly inserted into his pictures, problems about which Klimt had certainly never thought," wrote Klimt's painter colleague Josef Engelhard (1864–1941) in his memoirs, *Ein Wiener Mahler Erzählt: Mein Leben und Meine Modelle* (Vienna, 1943), p. 101.

48. As quoted in Nebehay, *Gustav Klimt Dokumentation*, p. 297; see above, n. 43.

49. Ibid.

50. As reported by the hostess and translator of Rodin's remark to Klimt, Berta Szeps-Zuckerkandl, *My Life and History* (New York, 1939), p. 181. Rodin passed through Vienna in June on his way back to Paris from a visit to Prague, where an exhibition of his works had been held. For more on Rodin's lengthy tour of the Klimt-Klinger Beethoven Exhibition, see Berta Zuckerkandl, "August Rodin in Wien (1902)" in Reinhard Federmann, ed., *Österreich intim, Erinnerungen 1892–1942* (Frankfurt, 1970), p. 58.

51. The wealthy Graz industrialist and noted art collector Carl Reininghaus was responsible for fending off the intended destruction of Klimt's *Beethoven Frieze*. He offered to buy the fragile work in its entirety and had it carefully removed in seven parts from the Secession walls afte r the exhibition was over. In 1915 Reininghaus sold the frieze to another Klimt admirer, August Lederer (whose wife, Serena, had been painted by Klimt in 1899), and in 1973 it was acquired by the republic of Austria. Over the next decade the work was extensively and successfully restored. In the summer of 1985 the entire frieze of seven panels was installed in a plaster reproduction of the original Secession showroom as part of the ambitious *Traum und Wirklichkeit* exhibition mounted by the city of Vienna. It has since been installed permanently in the basement of the newly renovated Secession building. For a richly illustrated his-

tory of the frieze and its related 148 drawings (given by Klimt as a gift to the Lederer family), see Marian Bisanz-Prakken, *Gustav Klimt: Der Beethovenfries* (Salzburg, 1977).

52. As given in Gerhard Winkler, *Max Klinger 1857–1920* (exhibition catalogue of the Leipzig Museum of Fine Arts for the fiftieth anniversary of the death of Klinger, 4 July–20 September 1970) (Leipzig, 1970), p. 55.

53. Elsa Asenijeff, *Max Klingers Beethoven: Eine Kunsttechnische Studie* (Leipzig, 1902), pp. 21, 22.

54. Klinger spent several years in Italy (from February 1888 to March 1893) with Rome as his headquarters studying classical sculpture, in particular examples of Roman polychromy.

55. According to Asenijeff, *Max Klingers Beethoven: Eine Kunst-technische Studie*, p. 4.

56. The fifty daughters of Danaus—the Danaidae—were forced to marry the fifty sons of Danaus's twin brother Aegyptus. At their father's command they (with the exception of one, Hypermnestra) murdered their husbands on their wedding night. Klinger thought of his Danaidae figure as the wife of Tantalus.

57. Klinger had inscribed Goethe's words "Wer frech ist, der muss leiden" ("Who is impudent, must suffer") near the figure of Venus in the plaster model of the throne, but this was not carried out in the bronze cast.

58. In the plaster model these small figures were given more specific and mythic identities (Prometheus and Ixion were identifiable), but in the final version they were made into general figures representing humanity.

59. Rodin's *The Thinker* dates from 1880, but Klinger was not aware of it at the time of his first working out of the Beethoven figure: "At that time [1887–88] Rodin's *Victor Hugo* and *The Thinker* did not yet exist," Klinger wrote, as cited in Winkler, *Max Klinger 1857–1920*, p. 55.

60. Asenijeff, *Max Klingers Beethoven: Eine Kunst-technische Studie*, p. 4.

61. See Albert E. Elsen's persuasive reading in *Rodin*, Museum of Modern Art exhibition catalogue (New York, 1963), p. 53.

62. Klinger had made a bronze Beethoven mask in the cire-perdue method some six years before the throne casting that more closely resembles the Klein life mask, see Asenijeff, *Max Klingers Beethoven: Eine Kunst-technische Studie*, p. 51. This bronze Beethoven face hangs on the wall of the sculptor's studio retreat in Grossjena, where I was able to study it in person recently (1983); the patina was left to develop naturally. Also in Klinger's Grossjena studio is a bronze replica, in a smaller size than the original marble, of the entire Beethoven torso (including arms and head), cast by the Gladenbeck firm in Lauchhammer. Several of these bronze torso casts were made with the artist's permission. A marble copy of the Beethoven torso, worked over by Klinger (see Fig. 171), is in the Boston Museum of Fine Arts and a somewhat disappointing white marble Beethoven bust carved by Klinger in 1907 especially for the Beethovenhaus in Bonn is on display in the ground floor Founders' Gallery there. Supported by a pedestal that doubles as a cravat and jacket collar, it presents the historical Beethoven (with drilled eye pupils) but without the drama of the Musikbibliothek Pe-

ters ex libris characterization Klinger had created earlier (Fig. 195).

63. As cited by Klinger's friend, Hans W. Singer, in *The Modern Cicerone: Dresden I: The Royal Picture Gallery*, trans. Martin Sampson (Stuttgart, n. d. [c. 1907]), p. 124. Until the present century it was generally held that the author of the Apocalypse (The Revelation of Saint John the Divine) was the same as three other New Testament personages: Saint John the "beloved disciple," Saint John the Evangelist—author of the Gospel of Saint John—and Saint John the Apostle.

64. Klinger had planned to surround Wagner, whose stark figure he seems purposefully to have purged of turn-of-the-century Bayreuthean mythologies, with a relief-decorated three-sided pedestal. The outbreak of World War I cut off his marble supply however and only studies for the allegorical surround exist.

65. Letter to Alexander Hummel of 31 December 1904, as cited in Winkler, *Max Klinger 1857–1920*, p. 57. Klinger's misgivings about a polychromatic Beethoven were taken up by his younger friend and colleague, the sculptor Georg Kolbe (1877–1947). In 1926–27 he modeled several versions of a monochromatically conceived three-figure Beethoven monument: in the first version a nude Beethoven was seated in thought before two female muses; in the final version Beethoven stands, advancing toward the spectator with his arms bent at the elbow and crossed in front of his torso protectively, fists clenched. In 1948 the ensemble was cast in bronze for the city of Frankfurt where it was unveiled in 1951; see the monograph by Alfred Wolters, *Georg Kolbe's Beethoven-Denkmal* (Frankfurt, 1951). Kolbe's heroic nudity and solemn expressiveness reflect the impact of Rodin, whom he had met and admired. Earlier, the Norwegian sculptor Gustav Vigeland (1869–1943) had created an equally Rodin-like heroic Beethoven (1905–6). It consists of a single figure with powerful frame bowed down like an Atlas figure, his arms lifted above his head to carry the weight of an invisible world.

66. The special room, attached to the south wall of the museum, displayed not only the Beethoven monument but also other sculptures by Klinger. Deeper inside the museum a large hall was devoted to Klinger's paintings. (This area was destroyed in World War II.) Over the years Klinger's Beethoven monument has developed a green sheen on portions of the marbles selected in the Pyrenees, notably the pedestal area nearest Beethoven's feet and on the head and outer wing surfaces of the eagle. One of the earliest writers on Klinger's Beethoven expressed the wish that the monument not be placed in a museum, but within the sound of Beethoven's music, "in the vestibule of a great concert house," see Franz Servaes, *Max Klinger* (Berlin, n. d. [1902]), p. 43. This desire was realized in 1981 when the New (third) Gewandhaus opened its doors: on permanent loan from the Leipzig Museum, the Beethoven monument now resides in the side foyer of the concert house, centrally set in a shallow, two-stepped hexagonal enclosure in the middle of the room, and certainly within the sound of Beethoven's music.

67. Ludwig Hevesi, *Acht Jahre Secession* (Vienna, 1906), p. 389, review published 17 April 1902, two days after the exhibition's opening.

68. See Bahr's ecstatic description addressed to the editor of *Die Zukunft* as given in Nebehay, *Gustav Klimt Dokumentation*, p. 295.

69. Recalled by Salten in a reminiscence published in 1936, see ibid., p. 285.

70. Eduard Pötzl, as quoted in ibid., p. 298.

71. See the account of his visit to Beethoven in September of 1826 by Samuel Heinrich Spiker (see chapter two, n. 114) in Sonneck, *Beethoven: Impressions by his Contemporaries*, p. 210.

72. Mahler, *Gustav Mahler: Memories and Letters*, p. 37.

73. Ibid.

74. Ibid. Neither was Alma Mahler much impressed by Klinger's personality as she and Gustav got to know him better. She continues sententiously: "He never said anything very much to the point, and so his company was no particular joy to us and we dispensed with it by degrees. He was a great drinker and his days and nights were invariably spent over the bottle, for which we had neither time nor inclination. He was the owner of a champagne factory and it cannot have done him much good." Ibid.

75. Reminiscence of 1936, as quoted in Nebehay, *Gustav Klimt Dokumentation*, pp. 284–85.

76. As late as 1913 Klinger was commenting on the intonation of *colors* he experienced at a performance of the Ninth Symphony, see letter of 25 May 1913 to G. Hirzel, as cited in Stella Wega Mathieu, *Max Klinger: Leben und Werk in Daten und Bildern* (Frankfurt, 1976), p. 52.

77. For the first modern writer to point to these musicial correspondences in Klimt's *Beethoven Frieze* see Fritz Novotny in Fritz Novotny and Johannes Dobai, *Gustav Klimt: With a Catalogue Raisonné of His Paintings* (London, 1968), p. 29.

78. As given in Blaukopf, *Mahler*, p. 249.

79. A plaster copy of Klinger's Beethoven even turned up in the art school of San Telmo in Málaga, where Picasso studied as a boy.

BIBLIOGRAPHY

Abraham, Gerald, ed. *Schumann: A Symposium*. London, 1952.

Abrahamsen, David. *The Mind and Death of a Genius*. New York, 1946.

Albrecht, Otto E. *A Census of Autograph Music Manuscripts of European Composers in America*. Philadelphia, 1953.

——. "Adventures and Discoveries of a Manuscript Hunter." *Musical Quarterly* 31, no. 4 (October 1945): 492–503.

Anderson, Emily, ed. and trans. *The Letters of Beethoven*. 3 vols. London, 1961.

Apponyi, Albert. *The Memoirs of Count Apponyi*. New York, 1935.

Arnim, Bettina Brentano von. *Ilius Pamphilius und die Ambrosia*. 2 vols. Berlin, 1857.

Arnold, Denis, and Fortune, Nigel, eds. *The Beethoven Reader*. New York, 1971.

Arnold, Elsie and Denis, eds. "The View of Posterity: An Anthology." In *The Beethoven Reader*, ed. Denis Arnold and Nigel Fortune. New York, 1971.

Asenijeff, Elsa. *Max Klingers Beethoven: Eine Kunsttechnische Studie*. Leipzig, 1902.

Badura-Skoda, Eva. "Der Bildhauer Anton Dietrich. Ein Beitrag zur Ikonographie Beethovens und Schuberts." In *Musik. Edition Interpretation: Gedenkschrift Günter Henle*. ed. Martin Bente, pp. 30–52. Munich, 1980.

Bahr, Hermann. *Gegen Klimt*. Vienna, 1903.

Barkan, Hans, trans. and ed. *Johannes Brahms and Theodor Billroth: Letters from a Musical Friendship*. Norman (Okla.), 1957.

Barth, Herbert; Mack, Dietrich; and Voss, Egon, eds. *Wagner, A Documentary Study*. New York, 1975.

Barzun, Jacques. *Berlioz and the Romantic Century*. 2 vols. 3rd ed. New York, 1969.

——, ed. *The Pleasures of Music*. 1952. London, 1977.

Beck, Dagmar, and Herre, Gritta. "Anton Schindlers fingierte Eintragungen in den Konversationsheften." In *Zu Beethoven: Aufsätze und Annotationen*, ed. Harry Goldschmidt. Berlin, 1979.

Beethoven-Monument in Heiligenstadt bei Wien (pamphlet). Vienna, 1863.

Bentley, Eric. *A Century of Hero-Worship*. Philadelphia, 1944.

Bergfeld, Joachim, ed., and Bird, George, trans. *The Diary of Richard Wagner 1865–1882: The Brown Book*. London, 1980.

Berlioz, Hector. *A Critical Study of Beethoven's Nine Symphonies*. 1862. Trans. Edwin Evans, Sr. 1913. London, 1958.

——. *Berlioz: A Selection from His Letters*. Ed. and trans. Humphrey Searle. 1966. New York, 1973.

——. *Berlioz: Evenings with the Orchestra*. Trans. Jacques Barzun. New York, 1956.

——. *Evenings in the Orchestra*. Trans. C. R. Fortescue. Harmondsworth (Middlesex), 1963.

——. *Memoirs*. 1932. Trans. Rachel and Eleanor Holmes; annotated and rev. trans. Ernest Newman. New York, 1966.

——. *Voyage musical en Allemagne et en Italie*. Paris, 1844.

Beyle, Marie Henri [Stendhal]. *Life of Rossini*. Trans. and annotated Richard N. Coe. New York, 1970.

Bisanz-Prakken, Marian. *Gustav Klimt: Der Beethovenfries*. Salzburg, 1977.

Blaukopf, Herta, ed., and Jephcott, Edmund, trans. *Gustav Mahler-Richard Strauss: Correspondence 1888–1911*. London, 1984.

Blaukopf, Kurt. *Mahler*. London, 1969.

Blunt, Wilfrid. *On Wings of Song: A Biography of Felix Mendelssohn*. New York, 1974.

Bory, Robert. *La vie de Franz Liszt par l' image*. Geneva, 1936.

——, ed. *Ludwig van Beethoven: His Life and His Work in Pictures*. London, 1966.

Boucourechliev, André. *Schumann*. London, 1959.

Bowen, Catherine Drinker. *"Free Artist": The Story of Anton and Nicholas Rubinstein*. New York, 1939.

Breidenstein, Heinrich Carl. *Festgabe zu der am 11. August 1845 Stattfindenden Inauguration des Beethoven-Monuments*. Bonn, 1845.

Breuning, Gerhard von. *Aus dem Schwarzspanierhause*. Vienna, 1874.

Burgess, Anthony. *Napoleon Symphony*. New York, 1974.

Burk, John N. *Clara Schumann: A Romantic Biography*. New York, 1940.

——, ed. *Letters of Richard Wagner: The Burrell Collection*. New York, 1972.

Burney, Charles. *General History of Music*. 4 vols. London, 1776–89.

Chan, Ann. "Beethoven in the United States to 1865." Ph.D. dissertation, University of North Carolina at Chapel Hill, 1976.

Chevigny, Bell Gale. *The Woman and the Myth: Margaret Fuller's Life and Writings*. Old Westbury (N.Y.), 1976.

469

Closson, Ernest. *L'élément flamand dans Beethoven*. 1928. Brussels, 1946.

Comini, Alessandra. *Egon Schiele's Portraits*. Berkeley, 1974.

———. *Gustav Klimt*. New York, 1975.

———. "In Praise of Creative Misinterpretation, or 'How a Little Bit of Schopenhauer Changed My Life.' " *Arts Magazine* 52, no. 11 (March 1978): 118–23.

———. *The Fantastic Art of Vienna*. New York, 1978.

———. "The Visual Brahms: Idols and Images." *Arts Magazine* 54, no. 2 (October 1979): 123–39.

———. "Through a Viennese Looking Glass Darkly: Images of Arnold Schönberg and His Circle." *Arts Magazine* 58, no. 9 (May 1984): 107–19.

Cooper, Martin. *Beethoven: The Last Decade 1817–1827*. London, 1970.

Courcy, Geraldine I. C. de. *Paganini the Genoese*. 2 vols. Norman (Okla.), 1957.

Cox, H. Bertram, and Cox, C. L. E., eds. *Leaves from the Journals of Sir George Smart*. London, 1907.

Dean, Winton, *Bizet*. 1948. London, 1975.

Debussy, Claude. *Debussy on Music*. Trans. Richard Langham Smith. New York, 1977.

Delacroix, Eugène. *The Journal of Eugène Delacroix*. Trans. Walter Pach. New York, 1937.

Deutsch, Otto Erich. *The Schubert Reader*. Trans. Eric Blom. New York, 1947.

Dilthey, Wilhelm. *Gesammelte Schriften*. 4 vols. Leipzig, 1925.

Doernberg, Erwin. *The Life and Symphonies of Anton Bruckner*. Toronto, 1960.

Dufet, Michel. *Das Drama Beethoven Erlebt von Bourdelle*. Paris, 1970.

Elsen, Albert E. *Rodin* (exh. cat.). Museum of Modern Art, New York, 1963.

Engelhard, Josef. *Ein Wiener Mahler Erzählt: Mein Leben und Meine Modelle*. Vienna, 1943.

Essers, Volkmar. *Johann Friedrich Drake*. Munich, 1976.

Ewen, Frederic, ed. and trans. *Heinrich Heine: Self-Portrait and Other Prose Writings*. Secaucus (N.J.), 1948.

Federmann, Reinhard, ed. *Österreich intim, Erinnerungen 1892–1942*. Frankfurt, 1970.

Fétis, François Joseph. *Biographie Universelle des Musiciens*. Brussels, 1837.

Fischer-Dieskau, Dietrich. *Schubert's Songs: A Biographical Study*. New York, 1977.

Friedlaender, Walter. *David to Delacroix*. 1930. Cambridge (Mass.), 1952.

Friedrich, Otto. *Before the Deluge*. New York, 1972.

Frimmel, Theodor von. *Beethoven im zeitgenössischen Bildnis*. Vienna, 1923.

———. *Beethoven-Studien I: Beethovens äussere Erscheinung. Seine Bildnisse*. Munich and Leipzig, 1905.

Gall, Hans. *Johannes Brahms: His Work and Personality*. 1961. Trans. Joseph Stein, New York, 1971.

———. *Richard Wagner*. 1963. New York, 1976.

Gavoty, Bernard. *Frederic Chopin*. New York, 1977.

Geiringer, Karl. "Brahms as a Musicologist." *Musical Quarterly* 69, no. 4 (fall 1983): 463–470.

———. *Brahms: His Life and Work*. 1935. 2nd ed., rev. and enl. New York, 1947.

Glück, Franz. "Prolegomena zu einer neuen Beethoven-Ikonographie." In *Festschrift Otto Erich Deutsch zum 80. Geburtstag am 5 September 1963*, eds. Walter Gerstenberg, Jan LaRue, and Wolfgang Rehm, pp. 203–12. Kassel, 1963.

———. "W. J. Mählers Beethovenbildnisse und seine Porträte anderer Persönlichkeiten." *Alte und Moderne Kunst* 6, no. 45 (1961): 11–16.

Glümer, C. von. *Erinnerungen an Wilhelmine Schröder-Devrient*. Leipzig, 1862.

Goldman, Albert, ed.; Spinchorn, Evert, intro.; and Ellis, H. Ashton, trans. *Wagner on Music and Drama*. New York, 1964.

Gotwals, Vernon, ed. *Joseph Haydn: Eighteenth-Century Gentleman of Genius*. Madison (Wis.), 1963.

Graf, Max. *Composer and Critic: Two Hundred Years of Musical Criticism*. 1946. New York, 1971.

Gregor-Dellin, Martin. *Richard Wagner: Eine Biographie in Bildern*. Munich, 1982.

Griepenkerl, Wolfgang Robert. *Das Musikfest, oder die Beethovener*. Leipzig, 1838.

Grillparzer, Franz. *Gesammelte Werke*. 20 vols. Vienna, 1923.

Grove, George. *Beethoven and His Nine Symphonies*. 1896; 3rd ed., 1898. New York, 1962.

———, ed. *A Dictionary of Music and Musicians*. 4 vols. London, 1878–90.

Grove's Dictionary of Music and Musicians. 5 vols. 3rd ed., 1927. New York, 1938.

The New Grove Dictionary of Music and Musicians. Ed. Stanley Sadie. 20 vols. 1980. Reprint with minor corrections. London, 1981.

Guglia, Eugen, ed. *Wien: Ein Führer durch Stadt und Umgebung*. Vienna, 1908.

Gutman, Robert. *Wagner: The Man, His Mind, and His Music*. New York, 1968.

Hallé, Charles. *The Autobiography of Charles Hallé*. 1896. Ed. Michael Kennedy. New York, 1973.

Hamburger, Michael. *Beethoven: Letters, Journals and Conversations*. New York, 1960.

Hanslick, Eduard. *Music Criticisms 1846–99*. Trans. and ed. Henry Pleasants. Baltimore, 1950.

Hellborn, Heinrich Kreissle von. *Franz Schubert*. Vienna, 1865.

Herbert, May, ed. and trans. *The Life of Robert Schumann Told in His Letters*. 2 vols. London, 1890.

Hertzmann, Erich. "The Newly Discovered Autograph of Beethoven's *Rondo à Capriccio*, Op. 129." *Musical Quarterly* 32, no. 2 (April): 171–95.

Heuffer, Francis, trans. *Correspondence of Wagner and Liszt*. 2 vols. 2nd ed., rev., 1897; New York, 1973.

Hevesi, Ludwig. *Acht Jahre Secession*. Vienna, 1906.

Hewett-Thayer, Harvey W. *Hoffmann: Author of the Tales*. Princeton, 1948.

Hiller, Ferdinand. *Aus dem Tonleben unsere Zeit*. Leipzig, 1868.

Hirth, Friedrich. *J. P. Lyser, der Dichter, Maler, und Musiker*. Munich, 1911.

Hrussoczy, Marie [Mariam Tenger]. *Beethovens Unsterbliche Geliebte, Nach persönlichen Erinnerungen*. Bonn, 1890.

Hüffer, Eduard. *Anton Felix Schindler* (Ph.D. dissertation). Münster, 1909.

Hughes, Spike. *The Toscanini Legacy*. 1959. New York, 1969.

Hugo, Howard E., ed. *The Portable Romantic Reader*. 1957. New York, 1972.

———, trans. *The Letters of Franz Liszt to Marie zu Sayn-Wittgenstein*. Cambridge (Mass.), 1953.

Huneker, James. *Franz Liszt*. New York, 1927.

Hürlimann, Martin, ed. *Besuch bei Beethoven*. Zurich, 1948.

Hutchings, Arthur, *Schubert*. Rev. ed. London, 1973.

Jacob, Heinrich Eduard. *Felix Mendelssohn and His Times*. Englewood Cliffs (N.J.), 1936.

———. *Johann Strauss, Father and Son: A Century of Light Music*. Richmond (Va.), 1940.

Jacobs, David. *Beethoven*. New York, 1970.

Jacobs, Robert L., and Skelton, Geoffrey, eds. and trans. *Wagner Writes from Paris.* . . . New York, 1973.

Josef Danhauser, Gemälde und Zeichnungen (exh. cat.). Graphische Sammlung Albertina, Vienna, March–May 1983.

Kalbeck, Max. *Johannes Brahms*. 8 vols. Berlin, 1904–14.

Kalischer, A. C., and Frimmel, Theodor, eds. *Beethovens sämtliche Briefe*. 2nd ed. (5 vols.). Berlin, 1908–11.

———, ed., and Shedlock, J. S., trans. *The Letters of Ludwig van Beethoven*. 2 vols. London, 1909.

Kennedy, Michael. *Mahler*. London, 1974.

Kern, O. J., and Uhde-Bernays, Hermann, eds. *Anselm Feuerbachs Briefe an seine Mutter*. 2 vols. Berlin, 1911.

Kerst, Friedrich, and Krehbiel, Henry Edward. *Beethoven: The Man and the Artist, as Revealed in his own Words*. New York, 1964.

Kinsky, George. "Zu Beethovens Heiligenstädter Testament." *Schweizerische Musikzeitung und Sängerblatt*, 14/15 '(1934) 519–20.

Kobald, Karl. *Beethoven: Seine Beziehungen zu Wiens Kunst und Kultur, Gesellschaft und Landschaft*. Vienna, 1946.

Köhler, Karl-Heinz; Herre, Grita, eds. *Ludwig van Beethovens Konversationshefte*. 8 vols. Leipzig, 1972–81.

Kolisko, Maria. *Caspar von Zumbusch*. Vienna, 1931.

Kolodin, Irving. *The Interior Beethoven*. New York, 1975.

Kropfinger, Klaus. *Wagner und Beethoven*. Regensburg, 1975.

XIV. Kunstausstellung der Vereinigung Bildender Künstler Österreichs Secession (exh. cat.). Vienna, April–June, 1902.

La Grange, Henry-Louis de. *Mahler*. Vol. 1. New York, 1973.

Lalor, John J., trans. *Life of Beethoven by Louis Nohl*. Chicago, 1896.

La Mara (Marie Lipsius), ed., and Bache, Constance, trans. *Letters of Franz Liszt*. 2 vols. London, 1894.

Lampadius, W. A. *The Life of Felix Mendelssohn-Bartholdy*. Trans. W. L. Gage. Boston, 1887.

Landon, H. C. Robbins. *Beethoven: A Documentary Study*. New York, 1970.

———. *Beethoven: A Documentary Study*. Abridged ed. New York, 1975.

———. *Haydn: A Documentary Study*. New York, 1981.

Lang, Paul Henry, ed. *The Creative World of Beethoven*. New York, 1971.

Langbehn, Julius. *Rembrandt als Erzieher, Von einem Deutschen*. 1890. 38th ed. Leipzig, 1891.

Larkin, Edward. "Beethoven's Medical History." In the Appendix to *Beethoven: The Last Decade 1817–1827*, by Martin Cooper. London, 1970.

László, Zsigmond, and Mátéka, Béla. *Franz Liszt par l'image*. Budapest, 1978.

Legouvé, Ernest. *Soixante ans de souvenirs*. 4 vols. Paris, 1887.

Leichtentritt, Hugo. *Music, History, and Ideas*. Cambridge, 1941.

Leitzmann, Albert, ed. *Ludwig van Beethoven: Berichte der Zeitgenossen, Briefe und persönliche Aufzeichnungen*. 2 vols. Leipzig, 1921.

Liebling, Leonard. *Richard Wagner and the Seamstress*. New York, 1941.

Lingg, Ann M. *Mephisto Waltz: The Story of Franz Liszt*. New York, 1951.

Liszt, Franz. *Life of Chopin*. Trans. John Broadhouse. London, 1879.

Litterscheid, Richard. *Johannes Brahms in seinen Schriften und Briefen*. Berlin, 1943.

Litzmann, Berthold. *Clara Schumann: Ein Künstlerleben*. 3 vols. Leipzig, 1902–8.

———, ed. *Letters of Clara Schumann and Johannes Brahms 1853–1896*. 2 vols. 1927. New York, 1973.

London, S. J. "Beethoven: Case Report of a Titan's Last Crisis." *Archives of Internal Medicine* 113 (March 1964) 442–48.

Ludwig, Emil. *Beethoven: Life of a Conqueror*. New York, 1943.

———. *Three Titans*. 1927. New York, 1930.

Lux, Joseph August. "Klinger's Beethoven und die Moderne Raum-Kunst." *Deutsche Kunst und Dekoration*. 10 (April–September 1902): 475–517.

MacArdle, D. W., and Misch, Ludwig, eds. and trans. *New Beethoven Letters*. Norman (Okla.), 1957.

Macdonald, Hugh. *Berlioz*. London, 1982.

Mahler, Alma. *Gustav Mahler: Memories and Letters*. 1946. Rev. ed. Seattle, 1971.

Marek, George R. *Beethoven: Biography of a Genius*. New York, 1969.

———. *Gentle Genius: The Story of Felix Mendelssohn*. New York, 1972.

Martner, Knud, ed. *Selected Letters of Gustav Mahler*. New York, 1979.

Mathieu, Stella Wega. *Max Klinger: Leben und Werk in Daten und Bildern*. Frankfurt, 1976.

May, Florence. *The Life of Johannes Brahms*. 2 vols. 1905. Enl. and illustrated ed. Neptune City (N.J.), 1981.

Mendelssohn Bartholdy, Felix. *Letters From Italy and Switzerland*. Trans. Lady Wallace. London, 1862.

Michotte, Edmond. *Richard Wagner's Visit to Rossini and an Evening at Rossini's in Beau-Sejour*. 1906. Trans. with an introduction and appendix by Herbert Weinstock. Chicago, 1968.

Mittig, Hans-Ernst. "Das Wiener Beethoven-Denkmal von Zumbusch und did Wende der Beethoven-Darstellung." *Alte und Moderne Kunst* 14, no. 104 (May–June 1969): 25–33.

———, and Plagermann, Volker, eds. *Denkmäler im 19. Jahrhundert*. Munich, 1972.

Moscheles, Ignaz. *Recent Music and Musicians*. Ed. Charlotte Moscheles. 1872. Trans. A. D. Coleridge. New York, 1873.

———, ed. *The Life of Beethoven including the Biography by Schindler, Beethoven's Correspondence with his Friends, Numerous Characteristic Traits, and Remarks on his Musical Works*. 2 vols. London, 1841.

Münz, Ludwig, and Künstler, Gustav. *Adolf Loos: Pioneer of Modern Architecture*. New York, 1966.

Musil, Robert. *The Man Without Qualities*. Vol. 1. New York, 1953.

Naiken, V. S. "Did Beethoven Have Paget's Disease of Bone?" *Annals of Internal Medicine* 74, no. 6 (June 1971): 995–99.

Nauhaus, Gerd, ed. *Robert Schumann: Tagebücher: Haushaltbücher*. 3 vols, 2 parts. Leipzig, 1982.

Nebehay, Christian M. *Gustav Klimt Dokumentation*. Vienna, 1969.

471

Nettl, Paul. *Beethoven Encyclopedia*. New York, 1956.

Newlin, Dika. *Bruckner, Mahler, Schoenberg*. London, 1978.

Newman, Ernest. *The Life of Richard Wagner*. 4 vols. 1933–47. London, 1976.

Niecks, Frederick. *Frederick Chopin as a Man and Musician*. 2 vols, London, 1888.

Niemann, Walter. *Brahms*. 1920. Trans. Catherine Alison Phillips. Reprint. New York, 1969.

Nietzsche, Friedrich. *The Birth of Tragedy and The Case of Wagner*. Trans. Walter Kaufmann. New York, 1976.

Nohl, Herman. *Die Weltanschauungen der Malerei*. Jena, 1908.

Nohl, Ludwig. *Beethovens Leben*. 3 vols. in 4. 1864. 2nd ed. (4 vols.) Vienna, 1909–13.

———. *Die Beethoven-Feier und die Kunst der Gegenwart*. Vienna, 1871.

Nottebohm, Gustav. *Ein Skizzenbuch von Beethoven*. Leipzig, 1865.

———. *Ein Skizzenbuch von Beethoven aus dem Jahre, 1803*. 1880. New York, 1970.

Novotny, Fritz and Dobai, Johannes. *Gustav Klimt: With a Catalogue Raisonné of His Paintings*. London, 1968.

Oberdorfer, Aldo, ed. *Giuseppe Verdi: Autobiografia dalle Lettere*. Milan, 1941.

Orel, Alfred. "Johannes Brahms' Musikbibliothek." In *Simrock-Jahrbuch*. Vol. 3. Leipzig, 1930–34. Reprinted in Kurt Hofmann. *Die Bibliothek von Johannes Brahms: Bücher und Musikalienverzeichnis*, pp. 147–48. Schriftenreihe zur Musik, Hamburg, 1974.

Perényi, Eleanor. *Liszt: The Artist as Romantic Hero*. Boston, 1974.

Pleasants, Henry, trans. and ed. *The Musical Journeys of Louis Spohr*. Norman (Okla.), 1961.

Prawer, S. S. *Caligari's Children: The Film as Tale of Terror*. Oxford, 1980.

Reed, John. *Schubert: The Final Years*. New York, 1972.

Reich, Nancy B. *Clara Schumann: The Artist and the Woman*. Ithaca, 1985.

Reichardt, Johann Friedrich. *Vertraute Briefe, geschrieben auf einer Reise nach Wien und den österreichischen Staaten zu Ende 1808 und zu Anfang 1809*. 1809. Amsterdam, 1810.

Reik, Theodor. *The Haunting Melody*. New York, 1953.

Rellstab, Heinrich Friedrich Ludwig. *Aus meinem Leben*. 2 vols. Berlin, 1861.

Rilke, Rainer Maria. *The Notebooks of Malte Laurids Brigge*. 1910. Trans. M. D. Herter Norton. New York, 1949.

Ritter, Fanny Raymond, trans. and ed. *Music and Musicians. Essays and Criticisms by Robert Schumann*. London, 1877.

Robson-Scott, W. D. *The Literary Background of the Gothic Revival in Germany*. Oxford, 1965.

Rochlitz, Johann Friedrich. *Für Freunde der Tonkunst*. 4 vols. Leipzig, 1832.

Roessler, Arthur. *Ferdinand Georg Waldmüller*. Vienna, 1907.

———. *Josef Danhauser*. Vienna, n.d. [c. 1910].

Rolland, Romain. *Beethoven*. 1903. Trans. B. Constance Hull. London, 1927.

———. *Beethoven the Creator*. 1927. Trans. Ernest Newman. New York, 1929; 1964.

———. *Goethe and Beethoven*. Trans. G. A. Pfister and E. S. Kemp. New York, 1931.

Runes, Dagobert D. *Pictorial History of Philosophy*. New York, 1959.

Saint-Pulgent, Maryvonne de. "Brahms et Beethoven: pour en finir avec une légende." *L' Avant-Scène*. No. 53 (June 1983; *Johannes Brahms* issue), pp. 87–92.

Schauffler, Robert Haven. *Beethoven: The Man Who Freed Music*. 2 vols. New York, 1929.

———. *Florestan: The Life and Work of Robert Schumann*. 1945. New York, 1963.

———. *The Unknown Brahms*. New York, 1933.

Schindler, Anton Felix. *Beethoven As I Knew Him*. 1840; rev. and enl. eds., 1845 and 1860. Ed. Donald W. MacArdle; trans. Constance S. Jolly. New York, 1972.

———. *Biographie von Ludwig van Beethoven (Zweite, mit zwei Nachträgen vermehrte Ausgabe)*. Münster (Aschendorff), 1845.

Schlosser, Johann Aloys. *Ludwig van Beethoven: Eine Biographie*, Prague, 1828 [1827].

Schmidt-Görg, Joseph, and Schmidt, Hans. *Ludwig van Beethoven*. Hamburg, 1970.

Schober, Franz Ritter von. *Briefe über F. Liszt's Aufenthalt in Ungarn*. Berlin, 1843.

Schönzeler, Hans-Hubert. *Bruckner*. London, 1970.

Schorske, Carl E. *Fin-de-Siècle Vienna: Politics and Culture*. New York, 1980.

Schottky, Julius. *Paganinis Leben und Treiben als Künstler und als Mensch*. Prague, 1830.

Schrade, Leo. *Beethoven in France*. New Haven, 1942.

Schumann, Karl. *Das Kleine Liszt-Buch*. Hamburg, 1981.

Schumann, Robert. *Gesammelte Schriften über Musik und Musiker*. 4 vols. Leipzig, 1854.

———. *On Music and Musicians*. Ed. Konrad Wolff; trans. Paul Rosenfeld. New York, 1969.

Selden-Goth, G., ed. *Felix Mendelssohn: Letters*. New York, 1973.

Servaes, Franz. *Max Klinger*. Berlin, n.d. [1902].

Shirer, William L. *The Rise and Fall of the Third Reich*. New York, 1962.

Singer, Hans W. *The Modern Cicerone: Dresden I: The Royal Picture Gallery*. Trans. Martin Sampson. Stuttgart, n.d. [c. 1907].

Sitwell, Sacheverell. *Liszt*. 1934, Rev. ed. London, 1967.

Skelton, Geoffrey. *Richard and Cosima Wagner: Biography of a Marriage*. Boston, 1982.

Slonimsky, Nicolas, ed. *Lexicon of Musical Invective*. 1953. Seattle, 1972.

Smart, Sir George. *Leaves From the Journals of Sir George Smart*. London, 1907.

Solomon, Maynard. *Beethoven*. New York, 1977.

Sonneck, O. G., ed. *Beethoven: Impressions by His Contemporaries*. 1926. New York, 1967.

Specht, Richard. *Johannes Brahms*. 1928. Trans. Eric Blom. London, 1930.

Stefan, Paul. *Gustav Mahler—Ein Bild seiner Persönlichkeit in Widmung*. Munich, 1910.

Steichen, Dana. *Beethoven's Beloved*. New York, 1959.

Sterba, Editha, and Richard M. D. *Beethoven and His Nephew*. New York, 1954.

Stern, Fritz. *The Politics of Cultural Despair: A Study in the Rise of the Germanic Ideology*. Berkeley, 1961.

Strunk, Oliver. *Source Readings in Music History: The Romantic Era*. New York, 1950.

Szeps-Zuckerkandl, Berta. *My Life and History*. New York, 1939.

Thayer-Forbes. *Thayer's Life of Beethoven*. Ed. Elliot Forbes. Princeton, 1970 (orig. vols. taking Beethoven's life up to 1817 by Alexander Wheelock Thayer published 1866–79).

Tolstoi, Leo. *The Works of Leo Tolstoi*. New York, 1928.

Tovey, Donald Francis. *Essays in Musical Analysis*. 6 vols. London, 1939.

Toye, Francis. *Giuseppe Verdi: His Life and Works*. New York, 1946.

———. *Rossini: A Study in Tragi-Comedy*. 1934. New York, 1947.

Trevor-Roper, Patrick. *The World Through Blunted Sight*. London, 1970.

Turner, W. J. *Berlioz: The Man and His Work*. London, 1934.

Tyson, Alan, ed. *Beethoven Studies*. New York, 1973.

———. "Ferdinand Ries (1784–1838): The History of His Contribution to Beethoven Biography." *19th Century Music* 7 (1984): 211–12.

———. "Sketches and Autographs." In David Arnold and Nigel Fortune, eds., *The Beethoven Reader*, pp. 443–58. New York, 1971.

Vergo, Peter. *Art in Vienna 1898–1918*. London, 1975.

Visani, Maria Cionini. *Toulouse-Lautrec*. New York, 1971.

Voynich, E. L., trans., and Opieński, Henry, coll. *Chopin's Letters*. 1931. New York, 1973.

Wagner, Cosima. *Cosima Wagner's Diaries*. Trans. Geoffrey Skelton. 2 vols. New York, 1978–80.

———. *Die Tagebücher*. Ed. Martin Gregor-Dellin and Dietrich Mack. 2 vols. Munich, 1976–77.

Wagner, Richard. *Beethoven*. Trans. Edward Dannreuther. 3rd ed. London, n.d. [1800?].

———. *Dichtungen und Schriften*. 10 vols. Frankfurt, 1983.

———. *Mein Leben*. 2 vols. 1911. Munich, 1963.

———. *My Life*. 2 vols. New York, 1911.

Wagner-Rieger, Renate. *Wiens Architektur im 19. Jahrhundert*. Vienna, 1970.

Walker, Alan. *Franz Liszt: The Virtuoso Years 1811–1847*. Vol. 1. New York, 1983.

Walter, Bruno. *Gustav Mahler*. 1957. New York, 1974.

Warrack, John. *Carl Maria von Weber*. New York, 1968.

———, ed., and Cooper, Martin, trans. *Carl Maria von Weber: Writings on Music*. Cambridge, 1981.

Weber, Max Maria von. *Carl Maria von Weber: Ein Lebensbild*. 3 vols. Leipzig, 1864–66.

Wechsberg, Joseph. *Schubert: His Life, His Work, His Time*. New York, 1977.

———. *The Waltz Emperors: The Life and Times and Music of the Strauss Family*. New York, 1973.

Wegeler, Dr. Franz G. *Nachtrag zu den biographischen Notizen über Ludwig van Beethoven*. Koblenz, 1845.

Wegeler, Dr. Franz Gerhard, and Ries, Ferdinand. *Biographische Notizen über Ludwig van Beethoven*. Koblenz, 1838.

Wellek, René, and Warren, Austin. *Theory of Literature*. 3rd ed. New York, 1962–63.

Werner, Eric. *Mendelssohn: A New Image of the Composer and His Age*. New York, 1963.

Wierzynski, Casimir. *The Life and Death of Chopin*. New York, 1949.

Willetts, Pamela J. *Beethoven and England: An Account of Sources in the British Museum*. London, 1970.

Winkler, Gerhard. *Max Klinger 1857–1920* (exh. cat. of the Leipzig Museum of Fine Arts for the fiftieth anniversary of the death of Klinger, 4 July–20 September 1970). Leipzig, 1970.

Wolters, Alfred. *Georg Kolbe's Beethoven-Denkmal*. Frankfurt, 1951.

Young, Percy M. *Beethoven: A Victorian Tribute Based on the Papers of Sir George Smart*. London, 1976.

INDEX

476

478